Business & Administration

Student Handbook
Level 3

Published by CfA

© CfA 2011

Registered charity number 1095 809

Published 2011

First published 2005

ISBN 978-0-9567738-2-1

All rights reserved.

CfA is committed to providing and promoting relevant business skills and knowledge to all types of organisations, to make sure employees have the required skills to excel and develop throughout their careers.

Cover design by Consider Creative
Additional graphics and design by Method UK and AyDesignWorks
Printed and bound by Mail Options Ltd.

Microsoft product screen shots reprinted with permission from Microsoft Corporation.

www.cfa.uk.com

Introduction

INTRODUCTION

The Council for Administration (CfA) is the leading government-recognised standard setting organisation for business skills. The CfA has represented over 10 million UK employees to date. As the leading authority on providing and promoting both business skills and knowledge, the CfA can make sure that employees from all types of organisations have the required skills to excel and develop throughout their careers. The CfA, in collaboration with its partners, develops standards, qualifications and apprenticeship frameworks for the following 'business skills @ work' across the UK:

Business & Administration	Industrial Relations
Consultancy & Business Support	Languages & Intercultural Working
Contact Centres	Management & Leadership
Customer Service	Marketing
Enterprise	Recruitment
Governance	Sales
HR	Small Business

The new Level 3 Business & Administration units in this Student Handbook will provide the learner with various resources to equip them with the skills and knowledge to achieve the units they have chosen in their Business & Administration vocational qualification. This book covers all the Level 3 units that are offered within the new:

- Qualifications and Credit Framework (QCF) Rules of Combination (RoC), called the QCF National Vocational Qualification (NVQ)

- Scottish Vocational Qualification (SVQ) qualification structures

- Apprenticeship frameworks

The new Business & Administration vocational qualifications offer greater flexibility of choice of units at different levels within their structures than in previous qualification. The Level 3 qualification structures will offer the choice of units at Level 1, Level 3 and Level 3.

Difference between unit titles in the QCF NVQ and the SVQ
The QCF NVQ was introduced into England, Wales and Northern Ireland during 2010. The NVQ is a **credit based** qualification, whereas the SVQ is a **unit based** qualification. The QCF NVQ also allows for up

to three different sizes of qualifications based on the number of credits needed to achieve the qualification. This has meant that some units are structured and titled differently across the two qualification frameworks. This applies to the following Level 3 units:

Type of unit	NVQ	SVQ
Mandatory / Optional	Manage own performance in a business environment	Agree how to manage and improve own performance in a business environment
Mandatory /Optional	Improve own performance in a business environment	
Mandatory	Work in a business environment	Undertake work in a business environment
Mandatory	Communicate in a business environment	Prepare to communicate in a business environment
Optional	Solve business problems	Plan how to solve business problems
Optional	Archive information	Provide archive services

The CfA, working with its stakeholders, has worked towards agreeing that the completion of different combinations of units toward achieving a vocational qualification is comparable across the four nations of the UK.

Structure of the Student Handbook
Each chapter within the Student Handbook has been structured into six parts, represented by the following icons:

Knowledge
This section covers the underpinning knowledge the learner will need to apply as they develop the skills to be recognised as competent in the unit of learning they are aiming to achieve. There are **activities** to complete throughout this section to test the learner's understanding of knowledge concepts.

Testing your Knowledge
This section follows up on the **activities** found in the previous section with more questions testing the learner's understanding of knowledge concepts.

Skills
This section focuses on the application and performance of skills in the workplace. The learner will be expected to apply the knowledge in the performance of their job to be recognised as competent. There may also be **ACTIVITIES** to complete throughout this section to test the learner's application of skills.

Testing your skills
This section asks questions about the application of skills in the workplace to make sure the learner will be competent to complete their job aims and objectives.

Ready for assessment?
This section allows the learner to recognise if they feel they are ready to be assessed.

Links to other units
This section reminds the learner that evidence gathered in support of the achievement of a unit may also be used to evidence requirements in other units and vice versa.

The **activities**, **testing your knowledge** and **testing your skills** sections allow the learner to generate evidence towards achieving competence in the units.

We wish you every success in the pursuit of your learning.

CONTENTS

1 Agree a budget

AGREE A BUDGET

'Agree a budget' is an <u>optional unit</u> which may be chosen as one of a combination of units to achieve either a Qualifications and Credit Framework (QCF), National Vocational Qualification (NVQ) or Scottish Vocational Qualification (SVQ).

The aims of this unit are to:

- Understand how to develop budgets
- Be able to agree a budget

To achieve the above aims of this unit, learners will be expected to provide evidence through the performance of work-based activities.

Knowledge
Purpose and types of budgets
A budget is a plan that shows the amount of money that an organisation intends to spend within a specified period of time. It expresses the money value in whatever currency an organisation is budgeting the future human and material resources requirements identified in action plans - the budget acts as a road map to carry out an organisation's objectives, strategies and assumptions. The budget will identify sources of revenue or income and expenditure, e.g. salaries, benefits, supplies and travel. Therefore, it is a financial document used to project future income and expenses. In planning a budget, potential use of resources should be aligned with an organisation's strategic plan. The process of budgeting will cascade down through each department or division of the organisation from the strategic plan. A budget can communicate an organisation's values and identify its priorities. The budget can then be used to determine if resources are being appropriately and beneficially used to achieve the organisation's mission and objectives.

Other goals that a budget can achieve for an organisation include:

- **Control and evaluation** - Having a budget allows a company to have a certain degree of control over costs. A budget gives a company a benchmark by which to evaluate its business units, departments etc., and individual managers. Unfortunately, the latter purpose can cause employees to have negative feelings about the budgeting process because their jobs may be dependent on meeting certain budgeting goals. This is especially true in companies when budgeting is a top-down process, rather than participative

- **Planning** - Arguably the main purpose of a budget. Planning a budget allows a business to take stock of revenue and expenses from the previous period, and judge where the business will be in future periods. It also allows organisations to add and remove products and services from its plan for the future period. Planning a master budget allows senior management to gain a picture of the entire business so they are better able to prioritise their business plans

- **Communication and motivation** - Budgets allow management to communicate goals so resources can be coordinated and focused in key areas. Budgets also allow an organisation to motivate its employees by involving them in the planning of a budget, where possible. When an employee is involved in creating their department's budget, that employee will be more likely to strive to achieve the goals of the budget

A budget is also an important step in overall business strategic planning.

• ACTIVITY 1

What is a budget and what is it designed to achieve?

The budgeting process is carried out by all types of business regardless of size, as any organisation will need to estimate whether they can continue to operate within its projected income and expenses. A budget may be prepared using paper and pencil; a computer, using a spreadsheet program like Excel, or with a financial application designed specifically to meet the needs of budgeting drawn up by the organisational objectives. The process for preparing a budget for a specified period of time includes:

- Listing all sources of income, e.g. government grants

- Listing all required, fixed expenses, e.g. salaries, rent, mortgage, utilities, telephone

- Listing other possible and variable expenses, e.g. use of consultants for specific projects

Most organisations will have a master budget or profit plan for the upcoming year. It is common that budgets prepared for the next accounting year will be prepared and reported quarterly or monthly. It is also typical that the annual budget will not be changed once the actual year begins. In rare circumstances the annual budget might be revised, but only when a business environment has radically changed. The master budget will include a projected income statement and balance sheet. The master budget will identify operating budgets, e.g. a sales budget, production budget, marketing budget, administrative budget, and budgets for each department in an organisation. Every constituent part of an organisation will have an operating budget, which is the blueprint for the core functions it will perform over the life of the budget. Each constituent part of an organisation may be asked to identify resources in its operating budget that will be transferred to the organisation's capital expenditure budget, which includes the resource plans for building or renovating new facilities, buying major pieces of equipment or improving the an organisation's infrastructure. There will also be cash budgets.

• ACTIVITY 2

What is a cash budget?

Other types of budgets include:

Rolling budgets
Also known as a continuous budget, a perpetual budget or a rolling horizon budget - always provide for a budget that will look ahead for one full year. A rolling budget could use three-month periods or quarters instead of months. An organisation may have a five-year rolling budget for capital expenditures. In this case a full year will be added to replace the year that has just ended. This means that an organisation will always have a five-year planning horizon.

Static budgets
Are budgets that do not change as volume changes, e.g. if it is estimated that sales commission will be £200,000 for the year, it will remain in the budget even if sales commissions have reached £4 million. However, the sales department may have a flexible budget. In the flexible budget, the sales commission expense budget might be expressed as 5% of sales. In this instance, the department's budget for sales commission expenses will be £200,000 when actual sales are £4 million, but it will decrease to £150,000 when actual sales are £3 million,

and the budget will increase to £300,000 when actual sales are £6 million, and so on.

Flexible budgets

Are budgets that adjust or accommodate changes in the volume of activity. The flexible budget is more sophisticated and useful than a static budget. For example, suppose an HR department estimates the cost of its service is £100 per day. It also knows that the office supervision, depreciation and other fixed costs are approximately £40,000 per month - 20 working days. The office has 50 employees working on a full-time contract of a five-day week. Based on this information, the flexible budget for each month would be £40,000 + £100 x 50 x 20 (£100,000) = £140,000. If, as a result of redundancies to the department, the number of employees working in the HR department decreased to 40 and then 30 employees over two consecutive months, then the flexible budgets for those two months would be £120,000 and £100,000, respectively. The flexible budget provides a better opportunity for planning and controlling than a static budget.

A budget should be flexible enough to enable the organisation and its constituents to take advantage of unexpected opportunities and cope with fluctuations in planned resources which have not been anticipated. Good managers recognise that a budget is only a guide and that it cannot be so rigid that it prevents timely action when needed. Budgeting is the process of matching planned uses to available resources.

• ACTIVITY 3

What are the advantages and disadvantages of a flexible budget over other types pf budgets?

During the specified period of time within which an agreed budget will operate, the budget is a tool for monitoring and controlling the generation and use of resources. By comparing actual results with the budget plan, an organisation can make adjustments to the budget. The budget also provides the foundation for future budgets and is a valuable tool for evaluating the accuracy of the planning assumptions it has made.

 The basis of any budget is estimating the amount of resources an organisation needs to deliver its services and the costs of those resources. For example, a project will need to identify the amount of time it will take to achieve its aims and purpose. Initially, consideration will be given to the amount of time to complete the project. Within this time, how many people will need to be involved in each stage of the milestones of the project? Within each milestone, identify the resources required to complete a milestone. From this, the project manager responsible for drawing up the budget can determine the number of people involved over the life of the project, which can be accounted for in total salaries. They can then make an estimate of the resources each team within the project will need to complete their tasks to arrive at an estimated total budget for the project.

Estimating budgets

Trying to estimate the income and expenditure / costs for a budget is an essential function of managers to make sure they are able to continue to make responsible decisions and maintain control of their department / team. Cost estimates will need to be made to assist with pricing decisions. The estimator should have a good working knowledge of the way the organisation's cost accounting system operates. There are four major costs that need to be considered when agreeing a budget:

- **Fixed costs** - Are expenses that do not vary because of other transactions but remain constant over specified periods of time, e.g. rent. Fixed costs are generally fixed in the short term

- **Variable costs** - Are expenses that change in proportion to the activity of a business. A variable cost is the sum of marginal costs of all units produced. It can also be considered as a normal cost. Variable costs are generally fixed in the long run

- **Direct costs** - Are expenses that can be identified with a specific cost centre or cost object, e.g. a department, process or product. Direct costs, e.g. materials, fuel or power, vary with the rate of output but are uniform for each unit of production, and are usually under the control and responsibility of a department manager. A direct cost is also known as a direct expense, on cost, operating cost, prime cost, variable cost or variable expense, which are grouped under variable costs

- **Indirect costs** - Are expenses that arise from joint usage and are difficult to identify with a specific cost object or cost centre, e.g. advertising, maintenance. Indirect costs are usually constant for a wide range of output and are grouped under fixed costs

• ACTIVITY 4

What are the different costs that need to be considered when estimating a budget?

 Estimating expenditures for a business is not just about making guesses. Though it is not an exact science, past data and previous experience can be used to make an educated estimate, creating a more realistic budget. The estimator will use a good degree of subjective judgement when making decisions about the budget. Judgements made need to be as accurate as possible. Past data that can be used includes, using receipts, credit card bills and purchase order books from previous years to track any increases and calculate the percentage increase, which can then be projected into the future. Another approach is to track spending for a month or two, identifying all expenditure that has been made in the organisation or department. This will provide a sense of the organisation's expenditure in the future. It may also provide a valuable aid to minimising or eliminating wasteful or unnecessary expenditure.

A budget is only successful if the estimates of income and expenses are feasible. The steps involved in making an educated estimate are as follows:

- **Start with what is known** - e.g. the rent of a building is constant over a year, so is a known expenditure. If there is an item of expenditure that is constantly happening every month for six months, use this to estimate the next six months expenditure activity for this item

- **Anticipate increased / decreased expenses due to external economic factors** - e.g. the Bank of England raising interest rates. Use percentage changes if money values are not known

- **Review previous data of expenditures** - The more data that can be collected the better the educated estimate will be, because patterns can be cyclical and may repeat themselves

- **Overestimate, if necessary** - It is better to have more money for expenses than to fall short. For example, if public relations' expenses have been averaging £1,650 per month, then increase this expense to £1,800 per month

- **Research similar businesses** - Ask other professionals or other businesses what they would estimate for their expenses. Not all businesses are alike, but there are similarities. Small businesses can be extremely volatile, as they are more susceptible to industry downturns. Do not be too specific, but look for average amounts

- **Break a project into stages or milestones** - Which correspond to the deliverables, which is broken down further into specific tasks, estimating the man hours that will be spent on each task. Add additional management hours or a contingency, depending on the approach to the project. Business development costs should be spread across each of the stages of the project

• ACTIVITY 5

What are the steps that can help to make an educated estimate of a budget?

There are four types of estimators with different styles for estimating income and expenditure which will have an impact on the final budget, which are:

- **Optimistic** - Where income and expenditure is overestimated

- **Pessimistic** - Where income and expenditure is underestimated

- **Inconsistent** - Where income and expenditure is estimated ranging from the optimistic to the pessimistic

- **Accurate** - Where income and expenditure is consistently estimated at about the correct levels

The best way to make educated estimates on expenditure is to know as much as possible about what needs to be paid out of the business. Expenses are not always precise. There will be occasions when expenditure is required for an unforeseen circumstance. So, if possible, always allow for a little extra for unexpected circumstances. Expecting the unexpected will help in preparing for those expenses which have not been planned for. Always build some degree of flexibility into a budget. There are two main areas to analyse when reviewing a budget:

Actual income

Each month compare actual income with the budget. To do this:

- Analyse the reasons for any shortfall, e.g. decrease in sales of a product
- Consider the reasons for a particularly high turnover, e.g. if targets were too low
- Compare the timings of income with projections and check that they fit

Actual expenditure

Regularly review actual expenditure against the budget, which will help to predict future costs with greater reliability, which can be done by:

- Looking at how fixed costs differ from the budget
- Checking variable costs were in line with the budget
- Analysing any reasons for changes in the relationship between costs and turnover
- Analysing any differences in the timing of any expenditure, e.g. check suppliers' payment terms

Analysing these variations will help to set future budgets more accurately and also allow a manager to action variations where needed.

Creating a budget

Creating a budget is for keeping an organisation's financial house in order. To create a budget it is important to provide as much detailed information as possible to guide the decision-making process. Ultimately, the end result will be able to show where your money is coming from, how much is there and where it is all going. To create a budget:

- **Make time for budgeting** - Investing quality time to create a comprehensive and realistic budget will make it easier to manage and ultimately be a more effective budget
- **Create realistic budgets** - Use historical information, business plans and any changes in operations or priorities to budget for overheads and other fixed costs. Make sure budgets contain enough information to easily monitor the key drivers of the business, e.g. sales, costs and working capital
- **Involve the right people** - Ask staff with financial responsibilities

within the business to provide estimates of figures for the budget, e.g. production costs. A more realistic budget can be achieved by balancing their estimates against those drawn up by the budget line holder. This involvement will give employees a greater commitment to meeting the priorities of a budget

- **Gather every available financial statement** - Which includes bank statements, investment accounts, recent utility bills and any information regarding a source of income or expense. The key for this process is to create a monthly average so the more information that can inform this the better

- **Record all sources of income**

- **Create a list of monthly expenses** - List all the expected expenses over a specified period of time

- **Break down expenses into two categories** - Fixed and variable costs

- **Total the income and expenses for a specified period of time** - If expenses are higher than the income look at variable expenses to find where they can be cut

Once a budget has been agreed, take some time to stand back from it and review all the cost decisions that have been made to make sure that they are realistic. As an organisation lives in a dynamic business environment, budgets should be reviewed regularly to make sure everything is financially on track, particularly if the business is growing and planning to move into new areas. An up-to-date budget enables managers to be flexible, manage cash flow and identify what needs to be achieved in the next budgeting period.

• ACTIVITY 6

What steps should be carried out to create a budget?

Negotiating a budget

There is very little difference in the negotiating strategy that needs to be undertaken to agree a budget. There will be a number of players involved in the decision-making process. Each one will be fighting for the supremacy of their budget lines which they will back up with facts to support their argument.

Negotiation takes place in three stages:

1. Preparation

The amount of time allocated to preparation will depend upon the complexity and importance of the budget being negotiated. There are five key issues to be identified when preparing to negotiate:

- What is the budget aiming to achieve?

- What are the priorities of the budget?

- How important is each stakeholder's contribution to the budget in relation to each other? Whose budget line is more important than others budget lines?

- What is each budget line's opening bid? This is going to be the best that each contributing budget holder can hope to achieve. This applies to all of the budget lines of the budget, which may apply to just a department or across the organisation. Once a budget line holder has stated what they are willing to accept, they will be negotiating towards less acceptable terms not better

- What is the budget line contributor's walk-away position? This is the least the budget line contributor is willing to accept

There will be a number of things a budget line holder wants to achieve. Generally, the negotiation process will not always fulfil all budget line holders' needs. There will be some compromising that will probably take place. Each budget line holder will need to identify the relative importance of each need and decide which they are prepared to concede to achieve the others. The budget line holder should try to establish what the other side's position is likely to be on similar issues and to establish some common ground from which the negotiation can start. Negotiations are best carried out in an atmosphere which encourages agreement. If negotiations are taking place face to face:

- Make sure to arrive on time

- Start the negotiation by confirming those areas that are already agreed

- Be seen to be listening to the other party

- Avoid making quick decisions

All budget line holders should find out what each budget line is hoping to achieve, which should be aligned to business plans so priorities can be identified and agreed. Normally, there will be some compromises that will need to be agreed between budget line holders. Having a good plan in place identifying the prioritised outcomes of a project or plan will present a more convincing argument than if figures are just being picked out of the air.

2. Discussion

The discussion stage should avoid starting with an argument. Arguments do not move negotiations forward. All sides should be suggesting solutions to overcome issues. This will help to move the negotiation into the bargaining stage, where one side offers to give up one of their needs in exchange for a concession from the other side, e.g. a budget line holder may decide to reduce their budget line if the other department worked more closely with them providing additional manpower. Each budget line holder should already have decided during the preparation stage the relative importance of their budget line and will argue to achieve it.

There are recognised negotiation strategies used by negotiators during negotiations; however, other negotiators will recognise them for what they are and will have developed countermeasures to combat them. Examples of well-known negotiation strategies and their counter strategies are:

- **Good cop / bad cop** - Where two members of a negotiating team adopt the role of one person who is difficult to negotiate with and another person who is looking for an agreement. This strategy is designed to make the opposing party accept the offer put forward by the 'good cop' because it is so much better than that being insisted on by the 'bad cop'. The counter strategy is to adopt a similar strategy

- **The builder strategy** - Where the strategy is to negotiate a budget that includes everything. The opposing party will want to include extra costs as they are incurred. The counter strategy is for the purchasing negotiator to make their specification extremely detailed

- **The double-glazing salesman ploy -** The opposing negotiators put forward what sounds like an attractive offer but impose a strict deadline on acceptance of the offer. The counter strategy is for the opposing negotiator to make it clear from the beginning what their time frame is for making the decision

- **The lesser of two evils -** The opposing negotiator gives the other negotiator a choice between two offers, one of which is so terrible that the other negotiator purchaser will accept the other which, although bad, is not as bad. The counter strategy is to refuse to accept either offer and defer to a higher authority in the organisation for agreement

- **The 'shirt off my back' approach -** The opposing negotiator convinces the purchasing negotiator that even their best offer is so unreasonable that they would be left in an impossible position if they accepted it. The counter strategy is for the purchasing negotiator to make their best offer and stick to it

The end of the discussion stage will aim to reach an agreement where all sides have a deal which is better than their walk-away position and as near as possible to their opening bid. It is possible that all parties may not be able to make an agreement, and so the process begins again. Make sure the terms of the agreement are minuted and signed by both parties so there can be no confusion over what was agreed.

3. Implementation - No negotiation is complete until an agreement has been fulfilled by all budget line holders, i.e. delivery of the final budget negotiated to achieve the priorities that each budget line holder has identified and agreed. Any failure to meet the agreed terms will require the reopening of negotiations.

Any failures during the negotiation process mainly occur in the preparation and implementation stages.

The following budget sets out what a budget may look like for a small firm in one financial year from 1 April to 31 March.

Category	Actual Inflows	Budget	Difference
Net Sales	385,400	300,000	85,400
Cost of Goods			
Merchandise Inventory, 1 April	160,000	160,000	0
Purchases	120,000	90,000	30,000
Freight Charges	2,500	2,000	500
Total Merchandise Handled	282,500	252,000	30,500
Less Inventory, 31 March	100,000	120,000	(20,000)
Cost of Goods Sold	182,500	132,000	50,500
Gross Profit	202,900	168,000	34,900
Interest Income	500	700	(200)
Total Income	**£202,500**	**£168,700**	**£33,800**
Expenses			
Salaries	68,250	45,000	23,250
Utilities	5,800	4,500	1,300
Rent	23,000	23,000	0
Office Supplies	2,250	3,000	(750)
Insurance	3,900	3,900	0
Advertising	8,650	9,000	(350)
Telephone	2,700	2,300	400
Travel and Accommodation	2,550	2,000	550
Dues and Subscriptions	1,100	1,000	100
Interest Paid	2,140	2,500	(360)
Repairs and Maintenance	1,250	1,000	250
Taxes and Licenses	11,700	10,000	1,700
Total Expenses	**£133,290**	**£106,850**	**£26,440**
Net Income	**£69,210**	**£61,850**	**£7,360**

• ACTIVITY 7

Using the above budget, separate out the fixed, variable, direct and indirect costs.

Testing your knowledge

1. What is the difference between revenue and expenditure?

2. What is the difference between a master budget and an operating budget?

3. What is the difference between an income statement and a balance sheet?

4. How important is estimating income and expenditure before agreeing a budget?

5. What is an educated estimate?

6. What are the four different types of estimators and how might their style of estimating affect a budget?

7. What are the three stages of negotiating?

Skills

Working out a budget is an important function for any organisation, and for the departments or divisions that make up the organisation. You will be working within a department or division which will have agreed a budget for the operational costs it will need to facilitate the achievement of the objectives it has set itself. If possible, participate in the planning and agreement of the budget with your manager. You may have overall responsibility for maintaining the budget on a weekly or monthly basis, where you may have to let your manager know that the budget is on course or identify overspends. You may also be involved in identifying the risks attached to a project that you may be involved in delivering. Risks are not static objects which once identified are permanent to a budget, as they will vary over the life of a project and its budget. A particular high risk attached to any budget is running over the stipulated time a project has been agreed to be completed. This may have implications for financial years and require working with your finance department to agree carrying forward a budget into the new financial year.

• ACTIVITY 8

Your manager has asked you to draw up a budget to replace the existing workstations and equipment for your department. Identify the total budget, breaking it down into its component parts to include fixed and variable costs, estimating what these will be and the time it will take to complete the work.

If you are working on a project team and have responsibility for delivering a milestone or part of a milestone, draw up your budget for this part of the project. Go over all the different types of cost that will be involved, how long it will take to deliver the milestone covered by the budget and the risks that the budget may undergo. Once you have completed your budget check through this with either your manager or the project manager and rationalise to them the choices that you have made for expenses. If they are not content with what you have estimated, negotiate with them until both of you are mutually satisfied. You will both want to make sure that the project achieves its aims, which can only be delivered by a realistic and appropriate budget. In times of recession and the rescaling of organisations to deliver more for the same, estimating a budget in the 21st century can be challenging.

Testing your skills

1. What financial resources did you use to plan budgets?
2. What did you do to evaluate and justify the costs of budgets?
3. What did you do to evaluate and justify associated risks?
4. How did you plan budgets?
5. How did you negotiate to achieve acceptance of your budget line?

Ready for assessment?

To achieve this Level 3 unit of a Business & Administration qualification, learners will need to demonstrate that they are able to perform the following activities:

1. Identified financial resources needed to achieve goals and objectives for agreeing a budget
2. Evaluated and justified costs and risks
3. Prepared a draft budget
4. Negotiated and agreed a budget

You will need to produce evidence from a variety of sources to support the performance requirements of this unit.

If you carry out the 'ACTIVITIES' and respond to the 'NEED TO KNOW' questions, these will provide some of the evidence required.

Links to other units
While gathering evidence for this unit, evidence may also be used from evidence generated from other units within the Business & Administration suite of units. Below is a sample of applicable units; however, most units within the Business & Administration suite of units will also be applicable.

QCF NVQ
Communications
Communicate in a business environment (Level 3)
Core business & administration
Evaluate and improve own performance in a business environment (Level 3)
Solve business problems (Level 3)
Work in a business environment (Level 3)
Work with other people in a business environment (Level 3)
Contribute to decision-making in a business environment
Negotiate in a business environment (Level 3)
Customer service
Deliver, monitor and evaluate customer service to internal customers

SVQ
Communications
Plan how to communicate in a business environment
Core business & administration
Solve business problems
Review and maintain work in a business environment
Support other people to work in a business environment
Contribute to decision-making in a business environment
Contribute to negotiations in a business environment
Customer service
Deliver, monitor and evaluate customer service to internal customers
Deliver, monitor and evaluate customer service to internal customers

2 Order products and servicess

ORDER PRODUCTS AND SERVICES

'Order products and services' is an <u>optional unit</u> which may be chosen as one of a combination of units to achieve either a Qualifications and Credit Framework (QCF), National Vocational Qualification (NVQ) or Scottish Vocational Qualification (SVQ).

The aims of this unit are to:

- Understand how to identify, select and negotiate the supply of services

- Understand organisational requirements and policies for the ordering and supply of products and services

- Understand how to monitor, evaluate and improve procedures for the ordering and supply of products and services

- Be able to follow organisational procedures for the ordering and supply of products and services

- Be able to maintain relationships with suppliers of products and services and deal with problems

- Be able to monitor, evaluate and make recommendations to improve the ordering and supply of products and services

To achieve the above aims of this unit, learners will be expected to provide evidence through the performance of work-based activities.

Knowledge

The process of ordering products and services that involves buying goods and services from appointed suppliers is called **procurement**. Most large organisations will probably have a procurement department with a team of legal advisers to support the drawing up of contracts and offer any legal advice when agreeing specifications. In smaller organisations, anyone could be involved in buying goods and services with no central point of contact. The procurement of products and services is more important in some organisations than in others. Purchases could involve external third parties or the purchasing department from within an organisation or someone within an organisation making specific purchases. Procurement can range from contracting an entire service, e.g. an external supplier to provide training, to purchasing small assets, e.g. office equipment, such as a laminator.

• ACTIVITY 1

What is procurement?

The procurement process spans the entire life cycle of a product or service from inception and design through to contract management and disposal of any redundant assets. The procurement process should deliver **high-quality services** which meet the current and future needs of the organisation and are based on **value for money**. An organisation may have agreed a **procurement strategy** from which **procurement policies** will have been developed, which they will expect employees to follow to make sure a quality service is achieved. A procurement strategy could aim to have any of the following aspirations:

- Make sure the process of procurement practice contributes to the effective use of resources
- Make sure procurement delivers year-on-year efficiencies and savings
- Make sure quality is measured by seeking feedback from customers
- Secure commitment to consistent and coordinated procurement when ordering products and services to achieve the delivery of high-quality, innovative and cost-effective services
- Encourage long-term thinking and commitment to a strategic approach to procurement issues
- Make sure that costing methods are used to assess and evaluate costs and benefits over the entire life of assets and services
- Establish a mechanism to link procurement action plans to the procurement strategy
- Promote the continuous improvement of procurement activity across the organisation
- Provide greater visibility and understanding of the role of the procurement function
- Develop skills and provide support for staff involved in procurement
- Promote and deliver sustainability, local economic development, equality and diversity objectives throughout procurement activities
- Continue to use and further develop procurement collaboration with other public bodies and partnering arrangements with suppliers in the public sector

- Recognise the contribution of procurement to achieving community, corporate, departmental and service objectives

- Raise awareness of the complex regulatory framework in which procurement operates

- Raise awareness of the risks involved in procurement, e.g. financial, legal, environmental, health & safety and reputation

• ACTIVITY 2

What purpose is served to the organisation by a procurement strategy?

As a result of having a procurement strategy in place, the procurement process could involve the following activities:

- Researching new sources of products, service and suppliers to meet the future requirements of the organisation

- Cooperating with other departments within the organisation

- Training staff

- Selecting the best available and most cost-effective suppliers and making sure appropriate service level agreements have been negotiated

- Maintaining relationships with suppliers which provide continuity of supply

- Monitoring market trends

- Negotiating with suppliers to achieve value for money

The process of procurement for any department will have agreed a **procurement budget** within which products and services will be purchased. The aim of the procurement budget, like most budgets, is to minimise or reduce costs to the organisation. The figure below shows some of the ways that costs can be reduced when purchasing products and services:

Figure 2.1. Reducing purchasing costs

An organisation's profits may be increased by improving purchasing activities and has more effect on the bottom line than by similar improvements in sales. An organisation with a profit ratio of 10%, which spends 50% of its turnover on products and services, can increase its profit margin by either increasing its turnover by 25% or by reducing its spending by 5% - every pound not spent is a pound extra profit, but every extra pound earned incurs costs and is therefore less than a pound extra profit.

• ACTIVITY 3

What strategies can be used to reduce costs in the purchasing of products and services?

An integral function of procurement is for purchasers to develop relationships with suppliers that are of mutual benefit to themselves and the supplier which should encourage the sharing of resources, e.g. technology, providing increased value to both parties. As overlapping interests are identified, additional efficiencies can be achieved, driving down the costs to the purchaser while maintaining the profit margin of the supplier. This kind of relationship will vary between purchasers and suppliers. According to Pareto's Law, 20% of suppliers will supply 80% of an organisation's needs - the customer relationship needs to be sustained and improved with this 20% of suppliers to realise the benefits from increased economies of scale.

When purchasing products or services the purchaser needs to determine which supplier or mode of supply will provide the **best value for money**. The concept of value for money is not restricted to price alone but needs to factor in the:

* **Contribution to the advancement of business / organisation priorities -** The aim should be to select sources of materials and equipment that have relatively low costs and where supply is easy to

secure. This will not always be achievable. Various factors that can be considered to achieve this include:

- The business / organisation priorities and its procurement guidance

- Rates and an evaluation of materials and equipment against selection criteria

- Limiting selection to only those suppliers that demonstrate agreed attributes

- Limiting selection to suppliers who have been pre-qualified, having met organisational priorities

- **Non-cost factors**, which include:

  - **Fitness for purpose:** the extent to which materials and equipment will deliver specified outcomes

  - **Technical and financial issues**

- Product-related factors include:

  - Technical performance, which needs to consider the 'duty' of materials or equipment

  - Reliability, to make sure customer expectations have been met with regard to functionality and performance, including contractual guarantee conditions

  - Economic life, to determine when materials and equipment become more economical to replace rather than to maintain. Action that would need to be taken to make this decision would be a cost-benefit analysis, management judgement, the degree of use and corporate policy

  - Maintainability

  - Supplier-related factors usually concern supplier capability, which includes the supplier's management capability, financial viability, technical expertise, methodology, systems, previous performance and capacity to complete the supply requirement.

- **Risk exposure,** which arises from the:

  - Purchaser organisation

  - Goods or services

  - Supplier

- Market
- **Benefits to be obtained from the purchase**
- **Availability of maintenance and support**
- **Compliance with specifications, where relevant**
- **Cost-related factors**, which will depend on the nature of the goods / services to be acquired, which should consider:
  - **Whole-of-life costs**, which include: acquisition costs, operating costs, maintenance costs, cleaning costs, alteration / refurbishment costs, support costs and disposal
  - **Transaction costs**, which include: establishing the need for the purchase, planning for the purchase, identifying sources of supply, approaching the market to seek supply, selecting suppliers, ordering and processing payments and managing relationships with suppliers

• ACTIVITY 4

What factors need to be considered to achieve value for money?

Value for money is not just about procuring the cheapest price but considering all the factors that may be hidden within the price of products or services. For an organisation to remain efficient and effective - of worth and value - it needs to make sure that the quality of products and services provided by suppliers is supplied:

- At the **agreed time**
- At the **agreed price**
- To the **agreed quality**
- In the **agreed quantity**
- With the **agreed supplementary support services**
- **Problem free**, or the supplier responds to purchase enquires quickly

Most organisations will endeavour to agree a **service level agreement (SLA)** with suppliers they contract with. A SLA is an agreement or contract that defines the service suppliers must provide. Essentially, the SLA is aiming to safeguard the performance that the purchaser expects to be delivered by a supplier of products or services. The SLA sets out the level of service to be delivered and its responsibilities and priorities. SLAs are **contractual obligations** and are often built into a contract. A SLA can be a complex document which should be well defined and drawn up and agreed with precision, highlighting the most critical components of the agreement so the strictest penalties can apply to these clauses. A SLA should identify the number of **performance reviews** that will be taken and specify the conditions that will initiate such reviews. A SLA will typically set out:

- The **service** being provided

- The **standards of service**

- The respective **responsibilities of supplier** and **purchaser**

- Provisions for **legal** and **regulatory compliance**

- Mechanisms for **monitoring** and **reporting** on the service

- **Payment terms**

- How **disputes** will be resolved

- Confidentiality and non-disclosure provisions

- Termination conditions

If suppliers fail to meet agreed levels of service, the SLA will usually provide for compensation. A SLA should be updated constantly as the needs of a business change, as different performance criteria may be required. Improvements in technology should also be taken into account when reviewing a SLA.

• ACTIVITY 5

What is a SLA and what is it used for?

Source products and services

Having specified the products or services that are required, it is then necessary to source the product. Some products will have been supplied on a continuous basis by the same supplier, perhaps perfectly satisfactorily, but the purchaser should be constantly on the alert for alternative sources that may reduce costs without compromising quality. While the final decision may often be to remain with the same supplier for regularly purchased items, the process of sourcing products and services should still be followed. Most organisations will probably have a list of suppliers that they use; however, if they do not or if a current supplier needs replacing, possible sources of suppliers can be found through the following means:

- **Recommendation** - Other buyers in an organisation or an employee's network of contacts with other organisations may be able to give details of suppliers that have satisfactorily supplied similar needs in the past

- **History** - There may be suppliers who have previously supplied1 an employee or the organisation with similar products or services

- **Registration with British Standards Institute (BSI) or similar** - The BSI website gives access to certificated and kitemarked organisations

- **Catalogues / price lists** - Most organisation's purchasing departments will have a library of useful material provided by potential suppliers

- **Trade directories** - Many trades and professions publish directories containing details of suppliers

- **Agencies** - Organisations whose sole business is to source potential suppliers for other organisations

- **The Internet** - Suppliers of products and services can be found on the Internet

Before selecting a supplier, contact should be made with a number of different suppliers from which an assessment of their service should be made before deciding on the supplier to contract with. When assessing the strength and weaknesses of a supplier, a purchaser could use the following criteria to make a choice:

- **Past performance** - The quality of service will already be known

- **Reputation** - Recommendations from others

- **Quality** - The potential supplier needs to consistently deliver to a level of quality that will satisfy the organisation. The purchaser should discuss a supplier's understanding of the specification and their past record in achieving similar quality with similar organisations

- **Quantity** - The potential supplier should be able to deliver the quantity of products or services that are required. Checks should be made of the financial stability of suppliers. A supplier who is not able to pay their bills on time will not be able to operate successfully

If a supplier ceases to trade before meeting their commitment to a purchaser, the organisation will be left searching desperately for a replacement at short notice

- **Timing** - Many organisations work to a 'Just-In-Time' (JIT) system, which reduces the need for investing money or space in holding stock. The purchaser will need to be confident that the chosen supplier can consistently supply resources

- **Service** - After-sales service is important. The availability of repairs and planned maintenance on plant and machinery or office equipment could override considerations of initial price. Before-sales service may also be important for some products and services. The purchaser will need to consider if the supplier is easy to contact or if quotations are delivered when promised or if technical support will be available. The purchaser will be looking for a reliable service

- **Price** - This may not always be the main choice for selecting a supplier. Consideration should be given to the total acquisition cost, taking into account all of the factors which add to the total cost, when comparing competing suppliers' quotations

• ACTIVITY 6

What should the purchaser / procurer investigate before making a choice of supplier?

The purchaser could also visit the supplier to gain an understanding of the scale of the supplier's operations to make sure they will be able to accommodate the purchaser's requirements. It is useful to order or request, free of charge, a small quantity of a product to test a supplier's suitability before committing  the organisation to using a supplier. If the purchaser has little or no previous experience of procurement, it is important to find the right supplier - the supplier who will meet all the needs of the organisation and provide the best value for money.

The first decision the purchaser will make is to decide if to place orders with a **single supplier** or to split orders across two or more suppliers.

This will depend on the types of products and services to be supplied to an organisation based on the considerations above when investigating potential suppliers. For example, there may be only one supplier able to meet the purchase specification in an acceptable time, at an acceptable price and with an acceptable level of service or an order for a quantity of products which would not be viable if split between two or more suppliers. However, the purchaser may wish to consider the following:

- Placing a whole order with one supplier may lead to the closure of the other suppliers and create a monopoly

- A single supplier may offer a better price based on quantity; however, placing orders with several suppliers could get a better price based on competition

- Orders with a single supplier may result in deliveries being made more easily as there is only one supplier to deal with; however, if an order is placed with several suppliers it will be protected from the risk of disruption of supply should something go wrong with one supplier's distribution

- A single supplier will be motivated to go out of their way to fulfil a purchase order, but on the other hand, they may become complacent and begin to fail to fulfil an organisation's requirements

Once the purchaser has selected a list of potential suppliers the purchaser will need to **negotiate** with the selected suppliers to make sure an organisation obtains the best value for money. Negotiations may be based on one issue or many, held on a one-to-one basis or between teams. The negotiations may be conducted over the telephone and concluded in a matter of minutes or they may be conducted face to face over a prolonged period.

Negotiation takes place in three stages:

- **Preparation** - The amount of time allocated to preparation will depend upon the complexity and importance of the negotiation. There are four key issues to be identified when preparing to negotiate:

  - What does the purchaser want to achieve?

  - How important is each of the purchaser's identified needs in relation to each of the others?

- What is the purchaser's opening bid? This is going to be the best bid the purchaser can hope to achieve which will be withheld for as long as possible before disclosing what the bid is. This applies to all of the conditions of the purchase, quality, quantity, timing, service and price. Once the purchaser has stated what they are willing to accept, they will be negotiating towards less acceptable terms not better

- What is the purchaser's walk-away position? This is the least a purchaser is willing to accept

There will be a number of things the purchaser wants to achieve. Generally, the negotiation process will not always fulfil all a purchaser's needs. The purchaser will need to identify the relative importance of each need and decide which they are prepared to concede to achieve the others. The purchaser should try to establish what the other side's position is likely to be on the same issues and to establish some common ground from which the negotiation can start. Negotiations are best carried out in an atmosphere which encourages agreement. If negotiations are taking place face to face:

- Make sure to arrive on time

- Start the negotiation by confirming those areas that are already agreed

- Be seen to be listening to the other party

- Avoid making quick decisions

The purchaser should try find out what the other side is looking for and encourage them to state their opening bid before stating theirs. This is because the purchaser will be hoping that the supplier's opening bid offers the purchaser a better deal than they were going to ask for. Normally, however, there will a gap between opening bids which will need to be negotiated.

- **Discussion -** The discussion stage should avoid starting with an argument. Arguments do not move negotiations forward. Both sides should be suggesting solutions to overcome problems. This will help to move the negotiation into the bargaining stage, where one side offers to give up one of their needs in exchange for a concession from the other side, e.g. the supplier may offer to reduce the unit price in exchange for a longer delivery time. The purchaser should already have decided during the preparation stage the relative importance of price and delivery and will be able to respond to this offer accordingly

There are recognised negotiation strategies used by negotiators during negotiations; however, other negotiators will recognise them for what they are and will have developed countermeasures to combat them. Examples of well-known negotiation strategies and their counter strategies are:

- **Good cop / bad cop** - Where two members of a negotiating team adopt the role of one person who is difficult to negotiate with and another person who is looking for an agreement. This strategy is designed to make the opposing party accept the offer put forward by the 'good cop' because it is so much better than that being insisted on by the 'bad cop'. The counter strategy is to adopt a similar strategy

- **The builder strategy** - Where the strategy is to negotiate a price that includes everything. The opposing party will want to include extra costs as they are incurred. The counter strategy is for the purchasing negotiator to make their specification extremely detailed

- **The double-glazing salesman ploy** - The opposing negotiators put forward what sounds like an attractive offer but impose a strict deadline on the purchaser's acceptance. The counter strategy is for the purchasing negotiator to make it clear from the beginning what their time frame is for making the decision

- **The lesser of two evils** - The opposing negotiator gives the purchasing negotiator a choice between two offers, one of which is so terrible that the purchaser will accept the other which, although bad, is not as bad. The counter strategy is to refuse to accept either offer and to go elsewhere

- **The 'shirt off my back' approach** - The opposing negotiator convinces the purchasing negotiator that even their best offer is so unreasonable that they would be left in an impossible position if they accepted it. The counter strategy is for the purchasing negotiator to make their best offer and stick to it

The end of the discussion stage will aim to reach an agreement where both sides have a deal which is better than their walk-away position and as near as possible to their opening bid. It is possible that both parties may not be able to make an agreement, and so the process begins again. Make sure the terms of the agreement are set out in a contract and signed by both parties so there can be no confusion over what was agreed.

- **Implementation** - No negotiation is complete until an agreement has been fulfilled, i.e. delivery of products or services negotiated at the price, time, quantity, quality and with the service agreed. Any failure to meet the agreed terms will require the reopening of negotiations. A wise procurer will make sure that penalties for failure to meet the obligations on the part of the supplier are included in the contract or purchase order

Any failures during the negotiation process mainly occur in the preparation and implementation stages.

Specifications

Although every purchase order will specify what is to be supplied, by when and at what price, formal detailed specifications are not drawn up for the majority of purchases. It is likely that the required product or service is commercially available from a number of suppliers at an acceptable price. The purchasing department simply selects their requirements from those available. Some products or services are more specialised, either technically or in terms of availability. It is a part of the purchasing department's responsibility to specify exactly what is required. Where national or international standards apply to the items being purchased, these are often used as the quality specification.

The purchasing department will liaise closely with other departments to determine the **final specification**. If the products are for resale, the marketing and sales departments will have a major contribution to make. If the product is for use in manufacture, the production department will be heavily involved. The purchasing department's role is to provide commercial expertise, advising what is available, to what timescale and at what price, to temper the purely technical expertise which would possibly specify the best possible product rather than the most commercially viable.

Specifications will usually state a 'tolerance', both in the quantity and quality of products to be supplied, as marginal costs can have a significant effect on unit price. The purchasing department will also remain in touch with changing situations and market prices. They will be able to advise when the specification of a product or service should be amended to meet new conditions.

• ACTIVITY 7

What is a specification and why is it required for purchasing products or services?

Purchase products and services

Most organisations will raise a **purchase order** to officially place a purchase order with a supplier. The purpose of the purchase order is to define what the purchaser is committed to accept and pay for. The goods receiving department will be given a copy of all purchase orders and instructed only to accept deliveries against an outstanding order. A copy is also often sent to the finance or procurement department with instructions that invoices should only be paid against an official order and delivery note. Purchase orders come in different forms, as they may be produced manually or electronically over the Internet; however, there should always be some form of agreement between the purchaser and the supplier.

In cases of high-value or complex purchases, a **contract** may be used as the purchase order. A contract may cover a number of orders over a period of time or a geographical area. Contracts are often renewed annually to allow the purchasing department to review the supplier's performance. It is a good idea to stagger the renewal dates of annual contracts to avoid being faced with renewing all contracts every December. Signatures on contracts and orders are binding on the organisation. In most organisations different levels of staff will have authority to sign contracts and orders based on the value of the contract or order.

The purchase of products and services is not complete until delivery has been satisfactorily made. The purchasing department will need to be advised of deliveries received against orders to track the supplier's performance against the original agreement or contract. Deliveries are checked against the purchase order and some form of goods received note produced. Often this will be raised electronically. Where goods do not meet the purchaser's specification, this will be noted by the receiving department and arrangements will need to be made with the supplier for their disposal. The **method of disposal** will depend on the agreement made between the purchaser and the supplier at the time of the order. Methods will include:

- Return to the supplier for credit

- Acceptance at a reduced price
- The goods being scrapped by the receiver and a credit note raised by the supplier

• ACTIVITY 8

What are the methods of disposal?

The next step in the procedure is the arrival of the invoice. This will be checked against the purchase order and the delivery note and, if everything is satisfactory, payment arranged. Invoice authorisation may be carried out by the accounts department or the purchasing department. There are circumstances in which the normal purchasing procedures will not apply. Processing large numbers of small orders is often not an efficient system, as the administration cost may be disproportionate to the value of the order. An organisation that operates from a large number of sites may place a blanket order with a supplier for an unspecified quantity of an item to be delivered as and when requested by any of the sites. Invoices will then be raised against the deliveries made quoting the blanket order number.

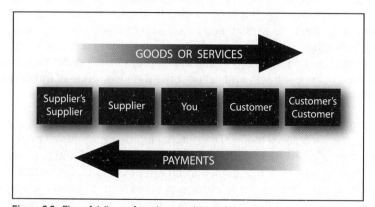

Figure 2.2. Flow of delivery of goods or services and payments

Large or complex projects may have a procedure designed especially to cover the purchasing of all the products and services required. For example, if a department was responsible for placing the order to design and build a hospital it will need technical support to produce specifications before it can source suppliers. The process often used in this situation is called **two-stage tendering**. The first stage is to invite unpriced technical bids from which a technical specification is prepared and used for the second stage in which complete priced bids are invited.

Sometimes there is a network of retailers, distributors, transporters, storage facilities and suppliers that are involved in the production, delivery and sale of a product to a consumer. This network is called a **supply chain**. The supply chain is usually made up of multiple companies who coordinate activities to set themselves apart from the competition. A supply chain has three key parts:

- **Supply** - Which focuses on the raw materials supplied to manufacturing, including how, when and from what location

- **Manufacturing** - Which focuses on converting these raw materials into finished products

- **Distribution** - Which focuses on making sure these products reach customers through an organised network of distributors, warehouses and retailers

While often applied to manufacturing and consumer products, a supply chain can also be used to show how several processes supply to one another, which can apply to Internet technology, finance and many other industries. A **supply chain strategy** defines how the supply chain should operate in order to compete in the market and evaluates the benefits and costs relating to the operation. The supply chain strategy focuses on the actual operations of the organisation and the supply chain that will be used to meet a specific goal.

Associated with a supply chain is **supply chain management (SCM)**. SCM is the control of the supply chain as a process from supplier to manufacturer to wholesaler to retailer to consumer. SCM covers the movement of a physical product, e.g. a microchip, through the chain as well as any data that goes along with the product, e.g. payment schedules, and the actual entities that handle the product from stage to stage of the supply chain. SCM involves coordinating this flow of materials within a company and to the end consumer. SCM can be divided into three main flows:

- The **product** flow includes moving goods from supplier to consumer and deals with customer service needs

- The **information** flow includes order information and delivery status

- The **financial** flow includes payment schedules, credit terms and consignment and title ownership arrangements

The three goals of SCM are to:

- Reduce inventory
- Increase the speed of transactions with real-time data exchange
- Increase revenue by satisfying customer demands more efficiently

• ACTIVITY 9

What is SCM and what does it aim to achieve?

Another form of customer-supplier relationship to be aware of is known as **reciprocity**. This is a system where organisation A buys from organisation B on the understanding that B will in turn buy from A. This has benefits in that both organisations have a market for their product, but the drawback is that it limits their choice of suppliers. It may make good sense from the sales department's point of view, but is unlikely to be the best solution for a purchasing department.

A form of customer-supplier relationship which may appear on the face of it to be relatively simple, but, in reality, is often complex, is the relationship between two companies within the same group of companies. The decision whether to purchase from an associated company rather than on the open market complicates the supplier selection process. On the one hand, inter-company purchases are beneficial to the group as a whole, as all of the profit from the transaction remains within the group. On the other hand, the relationship between the two companies can skew the competitiveness of the supply. Unless it is group policy that purchases are to be made from associated companies whenever possible, the purchasing department will probably treat them in the same way as any external supplier. Associated with the question of inter-company purchasing is the whole issue of **outsourcing**. In the same way that the purchaser will look at external suppliers in competition with potential suppliers from within the group, the purchaser should also consider whether services provided by other departments in the organisation could be supplied more efficiently from external sources.

• ACTIVITY 10

What is outsourcing in the context of procurement?

Problems can occur when the delivery date is not met. Purchasers will ordinarily blame the supplier for failing to carry out the agreement, but it is not always that simple. Sometimes the problem will be with the purchaser, who has allowed insufficient time for delivery, sometimes it will be with the supplier, who has quoted an unachievable delivery date in order to secure the order. Sometimes a problem is beyond the control of either party. There may be transport difficulties, industrial action, weather conditions or difficulties further along the supply chain. The first step to avoiding problems associated with late delivery is to make sure that the user department appreciates the **lead time** involved. Lead time is the minimum delay between placing the order and receiving the goods, which depends on the supply position - whether the goods have to be manufactured specially to meet the specification and the distance the goods have to travel. If the delivery date has taken into account the lead time, then it is reasonable to judge the supplier's performance on their ability to deliver the products or services on time. The supplier can then be advised that their performance will be taken into account when the selection of suppliers, to meet future requirements, is considered. There are two ways of measuring supplier performance in this area. The number of overdue deliveries as a percentage of total deliveries will give a simple ranking. A slightly more complicated measure is to consider how late deliveries are and weight the ranking accordingly. The choice between the two measures depends on whether the purchaser would rather have a number of slightly late deliveries or most deliveries on time and occasional deliveries very late.

Some organisations will have a section within the purchasing department whose responsibility is to **expedite** the receipt of products and services. Expediting should be a proactive task rather than a reactive, fire-fighting exercise. Those responsible for expediting should be in regular contact with suppliers between the placing of the order and the due date for delivery to continually check on the order's progress. This will allow the supplier to advise in advance where a problem has arisen which puts the delivery date in jeopardy. Action can then be taken either to assist the supplier to overcome the problem or to source the requirements elsewhere before the delay becomes critical. The true aim of the expediting section should be to make their work unnecessary. If the following standards can be regularly achieved the need to expedite will have been considerably reduced:

- User departments accept lead times
- Specifications are unambiguous
- Specifications are considered sacrosanct by purchasers
- The ability of suppliers to meet contracts is effectively checked prior to placing orders
- Suppliers do not offer what they know is unachievable
- Delivery dates are specified not implied
- Delivery dates are considered sacrosanct by purchasers
- Purchasers and suppliers understand and respect each other's needs

• ACTIVITY 11

What standards should be aimed for to eliminate the use of expediting?

The purchasing of products and services is an area which requires constant monitoring in order to make sure that all possible areas of inefficiency are eliminated. This includes internal systems and procedures as well as the selection and performance monitoring of suppliers.

Testing your knowledge

1. What is the role of a procurer?

2. Why is the contribution from improved efficiency in purchasing greater than that from an equivalent improvement in sales?

3. How does purchase price differ from total acquisition cost?

4. Describe the three phases of negotiation

5. Describe some common negotiation strategies and identify how they can be countered

6. Why are negotiations not complete until agreements are implemented?

7. What is the purpose of a purchase order?

8. What are the differences between a purchase order and a contract?

9. When is a purchase completed?

10. How does a supply chain work?

11. What is meant by 'lead time'?

12. What is the aim of expediting?

Performance

As someone looking after ordering products and services or procurement, you should keep abreast of the requirements of various departments in your organisation that you will be working for, as well as their feedback, to see if services from your suppliers can be improved. The bottom line of any organisation is always looking for ways of improving not just the price of goods and services but also the quality of service being provided by your supplier, and this can help to minimise costs. You should maintain a positive relationship with your supplier and have open communication with them. If you are not getting feedback from your stakeholders you could design a feedback form to impress on them the importance of making sure the service they receive is as agreed in the specifications or contracts signed between your organisation and its suppliers.

Make sure when you are agreeing specifications or contracts that they meet all the requirements that your organisation is looking to achieve for its business. Your specifications should outline the budget you will be working within to place different orders for the stakeholders in your organisation. Specifications are legal documents binding on both parties who sign them. These should be followed to the letter to make sure that service of delivery of products or services is always achieving value for money. Consider what the expectations of your organisation are for achieving value for money. You will need to make sure that this conforms to the ethical values that your organisation practises. Remember, there is more to value for money than just agreeing a good price, as you will need to consider other service requirements you want the product or service to deliver. Products and services should be procured conforming to the requirements of your organisation's relevant policies and procedures. As the person who looks after procurements, you are in the ideal position to feedback any issues you have found with the implementation of the policy or procedures. Value for money is also an internal organisation issue which you can contribute towards enhancing. Look for every opportunity in your work to increase value to the organisation by diminishing waste of any kind.

Specifications or contracts should outline exactly what both parties expect of each other. This relationship may be further strengthened by agreeing SLAs. Each of these documents aims to create a relationship of trust and delivery between parties. In this way, there should be no hidden agendas from any party. The specification or contract will have been negotiated openly between both parties who have signed the specification or contract.

• ACTIVITY 12

Evaluate the performance of a selection of your organisation's current suppliers. Write a report indicating where better value for money can be achieved through improving efficiency.

All specifications or contracts should be agreed by your organisation's procurement or legal department to make sure all clauses are relevant and can be achieved. Specifications or contract are the means by which you are able to assess the quality of delivery of the service with your suppliers. The service provided by your suppliers should be monitored on an ongoing basis. Decide, if the SLA has not done this, when it would be appropriate to have performance review meetings with your suppliers. Additional information about the supplier's performance should be collected from all your stakeholders who are directly involved in receiving this service. It is important for your reputation and the reputation of the organisation that you are seen to be maintaining these relationships.

• ACTIVITY 13

Your line manager has decided to replace all the office furniture in your department. You have been given the task of writing a specification for the replacement furniture covering the quantity, quality and features required. Liaise with the users to produce a specification. Source potential suppliers to meet this agreed specification. Compare their relative strengths and weaknesses. Obtain prices from each supplier. Consider whether one supplier or a number of suppliers would best suit your requirements. Write a recommendation on the supplier (s) to be used, justifying your reasons for selection. Raise dummy purchase orders for the supply of the office furniture. Consider whether staged deliveries or a one-hit delivery would be least disruptive for the department and take into account comparative total acquisition costs. Schedule the delivery as required.

It is inevitable that problems may occur from time to time. A measured approach should be taken to investigating why the problem has occurred. Do not jump to conclusions and blame the supplier immediately. A problem may have occurred which was beyond their control, e.g. traffic problems, a bomb alert. As with the negotiation process, it is important to work from a level of mutual respect. Do not assume anything that you cannot back with facts. Even if a problem has occurred which is beyond the control of your suppliers, take this as an opportunity to review your specifications or contracts, particularly if this problem recurs frequently. There may be other suppliers who are able to deliver a seamless service for your organisation.

• ACTIVITY 14

Your organisation has reviewed the financial services it receives. It has decided to evaluate alternative products and services with a view to implementing changes in the future. Identify the range of financial products and services that are needed in your organisation. Carry out research to identify and cost alternative solutions for your organisation, making sure you point out the benefits for each recommendation.

The benefits from evaluating the quality of service provided by your suppliers can be felt across various aspects of a business, which include:

- Minimising disruption to the service being provided to employees
- Valuing employees by making sure service is delivered as agreed
- Maintaining good business relationships with external suppliers
- Maintaining good business relationships with internal suppliers
- Rationalising and minimising costs to the business
- Improving the quality of service provided by all suppliers

An evaluation of the delivery service of your suppliers should be carried out using data and information that is recorded and backed up with documentary evidence. You could keep incident reports which will outline the issues involved and should be date stamped. Incident reports are helpful for identifying patterns of the service being provided by suppliers. Having documentary evidence will also help to negotiate more advantageous services, goods or prices to the organisation. Issues or incidents should be investigated thoroughly to correctly identify the source of the service issues, e.g. frequency of problems.

Testing your skills

1. How have you developed mutually beneficial relationships with suppliers?

2. How have you specified products and services?

3. Why should you consider changing suppliers whenever a new order is raised?

4. Who do you liaise with when specifying products and services?

5. What sources are used to identify potential new suppliers and how are they assessed?

6. How have you investigated potential new suppliers?

7. What level of authorisation do you have for raising a purchase order in your organisation?

8. How do you deal with unsatisfactory products in your organisation?

9. When would you raise blanket orders?

10. What is your organisation's policy on inter-company purchasing?

Ready for assessment?
To achieve this Level 3 unit of a Business & Administration qualification, learners will need to demonstrate that they are able to perform the following activities:

1. Used available information to keep up to date with products and services in own area of work

2. Agreed a budget and specification for products and services to be ordered

3. Identified sources of products and services that met the quality specifications of the organisation

4. Selected the product or services which represented best value for money

5. Procured products or services following organisational procedures

6. Negotiated with selected suppliers to reach an agreement which offered good value for money and which was acceptable to both parties, within limits of own authority

7. Agreed a contract for the supply of products or services, within limits of own authority

8. Took actions to create and maintain partnerships with suppliers to improve quality and cut costs, within limits of own authority

9. Monitored the performance of suppliers in line with the terms of the contract

10. Dealt with problems as they occurred, seeking support from others, where necessary

11. Monitored the ordering and supply of products and services for effectiveness and efficiency

12. Evaluated the ordering and supply of products and services and identified areas for improvement

13. Suggested ways to improve effectiveness and efficiency and obtained better value for money for the supply of products and services

You will need to produce evidence from a variety of sources to support the performance requirements of this unit.

If you carry out the 'ACTIVITIES' and respond to the 'NEED TO KNOW' questions, these will provide some of the evidence required.

Links to other units

While gathering evidence for this unit, evidence may also be used from evidence generated from other units within the Business & Administration suite of units. Below is a sample of applicable units; however, most units within the Business & Administration suite of units will also be applicable

QCF NVQ
Communications
Communicate in a business environment (Level 3)
Make and receive telephone calls
Core business & administration
Evaluate and improve own performance in a business environment (Level 3)
Solve business problems (Level 3)
Work in a business environment (Level 3)
Work with other people in a business environment (Level 3)
Contribute to decision-making in a business environment
Negotiate in a business environment (Level 3)
Customer service
Deliver, monitor and evaluate customer service to internal customers
Deliver, monitor and evaluate customer service to external customers

SVQ
Communications
Plan how to communicate in a business environment
Core business & administration
Solve business problems
Review and maintain work in a business environment
Support other people to work in a business environment
Contribute to decision-making in a business environment
Contribute to negotiations in a business environment
Customer service
Deliver, monitor and evaluate customer service to internal customers
Deliver, monitor and evaluate customer service to external customers

3 Supervise an office facility

SUPERVISE AN OFFICE FACILITY

'Supervise an office facility' is an <u>optional unit</u> which may be chosen as one of a combination of units to achieve either a Qualifications and Credit Framework (QCF), National Vocational Qualification (NVQ) or Scottish Vocational Qualification (SVQ).

The aims of this unit are to:

- Understand how to provide, maintain and supervise an office facility that meets the needs of its users

- Understand how to deal with repairs and problems when supervising office facilities and equipment

- Understand the purpose of health, safety and security requirements in an office

- Be able to supervise an office facility

To achieve the above aims of this unit, learners will be expected to provide evidence through the performance of work-based activities.

Knowledge

Supervising an office facility is a complex and diverse function. The office supervisor has to develop and maintain office procedures and systems for:

People, which will include:

- Managing employees to help them meet their targets

- Developing employees - the more skills and knowledge employees have the more the office supervisor is able to delegate tasks to different people and overcome the boredom that comes from repetition

- Navigating office politics, to avoid conflict and limit the growth of personal jealousies to manage employees more easily

- Build an environment of trust, empowerment and confidence - making sure the psychological contract is adhered to by both the office supervisor and their employees

- Dealing with external suppliers of products and services

- Dealing with complaints from both internal and external customers

- Complying with health and safety regulations and security precautions for employees and visitors

- Communicating across different levels of the organisation
- Maintaining records, e.g. employee holidays, days off, breaks and attendance at training courses
- Managing staff budgets

Physical resources, which will include:

- Supplying equipment and technology
- Repairing equipment and technology
- Upgrading equipment and technology
- Providing, maintaining and upgrading manuals for using equipment and technology
- Complying with health and safety regulations and taking security precautions for equipment, technology and the office space
- Maintaining and upgrading contracts with external suppliers of equipment and technology
- Maintaining records, e.g. service level agreements, risk assessments, inspection dates, maintenance dates
- Managing budgets

• ACTIVITY 1

What is a psychological contract?

In both of these two areas, the office supervisor will have to anticipate problems, resolve problems and troubleshoot. The depth and breadth of these activities will vary depending on the size, location and type of office being supervised, e.g. a specific department with a large organisation or the whole unit of business if it is a small organisation. The office supervisor is not expected to work independently but will coordinate activities between different groups of employees within the office who they consider have the best skills and knowledge to achieve the required targets. The office supervisor will be expected to **delegate** functions and activities within the office.

Members of an office will be delegated the tasks they need to achieve by the office supervisor. The office supervisor will need to identify the employee's priorities so that the most important issues are dealt with first. Often **urgent** issues are mistakenly identified as **important** when the latter have little or no long-term bearing on the performance of the organisation. True priorities depend on having both urgency and importance. Juggling the urgent but unimportant tasks alongside the important but non-urgent is an important skill of the office supervisor. Once priorities have been identified, more specific, clear objectives can be agreed for each employee. Clear objectives will allow all employees to be assured that that they are seeking to achieve a carefully considered outcome. This makes it easier for them to plan a course of action to reach the agreed objectives. When setting objectives make sure they are achievable to maintain morale within the office.

Some tasks may need to be divided into smaller sub-tasks. This will depend on the complexity of the tasks involved. The subdivision and delegation of tasks is a good way of empowering employees with individual responsibility and authority and setting out a progression pathway for all the tasks to be achieved within a specified time and standard. Good delegation leads to:

- More time and space for the office supervisor to supervise employees

- A reduction in the delay to decision-making, positioning decision-making at the level where data and information is known to make the best decision

- The distribution of routine activities to employees

- Increased motivation of the office and individual employees

- More highly skilled office, empowering employees to take on added responsibility and greater authority

- A fairer division of labour within the office audience very quickly.

• ACTIVITY 2

What are the benefits that arise from good delegation?

When delegating to employees the office supervisor must decide:

- **What tasks to delegate -** Those tasks the office supervisor does not need to do, i.e. routine and repetitive tasks. Also, those tasks where the skills and knowledge of individual employees are better suited to achieve task outcomes. Always agree expectations with employees, i.e. quality and standards, and timescales of the tasks they have been delegated to achieve so they are aiming to achieve success

- **Who to delegate tasks to -** It is important to trust the employee to undertake the tasks they have been delegated to achieve the task to meet agreed expectations and timescales. However, this is also an opportunity to develop the skills and knowledge of individual employees by delegating to them tasks which will stretch their skills and knowledge to achieve the task - it must be a realistic expectation which the office supervisor will have to manage

- **How to give out tasks -** Employees will need to understand:

  - Why the task needs to be achieved

  - What they are expected to do

  - When they are expected to achieve the task

  - What authority they have to make decisions

  - What problems must be referred back

  - When to submit progress reports

  - How they will be supported and monitored What resources they will need to complete the task

- **How to support employees -** Development of employees - guidance, instruction and training - not only for them and the whole office but also for the organisation. Improving performance allows the office supervisors to build trust between themselves and their employees, which will enable them to delegate more complex tasks in the future

- **How to monitor progress of employees -** Employees will need to be monitored to make sure they are capable of achieving the delegated task to meet expectations and on time. It should be supportive without being oppressive and intrusive without being unduly interfering. It is a delicate balancing act which will vary from employee to employee and will require the office supervisor to customise their expectations to each individual employee. This can be achieved by scheduling meetings and agreeing one-to-one meetings with employees to monitor progress

- **Acknowledge achievement of the task -** Always thank employees for the commitment and energy they used to achieve their tasksaudience very quickly.

• ACTIVITY 3

What decisions are involved in delegating tasks?

Delegation is not about surrendering responsibility. The office supervisor will always be responsible for the achievement of the office's goals and objectives, and it is their responsibility to make sure employees are fully supported in the performance of their tasks. The office supervisor should always delegate by the results they expect. They can only know what to expect by making sure they have delegated tasks to the right employee. However, before the office supervisor is able to delegate tasks / activities they must have agreed a **plan** to supervise all office activities, which should also include creating **contingency plans** to identify potential problems.

The most successful way of completing an agreed task / activity is to plan what work needs to be carried out. Plan work to the last detail. The purpose of planning is to have a clear idea of what needs to be achieved. Planning requires information: what information is required, where to get it from, whom to speak to, what the timescales and deadlines are - are they realistic? How it is to be presented? Obtain as much detail about the work to be completed. The aim is to produce the most efficient piece of work as possible. Written plans have the benefit of involving the activity of writing and thinking about the work to be completed. It is a permanent record of what has to be done and provides a blueprint of activities that need to be completed in a logical order. If it is written down, other people have access in the event of absences and it can be easily referred to. Having a plan is taking accountability for the work that has to be completed.

• ACTIVITY 4

What is the purpose of contingency plans?

The key to planning work is **time management**. Time management is the art of organising and scheduling time in the most efficient ways to create more effective work and productivity. Time is a limited resource. It is not elastic. It cannot be stretched. There are techniques which can be used to make the most of the time envisaged to complete an agreed task / activity:

Prioritise tasks / activities

Make a list of things that need to be completed. This can be carried out using two methods:

- **'To do list'** - A 'to do list' will provide a precise list of **priorities** that can help to manage and eliminate problems that might occur. Important tasks / activities can be separated from trivial ones. Completing the 'to do list' should involve:

  - Writing down all of the tasks / activities that need to be completed

  - Breaking them down into smaller manageable tasks / activities, estimating how long each task / activity will take

  - Prioritising the tasks / activities. Create a system that categorises each task / activity, e.g. high, medium, low or important, action immediately, get more information, read, telephone. Priorities can also be described as 'must do' - be done today, 'should do' - be done sometime or 'could do' - be done when there is time

  - List the tasks / activities in order of priority

  - Build in contingencies, as things may take longer than estimated

Using a 'to do list' should be a routine that is followed every day. It could be created at the end of the day in preparation for the next day, or the first thing that is done at the beginning of the day.

- **Diary** - May be maintained using a paper or electronic system. Diary entries must be made clearly and accurately and changed as required. It should provide sufficient information about timing - start, begin - and the subject matter to discuss, to prepare for  the appointment. Use the diary as a system that not only records appointments but organises how time is used in the working day. Most importantly, keep it up to date. It is no good to anyone if the diary entries bear no relationship to what is actually going to go on

Whatever system is used, avoid the temptation to concentrate on just doing the easy tasks / activities first. Prioritise always. Review the 'to do list' and diary to make sure that time is being used and managed wisely.

Plan the day's tasks / activities

Set aside enough time for employees to do the 'must do' tasks - or however they have been categorised - by their agreed deadlines. Allow time for the 'should do' tasks and even the 'could do' tasks if possible.

Record the time to complete a task / activity
It helps to keep track of time and know when falling behind or shooting ahead of schedule.

Deal with disruption
If there is something important that has to be done, let employees know that focus and concentration needs to be applied to that task / activity for a certain length of time.audience very quickly.

• ACTIVITY 5

Why is it important to supervise the use of time effectively in an office? What tools could be used to organise the achievement of tasks / activities?

The plan will need to be updated. Always understand why a plan needs to be changed. Do not be tempted to agree to all requests without notifying everyone involved of the knock-on effects of a change of plan. If an agreed deadline cannot be met, it may be possible to extend the deadline, or it may be necessary to get additional help to complete the task. Give employees the opportunity to discuss new ideas for improving the way things could be done in the future.

Supervise office employees
Before an office supervisor can supervise the organisation of their office employees, they first need to organise themselves using time management techniques and other skills to organise work schedules, e.g. using an in- / pending- / out-tray system. Papers in the in tray need to be scheduled in the diary for the day planned to start work on them; papers in the pending tray need to be scheduled in the diary for the day that the further information is expected. Such systems will enable an office supervisor to organise their day so they can deal with the tasks that are scheduled to take place each day. Each day should follow a routine:

- Read incoming post and deal with each item using the in- / pending- / out-tray system

- Check the list of tasks to be completed that day

- Prioritise the tasks and decide if there are any that could be carried out by other office employees

- Build rapport with employees each day by speaking to them as they arrive in the office to find out if they have any concerns and discuss their priorities for the day. It may be appropriate to have a brief meeting each day, formal or informal, which will depend on the number of employees and the complexity of their tasks

- During the day review the list of tasks to be achieved and keep an eye on how the rest of the office is coping

- Check that everything that needs to be completed has been mailed out and it is in the out tray before the collection deadline

- Before employees leave for the day, check their progress against their priorities for the day

- Before leaving at the end of each day, reschedule any uncompleted tasks, take a brief look at tomorrow's list in case there is any preparation that needs to be done, then take a quick walk around the office to check that machines have been turned off and nothing confidential has been left on a desk

When supervising a new office, the office supervisor will need to put into place systems and procedures for every task. If taking over the supervision of an existing office, there will almost certainly be changes that the new office supervisor will want to make. In every office, systems and procedures will change which may create a number of problems:

- Employees feel changes have been implemented without consultation

- Some employees find it difficult to cope with change

- Changes, if not properly communicated, feel threatening

These problems often arise because of lack of planning. Office procedures that are going to be changed should go through three stages:

- **The idea stage** - Where the office supervisor or employee comes up with the idea for a new procedure or a change to an existing procedure. At this stage it will probably be a fairly vague concept, but this is the point at which the office supervisor should check that there are no strong organisational reasons for not pursuing the idea, whether anybody else is already in the process of developing a similar idea, or whether anybody can suggest an even better idea

- **The research and development stage** - When the office manager will explore the idea, encouraging others to offer their input and look at the costs and benefits, timescales for implementation and any impact the change will have on other procedures or departments within the organisation

- **The executive stage** - When the procedure is put into place and evaluatedaudience very quickly.

• ACTIVITY 6

When changing systems and procedures what does the office supervisor need to consider?

Employees will be demotivated and feel disempowered if they believe they have no control over changes. Their initial reaction may be to feel that they will not be able to cope with the extra work or even that the whole idea is unworkable. The most important part of implementing new procedures is communicating them to the employees who will be using them. This should be a two-way process. Employees will often be able to suggest changes that the office supervisor has not thought of. As a result of changes to systems and procedures, employees may need to be retrained before the changes can be implemented. The office supervisor should match the current employee skills to the new skills requirements to identify any training needs for each employee. Training should be organised to take place before the start date of the implementation of new systems and procedures. This may be a good opportunity to multi-skill employees, as this will have two benefits to the office:

- Trained employees will be available to cover in the event of different types of absences

- Employees will feel they have benefited from the changes by receiving training in new skills and knowledge

All systems and procedures should be subject to continuous review in the evolving culture of globalisation that impacts on all organisations. Even with the best systems and procedures in place, work will not be carried out effectively unless an office has the right number of employees with the right skills. The office supervisor will prioritise the work of employees within their office to make sure that urgent work is completed to the required deadlines and routine work is not allowed to fall behind. Office supervisors should aim to delegate tasks / activities across employees in the office rather than favouring selected employees all the time, to enable a more homogenous office of skills and knowledge with employees who are able to step into different roles and responsibilities when colleagues are absent. This will empower employees, increasing office morale and provide training opportunities.

The office supervisor will have to agree a strategy for organising when employees can go on holiday, attend training etc. Wall planners are a helpful tool, to see who is doing what and when, when making these decisions. The strategy for signing-off time away from the office may be based on a 'hierarchy' for booking time off based on seniority, length of service or simply 'first come first served'; however, whatever strategy is used, it must be understood by all employees to avoid employees feeling aggrieved or attempting to exert pressure on others in order to get their own way.

For a plan to be successful the office supervisor will want to reassure themselves that tasks are being completed accurately and according to the agreed time schedule. To monitor office activity, targets will need to be set and agreed between the office supervisor and their employees. An office supervisor will not be able to monitor every individual task, so it may be practical to take a sample that is representative of each activity. Compare the result of the monitored task / activity with the agreed target and make sure each employee is given feedback. They will want to know that they have achieved their targets and, if they have not, they will need to know why and what they need to do to meet quality expectations.

Even the best-supervised office will have problems. These may be short-term problems - to be solved quickly or medium- and long-term problems - which will require more time and analysis to resolve. When tackling any problem, go through the following six stages to solve the problem:

- Identify the problem
- Define the effects of the problem
- Find the cause of the problem
- Identify possible solutions

- Choose between the solutions

- Plan the way forward

Each solution should be accompanied by the risk attached to implementing that course of action. It is important to check that, whatever the problem, the solution implemented does solve the problem. Consider whether an alternative action may solve the problem more effectively should it reoccur. The office supervisor should revisit their plan to see if the problem might have been avoided with better planning.

Complaints arise in any organisation from time to time. All complaints, e.g. from a customer, supplier, should be dealt with quickly. Ignoring complaints only worsens the situation, people feel ignored and powerless, which brings its own problems, as they then feel that they have to escalate the situation so that someone will listen to them. In an office environment there are bound to be conflicts between the different personalities. Employee's complaints against other employees are usually resolved informally between the two employees concerned. Where employees concerned cannot resolve the difficulty, perhaps another colleague can act as an informal mediator. If the complaint is more serious, it might have to go to a team meeting or the aggrieved person may want to speak to the office manager or invoke the company's complaints procedure. A complaint by an employee against the office supervisor can be more difficult to resolve because of the power imbalance between the two people. The office supervisor should aim to be approachable so employees feel they can approach them to resolve their complaint.

Sometimes, suppliers telephone the office to make some complaint, e.g. they have tried to deliver but could not. These complaints should be dealt with promptly and the agreed action to take should be clarified. It is very important to maintain a supplier's goodwill, as organisations never know when such goodwill could be crucial to their own survival. Goodwill should not be abused. Complaints made by customers should be dealt with the same level of promptness and politeness. However the complaint arises, it is important to remember that it is not personal, the customer is angry with the situation. Complaints that arise in the office should be resolved as promptly as possible before they escalate and get complicated. Most complaints are the least serious kind that are easily resolved by prompt and simple action.

• ACTIVITY 7

How should an office supervisor deal with complaints?

Allied to the above is the office supervisor being aware of the office politics and managing this so that problems do not arise. Office politics are a fact of business life which can be dealt with by considering some of the following options:

- **Look for hidden agendas** - Office politics tend to operate under the surface in hidden agendas. Uncover hidden agendas by watching how employees treat each other and how they are treated by others in the organisation

- **Find the power brokers** - Power brokers are employees who can help or hinder the progress towards achieving the goals and objectives of tasks / activities. Develop trust within the office environment and empower employees, to minimise the rise of office politics

- **Look for office melodrama** - Watch out for office melodrama that causes underlying tension between rival employees or management. Look for the causes of conflicts, power plays and difficult behaviour

- **Learn how to read office politics** - Get a realistic picture of how an office really operates and manage relationships between employees to minimise the rise of office politics

- **Study the organisation's culture** - Study the organisation's culture to learn when, where and how to make an impact with the right people who can help you achieve the agreed goals and objectives of delegated tasks / activities. This should be done ethically and in keeping with good morals and ethical personal values audience very quickly.

• ACTIVITY 8

What are office politics and how best can an office supervisor manage their impact on the achievement of tasks / activities in an office?

When making any decisions, make sure that they are scrupulously fair and that the decision can demonstrate that priority is given to the task of greatest benefit to the whole organisation. Always seek agreement rather than confrontation. Decisions should be informed by the urgency or importance of the task / activity rather than the seniority of employees.

Provide and maintain office equipment

Every office supervisor will have responsibility for drawing up and agreeing a budget for the products and services the office will require, e.g. office equipment, office repairs, and variable costs of telephones, postage and light and heat. The office supervisor will need to decide when to replace or repair office equipment and consider which would be most cost-effective for the office and their budget or agree how much stationery to order and balance between buying in bulk and taking advantage of economies of scale and finding the office space to store it. These will form part of the systems and procedures that the office manager will put in place to supervise the running of the office.

The office supervisor will have to decide how they wish to facilitate the administration of costs, e.g. set up cost centres for each aspect of the resources used by the office or one **cost centre** for the whole office. The office supervisor will need to know where particular cost units exist within their budget as these will be compensated for by the profits from other units in the office. The office supervisor will aim to cut out loss making units. A cost centre is how costs are structured to a specific department or section of an organisation. Costs are related to a location, function or items of equipment and apportioned to a cost centre to control the ebb and flow of budgets, e.g. an organisation that does printing may have many printing machines and will decide that each printing machine will be a cost centre in their own right. The purpose of a costing exercise is to determine which cost centre costs can be directed to. Only when costs cannot be attributed to a specific product are they to be charged to a cost centre. An organisation can also be divided into **profit centres**. A profit centre will look at the costs associated with running that centre and the revenues to calculate the profit. Dividing an organisation into profit centres makes it possible to identify the parts of the organisation that generate the profits and the parts that do not. audience very quickly.

• ACTIVITY 9

What is the difference between cost centres and profit centres?

A system will need to be agreed to supervise the control of office equipment to make sure that jobs are prioritised to meet agreed timescales and resources are used carefully so as not to produce waste. The office supervisor will need to consider what office equipment is necessary to run the office to meet the requirements of its **business plan**. The choice of office equipment should be decided by considering the **features of the equipment** that the office wishes it to perform. Types of office equipment that will need to be considered include:

- **Computers** - There is an enormous range of computer hardware on the market. The main factor in deciding what to purchase will be the applications that will be used, usually the more applications a computer has the more expensive it will be

- **Printers** - The main variables in printers to consider are speed and quality. If the printer needs to print high volumes with little concern about the quality of production, a printer with the highest pages per minute (ppm) would be a suitable choice. If the printing required is high quality in relatively low volumes, a printer with the highest dots per inch (dpi) would be the best printer

- **Photocopiers** - The features of photocopiers include speed, quality, collating documents, printing back-to-back, stapling, enveloping, enlarging and reducing. The choice of which photocopier to purchase comes down to how often these features would be used by employees within an office

- **Telephones** - There are many different telephone systems on the market. The choice of system will be determined by the features of the available telephones and how many of those features will be utilised within the office, e.g. a system with separate lines going to each desk or a smaller number of incoming lines with extension handsets on each desk

- **Fax machines** - These can be thermal or plain-paper machines. The disadvantage of thermal fax machines is that the fax copy will fade over time. A fax machine will require a dedicated telephone line. Some computers will have a fax function built into them, so this is also a feature that needs to be considered when purchasing a computer

- **Calculators** - Relatively cheap to buy; however, a computer or mobile phone will have this facility built into it so it may not be cost-effective to purchase a calculator; however, this will depend on the department, e.g. a finance department will benefit from having calculators with paper tabulating the series of costs they are making mathematical calculations with

- **Shredders** - These are important to manage the disposal of 'private and confidential' documents and control the proliferation of identity theft and industrial espionage. There are two types of shredders, straight-cut or cross-cut machines. The choice of shredder to use will depend on the level of security required within an office. Shredded paper can then be recycled in packaging

- **Franking machines and post scales** - They can be topped up electronically over a telephone line. The decision whether to have a franking machine will depend on the volume of post despatched. Franking machines have a monthly charge on top of the postage costs. The consideration in purchasing post scales depends on the type of post being sent. Most franking machines will have scales integrated into the system

Once the choice of office equipment has been decided, the office supervisor will need to investigate different models, different suppliers, cost and delivery dates etc. This will also be determined by the size of the budget for the office. Purchases of equipment will be made from either the 'Capital' budget or the 'Revenue' budget of the organisation. Generally, 'Capital' items are expected to be in use for more than 12 months while 'Revenue' items will be used within a shorter time. When selecting suppliers of products and services, the office supervisor will need to consider the following criteria:

- Price

- Customer service

- The technical support offered

The criteria for selection of office equipment will be dictated by its usage and the suppliers that can supply the selected pieces of office equipment. In some circumstances price will be all-important, in others service, while with others technical support may be crucial. There are no right choices, only choices that have to be made for the office equipment needed to run an effective office. When purchasing products or services the office supervisor needs to determine which supplier or mode of supply will provide the **best value for money**. The concept of value for money is not restricted to price alone but needs to factor the:

Contribution to the advancement of business / organisation priorities

The aim should be to select sources of materials and equipment that have relatively low costs and where supply is easy to secure. This will not always be achievable. Various factors that can be considered to achieve this include:

- The business / organisation priorities and its procurement guidance
- Rates and an evaluation of materials and equipment against selection criteria
- Limiting selection to only those suppliers that demonstrate agreed attributes
- Limiting selection to suppliers who have been pre-qualified having met organisational priorities

Non-cost factors

Which include:

- **Fitness for purpose** - The extent to which materials and equipment will deliver specified outcomes
- **Technical and financial issues**

Product-related factors

Which include:

- Technical performance, which needs to consider the 'duty' of materials or equipment
- Reliability, to make sure customer expectations have been met with regard to functionality and performance, including contractual guarantee conditions
- Economic life, to determine when materials and equipment become more economical to replace rather than to maintain. Action that would need to be taken to make this decision would be a cost-benefit analysis, management judgement, the degree of use and corporate policy
- Maintainability

Supplier-related factors

This usually concerns supplier capability, which includes the supplier's management capability, financial viability, technical expertise, methodology, systems, previous performance and capacity to complete the supply requirement.

Risk exposure

Which arises from the:

- Purchaser organisation

- Goods or services

- Supplier

- Market

- **Benefits to be obtained from the purchase**

- **Availability of maintenance and support**

- **Compliance with specifications, where relevant**

Cost-related factors

Which will depend on the nature of the goods / services to be acquired, which should consider:

- **Whole-of-life costs** - Which include: acquisition costs, operating costs, maintenance costs, cleaning costs, alteration / refurbishment costs, support costs and disposal

- **Transaction costs** - Which include: establishing the need for the purchase, planning for the purchase, identifying sources of supply, approaching the market to seek supply, selecting suppliers, ordering and processing payments and managing relationships with suppliers

Value for money is not just about procuring the cheapest price but considering all the factors that may be hidden within the price of products or services. For an office to remain efficient and effective - of worth and value - it needs to make sure that the quality of products and services provided by suppliers is supplied:

- At the **agreed time**

- At the **agreed price**

- To the **agreed quality**

- In the **agreed quantity**

- With the **agreed supplementary support services**

- **Problem free** or the supplier responds to purchase enquires quickly

Most offices will endeavour to agree a **service level agreement (SLA)** with suppliers they contract with. A SLA is an agreement or contract that defines the service suppliers must provide. Essentially, the SLA is aiming to safeguard the performance that the purchaser expects to be delivered by a supplier of products or services. The SLA sets out the level of service to be delivered and its responsibilities and priorities. SLAs are **contractual obligations** and are often built into a contract. A SLA can be a complex document which should be well defined and drawn up and agreed with precision, highlighting the most critical components of the agreement so the strictest penalties can apply to these clauses. A SLA should identify the number of **performance reviews** that will be taken and specify the conditions that will initiate such reviews. A SLA will typically set out:

- The **service** being provided

- The **standards of service**

- The respective **responsibilities of supplier** and **purchaser**

- Provisions for **legal** and **regulatory compliance**

- Mechanisms for **monitoring** and **reporting** on the service

- **Payment terms**

- How **disputes** will be resolved

- **Confidentiality** and **non-disclosure** provisions

- **Termination** conditions

If suppliers fail to meet agreed levels of service, the SLA will usually provide for compensation. A SLA should be updated constantly as the needs of a business change, as different performance criteria may be required. Improvements in technology should also be taken into account when reviewing a SLA.audience very quickly.

• ACTIVITY 10

What is a SLA and how should they be agreed and managed?

The office supervisor should aim to establish a good working relationship with their suppliers, maintaining a relationship with them over extended time periods. A regular customer can expect an efficient and effective service. While there may appear to be short-term benefits from switching suppliers to take advantage of special offers, established relationships have many advantages. If the organisation operates group purchasing arrangements with suppliers, it may put their terms in jeopardy if certain suppliers are not used.

The purchase of some 'Capital' items may be subject to the submission of tenders by potential suppliers. Tendering is a process by which acceptable suppliers are given the opportunity to offer a price for the supply of goods or services which will aim to meet the criteria set out by the tender document. Each supplier completes a tender document which is returned to the purchasing organisation in a sealed envelope by a fixed date. On the agreed date all tenders are opened and compared and the successful supplier identified. If the office supervisor is responsible for placing the orders they will need to make sure that the total cost is within the budget. The total cost may include delivery, insurance, VAT - if the organisation is not VAT registered - disposal of the existing equipment and the purchase of consumables. The office supervisor will also need to consider maintenance costs. Some items may benefit from a planned programme of maintenance; others can be repaired as required. It is important that all equipment is used and treated carefully, and as per the manufacturer's instructions, to minimise the cost of repairs and replacement.

All employees who are not familiar with using a new piece of office equipment should be offered training before using the office equipment, particularly if the equipment is dangerous or expensive. This may be provided in-house or outsourced to an external training provider. Some employers use distance learning or web-based learning to familiarise staff with new office equipment. Employees should also be trained to consider the next user of each piece of office equipment after they have finished using it, e.g. the photocopier, printer and fax machine all have ink and paper that can run out. The franking machine has credit which reduces with each run. From a health and safety perspective, the area around any machines and the machine itself should be left in a tidy manner.

Manage office facilities
The office supervisor needs to organise their office space effectively. Larger office spaces will cost more to run than smaller office spaces.

Underused office space needs to be used, e.g. if the headcount for an office has been reduced there may be ample space to set up a cubicle which could be rented to a freelance worker. The better option may be to move to a smaller office space, depending on the rental agreement with the leaseholder. Or an alternative option may be to share office space with another company. There should not be any problems with this as long as both companies are not in competition with each other. The office supervisor needs to make sure that the appropriate office facilities are in place to make the best use of them. Office equipment should be positioned so that it can be used without disrupting other employees. And training should be offered to make sure that employees are fully competent to use office equipment.

There is a lot of valuable equipment in the office which should only be used by employees who have been trained and authorised to use it. Damage may be caused by untrained employees or costs incurred through wastage, e.g. managing the use of photocopiers to make  sure that ink cartridges are used optimally. The office supervisor will also have to manage unauthorised use of office equipment for personal use or by employees from other departments within the organisation. Photocopiers can be programmed with different user codes so that costs can be correctly allocated across different departments. Always make sure there is a contingency plan to cover breakdowns, breakages or the replacement of office equipment.

While employees have responsibility for their own personal health, safety and security, the office supervisor has overall responsibility for their employees and visitors to an office. There are rules for health and safety, controlling hazardous substances and the safe use of equipment. The office supervisor needs to make sure that they are adhered to. Risk assessments should be carried out to identify hazards and risks, particularly those arising from the installation and use of new office equipment. An office should be organised to have adequate means of escape in the event of fire. Employees should be trained regularly in fire evacuation. Visitors should also be made aware of these precautions and alerted to the sound of the fire alarm and position of fire exits. All accidents, no matter how small, must be entered in an accident book. The office supervisor should also identify who to train as first aiders.

Security systems must be in place to protect the equipment, peripherals, consumables and information from theft. Office equipment can be marked with the organisation's name to deter theft and increase the possibility of recovering stolen property. A system requiring staff to sign out equipment they are removing from the premises will deter the possibility of staff theft. Where large amounts of expensive consumables are stored on the premises a stock control system may be  implemented to manage their distribution. To protect information from theft, paper files may be stored in locked cabinets. Electronic files should be password protected, particularly if they are 'private and confidential', and they should be stored so only authorised employees have access to them. Before leaving at the end of the day, the office supervisor should check that computers are switched off, all appropriate files and papers are secured and cabinets are locked and windows are closed and locked. They should then set any alarms before leaving the building.

The office supervisor should make sure that the business is run effectively by making sure the office has been organised to house its employees and office equipment so that they can be managed and used optimally.

Testing your knowledge

1. Why is it important to continually review systems and procedures?

2. What are the types of problems the office supervisor will need to resolve?

3. Why is good communication on systems and procedures vital to the well running of an office?

4. Why should employees be developed?

5. What are the benefits to the office supervisor of multi-skilled employees?

6. What factors need to be considered when deciding the technical specification of a new printer?

7. What criteria should be taken into consideration when selecting a supplier for replacement office equipment?

8. What would be the impact of failing to take the budget into consideration when making purchasing decisions?

9. What criteria should be taken into consideration when selecting a supplier for training on new office equipment?

10. Why is health and safety important in an office environment?

11. Why is it important to have a contingency plan in case of office equipment breakdown?

12. How does the office manager diplomatically prioritise the use of office facilities?

13. What factors need to be taken into consideration when deciding the best position for office equipment?

Skills

The office supervisor will need to agree all the components that make an office work effectively, from employees to equipment. It is not only making sure that they resources are in place, but that they are working effectively and achieving all the tasks / activities that have been delegated throughout the office. You will need to plan how you are going to pull all these resources together and supervise all the activities that support the optimal delivery of these resources. Your main role is one of a juggler walking a tightrope. You will always have to juggle different priorities and balance differing needs across the office to achieve all agreed goals and objectives.

Every office is in flux and nothing remains static. You will need to make sure that there are systems and procedures in place for the smooth running of operations in the office. These will need to be reviewed to make sure that they are still fit for purpose and aid the achievement of operational goals and objectives. Systems and procedures relate to both your employees, e.g. setting up appraisal meetings with all the employees you supervise, and office equipment, e.g. setting up maintenance schedules. The impact of the changing needs of the office will require you to make sure all your employees are fully up to date with changes that have been made so they are competent in carrying out their responsibilities.

• ACTIVITY 11

Review the systems and procedures for which you are responsible. Identify opportunities to make practical changes that will improve them. Draw up a plan to implement the changes, which will include the benefits you expect, total costs and the amount of time it will take for the plan to be cost neutral.

For all systems and procedures that you have agreed you need to make sure that they are all in place and working efficiently and effectively to support the work of your employees. You will need to make sure that you have:

- All the office equipment necessary for the running of your office

- Office equipment in good condition

- Office equipment that is maintained periodically

- Manufacturer's manuals and guidance documents for employees to follow to use office equipment and implement office procedures

- Contingency plans in place in the event of breakdowns, repairs and replacement of office equipment

- An office supplied with all the resources it needs to work effectively, e.g. stationery

- Office space that has been ergonomically organised to make sure of the health and safety of your employees and office equipment

- A secure officeaudience very quickly.

• ACTIVITY 12

Carry out a review of the existing facilities in your office. Identify where there is a need to replace, upgrade or remove any office equipment. Consider whether the repositioning of office equipment will improve the efficiency of the office. Write a report analysing your findings, making any recommendations.

A major role of the office supervisor is building and maintaining relationships with their internal staff, i.e. employees and external customers, e.g. suppliers. This is an integral part of your role. You will need to make sure that you create a work environment that is positive and conducive to maximising output from your employees. This includes tangible, e.g. office furniture, as well as intangible factors, e.g. your interpersonal skills, of which, communication is extremely important. You must be able to delegate and prioritise tasks / activities to the right employees which will also give employees the opportunity to develop their skills and knowledge. You will need to minimise and eliminate risks and hazards that the office may present to your employees and visitors. audience very quickly.

• ACTIVITY 13

Carry out a risk assessment of the area for which you are responsible. Cover risks associated with people, office equipment, office space, workflow, information, security, health and safety.

You will need to constantly review everything that is going on in your office. It is wise to have a logical and systematic approach to how you do this. The more you can make this an automatic function the easier it will be for you to organise and manage throughout each financial year. A financial year is probably a good measure to use to monitor the performance of your employees and office equipment.   audience very quickly.

• ACTIVITY 14

Ask your line manager to suggest a realistic budget for the replacement of the equipment currently in use in your office. Research the replacement requirements. Identify the range of alternative options. Make a selection based on your budget and the functions and features needed in your office. Ask your line manager to review your findings.

Testing your skills

1. What are the office systems and procedures that apply to your role?

2. How often have you reviewed your office systems and procedures?

3. What types problems have you encountered?

4. Why have you had to develop employees in your office facility?

5. What types of equipment are required in your organisation, and why?

6. How did you select the office suppliers your organisation has contracts with, if applicable?

7. What are the procedures for raising purchase orders within your organisation?

8. Who has the authority to sign purchase orders in your organisation?

9. Who is budget holder for office equipment in your organisation?

10. How have you improved the health and safety of your office facility, if applicable?

11. Who is responsible for health and safety in your office facility?

12. What are the security measures in place in your office facility?

Ready for assessment?

To achieve this Level 3 unit of a Business & Administration qualification, learners will need to demonstrate that they are able to perform the following activities:

1. Identified, agreed and provided facilities and equipment for an office facility to meet the needs of users, in line with agree budgets

2. Maintained facilities and equipment for an office facility to meet the needs of users

3. Supervised and monitored use of facilities and equipment for an office facility

4. Used and reviewed the facilities, systems and procedures of an office, having reported changes in requirements, as needed

5. Made sure the equipment in an office facility was working correctly

6. Identified repairs needed to the office facilities and equipment in an office and dealt with them or referred them, as required

7. Maintained relationships with suppliers and looked for opportunities to develop relationships

8. Made contributions to the review of an office environment in line with health, safety and security policy

9. Dealt with problems with facilities and equipment in an office facility, or referred, as required

10. Provided information and guidance to users on the facilities and equipment in an office facility

11. Explained priorities for the supply, maintenance and use of office facilities and equipment to users, as required

12. Monitored the use of office facilities

You will need to produce evidence from a variety of sources to support the performance requirements of this unit.

If you carry out the 'ACTIVITIES' and respond to the 'NEED TO KNOW' questions, these will provide some of the evidence required.

Links to other units

While gathering evidence for this unit, evidence **may** also be used from evidence generated from other units within the Business & Administration suite of units. Below is a **sample** of applicable units; however, most units within the Business & Administration suite of units will also be applicable.

QCF NVQ
Business resources
Agree a budget
Order products and services
Communications
Communicate in a business environment (Level 3)
Develop a presentation
Deliver a presentation
Core business & administration
Manage own performance in a business environment (Level 3)
Evaluate and improve own performance in a business environment
Solve business problems (Level 3)
Work with other people in a business environment (Level 3)
Contribute to decision-making in a business environment
Contribute to negotiations in a business environment
Document production
Design and produce documents in a business environment
Manage information and data
Analyse and report data

SVQ
Business resources
Agree a budget
Order products and services
Communications
Communicate in a business environment (Level 3)
Develop a presentation
Deliver a presentation
Core business & administration
Plan how to manage and improve own performance in a business environment
Review and maintain work in a business environment
Solve business problems
Support other people to work in a business environment
Contribute to decision-making in a business environment
Contribute to negotiations in a business environment
Document production
Design and produce documents in a business environment
Manage information and data
Analyse and report data

4

Develop a presentation

DEVELOP A PRESENTATION

'Develop a presentation' is an <u>optional unit</u> which may be chosen as one of a combination of units to achieve either a Qualifications and Credit Framework (QCF), National Vocational Qualification (NVQ) or Scottish Vocational Qualification (SVQ).

The aims of this unit are to:

- Understand the purpose of preparing for and evaluating a presentation
- Be able to develop a presentation

To achieve the above aims of this unit, learners will be expected to provide evidence through the performance of work-based activities.

Knowledge

What is a presentation?

A presentation is the practice of communicating information to an audience. It will generally require writing, in some form, for presentation to an audience. The presentation will always have a definite purpose for communicating information. The structure of the presentation will be developed according to the message that needs to be communicated and its audience requirements. An audience can be any group of more than three people. With more than three people, the presenter's attention is divided between members of the audience. Consequently, the presenter will need to have an organised approach to communicating the information. The presenter must aim to capture the attention of the audience and fully engage them in the information being shared with them. To do this competently, the presenter must develop the appropriate text and form of text from which they will deliver the presentation. The text of the presentation will form the backdrop against which information will be delivered to an audience.

• ACTIVITY 1

What do you consider are the most important aspects of developing a presentation? Explain why.

Types of presentation
A presentation may either be:

Formal
This will require a detailed plan of the information that has to be communicated. These types of presentations tend to be longer and offer more depth and breadth of the subject area being presented. Examples of formal presentations include: award ceremonies, conference contributions, training interventions, a sales presentation for customers or potential customers, a presentation to management about a suggested change in operations or procedures, a research presentation, a tender for a contract, a bid for funding, pitching new ideas.

Informal
This will require very little planning or no planning at all. Although, depending on the time given, a presenter will formulate some plan, even if given only a few minutes to respond to a request to present some information. These will be short presentations, with very specific and single subject areas to be presented. In many instances, the presenter will rely on their previous experience or expertise. An example of an informal presentation is a manager asking a project leader to update the Board of Directors at very short notice.

• ACTIVITY 2

What is the difference between formal and informal presentations?

Writing a formal presentation
The writing of a formal presentation can take many different forms. The form of the presentation will be determined by the type and style of presentation to be delivered. For example, the presentation may be read, verbatim, from a report. Decisions will be made about the content that should be written into the presentation.

The content of a presentation should be driven by the following elements:

Key message (s) to be communicated
Identify the key messages of the presentation. This should use considerable thinking time. It is the most important part of the presentation. Otherwise, the presenter will not focus their audience appropriately on the topic. The presenter may end up wasting their time and the time of their audience. Key messages should contain:

- The main action to change the audience's thinking

- Links to audience expectations (their experience and expertise)

- Examples the audience can relate to

Structure of the presentation
A presentation should aim to have three parts, which are:

- **Beginning -** Set out the aims of the presentation. Presentations are generally designed to change minds. An audience needs context. Describe briefly the journey the audience is going to travel in the presentation. Use Kipling's[1] 'six honest serving-men':

  - **What** we want to do. Set out the key message

  - **Where** we are now? Set out the background to the development of the key message and related topics

  - **Which** way we want to go? Set out the different approaches to the key message (s) that have been considered

  - **Why** we want to do it? Set out the rationale for the approach being taken

  - **When** we want to do it? Set out the timescales for implementing the key message (s)

  - **How** we want to do it? Set out how the key message (s) will be achieved

- **Middle -** At this stage of the presentation focus in more detail on the points raised in the 'Beginning'

- **End -** Summarise all the points of the key message that have been presented

---

1 Rudyard Kipling, from The Elephant's Child in the 'Just So Stories'

- **Workshops** - If the time available is more than the time you think you need, consider adding workshop activities, but only where these will genuinely add to the value of the presentation

Built into this structure should be a process of reinforcing the key message. This should be a subtle repetition of the key message (s) and the pertinent information that falls out of the key message (s). The structure should incorporate these four 'tell them' concepts:

- **Tell them** what you are going to **tell them**
- **Tell them**
- **Tell them** what you have told them
- Summarise what you **tell them**

• ACTIVITY 3

Who are Kiplings 'six honest serving-men'? How can they be used to develop a presentation?

Length of the presentation
This may be predetermined by the person who has asked for the development of the presentation. In this instance, the presentation will need to be written so it conforms to that person's expectations. Or it may be left to the presenter to agree. However, consideration will need to be given to the information that needs to be included. If this is more than the time allocated will permit, this should then be negotiated between the presenter and the chair of the event.

Detail of information to be presented
This will be determined by the level of knowledge the audience have of the topic being presented. Make sure there is not too much information. If there is too much information, an audience is likely to feel overwhelmed. They are liable to become disengaged and forget the key message (s). In developing the presentation, sufficient 'wiggle' room should be left for the presenter to respond to 'Q & A' - questions and answers. A presenter may take an informal approach to 'Q & A' and ask their audience to question them as they go along. Alternatively, it may formally be built into the presentation, e.g. before lunch, at the end of the presentation (plenary).

Aim for the key message (s) to be subdivided into a maximum of seven points / subject areas. This will make it easier for the audience to remember. If the key message (s) cannot be subdivided into a maximum of seven points / subject areas, rank the information. Discard any points / subject areas that fall below the seventh. Generally, this information will not really be necessary for the presentation.

Consideration should be given to the amount of statistical information that may be included in the presentation. It is a matter of finding the balance and how the statistic contributes to bringing the key message (s) alive for the audience. Too many statistics can disengage an audience very quickly.

• ACTIVITY 4

How much information in a presentation is too much information?

Use of language
The presentation should be written in language that will appeal to the audience, that will draw them into the world of the key message (s). Depending on the audience, language used may be highly technical, include use of jargon, acronyms, abbreviations, or non-technical, or a combination of both. If the former, a decision will need to be made on which points / subject areas need explaining to the audience. However, in a mixed audience, a balance regarding what is explained will need to be found, so as not to disengage those members of the audience who already have the technical knowledge or expertise. Use of similes and metaphors will bring a presentation alive, as it is generally something the audience can relate to. However, this will depend on the simile or metaphor used.

It cannot be overemphasised enough how important it is to develop a presentation that is free from any error, either in validity and reliability of content or accuracy of grammar and spelling. There is nothing more demoralising when delivering a presentation to find that a slide has been formatted incorrectly and is not consistent with the rest of the body of the presentation. An error will be so glaringly obvious to an audience, especially if it is found after lunch, when energy is low, when an audience can fixate on the error and pay less or no attention to the presenter or the content they are trying to communicate. All of the work that has gone into developing the presentation can be lost in a

moment with such glaring errors. The audience interprets such errors as a lack of care and even disinterest in the content. All presentations should be proofread from every perspective to make sure there are no errors. If possible, get someone to proofread the presentation who has no experience of the content. A fresh pair of eyes will have no preconceptions about the content and will be looking for meaning and comprehension to be clear. Particular care should be taken when there are last-minute changes to the content of a presentation to make sure that as new information is added to a presentation it does not have a negative impact of the formatting of the rest of the medium the presentation has been developed in.

Research the topic of the presentation

This should be a thorough search of available data. The level of research will vary depending on the experience and expertise of the presenter or the person preparing the presentation. These may be two different people, e.g. a director has thrown information to their PA and asked them to put together a presentation for them. Preparing a presentation provides different levels of learning opportunities for all participants, regardless of their knowledge of the topic to be presented. Information should be relevant and reliable. Gather as much information as appropriate in order to make a decision about what will be included. There is no need to be scrupulous in searching for information, as new ideas may come from  unexpected places. At this stage, gather together the relevant facts and figures that will inform an audience.

It is important that the presenter know at least as much as, and preferably more than, the audience about the subject areas being presented. Explore all possible sources of information before preparing a presentation so the presenter has as much information as possible, this will make them credible and inspire the audience with confidence.

While researching information for the presentation, be creative. Consider topics which may be tangential to the subject area (s), as they may create imaginative approaches to merging and melding together information.

Inclusion of presentation aids

Aids are used to enhance the presentation and help the presentation come alive. Aids are used to enhance the meaning of the message (s) being presented. Looking at something will break up the monotony of continued listening to a presentation. It gives the audience the opportunity of using different senses to assimilate information. Aids are a means of breaking up the energy at appropriate points of the presentation to achieve different levels of attention from the audience. Aids should be used sensibly and with a clear purpose. They should not be thrown in indiscriminately. Aids should be used to suit the audience.

Aids may be either:

Visual

These aids will be seen. Make sure the visual aid does not take over from the presenter. Use images, graphs, diagrams etc. that will help to enhance the meaning of concepts being presented in the presentation. The aids should complement the key message (s). Keep them simple. Use colour or monochromatic images. The use of colour is important.

Light backgrounds with dark colours have the most impact. This is especially important when making a presentation in a large auditorium. Black, blue, red and green are the most visually appealing colours and have a psychological impact on the audience:

- Black is the colour that presents the facilitator as serious, knowledgeable and professional. A no-frills choice for simple presentations

- Blue is the colour of trust and accessibility

- Red is the colour that infers the presenter is in charge. It can be used as a motivational tool to spur listeners and viewers to action

- Green is the colour of comfort, life and money. Presentations about increasing sales often include shades of green

- Other colours should be used as accents and accessories

When using visual aids, make sure they are:

- Appropriate, not silly

- Current and suit the key message (s)

- Clear, not grainy - some images do not enlarge well from the original source they have been downloaded from

- Obtained legitimately. Permission must be given from the copyright owner before the image can be used. Someone in the audience may be from the company or site where the image has been downloaded from

- Relevant. Images are used to enhance the presentation not just to fill it. An image is not a form of decoration to distract the audience

- Not too long - when using video clips. Use video clips for a maximum of two to three minutes. The attention span of an audience is very short. If there is a long video clip, split it up into smaller segments

When using images, make sure the screen will be large enough for the room or auditorium in which the presentation will be made. Zooming in and enlarging images to a full screen size gives a greater impact to the audience. It is also a way to focus in on a particular feature the presenter wants to emphasise.

Auditory

These aids will be heard. Auditory aids are a good way of attracting attention or changing the focus of attention. Be careful of the volume of sound that is going to be used. If it is too loud it may have the opposite effect than was intended. It can annoy the audience to have silly or grating sounds. Keep sound for transitions to a minimum, as this keeps the audience focused on the points being made. Audio clips should be kept short. During audio clips, members of the audience may stop paying attention or engage in conversations. Keep clips short and use them carefully throughout the presentation - it will have greater impact.

Kinaesthetic

This is a combination of visual and auditory, e.g. showing an audience how a new product works and then getting them to use it. Use the chosen presentation aids at the time they are needed. Showing the visuals too early may distract an audience.

Consideration should be given to what aids will most effectively enhance a presentation. These should be chosen when writing up the presentation. As members of an audience will have different preferences, learning preferences, for each of the different types of aids used, choose a combination of aids throughout the presentation. This should then engage all members of the audience with different levels of attention.

• ACTIVITY 5

What are the advantages and disadvantages of using different types of presentation aids?

Choice and preparation of handouts

Handouts should be prepared that contain all of the information that is included in the presentation. Handouts can provide background information for the audience or be used as an aide-memoire. Handouts are also a good way of providing information that the presentation has not been able to include. Handouts may take the following forms and will need to be written or prepared when writing the presentation:

- **Background information** - The audience should be given this information in advance, if they are to understand the presentation

- **Information which the audience needs during the presentation** - The audience should be given this on arrival at the presentation

- **Materials for workshops or discussions** - The audience should receive these at the appropriate time

- **Information to reflect or act on after the presentation** - The audience should be given this as they leave the presentation

Form of presentation

Once the purpose of the presentation has been agreed, a decision needs to be made about the form the presentation should be written in for delivery. Many people will think automatically of a PowerPoint presentation as the only or best means of recording the presentation text. However, a presentation may take different forms:

- **Written report** - This will be a full report, written to meet the agreed requirements of an organisation. It may be read verbatim as it has been written

- **PowerPoint** - This will use slides within the PowerPoint programme

- **Cards** - Synoptic information on cards which acts as a prompt, addressing key points of the presentation

- **Flip chart** - Similar to the use of 'cards'

• ACTIVITY 6

Which form of presentation would best accommodate the use of presentation aids?

Evaluating the written presentation
A presentation text may either be written by the presenter or prepared for the presenter. In either case, once the presentation text has been completed, it should be quality assured or evaluated by a third party. This will make sure that the information within the text addresses the key message (s). Discuss any changes that need to be made and amend the form of document to be used in the presentation.

• ACTIVITY 7

Design an evaluation template to test the quality of the text and content of a presentation.

Testing your knowledge

1. Which situations require a presentation to be developed?

2. What is the purpose of preparation when writing a presentation?

3. How is a presentation structured to engage an audience?

4. What is the purpose of making presentations interesting?

5. What aids can be used to enhance a presentation text?

6. What are the different forms a presentation may be written in?

Skills

A presentation is designed and written to be presented to an audience. For the purposes of a presentation, an audience can be made up of three or more people. The size of an audience will have implications on how you structure your presentation, the type of presentation aids you intend to use and where the presentation is to take place. Ascertain what it is the audience want to know. Think creatively about how you can shape the information so it appeals to your audience. Shape the presentation so it will engage the audience's mind in different ways, appealing to each individual member's style of learning. Use Honey and Mumford's learning styles[2] as a key to how you shape the presentation. Use the diagram below as a key to how you can shape the structure and form of the presentation you are designing.

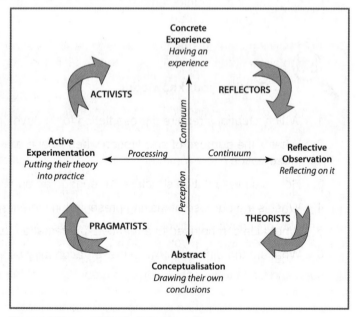

Figure 4.1. Honey and Mumford's learning cycle

2   http://www.nwlink.com/~donclark/hrd/styles/honey_mumford.html

Do you need to include workshops to engage the 'activists' and 'pragmatists', so they are doing something? ... or include 'theorists' actively into the decision-making process? Is there sufficient time for reflection of the key message (s) being communicated to the audience?

In agreeing to develop a presentation, your first step is to agree on the key message (s). If you are writing the presentation yourself, from an agreement you have made, there is little need to consult further on this. However, if you have been given a bundle of information by your senior manager to pull together a presentation for them, you should seek clarification from them of the key message (s) they wish to communicate. Do not waste your time trying to second-guess, go right to the horse's mouth. This will save you time and the embarrassment of getting it wrong at a later stage of development.

Your key message (s) may need to be sub-divided into different points of information. Use Kipling's 'six honest serving-men' to shape the structure of what it is you are going to say. Build into your structure the 'tell them' method of reinforcement, so the message (s) is indelibly printed on the minds of your audience as they leave the presentation.

Consider how long the presentation needs to be. If it is short, how will you include all the information that is needed? If it is too long, how do you stop the audience from getting bored? You should be aiming for Goldilocks' 'just right'. This is determined by good planning of the requirements of the presentation. The length of the presentation will determine the level of detail that you can include. How do you choose what should be in the presentation? How do you know if your choice of information, to the exclusion of another piece of information, is the correct choice? - If you are not sure, check with your manager. The length of the presentation will also help to inform you of the structure you need to develop. If it is a short presentation of five minutes, you will probably only have time to deliver one key message. Remember: it is not just a message that you are delivering - it is the meaning of the message! You need to make sure the audience will understand the message and leave the presentation with a good idea of the implications and impact of this new piece of information. Regardless of the length of your presentation, structure it so the key message (s) is clearly communicated, meaningfully, to your audience.

Tailor your presentation with the correct use of language. Make sure you use language that meets the anticipated level of understanding of your audience. Do not make it too flowery. Shy away from the use of too many figures of speech, e.g. similes, metaphors; allusions to classical or pop literature; foreign phrases, e.g. sine qua non, de rigueur or obscure words whose meaning may be unknown to most members of your audience. This will disrupt the reception of your message and disengage the audience. Suit the use of language to your audience.

Decide if you need to include 'presentation aids' to enhance the key message (s) you are trying to communicate. Why do you want to include a 'presentation aid'?

- To make your presentation more meaningful
- To help your audience remember your key message (s)
- To stimulate audience interest and participation in the presentation

Have you included 'handouts' to consolidate the key message (s) you are communicating? Do you need to include 'handouts'? If your presentation is only being developed to be delivered to a few people for five or 10 minutes, is there the need to offer 'handouts'. In preparing 'handouts', make sure the quality of reproduction is good. Consider the following:

- choice of type face
- clarity of images used
- colour or monochrome choice of images
- smudging in the copying of a 'handout'
- sufficient number of 'handouts', so all members of the audience have a copy, if not more for them to take back to their colleagues
- paper quality

Throughout all of the decision-making processes which help to inform the development of your presentation, you will 'research' the content of the presentation. Research is perhaps the single most important element that goes into developing and shaping the structure and form of your presentation. You must present the correct message that:

- Backs up the key message (s)
- Encourages your audience of the necessity to embrace the key message (s)

One piece of incorrect information and you will undermine the message (s) you are trying to encourage your audience to understand, use and communicate to others. Research will help to provide your mind with the creativity to bring disparate ideas together to make a meaningful whole concept.

Having completed all of your research and written it up, how are you going to present this information? If not reading a report verbatim, do you use PowerPoint, cards, a flip chart etc? This will depend on the size of your audience and the facilities available to you when you are making the presentation. PowerPoint is a popular medium of choice. However:

- Do not use too many slides - this could lead your audience to 'death by PowerPoint'

- Make sure slides are legible for the size of the room

- Design the content of the slide so that it prompts the facilitator to expand on points, so they are not just reading all the bullet points or narrative

- Make sure 'effects' are appropriate and work

- Design sentences to be written as bullet points, in large type, so they are:

  - Easy to read

  - Target key ideas

  - Easier for the audience to remember

Are you sure that the presentation you have developed and written is the best it can be, i.e. is the key message (s) clear so it reaches its audience? Check, check and check again. Ask colleagues to read through your text to make sure your meaning is clear. If you are developing a presentation for your manager, they will also make a final check and probably incorporate their own ideas. Use all this feedback to redevelop what you have already prepared. Sometimes getting bits wrong can led to improving the presentation when you are taking on board feedback.

• ACTIVITY 8

Design, develop and write up a presentation to be delivered to an audience for:

1. Five minutes (using cards)
2. Fifteen minutes (for a training programme)
3. Thirty minutes (PowerPoint)

 Testing your skills

1. Has the presentation been agreed?

2. How did you plan the presentation?

3. What type (s) of audience is the presentation being developed for?

4. Is the structure, content, style and timing of the presentation relevant to the key message (s) and audience?

5. How much research did you undertake to build the content of your presentation?

6. What type of 'presentation aids' and 'handouts' did you use, and why?

7. At what stage did you have the presentation evaluated for clarity, accuracy etc?

8. Who evaluated the presentation?

9. What changes have been made as a result of the feedback from the evaluation?

10. What did you learn as a result of the evaluation?

Ready for assessment?

To achieve this Level 3 unit of a Business & Administration qualification, learners will need to demonstrate that they are able to perform the following activities:

1. Agreed the purpose, content, style and timing of the presentation

2. Planned the presentation

3. Researched the presentation

4. Prepared the presentation to achieve its purpose

5. Used appropriate aids to enhance the presentation

6. Produced presentation handouts

7. Obtained feedback on the presentation

You will need to produce evidence from a variety of sources to support the performance requirements of this unit.

If you carry out the 'ACTIVITIES' and respond to the 'NEED TO KNOW' questions, these will provide some of the evidence required.

Links to other units

While gathering evidence for this unit, evidence **may** also be used from evidence generated from other units within the Business & Administration suite of units. Below is a **sample** of applicable units; however, most units within the Business & Administration suite of units will also be applicable.

QCF NVQ
Communications
Communicate in a business environment (Level 1)
Communicate in a business environment (Level 2)
Communicate in a business environment (Level 3)
Deliver a presentation
Document production
Produce text from notes using touch typing (20 wpm)
Produce text from notes using touch typing (40 wpm)
Produce text from notes using touch typing (60 wpm)
Produce documents in a business environment
Produce text from notes
Manage information and data
Organise and report data
Research information
Analyse and report data

SVQ
Communications
Understand how to communicate in a business environment
Prepare to communicate in a business environment
Communicate in a business environment
Deliver a presentation
Document production
Produce text from notes using touch typing (20 wpm)
Produce text from notes using touch typing (40 wpm)
Produce text from notes using touch typing (60 wpm)
Produce documents in a business environment
Produce text from notes
Manage information and data
Organise and report data
Research information
Analyse and report data

5

Communicate in a business environment

COMMUNICATE IN A BUSINESS ENVIRONMENT

'**Communicate in a business environment**' is a mandatory unit which may be chosen as one of a combination of units to achieve either a Qualifications and Credit Framework (QCF), National Vocational Qualification (NVQ) or Scottish Vocational Qualification (SVQ).

The aims of this unit are to:

- Understand the purpose of planning communication
- Understand how to communicate in writing
- Know how to communicate verbally
- Understand the purpose of feedback in developing communication skills
- Be able to plan communication
- Be able to communicate in writing
- Be able to communicate verbally
- Be able to identify and agree ways of developing communication skills

To achieve the above aims of this unit, learners will be expected to provide evidence through the performance of work-based activities.

Knowledge

What is communication?

Communication is an **action**. It is the process of transmitting or transferring information from one body to another body - a body may be one person or a collection of people. The purpose of communication is to **achieve something**. The process of communication will always require a minimum of two people - one person who **sends** the **message** and one person who **receives** the message.

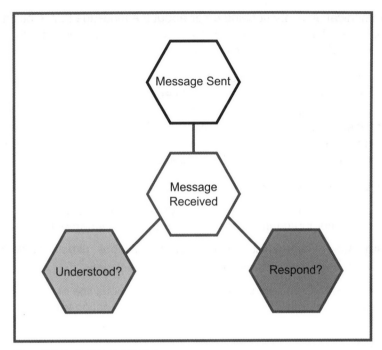

Figure 5.1. Cycle of communication

The act of communication may take the form of:

- **Informing -** Where information is shared, e.g. a change of address, a meeting will take place at a certain time and location. This is **one-way** communication, where a response is not generally required from the receiver

- **Calling to action -** Where someone is asked to do something, e.g. to have a report completed by a certain date. A call to action can either occur through a **direct request** or it can be **implied**. For example, a line manager says to their employee, 'I think that could be done in 10 minutes.' This is not a direct request to have it done in 10 minutes. However, there is the implication to get it done within 10 minutes. This is **two-way** communication, where the receiver is asked to respond to the communication

In business, these forms of communication are not always clearly separated. If a manager shares a story with their employee about a problem they are having, do they want the employee to be aware of the problem or do they want the employee to do something about it?

Communication is about being **clear** about the message that is being transmitted. The sender wants to make sure that their message is **understood** without any misunderstandings.

Communication is the lifeblood of a business. As a business is made up of many different parts, e.g. departments and teams that may be on many different floors of a building or geographical locations, for it to work effectively, to let each part know what is going on both within and outside of the organisation, each part of the business needs to be able to connect to other parts of the organisation to get things done.

The methods by which people communicate are:

- **Formal** - Communication delivered through 'official channels', e.g. a written memorandum from a manager to their department
- **Informal** - Communication delivered on the 'hoof', usually by word of mouth, e.g. about a director visiting the organisation
- **Diagonal** - Communication which has no obvious line of authority, e.g. team members requesting or sharing information with one another
- **Vertical** - Communication which may be top down or bottom up - from the organisation, usually via directors and managers, to its employees or from the employees to the organisation, e.g. instructions and policies sent from the Board of Directors to the employees for implementation
- **Verbal** - Communication which involves using the voice, e.g. speaking over the telephone, face to face, in a discussion, debate, interview, presentation
- **Non-verbal** - Communication where there is no use of the voice, e.g. eye contact, body language, use of sign language and signs
- **Visual** - Communication that is displayed to appeal to the eye, e.g. PowerPoint slides, public notices, advertisements
- **Written** - Communication that uses accepted symbols, e.g. the alphabet, in the written form, e.g. emails; telephone messages; letters
- **Internal** - Communication distributed to employees within an organisation, e.g. company intranet, tannoy, bulletins - email or hard copy
- **External** - Communication distributed to external customers and other stakeholders, e.g. shareholder meetings, company Internet

• ACTIVITY 1

What is the purpose of communication? What forms can communications take?

Written communication

The aim of written communication is to express ideas effectively, i.e. to transmit information **appropriately** and **accurately**. To do this, the sender will need to consider all aspects of **language**. Language is a **set of rules** for facilitating the transmission of ideas. Ideas need to be meaningful and written well if the receiver is going to understand the message being sent to them. Language rules to consider when writing are:

Style

Words

Use **short** words or words that are more **approachable**, e.g. 'distribute' rather than 'dissemination'. Try to avoid words that the receiver may not understand - the use of jargon, words that are specific to subject areas; acronyms, e.g. QCF and abbreviations, e.g. esp. The sender should not take it for granted that the receiver will have the same level of understanding as the sender.

Phrases

Try not to use a **hackneyed phrase** when a **single word** will do, e.g. the phrase 'it is the considered opinion' can be replaced by 'we / I think'. Use **short phrases** and try not to have more than **one phrase** to a sentence, as this may confuse meaning.

Sentences

Create sentences that are **short** - see plain English . However, if an idea needs many words to make it meaningful, use them. If a sentence uses a conjunction, such as 'and', 'but' etc., could the sentence be split into two separate sentences? Use different lengths of sentences in a paragraph to interest the reader and hold their attention.

Paragraphs

These break up the text. Paragraphs should try to develop one idea or be a continuation of another idea. Use short paragraphs rather than long ones, but always create a paragraph that will clearly transmit its meaning to the reader.

Layout

To make the message more accessible and increase ease of reading, use: Headings, Breaks, Indentation, **Bold type,** *Italics,* Underline, Colour. These different layout styles can be used together.

Format

There are many different forms of written communication, but for business purposes we will consider the following:

Letters

Letters are a formal approach to communicating and are generally written on headed paper. An organisation may expect its employees to use a template, which will automatically prompt specific information to be written.

Emails

Emails are considered to be the main format for communicating within a business today. Emails are sent both internally and externally. Emails can be a less formal way of writing. They are quick to write. They can elicit a quick response from the receiver and they are inexpensive to send. However, an email message is easy to delete from a personal computer (PC), so valuable information can be lost easily. Because it is such an easy form of communication, inboxes may overflow with messages, which will then need to be managed.

Reports

Reports may range in both the level of formality and size. Most will be prefaced with an 'executive summary', followed by various headings which will be dependent on the content of the report. An organisation may expect the content of a report to follow the organisation's '**house style**'.

Spelling, punctuation and grammar

Spelling

When using the written form of communication, it is important to make sure that words are spelled correctly. However, this may be more difficult than it sounds, due to the influence of 'text messaging' or Americanised spelling. Protocols will be in place within an organisation for acceptable use. Spelling shows that the sender is careful about what they are writing. Incorrect spelling may confuse the reader. It may also cause the receiver to dismiss the message if there are too many spelling mistakes

• ACTIVITY 2

Underline the correct spelling of the word.

1. Renisance	renaissance	renaissence
2. Abundant	abundent	abundint
3. Accessable	accessuble	accessible
4. Retoric	rhetoric	rhetorick
5. Brochure	brocher	broshure
6. Collegate	collegiate	colegiate
7. doublely	dooublly	doubly
8. Plagiarism	plagerism	plagarism
9. Behaviour	behavure	behavior
10. Abriviate	abbreviate	abbriviate

The English language is more eccentric than almost any other language. It is the hardest language to learn because spelling is not consistent, i.e. there are so many different spelling rules. Some words that look the same and sound the same may have one letter that changes their meaning, e.g. 'stationery' and 'stationary', the former refers to pens and pencils, while the latter is about standing still, not moving.

3• ACTIVITY 1

Underline the correct word:

1. The manager received payment in *lieu / loo*.

2. The team's thinking had to be *reigned / reined* in during that manager's *reign / rein*.

3. The manager was on a *role / roll* because of his *role / roll*.

4. It was a *complement / compliment* the *complement / compliment* they had been given.

5. They have to *review / revue* the report before the Christmas party *review / revue*.

6. It was not the *root / route* to go to get at the *root / route* of the problem.

7. *Who's / whose* who in *who's / whose* opinion.

8. There was no *descent / dissent* as a result of the *descent / dissent* of language being used.

9. *It's / its* the truth though *it's / its* time is not right.

Punctuation

Punctuation marks are a set of symbols used in writing to structure a sentence. Punctuation helps the reader to understand the message, making the written communication more meaningful and come alive from the printed page. Common symbols used in English are the following:

Capital, or **upper-case, letters** are used to:

- Begin sentences

- Indicate proper names, e.g. 'John', 'France', 'America'

- Begin titles, e.g. 'Mr', 'Mrs', 'Sir'

- Begin days of the week, e.g. 'Wednesday', 'Saturday'

- Begin months of the year, e.g. 'June', 'August'

- Indicate acronyms, e.g. 'MoU (Memorandum of Understanding)', 'ToR (Terms of Reference)', 'NOS (National Occupational Standard)'

Commas are used:

- To separate words in a list, e.g. 'printers, photocopiers, computers and scanners'. A comma is not used before the 'and'

- Before speech, e.g. Margaret said, 'I would like the work finished before the end of the day'

- In pairs, to indicate the part of a sentence that can be removed without changing its meaning, e.g. 'Mr Jones, scratching his head, answered the question'

- To indicate pauses in sentences, e.g. 'I must finish photocopying my friend' means something different from, 'I must finish photocopying, my friend'

Semi-colons are used to:

- Separate items in a list, e.g. 'the business has offices in London, England; Cardiff, Wales; Madrid, Spain and Paris, France'

- Emphasise contrasts, e.g. 'John preferred to write the presentation; Adam preferred to deliver the presentation'

- Link statements together, e.g. 'He wanted to get a job; his rent wouldn't be paid if he didn't'

- Add emphasis, e.g. 'Sandra answered the telephone; it was her boss; she knew she was in trouble'

Colons are used to:

- Introduce lists, e.g. 'The supervisor asked for information on: sales, purchases, stock levels and wastage'

- Separate two parts of a sentence where the second part explains the first, e.g. 'Sales had improved during February: it was the busiest week of the month so far that year'

Hyphens are used:

- To avoid doubt, e.g. words such as 'co-respondent', 're-formed', 'coordinate'

- When linking two nouns, e.g. 'Southampton-Crewe train' or two adjectives, e.g. 'Austro-Hungarian fall out'

- When a noun phrase is used to qualify another noun, e.g. 'A self-closing door is self closing; a three-drawer filing cabinet has three drawers'

- For certain prefixes, e.g. 'un-British', 'anti-hunting'

- To indicate words are to be spelled out, e.g. 'C-R-E-W-E'
- To avoid difficult looking compound words, e.g. 'coattail', 'belllike', 'deice', look better as 'coat-tail', 'bell-like' and 'de-ice'

Brackets are used:

- In a similar way as a pair of commas, as they separate a phrase within a sentence that could be removed without altering its meaning, e.g. 'Mrs Wentworth (the new Managing Director) will visit the office next Wednesday'

Full stops are used:

- To indicate the end of a sentence
- After initials or abbreviations, e.g. 'D. J. Campbell'

Exclamation marks are used:

- In place of a full stop to indicate an exclamation, e.g. 'The manager raced into the office shouting!'

Question marks are used:

- In place of a full stop to indicate a query, e.g. 'What time should I make the meeting for next week?'

Quotation marks or 'inverted commas' are used:

- To indicate speech, e.g. Peter said, 'I want you to work on the reception desk tomorrow'
- To indicate a quote from another source, e.g. The letter from the customer says: 'I sent the cheque on Wednesday'

•ACTIVITY 4

Punctuate and correct the following:

The manager was later every mourning it was never there fault

Its always a matter of opinion for times they had been later it wasn't fair

The order included office equipment of pcs scanners laminate machine printers etc. they arrive late

There time was taken for granted they worked such longe ours

It was to bad too of them had been over the limit too ere is human

Were here to do the right thing all ladies clothing should be kept down stairs

No enoughs enough it has to stop now or your dismissed from the company

The managers unability to do it correct coursed the unit a grate deal of problems

Its owner is gone it's the last straw as its not enough

Thyme and tyde wait for no man

Informaton is available 9 and 5 you can get it from the managers office

Apostrophes are used:

- In place of missing letters, e.g. 'mustn't' = must not; ''til' = until; ''phone' = telephone; 'S'ton' = Southampton

- To indicate possession

Possessive apostrophes follow certain rules:

- Where the noun is singular - The apostrophe comes between the noun and the 's', e.g. 'Ali's book' = the book that belongs to Ali

- Where the noun is singular but ends in 's' - The apostrophe still comes between the noun and the additional 's', e.g. 'The class's teacher' = the teacher of the class

- Where the noun is plural and ends in 's' - The apostrophe comes after the 's' and there is no additional 's', e.g. 'ladies' bags' = the bags that belong to the ladies

- Where the noun is plural and does not end in 's' - The apostrophe comes between the noun and the 's', e.g. 'men's room' = the room for men

- However, there is one exception to these rules - The word 'its'. If you mean 'it is' or 'it has', then the correct usage would be 'it's', because you are replacing the missing letters with an apostrophe. If you mean 'belonging to it', then the correct usage is 'its', without the apostrophe

Each of the above symbols are used for specific purposes within a sentence to improve its meaning and make it easier for the reader to understand.

Grammar
The purpose of good grammar is to make 'meaning' clearly understood. This can be achieved by dividing up what is being communicated into **paragraphs** and **sentences**:

A **sentence** is a set of words which make a complete statement. Sentences must start with a capital letter and end with a full stop, exclamation mark or question mark. Sentences can be of almost any length. For clarity, they should be as short as possible - see plain English - but as a minimum they must contain a subject and a verb. Sentences are broken down into parts of speech. There are many different parts of speech in the English language. The main ones are:

- **Nouns -** A noun is the name of a person, place, thing, day of the week or month of a year, e.g. 'Jeffrey', 'Isle of Man', 'Thursday'

- **Pronouns -** A pronoun is a word used in place of a noun, e.g. 'he', 'she', 'it', 'they'

- **Verbs -** A verb is a word that shows action, e.g. 'watching', 'playing', 'worked', 'ran'

- **Adverbs -** An adverb is a word that adds to a verb, generally with an '-ly' at the end, e.g. 'slowly', 'quickly'

- **Adjectives -** An adjective is a word that describes a noun, e.g. 'big', 'small', 'hollow', 'light'

- **Prepositions -** A preposition is a word that shows how one noun relates to another, e.g. 'towards', 'between', 'beside'

- **Conjunctions -** A conjunction is a word that joins two other words, e.g. 'and', 'but', 'so', 'then', 'therefore'

A **paragraph** is a collection of sentences about a single subject which contain two or more sentences, though they may contain a single sentence in order to emphasise a point. They can be as long as it is necessary to complete the subject. When a new subject is introduced, a new paragraph starts on the line below.

• ACTIVITY 5

Using emails or letters that you have written, check through them to analyse if the correct grammar has been used. Check to make sure that sentences and paragraphs are correctly formed

Plain English

Plain English, also known as 'plain language', describes language that focuses on clarity, brevity and the avoidance of technical wording. It seeks to use a writing style that readers can understand after just one reading. It uses only as many words as are necessary. It combines forms in English that are clear, concise, direct and natural. Plain English seeks to achieve the following principles:

- Clarity

- Simplicity

- Appropriateness to the audience - considering who they are and what relationship you want to have with them

- Directness

- Being personal

- Uses informal language, when appropriate

- Uses common, everyday language

- Accessibility to a wide audience

- Explains technical words in simple language

- Attempts to interest readers and hold their attention

- Relies heavily on simple sentence structures

- Generally avoids using the passive voice

- Is respectful of the reader

How to write plain English

Plain English can be written without being patronising or oversimplified. It is **not**:

- Reducing the length of a message or changing its meaning

- Banning new words, killing off long words or promoting completely perfect grammar

- Letting grammar slip

- Amateurish

- As easy as we would like to think

The main advantages of plain English are:

- Speed - It is faster to **write** and **read**

- Understanding - The message comes across more easily and in a friendlier way

When writing plain English, consider the following guidance:

- **Keep sentences short -** Keep an average sentence length of 15 to 20 words. This does not mean making every sentence the same length. Be punchy. Vary writing by mixing short sentences with longer ones. Stick to one main idea in a sentence, plus one other related point if needed. Most long sentences can be broken up into smaller ones

- **Use active verbs -** Plain English uses the active voice, crisp and professional, more than the passive voice, stuffy and bureaucratic. There are three main parts to almost every sentence:

  - A **subject -** The person, group or thing doing the action

  - A **verb -** The action itself

  - An **object -** The person, group or thing that the action is done to

By using the following example: 'John wrote the report', we can see that the **subject** is John - he is doing the writing; the **verb** is wrote; and the **object** is the report - it is being written. This is the simplest form of a sentence structure, though sentences can have more words in them. Using a passive verb reverses the order, i.e. **object** then **verb** then subject, e.g. 'The report - **object** - was written - **passive verb** - by John - **subject**. By making a sentence passive, more words are introduced into the sentence, which makes it clumsier.

Passive verbs cause several problems, as they:

- Can be confusing

- Often make writing more long winded

- Make writing less lively

Passive verbs are good to use:

- To make something less hostile

- To avoid taking the blame

- When the person or doer is not known

- If it simply sounds better

Aim to make about 80-90% of verbs active.

- **Use 'you' and 'we'** - Try to call the reader 'you', even if the reader is only one of many people you are talking too. Similarly, always call the organisation 'we'. There is nothing wrong with using 'we' and 'I' in the same letter

- **Use words that are appropriate for the reader** - Say exactly what is meant, using the simplest words that fit. This does not necessarily mean only using simple words – just words that the reader will understand. Decide which are the most suitable words to use. The use of jargon should be limited to a group of people who will understand its meaning. It can be a useful form of shorthand. Try to avoid using specialist jargon when addressing the general public

- **Do not be afraid to give instructions - Imperatives - commands** are the fastest and most direct way of giving someone instructions. If a command sounds too harsh, add 'please' where appropriate. Not using 'please' could result in a refusal to carry out the command. However, a command can tend to use the passive voice

- **Avoid nominalisations** - A **nominalisation** is a type of abstract noun - the name of something that is not a physical object, such as a process, technique or emotion. For example, 'We had a discussion about the report' becomes, 'We discussed the report'. Nominalisations are formed from verbs, e.g. 'completion', from the verb 'complete'. Nominalisations are often used instead of the verbs they come from. Because they are merely the names of things, they sound as if nothing is actually happening in the sentence

- **Use lists where appropriate** - Lists are excellent for splitting information up. There are two main types of list:

  - A list that is a continuous sentence with several listed points picked out at the beginning, middle or end

  - A list of separate points with an introductory statement - like this list

In the list above, each point is a complete sentence, as they both start with a capital letter and end with a full stop. With a list that is part of a continuous sentence, put semicolons after each point and start each with a lower-case letter. The next to last point has 'and' after the semicolon. Make sure each point follows logically and grammatically from the introduction. Use bullet points in lists. These are better than numbers or letters, as they draw attention to each point without giving extra information. See the example above

- **Apologising** - If you are replying to a tricky letter or a complaint, or are dealing with a difficult problem, empathise with the reader. Be professional, not emotional. Even if you have to be firm, be as helpful and polite as possible. If apologising, do so early. Apologise completely and concisely, sympathetically and sincerely

- **Destroying myths**
  - A sentence can start with **and, but, because, so** or **however**
  - Split infinitives are allowed
  - Sentences can end with a preposition
  - The same word can be used in a sentence twice if a better word cannot be found

- **Examples of alternative words** - Additional - **extra**, advise - **tell**, applicant - **you**, commence - **start**, complete - **fill in**, comply with - **keep to**, consequently - **so**, ensure - **make sure**, forward - **send**, in accordance with - **under / keeping to**, in excess of - **more than**, in respect of - **for**, in the event of - **if**, prior to - **before**

• ACTIVITY 6

Write this paragraph in plain English.

It was prestidigitation taken to the highest level of extravagance which could not have been foreseen by any of the people who were attending the meeting. Entering like a popinjay they rounded on everyone present, using a voice that would shatter glass. They had with them, a stapler, some paper clips, paper and fountain pens, in which they were going to use to make a collage for the presentation. No one else had deigned to think of those components as they were so out of left field. Still we were grateful they had arrived as they had not been seen at any of the last four meetings and no one was sure if what had been agreed at the first meeting was going to be completed in time if at all and the time was fast approaching when the team needed to see some results. Now that they had arrived it might be easier to complete the task and get the report with the collage to the right person and guarantee a good bonus which we could all use imbibing right royally from one weekend to another weekend. The conception of what they had done was breathtaking in its audacity.

What is 'netiquette'?

'Netiquette' is the writing etiquette used to write electronic communication such as email, bulletin boards etc. The methods of electronic communications differ from written communication in the following ways:

- **Speed** - Electronic messages are quicker to create, send and respond to. Speed can often change the writing style and formality of the written communication. These changes can lead to misinterpretation of messages

- **Permanence** - Electronic messages are easy to store online. Electronic communications can be altered without knowing whether it is the original or not. They may also be reformatted and then printed as more formal or 'official' correspondence

- **Costs** - There are no visible costs for sending electronic messages to people over a variety of geographical locations

- **Accessibility** - A means of direct communication. However, senders / recipients can get overburdened with the quantity of electronic messages being communicated

- **Security** and privacy - Access electronically stored mail and files. However, these are open to hacking if insufficient firewalls have been put in place by the organisation

- **Sender authenticity** - Verify the sender of a message. A systems administrator can return messages if they have been incorrectly addressed. Only the recipient of the message can read it, so it will sit unopened online until accessed

Some guidelines to consider when writing electronic communications:

- Use the appropriate formality - Electronic communication tends to lead to an informal writing style. Electronic communication is just as permanent as paper documents. They may be read by more individuals. Take time to make sure no electronic communication embarrasses you later. Minimise spelling mistakes. Make sure that the communication message is easy to read and understand

- **Keep paragraphs and messages short and to the point**

- Shorter paragraphs have more impact. They are more likely to be read by busy people

- **Format messages for easy reading**

- White space is not wasted space. It greatly improves clarity. Do not overuse font styles - Bold etc., as they loose their power. Use the same case as you would in a traditional letter - avoid use of all text in UPPERCASE, as it is more difficult to read and looks like shouting. Use of all lower case slows down reading, use a traditional typeface instead, e.g. Times New Roman; use a type size of no less than 10 points, preferably 12, and a line length of 40 to 60 characters

- **Use descriptive subject titles** - Use the subject line to describe the content of the message. This allows the receiver to decide when to read the message

- **Monitor the use of humour and sarcsm -** There is no voice or body language to observe in an electronic message. This can lead to a misinterpretation of the message. Subtle humour tends to get lost - make sure that people realise the message is trying to be funny

- **Be careful with expressions of ager -** Messages can often be misconstrued and generate unexpected angry responses. As electronic communication allows the recipient to respond immediately to a message, it can sometimes lead to a hasty response. If a message creates negative emotions, set it aside and reread it later, or ask for feedback on its content from a colleague. Take time to calmly respond to the message for fear of misunderstanding or misinterpreting the message. Ask for clarification on inflammatory statements. Be aware of using exclamation marks and upper-case text, as they may be misinterpreted. For example, use of upper case could be interpreted as 'shouting'

- **Be careful of criticising others** - Messages can be circulated very freely, so be careful with comments made about other people and yourself

- **Limit the distribution of mesages** - Do not 'cc' people in unnecessarily

- **Signaures** - Keep them short. Do not include graphics. Sometimes it is appropriate to add other information about upcoming activities of the organisation

Any piece of written communication should conform to all of the above rules and principles, whatever form is used. It is the responsibility of the sender to make sure that the written communication will be **understandable** to the receiver, allowing for no ambiguity. Any form of communication that is sent is an example of the branding of the organisation, of the expectations that the organisation has for expressing itself. Communication should be honest and open. The communication must aim not to distort the message. Communications are exchanged between employees in an organisation and external customers outside of the organisation. Distorted information can lead to rumour and innuendo, undermine the credibility of the sender and that of the organisation. It can also lead to uncertainty, anxiety and the lowering of morale and motivation.

> Think like a wise man but communicate in the language of the people.
> *- William Butler Yeats*

Urgent or important

Lots of things are 'important', but they are not always 'urgent'. They are not the same thing. Some communication becomes 'urgent' because it has been delayed or forgotten. Some tasks can be both 'important' and 'urgent'. Many communications are not nearly as 'urgent' as the communicator believes them to be.

To help differentiate between 'urgent' and 'important' a decision needs to be made about the priority of the communication. The decision when to complete communication can be informed by the **important / urgent matrix**

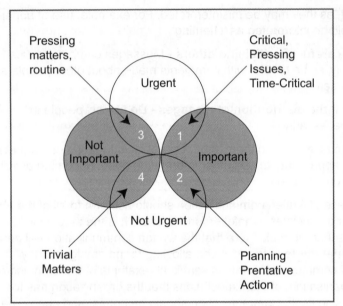

Figure 5.2. Important / urgent matrix. Stephen R. Covey, 1989, The 7 Habits of Highly Effective People

The matrix shows that not all communications will have the same level of 'urgency' or 'importance' as others.

Box 1
Represents things that are both 'urgent' and 'important'. This box requires some time to think about the method and content of the communication, e.g. senn emailemail to lorry drivers about road conditions to help them meet their daily deadlines.

Box 2
Represents things that are 'important, but not urgent'. This box is all about 'quality'. This box provides the communicator with the 'opportunity' to reflect, though still on a time schedule, to see how things can be improved. Attending to these types of communication minimises Box 1 communications.

Box 3
Represents things that are 'urgent, but not important'. The 'urgent' creates the illusion of 'importance'. Many telephone calls, meetings and drop-in visitors fall into this box. A lot of time can be spent in this box meeting other people's priorities, overestimating them as 'urgent' and 'important'.

Box 4

Represents communication that is 'not urgent and not important'. This is a box of activities which should be avoided if careful attention has been given to the purpose of the communication.

Sometimes what is important or urgent to the sender may not be to the receiver. Be clear about instructions when sending any form of communication, so the responder has a clear idea of when a response is required.

Storing written communication

It is important to **keep a record** of written communication. This provides proof to interested parties about when the communication was completed and sent. It also provides proof of the content of the written communication. It is also a statutory obligation under the **Freedom of Information Act 2000** (FOIA) to make certain documents available to the public, if requested. There are two methods by which written communication can be filed and stored, which are:

Manual storage systems

This involves keeping copies of written communication in the following formats:

- **Files**

- **Shelves / cupboards**

- **Cabinets / drawers**

Each of these formats may use security devices to keep confidential information safe

Electronic storage systems

These involve storing communication on a server which may use devices, such as:

- **PCs -** Desktops, laptops, notebooks, palmtops etc.

- **Handsets -** BlackBerrys, iPods etc. Handsets can be programmed to store important information. Likewise, removable memories, such as diskette, almost obsolete, compact disc (CD) and flash drives can be used as backups to store relevant information for future use

- **Microfilm -** Important and confidential information can be recorded onto tapes / films

Verbal communication

Verbal communication is composed of **sound** and **speaking** - using words and language. It is face-to-face communication. It may be **formal**, e.g. an appraisal meeting, or **informal**, e.g. a quick head-to-head. The use of spoken language can reflect class, profession and other social factors. As with written language, there will always be a purpose for verbal communication. Speaking can either be:

- **Interpersonal** - Most forms of verbal communication fall into this category. The speaker should avoid offending the receiver in the choice of language they use and tailor it to the receiver's needs and expectations

- **Public** - Verbal communication that takes place in a public setting, where a speaker is aiming to persuade, inform, inspire or motivate a large body of people

> Say what you mean, and mean what you say,
> but don't say it mean!

When communicating verbally, the speaker needs to consider the **content** and choice of **words** they wish to use. What is being said will affect how well it is received and understood, so sensory words should be used to help convey the meaning. Sensory words create a 'picture', a 'sound' or a 'feeling'. They are particularly useful if the speaker is trying to persuade the listener to agree. There are three main types of sensory words:

- **Seeing** - 'I see what you mean', 'I can imagine'

- **Hearing** - 'I hear what you say', 'I hear you loud and clear'

- **Feeling** - 'I feel good about what I hear'

Choose words that will put the message across the way that the speaker wants. If the speaker is not sure of how their choice of words will be interpreted by the listener, use a mixture of sensory words.

The **tone** of voice of the speech. The tone of voice will convey the way the speaker feels about what they are saying:

- Excited

- Angry

- Distressed

- Tired

- Happy

- Positive

To improve the tone of the voice:

- Make sure that breathing is from the diaphragm. Sit up straight. Taking deep breaths will lend body and warmth to the sound of the voice

- Drink lots of water to keep the voice lubricated and sounding pleasant

- Avoid caffeine. It is a diuretic

- Use gestures to make the voice sound energetic, especially if tired. Gestures will give the voice additional power, helping to emphasis words / phrases

- Smile, as this will automatically warm the tone of the voice

- Exercise the range of the voice to reach different tones. Deeper tones offer more credibility than higher-pitched voices. Get feedback on the tone of your voice. Ask a trusted colleague. Remember, your voice sells people on your knowledge level and professionalism. It helps you to gain their support when difficulties arise

The volume of speech. The volume used - loud / quiet - will depend on the audience - size / composition etc. - and the size of the room / venue.

The **clarity** of speech. Speaking clearly helps to make sure that the message is heard accurately, particularly if speaking in a language or accent that is unfamiliar to the listener.

The **speed** of speech. The listener's level of understanding needs to be considered when choosing the speed of the speech.

Unlike written communication, during the process of verbal communication, whether actively speaking or listening, the speaker is also using their body to communicate meaning. This is also known as body language. Body language sends out messages whether you are speaking or not. Messages may be sent by the body on purpose or accidentally. The way people sit, stand, fold their arms, use facial expression etc., can have an affect on how verbal communication is interpreted. Body language can either add to or take away from what is being said. When speaking, positive body language involves:

- **Face -** A major source of expression, the face can express many emotions, such as happiness when smiling. But remember that a person can say one thing when their face express something different. If the words do not match the face, question the meaning of the vocal word or expression

- **Eyes** - Most people will make eye contact first. Eye contact can be used to make visual contact, avoid visual contact, express feelings based on the intensity and length of eye contact etc. People generally make eye contact to make a connection - they are more likely to be telling the truth. When a person averts their eyes to the left it means they may be lying. If their eyes wander, the person may be feeling uncomfortable with revealing their true feelings. If a person maintains uncomfortable levels of eye contact they may be trying to impose their will

- **Posture** - Posture is how different parts of the body - head, arms, legs etc., are being held. They can work separately or together. If a person leans in towards you, they might be expressing interest in what you are saying. Leaning away shows that they may want to get away or are not interested in what is being said. Poor posture, e.g. slumping, can show a person 'protecting' their heart or silencing themselves. Look for aggressive or dominating postures, such as speaking and standing over a person while the other person is sitting

Gestures

Can be related to verbal communication or unrelated to verbal communication. For example, waving to say 'hi' without a verbal cue. Gestures can be used to emphasise a key point during a speech or presentation. Examples of arm gestures include:

- **Crossing arms -** Defensive position:
  - When you are talking, this could mean that they may not agree with what you have said and may doubt or suspect you. They may have a bad impression of you and may not wish to continue talking with you. It may also depict arrogance or defensiveness
  - When they are talking, this could mean that they may be hiding something from you, or may even be lying. A person engages in this protective posture when they feel anxious or nervous
  - They may be protecting themselves from verbal attack to maintain their composure
  - They might just be feeling cold

- **Shaking hands**
    - Firm grip: is associated with confidence or power - palms pointing downwards in most cases
    - Wilting or soft grip: is associated with being nervous, tense or shy - palms pointing upwards in most cases
- **Hands in pockets -** Which could be interpreted as:
    - Nervousness, anxiety or being uncomfortable with the situation
    - Deviousness: hiding something
    - Restrained: holding back from participating in a situation
    - Bored or uninterested
    - Lacking confidence
- **Clenching a fist -** Which could be interpreted as:
    - Frustration
    - Anger
    - Resistance
    - Defensiveness
    - Confidence
- **Deception -** Which could be exhibited by:
    - Physical expression which is limited and stiff, with minimal arm and hand movements
    - Avoiding making eye contact
    - Hands touching the face, throat and mouth. Likely to touch or scratch the nose or behind the ear, whereas not so likely to touch the chest / heart with an open hand
    - Timing and duration of emotional gestures and emotions are off normal pace and may stop suddenly
    - Timing is off between emotions, gestures / expressions and words
    - Gestures / expressions not matching the verbal statement
    - Expressions that are limited to mouth movements when someone is faking emotions, instead of expressing through the whole face

- **Voice** - It is also an integral part of non-verbal communication. The tone of voice, volume, emotion, pace etc., all influence the messages being sent as part of body language. Deception can be identified by:
  - The use of words to answer a question
  - A statement with a contraction is more likely to be truthful
  - No direct statements. Imply answers instead of denying something directly
  - Adding unnecessary details to convince. Not comfortable with silence or pauses
  - Leaving out pronouns and speaking in a monotonous tone
  - Garbled words and speech
  - Syntax and grammar may be mismatched. Muddling of sentences

Just because someone exhibits one or more of these signs does not make them deceptive.

- **Movement** - Whether using the entire body or just part of the body, movement is flexible and commanding. For example, moving toward another person may send a message of dominance or assertiveness; moving away from another person may send a message of avoidance or submission

- **Touch** - A powerful element of body language which is capable of communicating so many different messages. It can also be interpreted in many different ways. Touch is generally divided into four main categories: friendship, professional, social and intimate

- **Appearance** - Physical appearance includes clothing, neatness, body shape and anything else that provides visual messages and cues to other people. Dress appropriately to meet the purpose of the verbal communication

Some of the greatest differences in body language interpretation occur between different cultures. These variations can range from what is considered appropriate in formal versus informal situations, as well as professional versus personal situations. Gestures are a form of body language that can have entirely opposite meanings in different cultures. If you hold up two fingers with the palm facing outward in a 'v' sign, it means victory, or peace, in the US. But in the UK, when the palm is facing inward, it has a more derogatory meaning. If a meeting is being convened with people from different cultures, research their expectations beforehand to make sure there are no misinterpretations of body language etc.

Telephone communication is similar to face-to-face communication, except that the speaker is unable to see the person they are speaking to, so they are unable to interpret body language. The tone of voice, volume, clarity and speed are equally as important when speaking on the telephone. The way in which telephone calls are made and answered is very important. Callers will base their impression of the speaker and the organisation on what they hear. The speaker is aiming to make a friendly but efficient impression. Smile when answering the telephone - the listener will hear it! Avoid answering the telephone when you are eating, chewing gum or yawning. When making a call, always state the reason for the telephone call. Make sure that all of the information that is needed to communicate, or potential questions that need to be asked, are prepared in advance. Make a list of important points to communicate. Take notes of important points of the conversation that need to be acted on after the telephone conversation has ended. This will help the speaker to get the message across clearly. All telephone calls must be treated as important. Answering the telephone is not an interruption to work - it is a part of work! Callers will form an impression of the organisation from the way the telephone is answered. Be polite, receptive and let the caller know they are being listened to. When communicating information keep it relevant and accurate. If receiving information have a pen and paper ready to make notes when necessary.

• ACTIVITY 7

Here is a list of some sensory words: harmonise, move, speak, voice, imagine, touch, search, image, sound, picture, tone, grasp, hate, tune in to, accent, appearance, celebrate, fight, blunt, colour and show.

Place them in the correct category.

Seeing	Hearing	Feeling

We have two ears and one mouth so that we can listen twice as much as we speak
- Epictetus

Listening

The purpose of verbal communication is to communicate with another person or group of people. In order to do this, the person or group of people need to listen to the message. If the listener does not listen to what someone is saying, the speaker is wasting their time saying it. There is more to listening than simply being within hearing distance. There are two types of listening:

Active listening, which is making an effort to hear and understand. It is:

- Appearing involved
- Leaning towards the speaker
- Making eye contact
- Mirroring the speaker's facial expressions
- Nodding or shaking the head
- Paying attention
- Responding with 'mm', 'yes', 'okay', 'really'

Passive listening, which is hearing without taking in what is being said. It is:

- Listening but not hearing

- Switching off

- Slouching

- Not making eye contact

- Having an impassive expression

- Moving about restlessly

- Appearing disinterested

- Making no response

Actively listening gives the listener the opportunity to contribute meaningfully to the discussion or conversation. It allows the listener to contribute by asking questions when the meaning is not clear or they want to find out more information. There are several different types of questions:

- **Open questions** - Open questions are used if more information is needed. These are very useful for getting others to talk and share opinions, ideas and information

- **Closed questions** - Closed questions can be very specific and precise, which are used to elicit a 'yes' or 'no' answer. Closed questions would be used for getting accurate, factual information

- **Funnel questions** - Funnel questions are a combination of both open and closed questions, starting with an open question - starting wide. The response is then listened to and then further 'refined' enquiries are made, with each question getting narrower and narrower, until a closed question gives a specific and precise answer

- **Comparative questions** - These ask a person to think about two different situations and then compare them. Comparative questions are very good for revealing what matters to someone and what they value

- **Short questions** - These are used so that the speaker keeps receiving information from the other person who is doing the talking. For short questions, use Kipling's six friends: 'what', 'who', 'when', 'how', 'where' and 'why'. The question that is most probing is 'Why?' Handle these questions sensitively and assertively, otherwise the listener interpreting a short question may see this as a sign of aggression

- **Absence of a spoken question - pause or silence** - Sometimes the best response is no response. During the pause / silence, the speaker should maintain supportive eye contact and positive body language as they wait for a reply. This is an approach that can be used in a sensitive situation. This can sometimes be a difficult response to make, as a silence that goes on too long may be embarrassing and undermine the rapport that has been built up. However, the use of the pause / silence can also provoke the other person to speak out and reveal more information

- **Summarising questions** - These are great for checking out whether messages are being understood as you intended them to be

• ACTIVITY 8

Which of the following questions are either open or closed questions? Tick the correct box.

	OPEN	CLOSED
1. How many miles should I travel?		
2. Is it early or late?		
3. When is it due to arrive?		
4. Will it be repaired tomorrow?		
5. How should they get there?		
6. What is the different between red and rouge?		
7. When it's done it's done?		
8. Where can I find the manager?		

Contributing to and leading a discussion
Most discussions will focus on exchanging knowledge, ideas and opinions on a particular subject within a group of more than two people. The discussion aims to promote the sharing of and increasing understanding of a subject. Each participant needs to be engaged in the discussion to affect changes in attitude. Leading a discussion can take two approaches:

Directive
This is planned before the discussion to get the group to think about certain aspects of the subject. Discussion will be directed towards achieving particular conclusions.

Non-directive
This may be instigated by the discussion leader but is allowed to take a

free course. The leader will chair the discussion to help it flow, but not steer it so that they can achieve a specific conclusion. Non-directive discussions explore ideas or promote group feeling with no measurable outputs.

The choice of approach, or combination of approaches, will depend on the purpose of the discussion. The discussion leader will help to form a valid conclusion, using a minimum amount of guidance and maintaining control as they stay in the background. The control that the discussion leader exercises should be based on their skills not their position. The chief skills needed to lead a discussion are:

- Active listening

- Use of correct form of questions

- Coordination of the discussion efforts

The discussion leader will aim to:

- **Create an environment of participation** - People may not participate in a discussion for different reasons: unfamiliarity, fear of criticism or reproach, ignorance, lack of interest, inability to think quickly or speak fluently, shyness, resentment of a group member etc. Treat the members of the discussion as individuals and frame the style of approach so that it draws on the resources of the group, altering the pace when required. People may have hidden agendas, which could delay or derail discussion. Consider all aspects, using all points of view and evaluating possible answers

- **Promote discussion** - Discussion can be promoted by different methods, e.g. a provocative question, a case study

- **Control and involvement** - The discussion leader uses three main tools to control a discussion: **silence** - use it to allow independence of thinking within the discussion; **questions** - directed at individuals, using the appropriate form; non-threatening; and **summaries** - clarify but do not put words in people's mouths

Recognise the personalities that will need to be managed:

- The **quarrelsome** person. Do not let them monopolise

- The **positive** person. A helpful addition to the discussion, they should be used a lot

- The **know-all**. Let the group deal with their theories

- The **talkative** person. Limit their speaking, but interrupt tactfully

- The **shy** person. Involve them by asking non-threatening questions. Give credit where possible

- The **un-cooperative** person. Recognise their knowledge and experience and use them

- The **uninterested** person. Involve them by asking them what interests them most about their work

- The **snob**. Use the 'yes - but' technique and minimise criticism

- The **persistent questioner**. Do not get trapped by them. Park a response until later in the discussion / at the appropriate time

Evaluation of communication

Evaluation is a way of checking to see how things have been done or performed. The aim of evaluation is to learn and improve processes and performance. When evaluating the quality of communication skills, evaluation may either be carried out:

- **Subjectively** - This would be achieved through self-evaluation. Self-evaluation involves reviewing regular tasks to confirm that the most efficient methods are being used to complete them

- **Objectively** - This would be achieved through inviting an independent third party to evaluate. The independent evaluator will, generally, have had nothing to do with the person who is being evaluated. Objective evaluation involves asking people for feedback on tasks they have completed. They will be able to give feedback on whether their requirements are being satisfied and give suggestions on how to complete the task in an easier way. There are two types of objective evaluation:

  - **Formative evaluation** looks at the way things are being done at present to judge whether the right things are being done in the right way. Formative evaluation is used to assess all of the things that are done on a day-to-day basis to see if there are any improvements that can be made

  - **Summative evaluation** looks at a project after completion or after amendments have been put in place to judge their efficiency, effectiveness, impact and sustainability. Summative evaluation is a more formal process - the evaluation is focused on a specific project or change of process. This can be done by seeking structured feedback from everybody involved, possibly by the use of a questionnaire or feedback form, in order that the feedback is received in a manner that allows it to be analysed. This provides an evaluation that includes credible and useful information on the level of achievement and the effective use of resources

Evaluation of communication helps the communicator to move from a position of unconscious **incompetence** to unconscious **competence**. Sue Bishop[1] has identified four stages in this process:

- **Stage 1 - Unconscious incompetence -** Where the communicator has no idea of the impact their communication is having on third parties

- **Stage 2 - Conscious incompetence -** Where the communicator has some idea that their communication skills are letting them down

- **Stage 3 - Conscious competence -** Where the communicator has some idea of the effect of their communication skills, but still needs to think about how to communicate more effectively

- **Stage 4 - Unconscious competence -** Where communication is second nature to the communicator, and they do not have to think about what they are writing or saying

While someone may have excellent communication skills, these skills are never perfect. Communication skills can always be improved. Evaluation is the means of identifying how communication skills can be improved.

As communication skills improve towards 'unconscious competence', the communicator will find they are able to build and maintain **rapport**. Rapport is about empathising with the correspondent of the communication. This will lead to a more meaningful communication by creating an environment of trust and confidence. Rapport is a natural trait which people use to a greater or lesser extent, depending on their personality. People tend to get on with each other better if they like one another, and vice versa. However, in a business environment, often there is no choice about the people being communicated with.

Communication can often take place between people who have never met each other before. In this situation it is beneficial for all of the communicators to create an environment of trust and confidence by converting a stranger to the status of a friend. This can be achieved by a Neuro Linguist Programming (NLP) technique called **mirroring**. The communicators mirror, as with active listening, all behavioural elements that they have noticed in the person they are conversing with and build them into the discussion / conversation as a means of achieving

---

1   Sue Bishop, 1997, The Complete Guide to People Skills. Gower Publishing Company

a successful verbal communication, e.g. gesture; posture; use of language; voice - tone, volume.

> The most effective way to achieve right relations with any living thing is to look for the best in it, and then help that best into the fullest expression
>
> *- Allen J. Boone*

In aiming to achieve successful communication, the communicators, both transmitter and receiver, should summarise the progress of their discussion as a continuing means of building and maintaining rapport. A **summary** is a tool for accurately repeating back ideas and information that have been shared in a discussion or conversation. This helps to reinforce what has been discussed. A summary of the discussion can highlight areas of agreement or disagreement. If there are areas of agreement, summarising the points helps to build and maintain the rapport that is being created between the communicators. If there is disagreement, it is advisable to air any issues at the earliest opportunity, so they do not undermine the established rapport. Disagreements should be resolved to help move the discussion forward. If there is a meeting following an agenda, the agenda items will help to summarise the outcomes of each agenda point discussion. Questions may be used to summarise the content of discussions and also clarify meaning and understanding. Summarising can confirm and / or clarify key points and common ground. It will encourage all communicators to explore new information and any perceived contradictions.

A summary is not used in normal day-to-day conversation, but is a necessary tool for increasing the understanding of ideas and information in a business environment. A summary is not a statement of facts, it is a summing up of expressed ideas and information in a way that makes them come alive for the listener and corroborates what the speaker has said. It creates the opportunity to correct any misunderstanding and helps to reinforce openness and honesty in the communication process. Summarising is a valuable tool for any communicator and is a great way of testing active listening. If the communicator is unable to accurately summarise what has been said, they have probably been passively listening to what has been going on, which is an example of inappropriate behaviour.

> To effectively communicate, we must realise that we are all different in the way we perceive the world and use this understanding as a guide to our communication with others.
>
> *- Anthony Robbins*

Testing your knowledge

1. What are the different methods of communication?

2. When would written communication be used?

3. What are the elements of language that need to be used with written communication?

4. How does the use of language change depending on the form of written communication?

5. Why is the format of written communication important?

6. How is plain English written?

7. Why use netiquette?

8. Why is it important to check written communication before sending it?

9. What is the difference between 'urgent' and 'important' communication?

10. Why store written communication?

11. What elements are used by a speaker to present verbal communication successfully?

12. What is 'active listening'?

13. How does rapport improve communication?

14. Why is summarising so important in verbal communications?

15. Why should communication skills be evaluated?

Work-based performance

Once you have agreed the purpose and methods of communication, set about writing it or contributing to verbal discussions.

Written communication

When setting out to create a piece of written communication, look for information that will support the argument you intend to write. Sift through alternative arguments and select the most appropriate information - make sure you are positive that it will hold up to scrutiny and suits the purpose of your written communication. Find some examples of what other people have written on the same subject area, you can use them as a guide to compose your written communication. Once you have assembled these, the information that you have selected must be organised, structured and formatted appropriately, i.e. it meets the intended purpose of the written communication.

Shape the communication so that it follows a logical order, building on the arguments that you want to investigate and communicate. It could just respond to a piece of written communication that has been sent to you. In the same way as composing a new written piece, answer it logically, following the layout - as you are responding to the person who wrote it, their layout is the form that they like - this method helps to build rapport and bridge understanding between you and the recipient. Mirror their style while still retaining your personality. Correct any formatting and punctuation issues etc., while not appearing obvious, you are not a schoolteacher and that is not the purpose of the communication. However, you do want it to be a fully formed and accurate written piece of communication.

Compose the written communication using the relevant forms of language - grammar, punctuation and spelling. You never know who they are going to share this with. **Remember**, all forms of communication are an opportunity to promote the values of your organisation. Make the best impression by getting it right the first time. Make sure you only use 'text' spelling if it is appropriate, i.e. casual communication with someone you know well. Use it appropriately! Check your computer to make sure your 'spell check' is in English and not American, if that is the organisation requirement.

• ACTIVITY 9

Here is a group of words which show both English and American spelling. Put either E, English, or A, American, in the column next to the word to show how it is spelled in that country.

Honour		Holor	
Specilization		Specialisation	
Furore		Furor	
Specialty		Speciality	
Theater		Theatre	
Tidbit		Titbit	
Manoeuvre		Maneuver	
Enrollment		Enrolemnt	
Emphaize		Emphaise	
Civilize		Civilise	

Write your communication so that it answers any questions requesting information or further information. Make sure that it is written in time to meet the request of the person to whom you will be responding to. If you are unable to make the deadline, give them a quick call to let them know. Write in a style that suits the purpose of the written communication - formal, informal or colloquial.

If writing a letter, make sure that it is printed using paper with the company letterhead on.

When using your PC to write an email, make sure you use a format that will energise the recipient's interest and get them to respond. Use language that is as formal as it needs to be - take your lead from the original email and, when you compose it, make sure that you get to the point, stick to the point and make it short.

When you are writing, monitor your mood so that it does not overly influence the tone of your writing. If angry or annoyed, this may show through in your writing. If too upbeat, your tone of delivery may be too frivolous. **Remember** the purpose of the written communication at all times.

Remember the principles of plain English and use them to make your written communication appeal to the person to whom you are writing to - simple, simple, simple! Keep to short, pitchy, punchy sentences. Use the active voice - it will appeal more to the recipient of any form of written communication. Minimise the use of nominalisations. List things where possible, unless a narrative form is required throughout. What examples of plain English did you use? Make a final check of the written communication before sending it out. If it is important, check with your supervisor / manager before sending it out. Look at any corrections that have been made - what can you learn from them? Why were the corrections made? Check with someone if you do not understand why the communication had to be corrected.

Once the written communication has been sent, file a copy of it in the appropriate filing system.

Verbal communication
Agree the purpose of the verbal communication you will contribute to. How did you achieve it? Research the subject matter before you contribute to the discussion, making sure you understand what is going on and can contribute meaningfully to the discussion. Check with your supervisor or work colleagues for further information before the verbal exchange takes place. Be prepared to provide the correct information to contribute meaningfully to verbal discussions. Begin to think about the contribution you are going to make and how to formulate arguments for presentation. This will help to stimulate the discussion. Aim to move the discussion forward so that it reaches a constructive, if not amicable, conclusion. While striving to achieve a positive outcome is always good practice, in some cases it may not be achieved. If things are not going the way you anticipated and you are not sure about what to do, seek assistance from colleagues who may be present, or ask to adjourn the discussion and seek advice from colleagues on how to move forward.

Throughout a discussion, actively listen to what is being discussed - do not just hear sounds being made. The correct choice of words is what will help you to contribute to a face-to-face discussion or a conversation on the telephone. Do not hesitate to ask if you are not sure about something, or make a note of it and ask for clarification after the discussion if you feel your question may distract from the theme of the discussion. If you did not hear something, ask for it to be repeated - do not leave yourself out of the discussion or lose track of what is being discussed. Hear it and actively listen to what you have heard. Keep the conversation alive for you and your fellow contributors. Give yourself time to make a response and make sure that your contribution meets your objectives.

Make sure your body language is positive and interested in the discussion. Note examples of negative and positive body language that other people use in discussion or conversation. To achieve the outcomes you are looking for, use those that you think will energise a discussion and keep it alive. Monitor the effects of both your own and other people's body language during the discussions. Use the tone of your voice with colour. Make sure that you do not raise your voice when you become passionate about a particular topic. Observe people from other cultures and modify your body language and use of vocal language so that it does not cause offence.

Summarise ideas and points of information as a means of increasing understanding and building rapport.

Evaluation of communication skills
Look at the different methods of communication that you carry out regularly, for instance - attending a team meeting, a one to one with your manager, dealing with incoming mail, dealing with making and receiving incoming telephone calls etc. Did you carry out an evaluation of your communication skills? Who carried out the evaluation? How did you evaluate your communication skills? What did you learn from the evaluation of your communication skills? How have you improved your communication skills as a result of the evaluation? How was the information of the different evaluations recorded?

Testing your skills

1. Why have you used different methods of communication?

2. How has your written communication been formatted to meet specific purposes?

3. What language did you use in the written communication?

4. How many spelling mistakes were made?

5. How did you punctuate the written communication?

6. What did you have to change as a result of checking the written communication?

7. What filing system did you use to store the written communication?

8. How do you know that your verbal communication contributed to the discussion?

9. How did your contributions change to adapt to different audiences and situations?

10. What kinds of questions did you ask, and why?

11. How did you lead a discussion?

12. What did you notice about other people's body language?

13. How did you seek feedback to improve your communication skills?

Ready for assessment?
To achieve this Level 3 unit of a Business &
Administration qualification, learners will need to
demonstrate that they are able to perform the following
activities:

1. Agreed the purpose, content, style and format of the written communication

2. Agreed the final written communication before sending it

3. Agreed what is 'urgent' and 'important' before responding to written communication

4. Met deadlines for responding to written communication

5. Contributed ideas that adapted to the discussion

6. Used questions to contribute to discussions

7. Summarised the discussion at appropriate times

8. Reflected on the outcomes of the communication

9. Learned lessons for improving communication skills

You will need to produce evidence from a variety of sources to support the performance requirements of this unit.

If you carry out the 'ACTIVITIES' and respond to the 'NEED TO KNOW' questions, these will provide some of the evidence required.

Links to other units

While gathering evidence for this unit, evidence **may** also be used from evidence generated from other units within the Business & Administration suite of units. Below is a **sample** of applicable units; however, most units within the Business & Administration suite of units will also be applicable.

QCF NVQ
Communications
Use electronic message systems
Use diary systems
Take minutes
Develop a presentation
Deliver a presentation
Document production
Produce documents in a business environment
Design and produce documents in a business environment
Prepare text from notes
Prepare text from notes using touch typing (40 wpm)
Prepare text from notes using touch typing (60 wpm)
Prepare text from recorded audio instruction (40 wpm)
Prepare text from recorded audio instruction (60 wpm)
Prepare text from shorthand (60 wpm)
Prepare text from shorthand (60 wpm)

SVQ

Communications

Use electronic message systems

Use diary systems

Take minutes

Develop a presentation

Deliver a presentation

Document production

Produce documents in a business environment

Design and produce documents in a business environment

Prepare text from notes

Prepare text from notes using touch typing (40 wpm)

Prepare text from notes using touch typing (60 wpm)

Prepare text from recorded audio instruction (40 wpm)

Prepare text from recorded audio instruction (60 wpm)

Prepare text from shorthand (60 wpm)

Prepare text from shorthand (60 wpm)

6

Deliver a presentation

DELIVER A PRESENTATION

'**Deliver a presentation**' is an <u>optional unit</u> which may be chosen as one of a combination of units to achieve either a Qualifications and Credit Framework (QCF), National Vocational Qualification (NVQ) or Scottish Vocational Qualification (SVQ).

The aims of this unit are to:

- Understand the purpose of preparing for and evaluating the delivery of a presentation
- Understand the techniques used in enhancing a presentation
- Be able to prepare for the delivery of a presentation
- Be able to deliver a presentation
- Be able to evaluate a presentation

To achieve the above aims of this unit, learners will be expected to provide evidence through the performance of work-based activities

Knowledge
What is delivering a presentation all about?
Delivering a presentation is all about selling. It is not just about selling the new key message (s). Embedded within the key message (s) will be ideas, concepts and products that are to be sold to the audience. These need not necessarily be new. The aim of the presentation may be to reinforce current ideas, concepts and products. To successfully achieve the aims of the presentation, and gain audience buy-in, the presenter must sell the ideas, concepts and products through their presentation skills.

Before delivering a presentation, the presenter will have developed their presentation. The presentation will have specific aims and objectives that they want to achieve. If the presenter does not have clear aims and objectives they will not guide their audience to where they need to go. Delivering a presentation is like taking a journey with several stopovers. To deliver the audience to their final destination, the presenter needs to guide them every step of the way. The audience should leave the venue understanding the key message (s) and be enthusiastic to implement them.

The presentation has been developed to address the specific needs of an audience. The audience may willingly choose to attend a presentation or they may have been told to attend a presentation, e.g. by their line manager. The dynamics of an audience's motivation for attending a presentation are very important. They are continually in flux. They will have an effect on how the presentation will be delivered and received. The audience's dynamic is something the presenter will need to monitor constantly throughout the delivery of their presentation. Throughout the delivery of a presentation, the presenter will need to monitor their pitch, pace and volume in order to adapt them to make sure their audience is following them.

• ACTIVITY 1

What is the purpose of delivering a presentation?

A presentation will, generally, be delivered from a pre-prepared written presentation which will, generally, have been researched and developed by the presenter. The written presentation can take many forms, see unit **Develop a Presentation**. However, bottom line, the presenter must know their subject. If the presenter does not know their subject, how will they sell it? How will they make a sale to their audience? It is the aim of the presenter to keep the audience focused and interested in the subject matter they are delivering. It is important that the presenter knows at least as much as, and preferably more than, their audience about the subject you are presenting. If in doubt about the depth of knowledge required to deliver a presentation, explore all possible sources of information before preparing the presentation. The delivery of a presentation becomes truly challenging if the presenter has not prepared to take their audience on the journey to the expected final destination. The more prepared a presenter is, the more the presenter is able to be flexible, energetic and enthusiastic in their delivery. A presentation does not need to be memorised. Memorising introduces an unnecessary element into the presentation which distracts the presenter. It deprives the presenter of life and energy, as they strive to remember exactly what they have learned. It is not a concert. Memorising also makes it more difficult for the presenter to adapt to the changing circumstances of what the audience wants.

To deliver a presentation, the presenter is put on public display. The presenter is the focus of attention of the audience. The audience will listen to what the presenter has to share with them. The audience will respond to the content of the presentation and to the presenter themselves - their voice, their body, their gestures. Making a good presentation is more than just about preparing an excellent written presentation. To make an impact on the audience the presenter will need to develop a delivery style that is lively, responsive, interesting and delivered creatively.

A presenter will have been a member of an audience at some time in their working life. As a starting point, to encourage and inspire the presenter's confidence and understanding, they should think about how a presenter they have seen in the past:

- Grabbed their attention

- Stimulated their imagination and creativity

- Engaged their attention

A presentation is about the partnership formed between the presenter and audience. Both have a responsibility to achieve a successful presentation. However, the presenter is in the driving seat, as they know what the key message (s) is to be delivered.

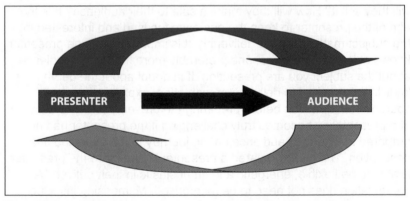

Figure 6.1. Presentation cycle

The presenter should always be focused on the audience. The presenter must make the sale! Otherwise, everybody's time has been wasted! If the presenter has made all the necessary preparations in developing the presentation, they should be more than prepared to deliver the presentation and focus their attention solely on the audience, not on themselves. The last thing the presenter needs to focus on is themselves. Be natural and allow those character traits that will facilitate the presentation to shine through. These character traits will vary and adapt to the subject matter and the size of the audience. However, consider and plan how they might be used during the preparation of the presentation. They may change once the delivery of the presentation is being rehearsed.

• ACTIVITY 2

Explain the presentation cycle.

Remember the **five Ps**: **p**lanning and **p**reparation **p**revent **p**oor **p**erformance.

Focus of attention

The size and membership of an audience will have an effect on how a presentation will be delivered. The size of an audience can be:

Small

An audience of less than 10 people. The presenter will be in close proximity to the audience. The focus of attention will need to move from each individual person, making eye contact with each person. Try not to focus too much attention on one person, as this will disturb the dynamic of the group. They may feel that someone is the favourite and switch off. The presenter could deliver from a sitting position. This will help their confidence, as it will not be so obvious that they are the centre of attention, as it will feel as if they are one of the group. Such informality could help to stimulate the interest of the group.

Medium

An audience of between 10 and 25 people. Less personalised than a small group of people, the presenter's focus of attention will chunk small groups of people together. The presenter's focus will dart from one person to another within these small groups. The presenter should try not to dwell too often on the same group. As it is a larger group, to get the key message (s) across, the presenter will probably stand. However, sitting is equally fine if the room is configured so all members of the audience can see and hear the presenter.

Large

An audience of more than 25 people. This size of this audience requires careful management. The presenter will need to make sure that all members of the audience can hear and see the presentation. As the audience knows it is large, they will not expect individual focus of attention. It is helpful to scan the audience and find faces exuding positivity and confidence. The presenter can use this positivity and confidence as an anchor to return to - this will stimulate the presenter's energy and confidence. However, the presenter should roam around the room engaging different groups of the audience. The presenter is an antenna and should scan the room to see where attention is waning, confused, bored etc. From this scan and evaluation, the presenter can then modify the delivery of their presentation.

Length of presentation

The presentation will have been developed taking its length into consideration. The length of a presentation will be determined by the key message (s) to be communicated to an audience. This will have an impact on the pace - the speed - with which the presentation is delivered. Pace is important to monitor to make sure the audience is still paying attention, understand what is being communicated and are not distracted. Pace of delivery will be determined by the length of a presentation, namely:

Short

This may be from 1 minute to 10 minutes. This is usually a very contained key message (s) that needs to be communicated. It may be just one message. Little reserves of energy are needed. Information does not need to be chunked up. No consideration needs to be given to the use of breaks and length of segments of the presentation. Attention is very specifically focused for the audience.

Medium

This may be from 10 minutes to one hour. Quality of tone of voice needs to be monitored to make sure it is still vibrant and loud enough. As a few key messages may be delivered with the content, the presentation may need to be chunked into smaller sections to aid the attention and understanding of the audience. Consideration should be given to using five-minute breaks or comfort breaks, toilet breaks, at an appropriate time in the presentation.

Long

This may be from a half-day event and upwards. There is a lot of pressure on both the presenter and audience to stimulate and maintain attention. In this situation, there will be breaks between pieces of information. This will help both the presenter and audience to recharge their energy for their different functions. Both parties need to keep their energy levels receptive to the assimilation of information and stimuli.

> Always make sure that the presentation finishes on time!

The venue

As with all the components that go into making a successful presentation, the selection of the venue is very important for both the presenter and audience. When deciding on a venue, consideration should be given to the following:

- **Dimensions** - Height, depth and breadth of the space. If a room is too small for the size of the audience invited to attend, it will make them feel uncomfortable. This will make it difficult for them to concentrate. If the room is too large, interaction with the audience is more difficult and has to be managed carefully by the presenter. If the room is an awkward shape it may impede sight and hearing. An audience may feel uncomfortable and become distracted with odd-shaped rooms

- **Room environment** - The temperature of the room needs to be monitored throughout the presentation. This can be done either directly, through a request from the audience, or indirectly, with the presenter observing the audience's behaviour. Ask them if they would like the temperature changed. If the temperature is  not to the audience's liking they become distracted. Temperature will change with the number of people in a room. If may be advisable to turn the temperature down after lunch, when people have eaten, as warmth encourages drowsiness. The decor of a room should also be considered. If it is too dark or has no natural light, it may influence the mood of the audience towards negativity and they will become distracted

- **Room layout** - The layout of the room should be determined by the type of key message (s) the presenter is aiming to deliver and what expectations the presenter has of working with the audience, see Unit 22, **Plan and organise an event** for detail of different room layouts

- **Facilities** - Consideration should be given to:

  - Access for disabled delegates

  - Number of toilets and access from the main presentation room

  - Refreshment availability

  - Stage availability, if required

  - Audio-visual equipment

  - Venue support

Personal delivery of the presentation
A good presenter needs to dress to suit the occasion and the audience. If it is a formal presentation with a large number of people in the audience, this will probably require formal attire. If it is a smaller group, the presenter could dress more casually. The presenter is always striving to engage the audience and get their buy-in. To that end, the presenter should be assertive, confident and in charge, but not aggressive. An assertive attitude can be achieved through:

Posture
Different postures create different moods. Match physical behaviour to the objectives underpinning the presentation. A formal, upright and still posture will create a very different atmosphere from a relaxed and active one. Whatever the posture, match it to the mood of the room as the presentation changes. Be consistent with each mood.

Presence
Fill the space. The presenter should not apologise for their presence, 'I don't really want to be here.' Limit the use of 'sorry', unless the situation demands it, e.g. 'we have an audio-visual malfunction.' Try not to hide behind a lectern or desk. If the presenter is confident in themselves, they have prepared, the audience will be confident in them. The presenter must be confident that the audience wants to listen to them.

They have something interesting to tell them. The presenter should not be afraid to wait for an audience to settle down before starting the presentation. It is the presenter's time to lead - only they know where they need to take the audience.

Making contact with the audience

Make contact with the audience, as this will maintain an audience's interest. It encourages the audience to believe that the presenter is genuinely interested in talking to them. Make contact with an audience through:

- **Eye contact -** Eye contact is a part of everyday communication. An audience needs this from a presenter or they will feel uncomfortable and not trust them. Eye contact gives an audience a sense of involvement in the presentation. It helps to convey the presenter's objectives on a personal level. Shift eye focus around the room, not so that you look nervous, but to help involve as many people as possible in the presentation. The floor and ceiling do not have eyes, so do not engage with them - focus your contact on the eyes of your audience

- **Gestures -** Use gestures in a natural way - they should be controlled and precise. Do not be afraid to gesture. Gesture when welcoming an audience or to add emphasis. Use open gestures which move away from the body, extending them out to the audience. This helps to break any division between the presenter and audience. Gestures are an extension of the presentation, use them to engage the audience and enhance their listening and understanding of the key message (s). Avoid pacing and walking around unless this is a purposeful part of the presentation. Do not block visuals with your body

- **The voice -** This is the personal equipment that will most immediately engage an audience. Make sure that the audience can hear the presenter. The human voice is a very flexible and powerful tool. It can be used in many different ways by modulating:

  - **Volume:** go for the **'Goldilocks' principle'** - not too loud and not too soft, but just loud enough to be heard clearly so the audience can follow the presentation. Use volume to emphasise a point. Add energy to a presentation, by using colour in the voice, to direct attention to the presentation

  - **Pace:** speak at a rate that makes it easy for the audience to follow. Using the **'Goldilocks' principle'** - if too quick or too slow the audience will have problems following the presentation. To add dynamics to the presentation, change the pace of delivery. Faster speech can convey enthusiasm, while slower speech might add emphasis or caution

- **Pitch**: use different notes / tones in your voice, from high to a low pitch. Pitch is used to identify an action, e.g. pitch will rise when asking a question; it will lower when sounding severe

- **Use of language**: the human voice sets the human race apart from all other species. Use language to involve the audience and develop and sustain that relationship. Ask questions by using 'we' or 'us', which will include them in discussion and explorations, e.g. 'We can see that ...', 'What can we learn from this?', 'This shows us that ...'. Use language that is welcoming throughout the presentation. Only use humour if you know it will work and it is appropriate to the situation. Humour needs to be relaxed and confident. If used inappropriately, it will only heighten a sense of awkwardness and anxiety, particularly if these are already present

It is a good idea to have some liquid on hand to quench thirst, if speaking for a long time. However, be careful not to gulp ice-cold water before starting, as this constricts the throat and affects the quality of the voice. Drink a warm, not hot, cup of tea to relax the throat and ease the speaking voice.

And breathe, breathe, breathe - steadily and deeply! The breath affects the quality of the voice and the ability to speak clearly and for extended lengths of time. Anxiety will produce fast and shallow breathing. Try to take a few deep breaths before making a presentation. Make a conscious effort to slow breathing down and take in more air with each breath. Do not be afraid to pause or slow down and take a breath. If the presenter is not breathing comfortably the audience will feel their discomfort.

• ACTIVITY 3

How can the voice be used to deliver a successful presentation?

Communicating the information

At the beginning of the presentation, after welcoming delegates to the presentation, the first thing that needs to be tackled is what is called 'housekeeping'. The presenter will need to find out from the venue hosts where the fire exits are, whether a fire drill is due and where the toilets are. Arrange for music to play as delegates arrive and leave the venue to create a more relaxed mood, if that is appropriate to the tone of the presentation. Switch the music off before beginning the presentation. Remind delegates to switch off their mobile phones to minimise interruptions and maintain focus throughout the presentation.

The next thing to do is go through the agenda of events for the presentation. If the presentation is long and will take up a whole day, make sure that refreshments will be provided for morning / afternoon tea and lunch. If there are any changes to the running of the presentation, this is the time to tell the audience.

Once the presenter has completed these introductions they can focus on the central themes of the presentation. At this time the presenter has made decisions and is confident about:

- What they are going to talk about
- Who they are going to talk to
- How long they are going to talk
- Where they are going to talk
- When they are going to talk
- What presentation aids will be used - the longer and more complex the presentation the more need there is for visual aids. A technical or all-day presentation will certainly need some visual aids and audience participation - workshops
- What equipment will be needed

The presenter is now in a position to deliver the information. The aim of any presentation is to gain buy-in from an audience, to gain their trust and confidence, so everyone can relax and enjoy the presentation. To do this, the presenter should use the following process to reinforce information as it is delivered throughout the presentation:

Tell them what you are going to tell them
Emphasise the importance of the key message (s) by repeating it several times during the presentation. Do not appear to be obviously repetitious, but skilfully build this into the delivery. Develop snappy phrases. Only deliver essential information. At the beginning of the presentation outline and contextualise what will be shared with the audience. The introduction, which all audiences will need regardless

of the experience and expertise they bring to the event, should start with what the presenter knows the audience knows. This will make everyone feel more comfortable. Outline the arguments that support the key message (s) in a logical fashion - create a storyline. After presenting the arguments that support the key message (s), recap these points at the end of the presentation. Then tie this up with a conclusion, re-emphasising the key message (s). The presenter should aim to educate the audience, not impress them - that is a by-product of the presentation, if at all. Too much detail should be avoided at the beginning. Make it simple. Express it simply.

Tell them
Present the essence of the key points skilfully. This is where most time will probably be spent -the middle of the presentation - but it may not be the part that an audience will remember most. Present arguments for and against the key message (s). Make it simple. Express it simply.

Tell them what you have told them
At the end of the presentation, it is a good idea to recap the key message (s). Provide a summary which breaks down all the key messages. The summary will usually be the conclusion to the presentation, which may suggest further work. If appropriate, you can invite the audience to ask questions at this point. Make it simple. Express it simply.

Limit the use of technical words, abbreviations, acronyms or use of jargon. If only one member of the audience does not understand a technical term, either remove it from the presentation or explain it in non-technical language. The difficulty there is that all the other members of the audience who understood these terms will lose interest while they are being explained.

Remembering the presentation
The final thing to prepare is a way of remembering everything the presenter wants to present. Find a way of making notes to support the presentation style.

Write down everything the presenter is going to say
This is a dangerous approach, as the presenter will read their script, which disengages the audience. It also loses contact - particularly eye contact - with the audience. The presenter focuses more attention on finding their place rather than communicating the key message (s). Reading can also make the presenter's voice sound monotonous,

removing energy and enthusiasm from the delivery.

Write as little as possible while covering everything that needs to be said. This can be achieved through either:

- **PowerPoint** - Using PowerPoint slides to make a presentation. The PowerPoint slides will act as an aid to remind the presenter of the points to be made throughout the presentation. The presenter should avoid just reading the slides, speaking to the slides and facing away from their audience. The audience will not hear what the presenter is explaining to them. The audience can stay at home to read PowerPoint slides, they do not need the presenter to read them to them. Audiences often ask to see the previous screens. Practice being able to navigate forwards and backwards through the PowerPoint slides

- **Plain cards** - Write the keywords down, two or three to a card. This allows the presenter to find their place and maintain eye contact with the audience all at once. Connect the cards together with a tag or a piece of string so that they do not get out of order. Cards are preferable to paper as card does not shake if the presenter is nervous

- **Chalk and talk** - Present with only the aid of a whiteboard or flip chart to write on. You may also add audio-visual aids

- **Learning the presentation** - Learning is fine until the audience interrupts the presentation with something that has not been scripted or unforeseen circumstances distract the presenter's attention. Always have some form of notes that keep the presentation on track. Learning a script robs the presenter of energy and enthusiasm

> Single out the sources of remembering the presentation so that they lead to confident spontaneity!

Presentation resources

There are a number of resources available for a presenter to use to highlight and focus on particular parts of the presentation. These resources include:

Equipment

Decide what will be needed. Make sure it is available and will work in the venue of the presentation. Find out who is responsible for providing the equipment. Arrive early on the day of the presentation to make sure all the equipment is in place and working properly - rehearse how it works if the audio-visual person is not doing this. Go over the equipment with the venue audio-visual specialist. Equipment may include the following items:

- Laptop, projector or screen

- Internet access

- Overhead projector or screen

- Flip chart and pens

- Whiteboard and pens

- Delegate packs, writing paper and pens / pencils

The type and amount of technology introduced into a presentation will depend on how much confidence the presenter has using it. If using advanced technology which the presenter is not fully conversant with, this could detract the presenter from their ability to present the information. However, many presentations are enhanced when information technology is used. If unable to deal with the technology and the delivery of the presentation at the same time, ask a colleague to help control the equipment and press the buttons as the presenter requires them.

If using a remote control, do not hide at the back of the room with the projector. The presenter should be at the front projecting to the audience. The presenter should be careful about wandering around the room. Avoid using a laser pointer, as they are generally too small to be seen effectively. If the presenter is nervous, the dot may be hard to hold still in their shaking hands.

Presentation handouts
Prepare handouts containing all of the information that has been included in the presentation. These will act as an aide-memoire to the audience, along with handouts covering any more detailed information which may not be included in the presentation.

> Always have a **contingency** or **back-up plan** for
> the possibility of equipment breaking down.

Rehearsing the delivery of the presentation

To make sure that the presentation runs as successfully as it can, rehearse the presentation so that it comes off with ease. This will prepare the presenter for the unexpected. Do more than practise reading through the presentation material. Rehearse the presentation out loud, accompanied by the medium being used to display information, such as PowerPoint slides. Play around with different volumes, pitch etc. Familiarise yourself with the main thrust of the arguments and explore how the individual elements of the presentation fit together. This will help the presenter keep to objectives and avoid distractions when it comes to the actual delivery. If possible, get someone to listen to the delivery of the presentation. If the presentation can be rehearsed in the venue, sit someone to listen to the presenter at the back of the room so the presenter can practice speaking loudly and clearly. Ask the listener for honest feedback about the presenter's presentation skills. Make changes where necessary and run through the whole presentation again, accommodating any suggested and agreed changes. Repeat this process until the presenter is comfortable and confident with the presentation. Get used to hearing your own voice filling a room. Familiarise yourself with the words and phrases in your presentation.

Whatever forms of presentation the presenter gives, it is vital to rehearse it and check timings. What looks like a good hour's worth of material on paper may prove to last only 20 minutes in practice. Create milestones that will warn the presenter if they are in danger of overrunning or finishing early. This will allow the presenter to tailor devices, such as encouraging or discouraging questions or debate among the audience to extend or contract the time. The presenter needs to keep a subtle eye on the time to make sure the presentation does not overrun.

The more familiar the presenter is with their presentation the more they will be to inspire their audience's trust and confidence.

• ACTIVITY 4

What needs to be done to make sure that the appropriate equipment has been selected?

Presentation evaluation forms

Prior to meeting the audience, the presenter starts off the process of delivering the presentation by rehearsing it to make sure it delivers what it says it is going to do. Once the audience has heard the presentation, they are usually given the opportunity to evaluate it in the form of a 'feedback form'. This is an objective means of evaluating. Subjectively, the presenter can monitor their performance throughout the presentation. In this way, the two forms of evaluation provide a balanced view.

Most organisations will use standard evaluation sheets to obtain feedback from the audience on the presentation. Make sure there will be sufficient evaluation forms available on the day for everyone in the audience. If there is no standard form, design one, as it is the best way to improve the presentation and presentation technique. Design the feedback form to capture quantitative and qualitative data. The feedback should cover:

- An overall rating of the presentation - Use **Likert scales** for quantitative data, if necessary
- Whether the venue was good, including refreshments, accessibility etc
- Whether the attendee's aims were met
- What the attendee learned from attending
- Which areas of the presentation were particularly useful and which were not particularly worthwhile
- Any way in which the presentation could be improved in the future

More specific feedback will depend on the type and purpose of the presentation and the audience.

• ACTIVITY 5

Design an evaluation form that will enable you to collect relevant feedback on your presentation skills

Make an impression

It may help to remember these five steps to making an impressive presentation:

- Purpose - Know why you are making the presentation
- Research - Know what you are going to say
- Individual - Make the presentation memorable
- Meaningful - Tell them something they did not know
- Enthusiasm - If you do not care, why should they?

These five points are captured in the acronym 'PRIME'. Follow these five steps to help make an impressive presentation. It is also necessary to take steps to avoid the pitfalls that undermine the presenter's life. The most common obstacles that will be encountered are captured in the acronym SHELF:

- Script - Do not be tempted to simply read your notes
- Handouts - These can disrupt your flow
- Ennui - Do not reveal your lack of interest
- Lack of belief - Do not let them know you do not believe
- Flannel - Do not waffle to fill the time

Aim for a maximum of seven points for the audience to remember.

Testing your knowledge

1. What are the situations that would be used to deliver a presentation?

2. What are the elements that go towards making a successful presentation?

3. What checks need to be carried out at the venue prior to the delivery of a presentation?

4. Why is it important to make the delivery of a presentation interesting?

5. What types of equipment could be used when delivering a presentation, and how are they used?

6. What are the advantages of using card rather than paper for writing keywords?

7. When should handouts be distributed at a presentation?

8. Why should a presentation be rehearsed prior to delivering the presentation?

9. What is meant by the acronym PRIME?

10. What is meant by the acronym SHELF?

Skills

The most difficult presentation you will ever make will be the first one. You will not know what to expect, what will work well or what to avoid. After making your first presentation make sure you have given the audience the opportunity to evaluate your performance and, most importantly, act on their comments. You will then have some data to use when preparing your subsequent presentations. Always gather feedback from your audience so you can go on improving your presentation skills.

• ACTIVITY 6

Attend a professionally delivered presentation. This could be a public lecture at the town hall, a sales presentation for an overseas property or a lecture at your local college. Make notes on what the presenter did so you can start to improve your own presentation skills.

If you are unfamiliar with the venue try to visit it before the event to check that there are no problems, such as health and safety issues, access to electricity or Internet connections or insufficient space for the size of the audience. Introduce yourself to the venue manager and any staff who will be working in the room where you will be making your presentation, e.g. audio-visual engineer. The audio-visual engineer is an important person. They will be in charge of all your equipment. They will be in charge of making sure the resources work so that your presentation is delivered as smoothly as possible.

On the day of the presentation arrive at least half an hour before you are due to start. This will allow you to make the following checks:

- All materials that will be handed out to the audience have arrived, e.g. delegate packs and handouts, advertising material, feedback forms

- The venue host / manager confirms that everything is in working order

- The venue staff who will be working with you are in and that all equipment is working correctly

- All 'housekeeping' requirements

- Refreshments are available and breaks will be taken at the correct time

- The room temperature

- The room layout has been completed as agreed

- All clocks give the same time

- Familiarise yourself with the room: the stage and any furniture that will be used on it, if there is one, microphones - table or personal

Once these checks have been completed run through the presentation in your mind. Reassure yourself that you are well prepared. Remember that first impressions are lasting impressions, so use positive body language:

- If possible, be in the room before your audience arrives. This will put you 'in charge' from the start

- Familiarise yourself with the audience

- Communicate a positive posture, i.e. stand up straight, keep your head up. Do not hold your arms across the front of your body, as this will be seen as defensive

- Be careful not to always position yourself behind a table or desk. This will create a barrier. If you feel the need for support, stand in front of a piece of furniture and lean against it without slouching. Or hold something, as a kind of security blanket. Or adopt what is natural for you when communicating to an audience

If there have been transport problems and a decision has been taken to delay the presentation (s), make an announcement to the audience.

Mingle with the audience to get a feeling for the mood of the delegates.

Start your presentation by welcoming the audience and introduce yourself - if you are not already known to all of the audience. If you are feeling confident, you could introduce a bit of humour. Introduce any other members of staff from the organisation who will be available throughout the presentation (s) to assist the audience. Go through any 'housekeeping' that the audience needs to be aware of. Introduce the agenda for the day. Outline the main purpose of the day. Identify the aims and objectives.

Tell them, the audience, what you are going to tell them, how long it is going to take and the protocol for answering questions, i.e. whether you welcome questions throughout the presentation or will have a plenary session at the end? The response you receive from the audience at this stage will set the tone for the whole presentation, so it is important that you get into your stride straight away.

During your presentation, ask rhetorical questions that you can then answer, e.g. 'How do we know this was true?' or 'So, what does this prove?'. At the end of your talk give the audience an opportunity to ask questions or to clarify detail - this encourages them to engage with and take ownership of your material. The use of questions is an important tool. Questions involve your audience's mind in a more stimulating way than simply asking them to sit and listen to you talk. Draw an audience in with clear and focused questions.

Do not let the thought of your body language or members of the audience's body language distract you. If you are normally expressive and use hand gestures in everyday conversation, they will generally appear natural if you use them during your presentation. Try to avoid hand-to-face gestures, such as rubbing your nose, as these indicate that you are unsure of your subject or are being less than honest.

When you tell them, the audience, what you are going to tell them - it will reinforce in your mind the points you need to cover. You now need to move on to giving them the information that is the purpose of their attendance. There are a number of techniques which will help you to deliver your points:

- Short sentences are easier to absorb

- Simple sentences containing only one idea are better than complex sentences

- Be precise, but avoid sounding too prepared

- Use metaphors to illustrate ideas

- Maintain eye contact with everyone in the room

Do not attempt to put all of the information onto one slide. Use the slide to list the main points you are aiming to cover. Expand on each point either verbally or by using visual aids. Avoid using too much animation or colour, as this will distract the audience from listening to what you have to say. Do not walk between the projector and the screen while the projector is operating. Project clearly and loudly, enough to be heard at the back of the room without being uncomfortably loud for those close to you or close to the speakers, if you are using a microphone.

Throughout the presentation keep one eye on the clock, but do not be too obvious about it, as this will disengage the audience. If you have placed milestones in your notes you will be able to judge whether you need to accelerate or decelerate your delivery. Avoid the temptation to do this by speaking more quickly or more slowly, as either will risk losing the audience's attention. Always have a contingency plan in mind so that you know which areas you can reduce or remove completely from the presentation if you need to save time and which areas you can expand on if you have too much time. Unless you are a natural, it is probably safest to avoid humour. This does not mean you cannot add a light touch to the proceedings, but jokes have a nasty habit of either not being funny, which will embarrass you, or being found offensive by at least one member of the audience, which will embarrass them.

At some point during the presentation, or at the end of the session, you will have to deal with questions. Be prepared for this section of the presentation in advance. Although you cannot anticipate every question you may be asked, you can be ready for certain types of question:

- The question that tests your expertise. The questioner asks you to explain in greater depth

- The question that demonstrates the questioner's expertise. No real response is required, the purpose of the question is to 'show off', but you can acknowledge their contribution, e.g. 'Good point' or 'I am glad you brought that up'

- The question that aims to correct an assertion that you have made. The questioner is, in essence, saying that you are wrong. Remain cool and do not take it personally, but thank them for their contribution and the help they have given you

- The question that seeks justification. The questioner does not want to believe what you are saying. Probably the most difficult of questions, almost a no-win situation. Play it by ear and be professional in your response

- The question that comes too early. The questioner is raising a point that you fully intend to answer later in the presentation. These types of question can always prompt a humorous reply, e.g. 'You are getting ahead of yourself'

- The question you cannot answer. Acknowledge it. And let the audience know that you will find out the answer and get back to them

Obviously, the way that you deal with each question will depend on the circumstances. If answering the question at that stage would seriously disrupt your plan for the presentation, offer to 'park' the question and come back to it at the end if it still has not been answered. Confirm with the questioner that they are happy for this to happen.

Bring the presentation to a close by 'telling them what you have told them'. Review the main points that you want the audience to remember. Avoid the temptation to go through all the arguments again. Thank your audience for attending and listening and, if they are leaving at this point, wish them a safe journey. Remember to ask them to complete the evaluation form and, preferably, leave the forms on tables etc at the end of the event - a reminder could be given to the audience during a session from half way through the day.

• ACTIVITY 7

Negotiate with your line manager a presentation that you can deliver to colleagues or members of staff. Prepare the presentation and make plans to present it in an agreed location. Once your line manager has approved your draft presentation and plans, invite your audience and deliver the presentation. Obtain feedback from your audience using your own or your organisation's feedback form

On receiving the evaluation forms, look at the feedback objectively. This may be something that is done back in the office. If a single member of the audience is critical of an aspect of your presentation, which the rest of the audience found satisfactory or better, you probably do not need to take too much notice. However, every remark has a kernel of truth, so explore the kernel to see what you can take away from it. If most of the audience is critical, the chances are you need to reconsider the way you handle that aspect in the future. This applies equally to the content of the presentation. While the feedback form is an objective means of evaluating your performance subjectively, self-reflect on your own performance and makes notes at an appropriate time.

• ACTIVITY 8

Ask your audience to complete an evaluation form. Evaluate the feedback. Write a report explaining how you would amend the presentation in light of the comments that have been made. What personal presentation skills could you improve?

Any presenter, regardless of how experienced they are at presenting, will be nervous to a lesser or greater extent. If you were not a little nervous, something would be wrong. Nerves are a positive thing, without them your presentation could be flat and uninteresting. Nerves keep you on your toes. The key is to control your nerves and make them work for you. Go into the presentation with a positive attitude. If you have been asked to make the presentation it is because you are the best person for the job. Speak clearly and confidently. Do not be afraid of pausing to collect your thoughts - you are in charge. The audience cannot go anywhere without your guidance.

Sure-fire tools for success:

Do:

- Check your **plans**
- Check your preparations
- **Engage** your audience by **involving** them and **responding** to them
- Be **positive** and project **confidence** and **enthusiasm**
- Maintain **eye contact**
- Respond to **questions** immediately
- Establish **next steps**

Do not:

- Worry about being **nervous** - use nerves positively
- Read or learn a **script**
- Speak too **quickly**, too **loudly** or at the same **pace**

> It's natural to have butterflies in your stomach - getting them to fly in the right direction is the art!

Testing your skills

1. How do you make sure that your gestures are natural and appropriate while delivering a presentation?

2. Why should you arrive at the venue early?

3. What techniques can you use to deliver information?

4. How much information should you include on visual aids?

5. How do you use milestones in timing the delivery of a presentation?

6. How do you bring a presentation to a successful close?

7. Why is it important to have a contingency plan for adjusting the timings of the presentation?

8. What do you do if your equipment breaks down?

9. What feedback are you looking for from an audience?

10. How do you handle difficult questions?

11. How do you evaluate audience feedback objectively?

Ready for assessment?

To achieve this Level 3 unit of a Business & Administration qualification, learners will need to demonstrate that they are able to perform the following activities:

1. Agreed the purpose, content, style and timing (s) of the presentation

2. Planned the delivery of the presentation

3. Chose equipment and planned how to use the equipment's features to best effect

4. Prepared the presentation to achieve its purpose

5. Obtained audience feedback on the content and delivery of the presentation

6. Rehearsed the timing (s) of the presentation

7. Produced presentation handouts

8. Checked equipment and resources

9. Circulated presentation handouts and materials

10. Addressed the audience by speaking clearly and confidently

11. Made the presentation and summarised the key points

12. Used the equipment effectively, dealing with any problems that may have occurred

13. Provided the audience with the opportunity to ask questions

14. Responded to questions in a way that met the audience's needs

15. Collected feedback on the delivery and content of the presentation

16. Evaluated the presentation and identified improvements

You will need to produce evidence from a variety of sources to support the performance requirements of this unit

If you carry out the 'ACTIVITIES' and respond to the 'NEED TO KNOW' questions, these will provide some of the evidence required

Links to other units

While gathering evidence for this unit, evidence may also be used from evidence generated from other units within the Business & Administration suite of units. Below is a sample of applicable units; however, most units within the Business & Administration suite of units will also be applicable.

QCF NVQ
Communications
Communicate in a business environment (Level 2)
Communicate in a business environment (Level 3)
Develop a presentation
Document production
Produce text from notes using touch typing (20 wpm)
Produce text from notes using touch typing (40 wpm)
Produce text from notes using touch typing (60 wpm)
Produce documents in a business environment
Produce text from notes
Manage information and data
Manage information and data
Organise and report data
Research information
Analyse and report data

SVQ
Communications
Prepare to communicate in a business environment
Communicate in a business environment
Develop a presentation
Document production
Produce text from notes using touch typing (20 wpm)
Produce text from notes using touch typing (40 wpm)
Produce text from notes using touch typing (60 wpm)
Produce documents in a business environment
Produce text from notes
Manage information and data
Manage information and data
Organise and report data
Research information
Analyse and report data

7 Manage own performance in a business environment

MANAGE OWN PERFORMANCE IN A BUSINESS ENVIRONMENT

'**Manage own performance in a business environment**' is a mandatory unit which may be chosen as one of a combination of units to achieve either a Qualifications and Credit Framework (QCF), National Vocational Qualification (NVQ) or Scottish Vocational Qualification (SVQ).

The aims of this unit are to:

- Understand how to plan work and be accountable to others
- Understand how to behave in a way that supports effective working
- Be able to plan and be responsible for own work, supported by others
- Behave in a way that supports effective working

To achieve the above aims of this unit, learners will be expected to provide evidence through the performance of work-based activities.

Knowledge

Every organisation will have different expectations about how they expect their employees to work. Supervisors / managers will be trained and have the experience and expertise to manage their employees effectively. They will expect their employees to perform in ways that are productive. The culture of work has changed over the past few years because of the economic environment. Employees are being asked to work more hours for the same pay to increase productivity. In some cases this is interpreted as working longer and longer hours, which some people do. However, there is a work-life balance that needs to be struck. So instead of working longer hours, work smarter.

Each employee will have their own specific roles and responsibilities which they will carry out in their daily operations. These responsibilities will include:

- **Performing tasks / activities** - These could occur at specific appointed and agreed times throughout a day, week, month, year, or as they occur. As with real life, not everything goes to plan. There are times when some tasks / activities will appear to be unreasonable and cause frustration. However, a manager will ask an employee to undertake a task / activity when they know they will be able to accomplish it. This does not mean that it will be easy, as some tasks / activities will be given to develop workplace skills, knowledge and confidence. It may appear to be unfair, but such a perception probably comes from not feeling confident enough to complete the task / activity

- **Being accountable** - For own work and taking responsibility for successfully completing it to the agreed requirements. Keep in contact and report any problems to the manager. The employee must take ownership of the task / activity they have been asked to complete. This will involve working with others to plan how the task / activity will be completed. In a new task / activity, when the requirements of the task / activity may not be clear, mistakes may happen. Plan well with colleagues and make decisions to minimise mistakes. Resolve problems when they occur with the supervisor / manager. And communicate. Meetings to discuss progress or problems are an opportunity to update progress and offer new ideas to improve the way things are done. Personal feelings may also be discussed with the supervisor / manager which will help the employee to:

  - Get on better with other people

  - Get to know more people

  - Learn new skills

  - Learn to make better decisions

  - Move on to more interesting tasks

- **Working within a team or teams** - Working as part of a team can be challenging. People are working with different personalities, skills and knowledge. However, it is the responsibility of an employee to behave in a professional and courteous manner, at all times, despite their personal feelings. Working in a team opens up opportunities to develop new skills and knowledge. The team provides lots of learning opportunities, as members of the team can learn from each other and guide one another

It is the way that an employee deals with different situations that will decide how much they enjoy their time at work.

Planning work

The most successful way of completing an agreed task / activity is to plan what work needs to be carried out. Plan work to the last detail. The purpose of planning is to have a clear idea of what needs to be achieved. Planning requires information: what information is required, where to get it from, whom to speak to, what the timescales and deadlines are - are they realistic? How it is to be presented? Obtain as much detail about the work to be completed. The aim is to produce the most efficient piece of work as possible. What is the best way of planning work? Write it down. Written plans have the benefit of involving the activity of writing and thinking about the work to be completed. It is a permanent record of what has to be done and provides a blueprint of activities that need to be completed in a logical order. If it is written down, other people have access in the event of absences and it can be easily referred to. Having a plan is taking accountability for the work that has to be completed.

The key to planning work is time management. Time management is the art of organising and scheduling time in the most efficient ways to create more effective work and productivity. Time is a limited resource. It is not elastic. It cannot be stretched. There are techniques which can be used to make the most of the time envisaged to complete an agreed task / activity:

Prioritise tasks / activities. Make a list of things that need to be completed. This can be carried out using two methods:

'To do list'

A 'to do list' will provide a precise list of priorities that can help to manage and eliminate problems that might occur. Important tasks / activities can be separated from trivial ones. Completing the 'to do list' should involve:

* Writing down all of the tasks / activities that need to be completed

* Breaking them down into smaller manageable tasks / activities, estimating how long each task / activity will take

* Prioritise the tasks / activities. Create a system that categorises each task / activity, e.g. high, medium, low or important, action immediately, get more information, read, telephone. Priorities can also be described as 'must do' - be done today, 'should do' - be done sometime or 'could do' - be done when there is time

- List the tasks / activities in order of priority

- Build in contingencies, as things may take longer than estimated

Using a 'to do list' should be a routine that is followed every day. It could be created at the end of the day in preparation for the next day, or the first thing that is done at the beginning of the day.

Diary

May be maintained using a paper or electronic system. Diary entries must be made clearly and accurately and changed as required. It should provide sufficient information about timing - start, begin - and the subject matter to discuss, to prepare for the appointment. Use the diary as a system that not only records appointments but organises how time is used in the working day. Most importantly, keep it up to date. It is no good to anyone if the diary entries bear no relationship to what is actually going to go on.

Whatever system is used, avoid the temptation to concentrate on just doing the easy tasks / activities first. Prioritise always. Review the 'to do list' and diary to make sure that time is being used and managed wisely.

> Nothing is particularly hard if you break it down into small jobs.
> *- Henry Ford*

Plan the day's tasks / activities

Set aside enough time to do the 'must do' tasks - or however they have been categorised - by their deadlines. Allow time for the 'should do' tasks and even the 'could do' tasks if possible.

Record the time to complete a task / activity - It helps to keep track of time and know when falling behind or shooting ahead of schedule.

Deal with disruption - If there is something important that has to be done, let colleagues know that focus and concentration needs to be applied to that task / activity for a certain length of time. Avoid needlessly disturbing those people involved in the task / activity at that time.

Control the telephone - List the calls that need to be made and set aside a specific time to complete these telephone calls. Make sure the telephone call is focused and achieves what needs to be achieved as quickly as possible.

• ACTIVITY 1

Why is it important to manage your time effectively? What tools could you use and why?

 Sometimes it may feel like time is getting away from you, that there is no control over time. For example, a supervisor / manager may require a task to be completed immediately. Respond with understanding and respect. Discuss what needs to be done and find out if the priority for completing the task / activity is realistic. Establish that re-routing to another task / activity will have a knock-on effect to the current task / activity. The plan will need to be updated. Always understand why a plan needs to be changed. Do not be tempted to agree to all requests without notifying a supervisor / manager of the knock-on effects of a change of plan. By agreeing to do any and everything, without any thought of the knock-on effects the change of plan requires, means that a task / activity will not be completed to the agreed time. If an employee continues to do this they will be in danger of earning the reputation of being unreliable.

If an agreed deadline cannot be met, let the supervisor / manager know as soon as possible. It may be possible to extend the deadline, or it may be necessary to get help with completing the task. If a problem is reported sooner, rather than later, action can be taken. Carrying on hoping that it will sort itself out undermines the plan of work. The plan becomes obsolete. When it is obvious that the deadline will not be met it may be too late to do anything about it. Supervisors / managers would prefer that help is asked for when something can be done about it rather than leaving it till the last minute and putting a lot of unnecessary stress and tension on the team. No one likes to be asked to take over a backlog of work which has not been completed because an employee has been unwilling to admit to it being a problem.

> If you have a job without any aggravations, you don't have a job.
> - *Malcolm S. Forbes*

Always make sure the authority to change something has been given by the appropriate person. Do not change the way things are done without asking first. It is quite possible things are done the way they are done 'because we've always done it that way'. On the other hand, it is also possible things are done that way for very good reasons. Changes may have consequences that an employee cannot see. These could be legal or financial. Discuss new ideas for improving the way things could be done in the future with a supervisor / manager, to make sure someone is aware of this new thinking.

Realistic objectives

Planning is used to establish a baseline of the work that needs to be completed. The demands of the workplace are fluid and demanding. Make sure that the plan is linked to clear and realistic objectives, objectives which have a clear target. Objectives should be agreed to be achieved within the required time frame. Objectives have the advantage of:

- Clearly identifying what needs to be done and when

- Organising tasks / activities

- Focusing on what is essential

- Eliminating what is irrelevant

- Coordinating tasks / activities

- Establishing and maintaining personal discipline with which to approach work

It is important to make sure that objectives remain applicable to the task / activity. Objectives should be linked to the needs of the business. Objectives may come in different forms:

- **Personal objectives** - What needs to be done to develop people

- **Outcome objectives** - Short-term objectives to change attitudes, knowledge or behaviour

- **Impact objectives** - Long-term objectives which identify the impact of tasks / activities

- **Process objectives** - What needs to be done and how it needs to be done. Focus on people and their interrelationships as they go about tasks / activities

A proven method of writing objectives is following the SMART acronym. The acronym has been attributed to the work of Peter Drucker in this theory 'Management by Objectives'. The acronym means:

- **S**pecific. Make sure that the objectives are clear and well defined. The people performing the task / activity know what is expected of them, while the manager is able to monitor performance and progress against the objectives

- **M**easurable. Make sure that the objectives can monitor progress and completion of tasks / activities

- **A**chievable / **A**ppropriate. Make sure that everything is in place to complete the task / activity, e.g. people have the right skills, have enough / correct resources

- **R**ealistic / **R**elevant. Make sure that the objectives are valuable - aligned with strategies and higher goals - and add value

- **T**ime bound. Make sure that the objectives let people know when a task /activity has to be completed by. A time gives a sense of urgency to the task / activity

When writing SMART objectives choose active verbs to describe the objective. Active verbs are more observable, have a greater intensity and are more motivational.

Objectives are created to give direction to a task / activity. In most cases, objectives will be set for more than one person. Objectives may be set individually, by a committee or by members of a team. If people involved in a task / activity are not in agreement about the objectives, e.g. they think the time requirement is too short, this will need to be negotiated to reach an agreement about the objective. People want clarity and, above all, to succeed. Negotiation in this context is not referring to big time 'wheeling' and 'dealing', but gaining agreement of what needs to be done within acceptable limits. If objectives have been created SMARTly, the need to negotiate should be minimised. However, if there is disagreement about objectives:

- Find out what the issues are

- Openly discuss the issues

- Implement the objectives

In this negotiation situation everybody is on the same side. Everybody wants to complete the task / activity successfully - nobody wants any problems.

Objectives should be routinely reviewed to make sure that they are still SMART and relevant to the task / activity. If this does not happen problems may occur. Problems can occur in the following areas:

- **Planning**
  - Not appropriate to the tasks / activities to be completed
  - Unrealistic objectives
  - Unrealistic time frames
  - Inappropriate priorities
  - Inappropriate budget
  - Insufficient human and physical resources

- **Human resources**
  - People being used for the wrong tasks / activities
  - People do not have the relevant skills and knowledge or use resources incorrectly
  - People not following instructions correctly
  - People may not report problems
  - People not knowing who to report to in the event of a problem
  - Team composition
  - Motivation

- **Physical resources**
  - Either too much or too little
  - Costs
  - Logistics

- **Technical**
  - Computers or their programs breakdown
  - Machinery breaks down

A problem should be resolved at the earliest opportunity. As can be seen from the above list, there are many different forms that a problem can take. However, the problem has to be resolved. Dealing with a problem can consist of the following stages:

- Acknowledge that there is a problem
- Look at the impact the continuation of the problem will have

- Consider options about how best the problem can be resolved
- Decide which option would be best to resolve the problem
- Implement the agreed option to solve the problem
- Review the solution

If a problem is not solved promptly it can escalate to a crisis. In either case, a problem may then become a cost to the organisation, either financially or to its reputation - both of which should be avoided at all costs.

• ACTIVITY 2

What is a SMART objective? How and why are objectives agreed?

Any change to the objectives of a task / activity should be reported to all who are involved in that task / activity. If not sure about the impact of a change, work with the supervisor / manger or other members of the team, if working in a team, to resolve and agree the change. There is nothing wrong with change. There is something wrong with change if no one knows there has been a change and what the impact of that change is on the task / activity. If there is a change in plan let people know as soon as possible. Then people can replan what needs to be done and see if there is a new approach to be taken. People are not mind readers and they can only do what they have agreed to do. It is important that people are given new instructions in good time. People may be working in an organisation that uses matrix management, so employees work in different teams in different departments reporting to different managers. They will have to let a lot of people know if there are changes to one task / activity that will affect working on other tasks / activities at the same time.

The same can be said for mistakes. Mistakes can happen. Even with the best plan in the world, mistakes can happen. If a mistake is made, acknowledge it immediately, and most people will be willing to help sort it out. If a mistake is covered up, when the truth is uncovered, there will be little sympathy for the employee. Mistakes are much more easily put right immediately than they are further down the line. Admitting to a mistake is the first step towards learning from them. One of the ways that civilisation has advanced is by learning from mistakes. Thomas Edison discovered how to make the electric light bulb from making 2,000 mistakes. However, a mistake is not always considered a virtue by an organisation.

To learn from a mistake, responsibility must be acknowledged for making the mistake. Aim to acknowledge a mistake with ease and minimise apportioning blame. Blame is a game that inflames shame. But admitting to making mistakes is not easy. The implication is that the mistake is a reflection of us, our worth, and no one likes to think of themselves as worthless.

Learning from mistakes requires three things:

- Identify interesting mistakes

- Self-confidence to admit to a mistake

- Courage to make changes

There are four main types of mistakes:

- **Stupid** - Absurd and unexpected things that happen

- **Simple** - Mistakes that are avoidable but the sequence of decisions made inevitable

- **Involved** - Mistakes that are understood but require effort to prevent

- **Complex** - Mistakes that have complicated causes and no obvious way to avoid next time

The first two types of mistakes are uninteresting and do not lead to deep learning, and should be easy to correct. Involved mistakes require significant change, things to avoid doing, thinking etc., in the future. These are mistakes made through either habit or nature. However, as change is difficult, the same involved mistakes can be made over and over again. Overcoming involved mistakes is taking the responsibility to change. The more complex a mistake is the more patience is required to resolve it to gain an objective understanding of the complex mistake and compare it across different perspectives, especially if there are other people involved. Break down what happened and slowly go through each event. Questions will arise which may not have been considered before. Work backwards, forensically, before the mistake was made, to review all the contributing factors that lead to making the mistake. When reviewing a mistake, consider:

- Probable sequence of events

- Small mistakes that may have led to a larger one

- Erroneous assumptions made - could it have been identified earlier?

- Goals
- Information - was it complete?
- What could be done differently if in the same situation again

Review a mistake and break it down into smaller units to see where the mistake could have been rectified. While it may appear as though the world has caved in, it has not!

• ACTIVITY 3

What should be considered when reviewing mistakes, to make changes for the future?

Policy, procedures and codes of practice

An organisation will have created many different policies, procedures and processes for completing most of its tasks / activities and for managing its people, the place and the products it has designed and developed. A policy is a document that sets out the course of actions an organisation's employee should follow. A policy will then develop procedures and processes which will identify how individual tasks / activities should be done. Policies, procedures and processes have been developed for employees to make sure that behaviours and products are consistently completed to the same accepted standards and quality. A Human Resources department will have created policies for managing the people within the organisation, e.g. policies and processes on the recruitment and selection of employees. They will also have policies and procedures on health and safety. Most of these are designed to conform to legal requirements. The delivery of products will be shaped by a delivery process based on industry good practice, some of which will have codes of practice that will need to be adhered to.

A code of practice is a set of guidelines and regulations to be followed by members of a profession, trade, occupation, organisation etc. As with instructions, these should be respected and consulted before entering into areas of work that the employee may be unfamiliar with. A code of practice can provide guidance and lay down expected standards, conduct and practice that should be achieved within specific sectors. They may provide support by giving advice and guidance based on real-life experience. Codes of practice may include acts of parliament, e.g. the Data Protection Act 1998; however, the actual code of practice may not necessarily be binding in law.

• ACTIVITY 4

What is the difference between a policy, procedure and process and a code of practice?

Behave in a way that supports effective working

Every organisation expects to produce quality products. Quality products are designed to offer the customer consistency. An employee will work in an organisation implementing standards that will work towards achieving consistency of output. Consistency engenders confidence and trust in an organisation's products, whether they are internal products, e.g. an organisation's employees, or external products, e.g. finished goods.

An organisation has designed its appraisal system specifically to measure the standard of performance its employees are achieving. This includes behaviour and attitudes. There is a wide difference between an employee doing what they have been told to do and an employee who goes out of their way to achieve the highest possible standard. Aim to achieve above the set standard and achieving the required standard will be easy. By taking on a challenge an employee shows that they are:

- **Adaptable** - they are not set in a routine

- **Prepared** - to embrace change

- **Focused** - on the needs of the business

- **Competitive**

  The three great essentials to achieve anything worthwhile are, first, hard work; second, stick-to-itiveness; third, common sense.
  - Thomas Edison

Nothing remains the same. The world is in a constant state of flux. This is the same for the world of business. For an organisation to remain profitable and keep up with the times, it constantly reviews what is going on around it. Not only locally but compared with what is happening in other countries throughout the world. An organisation has to remain competitive or it will go out of business. To remain competitive, expected standards may need to change within the organisation. This may have an effect on the way tasks / activities will need to be performed in the future. Most organisations will try to manage the forces of change, but sometimes they are out of the control of the organisation, e.g. the effects of a disaster, new technology, new products. This could affect the way employees will work in the future. Change may provide new challenges. Challenges may be perceived as either an opportunity or a threat, depending on the employee interpreting the effects of change. The organisation is not changing on purpose but has a purpose for changing. Change is never easy, but the approach an employee takes to embracing change can be easy. It can be positive and provide a motivational force to help others accept the nature of change.

• ACTIVITY 5

What is change and why is it important in an organisation?

If colleagues are struggling to cope with the new situation, an employee can offer to help them in any way that they can. Remember, it is important to be honest about how much help can be given. Focus should always remain on maintaining the agreed standard of work, so tasks / activities must continue to be completed to the agreed or new standards and timescales. As such, change may require employees to be trained in new ways of working. If there is any doubt about the expected standard that needs to be achieved, ask the supervisor / manager for their advice. Change is an opportunity to learn new things. However, the force of change can place a lot of pressure on individuals or the team.

Workplace pressure is something that needs to be monitored and managed. Because of the increasing need for business to remain competitive, more demands are being placed on a business's workforce. Some people thrive on working under pressure; however, normally too much pressure can be stressful. How much is too much pressure? This will vary on the individual and the coping mechanism that they use and know works for them. So how can high levels of pressure be dealt with?

- **Make things happen, do not just do things**

- Write it down, do not just have mental pictures - Make the pressures tangible, so they can be managed

- **Discipline** - Plan well using 'to do lists' and diaries. It will add clarity to what needs to be done throughout the day   .

- **Personal responsibility -** Be pragmatic. Do not carry the weight of the world on your shoulders, e.g. do not take on responsibility for worrying about other people meeting their deadlines on time

- **Feedback -** Let the supervisor / manager know how things are going. Work is not a zoo, so do not behave like an ostrich

- **Communication -** Keep people informed with the right levels of information at the right time

- **Fitness -** A healthy mind and a healthy body

- **Empathy -** Pressure comes from above and below. Consider the pressure that a supervisor / manager may be under to achieve the outcomes of a task / activity

- **Pause and breathe -** Take some moments to relax and chill out

Pressure in the workplace needs to be minimised so that it does not lead to an unhealthy workforce. Stress, if not managed, can lead to behavioural and physical problems from people in the workplace. It is about managing mental energy and perception. How is resilience built and maintained?

> All pressure is self-inflicted. It's what you make of it or how you let it rub off on you.
>
> *- Sebastian Coe*

Pressure can also arise when things do not go according to plan. An employee aims to succeed, however, sometimes there are unforeseen circumstances that undermine these best intentions. At such times, remain resilient. Resilience is the skill of remaining buoyant in the face of adversity to continue to move forward. Strategies that can be employed to remain resilient include:

- **Positivity -** Things can go wrong, but turn the wrong into a right by expecting disruptions and then think about what can be done to overcome them

- **Focus -** Keep in the moment. Stick to the agreed objectives and try to avoid distractions

- **Flexibility -** Recognise that diversity is a part of the make-up of the workplace, which can create contradiction. Acknowledge differences and work with them rather than against them

- **Acting not reacting -** Invent, reinvent but do not vent!

- **Conserving energy** - Identify what is important to achieve and do not let any adverse effects of the first four points listed above cause a distraction

Aim to keep going rather than fall into decline.

• ACTIVITY 6

How are 'pressure' and 'resilience' related?

Working within an organisation is like working in a beehive. Each employee has different functions to deliver; each employee will have different levels of skills and knowledge and each employee will have greater or lesser experience of working for the organisation. At some stage every employee is new. This may happen on joining an organisation or being promoted to another team within the organisation. With each introduction to new ways of working, the employee is expected to grasp the new culture. Culture is the 'way we do things round here', the shared values and beliefs that employees are expected to embrace and practise. These may be either:

- **Explicit**, clearly set down. An organisation may have specific requirements about **personal appearance**, dress and personal hygiene, e.g. wearing formal attire at all times, company uniform, polished shoes, well-kept hair. Personal appearance brands the organisation and is a means of impressing its customers through their employees' attitude. Consideration must be given to how employees behave towards one another. 'Do unto others as you would have them do unto you' is a good phrase to practise. Be polite. Be honest. Respect others. By behaving in these ways the employee almost contracts the person with whom they are communicating with to behave in the same way, almost mirroring their behaviour. Employees should expect to be able to work in an environment that is positive and encourages growth and have the right to be themselves, within reason - the organisational requirements. If an employee is at such variance with these requirements it would be best to move on to another organisation where that culture respected their attitude and behaviours

- **Implicit**, picked up from observation, e.g. going out to lunch on a Friday where important bits of information are shared between employees in a relaxed atmosphere

• ACTIVITY 7

Why do organisations have different cultures?

If an employee is behaving in a way that goes against company expectations, find out about how long they have been with the organisation - they may not know how they are meant to behave. If an employee is new to the organisation, remember it is not easy fitting into somewhere that is new, where there is no experience of working in that new work environment. Make allowances for the fact that they are probably feeling nervous and uncomfortable. Do not jump to conclusions about either their abilities or their attitude. Get to know them and, till then, give them the benefit of the doubt. The support that an employee can give another employee or group of employees is important because it:

* Increases respect from employee to employee

* Reinforces the skills or knowledge that are being passed on in the person who is lending support

* Encourages people to reciprocate

* Creates a work environment of trust and sharing

Supporting other people in the workplace can either be done formally or informally. Formal approaches to supporting other people can be through coaching or mentoring. An informal approach to supporting people can take place through assertive behaviour. Assertiveness in the workplace is all about respecting the rights of other people in the organisation. It means there is no need for passive people - those who only  want to hear good things said about themselves and will do anything to please or aggressive people - those who do not want to listen to other people and dominate situations with their will. An assertive person will strive to actively listen to what is going on. They will focus on achieving agreed objectives in a way that respects the rights of all those involved in achieving an objective. Not only will an assertive person actively listen but they will listen to what they can see in the non-verbal cues that the people they are working with are communicating.

Assertive behaviour is:

- **Stating what you want**
- **Standing up for what you want**
- **Opposing arguments when necessary**
- **Aiming for a win / win resolution**

Assertive behaviour can be enhanced by:

- **Being ready to meet assertiveness from others**
- **Preparing responses**
- **Gathering all the information required before joining a discussion**
- **Using open questions in the discussion**

• ACTIVITY 8

Identify non-verbal behaviour that an assertive person would use to behave respectfully towards others.

Respect and consideration should be shown equally to the employer as well as other employees by being honest and ethical in the way they are dealt with. This does not only mean by not stealing from them, but also by being punctual, only taking days off when genuinely unwell, doing the job to meet the standards expected etc. An employee will need to continue to:

- Communicate effectively
- Be positive
- Volunteer for extra responsibility
- Be loyal to colleagues
- Accept constructive feedback
- Get on well with everybody in a professional manner
- Treat the employer with honesty and respect

It is a constant juggling act to achieve all these expectations, given how quickly things can change. Strive for perfection and judge imprecation as passing frailties.

The price of success is hard work, dedication to the job at hand, and the determination that whether we win or lose, we have applied the best of ourselves to the task at hand.

- Vince Lombardi

Testing your knowledge

1. What is required to make a realistic and achievable plan?

2. Why should a plan have realistic objectives?

3. What are SMART objectives?

4. Why skills are required to negotiate a realistic target?

5. What sort of problems can occur in the workplace?

6. When a plan is revised, what needs to be done?

7. How is a problem resolved?

8. What is a work standard?

9. Why create 'high' standards?

10. Why take on a challenge in the workplace?

11. Why keep people informed about progress?

12. Why is change important to an organisation and its employees?

13. What is culture in the context of business?

14. How is work pressure managed to minimise stress in the workplace?

15. What is the difference between assertive and aggressive behaviour?

16. How is resilience maintained in the face of adversity?

17. Why treat colleagues with honesty, respect and consideration?

18. Why help and support others to the best of your ability?

Skills

Taking accountability for the planning of your own work involves understanding what the environment of your work is. It means finding out the expectations for achieving an agreed standard of work, whether that be in terms of behaviour or the final product that is expected to be produced.

Identify all the roles and responsibilities you will have to perform. Confirm with your supervisor / manager what the difference is between roles and responsibilities. Go through all of your responsibilities. Find out the tasks that you will have to do to complete your responsibilities. Find out who you need to report to if you are working across teams. Find out who you will be working with who can help you. If possible, enlist a coach or mentor to assist you with making decisions. Find out which of the tasks are routine - part of your daily, weekly or monthly practice - and the time when they are expected to be completed by. Factor these into your 'to do list' and diary. Find out the timescales for completing the tasks that are not routine. Take ownership of these responsibilities quickly, but not to the extent that they become automatic and you make mistakes.

When you start a task / activity, consider the amount of planning that needs to be done. Sit down, either by yourself or with members of your team, and work through what needs to be achieved. Determine the target and then draw up the objectives for achieving the target. Objectives are bite-size tasks / activities that keep you on track and warn you where there might be a problem. Remember to negotiate the objectives with members of the team if you do not all see eye to eye on what the objectives should be. Make sure the objectives are SMART objectives. Once you have established the objectives, list them in priority. What needs to be done first to allow the next objectives to be completed? If necessary, break down each of the objectives into smaller chunks of work so that it is more manageable. Give each of the chunks a time limit to complete which fits in with the overall time objective for completing the objective and the task / activity. Confirm and agree the working plan with all those involved in the task / activity. Implement work methods following either verbal or written instructions, or both. Make notes or create a checklist to remember what needs to be done and the order things need to be done in.

Make changes to the plan when necessary. Make sure that if any changes have been made to the plan that all members of the team involved in the change are aware that it has taken place and can accommodate anything new that has to be done. Set about agreeing realistic objectives as a result of the changes to achieve the desired target. Continue to review objectives and the desired target for the task / activity to make sure that you are on schedule or decide on contingencies that need to be in place. If objectives change because of pressure of work, make sure those you are working with know and can adapt to the agreed change. If the change is not achievable, discuss this with your supervisor / manager and agree an alternative approach. If you encounter any problems go through how to resolve the problem so you can get back on track with the task / activity. If you are not sure, ask for advice from your supervisor / manager or a trusted member of the team you are working with. It is better to fix it right than fix it wrong and make the problem worse.

Remember, mistakes are bound to be made. Learn from them. How could you have done it better? Where did things go wrong for the mistake to have happened in the first place? Could this have been avoided? Were you not actively listening to what was going on around me? Did you continue to make the same mistake? If so, what do you need to do to change your thinking and approach to your work? Watch others in the task / activity to see what you can learn from them. Always reflect on the mistakes you have made and make the changes required so it does not happen again. Learn from your supervisor / manager what kind of culture you work in. Is it a culture of blame, where it is difficult to make mistakes? This will affect the way work with others in the team. Create checklists for yourself and reminder notes. Notice the behaviour of others towards you when you make a mistake. Is it generous or not? Watch how other people behave and ask why some behaviours are favoured above others. You will want to complete the task / activity as soon as possible, so focus on how and what you can learn as you complete your objectives towards achieving your targets. Find out all the procedures that you have to follow. Make sure you understand why the procedures are in place. Is it technological? Is it legal? Is it health and safety? Is it cultural - how we do things round here? Look through the codes of practice that you will need to implement, if appropriate.

• ACTIVITY 9

Look at some of the policies and codes of practice that your company has created. Why have they been created? What do you notice about the way they have been structured? What codes of practice, if any, does you organisation need to comply with?

Once you have a good feel and understanding of what it is you will be doing in your job, make sure you are performing to the required standard. Find out what the standard (s) is and work towards achieving it / them. Find out from your supervisor / manager if there are National Occupational Standards (NOS) for the sector you work in and use them as a guide to managing your performance. Finish your work so that it has clearly achieved the agreed objectives within the agreed time and to a high quality. Make sure you are able to respond unequivocally to your supervisor / manager if asked what you are doing, how you are doing it, when you are doing it, why you are doing it, where you are doing it and who you are doing it with.

Grow with your job and take on more and new challenges. Challenge yourself with the standard of work that you are expected to complete. Aim higher than the expected standard to achieve what is expected of you. For example, aim to complete a task / activity in less time than agreed in the objective. It is always good to have more time on your side. Earn a reputation for getting the job done ahead of time. Make sure you have enough knowledge and skills under your belt to take on new challenges. Do not run before you can walk! It is good to be ambitious, but make sure it does not antagonise others that you work with. Recognise that your way of working is not everyone else's way of working. Adapt and adopt. Learn what is effective for others may not be effective for you and understand why that is the case. We are not all the same. We deal with the same things in life but we all deal with them differently. Respect difference and learn from it. Learn to be assertive in your work. Remind people of who you are and do not allow yourself to be bullied. This is not acceptable in the workplace.

• ACTIVITY 10

Monitor everything that you do in a week at work to see if you can maximise more of your time with the work you have to do. Create a diary and put in the start and finish time of each task / activity you do and what you do within that time. You may find at the end of the week that you spend a lot of time on the telephone - is that appropriate or not? Review what you have done and see if there is anything that you can cut out or overhaul.

If you notice something has changed, be prepared to take on board the new ways of working. Be positive about the change. Find out about why the change has come about. Add to the discussion within your group how you can all make the change work with the minimum of fuss. It is achievable. It is all about attitudes.

• ACTIVITY 11

Write a list of changes that have happened in your workplace in the past three months. What was the effect of these changes? What part did you play in these changes? Did the change go smoothly?

Whether it is from noticing problems or mistakes or dealing with people in your day-to-day tasks / activities, you are probably having to cope with the pressure of work at some time. Pause, think and take stock. The last thing you want to do is to stress yourself to inaction. Remain positive and actively listen to what is going on around you. Make adjustments where they need to be made and relieve pressure. Take charge of any setbacks, do not let the setbacks take charge of you. Refocus and replan - that is what plans are for. Plans are not made in stone. They are only there as a guide to get you through what needs to be done, when you know everything that needs to be done. If what needs to be done changes, change the plan and objectives. You may not always agree with the change. Be assertive in your behaviour; argue constructively for your opinion; work with others to make it happen. You really never need to raise your voice or get angry. Adopt an ethical approach to everything that you do and you will not fall foul of anything or anyone. Well, you might, if dealing with a disreputable character who does not share an ethical approach to work. Treat others as you would have them treat you. Support other people you are working with. Sometimes this is not easy as you will not want to jeopardise your own work by taking on more responsibilities in supporting other people. Supporting other people can also take the form of shadowing their work, or coaching them to assist them with their development. When supporting others, it can be a two-way learning process. It is an enriching experience.

Testing your skills

1. Who have you agreed your work plan with?

2. How did you agree SMART objectives? What negotiation skills did you use, if this was appropriate?

3. Who do you keep informed about progress?

4. When do you report that deadlines may not be achieved in the agreed time?

5. How have you resolved your problems?

6. What codes of practice and procedures are relevant to your work?

7. What is the importance of behaving responsibly at work?

8. What pressures have you had to cope with and how did you do this?

9. How have you dealt with aggressive behaviour?

10. What are the standards which you work by?

11. How do your standards go beyond what is expected of you?

12. How have you made change work positively for you, your team and the organisation?

Ready for assessment?
To achieve this Level 3 unit of a Business & Administration qualification, learners will need to demonstrate that they are able to perform the following activities:

1. Negotiated and agreed realistic objectives and targets

2. Prioritised targets

3. Achieved timescales for their own work

4. Planned how to make best use of all resources to achieve the plan of work

5. Agreed and took responsibility for their own work

6. Followed the correct procedures for dealing with problems

7. Kept others informed of any changes to the work plan in time

8. Renegotiated timescales and deadlines in time

9. Followed agreed guidelines, procedures or codes of practice

10. Set a high standard and commitment to achieving their high standards

11. Showed a willingness to take on challenges

12. Adapted to change readily

13. Treated other people with honesty, respect and consideration

14. Helped and supported other people

You will need to produce evidence from a variety of sources to support the performance requirements of this unit.

If you carry out the 'ACTIVITIES' and respond to the 'NEED TO KNOW' questions, these will provide some of the evidence required.

Links to other units

While gathering evidence for this unit, evidence may also be used from evidence generated from other units within the Business & Administration suite of units. Below is a sample of applicable units; however, most units within the Business & Administration suite of units will also be applicable.

QCF NVQ
Communications
Communicate in a business environment (Level 3)
Make and receive telephone calls
Core business & administration
Evaluate and improve own performance in a business environment (Level 3)
Solve business problems (Level 3)
Work in a business environment (Level 3)
Work with other people in a business environment (Level 3)
Contribute to decision-making in a business environment
Negotiate in a business environment (Level 3)
Customer service
Deliver, monitor and evaluate customer service to internal customers
Deliver, monitor and evaluate customer service to external customers

SVQ
Communications
Plan how to communicate in a business environment
Core business & administration
Solve business problems
Review and maintain work in a business environment
Support other people to work in a business environment
Contribute to decision-making in a business environment
Contribute to negotiations in a business environment
Customer service
Deliver, monitor and evaluate customer service to internal customers
Deliver, monitor and evaluate customer service to external customers

8

Evaluate and improve own performance in a business environment

EVALUATE AND IMPROVE OWN PERFORMANCE IN A BUSINESS ENVIRONMENT

'Evaluate and improve own performance in a business environment' is a <u>mandatory unit</u> which may be chosen as one of a combination of units to achieve either a Qualifications and Credit Framework (QCF), National Vocational Qualification (NVQ) or Scottish Vocational Qualification (SVQ).

The aims of this unit are to:

- Understand how to evaluate and improve own performance

- Be able to evaluate and improve own performance using feedback from others

- Be able to use evaluation of own performance to agree, develop and use a learning plan

To achieve the above aims of this unit, learners will be expected to provide evidence through the performance of work-based activities.

Knowledge

In the competitive world of business of the 21st century, continuous improvement and development is the key to survival. For a business to survive it must remain competitive and profitable. It must develop. It cannot afford to stand still. Globalisation and new working practices force businesses to evaluate where they are and make changes to maintain and improve their competitive edge, or else they will go out of business. As an integral resource of any business, this means that each of its employees will be expected to improve their performance to contribute towards sustaining the business.

From the moment an employee has been offered a position of work in an organisation they have taken their first step towards improving their performance. Once they have attended their first induction meeting they have taken their next step towards improving their performance. Each of these steps will contribute towards an employee consolidating their skills, knowledge and attitudes. They are adding value to the business. In any business that considers itself a 'learning organisation' there should be a learning strategy that encourages its employees to embrace 'lifelong learning'. This new learning can then be applied to the business and to appropriate aspects of an employee's life.

As with life, working in a business is all about continually learning: evaluating, observing, absorbing, questioning, adapting and re-evaluating.

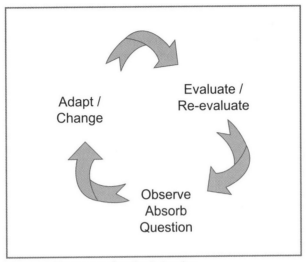

Figure 8.1. The process of continually learning

One of the aims of an organisation should be to develop the full potential of its employees, who need to:

- Stay employable throughout their lifetime

- Learn methods and techniques to do specific jobs

- Extend their capabilities

- Remain motivated and attracted to a job

- Develop their career

> Success in the marketplace increasingly depends on learning, yet most people don't know how to learn
> - *Chris Argyris*

Learning to work and working to learn is a cycle that continues throughout an employee's career. However, the opportunity to learn is influenced by two factors: the work environment - does it encourage learning by providing a time and a place to learn? and the approach the employee takes towards learning - their learning style, motivation to learn, ambition, interests, ability.

Learning can be undertaken either formally, e.g. in a classroom of a technical college, or informally, e.g. sitting with a colleague in the workplace picking up skills and knowledge.

The learning process will involve two parties - the person who is giving the learning and the person who is learning from them. For the provider of learning to know whether their learner is <u>actually</u> learning, they will have to question their learner and offer them feedback to encourage and reassure them that their learning is moving in the right direction.

• ACTIVITY 1

What steps are involved in continuously improving individual performance?

Feedback
Feedback is information that is structured to be delivered to a person about the impact and implications of their performance. Good-quality feedback is an important ingredient in building constructive relationships and in getting jobs done well. Feedback is an essential part of learning. It helps learners to maximise their potential at different stages of learning, raise awareness of strengths and weaknesses and areas for improvement and identify the actions that need to be taken to improve performance. Feedback is given to confirm that learning has taken place. Feedback can come from a number of sources:

- Supervisors / managers
- Team leaders
- Colleagues / team members
- Other people working in a project
- Friends
- People met at learning events
- Customers

Feedback can be either informal - a discussion between a supervisor / manager and their employee - or formal - part of an appraisal interview. Feedback is a valuable tool both for the learner and the person providing feedback. Learners may think they are doing well and have no areas that need improving - this rarely happens, except in the mind of the employee - but there is always something that can be improved.

If feedback is not offered to an employee it may send out a message that the employer does not care, leading to a loss of commitment and undermining of trust in the business. Feedback is offered to:

- **Influence** someone to change their approach

- **Recognise and reward** effort

- **Improve the quality** of work

- **Build and maintain relationships**

- **Clarify expectations**

- **Motivate**

Feedback can take different forms:

Formal
- **360-degree feedback** -This is where managers, colleagues, customers etc., all give feedback - often anonymously in writing

- **Mentoring -** Is a partnership between two people - mentor and mentee. It is based upon mutual trust and respect to support and encourage employees to manage their own learning to maximise their potential, develop their skills, improve their performance and become the person they want to be. It is a powerful personal development and empowerment tool. The mentor is a guide who helps the mentee to find the right direction and develop solutions to career issues and progression. The mentor helps the mentee to believe in themselves, which boosts their confidence, and provides guidance and encouragement. The mentee can explore new ideas in confidence, giving them the chance to look more closely at themselves, their issues, opportunities and what they want in life.

- **Coaching** - Is an equal partnership, where the person being coached sets goals and the coach coaches them to find the best way to reach their goals. Coaching is not about giving advice or telling someone what to do. It is about offering more questions than answers, challenging the person being coached to consider new perspectives and different approaches at work. A coach is a facilitator, who focuses on helping another person excel. It is a journey towards self-discovery and self-improvement. A coach may use questionnaires, feedback from co-workers and direct observation of the employees in their work environment to assess their leadership and management style. The coach will then, through one-to-one coaching sessions, challenge the employee with hard and uncomfortable questions to increase their self-awareness and lead them to new insights about their own behaviour. A coach does not tell the employee how to do things.

Informal
- **Mentoring**

> **• ACTIVITY 2**
>
> What is the difference between mentoring and coaching? Why is feedback given to employees?

Feedback should be welcomed and encouraged. The important thing about feedback is that it should be constructive and be given by a credible person, a person that is respected by the employee. Encouraging feedback sends a signal to the supervisor / manager and the organisation that the employee cares about what they are doing, is interested in cultivating an approach to lifelong learning, that they may have talent that needs to be nurtured and grown, that they may be promotion material, that they could be given more demanding work to do, which would stretch them, and that they want to develop a career within the business. The empowered employee must determine how often and with whom they are going to encourage feedback from. Feedback is only one form of the objectives that an employee must achieve in their work.

It is good for an employee to hear where they have done well, but it is more constructive when they hear where there are areas that they can improve their performance. This will help them to confidence and give them the will to improve. Feedback should provide the employee with a full summary of how things can be improved, explaining:

- The task
- The skills, knowledge and attitude / behaviour that were required to complete the task
- Why the task had to be done that way
- Where the employee did not meet these requirements - identifying the gaps

Once the employee fully understands this, a learning plan can be agreed to bridge the gaps.

Feedback is the breakfast of champions.

- Ken Blanchard

Feedback can improve an employee's confidence, self-awareness and enthusiasm for learning. Good feedback should be:

- Descriptive - set out expectations
- Focused on performance
- Clear and direct
- Balanced
- Specific
- Timely
- Regular
- Able to offer a solution

• ACTIVITY 3

Why is feedback given to employees?

Barriers to feedback

Feedback is not always easy to receive. The feedback may be perceived as being based on incorrect assumptions. Both parties involved in the feedback process will need to work through negative perceptions. Receiving corrective feedback may be difficult because the employee may:

- Want to rationalise what went wrong - as they may feel uncomfortable
- Feel their self-worth is undermined by suggestions for improvement
- Have had previous experiences where feedback was unhelpful or unjustified

Be realistic about the feedback process. It is not always an easy experience for anyone. So be wary of:

- Being defensive
- Trying to prove that the person giving feedback is wrong
- Justifying the original performance

- Dismissing the feedback
- Attacking the speaker
- Feeling something has to be done to change your whole self
- Feeling helpless to do anything about the feedback
- Generalising the message and feeling bad about everything or feeling perfect about everything

Improve the feedback process by:

- Using questions to find out the issue behind the criticism
- Being clear about what would help
- Helping the person giving the feedback understand what is wanted

• ACTIVITY 4

What behaviours need to be monitored when receiving feedback?

Appraisals

Appraisals are an important opportunity for supervisors and staff to discuss performance. They should be seen as a joint problem-solving exercise in which opportunities will be identified. The outcome of an appraisal will be a development plan which will identify what you need to do in order to achieve an acceptable level of performance and what opportunities there are for you to fulfil your potential.

From time to time feedback will be given formally in an appraisal meeting. An appraisal may be carried out to:

- Identify how well the job is being done
- Identify strengths and weaknesses
- Reward employee contribution to achieving objectives
- Motivate
- Identify learning and development needs
- Identify potential

Appraisals are an important opportunity for supervisors and staff to discuss performance. They should be seen as an opportunity to resolve any problems. Following an appraisal a learning plan will be agreed. Appraisals are usually held annually.

Learning plans

A learning plan is a set of personal targets that have been agreed between an employee and their supervisor / manager to achieve over a specified period of time. It is also a means of recording achievement. It keeps the employee on track towards achieving where they want to be in their work and life. It helps an employee take more control of their future, by reminding them what they have learned, achieved and enjoyed. It helps to increase confidence, abilities, employability and enables them to get more out of life.

A learning plan will usually be drawn up between the employee and the employer after the appraisal interview. The learning plan will identify:

- Learning objectives that are tied to specific work

- Milestones, with expected outcomes that can be reviewed and amended

- A review of any successes / failures and a description of why

- Areas needing improvement

- Opportunities for further growth

- And commit to actions that address these needs or opportunities by building relevant knowledge, skills or other qualities

- A well-written learning plan will:

- Motivate. Do not forget the importance of self-motivation

- Build self-esteem

- Concentrate on the right parts of the learning plan

- Focus on what is being done well

- Recognise how to avoid time-wasting activities

- Negotiate deadlines more realistically

- Get evidence of performance, or for any qualifications being worked toward achieving

- Improve performance of the employee and others

- Increase areas of responsibility

- Develop administration skills
- Develop management skills
- Address development needs

What is the purpose and benefits of testing out possible improvements to own work?

The content of a learning plan can be agreed using a **SWOT analysis**. A SWOT analysis is an analytical tool which can be used in many different contexts across the life of an organisation to guide its growth and development. SWOT is a mnemonic, where each letter of the mnemonic means something:

Internal in origin, influenced by the employee

- **S = Strengths**, which are helpful to achieve objectives
- **W = Weaknesses**, which are not helpful to achieving objectives

External in origin, influenced by the business, usually outside the control of the employee

- **O = Opportunities**, which are helpful to achieve objectives
- **T = Threats**, which are not helpful to achieving objectives

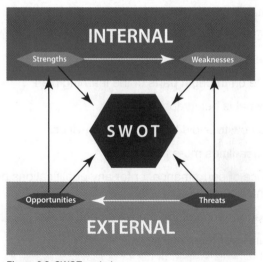

Figure 8.2. SWOT analysis

In the context of a learning plan, an employee can review their performance by working with their supervisor / manager through each of the elements of the SWOT analysis to give them a picture of where the employee is and where they want to be, from which a learning plan can be agreed. Some simple rules for using SWOT analysis successfully include:

- Be **realistic** about the strengths and weaknesses identified

- Distinguish between where the employee is **today** and where they could be in the **future**

- Always be **specific**

- Consider the skills and knowledge compared to the **past**, to see how much they have changed

- Keep it **short** and **simple** - avoid complexity and over analysis

Use the activities identified in the development plan to improve how work is carried out. Check regularly that the plan is being followed. Evaluate the effectiveness of the actions that have been taken. Review the plan with the supervisor / manager between appraisals. Amendments can then be jointly agreed and steps taken to achieve the new objectives. When looking at ways of improving and developing:

- Always confirm important information

- Work, if possible, with successful people who reflect positively on what an employee is doing

- Keep in touch with people; they may be useful in the future

- Do not put off making unpopular decisions

- Offer to find out information if it is unknown

- Manage stress

- When negotiating, always have something in reserve

Progression in a job is something that needs to be carefully considered. It will generally mean added responsibility and taking on the management of staff.

Evaluate own work
It is very important to look back at how effective performance and improvements have been. To evaluate own work consider:

- What went well? What could be done to make the performance /

improvement easier next time? What was done best in the piece of work?

- What part of work would it be best to improve?

- What caused problems? Were the instructions about what was needed to do clear? Were any of the instructions misunderstood? Why were they misunderstood? What could be done to prevent it from happening again? Were there things that could have been done to avoid the problems?

Career progression routes
The best kind of development is self-development. Organisations may have limited resources - finance, space, people etc., to focus on all the expressed and unexpressed needs of the employee. Increasingly, employees have to manage their own development beyond the resources that an organisation can offer. An employee joins a business to work. Depending on the employee, they may develop a passion for the job and want to explore it in further depth. They see themselves progressing and developing a career.

> If the career you have chosen has some unexpected inconvenience, console yourself by reflecting that no career is without them.
> *- Jane Fonda*

The opportunity to develop a career comes mainly from the employee, who will consult with the employer on the practicality of their plans. Aim to upgrade skills and knowledge. The potential benefits that can come from self-development are:

- New and improved skills, knowledge and behaviours

- The ability to cope more readily with change

- Enhanced interpersonal skills

- Greater self-awareness

- Better understanding of learning

- Increased confidence

- Increased self-reliance

Opportunities to progress come from:

- **Promotion -** Either within an organisation or moving to a new one

- **Transfer** - Within the organisation on site or to a new site

- **Secondment or outplacement** - Essentially a transfer to another organisation for an agreed contract of time

- **New job** - Leaving a current employer to work with a new employer

To help with progression within an organisation:
- Learn about and embrace its **culture**

- Identify and work towards achieving some **short-term objectives**

- **Network** - internally and externally

- **Develop** self-reliance

Giving constructive feedback

Feedback can be given two ways: through constructive feedback or through praise and criticism. The latter is not the most appropriate form, as it is based on personal judgments, where information given to the employee is vague and focused on the person rather than what they have done. It is also based on feelings. Constructive feedback is information specific, issue focused and based on observations. There are two kinds of constructive feedback:

Positive feedback is information given to an employee about a job well done.

Negative feedback is information given to employee about where they need to improve. Negative feedback looks at how performance can be improved.

When giving feedback the appraiser should think about:

What is going to be discussed?

Identify the issue that the feedback will focus on. Be specific by using 'I', as this keeps the appraiser focused on the issues.

How the feedback is given

A one-to-one meeting specifically agreed to discuss performance issues so it reinforces the relationship between the appraiser and the person being appraised. Deliver direct messages. Get to the point. Be straightforward. Avoid 'need to' phrases, as they imply that something did not go well. Be clear about what happened. Be sincere. Avoid giving mixed messages. Express appreciation when giving positive feedback. Express concern when giving negative feedback, not criticism. The person receiving negative feedback needs to know that performance can be improved. Give face-to-face appraisals. Make observations, not interpretations, as they are more factual and non-judgmental. Focus on behaviours. Seek the individual's opinion regarding the cause of events. Allow the individual to decide what happened and why. Encourage corrective action rather than reprimanding.

When to give the appraisal
As soon as possible, in real time, and close to the performance issues that are going to be discussed. When giving negative feedback use cool-down time to prevent an issue from becoming inflamed.

How often?
Regularly, and at agreed, scheduled times

When delivering an appraisal interview, be positive and objective. Deliver a 'praise sandwich', which highlights the things that have been done well at the beginning and end of the feedback and points out the areas for improvement in the middle. When giving formal feedback or carrying out an appraisal, effective planning is essential.

At an appraisal meeting most of the talking should be done by the person being appraised and the listening by the person giving the appraisal. Remember that good listeners concentrate on what the speaker is saying, do not interrupt, ask questions to clarify issues and demonstrate understanding without interrupting the flow of the speaker.

• ACTIVITY 6

How can an employee prepare for an appraisal?

The person being appraised should be given the opportunity to self-assess prior to the meeting to consider:

- Their achievements against previously set objectives
- Reasons for non-achievement of objectives
- Their training needs
- Their own aspirations
- Where they feel support is needed

The appraiser should prepare by:

- Reviewing the individual's performance
- Reviewing progress against the previous development plan

- Collating evidence to support the intended feedback
- Considering training opportunities
- Considering the individual's potential to progress
- Considering where support can be offered

During the meeting ask open questions. This will allow the employee to expand on their answers and open up more specific information on what happened and why. The appraisal should look at performance over the whole period under review, recognise the person's achievement and produce a development plan which the individual is able to agree with.

> Because that's just the way it is, and don't sleep on what you did before, you know, because it cannot hurt you, but you can find yourself sleeping on something that happened in the past, but you dare to progress and there is always room for progression.
> *- Thierry Henry*

Testing your knowledge

1. What is the purpose of continuously improving work?
2. What is feedback?
3. How should negative feedback be handled?
4. Why is feedback important to continuously improve work?
5. Why should feedback be encouraged and offered?
6. What preparations should be made prior to an appraisal meeting?
7. What is career progression?
8. Why should employees develop their skills and knowledge?
9. What can a learning plan be used for?
10. How is a learning plan developed for others?
11. What are the benefits of continuous learning and development?
12. What is self-development?
13. What career progression routes are available to an employee?

Skills

The only way you will know if what you are doing is any good, of value to the team and the organisation, is if someone tells you. Make it part of your working plan to improve - to do everything that you do today better tomorrow. This will not only be fulfilling to you but appreciated by your supervisor and the organisation that you work for. So aim to improve, but do it incrementally. Have a plan and work towards achieving it.

Remember the last time that you were given feedback - did you volunteer for it or was it part of a process? How often is feedback given to you in either situation? Is it enough? Do you feel like you are moving forward? Is the pace of movement too slow, too quick etc? How did you feel when you were given the feedback? If feedback is given in a positive environment it should be easy to accept if it is specific and clearly describes what has to be changed and the reason for the change. Everybody, including you, wants to get better and add value to the business.

Look at ways of using the feedback to impact on all areas of your work. If the scope of the feedback can be applied more generally, use it. Try not to look at things in isolation but take a helicopter view. Look at ways where the feedback can improve the way you work with other people, the way you support other people, the way you generally take direction from other people and how you are managed by other people. Review your behaviours and attitudes, as these are always the hardest areas to feedback on, both for the person giving the feedback and the person receiving. Feedback can be interpreted very personally, and sometimes that is right, but try to take an objective view and look at how the feedback is contributing to adding value to you, the job and the organisation. Once you have been given the feedback, how did you use it? Did you use it immediately or did you review it to make it work for you?

Develop a plan to encourage feedback of your work. It needs to fit organically into the management of your skills and knowledge and with your feedback person's schedule. Do not request too much feedback, as this may antagonise a busy manager. You may also not have time to do what is required as a result of the feedback, as it may jeopardise the completion of your agreed objectives. Always be realistic about what you can and cannot handle.

How much of the feedback that you have received has gone towards the development of your learning plan - also called a development plan? Agree the learning plan with your supervisor / manager. Make sure that it is realistic and achievable. There is nothing worse than having a plan which you do not or cannot achieve, as this is demoralising and can undermine your confidence. Once you have agreed your learning plan make it an organic part of your work. Use it to inform the way that you undertake your work and improve your performance. Remember, work can be a volatile environment with things changing all the time. Be prepared for the impact of change. Review your learning plan to make sure that it remains relevant - change it when it needs to be changed. How often do you look at your learning plan? How often do you review your learning plan? Do you have a learning plan? Continue to update the learning plan with ideas and potential alternative routes to learning.

The best person to develop your skills and knowledge is you. If your organisation does not have a system of learning plans, create one for yourself. Set out the objectives that you want to achieve in the short, medium and long term. Look at what you will need to do in each of these time spans. Once you know what you will need to do, look for any gaps which will stop you from achieving your objectives. Plan to put the required learning in place to cover these gaps. Monitor your learning through discussion with your supervisor / manager. Make any changes to your learning plan as a result of these discussions. Look at ways of undertaking further learning. Remember, this does not necessarily need to take place in the workplace but could be done through studying to complete a qualification. Has your organisation helped to fund this qualification?

Use self-evaluation to monitor the progress you are making as a result of the objectives identified in your learning plan. Improve and update them when necessary. Merge the feedback you have received from other people with your self-evaluation as a means of confirming or disconfirming what you have decided. If unclear, seek further advice from your supervisor / manager. How has long-term planning affected the choice of learning interventions that you have considered? Do you have short-, medium- and long-term learning objectives, a step process, that you have agreed with your supervisor / manager?

• ACTIVITY 7

What tools does your organisation have to help with the development of a learning plan?

Develop strategies to identify further areas for your learning and development. Use your networking skills to find out what is going on in other parts of your organisation which you might find interesting to pursue. Broaden your reading to subject areas that your career could move towards. Attend meetings or conferences to open up opportunities to develop your learning. Research these new areas of work to see what you feel about them. Is shadowing someone for a few hours a viable thing to do to find out more information? Do they fit into your overall career plan?

• ACTIVITY 8

Complete the following self-appraisal by ticking the most appropriate box against each skill. For each tick in the 'training needs' column identify an action that you can take.

Skill	Can do	Training needs	Actions to be taken
Speak at meetings			
Join in discussions			
Answer the telephone			
Make telephone calls			
Give a talk			
Write a report			
Write a memo			
Research information			
Prioritise tasks			
Delegate			
Deal with disruption			
Say 'no' if necessary			
Admit mistakes			
Put forward ideas			
Accept feedback			
Motivate yourself			
Set high standards			
Accept new challenges			
Embrace change			

Show the completed self-appraisal to your supervisor to check that they agree with your findings.

• ACTIVITY 9

Your supervisor / manager has advised you that a new member of staff is to start work in your department next week and has asked you to carry out their induction to the whole organisation. Prepare a checklist of all the things that you will need to cover. Do not forget things like toilets, staff rooms, arrangements for lunch etc.

Testing your skills

1. How have you improved your overall performance?
2. Why should feedback be encouraged?
3. What feedback was difficult to receive, and why?
4. What feedback was great to receive, and why?
5. What changes have you made to your performance as a result of feedback?
6. How did you agree and accept the learning plan that you used to improve your work?
7. How have you followed your learning plan?
8. How have you evaluated and continuously improved your overall performance?
9. What training opportunities have been available to you?
10. What have you done to find further learning?
11. What opportunities for leaning and development have been available to you and others?
12. What opportunities for career progression have been available to you and others?

Ready for assessment?
To achieve this Level 3 unit of a Business & Administration qualification, learners will need to demonstrate that they are able to perform the following activities:

1. Encouraged and accepted feedback from other people

2. Evaluated own work

3. Used feedback from other people to identify where to make improvements

4. Identified ways to improve work, consistently put them into practice and tested how effective they were

5. Identified where further learning and development could improve performance

6. Developed and followed through a learning plan that met own needs

7. Reviewed progress against their learning plan

8. Updated plans for improvement and learning

You will need to produce evidence from a variety of sources to support the performance requirements of this unit.

If you carry out the 'ACTIVITIES' and respond to the 'NEED TO KNOW' questions, these will provide some of the evidence required.

Links to other units

While gathering evidence for this unit, evidence may also be used from evidence generated from other units within the Business & Administration suite of units. Below is a sample of applicable units; however, most units within the Business & Administration suite of units will also be applicable.

QCF NVQ
Communications
Communicate in a business environment (Level 3)
Core business & administration
Manage own performance in a business environment (Level 3)
Solve business problems (Level 3)

SVQ
Communications
Communicate in a business environment
Core business & administration
Solve a business problem

9 Work in a business environment

WORK IN A BUSINESS ENVIRONMENT

'**Work in a business environment**' is a <u>mandatory unit</u> which must be chosen as one of a combination of units to achieve either a Qualifications and Credit Framework (QCF), National Vocational Qualification (NVQ) or Scottish Vocational Qualification (SVQ).

The aims of this unit are to:

- Understand the purpose and benefits of respecting and supporting other people at work

- Understand how to maintain security and confidentiality at work and deal with concerns

- Understand how to assess, manage and monitor risk in the workplace

- Understand the purpose of keeping waste to a minimum in a business environment and the procedures to follow

- Understand procedures for the disposal of hazardous materials

- Understand ways of supporting sustainability in an organisation

- Be able to respect and support other people at work in an organisation

- Be able to maintain security and confidentiality

- Be able to assess, manage and monitor risk

- Be able to support the minimisation of waste in an organisation

- Be able to follow procedures for the disposal of hazardous waste in an organisation

- Be able to support sustainability in an organisation

To achieve the above aims of this unit, learners will be expected to provide evidence through the performance of work-based activities.

Knowledge
We live in a world of finite resources. The world is coming under increasing pressure, as the earth ages, to support more people with these finite resources. Employees working in an organisation will be inducted to understand the vision and ethos of how the organisation expects them to behave and undertake the responsibilities of their job. Much of this will be covered in the legal contract an employee signs; however, there will be expectations placed on an employee which are also covered in the 'psychological contract' shared between the employee and the organisation. The 'psychological contract' has no legal standing, but is a powerful ethos of expectations built between the employee and the organisation. The mix between the 'legal contract' and the 'psychological contract' underpins how an employer and employee contribute to the values and productivity of a business. Three important areas that this covers are:

- **Supporting sustainability** - Organisations need to manage their business to sustain their future by devising policies and processes to manage an 'environmentally friendly' workplace. Organisations also seek to reduce their carbon footprint by managing waste, hazardous materials and recycling to sustain their internal economy and the rest of the world. By supporting sustainability the employee and the organisation aim to enhance their community at work

- **Supporting diversity** - Organisations need to determine how they manage the selection and organisation of their employees that takes into consideration the different cultural values that each employee brings to an organisation, which can add a new dimension to how organisations can achieve their aims and goals

- **Maintaining security and confidentiality** - Employees, the physical premises and information about all aspects held by a business should be protected at all times from threat of loss or violence

Support sustainability
Increasingly within the global economy, many organisations seek to operate in an environmentally friendly way. This has an impact on the way all employees will work to achieve, maintain and build an environmentally friendly organisation which can be achieved by aiming to:

- Reduce wasting energy, e.g. using light bulbs which are more energy efficient
- Recycle different types of resources
- Use low-emission vehicles etc.
- Increase reliance on public transport
- Use technology more efficiently in the work environment, e.g. switch off the computer and computer screen at the end of the working day

• ACTIVITY 1

What is sustainability in the context of an organisation?

Organisations seek to be environmentally sensitive by providing a place of work that is considerate of the environment. They will seek to do this by creating a sustainable work environment that:

- Actively seeks to minimise climate change, e.g. through energy efficiency and the use of renewable material
- Protects the environment, by minimising pollution on land, in water and in the air
- Minimises waste and disposes of it in accordance with organisational procedures
- Uses natural resources efficiently, encouraging sustainable production and consumption
- Protects and improves bio-diversity, e.g. wildlife habitats
- Enables a lifestyle that minimises negative environmental impact and enhances positive impacts, e.g. reducing noise pollution and dependence on cars
- Creates cleaner, safer and greener neighbourhoods, e.g. by reducing litter

• ACTIVITY 2

How can an organisation create a sustainable work environment?

Waste can be caused in the following areas in an organisation:

- **Time -** Due to employees engaged needlessly doing personal tasks, using social networks, poor decision-making, being unproductive due to poor management direction etc.

- **Office resources and materials** - Due to theft, excessive use of printing when not required, personal use of printers and other supplies by employees etc.

- **Office technology** - Due to energy being wasted leaving lights and personal computers (PCs) turned on at night when no one is there, keeping heat or air conditioning turned too high or low, inefficient use of company vehicles etc.

The purpose of managing waste is to promote the economic use of materials / resources and methods so that waste is minimised. Any waste produced in an organisation should be reused, recycled or recovered in some other ways before disposing of any waste. Currently, it is claimed that there is a cost of £15 billion to British industry because of bad waste practices. By minimising waste in the workplace, significant financial savings can be made, as well as reducing the impact of the business on the environment. The key areas of potential physical waste are:

- Misuse
- Extravagance
- Rework
- Shrinkage

• ACTIVITY 3

What are the key areas of potential physical waste?

Waste can be reduced in the workplace by implementing the following practices:

- **Paper consumption** - Can be reduced by using double-sided photocopying, 'waste' sheets as scrap paper and email wherever possible, only printing off emails when necessary. Post visual reminders around the organisation reminding employees to consider alternatives to producing waste

- **Publications** - Try not to over-order, or consider publishing electronically

- **Amnesty days** - The aim of which is to give up items that can be reused elsewhere and to identify wastes that can be recycled. It also raises employee awareness about how much waste is unnecessarily produced

- **Negotiate waste packaging with suppliers** - Encourage suppliers to recover and reuse packaging a number of times before disposal. Make the best use of the available recycling facilities to minimise waste. Make sure contracts are in place to recycle glass, fluorescent tubes, paper, aluminium cans, plastics, toner cartridges, batteries, IT and electronic equipment and mobile phones

- **Recycle** - This is reprocessing used materials that would otherwise become waste. Recycling breaks down waste to reproduce new products, whereas reuse is about collecting waste to be cleaned, refilled and resold. Recycling prevents waste from being sent to landfill sites or burned by incinerators; it reduces the consumption of new raw materials and requires less energy than producing new products. Common materials that can be recycled include:

  - Glass

  - Paper

  - Aluminium

  - Asphalt

  - Steel

  - Textiles

  - Plastic

  - These materials can be used in either manufacturing industries, pre-consumer waste, or thrown away by consumers, post-consumer waste. The recycling of waste requires a system to sort the waste. Recycling leads to reducing the amount of new materials required for production, or to change the way manufacturers use resources, the amount of waste going to landfill sites or incinerators, and it saves money, e.g. recycling of aluminium saves 95% of the carbon dioxide emissions compared to refining new metal. The purpose of recycling is to change the way industrial societies behave to maintain the planet's resources for posterity

• ACTIVITY 4

How is waste generated in an organisation and what can be done to minimise this?

There are some materials that cannot be recycled or, as waste, need to follow special procedures for disposing of them. These are called hazardous materials. Hazardous materials should be disposed of safely following these procedures:

- Identify the hazardous substances in the workplace and the potential risks they pose to people's health or the environment

- Decide what precautions are needed to eliminate the risks

- Eliminate the hazardous substances wherever possible or control exposure to protect the health of the environment

- Implement control measures or procedures which employees use consistently to avoid any risks to health

- Monitor exposure

- Implement health surveillance, e.g. medical checks for employees

- Prepare plans and procedures to deal with accidents, incidents and emergencies

- Train and supervise employees to make sure that their health is not damaged when using or when coming into contact with hazardous substances

Examples of hazardous wastes include:

- Asbestos

- Lead-acid batteries

- Used engine oils and oil filters

- Solvents and solvent-based substances

- Chemical waste

- Pesticides

- Fluorescent light tubes

- Computers

- Medicines

• ACTIVITY 5

What precautions should be taken to make sure 'hazardous' materials do not adversely affect employees in an organisation?

Legislation that covers the management of waste and hazardous materials are:

- The Environmental Protection Act

- Hazardous Waste (England and Wales) Regulations 2005

Managers are duty bound to make sure hazardous waste is correctly identified at each stage of production. They must implement procedures to protect the health of employees and contractors who transport or dispose of waste. This is covered by the **Health and Safety at Work Act 1974** and the **Control of Substances Hazardous to Health Regulations (COSHH) 1999 (SI 1999 No. 437)**.

Office equipment and technology is the fastest-growing energy consumer. However, it can be reduced using energy-saving measures, e.g. turning on power-saving modes on PCs and laptops, switching equipment off overnight, attaching timers to light switches, making sure windows are closed in winter, using different lighting bulbs. The **Carbon Trust** estimates that most businesses can make vast savings, e.g. in the service sector it could reduce energy bills by an estimated 20-30%.

Most businesses waste energy through unnecessary use of equipment and technology. This can be overcome by:

Training employees to use equipment correctly or retrain them to do so
e.g. cutting or drilling into raw materials using accurate measurements or double-sided printing and low toner setting on office printers.

Installing low-cost equipment
e.g. motion-sensor controlled lighting, replacing current equipment with equipment which has a lower consumption of energy, making equipment more energy efficient.

Maintaining equipment regularly
A maintenance schedule should be in place to make sure equipment is maintained, at a minimum, to meet the guidance given by a

manufacturer's operating instructions. Maintenance could be carried out more often if a risk assessment has stated that it should. The purpose of maintenance is to minimise risks to the organisation by identifying problems before they happen, e.g. prevent blockages, leaks or breakdowns. Some types of equipment require examinations by law. These will usually be undertaken by a thorough examination by a competent person, in addition to normal repair and servicing. Certificates and records of such checks will be issued which sets out the findings of the inspection and recommends repair work that needs to be carried out to correct any faults. Equipment should also have safety devices surrounding them, where appropriate. This could include devices such as guards, alarms, safety cages and warning signs. When any equipment is being checked or repaired it should be turned off and isolated so it cannot be started in error. Most equipment comes with guidelines for maintenance, including advice on how to carry out equipment checks safely. Many businesses find it useful to establish documented procedures for maintenance and repair work. Warning signs should be issued as a visible reminder that equipment is temporarily out of use and / or a lock-out system, i.e. the person doing the maintenance work has a key that prevents the equipment starting up while they work on it.

Changing processes to reduce waste
Using bottom-up approaches, e.g. reducing the cost and environmental impact of office printers, can be achieved by employing different strategies:

- Change fonts by using a thinner-lined typeface, e.g. Century Gothic, requires less ink or toner, which could reduce costs to an organisation by 10%

- Extending the life of ink and toner cartridges. Many toners and cartridges are configured to stop printing until the cartridge is changed. Most of these cartridges still have a lot of ink left in them. A way to extend the life of the cartridge is to cover the tiny window in toner cartridges with a piece of tape, fooling the optical sensor into thinking the cartridge is always full

- Use less paper by using the duplex function when printing, which can cut costs by up to 38% and minimise the waste that an organisation produces

Using top-down approaches, e.g. outsourcing printing services and the management of office printers and copiers to an external supplier. This method employs **managed print services** and has the advantage of using up-to-date technology. This can cut costs by up to 30%.

The European Union document **Handbook on Green Public Procurement** sets out further strategies that can be employed to reduce cost and limit damage to the environment:

- **Effectively storing and handling finished goods**

- **Minimising the packaging used on finished goods**

- **Taking an innovative approach to use technology** and other methods to work more efficiently

When purchasing materials or equipment, determine which supplier or mode of supply will provide the **best value for money**. The concept of value for money is not restricted to price alone but needs to factor the:

Contribution to the advancement of business / organisation priorities

The aim should be to select sources of materials and equipment that have relatively low costs and where supply is easy to secure. This will not always be achievable. Various factors that can be considered to achieve this include:

- The business / organisation priorities and its procurement guidance

- Rates and an evaluation of materials and equipment against selection criteria

- Limiting selection to only those suppliers that demonstrate agreed attributes

- Limiting selection to suppliers who have been pre-qualified, having met organisational priorities

Non-cost factors

Which include:

- **Fitness for purpose** - The extent to which materials and equipment will deliver specified outcomes

- **Technical and financial issues**

Product-related factors

Which include:

- **Technical performance** - Which needs to consider the 'duty' of materials or equipment

- **Reliability** - To make sure customer expectations have been met with regard to functionality and performance, including contractual guarantee conditions

- **Economic life** - To determine when materials and equipment becomes more economical to replace rather than to maintain. Action that would need to be taken to make this decision would be a cost-benefit analysis, management judgement, the degree of use and corporate policy

- **Maintainability**

Supplier-related factors
Usually concern supplier capability, which includes the supplier's management capability, financial viability, technical expertise, methodology, systems, previous performance and capacity to complete the supply requirement.

Risk exposure
Which arises from the:

- Purchaser organisation

- Goods or services

- Supplier

- Market

Benefits to be obtained from the purchase

- Availability of maintenance and support

- Compliance with specifications, where relevant

Cost-related factors
Which will depend on the nature of the goods / services to be acquired, which should consider:

- **Whole-of-life costs** - Which include, acquisition costs, operating costs, maintenance costs, cleaning costs, alteration / refurbishment costs, support costs and disposal

- **Transaction costs** - Which include, establishing the need for the purchase, planning for the purchase, identifying sources of supply, approaching the market to seek supply, selecting suppliers, ordering and processing payments and managing relationships with suppliers

• ACTIVITY 6

What is value for money and what needs to be considered when making this judgement?

Support diversity

As the EU expands or as the world contracts, more and more people from different backgrounds and different countries will enter the British employment market. Many organisations conduct their business globally, with different offices located throughout the world. This offers their employees the opportunity to be transferred to different countries.

Employment no longer caters for a clearly defined single group of people. It is a mix of people from different races, nationalities and religions. When people from diverse backgrounds enter an organisation they bring with them their experience of different cultures and values. Diversity refers to the different human qualities exhibited from different groups of people. Diversity in the workforce means employing people without discrimination on the basis of gender, age and ethnic or racial background. Diversity also relates to issues of:

- Disability
- Religion
- Job title
- Physical appearance
- Sexual orientation
- Nationality
- Multiculturalism
- Competency
- Training
- Experience
- Personal habits

Diversity is to be valued because it adds richness to an organisation. However, it also adds challenges. Policies and procedures in organisations should focus on developing effective working relationships with a diverse workforce. To achieve effective working relationships in a diverse community of people, an organisation needs to focus on similarities rather than differences. Building relationships from within a diverse community of people is critical for the success of any organisation in the 21st century. Different points of view can be invaluable to an organisation as they can provide opportunities that a business may not have considered in the past. An organisation with a diverse workforce has a greater pool of experiences to work with to produce ideas for products that cater to different cultures.

• ACTIVITY 7

Why is diversity an important component of a business environment?

Organisations, irrespective of size, that employ a diverse workforce are in a better position to understand the demographics of its customers. This gives them the advantage of being able to increase market share by reaching out to new markets and new customers. An organisation that supports a diverse workforce is also better able to address employee satisfaction and retention issues. It also has a larger pool of potential employees from which it can select to join the organisation. Organisations should seek to promote inclusion so the organisation can take advantage of the wide range of experiences within the organisation.

Valuing diversity means creating a workplace that respects and includes differences. It recognises the unique contributions that employees with many types of differences can make, and creates a work environment that strives to maximise the potential of all employees. Employees working in an organisation should respect, honour and appreciate the differences that a diverse workforce can add to help achieve the goals and ambitions of any organisation of any size. It is important to acknowledge similarities and likenesses to foster an understanding and appreciation of diversity in the workplace.

There are a number of strategies that can be used to increase sensitivity towards the needs of others in an environment which encourages diversity:

Increase awareness of what others might be experiencing
Be careful not only about the words used, but also about not saying anything at all. Be thoughtful and tactful about expressing awareness of another employee's actions and reactions or of others' actions or reactions.

Do not assume
It makes an ass of 'u' and 'me'. Assumptions are often mistaken because we rarely understand the complexities of another person's life. Avoid labelling a person, but imagine why they act the way they do or say the things they do.

Respect others
Our status - marital, financial or social - does not define us, so it should not determine the way we treat others. If you start to feel irritated, stop yourself from saying anything. Think to yourself that there is a reason this person is acting the way they are acting, and that you should respect how they feel at the moment, even if it bothers you.

Show understanding and avoid gossip

Resist taking offence
Everyone deals with something difficult and we all have weaknesses. Some deficits are more obvious than others, but everyone must overcome some obstacles. Help to build each other up.

Empathise - Do not let one encounter ruin the perception of that person
For example, just because someone seemed to be in a bad mood when spoken to, it does not mean they are constantly angry and depressed.

Do not let your insecurities or beliefs get in the way
e.g. it is common to meet people with different beliefs, likes and dislikes than you, so do not be put off if the person you are talking to does not like something you do, or likes something you do not.

The benefits that can be derived to the business / organisation as a result of promoting and managing diversity in the workplace include:

- Incorporating other groups of people into jobs which may have been selected from people of a certain ethnicity or gender

- Creating a workplace that is more functional and able to adapt quickly to market conditions

- Creating a workplace that understands the multiple cultures and beliefs of customers, allowing for a targeted service

- Employees taking the benefits home with them, which they can use to increase their understanding of relationships in their private life recognising and celebrating the differences which exist in different backgrounds

- Increasing productivity and profitability from investing in a larger pool of talent, which can provide a competitive edge in a business / organisation

- More innovative and creative ideas are a distinct result

- Lowering absenteeism rates

- Lowering employee turnover costs and decreasing liability in discrimination lawsuits

- Reflecting current business expectations and their environment, as this represents different populations

- Increasing marketplace understanding

- Improving global relationships

Organisations should aim to be an inclusive organisation. An 'inclusive' organisation seeks to reflect the needs and aspirations of all employees by respecting and valuing difference and promoting equal opportunity for all. Equal opportunity is a commitment to minimise and eliminate barriers to participation in an organisation's activities. An organisation provides a culture of 'equal opportunities' to offer equal treatment to its internal and external customers, where everyone has the right to be treated with respect and dignity.

• ACTIVITY 8

Why should employees behave more sensitively towards other employees in an organisation?

Organisations will usually have policies and procedures that cover equal opportunities in the workplace, where all types of customers are expected to:

- Treat others fairly. Appreciate that first impressions can be misleading. Give people the opportunity to be discovered

- Learn from others

- Not support people who treat others unfairly

- Support equal-opportunity programmes

For example, people with disabilities or the elderly may require help with access to the building; visitors, of either gender, may require crèche facilities for their babies or small children; hearing-impaired colleagues may need more visual aids.

•ACTIVITY 9

What are the advantages and disadvantages of having an 'equal-opportunities' programme?

Organisations have equal-opportunity programmes designed to:

- Improve team success through respect and dignity for all by making sure employees are judged on their abilities and past performance. This is covered by an organisation's policies on recruitment, promotion training, benefits and dismissal
- Reduce stress levels and absenteeism
- Improve safety performance
- Reduce the costs of recruiting new staff
- Increase sales by making staff more committed
- Widen the customer base
- Homogenise behaviour in the workplace

For an organisation, equal opportunity is about good business practice and can:

- Reduce costs
- Improve efficiency
- Lower staff turnover
- Improve customer relations

An organisation will aim to make their equal-opportunity policies more successful by:

- Managing **discrimination** and **harassment** in the workplace
- Treating all employees equally
- Providing appropriate advice and training
- Offering flexible working time
- Handling complaints promptly

It does not necessarily matter if an employer intended to discriminate. It is the effect of the discrimination which is important. There are two types of discrimination:

- **Direct -** Direct discrimination happens when people are treated less favourable because of their gender, ethnicity, sexual orientation etc. For example, selecting a male for the supervisor's position ahead of a better qualified female because the majority of the staff are male and the supervisor has always been a male

- **Indirect -** Discrimination which takes a more subtle form where a provision or condition that appears neutral actually disadvantages a person or group of people. For example, when a rule states that everyone applying for a job must have attended a public school when there is no good reason for this

• ACTIVITY 10

What is the difference between discrimination, harassment and victimisation?

Harassment, on the other hand, is an unwelcome or offensive remark, request or other act that discriminates against a person by harming their job performance or satisfaction. Sexual harassment is a criminal offence. Other types of harassment that may be judged as criminal include:

- Offensive jokes, remarks or insults based on ethnicity, nationality or other characteristics

- Bullying

- Threats, verbal or physical abuse

- Threatening or discriminating against someone for reporting a breach of the law

Victimisation may occur in many different ways, e.g. when an employee:

- Has made a complaint about being discriminated against or harassed

- Has made a complaint about discrimination or harassment

- Intends to act as a witness or give evidence in support of another employee that relates to a complaint about discrimination or harassment

- May have been refused requests for time off
- May have been denied promotion or training
- May have been ignored by their manager or colleagues
- May have been criticised continually for their work
- Is gay and has been treated less favourably, having previously made a complaint of discrimination

Employees can be compensated for cases of victimisation. An organisation should have a clear process for complaint or grievance where discrimination has occurred. If an employee is being discriminated against or harassed they should approach either their manager or the organisation's diversity and inclusion manager. Any behaviour that discriminates against an employee in any form is unacceptable behaviour.

There used to be many parliamentary acts that covered discrimination in its many forms. However, from October 2010 all of these acts will be subsumed into one act, called the **Equality Act 2010**. The Equality Act aims to:

- Provide a new cross-cutting legislative framework to protect the rights of individuals and advance equality of opportunity for all
- Update, simplify and strengthen previous legislation
- Deliver a simple, modern and accessible framework of discrimination law which protects individuals from unfair treatment and promotes a fair and more equal society

The provisions in the Equality Act will come into force at different times to allow time for the people and organisations affected by the new laws to prepare for them. The Equality Act will

introduce new laws to help narrow the gender pay gap and strengthen anti-discrimination legislation. It will also consolidate the numerous pieces of existing discrimination legislation into one act. The Equality Act is the most far-reaching discrimination legislation for years which:

- Will allow employers to take further positive action in favour of women and minorities at the recruitment and promotion stage
- Gives wider powers to employment tribunals
- Bans 'gagging clauses' on pay

- Will require some organisations to publish diversity and gender pay statistics

• ACTIVITY 11

What are the major differences between the Equality Act 2010 and previous specific legislation to do with prejudice in the workplace?

The Equality Act has 16 parts:

- Part 1 Socio-economic inequalities

- Part 2 Equality: key concepts

- Part 3 Services and public functions

- Part 4 Premises

- Part 5 Work

- Part 6 Education

- Part 7 Associations

- Part 8 Prohibited conduct: ancillary

- Part 9 Enforcement

- Part 10 Contracts etc.

- Part 11 Advancement of equality

- Part 12 Disabled persons: transport

- Part 13 Disability: miscellaneous

- Part 14 General exceptions

- Part 15 Family property

- Part 16 General and miscellaneous

The Equality Act replaces previous legislation which covered age, race, gender, disability etc., in such acts as:

- **The Sex Discrimination Acts 1975 and 1986**

- **Race Relations Act 1976**

- **Disability Discrimination Act 1995**

- **Employment Rights Act 1996**

- **Employment Equality Regulations 2003**
- **Employment Equality (Age) Regulations 2006**
- **Health and Safety at Work Act 1974**

 Equal opportunity at work involves the attitude of people about colleagues who are different from themselves. This makes the best use of the organisation's human resources. Equal-opportunity policies have the potential to bring out the best in people and transform an organisation.

Maintain security and confidentiality

Organisations need to make sure that their employees, buildings and facilities, and the intellectual property that they create, are free from risk or danger. An organisation needs to make sure that these dimensions of its business are kept safe. An organisation needs to minimise the threat to these areas by devising policies and procedures that cover:

- **Security and security risk management** - e.g. to cover buildings and their external perimeter, the design of an office space. Also to recognise signs of drug and alcohol abuse in the workplace and the dangers that this can represent

- **Intruder detection** - e.g. an alarm system for the building or control of access to the premises by visitors, defining where visitors can and cannot go. This may involve employing the services of security personnel or installing closed-circuit television (CCTV) cameras, alarms etc., or having locked access doors for certain staff members to access only. An organisation may also carry out regular security checks

- **Conference security** - e.g. work with an external event provider to make sure its delegates are kept safe

- **CCTV**

- **Company hospitality** - e.g. prevent overlooking or overhearing of confidential and important information

- **Bomb threats**

- **Fire and flood** - A major risk to premises is fire. The priority must be to prevent fire and to reduce the damage if one starts. To prevent fire:

  - Report any faulty equipment or wiring

- Switch off any faulty equipment until it has been repaired
- Do not put papers, clothing etc., near heaters or equipment that gets hot
- Switch off all equipment at the end of the day

- To minimise the effect of fire:
  - Do not block fire doors or fire exits
  - Do not prop fire doors open
  - Know where the fire exits are
  - Take fire drills seriously
  - Know where fire fighting equipment is and how to use it
  - Know how to raise the alarm

- Know where employee assembly points are to facilitate - completion of the roll call
  - Leave the building immediately by the nearest fire exit
  - Do not stop to pick up personal possessions
  - Re-enter the premises when given the all clear by the fire officer

- I.T. - Keeping confidential information safe or destroying confidential information

- **Contingency planning**

• ACTIVITY 12

What is contingency planning?

Security procedures should be in place to protect the employees of an organisation. The procedures should be followed by both internal and external customers, e.g. contractor and maintenance people, clients, visitors. Anything suspicious should be reported immediately to the appropriate person.

The development of these policies and procedures and the physical protection afforded by the physical resources of an organisation's building will equip the organisation and its employees with the physical and psychological defences to reduce the likelihood of these threats. By maintaining security and confidentiality an organisation:

- Reduces and eliminates threats to its reputation
- Manages and minimises costs to the business of systems upgrades
- Remains responsive to emerging risks
- Increases confidence in the business by internal and external customers
- Provides a safe organisation and a culture that looks after the community of people it interacts with

This will vary from organisation to organisation and their scale of implementation will depend on the size of an organisation. Most crimes are directed towards employees or offices that have little or no security in place.

Organisations should aim to reduce threats to its business by assessing its security needs to prevent the many forms of crime by asking the following questions:

- Do the available security resources, policies and procedures meet the potential threat?
- What is the prevailing attitude toward security?
- Who is responsible for the overall security programme?
- How are security policies enforced?
- What are the possible targets?
- When was the current emergency preparedness plan developed, including fire, power failure, bomb threat and other types of physical disaster?
- What resources are available locally?
- How rapid are the response times for fire, police and ambulance?
- What kind of physical security systems and controls are presently used?
- Are employees sufficiently trained to understand the threats to security and confidentiality, e.g. are telephone numbers publicised, contact persons identified and employees drilled in the event of threats?

There are various procedures that can increase an organisation's security. An organisation may:

- Install key-card access systems

- Issue access control badges

- Upgrade perimeter control systems with intercoms and closed-circuit monitoring devices

- Keep master and extra keys locked in a security office. There should be a system in place to record who has access to keys, which will cover access to a keyholder if a problem happens outside of working hours. A list of keyholders should be held by the police or a private security company. Keys to internal doors, cabinets, safes etc., should be removed from a building at night

- Develop crisis communication among key personnel and security office

- Have a back-up communication system, e.g. a two-way radio

- Design executive offices near the inner core of the building to provide maximum protection and to avoid external surveillance

- Organise office space so visitors who are not escorted can be easily noticed

- Staff follow strict access control procedures without exception

- Keep important papers locked in secure cabinets or password protected

- Keep offices neat and orderly to identify strange objects or unauthorised people more easily. Rearrange office furniture etc., so that employees in daily contact with external customers are surrounded by natural barriers, e.g. desks, countertops, partitions, to separate employees from external customers

- Empty rubbish bins often

- Open packages and large envelopes in executive offices only if the source or sender is positively identified

- Keep all types of cupboards locked at all times

- Protect crucial communications equipment and utility areas with an alarm system

- Avoid stairwells and other isolated areas during an emergency

- Close and unlock, unless the contents of a room are valuable, internal doors to prevent the spread of fire

- Do not work late alone or on a routine basis

- Keep publicly accessible washroom doors locked and set up a key control system. If there is a combination lock, only office personnel should open the lock for visitors

- Post a security guard at the main building entrance

- Install a metal detector or CCTV camera to monitor people entering all building entrances

- Brief employees on steps to take if a threatening or violent incident occurs

- Establish code words to alert co-workers and supervisors that immediate help is needed

- Provide an under-the-counter duress alarm system to signal a supervisor or security officer if a customer becomes threatening or violent

• ACTIVITY 13

What should an organisation's security policy and procedure cover?

- Prevent burglary and theft by:
- Locking external doors and windows
- Removing vulnerable items from view
- Using any security devices available
- Making sure that safes are left open at the end of business to minimise damage by burglars

In the event that a burglary has happened:

- Telephone the police by dialling 999
- Contact the appropriate manager or the security officer
- Do not disturb any evidence

If an employee observes a theft taking place, or is suspicious of one taking place, they should:

- Watch until they are sure a theft has taken place
- Ask a colleague to alert security or a manager
- Try to keep the thief under constant observation

- Do not give the thief the opportunity to pass on the stolen items to anyone else

- Avoid confronting the thief, as this may lead to violence

- Take a detailed description of the thief

- Keep a safe distance from the thief

- Avoid any risks

• ACTIVITY 14

What should an employee do if they suspect a theft if taking place?

There is no such thing as a typical criminal. They come from all walks of life, cultures and ages. People who are intent on stealing from others will be creative. They may steal from offices, hotels, leisure centres etc. Some criminals may be employees working in the organisation who may feel that stealing from a large organisation is not really theft, as nobody suffers. However, the cost of theft is passed on to the customer of the organisation through higher prices or higher charges. It also increases insurance premiums. A further effect of theft is that there is less profit available in the organisation to pay wages and salaries. An organisation can reduce the risk to property being stolen by:

- Marking expensive equipment with the organisation's name

- Keeping a record of serial numbers of equipment

- Changing the codes used to access areas regularly

Employees can assist in this process by:

- Not leaving valuable equipment unattended

- Not assuming things will not be stolen if they are not considered valuable

- Signing in and out portable equipment

Under the **Police and Criminal Evidence Act 1984** an employee has the power of arrest; however, this does not give the employee the authority to search people, cars or premises - only the police have this authority. If an employee searches someone without their permission they could be accused of assault. An employee can ask the suspected thief to empty their pockets, handbag, briefcase etc., but they cannot insist the suspect complies with this request. Always make sure there is a third person present to act as a witness.

Remember: most thieves are opportunists. Get rid of the opportunity; get rid of the stealing! So:

- Do not take valuables to work unless absolutely necessary, when at work they should be locked away safely
- Keep handbags, wallets, mobile phones in a safe place and out of sight
- Challenge visitors found in an area of the building where they are not permitted

A major risk to employees is violence which may be perpetrated against them by an intruder, or external customers that they may be serving who become violent, who has been identified on the premises. In this situation:

- Remain calm and polite
- Ask them their business
- Walk away if threatened
- Be vigilant and alert
- **DO NOT** put anyone at risk
- **DO NOT** argue with them
- **DO NOT** be confrontational
- **DO NOT** chase after them

An organisation should consider different means of safeguarding its employees against violence by providing, as appropriate:

- Panic buttons
- Glass screens
- Two-way radios
- Improved training so employees know in advance what to do if they feel threatened
- Work schedules that avoid employees working alone

Confidentiality is about keeping customer, internal and external, and business information private. Many employees will work with information that is confidential. It is their responsibility to protect this information, to keep confidential any information concerning their customers and the business. What is seen and heard in the workplace remains in the workplace. No confidential information can be told to anyone outside the workplace. Confidential issues should only be discussed in areas where visitors or the public may not be able to overhear. No information should be given to customers without permission from the appropriate person. If confidential information is to be released, employees should make sure they follow organisational procedures before releasing information on request. Employees can only access files if given permission. No confidential material or files should leave a business.

• ACTIVITY 14

Why is it important to have policies and procedures about securing and safeguarding 'confidential' information?

One of the fastest growing types of theft is the theft of information, e.g. through industrial espionage. This may be commercial information or personal information. If confidential information is held on a computer it should be encrypted and protected by passwords. Hard copies of confidential information should not be left in plain sight on desks. Confidential information should be shredded before being disposed of or disposed of in the appropriate recycling bins. Personal information about living individuals, including customers, employees, suppliers etc., should

be held on computers or hardcopy covered by the organisation's policies and procedures that are governed by the **Data Protection Act 1998**.

If, at any time, an employee identifies a risk that is being imposed by lack of adherence to security or confidentiality, it should be reported to the appropriate person in line with organisational procedures. A breach of confidentiality will affect a business's reputation and cause financial loss. An employee can be dismissed if information is given out, either on purpose or by accident. Legal action may be taken against an employee or the organisation that reveals customer and business information.

Risk assessment
Every organisation is challenged by risks. It is an essential responsibility of any business to make sure it manages risk in the workplace appropriately. This means making sure the process of managing risk is visible and tangible to employees, is carried out repeatedly by appointed employees and is consistently carried out and followed through with recommendations to improve safety and security. There are many types of risks that can arise in an organisation, which include:

- Investment risk

- Budgetary risk

- Programme management risk

- Legal liability risk

- Health and safety risk

- Inventory risk

- Risk from <u>information systems</u>

To manage risks an organisation will undertake **risk assessments**. The purpose of a risk assessment is to remove risks entirely or to reduce risks to an acceptable level within the organisation. There is a legal requirement to protect employees as far as 'reasonably practicable'. A risk assessment should identify hazards - anything which has the potential to cause harm to people. As part of risk assessment, risks - the likelihood of the harm from a hazard being realised and the extent of it - are identified that may arise from identified hazards. A decision will then need to agree suitable strategies / measures to eliminate or control the risks. All decisions that relate to the findings of the risk assessment must be recorded. When completing a risk assessment make sure:

- Only one person is responsible for health and safety

- All event employees are briefed on the health and safety plan and risk assessment

- A logical process is followed. Ask "what if ... ?", thinking through the whole event to cover all elements of its organisation. Do not complicate it

A risk assessment has five steps:

- **1 - Identify hazards**. Identify how employees could be harmed by:

  - Walking around the workplace and looking at what could reasonably be expected to cause harm

  - Ask employees or their representatives what they think, as they may have noticed things that are not immediately obvious to the person completing the risk assessment

  - Check manufacturers' instructions or data sheets for chemicals and equipment, as these can identify hazards and put them in context

  - Review accident and ill-health records - these often help to identify the less obvious hazards. Also, consider long-term hazards to health, e.g. high levels of noise or exposure to harmful substances, as well as safety hazards

- **2 - Identify who may be harmed, and how**. For each hazard be clear about who might be harmed to help identify the best way of managing the risk. For each risk identified, identify how the group of employees might be harmed. Remember:

  - Some employees have particular requirements, e.g. new employees to the business, employees with disabilities

  - The public and visitors or peripatetic workers to the business, e.g. contractors

- **3 - Evaluate risks and identify existing precautions**, e.g. operational procedures. Decide what needs to be done about doing everything 'reasonably practicable' to protect employees from harm. Review what is already being done, think about the controls already in place and how well this has worked to date. Consider if there is more that can be done to upgrade to the required standard. Consider if a hazard can be eliminated completely. If not, how can risks be managed to eliminate harm? When controlling risks, apply the principles below, if possible in the following order:

  - Try a less risky option

  - Prevent access to the hazard

  - Organise work to reduce exposure to the hazard

  - Issue personal protective equipment

  - Provide welfare facilities, e.g. first aid

  - Improving health and safety does not need to be expensive.

- Involve employees to make sure what will be proposed will work and will not introduce any new hazards.

- **4 - Record findings and implement them**. Share findings with employees. If there are fewer than five employees nothing needs to be written down; however, it is useful to do so to review later. When writing down the results, keep it simple. A risk assessment must be suitable and sufficient. It needs to show:

  - A proper check was carried out

  - People who might be affected were involved

  - Significant hazards were addressed

  - The number of employees who could be involved were accounted for

  - The precautions are reasonable and the remaining risk is low

  - Employees or representative who were involved in the process

Agree a plan of action to deal with the most important things first. A good plan of action often includes a mixture of different things, such as:

- A few cheap or easy improvements that can be done quickly, perhaps as a temporary solution until more reliable controls are in place

- Long-term solutions to those risks most likely to cause accidents or ill health

- Long-term solutions to those risks with the worst potential consequences

- Arrangements for training employees on the main risks that remain and how they are to be controlled

- Regular checks to make sure that the **control measures** stay in place. Control measures will be required, i.e. the actions that need to be taken to remove the risk or reduce it to an acceptable level. Look for a simple or common-sense solution to the problem. It needs to be identified and make sure it is carried out every time that risk is present, i.e. identify the realistic actions that can be taken to reduce the risk. As there may be many solutions to contain a risk, select the most appropriate solution

- Clear responsibilities - who will lead on what action, and by when

- **5 - Review and update as required.** Few workplaces stay the same. Sooner or later there is new equipment, substances and procedures that could lead to new hazards. It makes sense to review the workplace on an ongoing basis, e.g. annually. Have there been any changes? Are there improvements still to be made? Have employees spotted a problem? What has been learned from accidents or near misses? Set a review date to make sure the assessment of risk in the organisation remains up to date

Managing risk brings together the best collective judgements of the individuals responsible for the strategic planning and day-to-day operations of organisations to provide adequate security and mitigation of risks. Every opportunity, when assessing risks, presents opportunities to review previous experience and learn from mistakes from judgements that may have been agreed and carried out.

Testing your knowledge

1. What is an environmentally friendly policy and what are its benefits to an organisation?

2. How is an organisation affected if it does not manage waste reduction?

3. What strategies can an organisation implement to manage the production of waste?

4. Why should equipment be maintained against manufacturers' requirements regularly?

5. What is energy efficiency?

6. What legislation covers hazardous materials?

7. What is 'inclusivity'?

8. What are the benefits derived from promoting diversity?

9. What are the benefits of the Equality Act 2010?

10. What is the difference between a 'hazard' and a 'risk'?

11. What are risk assessments and how often should they be reviewed?

12. What are the legal requirements surrounding the presence of risk to employees in an organisation?

13. What is a 'controlled measure'?

Skills

Supporting sustainability

As part of your induction to an organisation you should have been shown what the organisation's policies were about supporting sustainability and maintaining an environment which minimises the production of waste. This will vary in depth and breadth from organisation to organisation, depending on the sector that the organisation works in. At a minimum, you should be aware of how your organisation handles the disposal of waste, what waste it recycles, how it deals with hazardous materials and the signage it has to remind employees of their responsibilities around the organisation.

You should be aware of how to use equipment and technology effectively and efficiently so as to minimise the production of waste, e.g. not printing documents when it is not necessary, and saving on paper, or using colour when printing documents. Check equipment to make sure that it has been maintained regularly. If it has missed a maintenance check discuss this with your supervisor / manager. If the organisation recycles waste be aware of where the recycle bins are kept. Make sure that you follow the correct procedures for recycling.

• ACTIVITY 16

Devise a policy for managing sustainability in your organisation.

Supporting diversity

You will be working in an environment where you will be working with many different types of people. This not only covers people from different cultures, but also different gender, sexuality, intelligence etc. You will be surrounded by people who are different from you but who are as equally important to you in your work life as you are to them. Look at what makes you similar rather than what separates you by differences. Build on the similarities to bring you closer to your fellow team members and focus on the ambitions the team has for achieving its aims and goals. As you work with other people be aware of how they interact with you. Is it different from how they interact with other members of the team? Look at why you think there is a difference. Is this different way of being treated acceptable? What could you do to improve the way you get on with other people in your team and how they get on with you?

Question what you do not understand. Do not jump to conclusions when your opinions are based on observations which are not backed up by evidence. Look at the different backgrounds and cultures people come from to gain an understanding of what makes them tick. How are their values, customs and beliefs different from what you believe? Is there something that you can learn from any difference that you have identified? Get to know what your organisational policies are on working with others, e.g. its 'equal-opportunity' programme.

Rather than criticise, look to ways of conforming to the expectations of these policies, or question yourself as to why you find them difficult to conform to. Ask for feedback from you supervisor / manager if you are having problems. Seek out their guidance. Employ other behavioural strategies that increase your sensitivity towards the differences that other people you work with might have.

• ACTIVITY 17

Write an article for a newspaper about the delivery and promotion of 'diversity' in your organisation. Discuss this with you manager before submitting it to the newspaper.

Maintaining security and confidentiality

As an employee of an organisation you have a responsibility to make sure that the premises you work in are safe and protected. Make sure exits are not blocked, waste bins are not over filled etc. This will help to make sure that the exit from the building is not blocked, making it a safer environment to work in. Follow all organisational procedures for identifying suspicious material or behaviour and report your findings to the appropriate person. Make sure all doors are closed as they should be and locked appropriately. Make sure that you are aware of all the people who work in your work area, particularly in large organisations, so you can identify any strangers walking around which should be reported.

When working with confidential information make sure you follow organisational procedures for making sure that it is only given to or discussed by those with the appropriate security clearance. Avoid taking 'confidential' documents from the building unless you have prior permission to do so. Be careful not to discuss 'confidential' information outside the organisation - 'loose lips sink ships'!

Make sure if you have any concerns about security and confidentially that you share these concerns with the appropriate authority within the organisation.

Assess and manage risk

As part of your role you may be given responsibility for assessing risks at some level. This could be at an organisational level or more specific areas, e.g. a part of a project that you may be running or contributing towards achieving a milestone. The starting point for any risk assessment will be identifying the context within which the risk assessment has to take place. It is then a matter of identifying the hazards and risks that exist, either historical or new ones. If your organisation has a risk assessment template use this to marshal your findings before making any recommendations for remedial actions. You should make sure that you make a note of all your findings, especially if there are more than five employees involved. Working in a business environment is a very fluid experience, so be aware that things can change very quickly, which may bring new risks to a project etc. Within the context of your risk assessment, it would be best to monitor, on a regular basis, the environment to see if anything has changed which you need to be aware of. It is important to date the data that you have collected to keep a track of your monitoring activities, which will help you identify the information you need to make in your reports. As with any activity that you participate, learn from the experience to improve your performance. Identify if there are any areas that you need further development in and discuss these with your supervisor / manager.

• ACTIVITY 18

Create a template for assessing risk in your organisation. Show it to your line manager and ask them to give you feedback.

Testing your skills

1. How was your organisation's sustainability policy communicated to you?

2. What policies cover the use and maintenance of equipment and other technology in your organisation?

3. What are your organisation's policies on recycling?

4. What are your organisation's policies on hazardous materials?

5. What do you do if you observe someone being discriminated against?

6. What type of jokes could be interpreted offensively to various employees in the workplace?

7. What do the security policies cover in your organisation?

8. How do you deal with a burglary?

9. What process do you have to follow in the event of a fire in your organisation?

10. How do you maintain the security of property in your organisation?

11. How do you make sure 'confidential' information is stored securely in your organisation?

12. What tools have you used to assess and manage risk in your organisation?

13. What methods have you used to minimise risk in your organisation?

Ready for assessment?
To achieve this Level 3 unit of a Business & Administration qualification, learners will need to demonstrate that they are able to perform the following activities:

1. Completed work tasks alongside other people in a way that showed respect for:
   1.1. Backgrounds
   1.2. Abilitiesc
   1.3. Values, customs and beliefs

2. Completed work tasks with other people in a way that was sensitive to their needs

3. Used feedback and guidance from other people to improve own way of working

4. Followed organisational procedures and legal requirements in relation to discrimination legislation in own work

5. Kept property secure, having followed organisational procedures and legal requirements, as required

6. Kept information secure and confidential, having followed organisational procedures and legal requirements

7. Followed organisational procedures to report concerns about security / confidentiality to an appropriate person or agency, as required

8. Identified and agreed possible sources of risk in own work

9. Identified and agreed new risks in own work, as required

10. Assessed and confirmed the level of risk

11. Identified and agreed ways of minimising risk in own work

12. Monitored risk in own work

13. Used outcomes of assessing and dealing with risk to make recommendations, as required

14. Completed work tasks, having kept waste to a minimum

15. Used technology in own work tasks in a way that minimised waste

16. Followed procedures for recycling and disposal of hazardous material in own work tasks, as required

17. Followed procedures for the maintenance of equipment in own work

18. Reviewed own ways of working, including use of technology, and made suggestions for improving efficiency

19. Selected and used equipment and materials in own work in ways that gave best value for money

20. Supported other people in ways that maximised their effectiveness and efficiency

You will need to produce evidence from a variety of sources to support the performance requirements of this unit.

If you carry out the 'ACTIVITIES' and respond to the 'NEED TO KNOW' questions, these will provide some of the evidence required.

Links to other units

While gathering evidence for this unit, evidence may also be used from evidence generated from other units within the Business & Administration suite of units. Below is a sample of applicable units; however, most units within the Business & Administration suite of units will also be applicable.

QCF NVQ

Communications

Communicate in a business environment (Level 3)

Develop a presentation

Deliver a presentation

Core business & administration

Manage own performance in a business environment (Level 3)

Evaluate and improve own performance in a business environment

Solve business problems (Level 3)

Work with other people in a business environment (Level 3)

Contribute to decision-making in a business environment

Contribute to negotiations in a business environment

SVQ

Communications

Communicate in a business environment

Develop a presentation

Deliver a presentation

Core business & administration

Plan how to manage and improve own performance in a business environment

Review and maintain work in a business environment

Solve business problems

Support other people to work in a business environment

Contribute to decision-making in a business environment

Contribute to negotiations in a business environment

10 Contribute to decision-making in a business environment

CONTRIBUTE TO DECISION-MAKING IN A BUSINESS ENVIRONMENT

'**Contribute to decision-making in a business environment**' is an optional unit which may be chosen as one of a combination of units to achieve either a Qualifications and Credit Framework (QCF), National Vocational Qualification (NVQ) or Scottish Vocational Qualification (SVQ).

The aims of this unit are to:

- Understand the purpose and process of decision-making
- Understand how to prepare to contribute to decision-making
- Understand how to contribute to decision-making
- Be able to prepare contributions to decision-making
- Be able to make contributions to decision-making

To achieve the above aims of this unit, learners will be expected to provide evidence through the performance of work-based activities.

Knowledge

Decisions and the decision-making process

What is a **decision**? A decision is an act discriminating between alternative options and making a judgement about the best course of action to take. It is about making up one's mind. Decision-making is a cognitive process. It relies on thinking skills to understand pertinent data and information. It requires the use of thinking skills to draw from memory - decide from the past what is appropriate to the current situation; language - eloquent communication to influence the adoption of alternative approaches to reach a final decision and perception - able to recognise the worth of data and information that is appropriate to inform the decision-making process of the current situation. The decision-making process is a demanding process which calls upon a judgement to be made from competing sources of data and information. The decision-making process is fraught with paradoxes affected by the noise created from the internal, i.e. perceptual mental models, and external world, i.e. interference from the external environment that impacts on every person.

Making a decision is not difficult to do. It is something that everybody does every day from the minute they put their feet on the floor when they get out of bed. And it continues as they go about their everyday activities. The flow of life is managed throughout a day by the decisions that are made. Many of these decisions are made automatically, based on past experience and gut feelings or intuition. Decision-making in a business environment needs to take a more systematic, logical and objective approach to consider all the pertinent information that will optimise the best decision that can be made for the business. Decisions should consider all available information and be guided by the aims and objectives of the individual employee / team / management / organisation. There are competing demands that are placed on an employee in the decision-making process as they consider their role in the outcome which will be achieved by the decisions they make.

In a business environment decision-making should be rational and focused. In the course of a business day, employees will be faced with many situations that require decisions to be made, e.g. a manager has been asked by an employee if they can have an extended lunch break so they can have an eye test. To help the manager make this decision they may ask themselves the following questions:

- How much **time** is being requested?
- What impact will this have on the employee's work schedule?
- What impact will this have on the team?
- Is there any priority work that needs to be completed?
- What is the company policy?
- What will be the impact - **cost** - of the decision taken?
- Is there an **alternative**?

The decision that the manager has to make appears to be relatively straightforward - yes or no. But it can be seen from the number of factors the manager has to consider that it is not that straightforward. The manager, most importantly, will consider the time, cost and alternative decisions that can be made as well as any other information that will help the decision-making process. There is more to rational decision-making than meets the eye. It is a skill that will help problem-solving, time management and support leadership skills.

• ACTIVITY 1

What is a decision? What are the different types of decisions that can be made?

Making decisions and solving problems are related activities, as problem-solving always involves some form of decision-making. When solving a problem activity is focused on generating possible actions. In the decision-making process activity is focused on choosing from a selection of alternative possible actions. The aim of both processes is to come up with an action that minimises risk to the organisation through the choice of the proposed action to take. In trying to minimise the risk of a decision the decision-making process will aim to eliminate uncertainty.

As can be seen from the above example, decision-making is not easy. There will always be some conflicts or dissatisfaction involved in the decision-making process. The skill of decision-making is an essential tool for career progression within an organisation, as it will lead to success for individual employees and the team as a whole. The converse is equally true, so it is important for employees to develop their skill to make good decisions.

The above example requires a decision based on a decision-making process somewhere between making a simple and complex decision. Each type of decision requires a different approach to the decision-making process or different style. Simple decisions require a simple decision-making process. However, complex decisions will involve complex factors which will need to be carefully considered. Complex decisions are surrounded by:

- **Uncertainty** - Not all the factors surrounding the decision may be known

- **Complexity** - Many interrelated factors will need to be considered

- **High-risk impact** - There may be a significant impact of the decision that needs to be considered

- **Alternatives** - Each alternative decision has its own uncertainties and impacts that need to be considered

- **Interpersonal issues** - Predicting how other employees will react to the decision

The aim of good decision-making is to select from all possible alternative decisions the most positive decision that will have the least cost impact or losses on the business, e.g. less expensive, less aggravation, less stress. Sometimes, it appears that it would be easier not to make a decision! The process of good decision-making aims to make quality decisions which are consistent and will improve the work of all employees in an organisation. An effective decision-making process is required to improve the quality of what employees do in a business. Quality decision-making will lead to an improved decision-making processes. Decision-making that can lead to improved performance can be summarised in the following stages:

Identify and agree the purpose of the decision
Why does a problem need to be solved? What is the context within which the decision is being made? It is important to create a constructive environment within which all invited employees can attend to the decision-making process. To make a constructive environment:

- Define what needs to be achieved

- Agree how the final decision will be made

- **Involve the right people** - Consult appropriate stakeholders even if making individual decisions

- **Encourage people to contribute wholeheartedly to discussions** - The objective of the decision-making process is to make the best decision under the circumstances, which includes selecting the right people to be involved in the decision-making process

- **Ask the correct questions** - Identify what the true issue is to be investigated before making a decision

- **Be creative** - Think from different perspectives, as this will generate new ideas and alternative decisions which will encourage new styles of decision-making for all involved in the decision-making process

Gather all relevant information to help make a decision
What factors need to be considered from this information to make the right decision?

Identify the criteria to judge alternative decisions
What factors will form the basis for making a decision?

Generate ideas for alternative decisions

Use different methods to gather lots of different ideas. This is a critical stage when making a decision. More alternatives will lead to a more informed final decision which has considered all possibilities, even the absurd. Generating ideas is like mining, digging deeper and deeper to find that stream of gold! Some tools that can be used to generate ideas which can lead to alternative decisions are:

Methods of generating ideas:

- **Brainstorming** - Which facilitates the generation of lots of ideas. Group participants are encouraged to be as creative as possible without restriction. This results in more equal involvement from the group. The steps involved in brainstorming are:

  - Define questions, then ask group members to generate as many ideas about an issue as possible

  - Do not criticise any idea, regardless of how wild or crazy it appears

  - Do not discuss any proposed ideas until the brainstorming session is over

  - Encourage people expand on proposed ideas

  - Collect all the ideas together so all group members can view them

- **Reverse brainstorming** - Ask people to brainstorm how to achieve the opposite outcome from the one wanted, and then reverse the action

- **Charette procedure** - Gather and develop ideas from many stakeholders

Gather different perspectives through:

- **Reframing matrix** - Using the **4Ps** - product, planning, potential and people - to gather different perspectives

- **Concept fan** - If there are few options, or an unsatisfactory alternative to consider, this process approaches the decision from a wider perspective

- **Appreciative inquiry** - This approaches the factors from the point of view of what's 'going right', rather than what's 'going wrong'

Organise ideas - if there are a large number of them - through:

- **Affinity diagrams** - Which organises ideas into common themes

Finding ideas can be a taxing occupation. If ideas are not flowing freely find external inputs to stimulate the mind. These external inputs can break down mental defences and stimulate creativity. For an external input to be useful it should have a quality of diversity - get diverse inputs to stimulate the mind which will create connections between an input and the decision being formulated - and connections between some inputs you get and the decision being formulated. External inputs that may be effective to create ideas include:

- **Clean your workstation -** As this gives you the opportunity to break away from the workspace, which gets blood pumping in the body. It removes clutter, which allows greater focus

- **Agree a deadline -** As it forces focus on a goal, which gives scope and perspective

- **Use different mediums of expression -** Change can have a big impact on creativity

- **Define the situation clearly and focus on that**

- **Gather together lots of materials -** e.g. sources of information that will be needed to make a decision. Sometimes, looking at something differently will generate a new idea

- **Relax breathing, cool the nerves -** It takes a clear, cool mind to generate great ideas. Breathing gives decision-makers a sense of control and boosts confidence

- **Create a mind map -** Put down what is known and organise it. A mind map identifies what is known and what needs to be known

- **Ask a friend for advice**

- **Think with your eyes wide shut - as this will push away** visual distractions

- **Sleep on it**

- **Use a search engine**

- **Ask questions**

- **Play music**

- **Exercise**

- **Perspiration, not inspiration -** Thomas Edison said: "Genius is 1% inspiration and 99% perspiration." Eventually perspiration will lead to inspiration

• ACTIVITY 2

What is an external input and what strategies can be used to stimulate ideas?

- **Review and evaluate alternative decisions for cost impact -** Make sure alternatives are realistic by evaluating each alternative for:

    - **Risks:** as there is some degree of uncertainty in the decision-making process the risk needs to be manageable. Risks should be evaluated objectively through a risk analysis, which could be done using a **SWOT analysis**

    - **Impact:** evaluate the potential consequences of alternative decisions, which could be done using **De Bono's Six Thinking Hats method**

    - **Validity:** identify if resources are adequate, if the solution matches objectives and if the decision is likely to work in the long term, which could be done using **Starbursting** or **Force Field Analysis** or **Cost-benefit Analysis**

- **Make the decision -** Choose from the above-mentioned options and agree from alternative decisions the one that is the most appropriate to action. If this is not clear cut, an analysis of alternatives can be done using the following methods:

    - **Decision matrix:** brings divergent factors into the decision-making process in a reliable and rigorous way

    - **Paired comparison analysis:** evaluates the relative importance of disparate factors. This compares dissimilar factors and decides which ones should carry the most weight in making a decision

    - **Decision trees:** these help to choose between alternatives. They identify the likelihood of project success or a failure in the decision-making process

- **Check the decision -** Look at the decisions about to be implemented objectively for a final check to make sure the decision-making process has been thorough. The aim is to avoid any errors that may have crept into the decision-making process. Test all

the assumptions underlying the decision; make sure any decision-making errors, e.g. over-confidence, groupthink, have been identified and rectified and check through the structure of the decision

- **Communicate the decision and action it** - Explain to all stakeholders affected by the decision why that alternative decision was selected. Provide as much information so all stakeholders are fully informed to minimise any risks and promote the outcome of the decision to gain support for the decision

- **Review and evaluate the outcome of the decision taken** - What lessons can be learned from the decision taken and the decision-making process of all those involved in making the decision? This will lead to the development of decision-making skills in the future

• ACTIVITY 3

What steps are involved in the decision-making process?

The above is a blueprint for the decision-making process; however, for as many different people who inhabit the earth there are equally as many different **styles** of decision-making. So when making a decision an employee should:

- Only make decisions they are empowered to make

- Choose from an array of alternative decisions

- Avoid making snap decisions

- Make decisions with sufficient time to be informed by all factors that populate specific decisions

- Physically visualise decisions by writing everything down when considering all pertinent information to inform the decision-making process

> Making good decisions is a crucial skill at every level.
> - *Peter Drucker*

Barriers to making decisions

Howard Raiffa argues that it is not the decision-making process per se that guides us to make wrong decisions but the personal decision-making processes that each of us uses - it is the mind of the decision-maker that needs to be overhauled so it does not allow itself to be distracted by outmoded ways of thinking or unconscious ways of thinking. Some decisions are biased towards processes which may not be appropriate to every decision-making situation. On other occasions there may be irrational anomalies in the way people think. These will get in the way of making correct decisions as they are not based in real time, in the real situation or do not have the whole truth of the situation. Many people fail to recognise when they automatically make decisions based on these anomalous ways of thinking. When making decisions, help to reduce anomalous ways of thinking by carrying out the following:

- Source information and opinions from a variety of people to widen the frame of reference

- Exchange information with a variety of people so diverse opinions can be shared without resorting to the old familiar patterns of thinking

- Avoid being persuaded by someone else's strong perception of the situation

- Avoid maintaining the status quo and seek a selection of alternative decisions which should promote effortless and purposeful decision-making. Think of the goals aiming to be achieved, review how they are served by the status quo compared with change. Look at each possible alternative decision rather than wanting to 'play it safe'

- Set aside past actions and all the emotional, financial or other recourse baggage that may come with them. The more actions already taken on behalf of a choice or direction, the more difficult it is to change direction or make a different choice. Whenever time, money or other resources have been invested, or if personal reputation is at stake, it is more difficult to change decisions or courses of action

- Do not be afraid of making a mistake

- Make sure that you are confident about how to make a decision

- Follow prescribed decision-making processes

- Ask yourself if expert advice is relevant to the decision being discussed?

• ACTIVITY 4

What strategies can be used that aim to produce a good decision?

The best way to overcome any of these barriers is education - be aware of the different processes that work best for you and the different barriers that you face. Evaluate the situation, as there may not be any barriers to reaching a decision.

Sources of information for the decision-making process

To understand the environment within which a decision has to be made will mean looking at all the relevant sources of information, which also includes data. A full analysis of the decision area should be undertaken to understand the alternative decision that should be selected. Different relevant sources of information should be considered which are covered by the following areas:

Previous research carried out by the organisation

This will require previous research to have been stored accurately, e.g. in the organisation's library or archived conveniently to allow easy access. There is a good chance that most of the information will be freely available and held in the organisation's database or relevant spreadsheets. Information to address potential complex decisions will involve more time and a greater depth and breadth of sourcing. Research may have taken place in the past, which may be a good point to start the current information search. If the decision environment is internal to the organisation there should be sufficient internal information available from which to source relevant data and information.

Areas which cover potential complex decisions will normally require information to be sourced both inside and outside of the organisation.

Paper-based reference material

For example, books, industry / sector magazine articles, newspapers, brochures, leaflets, government papers. Each of these types of publication will have varying levels of relevance to the research proposal. These are shortcuts, saving time, to looking up information in reference books:

- **The preface** - An initial review to see if the source will be relevant

- **The publication date** - Tells the researcher how current the information is

- **The index** - Uses keywords

- **The contents** - Uses chapter headings
- **The bibliography** - Uses other books related to the same subject area

Electronic-based reference material
For example, using the Internet. The Internet holds information on almost everything; however, as there is so much information, it can be difficult to find exactly what is required. Use a good 'search engine', e.g. 'Google', 'Yahoo'. To narrow the search:

- Think of keywords that would appear in an article
- Avoid using lengthy combinations of keywords
- Start with seven words
- Spell the keywords correctly
- Use a 'thesaurus' to choose keywords
- Use lower-case letters

In all searches for information consider how it is going to be used, as it may be affected by copyright and confidentiality issues.

People
This may be an informal approach, where key members of staff are asked for their opinions, or a formal approach, where a questionnaire is specifically designed to ask questions to explore the decision area under investigation. Talk to everybody who may have useful knowledge. Work colleagues bring lots of information from their previous experience and expertise gained in other jobs, which may be applicable. It may be necessary to liaise with other departments to obtain information which they may hold in databases. All personal data will be subject to the **Data Protection Act 1998**.

When sourcing information, consideration will also need to be given to the following areas:

- The **volume** of information required - consider all types of information that will help and do not get sidetracked by irrelevant information

- The **depth and breadth** of information to be sourced
- **When** the information is required
- How the information should be **formatted**
- How the information should be **reported**
- If the information is relevant to its **intended audience**

Always remain focused on the purpose of the research and what it is aiming to achieve.

• ACTIVITY 5

What are the different sources of information that can be investigated in the decision-making process?

All information sourced should be:

- **Relevant** - Information that is applicable to the research
- **Valid** - Information is what it claims it is. It is the 'truth'
- **Reliable** - Information that is consistent

In undertaking the sourcing of information, always be guided by the environment within which the decision-making process will take place - what is to be achieved? The decision being sought may vary from the simple to the complex. The breadth and depth of information being sourced will be partly informed by the deadline that has been agreed to produce the information to reach a decision. If there is a lot of time, more sources of information will be searched for than if a short deadline had been agreed. By using participants involved in the decision-making process decisions will be made about the relevance of the information found and how to use it to reach a decision.

Contributing to the decision-making process
The decision-making process can be very challenging in the context of working with a group of people. Every person is equipped with an ego. Some people seek recognition and position and may want to establish their power and authority over the group. Other people may be highly critical, which can be disruptive to group discussions, and some people may feel overwhelmed by the force of the arguments. At the extreme end of the ego continuum some people will sit quietly and contribute little

to the decision-making process. Such groups of people can make poor-quality decisions. The decision-making process can get out of control and be very frustrating for everyone involved. The aim of the decision-making process is to make good-quality decisions within an environment which inspires everyone present to contribute to generating ideas and agreeing a final decision. It is aiming to avoid making decisions out of desperation. Desperate decisions are reactive. They are created and agreed in an environment where the group has not been able to rationally and logically respond to the situation. A desperate decision can lead to very negative consequences for an organisation, e.g. taking on clients that will not be productive, redundancies.

> Most discussions of decision-making assume that only senior executives make decisions or that only senior executives' decisions matter. This is a dangerous mistake.
>
> *- Peter Drucker*

Before embarking on the decision-making process make sure that everyone is in a positive frame of mind, as they will think more clearly. Depending on the nature of the decision to be made, there can be an element of fun, which will relax the group and lead to more productive discussions. Some steps that can lead to more productive discussions and good decision-making involve:

- **Establishing the cause and nature of the situation that requires the decision**. Take time to identify everything that is causing the situation that needs to be altered

- **Agreeing the optimal outcome and working towards achieving it**

- **Making sure the decision is in harmony with the organisation**. Review and evaluate the effects of any decisions that need to be made to make sure there are no negative impacts on the organisation, or at least minimises these impacts

- **Making sure the decision is in harmony with the organisation's core values and vision**

- **Reviewing the potential impact of the decision over time**

- **Taking an ethical and moral approach to the decision-making process, which maintains the integrity of all members of the group who have made and agreed the decision**

There are many techniques which can be employed to help facilitate a good decision-making process. This chapter will focus on the

Stepladder Technique. The Stepladder Technique is a technique developed by Steven Rogelberg, Janet Barnes-Farrell and Charles Lowe, in 1992, which manages how members of a decision-making group enter the decision-making process. It encourages all members of the group to contribute on an individual level before being influenced by someone else in the group. This technique produces a greater variety of ideas, encourages people to contribute to discussions and helps group members resist being overpowered by dominant members of the group. The technique involves using five steps, which are:

- **Step 1** - Before bringing the group together, introduce the situation to all members of the group. Give each group member adequate time to think about what needs to be done and to form their own opinions on how to best approach agreeing a decision

- **Step 2** - Establish a CORE GROUP of two group members to discuss the situation

- **Step 3** - Add a third group member to the core group. The third group member is asked to present their ideas to the first two members before hearing the ideas that have already been discussed in the CORE GROUP. All three group members discuss and establish their ideas and solutions before discussing their options together

- **Step 4** - Repeat **Step 3** and introduce a fourth group member to the group. Continue to repeat **Step 3** until all members of the group have been given time to discuss the situation as they are introduced to the group and present their ideas

- **Step 5** - Agree a final decision only after all group members have been introduced to the group and been given the opportunity to present their own ideas

The Stepladder Technique is a step-by-step approach that helps to make sure all group members get to participate in the discussions and are heard. All group members are given the opportunity to make their presence felt and feel valued to agree the final decision. When working in a group, to make sure that it works effectively it is wise to restrict membership of the group to no more than seven group members.

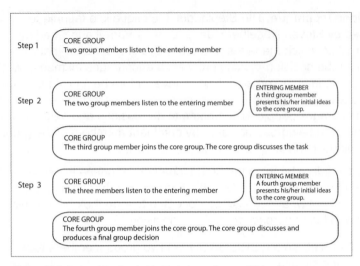

Figure 10.1. Steps of the Stepladder Technique - Source: Wikipedia

• ACTIVITY 6

What is the Stepladder Technique? What advantages does it give to individual members of a group?

To help group members remain focused and contribute to discussions there are some important questions they can ask to consolidate their thinking and keep them within the environment of the specific decision-making process:

- What influence will the decision have on the situation?

- When will the decision be made?

- Who will make the decision?

- What is at stake in the decision? From whom? What controversies or issues surround the decision?

- What is the history and context of the decision-making process?

- What other factors - values, politics, personalities, promises already made - will affect the decision-making process? What might happen to make the decision irrelevant or keep it from being made?

- To what extent has the outcome of the decision already been determined?

- What data and information are needed to support the decision-making process?

- How will it be known that the decision has been implemented as intended?

Decision-making techniques are used to minimise the effect of Groupthink. Groupthink is a phenomenon that occurs when the desire for group consensus overrides people's common-sense desire to present alternatives, critique a position or express an unpopular opinion. The desire for group cohesion effectively banishes good decision-making. Groupthink was conceived of by Irving Janis in 1972. He found that a lack of conflict or opposing viewpoints led to poor decisions, because: 1. alternatives were not fully analysed and 2. groups did not gather enough information to make an informed decision. An example of Groupthink is when a fault is known in a product but rather than fixing the fault and stimulating negative press the group goes ahead and launches the product. The symptoms of Groupthink are:

- **The group cannot fail** - Which creates excessive optimism that can lead to the group taking excessive risks

- **Collective rationalisation** - Where group members disregard warnings and do not reconsider their assumptions

- **Belief in inherent morality** - Where members believe in the rightness of their cause and therefore ignore the ethical or moral consequences of their decisions

- **Stereotyped views of out-groups** - Where the 'in-group' stereotypes the 'out-group' as the enemy, making responses to conflict appear unnecessary

- **Direct pressure on group members not in agreement** - Where group members are under pressure not to express arguments against any of the group's views

- **Self-censorship** - Where group members who feel doubts or differences from the perceived group consensus do not contribute them to the discussion

- **Illusion of unanimity** - Where the group majority view and judgements are assumed to be unanimous

- **Self-appointed 'mindpolice'** - Where group members protect the group and the leader from information that is problematic or contradictory to the group's cohesiveness, view and / or decisions

Groupthink can be avoided by using techniques or methods that promote an inclusive approach to the decision-making process, as already identified in this chapter, e.g. brainstorming.

• ACTIVITY 7

What is Groupthink? What are the symptoms which can help to identify if Groupthink is happening?

For the purpose of decision-making to work effectively group members need to contribute positively to the discussions. To do this group members need to listen to one another. If the listener does not listen to what someone is saying, the speaker is wasting their time saying it and showing no respect to the other group member offering their opinions. There are two types of listening to consider:

Active listening is making an effort to hear and understand. It is:

- Appearing involved
- Leaning towards the speaker
- Making eye contact
- Mirroring the speaker's facial expression
- Nodding or shaking the head
- Paying attention
- Responding with 'mm', 'yes', 'okay', 'really'

> We have two ears and one mouth so that we can listen twice as much as we speak.
> *- Epictetus*

Passive listening is hearing without taking in what is being said. It is:

- Listening but not hearing
- Switching off
- Slouching
- Not making eye contact
- Impassive expression
- Moving about restlessly

- Appearing disinterested

- Making no response

Actively listening gives the listener the opportunity to contribute meaningfully to the discussion. It allows the listener to contribute by asking questions when the meaning is not clear or they want to find out more information. There are several different types of questions that group members can use:

- **Open questions** - Open questions are used if more information is needed. These are very useful for getting others to talk and share opinions, ideas and information

- **Closed questions** - Closed questions can be very specific and precise, which are used to elicit a 'yes' or 'no' answer. Closed questions would be used for getting accurate, factual information

- **Funnel questions** - Are a combination of both open and closed questions, starting with an open question - starting wide. Listen to the response and refine enquiries with each question, getting narrower and narrower until a closed question gives a specific and precise answer

- **Comparative questions** - Ask a person to think about two different situations and then compare them. Comparative questions are very good for revealing what matters to someone and what they value

- **Short questions** - These are used to keep the speaker receiving and the other person talking, as well as making progress. For short questions, use **Kipling's** six friends: 'what', 'who', 'when', 'how', 'where' and 'why'. The question that is most probing is 'why'. Handle these questions sensitively and assertively, otherwise the listener interpreting a short question will see this as a sign of aggression

- **Absence of a spoken question using pauses / silence** - Sometimes the best response is no response, while the speaker maintains supportive eye contact and body language as they wait. This is an approach that can be used in a sensitive situation. This is a difficult response to make, as a silence that goes on too long may be embarrassing and undermine the rapport that has been built up. The use of pauses / silence could also provoke the other person to speak out and reveal more information

- **Summarising questions** - Used to check whether messages are being understood as they were intended

• ACTIVITY 8

What are the types of questions that can be used in a discussion during the decision-making process?

Most discussions in the decision-making process will focus on exchanging knowledge, ideas and opinions on a particular subject within the group. The discussion aims to promote the sharing of and increasing understanding of a situation. Each group member needs to be engaged in the discussion to affect the final decision that the group is aiming to agree on. As part of the group a group member should aim to:

Contribute to creating an environment of mutual respect
Group members may not participate in a discussion for different reasons: unfamiliarity, fear of criticism or reproach, ignorance, lack of interest, inability to think quickly or speak fluently, shyness, resentment of a group member etc. Treat fellow group members as individuals and frame contributions so that they draw on the resources of the group. Consider all aspects, using all points of view and evaluating possible answers to contribute to discussions.

Promote open discussion within the group
By actively listening and giving group members the opportunity to express their opinions without fear of criticism, which encourages group members to be less guarded in their responses and more open to sharing their ideas. There is no such thing as a bad idea and every idea is worthy of discussion.

Know when to get involved
Use the following skills to keep up to date with the discussions: silence - use it to allow independence of thinking within the discussion; questions - directed at group members, these should use the appropriate form and be non-threatening and summarise - clarify the discussion points but do not put words in people's mouth. During the discussion use these skills to encourage other group members to remain involved in the discussion.

Positively acknowledge responses from other group members
As this will fertilise the discussion and maintain involvement from group members.

• ACTIVITY 9

What should group members aim to do to contribute effectively to a discussion during the decision-making process?

Groups will be made up of different personalities, some of which can be identified as:

- The **quarrelsome** person, who tends to want to monopolise discussions
- The **positive** person, who keeps discussions moving
- The **know-all**, who feels they are the authority on every subject
- The **talkative** person, who does not know when to give other people a chance to contribute to discussions
- The **shy** person, who finds it difficult to contribute to discussions and who should be encourage to participate
- The **un-co-operative** person, who finds fault at every turn
- The **uninterested** person, who should probably not be at a decision-making discussion
- The **snob**, who may try to put other group members down
- The **persistent questioner**, who may need to use actively listening with greater skill

Working in a group is a very dynamic way of working. Different group members are vying to have their points of view valued. Group members need to be aware of the skills they can use to influence the direction of discussions by using the following techniques:

Evidence based responses
Respond with fact not fiction and try to recognise when personal opinion is being used.

Well-reasoned argument
Aim for healthy arguments and contributions to discussions. Get to know group members by actively listening to how they are engaging in discussions. Every response does not need to be a knee-jerk reaction given without the benefit of considering how it will accelerate discussions. Keep to the point and do not introduce irrelevant data or information into the discussion. Keep the discussion focused at

all times. It is not about scoring points against other group members. Keep responses relevant to the discussion, in real time - do not add a response to a discussion which was finalised 30 minutes ago. Also, do not blame group members and always look for a win / win solution that respects group members.

Assertiveness

Is a way of thinking and behaving that allows a person to stand up for their rights while respecting the rights of others. A person with an assertive attitude recognises that every person has rights: not only legal rights, but also rights to individuality, to have and express personal preferences, feelings and opinions. The assertive person believes in their rights and is committed to preserving those rights. An assertive person will know when their rights are being violated. The assertive person clearly expresses their rights / needs. They tend to face problems promptly and focus on solutions. Assertiveness can be enhanced using the following skills:

- **Assertive listening -** focuses on understanding other group members' points of view, understanding accurately what group members are saying and to let group members know that they have been understood. Understanding does not mean agreement

- **Listen for accuracy -** requires concentration and full attention to what other group members are saying. It is easier to listen for accuracy when relaxed. Take a few deep breaths to relax and clear the mind. Ask questions as they come up, especially if aiming to understand additional points other group members are discussing. Saying, 'um hum' or nodding the head slightly encourages other group members to continue talking

- **Body language -** in silent moments group members continue to communicate with their eyes, facial expression, posture, gesture and personal appearance. These non-verbal behaviours communicate who we are and how we feel. Other group members will make conclusions about a group member's sincerity, credibility and emotional state based on their non-verbal behaviour

It is the collective responsibility of every group member to participate in the decision-making process without bias to their position or rank within the group / organisation. This may apply equally to a group member who may abstain from discussions during the decision-making process. It is important that the rights of each group member to participate in discussions without bias are respected throughout the group. This could always be a principle for bringing together the group members for a specific decision-making process. Working collectively fosters a positive atmosphere within which group members feel able to contribute to a discussion without fear of negative criticism. The principle of collective responsibility generates an environment of freedom from which all group members feel that they have meaningfully contributed to the final outcome of the decision-making process.

> My job is to listen to ideas, maybe cook up a few of my own, and make decisions based on what's good for the shareholders and for the company.
> - *Philip Knight*

Testing your knowledge

1. What are the cognitive skills involved in the decision-making process?

2. What is the difference between decision-making and problem-solving?

3. What is the difference between a 'simple' and a 'complex' decision?

4. What is the value of generating new ideas in the decision-making process?

5. What is the difference between 'brainstorming' and 'reverse brainstorming'?

6. What is a 'concept fan'?

7. What are some of the barriers that hamper the decision-making process?

8. Explain the process of 'starbursting'?

9. Why are different sources of information explored in the decision-making process?

10. What is the difference between 'active listening' and 'assertive listening'?

11. What skills can be used to influence the course of discussion during the decision-making process?

12. How did you deal with difficult group members?

13. What is 'collective responsibility'?

Skills

In your organisation you will be called upon to make many decisions in your working day. These will range from the very simple, e.g. shall I do the photocopying now myself or get someone else to help me, to the very complex, e.g. placing an order which will take in the requirements of all departments of the organisation. Some decisions you will be able to agree independently, without having to refer to your manager or other people with the specific expertise to help you. Some decisions you will only be able to make in the company of others who will help you to clarify the situation.

Whatever form of decision you are trying to resolve you will need data and information of some kind to assist you with the decision-making process. You will need to make sure that you source the correct information to help with the decision-making process. This should be translated in the most meaningful form so all group members will understand the importance of the information. Information is gathered to help agree on a decision. It should be transparent and speak for itself.

You will need to consider all alternative decisions and, more importantly, how other group members got to a particular decision that you did not think of. What did they do which you had not considered? Was it more information? Or a more open approach to the decision-making process?

Observe how you interact in the decision-making process. What skills do you perform which helps to facilitate the decision-making process? What do you do when you do not agree with someone's point of view? How do you persuade them of the merit of your opinion? How do you contribute to establishing a positive environment within which the decision-making process can operate? Are there any specific methodologies or techniques that the chair of the meeting uses to facilitate a more open and inclusive approach to the decision-making process?

When discussing information and ideas from other members of the group look at how you structure your thinking to avoid outmoded ways of thinking or ways of thinking which are not appropriate to the situation under discussion. How did you alter your approach to your thinking, if this was the case in any of your decision-making experiences? Did you find it easy generating ideas to help make a decision? If techniques were used to generate new ideas, which ones have you found most beneficial? Analyse why you think they are beneficial so you can develop the way your mind works when taking part in the decision-making process.

Look at the way you frame yourself when influencing other group members to your way of thinking. Groups are made up of diverse groups of people who all think in different ways and may well have a particular style for making decisions. Are you aware that you have a particular decision-making style? Look at the composition of the group to see how the dynamic of the group operates. Look to change the way other group members may be undermining the group dynamic and use skills to influence the way they are performing. You are all in this together and it will require a concerted effort on the part of all group members to accept collective responsibility for any decision that has been agreed. At all times behave with respect towards all group members, even those you are passionately opposed to an agreed decision. Behave with integrity and make sure your contributions to the decision-making process are ethical.

Testing your skills

1. What information did you research which contributed to the decision-making process?

2. How did the information you presented influence the decision-making process?

3. What do you do to generate ideas during a discussion?

4. What do you do to clarify meaning for other group members during the decision-making process?

5. How do you contribute to discussions during the decision-making process?

6. How have you influenced final decisions being agreed?

7. What kind of questions have you used during decision-making processes?

8. How do you display assertive behaviour during the decision-making process?

9. How have you supported decisions that you did not agree with?

10. How would you describe your decision-making style?

Ready for assessment?
To achieve this Level 3 unit of a Business & Administration qualification, learners will need to demonstrate that they are able to perform the following activities:

1. Identified sources of information needed

2. Researched and collected information to add value to the decision-making process

3. Presented information to others and developed ideas, using accurate and current information

4. Made constructive, relevant and timely contributions to meetings, or other discussions, to contribute to making a decision

5. Provided additional information, when asked, to contribute to making a decision

6. Contributed to identifying and agreeing criteria for making a decision

7. Contributed to structuring ideas and information in a way that helps other people to understand their own ideas

8. Listened to other people's contributions, adapting own ideas as necessary

9. Contributed to reviewing information

10. Confirmed support for an agreed decision

You will need to produce evidence from a variety of sources to support the performance requirements of this unit.

If you carry out the 'ACTIVITIES' and respond to the 'NEED TO KNOW' questions, these will provide some of the evidence required.

Links to other units

While gathering evidence for this unit, evidence may also be used from evidence generated from other units within the Business & Administration suite of units. Below is a sample of applicable units; however, most units within the Business & Administration suite of units will also be applicable.

QCF NVQ

Communications

Communicate in a business environment (Level 3)

Make and receive telephone calls

Core business & administration

Evaluate and improve own performance in a business environment (Level 3)

Solve business problems (Level 3)

Work in a business environment (Level 3)

Work with other people in a business environment (Level 3)

Negotiate in a business environment (Level 3)

Customer service

Deliver, monitor and evaluate customer service to internal customers

Deliver, monitor and evaluate customer service to external customers

SVQ

Communications

Plan how to communicate in a business environment

Core business & administration

Solve business problems

Review and maintain work in a business environment

Support other people to work in a business environment

Contribute to negotiations in a business environment

Customer service

Deliver, monitor and evaluate customer service to internal customers

Deliver, monitor and evaluate customer service to external customers

11 Negotiate in a business environment

NEGOTIATE IN A BUSINESS ENVIRONMENT

'**Negotiate in a business environment**' is an <u>optional unit</u> which may be chosen as one of a combination of units to achieve either a Qualifications and Credit Framework (QCF), National Vocational Qualification (NVQ) or Scottish Vocational Qualification (SVQ).

The aims of this unit are to:

*   Understand how to prepare for negotiations

*   Understand how to conduct negotiations

*   Understand how to complete negotiations

*   Be able to prepare for negotiations

*   Be able to conduct negotiations

*   Be able to complete negotiations

To achieve the above aims of this unit, learners will be expected to provide evidence through the performance of work-based activities.

Knowledge
What is negotiation?
Negotiation is a process undertaken in all business environments. It usually involves at least two parties who come together to try to agree a mutually acceptable decision based on competing outcomes. Negotiating is usually about managing the level of compromise either party is willing to settle for as they oppose each other. Each party will have different outcomes that they are hoping to achieve. Therefore, negotiation can be a very adversarial practice. As such, it can be an intricate and lengthy process which is more than just collecting relevant information but using artful negotiation and interpersonal skills. For example, negotiations may involve parties from different cultures who have different customs and ways of doing business. Attitude - how others are dealt with when negotiating - should drive the negotiation relationship. Attitudinal characteristics of negotiation include self-awareness, self-belief and openness to other viewpoints. Skillful negotiators will analyse the other party's attitudes and moderate their behaviour and usual negotiating style to achieve a win-win situation where all parties are satisfied with the business solution.

Negotiation is required for business survival, growth and empowerment to help an organisation make the best financial and inter-company decisions. Negotiation is a valuable tool that will protect an organisation by promoting its brand and good name. Fruitful and positive relationships made throughout the negotiation process will create and promote a positive advertisement of an organisation which helps to sustain and keep an organisation growing and remaining competitive. Negotiation is about getting the very best deal for the organisation.

• ACTIVITY 1

What is negotiation and why is it important in the life of an organisation?

The principles of the negotiation process

Aside from the very commercial types of negotiation described above, negotiation can take place at many different levels within and between organisations and for many different reasons, e.g. an employee negotiating an increase in salary, a manager negotiating with another manager when an employee can be transferred to another division of the business. The process of negotiation normally covers the following stages:

Planning and preparation

Set the objectives aiming to be achieved in the negotiation, gather together relevant data and information - to discover where the opposing party's weaknesses are and decide on a negotiating strategy. Information is power and the more a negotiator has the more they are able to influence the settlement of the negotiation to their advantage. The more a negotiator knows about the members of the opposing party and their organisation, the better. Insufficient planning time may result in failure to negotiate a mutually beneficial agreement and raises feelings of hostility and frustration. The negotiator should make sure that, if necessary, all legal issues are covered before commencing with the opening of the negotiation. Planning should evolve a carefully designed blueprint outlining specifically desired results for both negotiating parties. The planning process should involve:

- **Clearly articulating objectives** - Identify issues that are not negotiable, 'must-have', which are predetermined prior to negotiation and are essential for a satisfactory agreement, and the issues that are negotiable, the 'nice-to-have', which are not essential to the settlement which can be conceded or used as trade-offs to reach a settlement or maintain a relationship. The key to negotiation is knowing the parameters of the negotiation prior to negotiation and the strategies to adopt. Those parties who ask for more typically get more ... and those with low targets typically underachieve. The negotiator should have a target they are aiming to achieve which they believe is realistic and have a good chance of achieving

- **Defining the issues worthy of negotiation** - Identify and prioritise all the issues of both negotiating parties into a comprehensive list. Some issues may have been resolved prior to the negotiation, which is fine, but be sure to identify any outstanding issues. Extract relevant information from the list to enhance the negotiating position

Planning increases negotiation success and helps to achieve solutions never thought possible. Prepare a strategy in line with the opposing party's behavioral style, if known. Having a strategy helps parties to relax, face fewer unknowns and reduce stress. Various strategies can be employed at this stage of negotiation:

- Give room for manoeuvre where concessions and bargaining can move towards reaching a settlement. Negotiations are completed between parties who seek mutual advantage, not unilateral victory. Both sides have to win something

- Give no room for manoeuvre, e.g. start the negotiation off with a final offer, which may cause a stalemate where no settlement can be reached and both parties walk away from the negotiation not having achieved their objectives. This may be counterproductive, as it gives the opposing party no room to negotiate

A good negotiator is someone who knows what they want as well as what they have. Try to determine the priorities of the opposing negotiator, discovering their needs, wants and interests. This will place the negotiator in a very good position to open the negotiations, identify the strength and value of the negotiator and the challenges that might be faced in the negotiation.

• ACTIVITY 2

What issues need to be considered when preparing and planning for a negotiation?

Opening

Negotiators reveal their initial bargaining positions to the opposing party. Both parties will have agreed a rationale for the approach they are taking to achieve a win-win settlement. They will set out their arguments to each other, listen and observe reactions and move forward as much as they can. Open realistically and move moderately. Take the opportunity to challenge the opposing party's current position; however, do not restrict their ability to move. Make no concessions of any kind at this stage of the negotiation.

It is important when opening the negotiation that the negotiation focuses on issues not personalities, e.g. in a sales negotiation focus on selling value and benefits to the customer. Do not mention price unless the customer asks or unless negotiating the price. This may appear manipulative and irresponsible but it is not. Consider opening with minor issues, as this will give the negotiator an early indication of how the opposing party negotiates. This knowledge can be used to benefit the negotiation of more important and major issues.

During the negotiation be aware of the opposing party's behavioral style, and adapt, perhaps using the **mirror principle** from **Neuro Linguistic Programming**. Frustration and anger may develop in the negotiation, not as a result of the topic or issues, but because of the opposing party's personality traits. Adopt an emotional distance with the opposing party and react unemotionally. The negotiating process can unleash emotions and short-cut rational processes where negotiators can lose sight of their original objectives. However, negotiators should always act professionally and free of emotional distractions, e.g. biases, perceptions, values, fear of being exploited, egos. Avoid getting personal. Many business negotiations are not about befriending the other side. Be courteous and kind. This does not mean developing a relationship outside of the negotiation. Do not express dislike of the opposing party.

Parties can get too caught up in the emotions of negotiation, sometimes exceeding the remit of their responsibility, promising things which they do not have the authority to offer. This may endanger the whole outcome of the negotiation and undermine the credibility not only of the negotiator but also of the organisation. Sometimes a negotiator can get too close to the deal and overlook important facts that may help move the settlement forward. Avoid entangling with relationship challenges during the negotiating process.

Fear of negotiation itself can become a barrier to the negotiating process: the fear of rejection or perhaps sounding too aggressive. The best approach to dealing with the emotional aspect of negotiation is to pause by taking a break to re-evaluate the situation. This will endow the negotiator with an aura of composure and confidence and also gives that negotiator control over all the critical points of the negotiation. Negotiators cannot arrive fully prepared for every eventuality of all emotional upheavals that may occur during the negotiation. Pausing also allows a negotiator more time to consider the issues and stall the opposing party from forcing a settlement. It also gives the negotiator time to consult with an expert about issues and avoid appearing weak and foolish pretending to possess expertise and knowledge that they do not have. This may harm a negotiators negotiating position. If there are any pauses in the negotiation avoid discussion of issues in public places where they can be overheard - 'walls have ears'.

Before opening the negotiation, and throughout the whole process, negotiators should compose themselves, sum up the climate of the negotiation and continually remind themselves of the following:

- What are the **goals** to get out of the negotiation? What does a negotiator think the other negotiator wants?

- What does each negotiator have that can be a **trade-off**? What do each have that the other wants? What is each comfortable giving away?

- If a settlement cannot be reached what **alternatives** can be offered? Are these good or bad? How much does it matter if a settlement is not agreed? Does failure to reach an agreement eliminate future opportunities? What alternatives might the other party have?

- What is the history of the **relationship**? Could or should this history impact the negotiation? Will there be any hidden issues that may influence the negotiation? How will these be handled?

- Who has what **power** in the relationship? Who controls resources? Who stands to lose the most if an agreement is not reached? What power does the other party have to deliver what is hoped for?

- What are the **expected outcomes** from this negotiation? What has the outcome been in the past and what precedents have been set?

- What are the **consequences** for the negotiator of winning or losing this negotiation? What are the consequences for the other negotiator?

- Based on all of the considerations, what are the possible **solutions** and compromises available?

• ACTIVITY 3

How can a negotiator manage the different kinds of emotions that may surface in a negotiation between opposing negotiators?

Bargaining
As both negotiating parties have different objectives, each negotiator will seek to:

- Determine the real agenda by asking why the opposing party has the particular needs that they have identified. Knowing the 'why' insures that both sides understand each other's positions

- Discover any weaknesses in the other party's strategy by listening and reading the signal the opposing party is sending, e.g. if the opposing party says, 'Let's think about that point', what they mean is, 'I am prepared to negotiate'; if they say, 'I shall consider your offer', what they mean is, 'I am going to accept your offer but I do not want to appear to cave in too early or be a light touch'

- Check that the information that has informed each negotiating position is correct by observing the opposing party's reactions

- Adjusting the negotiating position in light of the changing dynamics of the negotiation process

- Persuade the other party to abandon their position and accept the opposing position

- Make concessions to move towards achieving a satisfactory conclusion. Concessions should not be one sided but trade-off against a trade-off from the opposing party, e.g. 'If I concede "a" then I expect you to concede "b"'

• ACTIVITY 4

What other signals should a negotiator look out for during the negotiation?

Negotiator's positions are rarely as fundamentally opposed as they might initially appear. In an ideal situation, a negotiator will find that the other party wants what they are prepared to trade, and that the negotiator is prepared to give what the other party wants. If this is not the case and one party must give way, then it is fair for this party to try to negotiate some form of compensation for doing so. Ultimately, both parties should feel comfortable with the final settlement if the agreement is to be considered win-win.

Once an offer has been made do not make another offer if the first one has not been accepted. Wait for a counter-offer. Never give something up without getting something back. Do not be afraid to take a risk. Sometimes it is risky not to take a risk. Do not be bluffed by artificial deadlines or 'final offers'. And do not bluff, because if the negotiator cannot follow through they will lose their credibility. Negotiators should be careful not to attribute more strength to the other side than it possesses. In any negotiation, both sides are under pressure to perform. Sometimes negotiators can get what they want by calling it by another name, e.g. the opposing party does not subscribe to 'renegotiating' contracts but is okay with 'extending' contracts.

Negotiators should make time work for themselves, never revealing how much time they have to negotiate the settlement. Once that is done, some of the power of the negotiator is given away in the negotiation. If asked how much time a negotiator has to negotiate, answer by saying: 'I have as much time as it takes to successfully complete our negotiation.' This gives the negotiator flexibility to work within the negotiation process. The negotiator should go into the negotiation with options, e.g. if the negotiator's director has specified that negotiations should be completed by a certain date because of organisation strategy, do not let the opposing party know this information. If too much information is given away the negotiator loses some of their bargaining position. Having options empowers the negotiator and strengthens their position in the negotiation as they will be able to counter arguments and offers the opposing party might offer.

Use **Pareto's 80 / 20 rule**. Spend 80% of the time in the negotiation listening and 20% talking. Listening gives the negotiator the opportunity to gain further information, and remember, information is power. Use silence strategically during the negotiation. If the opposing negotiator offers something, refrain from saying anything and see what happens. Be non-committal about proposals and explanations - do not talk too much.

Most of the bargaining stage will be taken up with arguing, so clear thinking is required by negotiators so they can present their case and expose the weaknesses in the opposing party's argument. Consideration needs to be given to the manner of arguing. A negotiator will want to maintain a positive atmosphere within which a settlement can be reached. It would be divisive to continually browbeat the opposing party. Argument should be approached calmly and unemotionally. There are a number of **bargaining strategies** that can be used throughout the negotiation, which include:

- Making threats
- No negotiation under duress - it will reflect badly on you
- The direct bluff
- The leading question
- The piecemeal or 'salami' technique
- The 'yes, but ...' approach

Strategies a negotiator should avoid include:

- **Stonewalling -** Where they stay silent in the face of crisis
- **Whitewashing -** Where they minimise the effects of their actions
- **Smokescreening -** Where they conceal the truth
- **Setting a false front -** Where they enter the argument of negotiation under false pretenses
- **Block and blaming -** Where they distance themselves from the problems and blame someone else
- **Slash and burn -** Where they declare war against their critics

Always keep up-to-date notes of discussions and offers made throughout the negotiation.

• ACTIVITY 5

Describe the bargaining strategies that can be used in negotiation and when it would be appropriate to use them.

Closing

Deciding what 'trade-offs' are acceptable to either negotiating party to achieve the best win / win settlement. This may vary in strategies from pleading to losing one's temper. When and how a negotiation is closed will depend on the assessment of the strength of the opposing party's case and their determination to achieve it. Strategies that can be employed to close a negotiation include:

- Make a trade-off, preferably a minor one

- Agree a deal which may split the difference between the two opposing positions or bring something new to the table

- Offer the opposing party two courses of action to select

- Apply pressure if the final settlement is not accepted

- Summarise the negotiation, highlighting concessions offered and identifying the final settlement

The final settlement should be reached positively. Avoid being forced into making a final offer until you are ready. However, both parties will manipulate the situation to find out how close their opposing party is to making a final settlement. A final offer should be just that, a final offer. This is not the time for gamesmanship. If the negotiator is unable to make good on their final offer it will undermine their position and allow the opposing party to seek further concessions. The final settlement for any negotiator is the point to which they are willing to go. At this stage, the final settlement should be documented in a contract. Make sure the contract is specific in the clauses that have been agreed between the two negotiating parties.

• ACTIVITY 6

How should a negotiation be closed?

Negotiation styles

The style of negotiation will be governed by the desire to agree a final settlement which should try to create a win / win situation where both parties feel positive about the negotiation once it is over. This helps people to preserve good working relationships afterwards. Histrionics and emotionalism may be inappropriate because they undermine the rational basis of the negotiation and they appear to be manipulative; however, these may be strategies a negotiator may use to move the negotiation forward.

Styles of negotiation will depend on circumstances and vary with the beliefs and skills of the negotiator. There are a number of different negotiation styles, which can be summarised as:

Belief-based styles

Which range from a collaborative to a competitive approach to the negotiation. This approach is based on beliefs about people and how selfish or generous they are. The different approaches under this style range from concessional, lose / win, through collaborative, win / win, to competitive, win / lose, which will be motivated by either excessive consideration of others or of the self:

- **Collaborative negotiation** - The approach is to treat the relationship as an important and valuable element aiming to reach a win-win settlement. The negotiator will seek to be fair in their dealings with their opposing party, converting individual wants into a single problem and bringing both parties together to solving this problem. This frees negotiators from petty jealousies and personal attachment to their requirements so they can then take a more objective and equitable position from which they can act in a more collaborative way. It does not seek to be weak and giving in but offers transparency and trust by offering information before it is requested. If faced with a competitive negotiator the collaborative negotiator should be assertive

- **Competitive negotiation** - The approach is to treat the negotiation process as a competition that has to be won or lost. It is assumed by negotiators using this style that there is a fixed amount to be gained which both negotiators want, and if one person gains then the other person loses. The substance of what is being negotiated is the only real concern. Strategies employed are: 'what can I get?' The relationship between people in this approach is unimportant. The negotiators do not care about one another or what the other thinks about them as this may be interpreted as a sign of weakness which may be taken advantage of. The worst-case scenario of this approach is negotiators behaving aggressively and deceptively, using subterfuge to get what they want and ridding themselves of 'truth'. This is an approach that may just focus on the 'price'

- **Balanced negotiation** - This approach takes the middle way, balancing the use of elements from the competitive and collaborative approach. Negotiators struggle between the need to achieve their more immediate substantive goals while also keeping within their social norms and personal values, which will vary from society to society and culture to culture. It is important to understand the other negotiator's natural negotiating style, the boundaries within which they negotiate, so the negotiator can adapt their style to find an optimally effective solution

• ACTIVITY 7

What are the advantages and disadvantages of a win / win negotiation?

Professional styles
Used by seasoned negotiators and can be used in the following contexts:

- **Industrial relations** - Where confrontational bargaining is used. This is usually a highly charged situation which trade unions' negotiations are characterised by. Industrial negotiations are characterised by the overt use of power, threats and taking things to the edge, and over, with little use of gentle bargaining. Such negotiations may break down and have to resort to mediation and arbitration to reach a final settlement

- **Managing board negotiation** - Senior managers often have to negotiate among themselves for the limited resources of an organisation, e.g. budgets, employees. They must act together but they are also apart from one another in the departments that they must run. The style of negotiation of board members may be political using whatever forms of power a negotiator has working at this level of the organisation. Alliances and coalitions may be organised and favours are used to gain power and achieve goals. Open disagreement may be of benefit to the organisation in creating a healthy culture. Constructive criticism of alternative strategies can lead to a better way forward. This approach needs to be aware of the power plays that can be used to control negotiations and discredit other board members, which results in personal gain and company loss. Sometimes organisations indirectly reward this negative activity with bonuses

- **International negotiation** - Is about negotiation between countries. It also happens between individuals and companies. Large delegations will be well organised, where every person has specific expertise germane to the negotiation. In a complex negotiation, there may be multiple sub-negotiations going on at the same time. This type of negotiation can take a long time to negotiate due to the cultural sensitivities that need to be observed between opposing parties

- **Political negotiation** - Some political negotiation can take a friendly and collaborative approach; however, many negotiations are based on personal and political gains. Political negotiation makes most use of social power and a lot of horse-trading may take place before a final settlement is agreed

- **Selling and buying** - This may involve business-to-business negotiations and the role of the professional buyer, who is aiming to get the best deal available. Negotiators will be highly trained and have skills in negotiation

- **Hostage negotiation** - A hostage negotiation happens when a criminal or deranged person uses innocent people as bargaining chips. This is a highly complex form of negotiation which will have different characteristics from hostage situation to hostage situation

Contextual styles

Used in non-professional contexts where the people are not aware that they are negotiating or are not highly skilled at negotiation:

- **Domestic negotiation** - Includes all the negotiations that take place in the home environment, between partners, children or neighbours

- **Everyday negotiation** - Are negotiations people engage in every day. This can involve silent negotiations, e.g. walking along a street and avoiding others

- **Hierarchical negotiation** - Hierarchies may be domestic, in the home between parents / children; social, in the network of friends that surround people; and work related, where there are negotiations between the boss and the worker or the legal work contract and the psychological contract

- **Remote negotiation - This is
  negotiation** that does not take place
  face to face with the opposing
  party, e.g. telephone, email, letter.
  Agreement may be more difficult to
  achieve because negotiators are
  unable to check body language
  or use other elements of their
  communications skills optimally. It may take even longer to agree
  when using mediums of written communication, as each party waits
  for the other party to respond

Every negotiation situation will be different. The cornerstone of any
negotiation is doing the preparation and planning to give the negotiator
every opportunity of presenting their argument and responding to
the counter arguments presented by the opposing negotiating party
with expertise. It requires the negotiator to use the full gamut of their
interpersonal skills, foremost of which is communication. The negotiator
must be able to sum up and express their argument succinctly, clearly
and persuasively so the opposing negotiator is convinced to adopt the
counter argument.

At its heart, negotiation is about solving problems to the mutual
satisfaction of both negotiators. The negotiator needs to sufficiently
understand what the problem is to frame it in a way that it can be
resolved and its solution adopted into the final settlement of the
negotiation. This will also require the exercise of decision-making skills
throughout the negotiation.

Testing your knowledge

1. What are the four stages of the negotiation process?

2. Describe different kinds of negotiations

3. What should a negotiator remind themselves of at the opening of and throughout the negotiation?

4. What objectives should a negotiator aim to achieve during the bargaining phase of negotiation?

5. How can Pareto's 80 / 20 rule be used in the negotiation process?

6. What strategies should be avoided in a negotiation?

7. How can fear affect the negotiation?

8. What is negotiation style?

9. Compare and contrast the three styles of the belief-based styles of negotiation

10. What is the difference between belief-based and professional styles of negotiation?

11. Why are decision-making skills important in the negotiation process?

Skills

In your organisation you will be called upon to negotiate in many different ways and situations. These will range from very simple negotiation, e.g. 'If I work through lunch may I leave work early to get to a dental appointment?', to the more complex negotiation, e.g. agreeing the price of a product that you are hoping to sell. Some negotiations you will be able to agree independently without having to refer to your manager or other people with the specific expertise to help you. Some negotiations you will only be able to make in the company of others who will help you clarify the situation. In complex negotiations it is likely that you will be involved in the negotiation process, undertaking roles within the process rather than leading the negotiation, e.g. searching out relevant data and information that will allow the negotiation team and the lead negotiator to make the best decisions throughout the negotiation process. You will need to make sure that you source the correct information to help with the negotiation process. This should be translated in the most meaningful form so all members of the negotiating team will understand the importance of the information. It should be transparent and speak for itself. This information will form the basis for the negotiation brief from which all decisions about how to implement the negotiation process will be decided.

As a negotiator you will be expected to apply the following skills:

- Communication

- Leadership

- Decision-making

- Problem-solving

- Interrelationship

- Influencing

• ACTIVITY 8

What skills have you used to keep a negotiation running smoothly rather than getting bogged down in irrelevant detail? How would you apply these skills?

In preparation for the negotiation you will work with your team and decide what the purpose of the negotiation is - what are the objectives that you are seeking to achieve? This is a situation which is dependent on two sides reaching a decision which both parties will be happy with. As such, you and your team will only have half the story and you will need to interpolate from the information you have acquired what the other party potentially is aiming to achieve. Having this information will arm you and your team with the skills and knowledge to navigate your way through the negotiation process. You will need to identify what your minimum and maximum targets are - what are the possible trade-offs that you and the team are willing to accept? Consider the advantages and disadvantages of each trade-off and decide what you think is realistic. You should have agreed a number of alternatives from which you can trade-off and make concessions. This stage or preparation is very important to help all members of the negotiation team achieve a state of equilibrium where they can manage their emotions. Each negotiation situation is different and you may not know the different type of personalities that will be sitting opposite you throughout the negotiation process. You will not know the negotiation strategies that they are aiming to use, which may be opposite to what you and your team have agreed to employ. In all negotiation situations, never forget that if you need time to consider the impact of new and conflicting information, you can pause. You may also need this time to consult with your managers if you do not have the authority to make decisions at this stage of the negotiation process.

• ACTIVITY 9

How would you deal with an aggressive negotiator who keeps blaming you for all the problems happening in the negotiation?

Throughout the negotiation process you need to observe not only the members of the opposing party but yourself, so you keep your emotions in check. Always remain professional. What skills can you use to help facilitate the negotiation process? What do you do when you do not agree with someone's point of view? How do you persuade them of the merit of your position? How do you contribute to establishing a positive environment within which the negotiation process can operate? Are there alternative negotiating strategies you can use from the ones that have been agreed and when should they be employed? What can you do to keep the negotiation environment positive to facilitate a win / win settlement?

• ACTIVITY 10

What would you do if the negotiation was in stalemate?

You and the other members of your negotiating team are all in this together, so it will require a concerted effort on the part of all members of the negotiating team to accept collective responsibility for any decisions that have to be agreed. This is why it is so important to have a clear strategy, with alternatives as a back-up, when entering the negotiating process. As much as you have a plan, it can, and probably will, change throughout the negotiation process due to the dynamics of the opposing party. At all times behave with respect towards all group members, even those you are passionately opposed to. Behave with integrity and make sure your contributions to the decision-making process are ethical.

Throughout the negotiation process keep accurate records of what has been decided, as this is important when agreeing the final settlement and drawing up the contract, if relevant, so as to avoid misunderstandings.

Testing your skills

1. How have you been involved in the negotiating process in your current job?

2. What did you find difficult about your role in the negotiating process and how did you overcome this, if relevant?

3. How did you agree the objectives of the negotiations you were involved with?

4. How did you agree the bargaining strategies that you would employ throughout the negotiation process?

5. What problems did you encounter during the negotiation process? How were these resolved?

6. How did you use your skills to build a positive and constructive environment for the negotiating process?

7. How did you reach the final settlement of the negotiating process? What was your contribution?

8. How did you achieve a win / win settlement, if relevant?

Ready for assessment?
To achieve this Level 3 unit of a Business & Administration qualification, learners will need to demonstrate that they are able to perform the following activities:

1. Identified objectives to be achieved

2. Identified potential problems in negotiations and ways of overcoming them

3. Carried out negotiations within limits of own authority

4. Made proposals which met main objectives

5. Used negotiation strategies to obtain results that met minimum or agreed outcomes

6. Clarified other negotiator's understanding, and responded to their queries

7. Suggested solutions to deal with problems, if required

8. Referred the negotiation to others, when required

9. Carried out negotiations in a way that maintained goodwill and promoted a positive image of self and the organisation

10. Reached an agreement to the satisfaction of all those involved in the negotiations, where possible

11. Maintained records of the negotiations, if required

12. Completed negotiations in a way that maintained goodwill and promoted a positive image of self and the organisation

You will need to produce evidence from a variety of sources to support the performance requirements of this unit.

If you carry out the 'ACTIVITIES' and respond to the 'NEED TO KNOW' questions, these will provide some of the evidence required.

Links to other units

While gathering evidence for this unit, evidence **may** also be used from evidence generated from other units within the Business & Administration suite of units. Below is a **sample** of applicable units; however, most units within the Business & Administration suite of units will also be applicable.

QCF NVQ

Communications

Communicate in a business environment (Level 3)

Make and receive telephone calls

Core business & administration

Evaluate and improve own performance in a business environment (Level 3)

Solve business problems (Level 3)

Work in a business environment (Level 3)

Work with other people in a business environment (Level 3)

Contribute to decision-making in a business environment

Customer service

Deliver, monitor and evaluate customer service to internal customers

Deliver, monitor and evaluate customer service to external customers

SVQ

Communications

Plan how to communicate in a business environment

Core business & administration

Solve business problems

Review and maintain work in a business environment

Support other people to work in a business environment

Contribute to decision-making in a business environment

Customer service

Deliver, monitor and evaluate customer service to internal customers

Deliver, monitor and evaluate customer service to external customers

12 Solve business problems

SOLVE BUSINESS PROBLEMS

'**Solve business problems**' is an <u>optional unit</u> which may be chosen as one of a combination of units to achieve either a Qualifications and Credit Framework (QCF), National Vocational Qualification (NVQ) or Scottish Vocational Qualification (SVQ).

The aims of this unit are to:

- Understand business problems and their causes
- Understand techniques for solving business problems
- Understand factors that influence solutions to business problems
- Understand how to evaluate approaches to solving business problems
- Be able to recognise and analyse business problems
- Be able to plan and carry out own solution to business problems
- Be able to evaluate own solution to business problems

To achieve the above aims of this unit, learners will be expected to provide evidence through the performance of work-based activities.

Knowledge
Causes of business problems

A **business problem** occurs when there is an obstacle to achieving a desired objective. A business problem occurs when something that has been planned for has not happened as expected. Essentially, a business problem is about managing the effects of change. Business problems come in all shapes and sizes. As they can be very different from one another they required different approaches to resolve them. Business problems may be short, medium or long term. Some problems may contain problems within problems, from which the priority problem must be selected to be solved first. They will all require some form of decision-making; however, some business problems may not be solved, which will require a plan to be agreed with how to cope with this situation. It is clear that there is no one way to solve all problems. But a variety of approaches can be used to solve a business problem, depending on the type of problem to be solved. In analysing a business problem there are a number of tools that could be used to solve a problem.

The result of a business problem could have a positive or negative effect on a business, e.g. a business problem resulting in a negative effect would be if a delivery is going to be late due to a van breaking down. The customer tells the provider that they will take their business to another provider if they do not get the delivery on time. So the provider has various options to consider regarding how to solve the business problem:

- Get another driver to drive to the broken-down van

- Collect the parcel and deliver it to the customer

- Do nothing and lose the customer, which is not the best option

- Deliver the parcel late but agree with the customer to give them a full credit for the cost of the delivery or reimburse all costs as a result of the later delivery.

Something - a van breaking down - has got in the way of a planned situation - the delivery of a parcel - and this problem needs to be resolved. If the business problem is not resolved as soon as possible, it may become an even greater problem, a catastrophic business problem, e.g. the Enron scandal of 2001 in America, which resulted in Enron, and many other companies, closing down.

• ACTIVITY 1

What causes business problems?

Many business problems are more complex and easier to solve than the above example. With any business problem there may be a range of causes, and therefore time should be spent wisely on solving problems. There is no use spending many days solving an insignificant problem when there is a bigger, more demanding, problem to solve that demands an immediate response and a good solution. This principle is often expressed as the **80 / 20 rule**. Originally called the **Pareto Principle**, named after its inventor, for problem solving, this means that a few problems are vital - 20% - and many are trivial - 80%, so focus on the 20%, as these are the problems that really matter. Decide what business problems fall within the 20% and focus on solving these first.

A supervisor / manager may develop possible problem scenarios to help them develop a business plan. This would lead to a clearer picture of a business situation in order to minimise business problems from happening. Such **business forecasting** tries to minimise the level of disruption to a business.

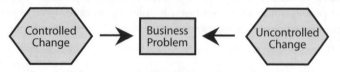

Figure 12.1. Cause of business problems: the winds of change

• ACTIVITY 2

What is the Pareto Principle and how does it provide a strategy for solving business problems?

Business is built around the **routinisation** of jobs. When business problems upset a routine they have a cost implication to a business, which all business strives to avoid. The cause of business problems are varied and many. To highlight just a few:

- **Uncontrolled change** - This occurs outside the control of the business. The business takes a reactive role in identifying what the business problem is and how best to solve it. These changes could come about through changes in government impacting on policy; legislation; environment; social upheaval; technology etc.

- **Controlled change** - This occurs as a result of a business re-evaluating an existing strategy or work plan etc. These changes could come either from within the organisation, e.g. the effects of change to other parts of a business that are looking at ways of becoming leaner, or from outside the organisation, e.g. deciding to launch a new product ahead of schedule when it hears that a competitor is about to launch a similar product

Each of these changes will upset the established routine for a plan of work. The plan of work, which would have included all tasks / activities that fell under the project, will have already been signed off, so an evaluation will have to take place to determine the effect of this change and see how much of a problem it may cause the business, so the business can resolve the business problem accordingly. When a business problem is found it is best to resolve it as soon as possible, so it does not increase costs to the business. A business problem will tend to maximise waste. One of the aims of business is to minimise waste through effective routinisation of work.

A problem understood is half solved.
- Albert Einstein

Identify a problem

Take a positive approach when solving a business problem. Approach the business problem with confidence and a desire to spend time and effort to find an appropriate solution to the business problem. To overcome or resolve a business problem, the business problem needs to be identified. Identifying or defining a business problem requires describing the business problem in detail. To identify the business problem, ask the following questions:

- What is the business problem?

- What happened?

- When did it happen?

- Where did it happen?

- How did it happen?

- Who was involved?

> Identify your problems, but give your power and energy to solutions.
> *- Anthony Robbins*

Write down what the business problem is. By writing the business problem down, it forces the problem-solver to think about the issues that need to be resolved. This could be achieved through a **brainstorming** session, which aims to promote a free flow of ideas. At this stage there should be no judgements about whether the idea (s) is good or bad, will work or will not work etc. It is important to create a relaxed environment to identify what the business problem is and collect lots of ideas. Analyse the current situation to understand why the business problem occurred:

- Check to make sure that the right questions to identify the business problem have been asked

- Make sure that there are no detours which only identify parts of the business problem

- Make sure that the business problem that has been identified is the correct one to solve

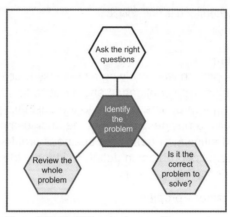

Figure 12.2. Identifying a business problem

The business problem needs to be explored in detail to identify what it is. This will help to determine which solution will be the most effective in resolving the business problem. Understand where the problem is coming from, how it came about, how it fits in with current developments and how it needs to be resolved - then solve it.

• ACTIVITY 3

What strategies would you use to identify a business problem?

Have a set of criteria to evaluate the proposed solution to see whether it is workable or not. Spend time analysing the business problem by reviewing the current situation and consider what needs to be changed. Continue to reassess the business problem so that it is still valid. People often discover that the business problem they really wanted to answer is very different from their original interpretation of it.

Symptoms and causes - analysing business problems
When analysing business problems agree what the **symptom** is and what the **cause** could be. Is a pain the problem, or is it a symptom of a more serious illness? Sometimes, the absence of a symptom may be just as significant as its presence. Having a pain from Monday to Friday, but not on Saturdays or Sundays, may identify its cause. The business problem must identify its cause or causes that will explain the symptoms. Understand all the known facts to deduce an underlying pattern. Generally, there will be a lot of solutions offered; however,

before deciding on a course of action, listen carefully to what is being suggested and then analyse the situation carefully before agreeing to a solution, as immediate solutions can be obvious or knee-jerk solutions may be highly inappropriate. Solutions can be expensive and time-consuming, so it would be prudent to make sure they are going to work and are the most appropriate solutions to carry out. In some cases the cause is known but the question may be what to do about it. There is always a choice of options to carry out. When looking at alternative options consider technical and human factors and risk. An analytical tools that can be used is:

Business process re-engineering (BPR) 20 questions

The process of rethinking through what a business does and how it does it. It accounts for all factors involved - cultural, technical, costs, skills, outcomes. There are many tools and techniques associated with BPR; however, a powerful tool is the '20 questions' tool. Identify a process and then proceed as follows:

1. **What** is being done? - what is being achieved

Why is it necessary?

What else could be done?

What else should be done?

2. **Where** is it being done?

Why there?

Where else could it be done?

Where else should it be done?

3. **When** is it done?

Why then?

When else could it be done?

When else should it be done?

4. **Who** does it?

Why this person/group?

Who else could do it?

Who else should do it?

5. **How** is it done?

Why this way?

How else could it be done?

How else should it be done?

It is important that the questions are asked in a sequence. Group 1 questions are asked first and group 5 questions are asked last. It is not important how the other groups are asked.

• ACTIVITY4

The following problems have been identified: the stationery cupboard is not easy to access and it does not provide all the resources required. There are a number of possible causes: sabotage, bad storage, long-term sickness, supplier delivered incorrect stationery items, pilfering of stock, small space, old stock and incorrect orders.

Pick one major problem and then list all the minor problems which contribute to this major problem.

1. Use cause and effect analysis to find solutions. Group the solutions into related sets and then organise them into a hierarchy. Or tabulate causes and effects using the words 'leads to' and 'caused by'. What is the best solution?

2. Use BPR 20 questions methodology to tackle the same problem.

The following checklist may be helpful when undertaking analysis to find solutions to business problems:

- Were any problems positively identified by managerial or supervisory staff?

- Is there any evidence of procedural difficulty?

- Are procedures and documentation satisfactory?

- Is there any duplication of effort or information?

- Are any processes redundant?

- Does the workload exhibit peaks and troughs? If so, are these in regular cycles?

- Are there bottlenecks in the system?

- Are any facilities underemployed?

- Are controls satisfactory?

- Would auditing the system be difficult?
- Does the system cope with exceptions?
- Are exceptions, inaccuracies and omissions excessive?
- Are files accurate and up to date? Do they need to be?
- If files are not up to date, what problems does this cause?
- Are there delays in the completion of work and in the production of information?

> When is a problem not a problem? When it becomes a challenge

Ways of solving business problems

As a result of identifying a business problem a number of solutions will have presented themselves. There may be a number of different ways of solving a particular business problem. When looking at different ways of solving a business problem, there is no fixed route to solving a business problem. Each business problem will be defined differently.

Create a number of solutions. Do not censor any of the possible solutions as they appear. Write them all down or, if brainstorming, use post-it notes and put these on a wall. If working in a group this should generate a number of possible solutions. Every solution is worthy of consideration. When making a decision about which way to solve a business problem, think about the following elements, as they will each have an impact on the way the business problem will be solved:

- **Time** - How long will it take? This will need to take into consideration the decision-making process to sign off the agreed way of solving the business problem

- **Resources** - How much resource - physical, human, technological - will be required?

- **Costs** - How cheap or expensive will it be?

- **Size of the solution** - What minimal solution will solve the business problem? How much of a compromise is the business willing to make?

- **Reputation** - What will be the impact on the business, both positive and negative?

- **Risks** - What will happen to the business if the business problem is not resolved?

Think about when a solution has to be signed off. Review the priorities about what must be done first to agree which solution should be adopted. If this is a solution that requires many parts to it, prioritise when each part needs to be accomplished. Use experience gained from other business problems to help shape thinking and see if past solutions or an adaptation of a past solution may solve the current business problem. Once all these elements have been agreed, plan how and when the business problem needs to be resolved.

Planning to resolve the business plan will require updating the original work plan, if it existed, depending on how large a piece of work is required as a result of solving the business problem. As with any business plan, agree what the purpose of the solution is aiming to achieve. Prioritise each stage of this work. Monitor each stage of the work to make sure it is achieving targets and objectives as agreed. Evaluate the success of the implementation of the solution to see if it has been effective in minimising a cost to the business.

> We can't solve problems by using the same kind of thinking we used when we created them.
> *- Albert Einstein*

Review and evaluate the problem-solving process
The dynamic of a problem can be very fluid and the causes / symptoms / issues of the problem that were first identified may have shifted, in essence, invalidating the problem-solving process that has been carried on. The solution will no longer be appropriate for solving that particular problem as the problem has changed. It is important to always review the work that is being carried when solving the business problem.

Plans may need to be reformulated to take account of changing factors. This should be done to minimise costs, resources and time and work within the accepted tolerances of the organisation and any appropriate legal framework that the business problem may impact on. As part of a continuing review process the following should be carried out:

- Identify that the cause (s) is current
- Identify a new cause (s) and a possible changed effect (s)
- Identify what has been learned from the process so far
- Identify alternative procedures that will solve the problem
- Monitor the effectiveness of decision-making in the process so far. This way? Or this way? Or this way?
- Identify an alternative that will solve the problem without causing other unanticipated problems
- Clarify that all individuals involved will accept the alternative
- Identify if the chosen alternative will be implemented
- Identify if the alternative fits within organisational constraints
- Identify procedures that will help to prevent similar problems in the future

Knowing when a business problem has been solved
The solution that resolves the business problem is often a compromise between conflicting needs. The successful solution to a business problem is the one that fits the ideal solution most closely. The successful solution will have optimised the required resources to resolve the business problem. The successful solution will have minimised any risks attached to the delivery of the solution. A business problem will be solved when it:

- Delivers the results that the solution promised to deliver
- Is able to deliver the benefits that the solution promised to deliver
- Has overcome all barriers to achieving the delivery of the solution
- Has been accepted by all the people involved in resolving the business problem, if more than one person was involved
- Has used available resources productively
- Has minimised the risks that the delivery of the business problem is aiming to achieve
- Meets legal and / or organisation policy
- Delivers the maximum acceptable result

Not all of the above may be appropriate in deciding when a business problem has been solved, as solutions will vary with the complexity of the business problem. A successful solution will be the one which will have maximised the advantages and minimised the disadvantages attached to the delivery of that solution, from all available solutions. For example, a successful solution may not impact on or be influenced by legal requirements.

• ACTIVITY 5

What are the best solutions to business problems?

A successful solution will be one that is methodical; is committed to solving the business problem; has used information accurately to solve the business problem, using analytical and creative thinking, and has made sure that it was effectively implemented.

Work with others to solve a business problem
Solving business problems can either take place individually or with a group of colleagues. In the latter context, this may happen **formally**, e.g. a meeting arranged to resolve a problem, or **informally**, e.g. a group of colleagues who meet when a problem comes up. At both formal and informal meetings, people share points of view until a consensus is agreed. Each member of the group will contribute towards resolving the business problem. When aiming to resolve a business problem it is best to use a group setting, as:

- A problem can be defined in many different ways

- Information about the problem is diverse

- It may be a specialised problem and a diverse approach may help to identify a solution

- The problem may impact on many different people

- There may be many different possible solutions to the business problem

- It may be a complex business problem

- A solution can only be implemented when it has been agreed to by others

The most suitable and relevant people should be involved in this process of sharing ideas.

Advantages of working with others:

- **Increased output** - The more people there are the more skills, knowledge and experience can be pooled to find a solution

- **Exchange of ideas** - Ideas are explored that may not have been considered by one person

- **Reduced bias** - A group can explore unrealistic ideas that personal prejudice may not have considered

- **Risk taking** - As more people are involved in the discussion, individuals are more willing to take risks in sharing their ideas

- **Commitment** - In a group, commitment is improved as a result of sharing a common purpose

- **Communication** - In a group, communication is improved due to the involvement and expertise this brings to the project

- **Better solutions** - A stimulating environment is created which encourages the discussion of diverse ideas which lead to more solutions and better solutions

Disadvantages of working with others:

- **Competition** - In a group, competition may undermine the problem-solving process because the perception of behaviours encourages negative behaviour

- **Conformity** - People will reduce their thinking to the agreed decisions, they will not want to upset the group or be seen as different

- **Lack of direction** - Where a meeting has been arranged with no effective direction in place to solve the business problem

- **Time** - Arranging a meeting can be a slow process. Having lots of different people adding lots of different ideas during the meeting can also take up valuable time

Problem-solving techniques

There are a number of well-known problem-solving techniques that are used within organisations. These techniques have established formal procedures for interrogating a problem and for solving it. They are planned approaches to solving problems. Some examples of problem-solving techniques are:

Appreciation
Developed by the military in the US, this is a drilling technique where the same question, '**so what?**' is continually asked until no more information can be extracted that will help to determine a solution to a problem. This is a very quick, efficient and reliable method.

Cause and effect diagrams or 'fishbone diagrams'
Used to focus on identifying the **cause** of a problem, these allow a deep exploration of every cause rather than the most obvious causes. This technique uses a hierarchy to rationalise the factors that contribute to the actualisation of a problem. Problems do not just happen - **cause** - and one thing leads to another - **effect**. It is a simple way of making sense out of what may be a confusing set of interrelated factors. It is a good technique to use with big problems or problems with complicated issues. An example of a 'cause and effect diagram' is an **Ishikawa diagram**. This technique uses **brainstorming** to gather information.

This is done in four steps:

1. **Identify the problem** - Write down the exact problem in a box on the left-hand side of a page. Draw a line from it across the page. This creates the spine of the fish and space to develop ideas either side of it

2. **Identify major factors** - Identify all the factors that added to the problem. Draw lines off the 'spine' for each factor and label them. Each factor looks like the bones of a fish

3. **Identify possible causes** - Identify possible causes that relate to each factor

4. **Analyse the diagram** - The diagram is complete, showing all possible causes of a problem. Investigate the most likely causes further. Use various tests to see if the assessments that have been made about the causes are valid

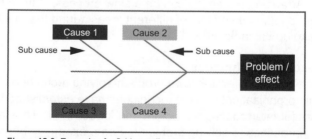

Figure 12.3. Example of a fishbone diagram

Affinity diagrams

Used to organise and make sense of a large amount of information as a result of interrogating a problem. An 'affinity diagram' is also known as the **'KJ method'**, after Kawakita Jiro, the Japanese anthropologist who developed it. This method looks at finding the relationships that exist between ideas.

Force field analysis

Used to analyse all the positive and negative forces acting on making a decision about a problem. This strengthens the forces supporting the decision and minimises the forces opposing the decision.

Edward de Bono, thinking tools

These tools have been developed by Edward de Bono, one of the world leaders on teaching thinking as a skill. Some tools he has promoted include:

Affinity Diagram

Figure 12.4. Example of an Affinity diagram

- **The APC tool** - This technique forces the mind to think about alternatives. Where A = Alternatives, P = Possibilities and C = Choices

- **The Ideal Solution method** - This technique lists the alternatives and then ignores them. This then identifies an 'ideal solution' and the 'alternatives' can be compared with the 'ideal solution'

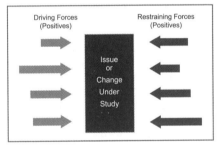

Figure 12.5. Example of a force field analysis diagram

- **The TEC framework** - A technique with strict time limits, e.g. five minutes. Where T = Target, E = Expand and Explore and C = Contract and Conclude. Using this technique focuses the mind to produce results

> Open your mind up to things that have no connection with the problem you're trying to solve: subscribe to an unusual magazine; spend a morning at an elementary school; go to work two hours early; test drive an exotic car; attend a city council meeting; try an Indonesian recipe.
> *Roger von Oech*

The reason for selecting any of the above problem-solving techniques will depend on either the type of problem that needs to be solved or the stage at which the business problem has had an effect on the plan of work. Most work within a business will be planned to achieve objectives. Once a business problem has been identified, and processes agreed to solve it, the problem-solvers must continue to review what has been resolved at each stage to solve the business problem. The process is circular. Checks should be made to make sure:

- What has been agreed is correct and still targets the identified business problem

- The alternative solutions address the identified business problem

- The chosen solution addresses the identified business problem

- The result of solving the business problem does actually solve the identified business problem

Any of the above problem-solving techniques can be used to review the approach taken to solve the business problem.

• ACTIVITY 6

Judith has been employed by the organisation for 20 years. She is continually late manning her post and, consequently, is never around when she is required to do a critical piece of work. She has a difficult personality and blames the transport system, her children, utilities going wrong in her house, not having a good relationship with her manager and having an uncomfortable chair and desk to sit at. She is the social secretary for the division and organises social events and the book club.

Use the scenario outlined above to answer the following questions:

1. What are the explicit business problems raised in the above scenario?

2. What is the most important business problem that has to be solved first?

3. Why has this business problem been given the highest priority to be solved?

4. What problem-solving techniques could be used to solve the business problems?

5. Who would need to be involved to resolve the most important business problem? Why?

Testing your knowledge

1. How does the type of business affect techniques that can be used to solve the problem?

2. What causes business problems?

3. How are business problems analysed?

4. What is brainstorming?

5. What are some of the problem-solving techniques created by De Bono? Explain when they could be used?

6. How could business plans be affected if the causes of the original business problem change during the analysis of the problem and its solution?

7. Why is it important to review the implemented solution of business problems?

8. How do we know if business problems are solved?

Skills

Something has gone wrong, or things have not gone entirely to plan. It is at this time when you might think there is a business problem. If the plan is to reach certain objectives at an agreed time, something needs to be done. However, nothing can be done until you identify that there is a problem and the nature of the problem before you can begin to solve it.

You have reviewed the situation and identified that there is indeed a business problem. What did you do to identify that a business problem existed? If something is not done to overcome the business problem, it could lead to even bigger business problems. You will now have to analyse why the business problem exists and identify the causes / symptoms / effects. You will need to separate these factors out to establish the true / real underlying cause of the business problem. Decide on the analytical tool that you would like to use to diagnose the business problem. Determine, from an initial review of the business problem, if it is something that you can handle on your own or if you will need the help of other people, including your supervisor / manager. Either option will have an impact on the way you go about identifying what the problem is. The more people involved in the process the more ideas are generated to help solve the business problem.

Your initial investigation is to discover what went wrong, why it went wrong and if there was anything that you could have done to prevent it from going wrong. Gather together as much information as you can about the problem - there can never be too much information. When did it happen? Who did it happen to? What happened exactly? How did it happen? Why did it happen? A business problem could be caused by technology, because of absences in the workplace or because the plan of work was not appropriate in the first place. There are lots of reasons why business problems happen. The trick is to minimise them by good work planning; however, things do happen over which no one has any control, e.g. a natural disaster. Does your business problem lie in the 20% of important business problems that should occupy your time and energy? How do you know that the business problem is in the 20% category?

If you are not sure how to approach solving the problem, ask colleagues or your supervisor / manager for advice and gather additional information. They may have the experience to help you. Use this help.

If there is an opportunity to work with others, take it. Learn from the experience and see how other people approach solving the business problem differently from you. Learn from this. Adopt and adapt what you find is most relevant to enhance your thinking in the future.

There are many different problem-solving techniques which can be used to solve business problems. Review possible choices of problem-solving techniques. If you are not sure of the value of using one technique rather than another, seek advice from your supervisor / manager. Work through the advantages and disadvantages of different problem-solving techniques. Once you have decided the problem-solving technique to use, begin your thinking from a very open position. Eliminate any preconceptions you may think of. If you have not fully identified what the problem is, preconceptions are only likely to send you down the wrong path and solve the wrong problem. There are many different ways of solving a business problem, which each business problem should help you to identify. Keep returning to what the business problem is to make sure your thinking is focused on resolving it and not some other business problem. From your analysis develop and justify the approach you are going to take to solve the business problem.

Plan how many people will be involved in the problem-solving working group. If having a brainstorming session, use post-it notes to jot down ideas. Collect the notes and start to categorise them. How will you categorise them? Which problem-solving techniques would be helpful for you to do this? It is important that no one makes any value statements about ideas; otherwise people will be reluctant to share their ideas. Judging ideas should not happen at the beginning of a thinking session. This is a time for letting all ideas to come to the surface. You still do not know what the solution is, so it would be premature to discount anyone else's ideas at this stage. After you have gathered a number of ideas you can select which ones you think will be most effective in solving the business problem. Get rid of the solutions that obviously will not work or are solutions for another problem. With the remaining solutions, analyse each one to see what the costs for implementing them will be to you, the team and the organisation. You will rarely work in isolation when solving a business problem, as you will want to take advice from people within the organisation who have come across a similar problem in the past. You will need to consider the impact the solution you have chosen will have. It has to meet the requirements of the plan of work and be of value to the organisation. The solution also has to remain current to the problem. Review the process you have taken to reach the proposed solution, identifying alternative solutions and confirming the solution will solve the problem.

Implement an action plan for resolving the business problem. Look at the knock-on effects of what this new plan will have to work practices. Agree these with the relevant stakeholders you are working with and, as appropriate, inform people of their new roles and responsibilities. Make sure people know why their roles / responsibilities are changing and make sure they review their new roles / responsibilities to make sure this is the correct course of action. If these people are unaware of the issues get them to review the new course of action, they might have a different perspective to add which has not been thought of before.

Always be disciplined and methodical in how you approach identifying and recognising when you think a problem has been solved. Solving a business problem is about minimising waste, and waste can be a costly factor. Waste can take different forms in terms of cost, resources, time etc. If working with a group of people, decisions that will be made will need to be agreed with by everyone or the majority view within the group. Be generous about this decision if it is not one that you agree with. Why do you not agree with it? Is the reason good enough to divert to an alternative solution? There will be other business problems which will not only be solved by you, but which you will influence in a group situation. Decide, with those you are working with to solve the business problem, how you think you will know when the business problem has been solved. Identify criteria appropriate to the specific business problem, use it as a checklist and keep returning to it to make sure you are still on the right course to solving the business problem appropriately. These criteria will vary from business problem to business problem.

Review the progress that is being made towards establishing the solution and the worth of alternative solutions. Always keep the problem in focus and remember that it is a dynamic concept open to change at any time. Monitor the conditions that surround the problem to make sure they still manifest the same causes and effects. Continue to evaluate the approach that is being taken in view of changing circumstances. Undertake a risk assessment of the chosen alternative to make sure it is cost-effective from every perspective. Evaluate the cost of implementing alternative solutions. Are they cheaper? What is the reason for not using alternative solutions?

Once the business problem has been resolved and the business plan is back on course, review the whole process of solving the business problem. Of the problem-solving techniques used, were they the best way of solving the business problem? If not, what ones would have been better? Why would they have been better? Were enough people involved in the brainstorming activities to solve the business problem?

Do not see what you want to see or expect to see, see what is really there, in context.

Testing your skills

1. How did you recognise when a business problem existed?

2. How did you identify it as a business problem?

3. What kind of information did you gather to help you identify what the business problem was?

4. How many other people did you discuss the business problem with?

5. Why did you work with the people you worked with when trying to resolve the business problem?

6. What contributions did you make to solve the business problem?

7. How did you analyse business problems?

8. Why did you use the problem-solving techniques that you used?

9. What criteria did you agree with others to recognise when a business problem was solved?

10. Did you have to agree your plan with someone or did you work alone?

11. Why did you work with the number of people you worked with to solve the business problem?

12. How effective was the support and feedback you got from others to help you solve the business problems?

13. What checks did you have in place to make sure progress was being made towards solving the correct business problem?

14. How did you review the approach to solving the business problem?

15. What lessons did you learn?

Ready for assessment?

To achieve this Level 3 unit of a Business & Administration qualification, learners will need to demonstrate that they are able to perform the following activities:

1. Recognised business problems

2. Confirmed own understanding of business problems

3. Identified reasons for business problems

4. Analysed business problems, having obtained additional information, as required

5. Worked with others to agree what the business problems were

6. Developed and justified an approach for solving business problems

7. Developed own plan to solve business problems

8. Identified ways of deciding when business problems were solved

9. Agreed own plan, with others as required

10. Carried out own plan to solve business problems, involving others as required

11. Used support and feedback from others to help reach a solution

12. Regularly checked progress towards solving business problems

13. Used feedback and progress reports to adjust the plan, as required

14. Confirmed business problems had been solved, with others as required

15. Evaluated own approach to solving business problems for their effectiveness

16. Evaluated own solution to business problems for their effectiveness

17. Evaluated alternative approach and solutions for possible effectiveness

You will need to produce evidence from a variety of sources to support the performance requirements of this unit.

If you carry out the 'ACTIVITIES' and respond to the 'NEED TO KNOW' questions, these will provide some of the evidence required.

Links to other units

While gathering evidence for this unit, evidence **may** also be used from evidence generated from other units within the Business & Administration suite of units. Below is a **sample** of applicable units; however, most units within the Business & Administration suite of units will also be applicable.

QCF NVQ

Communications

Communicate in a business environment (Level 3)

Make and receive telephone calls

Core business & administration

Evaluate and improve own performance in a business environment (Level 3)

Solve business problems (Level 3)

Work in a business environment (Level 3)

Work with other people in a business environment (Level 3)

Contribute to decision-making in a business environment

Negotiate in a business environment (Level 3)

Customer service

Deliver, monitor and evaluate customer service to internal customers

Deliver, monitor and evaluate customer service to external customers

SVQ

Communications

Plan how to communicate in a business environment

Core business & administration

Solve business problems

Review and maintain work in a business environment

Support other people to work in a business environment

Contribute to decision-making in a business environment

Contribute to negotiations in a business environment

Customer service

Deliver, monitor and evaluate customer service to internal customers

Deliver, monitor and evaluate customer service to external customers

13

Work with other people in a business environment

WORK WITH OTHER PEOPLE IN A BUSINESS ENVIRONMENT

'Work with other people in a business environment' is an optional unit which may be chosen as one of a combination of units to achieve either a Qualifications and Credit Framework (QCF), National Vocational Qualification (NVQ) or Scottish Vocational Qualification (SVQ).

The aims of this unit are to:

- Understand how to support an organisation's overall mission and purpose

- Understand how to work as team to achieve goals and objectives

- Understand how to communicate as a team

- Understand the contribution of individuals within a team

- Understand how to deal with problems and disagreements

- Understand the purpose of feedback when working as a team

- Be able to work in a team to achieve goals and objectives

- Be able to deal with problems in a team

- Be able to share feedback on objectives in a team

To achieve the above aims of this unit, learners will be expected to provide evidence through the performance of work-based activities.

Knowledge

The most essential ingredient that any organisation must have to succeed is to have a clear purpose for its existence. There are various purposes an organisation may have, e.g. a profit, to offer products and services to achieve financial returns, or not-for-profit, to organise and deliver social reforms; however, the purpose or an organisation will vary depending on the nature of the organisation.

An organisation is energised by its purpose when it is aligned to achieving specific goals. An effectively run organisation needs to have the following tools in place to identify how it will achieve its purpose:

- **Mission statement -** So its customers understand why it is delivering its business in a particular sector. A mission statement should address concepts such as the moral / ethical position of the business, its public image, its target market, its products / services, its geographic sphere and its expectations of growth and profitability

- **Vision statement** - So its customers understand where the organisation wants to be within certain timescales

- **Values statement** - Which sets out the behaviours that it will need to achieve its purpose

- **Strategies and business plans** - Which will set out how the organisation aims to achieve its purpose

- **Financial plans** - Which will set out the targets the organisations is aiming to achieve

• ACTIVITY 1

How can a mission statement and value statement be used to help achieve aims and objectives agreed within a job role?

These tools will identify for people whether they want to be a part of the business of a particular organisation, either as internal or external customers. They will also be motivated by an organisation's size, e.g. a multi-national company or a small business. An organisation's internal customers, their employees, will use these tools to decide if they want to work for this type of organisation. An organisation's most important resource is its employees. How an organisation organises it employees is integral to achieving its purpose.

At an **individual level**, employees will need to be aware of what it is they have been specifically selected and employed by the organisation to do. They will need to know how their role fits into the structure of the organisation, e.g. what department they work in and how this contributes to achieving the organisation's goals. An employee will need to establish what it is they need to do on a day-to-day basis, what they are responsible for and the limits of authority they have for achieving their responsibilities. There will be specific **policies and procedures** that an employee will need to follow, e.g. human resource policies covering diversity and 'equal opportunities' in the workplace. Policies and procedures are an employee's compass for navigating the behaviours that they will need to adapt to or adopt as they work within the culture of the organisation. As an employee is always implementing and working with an organisation's policies and procedures, they have first-hand knowledge of how effective these policies and procedures are. As such, an employee can provide feedback to their supervisor / manager about what is not working as effectively as it could or should do and offer some recommendations to improve them. Such feedback may impact on an organisation's mission statement or value statement. As with all aspects of life in an organisation, it is fluid and should respond to the demands of the workforce supplying goods and services to different types of customers outside the organisation.

Mission and value statements provide the blueprint for employees to understand what the organisation is aiming to achieve and how it aims to achieve its agreed missions. Employees are ambassadors of an organisation and are expected to fulfil the promise the organisation gives its customers. Employees are the front line for making sure that an organisation delivers on its promises. Employees should utilise the values espoused by their organisation to protect, promote and improve their organisation's reputation and image in the wider community. There may be many images an organisation promotes, e.g. vehicle livery, uniforms, shop displays etc., through the services it supplies. Employees will need to keep up to date with changing organisational images to make sure they promote them in the appropriate way. An employee is always on show and someone is always observing how employees perform and behave, whether on purpose, e.g. mystery shoppers, appraisals, or by accident.

 At a **collective level**, no employee works independently. Most employees will be organised into teams to achieve specific objectives. An employee may be a member of more than one team at any one time, which is increasingly the case as organisations opt to work within the principles of **matrix-management**, e.g. a member of the production team carrying out stocktaking while working with the management team to arrange for additional staff to help. There are many different types of teams which can be established within a business, which may have two different timescales:

Temporary
- **Task Force - functional teams -** Formed to investigate a specific issue or problem. Usually from the same hierarchical level within the organisation

- **Problem-solving Team -** Formed to solve a specific problem. Usually 5-12 employees who meet to improve quality, efficiency and the work environment, e.g. an HR group

- **Product Design Team** - Formed to design a new product or service
- **Committee** - Formed to act on some matter

Permanent
- **Work Group** - A group that receives direction from a specific leader

- **Work Team or Self-Directed Work Team / Self-Managed Work Team** - An ongoing group who share a common mission, collectively managing their own affairs within agreed parameters. Usually 10-15 employees who are usually self-selected and evaluate each other's work

- **Quality Circle** - Which is a group from the same functional area who meet regularly to uncover and solve work-related problems and seek work improvement opportunities

• ACTIVITY2

What function does a quality circle provide for an organisation?

All of these different types of teams may also be organised into **virtual teams**. Virtual teams allow members of a team to function online without the hindrance of geography or time constraints. However, they have the disadvantage of not allowing team members to observe non-verbal communication.

Employees come together and are organised to work in teams to achieve something much bigger and work more effectively than would be achieved by working independently as an individual. Working in a team provides the opportunity to bring together different strengths, which can compensate for different weaknesses. Strengths and weaknesses present a strong 'synergy' of individual contributions from each team member: experience, expertise, knowledge, skills, personalities etc., which are focused towards achieving the same short, clear team aims and objectives.

A team's aims and objectives should be managed so that they:

- Clearly identify who is doing what, by when, and avoid the conflict of overlapping authority

- Build trust within the team by creating an atmosphere of honesty and openness

- Involve the whole team in the decision-making process, which will promote a sense of ownership from within the team. Ownership will lead to commitment to the team's aims and objectives

- Identify clear lines of communication so all members of the team are kept fully informed

• ACTIVITY 3

What should be done if a team's aims and objectives are no longer appropriate for the completion of a project?

There are many rewards to be achieved from working as a team; however, it also presents many challenges. There are many opportunities for problems, e.g. different personalities may cause problems or similar personalities may start vying to dominate the team. Even if aims and objectives are clear, there may be lack of agreement on how they will be achieved; there may be little trust within the team which blocks communication and can lead to loss of coordination by individual team members etc. For a team to work effectively and achieve positive results it needs to have a good leader who can bring the above elements together.

As teams are a collective of individuals, it is important that each member of the team recognises how they can support the achievement of the team's aims and objectives. This can be done through:

Communication
Communicate, communicate and communicate! A team member can never communicate enough. A team member should not isolate themselves by bottling up unexpressed emotions / ideas / problems, as this will undermine both themselves and what the team is aiming to achieve. Make points by being assertive rather than aggressive. Effective teams are those where all team members feel able to talk to each other openly whenever they have anything to say, and in a positive environment of mutual trust. Team members will communicate using a combination of:

- **Written communication -** Written forms of communication will be used to set out ideas about how the team is going to achieve its goals, agree plans, set up milestones so team members know what is expected of them etc.

- **Verbal communication** - Verbal communication uses the spoken word; however, team members will also take cues from non-verbal communication - what the body is saying when speaking, e.g. gesturing, posture. Team members should be aware of how they use their voice, e.g. volume, pitch, tone. Communication is a two-way process. It is important to **actively listen** to what other team members are saying. Clarify meaning by asking questions, either **closed**, usually receive a 'yes' or 'no' response, or **open**, usually do not receive a 'yes' or 'no' response, questions depending on what the team member is aiming to understand

• ACTIVITY 4

What is 'active listening'?

Working effectively with people is a skill that team members will need to do all the time. This is true not only of working in a team but also working with anybody else inside or outside of the organisation. Cooperating with others creates a harmonious work environment which enables team members to achieve more, which makes work more enjoyable.

> Speak up, speak out, but do not speak down!
> Write up, write out, but do not write off!

• ACTIVITY 5

What are the major differences between verbal and oral communication?

Taking responsibility
Eliminate 'blame' from a team's vocabulary. Identify a delay or assist a team member who might be delayed so it becomes a shared responsibility of the team to overcome.

Supporting team members' ideas
Take account of other team members' ideas rather than discount them out of hand, as this shows interest not only in individual members of the team but in the team ideal.

Framing the context of how the team will work

Team members should recognise that they are not working alone. They are working interdependently with other members of the team. Team members should show respect to other members by attending team meetings on time - implement the principles of good time management - and always be prepared to contribute positively to the aims of the meeting. If a team member is going to be late they will need to let another member of the team know. Team members should behave positively, as being in a team creates a new culture of working. Team members will have different attitudes, behaviours which need to be appreciated, understood and worked with. All members of a team will modify their behaviour appropriately towards other members of the team. Agree to offer criticism in a positive fashion by being polite.

Humility

Team members should be discrete rather than conceited about the success of their contribution to the team's achievements. Avoid creating tension in the team by recognising that other team members will know when individual team members are doing well.

Active involvement

Share suggestions, ideas, solutions and proposals with team members. Take the time to help fellow teammates, no matter what the request.

• ACTIVITY 6

What is the purpose of 'active involvement' and why is it important to achieving a cohesive team?

There is no employee working in any organisation who has not at some time in their life been a member of a team, e.g. they will have been a member of a family or played sports where they were a team member. The whole organisation is one big team that should override any internal divisions between departments. When people work effectively together the business will thrive. If people are working against each other it will cause friction and nothing effective will be achieved. If passing a telephone that is ringing and there is nobody else free to answer it, pick it up and take a message. The truly great teams are those that are committed to excellence in everything they do. The goal is to achieve at the highest level; a commitment which is sustained by all members of the team and at every level of the team.

From the outset of the formation of a team, the level of quality the team is aiming to achieve should be agreed by all members of the team. The team should know how they work with one another and take care of each other. Team members need to be perceptive, empowering and innovative by setting achievable goals for each member of the team and agree ways of getting there so the whole team has the same expectations. A team should aim to link what needs to be achieved by their team to the overall goals of what the organisation is aiming to achieve. Celebrate the **diversity** that the members of a team bring to the composition of a team and use those different skills and knowledge to help team **growth and support** one another. Above all, keep the communication channels open at all times. As expressed previously, team members can never communicate too much or listen too much.

Diversity

Employment no longer caters for a clearly defined single group of people. It is a mix of people from different races, nationalities and religions. When people from diverse backgrounds enter an organisation they bring with them their experience of different cultures and values. **Diversity** refers to the different human qualities exhibited from different groups of people. Diversity in the workforce means employing people without discrimination on the basis of gender, age and ethnic or racial background. Diversity also relates to issues of:

- Disability

- Religion

- Job title

- Physical appearance

- Sexual orientation

- Nationality

- Multiculturalism

- Competency

- Training

- Experience

- Personal habits

Diversity is to be valued because it adds richness to an organisation. However, it also adds challenges. Policies and procedures in organisations should focus on developing effective working relationships with a diverse workforce. To achieve effective working relationships in a diverse community of people, an organisation needs to focus on similarities rather than differences. Building relationships from within a diverse community of people is critical for the success of any organisation in the 21st century. Different points of view can be invaluable to an organisation as they can provide opportunities that a business may not have considered in the past. An organisation with a diverse workforce has a greater pool of experiences to work with to produce ideas for products that cater to different cultures.

Employees working in an organisation should respect, honour and appreciate the differences that a diverse workforce can add to help achieve the goals and ambitions of any organisation of any size. It is important to acknowledge similarities and likenesses to foster an understanding and appreciation of diversity in the workplace. There are a number of strategies that can be used to increase sensitivity towards the needs of others in an environment which encourages diversity:

- **Increase awareness of what others might be experiencing** - Be careful not only about the words used, but also about not saying anything at all. Be thoughtful and tactful about expressing awareness of another employee's actions and reactions or of others' actions or reactions

- **Do not assume** - It makes an ass of 'u' and 'me'. Assumptions are often mistaken because we rarely understand the complexities of another person's life. Avoid labelling a person, but imagine why they act the way they do or say the things they do

- **Respect others** - A person's status - marital, financial or social - does not define them, so it should not determine the way people are treated. If an employee feels irritated by other team members they should stop themselves saying anything. They should think to themselves that there is a reason this person is acting the way they are acting, and that they should respect how they feel at the moment, even if it bothers them

- **Show understanding and avoid gossip**

- **Resist taking offence** - Everyone deals with something difficult and we all have weaknesses. Some deficits are more obvious than others, but everyone must overcome some obstacles. Help to build each other up

- **Empathise - Do not let one encounter ruin the perception of that person**
  For example, just because someone seemed to be in a bad mood when spoken to, that does not mean they are constantly angry and depressed

- **Do not let your insecurities or beliefs get in the way** - For example, it is common to meet people with different beliefs, likes and dislikes than you, so do not be put off if the person you are talking to does not like something you do, or likes something you do not

The benefits that can be derived to the business / organisation as a result of promoting and managing diversity in the workplace include:

- Incorporating other groups of people into jobs which may have been selected from people of a certain ethnicity or gender

- Creating a workplace that is more functional and able to adapt quickly to market conditions

- Creating a workplace that understands the multiple cultures and beliefs of customers, allowing for a targeted service

- Employees taking the benefits home with them, which they can use to increase their understanding of relationships in their private life recognising and celebrating the differences which exist in different backgrounds

- Increasing productivity and profitability from investing in a larger pool of talent, which can provide a competitive edge in a business / organisation

- More innovative and creative ideas are a distinct result.

- Lowering absenteeism rates

- Lowering employee turnover costs and decreasing liability in discrimination lawsuits

- Reflecting current business expectations and their environment, as it represents different populations

- Increasing marketplace understanding

- Improving global relationships

There used to be many parliamentary acts that covered discrimination in its many forms. However, from October 2010 all of these acts will be subsumed into one act, called the **Equality Act 2010**. The Equality Act aims to:

- Provide a new cross-cutting legislative framework to protect the rights of individuals and advance equality of opportunity for all
- Update, simplify and strengthen previous legislation
- Deliver a simple, modern and accessible framework of discrimination law which protects individuals from unfair treatment and promotes a fair and more equal society

The provisions in the Equality Act will come into force at different times to allow time for the people and organisations affected by the new laws to prepare for them. The Equality Act will introduce new laws to help narrow the gender pay gap and strengthen anti-discrimination legislation. It will also consolidate the numerous pieces of existing discrimination legislation into one act. The Equality Act is the most far-reaching discrimination legislation for years which:

- Will allow employers to take further positive action in favour of women and minorities at the recruitment and promotion stage
- Gives wider powers to employment tribunals
- Bans 'gagging clauses' on pay
- Will require some organisations to publish diversity and gender pay statistics

The Equality Act has 16 parts:

- Part 1 Socio-economic inequalities
- Part 2 Equality: key concepts
- Part 3 Services and public functions
- Part 4 Premises
- Part 5 Work
- Part 6 Education
- Part 7 Associations
- Part 8 Prohibited conduct: ancillary
- Part 9 Enforcement
- Part 10 Contracts etc.
- Part 11 Advancement of equality
- Part 12 Disabled persons: transport

- Part 13 Disability: miscellaneous
- Part 14 General exceptions
- Part 15 Family property
- Part 16 General and miscellaneous

The Equality Act replaces previous legislation which covered age, race, gender, disability etc., in such acts as:

- **The Sex Discrimination Acts 1975 & 1986**
- **Race Relations Act 1976**
- **Disability Discrimination Act 1995**
- **Employment Rights Act 1996**
- **Employment Equality Regulations 2003**
- **Employment Equality (Age) Regulations 2006**
- **Health and Safety at Work Act 1974**

Team composition
Successful teams are made up of diverse people with complementary abilities. In all teams there will be a leader, although they may not have been appointed as such. In fact, the leadership role may change from member to member depending on the situation. Leadership depends on power, which can be found in different people in different situations and at different times. Other roles within the team will involve:

- **The innovator** - Who comes up with new ideas
- **The peacemaker** - Who mediates between people
- **The coordinator** - Who takes the ideas and gets on with achieving the team's goals
- **The analyst** - Who keeps the team on track and sees the overall picture
- **The dissenter** - Who disagrees with the majority view and keeps the team open-minded

• ACTIVITY 7

What is the difference between team members who are described as 'analysts' and 'innovators'? How can each role advance the aims and objectives of a team?

A team member may take on more than one role while working in a team. A team member may also change roles as the team grows. It is important for team members to recognise what their specific abilities are, and the abilities of other team members so they can be used where they are most effective to achieve the team's goals. Team members must be supportive of the diversity that the team is composed of. Differences can bind a team together, with each team member contributing positively with their skills to achieving the team's goals. Team members can **empower** one another to succeed by recognising other team members' skills and celebrating them as a team when milestones are achieved. In some organisations teams are organised competitively to motivate the team members to achieve goals. This needs careful handling as it can have a negative effect. Team members can become demotivated if their team is consistently unsuccessful, or if teams do not cooperate with each other in an attempt to 'win'. However, regardless of why teams are formed, they will all focus on achieving team goals.

> A team with a star player is a good team, but a team without one is a great team.
> - *Author unknown*

Team problems

Teams will be organised to achieve specific purposes; however, despite how well they may be organised and constituted, problems will arise. If there is a clear plan of how the team is going to achieve its goals, it should be able to anticipate difficulties before they happen and work out a solution so that the difficulty does not become a problem. Approach problem-solving by identifying what the problem is, why it happened, what should be done to resolve it, implement the problem-solving initiative and then evaluate the outcome of the implementation. Team members may approach problems to do with:

- Clash of team members' **personalities**

- **Goals not clearly defined**

- Team **responsibilities not clearly defined**

- **Changing circumstances** of the organisation

- **Poor leadership**

- Team members having **insufficient skills and knowledge** to do what they have been tasked to achieve

- **Insufficient time** to complete tasks

- **Poor communication** as a result of misunderstandings. These problems should be tackled by direct communication with the team member involved. If the problem is too difficult, a supervisor / manager should be consulted

- **Lack of motivation.** Team members should keep focused on what they need to achieve and contribute positively to the team going forward. Seek assistance when required and offer assistance if fellow team members require help

- **Poor feedback.** It is important that all members of the team know whether they are meeting those objectives or not. Team members should be aware of how well they are performing within the team and meeting expectations. Feedback encourages team members to give of their best by making sure of mutual satisfaction and improvement. Feedback should provide the team members with information on their strengths and weakness which is fair and offered without bias or favouritism. Feedback is given to reward team members with praise and identify any development opportunities which a team member should do. Areas of feedback to team members may cover their approach to how they have:

  - Achieved team goals

  - Taken ownership of their responsibilities

  - Worked collaboratively with others

  - Added value to the achievement of the team's goals

  - Managed their time to achieve team goals

  - Communicated with others, within and outside the team

  - Been committed to achieving the team goals

• ACTIVITY 8

Why should problems that occur in a team be resolved as quickly as possible?

Give and receive feedback

Feedback is information that is structured to be delivered to team members about the impact and implications of their team performance. Good-quality feedback is an important ingredient in building constructive relationships and in getting jobs done well. Feedback helps team members to maximise their potential, raise awareness of strengths and weaknesses and areas for improvement and identify the actions that need to be taken to improve performance. Feedback is given to confirm that team members are meeting the aims and objectives of the team. Feedback can come from a number of sources:

- Supervisors / managers
- Team leaders
- Colleagues / team members
- Other people working in a project
- Customers

Feedback can be either **informal** - a discussion between a supervisor / manager and their team members - or **formal** - part of an appraisal interview. Feedback is a valuable tool both for team members and the person providing feedback. Team members may think they are doing well and have no areas that they need improving - this rarely happens, except in the mind of the team member - but there is always something that can be improved. If feedback is not offered to a team member it may send a message that the team or project leader does not care, which can lead to a loss of commitment and undermining of trust in the work of the team. Feedback is offered to:

- **Influence** someone to change their approach
- **Recognise and reward** effort
- **Improve the quality** of work
- **Build and maintain relationships**
- **Clarify expectations**
- **Motivate**

Feedback can take different forms:

Formal

- **360-degree feedback** - This is where managers, colleagues, customers etc., all give feedback, often anonymously and in writing

- **Mentoring** - This is a partnership between two people - mentor and mentee - which is based upon mutual trust and respect to support and encourage team members to manage their own learning to maximise their potential, develop their skills, improve their performance and become the person they want to be. It is a powerful personal development and empowerment tool. The mentor is a guide who helps the mentee to find the right direction and develop solutions to career issues and progression. The mentor helps the mentee to believe in themselves, which boosts their confidence and provides guidance and encouragement. The mentee can explore new ideas in confidence, giving them the chance to look more closely at themselves, their issues, opportunities and what they want in life

- **Coaching** - This is an equal partnership, where the person being coached sets goals and the coach coaches them to find the best way to reach their goals. Coaching is not about giving advice or telling someone what to do. It is about offering more questions than answers, challenging the person being coached to consider new perspectives and different approaches at work. A coach is a facilitator, who focuses on helping another person to excel. It is a journey towards self-discovery and self-improvement. A coach may use questionnaires, feedback from co-workers and direct observation of team members in their work environment to assess their contributions to the way they work in a team. The coach will then, through one-to-one coaching sessions, challenge the team member with hard and uncomfortable questions to increase their self-awareness and lead them to new insights about their own behaviour. A coach does not tell the employee how to do things

Informal

- **Mentoring**

• ACTIVITY 9

Why is feedback given to team members?

Feedback should be welcomed and encouraged. The important thing about feedback is that it should be constructive and be offered from a credible person, a person that is respected by the team members. Many organisations work with the principles of matrix management, so feedback may come from a number of different people within the organisation. Encouraging feedback sends a signal to the supervisor / manager and the organisation that the team member:

- Cares about what they are doing

- Is interested in cultivating an approach to improving the way they and the team works

- May have talent that needs to be nurtured and grown

- May be considered for promotion

- Could be given more demanding work to do which would stretch them

- May want to develop a career within the business

The empowered team members must determine how often and with whom they are going to encourage feedback from. Feedback is only one form of the objectives that a team member must achieve in their work.

> Feedback is the breakfast of champions.
> *- Ken Blanchard*

It is good for team members to hear where they have done well, but it is more constructive when they hear where there are areas that they can improve their performance. This will help them to gain confidence and give them the will to improve. Feedback should provide team members with a full summary of how things can be improved, explaining:

- The task

- The skills, knowledge and attitude / behaviour that were required to complete the task

- Why the task had to be done that way

- Where team members did not meet these requirements - the gaps

Once team members fully understand this, a learning plan can be agreed to bridge the gaps. Feedback can improve team members' confidence, self-awareness and enthusiasm for learning. Good feedback should be:

- Descriptive - set out expectations
- Focused on performance
- Clear and direct
- Balanced
- Specific
- Timely
- Regular
- Able to offer a solution

• ACTIVITY 10

What is the best form of feedback to give and receive for team members?

Barriers to feedback

Feedback is not always easy to receive. The feedback may be perceived as being based on incorrect assumptions. Both parties involved in the feedback process will need to work through negative perceptions. Receiving corrective feedback may be difficult because team members may:

- Want to rationalise what went wrong - as they may feel uncomfortable about the situation
- Feel their self-worth is undermined by suggestions for improvement
- Have had previous experiences where feedback was unhelpful or unjustified

Be realistic about the feedback process. It is not always an easy experience for anyone. So be wary of:

- Being defensive
- Trying to prove the person giving feedback is wrong
- Justifying the original performance
- Dismissing the feedback
- Attacking the speaker
- Feeling something has to be done to change your whole self

- Feeling helpless to do anything about what has been feedback
- Generalising the message and feeling bad about everything or feeling perfect about everything

Improve the feedback process by:

- Using questions to find out the issues behind the criticism
- Being clear about what would help
- Helping the person giving the feedback understand what is wanted

To overcome problems always look to what it is the team is aiming to achieve. A team is never static; a team will evolve and build on itself as a result of the normal elements of change that are experienced in an organisation. Team building is a never-ending process which builds on the success of a team and recognises its weaknesses and overcomes them by taking action. As a team, always focus on producing work to the required standard and by the agreed deadlines.

Testing your knowledge

1. What is it important to know what the purpose of an organisation is?

2. Why are 'mission' statements written?

3. Why is it important to promote 'organisational values' to external customers of an organisation?

4. What are the different types of images an organisation displays?

5. Why is it important to have a positive attitude?

6. How should a team member receive difficult advice and feedback?

7. What are the important factors involved in building a successful team?

8. Why are the best teams made up of a diverse group of people?

9. What are the different types of questions that can be used to illicit information?

10. Describe the different roles a team can be made up from.

11. What is the difference between mentoring and coaching?

Skills

You should be aware of the purpose of your organisation. Your team goals should be aligned in some way to the overall organisation purpose. Gather together information about your organisation's mission statement, value statement and any other business plans that you may have access to. Discuss these with team members as well as your supervisor / manager if you need to clarify your understanding. The mission and values of the organisation should be developed as part of your behaviour - there will be some changes that you will need to consider to work effectively in the culture of whatever organisation you work in. Every organisation will have a different culture - the way they do things differently from other organisations. Some will be explicit, like the expectations that will come from the policies and procedures you need to implement, but others will be implicit, which you will observe as you work with colleagues and different team members. These behaviours should not only be exercised within the organisation but also to external customers. If you are not sure about organisational policies and procedures, check with your supervisor / manager. These policy documents will help you to promote the image of the organisation and protect its reputation. As you implement the policies and procedures that fall out of the mission and value statement, remember that you are not just a robot blindly doing what you are told to do. Look at what you are doing and consider if there are more effective ways of carrying out the tasks you have been commissioned to carry out. Think about alternative ways of working and recommend these to your supervisor / manager.

• ACTIVITY 11

Review your ability to develop productive working relationships with your line manager. Agree an action plan to improve your own and your team's performance.

The most important function a team should accomplish is agreeing on what it is aiming to do and identifying how each team member will contribute towards achieving the goal (s). Once you have been assigned your role within the team, check:

- Who the leader of the team is and the chain of command

- The programme of meetings

- What exactly you have to do

- When you need to achieve the allotted tasks

- How you need to complete the tasks - the standard and level of excellence you should be working towards achieving

- Who you will be working with specifically on your tasks, if anyone

- Who to report to in the event of problems, if you cannot resolve them yourself

- The budget you will work with, if appropriate

Your first task should be to consider how you can contribute positively to achieving the goals for which the team has been assembled. Continue to work collaboratively - find opportunities to support others, not only to be of help but to increase your learning of the team's project - clearly, concisely and to add value to the tasks you have been asked to complete. Being in a team is an opportunity to do a stocktake of your skills and knowledge. Are you equipped to complete the tasks for the team that you have been asked to complete? Find learning opportunities to advance your skills and knowledge when in a team.

Perhaps the greatest skill to use in a team to help it work more effectively is using good communication skills. Improving your communication skills is a timeless experience, as there are always opportunities that can be found that will challenge the way you need to respond positively, and if not positively, adopting a tone that projects a caring attitude to the different forms of communication that you will receive.

Being a member of a team means that you will no longer be working alone. You will be working with different people, with different skills and knowledge, personalities, behaviours, attitudes etc. It will be a diverse environment which you will need to be a part of. Rather than consider the differences that may separate members of a team, consider the differences that may pull the team together. Diversity in a team is something to be celebrated. It is an opportunity to learn different ways of thinking and approaching your work which may be more effective than what you have normally done in the past. If problems or disagreements occur when working in a team, communicate what they are and aim to resolve them. If you cannot resolve problems or disagreements by yourself, work them out within the team, or if the problem is of a sensitive nature, discuss the problem with either your team leader or your supervisor / manager.

Working as a member of a team is a great learning opportunity, as you will be working with lots of different people who will do things differently from you. Learn from differences. Make sure you are receiving feedback on the quality of your performance. This should form part of your appraisal process, if your organisation carries out this function. Always try to find ways of improving how you work in an organisation so as to be meaningful and add value.

• ACTIVITY 12

Draw a diagram showing your internal and external networks of contacts within and outside the organisation. Draw lines to make connections between these stakeholders. Where do you see weaknesses within your network of contacts and how could you improve them?

Testing your skills

1. What are the organisational policies and procedures that you must work with to achieve the goals of your team?

2. What roles have you played in the teams you have been a member of?

3. How do you contribute to the agreement of your team's goals?

4. How do you work sensitively and supportively with other team members?

5. What skills and knowledge have you used to achieve the tasks you have been given in your team?

6. How have you dealt with diversity working in your team?

7. How do you deal with disagreements between team members?

8. What has empowered you when working in a team?

9. How do you accept negative feedback?

10. What communication have you given which was misinterpreted? How did you resolve this?

11. How do you agree quality measures with your team?

12. What do you do if someone is not supporting the achievement of the team's aims and objectives?

Ready for Assessment?
To achieve this Level 3 unit of a Business & Administration qualification, learners will need to demonstrate that they are able to perform the following activities:

1. Worked in a way that supported your organisation's overall mission

2. Followed policies, systems and procedures relevant to your job

3. Contributed to improving objectives, policies, systems, procedures and values in a way that was consistent with your role

4. Put your organisation's values into practice in all aspects of your work

5. Sought guidance from others when unsure about objectives, policies, systems, procedures and values

6. Communicated effectively with other people in a team

7. Shared work goals, priorities and responsibilities with a team

8. Agreed work objectives and quality measures with a team to achieve a positive outcome

9. Made sure work goals and objectives were achieved in a way that made best use of all abilities in a team

10. Provided support to members of a team, as required

11. Showed respect for individuals in a team

12. Made sure the team produced quality work on time

13. Identified problems or disagreements in a team

14. Resolved problems or disagreements, referring them if required

15. Shared constructive feedback on achievement of objectives with a team

16. Received constructive feedback on own work

17. Shared feedback on achievement of objectives to identify improvements in own work and that of the team

You will need to produce evidence from a variety of sources to support the performance requirements of this unit.

If you carry out the 'ACTIVITIES' and respond to the 'NEED TO KNOW' questions, these will provide some of the evidence required.

Links to other units

While gathering evidence for this unit, evidence **may** also be used from evidence generated from other units within the Business & Administration suite of units. Below is a **sample** of applicable units; however, most units within the Business & Administration suite of units will also be applicable.

QCF NVQ

Communications

Communicate in a business environment (Level 3)

Develop a presentation

Deliver a presentation

Core business & administration

Manage own performance in a business environment (Level 3)

Evaluate and improve own performance in a business environment

Solve business problems (Level 3)

Work with other people in a business environment (Level 3)

Contribute to decision-making in a business environment

Contribute to negotiations in a business environment

SVQ

Communications

Communicate in a business environment

Develop a presentation

Deliver a presentation

Core business & administration

Plan how to manage and improve own performance in a business environment

Review and maintain work in a business environment

Solve business problems

Support other people to work in a business environment

Contribute to decision-making in a business environment

Contribute to negotiations in a business environment

14

Supervise a team in a business environment

SUPERVISE A TEAM IN A BUSINESS ENVIRONMENT

'Supervise a team in a business environment' is an <u>optional unit</u> which may be chosen as one of a combination of units to achieve either a Qualifications and Credit Framework (QCF), National Vocational Qualification (NVQ) or Scottish Vocational Qualification (SVQ).

The aims of this unit are to:

- Understand the purpose and benefits of teamwork

- Understand the purpose of communication in teams and how to do so

- Understand the purpose of planning work with teams and how to do so

- Understand the value of people in a team and how to respect and support them

- Understand the purpose and benefits of assessing and evaluating the work of a team and how to do so

- Be able to supervise a team

- Be able to assess, evaluate and improve the work of a team

To achieve the above aims of this unit, learners will be expected to provide evidence through the performance of work-based activities.

Knowledge

The purpose of a team

A **team** is a unit of employees that have been specifically brought together to achieve agreed **goals** and **objectives** within an organisation. The team should work together to agree the goals and objectives that it will work to achieve. It is important for all team members to be involved in this process to give them a sense of **ownership, empowerment** and **team identity**. This will give a team a strong **sense of purpose** which is shared and understood by all team members. This identity has the benefit of not only achieving the tasks for which the team has been created to achieve, but also provides an environment that encourages greater **creativity, cooperation, coordination** and **cohesion**.

The team supervisor will have the task of leading and managing this group of individual employees. As part of their role the team supervisor will need to balance the aims and objectives of:

* The **organisation** - Organisations can be very large and impersonal, providing little scope for interaction between employees

* The **team** - As smaller groups of employees a team possesses the potential to satisfy shared psychological needs by contributing to the agreement of goals and objectives which they will all work towards achieving by playing a variety of different roles within the team, as long as there is no ambiguity or overlapping of responsibility

* **Individual team members** - Where each team member will build a stronger sense of identification, have greater task interdependence and the opportunity to undertake more differentiated and specialised roles within the team. Each team member has a number of objectives they are aiming to achieve, which includes personal objectives, professional objectives, project objectives and organisational objectives. It is the  role of the team supervisor to manage these competing objectives to achieve the purpose for which the team has been created. It is up to the team supervisor to provide a stimulating environment within which team members can work to balance and integrate each of their different types of objectives. When establishing a team, the team supervisor should:

- Identify team members willing to be lead and follow

- Check access to necessary resources

- Find out what team members are thinking

- Discuss ideas with all team members

- Encourage team members to build rapport with each other

- Set realistic goals for the team

- Recognise and reward achievement of those goals

• ACTIVITY 1

What is a team created to achieve and how can employee objectives be managed against organisational and team objectives?

Characteristics of a team supervisor

The team supervisor will have the **authority** to coordinate the activities of a team and will take the lead in the final decision-making process. The authority exercised by the team supervisor should be:

- Firm but also flexible, to enable team members to perform at their best

- Competent, to allow teams to comply when conditions demand it, e.g. emergencies

- Inspired to empower team members to apply their expertise when appropriate

- Questioned when decisions have no clear right answers

The team supervisor should have the ability to **lead** their team by guiding, directing and influencing their team members. A good team supervisor should lead their team with authority to get the best out of their team. Good leaders should have the following characteristics:

- To envisage a vision to lead the team into the future

- To communicate effectively

- To welcome challenges

- To continually challenge the status quo

- To differentiate between fact and fiction to enable clarity of decision-making

- To accept responsibility and empathise with team members

- To complete tasks

- To accept criticism

- To build and earn respect

- To actively listen to team members encouraging them to improve their performance - motivational techniques - and being sensitive to their needs

- To inspire a team to follow through example and give credit where credit is due

These characteristics can be bundled together to identify different **styles of leadership**, which include the following:

- **Dictatorial** - Where a team will be told what to do without being given the opportunity to contribute to the decision-making process. Can be used when urgent action is required and there may be no time to debate issues. This is not an inclusive form of leadership; however, some teams will prefer to simply be told what to do

- **Laid back** - Where the team leader can empower the team by delegating authority to them. This style may get the best performance from a team of capable and experienced experts in their field. Interfering with their routines without good reason can have an adverse effect

- **Egalitarian** - Where the team is encouraged to participate and discuss issues while the control remains with the leader. The team supervisor will need to make sure that the team does not end up constantly discussing issues rather than deciding outcomes

• ACTIVITY 2

What would be the effect on a team if they were given no opportunity to influence the way the team works?

A team will generally be created to achieve **positive outcomes**. To that end teams should be organised to work with:

- **Clearly defined team goals** - All team members should understand its purpose and goals for it to work well. If there is any confusion or disagreement the team needs to work on resolving these issues. All team members should be in agreement over the team's purpose and have a clear vision of what it is aiming to achieve. The purpose of the team should meet the goals and objectives of the team

- **A team plan** - Which will identify the type of advice, assistance, training and other inputs and materials it may need. A plan gives the team a schedule and an identification of 'milestones' to be achieved

- **Clearly defined team roles** - Team roles should be apportioned to meet the strengths of each individual member of the team. Roles should be flexible to provide learning opportunities to enhance individual performance. All team members should have a clear idea of their tasks and responsibilities. According to **Belbin**, there a number of roles that team members can perform:

Action	Roles	Description
Doing / action oriented	Implementer	**Advantage - A:** well organised, predictable and practical - gets things done **Disadvantage - D:** may be slow, inflexible and resist change
	Shaper	**A:** lots of energy and action and challenges others to improve **D:** may be insensitive and argumentative
	Completer / Finisher	**A:** resolves all issues thoroughly to make sure everything works well down to the smallest detail **D:** may worry too much and find it difficult to delegate
Problem-solving / thought oriented	Plant	**A:** creative innovator who comes up with new ideas and approaches **D:** may communicate poorly and ignore details
	Monitor / Evaluator	**A:** objectively analyses and evaluates ideas the team comes up with, seeing the big picture **D:** may appear detached and is sometimes a poor motivator
	Specialist	**A:** expertise in key areas to solve problems **D:** may only focus on own area of expertise
People oriented	Coordinator	**A:** respected leader who helps others to focus on their task **D:** may be perceived as controlling and manipulative
	Team worker	**A:** cares for team members and the team: a good listener and works to resolve social problems **D:** poor decision-makers and lack of commitment
	Resource / Investigator	**A:** explores new ideas and possibilities with energy and with others: a good networker **D:** overly optimistic and may lose enthusiasm quickly

These roles are not fixed roles designated to team members permanently, nor are they to be performed exclusively by one team member, as team members may have the ability to perform more than one role at any time within the team. The team supervisor must analyse which mix of roles will best suit each team member to contribute towards achieving a harmonious team.

- **Clear communication** - Communication channels should remain open at all times, allowing for positive and productive discussions. An effective team is one which is kept fully informed of all decisions that have been made

- **Beneficial team behaviour** - Team members should be encouraged to use skills and knowledge that contribute towards realising the goals and objectives of the team

- **Well-defined decision-making procedures** - Teams should be encouraged to take a consensual approach to the decision-making process

- **Participation** - Every team member should participate in discussions and decision-making to achieve the goals and objectives that they have all agreed to work towards achieving

- **Ground rules** - Teams should agree how they want team members to work, establishing processes and procedures which should continually be reviewed and revised to make sure they drive the team towards achieving their goals and objectives

- **Awareness of the group process** - Team members should be aware of how the team works together

- **Use of the scientific approach in teamwork** - Valid and reliable data should be used for problem-solving and decision-making to make sure facts drive final outcomes

• ACTIVITY 3

What is the difference between Belbin's 'thought-oriented' and 'people-oriented' team roles?

Team communication skills

As discussed above, having clear communication is very important for a team to enable it to achieve its goals and objectives. The supervisor will need to make sure that data and information both given and received is in a form that is best suited to the tasks to be completed. Most team supervisors will communicate verbally. However, it is equally important for the team supervisor to listen. Some communication techniques that can be used to enhance the quality of communication are:

- **Launching** - Specify and highlight the main point (s) that the team members need to be made aware of. If there is more than one main point, deal with them individually, one at a time

- **Tempo** - Monitor the team member's reception of information and match the tempo of delivery to the team member's response. Allow team members to ask questions to clarity any points of information

- **Recap / summarise** - Summarise information that has been given to team members throughout a discussion to confirm their understanding and decisions that might have been made and the impact these will have on each individual team member's actions. Confirm with each team member their understanding. At the end of any team meeting always summarise what has been agreed, what actions are to be taken and by whom

- **Receiving** information

- **Prejudice** - Anyone working in organisations will have some pre-formed view about almost any subject which will influence the way information is received. It is important to recognise these • personal prejudices and work against them to make sure decisions are made fairly

- **Body language** - The person (s) listening to team members will interpret the body language of the speaker according to their own experience. In a multi-cultural society this can lead to misunderstanding, as body language varies between people of different cultural groups. As a team supervisor, be aware of own body language as well as another speaker's body language, as this will affect the communication process

- **Tone and pitch of voice** - A speaker's tone and pitch of voice may offer more information about what they mean rather than the actual words they are using. The true feelings of the communicator may be communicated more through the way they say things and the pitch of their voice than the substance of what they are talking about

• ACTIVITY 4

When listening to a team member, aside from what is being said, what else should a team supervisor evaluate to fully understand what is being communicated?

A good team supervisor will communicate regularly with their team to encourage active participation in decision-making. Every team will be made up of team members with different skills, knowledge and energy levels which will offer different levels of confidence, commitment and ability. Each team member will need to be approached individually through:

- **Coaching** - Team members who are totally committed but not yet fully competent, because of insufficient experience or training in the particular task, will need coaching more than encouragement

- **Mentoring** - Team members who have been a part of the team for some time but are still not fully competent will need mentoring. This will involve continuing the close supervision of their work, encouraging and praising them

- **Encouragement** - When team members reach a satisfactory level of competence they will need less coaching but will still welcome encouragement to improve their self-confidence. At this point, a team member should be involved in the decision-making process

- **Responsibility** - When team members are competent and their confidence has grown sufficiently to work entirely on their own, they can be given tasks to complete with little supervision

Delegation of team priorities
Having established the team, team members will need to be delegated the tasks they need to achieve. The team supervisor will need to identify the team's priorities so that the most important issues are dealt with first. Often **urgent** issues are mistakenly identified as **important** when the latter have little or no long-term bearing on the performance of the organisation. True priorities depend on having both urgency and importance. Juggling the urgent but unimportant tasks alongside the important but non-urgent is the real skill of a team supervisor. Once priorities have been identified, more specific, clear objectives can be agreed for each individual team member. Clear

objectives will allow all team members to be assured that that they are seeking to achieve a common outcome. This makes it easier for them to plan a course of action to reach the agreed objectives. When setting objectives make sure they are achievable to maintain morale among team members.

Some tasks may need to be divided into smaller sub-tasks, which will depend on the complexity of the tasks involved. The subdivision of tasks is a good way of empowering team members with individual responsibility and authority and setting out a progression pathway for all the tasks to be achieved within a team activity. Sub-tasks can be **delegated** to individual team members or smaller groups of team members. Good delegation leads to:

- More time and space for the team supervisor to manage the team

- A reduction in the delay to decision-making, positioning decision-making at the level where data and information is known to make the best decision

- The distribution of routine activities to team members

- Increased motivation of the team and individual team members

- More highly skilled team members, empowering team members to take on added responsibility and greater authority

- A fairer division of labour through the team

• ACTIVITY 5

What are the benefits that arise from good delegation?

When delegating to team members the team supervisor must decide:

- **What tasks to delegate** - Those tasks the team supervisor does not need to do, i.e. routine and repetitive tasks. Also, those tasks where the skills and knowledge of individual team members are better suited to achieve task outcomes. Always agree expectations with team members, i.e. quality and standards, and timescales of the tasks they have been delegated to achieve so they are aiming to achieve success

- **Who to delegate tasks to** - It is important to trust the team member to undertake the tasks they have been delegated to achieve the task to meet agreed expectations and timescales. However, this is also an opportunity to develop the skills and knowledge of team members by delegating to them tasks which will stretch their skills and knowledge to achieve the task - it must be a realistic expectation which the team supervisor will have to manage

- **How to give out tasks** - Team members will need to understand:
  - Why the task needs to be achieved
  - What they are expected to do
  - When they are expected to achieve the task
  - What authority they have to make decisions
  - What problems must be referred back
  - When to submit progress reports
  - How they will be supported and monitored
  - What resources they will need to complete the task

- **How to support team members** - Development of team members - guidance, instruction and training - not only for them and the team but also for the organisation. Improving performance allows the team supervisors to build trust between themselves and their team members, which enables them to delegate more complex tasks in the future

- **How to monitor progress of team members** - Team members will need to be monitored to make sure they are capable of achieving the delegated task to meet expectations and on time. It should be supportive without being oppressive and intrusive without being unduly interfering. It is a delicate balancing act which will vary from team member to team member and will require the team supervisor to customise their expectations to each individual team member. This can be achieved by scheduling team meetings and agreeing one-to-one meetings with team members to monitor progress

- **Acknowledge achievement of the task** - Always thank team members for the commitment and energy they used to achieve their tasks

• ACTIVITY 6

What decisions are involved in delegating tasks?

Delegation is not about surrendering responsibility. The team supervisor will always be responsible for the achievement of the team's goals and objectives, and it is their responsibility to make sure team members are fully supported in the performance of their tasks. The team supervisor should always delegate by the results they expect. They can only know what to expect by making sure they have delegated tasks to the right team member.

Building cohesive teams

A team should be established with the right mix of skills and knowledge to function to achieve its agreed goals and objectives. To achieve a cohesive team, the team supervisor will need to **motivate** team members and maintain different levels of motivation for each team member. Motivation can be described as the will to act. People are motivated to do something if they think it will be worth their while. If any  team member lacks motivation the whole team effort suffers. Different people are motivated in different ways. The team supervisor will need to recognise what motivates different employees within their team in order to tailor the rewards to offer to meet an individual team member's values. People can fall into one of three patterns of behaviour:

- **Determined and forceful** - People who are driven to achieve and are challenging to lead. The best way to motivate them is to organise team objectives so that these individuals' achievements stand out while contributing to the overall goals

- **Considerate and loyal** - People who are motivated by the success of others rather than any personal glory. They are motivated by the team's achievement and are usually involved heavily in tidying up the details for the go-getters who are racing ahead dealing with the big picture

- **Logical and systematic** - People who are best working alone within the framework of the team. They are motivated by the completion of the task whether or not they are given any recognition for it. They can be allocated the more complex tasks in the knowledge that they will simply get on with the job until it is completed. Avoid the temptation to push them into group activities against their will

The team supervisor needs to recognise which of the above groups individual team members fit into to enable them to allocate tasks appropriately to make full use of their creativity and innovation and allow each to fulfil their true potential. Team motivation can be improved by:

- Encouraging social interaction between the members of the team

- Emphasising the importance of the team as a whole

- Emphasising the importance of every individual

- Providing clear objectives

- Informing the team of the progress they are making

- Acknowledging the achievements of the team and individuals

• ACTIVITY 7

How can team motivation be improved?

It is the role of the team supervisor to encourage understanding between team members. Understanding enhances the sense of purpose and unity among the team. Open discussion between all those involved is the key to fostering understanding. The challenge is to allow the discussion to air differences of opinion and to manage any conflict caused. This is best done by a team supervisor who sets a personal example, who does not take offence if their views are contradicted or who falls back on their position to settle any dispute.

The benefits of creating a forum where opinions can be freely stated without the loudest voice dominating are that everybody's ideas will be heard and it encourages loyalty and commitment to the team. To prevent the discussion degenerating into chaos, ground rules will need to be set and agreed. The team supervisor will act as the moderator between other team members so that everyone gets a fair hearing. To facilitate positive discussions the team supervisor may need to undertake some of the following functions:

Chair the discussion
This involves making sure that the discussion is not dominated by one person or a few people. Inform all members of the team that only one person is allowed to speak at a time and that nobody should speak until you invite them to. Try to ensure that everybody who wishes to gets a fair opportunity to air their views. Look out for those team members who give signs that they have something to say, but do not want to put themselves forward, and invite them to contribute. It is better to frustrate

those who have a lot to say and have to wait their turn to say it than to miss the contribution of those who are not forceful enough to take their turn.

Restate people's comments

If the discussion goes off track, restate the position reached by relating the off-track issue to the point that is under discussion. If those who brought up the off-track issue wish to have it discussed fully they should be allowed to raise it after discussion of the main topic is completed. There will also be occasions when it is necessary to paraphrase what one team member has said so that other team members can fully understand it, particularly in the use of jargon or specialist knowledge.

Mediate between participants

From time to time, team members become heated in their views and it will be necessary to encourage them to withdraw from the discussion while they regain their composure. Ask other team members to give their views on the matter under discussion so that the 'heat' is taken out of the situation. There is a risk that a team member will attempt to change the subject in order to divert attention from the confrontation, but, as mediator, do not allow this to happen or the dispute will simply resurface later - refocus the discussion to the issue under debate and away from the personalities in dispute. The whole team must then find a solution which is acceptable to all.

Diversity in teams

Diversity not only applies to the components that go to make up a multi-racial society like Great Britain, e.g. race, gender, sexual orientation, disability, but is also refers to the different human qualities exhibited from different groups of people that make up a team.  Diversity in a business environment means working with different people without discrimination on the basis of:

- Gender

- Age

- Ethnic or racial background

- Disability

- Religion

- Job title

- Physical appearance

- Sexual orientation

- Nationality

- Competency

- Training

- Experience

- Personal habits

Diversity is to be valued because it adds richness to an organisation and a team. However, it also adds challenges. Policies and procedures in organisations should focus on developing effective working relationships with a diverse workforce. To achieve effective working relationships in a diverse community of people, an organisation needs to focus on similarities rather than differences. Building relationships from within a diverse community of people is critical for the success of any organisation in the 21st century. Different points of view can be invaluable to an organisation as they can provide opportunities that a business may not have considered in the past. An organisation with a diverse workforce has a greater pool of experiences to work with to produce ideas for products that cater to different cultures.

• ACTIVITY 8

What is diversity and why should it be valued in teams?

 Employees working in an organisation should respect, honour and appreciate the differences that a diverse workforce can add to help achieve the goals and ambitions of any organisation of any size. It is important to acknowledge similarities and likenesses to foster an understanding and appreciation of diversity in a business environment. There are a number of strategies that can be used to increase sensitivity towards the needs of others in an environment which encourages diversity:

- **Increase awareness of what others might be experiencing** - Be careful not only about the words used, but also about not saying anything at all. Be thoughtful and tactful about expressing awareness of another employee's actions and reactions or of others' actions or reactions

- **Do not assume** - Assumptions are often mistaken because we rarely understand the complexities of another person's life. Avoid labelling a person, but imagine why they act the way they do or say the things they do

- **Respect others** - A person's status - marital, financial or social - does not define them, so it should not determine the way people are treated. If an employee feels irritated by other team members they should stop themselves saying anything. They should think to themselves that there is a reason this person is acting the way they are acting, and that they should respect how they feel at the moment, even if it bothers them

- **Show understanding and avoid gossip**

- **Resist taking offence** - Everyone deals with something difficult and we all have weaknesses. Some deficits are more obvious than others, but everyone must overcome some obstacles. Help to build each other up

- **Empathise** - Do not let one encounter ruin the perception of that person, e.g. just because someone seemed to be in a bad mood when spoken to, that does not mean they are constantly angry and depressed

- **Do not let personal insecurities or beliefs get in the way** - e.g. it is common to meet people with different beliefs, likes and dislikes, so a team supervisor should not be put off if the team member to whom they are speaking to does not like something the team supervisor does or likes something the team supervisor does not

The benefits that can be derived to the business / organisation as a result of promoting and managing diversity in teams include:

- Incorporating other groups of people into jobs which may have been selected from people of a certain ethnicity or gender

- Creating a business environment that is more functional and able to adapt quickly to market conditions

- Creating a business environment that understands the multiple cultures and beliefs of customers, allowing for a targeted service

- Team members taking the benefits home with them, which they can use to increase their understanding of relationships in their private life, recognising and celebrating the differences which exist in different backgrounds

- Increasing productivity and profitability from investing in a larger pool of talent, which can provide a competitive edge in a business environment

- Resulting in more innovative and creative ideas

- Lowering absenteeism rates

- Lowering employee turnover costs and decreasing liability in discrimination lawsuits

- Reflecting current business expectations and their environment, as it represents different populations

- An increase in marketplace understanding

- Improving global relationships

• ACTIVITY 9

What are the benefits of team diversity?

If team members are behaving in a way that goes against team expectations find out about how long they have been with the organisation - they may not know how they are meant to behave. If a team member is new to a team, remember it is not easy fitting into something that is new, where there is no experience of working in that new work environment. Make allowances for the fact that they are probably feeling nervous and uncomfortable. Do not jump to conclusions about either their abilities or their attitude. Get to know them and, until then, give them the benefit of the doubt. The support that a team member can give another team member is important because it:

- Increases respect from team member to team member

- Reinforces the skills or knowledge that are being passed on in the person who is lending support

- Encourages team members to reciprocate

- Creates a team environment of trust and sharing

Supporting team members can either be done formally or informally. Formal approaches to support team members can be undertaken through coaching or mentoring. An informal approach to supporting team members can take place through **assertive behaviour**. Assertiveness in the workplace is all about respecting the rights of team members. It means there is no need for passive - people who only want to hear good things said about themselves and will do anything to please - or aggressive - people who do not want to listen to other people and dominate situations with their will - team members. An assertive team member will strive to actively listen to what is going on. They will focus on achieving agreed objectives in a way that respects the rights of all those involved in achieving a task objective. Not only will an assertive team member actively listen, but they will listen to what they can see in the non-verbal cues that the team members they are working with are communicating.

Assertive behaviour is:

- **Stating what is aiming to be achieved**
- **Standing up for achieving agreed goals and objectives**
- **Opposing arguments when necessary**
- **Aiming for a win / win resolution**

Assertive behaviour can be enhanced by:

- **Being ready to meet assertiveness from other team members**
- **responses**
- **Gathering all the information required before joining a discussion**
- **Using open questions in the discussion**

Respect and consideration should equally be shown to team members by being honest and ethical in the way they are dealt with. This does not only mean by not stealing from them, but also by being, e.g. punctual, only taking days off when genuinely unwell, doing the job to meet the standards expected. A team member will be expected to:

- **Communicate effectively**
- **Be positive**
- **Volunteer for extra responsibility**

- **loyal to colleagues**
- **Accept constructive feedback**
- **Get on well with everybody in a professional manner**
- **Treat the employer with honesty and respect**

• ACTIVITY 10

What is the difference between assertive behaviour and aggressive behaviour?

Team problems

Teams will be organised to achieve specific purposes; however, despite how well they may be organised and constituted, problems will arise. If there is a clear plan of how the team is going to achieve its goals and objectives, it should be able to anticipate difficulties before they happen and work out a solution so that the difficulty does not become a problem. Approach problem-solving by identifying what the problem is, why it happened and what should be done to resolve it. Then implement the problem-solving initiative and then evaluate the outcome of the implementation. Team problems may occur to do with:

- Clash of team members' **personalities**
- **Goals and objectives not clearly defined**
- Team **responsibilities not clearly defined**
- **Changing circumstances** of the organisation
- **Poor leadership**
- Team members having **insufficient skills and knowledge** to do what they have been tasked to achieve
- **Insufficient time** to complete tasks
- **Poor communication** as a result of misunderstandings - these problems should be tackled by direct communication with the team member involved. If the problem is too difficult, a supervisor / manager should be consulted
- **Lack of motivation** - Team members should keep focused on what they need to achieve and contribute positively to the team going forward. Seek assistance when required and offer assistance if fellow team members require help

- **Poor feedback** - It is important that all members of the team know whether they are meeting those objectives or not. Team members should be aware of how well they are performing within the team and meeting expectations. Feedback encourages team members to give of their best by making sure there is mutual satisfaction and improvement. Feedback should provide the team members with information on their strengths and weakness which is fair and offered without bias or favouritism. Feedback is given to reward team members with praise and identify any development opportunities which a team member should do. Areas of feedback to team members may cover their approach to how they have:

  - Achieved team goals

  - Taken ownership of their responsibilities

  - Worked collaboratively with others

  - Added value to the achievement of the team's goals

  - Managed their time to achieve team goals

  - Communicated with others, within and outside the team

  - Been committed to achieving the team goals

Where conflict arises between team members outside of the discussion situation there are four ways to deal with it:

- **Use leader authority** - Simply tell one of the team members they are wrong and they will have to accept that the other is right

- **Find a compromise** - Identify a situation that will fully satisfy neither but which both will accept rather than acknowledging the other's position

- **Find common ground** - Identify a situation that will enable both team members to achieve at least part of their goal by emphasising the common ground, although this situation may be artificial with issues surfacing at a later time

- **Solve the problem** - The team defines the problem, develops alternative solutions and debates their merits, they then reach an agreement on the chosen action and its implementation

The first method very rarely works, as the 'loser' will resent interference while the 'winner' will get little satisfaction out of such an easy victory. They will have made no progress towards persuading their protagonist that their view was correct. A compromise will often seem the easy solution, but is unlikely to be satisfactory over the long term, as both will feel they have not achieved their goal and will raise the issue again at a later date. The ability to find common ground often produces the best long-term solution.

Assess team effectiveness

Teams need to be assessed to see how well they are achieving the agreed goals and objectives. To that end, the team will need to:

- Identify where things are going wrong in order to put them right

- Know what is going well to continue to pursue their tasks confidently

Teams need to check they are performing in ways they need to. A simple framework that can be used to assess performance is called **PERFORM**, which is an acronym for the seven dimensions that need to be assessed:

- **Productivity / outcomes** - This is the most important of the dimensions because it is about assessing if the tasks are achieving their goals and objectives. It can be useful to gather data through surveys / complaints etc., to make an accurate assessment. However, teams are often very insightful and honest with themselves about whether they are achieving their agreed goals and objectives as fast as they need to and to the agreed standard

- **Empathy** - Considers whether team members feel comfortable with each other. If they do not, it can drain energy and creativity, which affects performance. Empathy is strongly related to the ability of the team to communicate effectively about difficult issues and to feel comfortable with each other

- **Roles and goals** - Considers if team members know their roles and how they fit in with others' roles in the team. Team tasks must be clear about who has responsibility for achieving tasks, goals and objectives

- **Flexibility** - Considers whether the team is responsive to outside influence and contribution. Some teams develop a rigid 'fortress-like' way of operating which can limit its functioning. Team members should ask themselves:
  - How do they respond when the goalposts are moved?
  - Much communicating do they do with teams around them?
  - Do they listen and respond as well as tell?

- **Openness** - Considers to the quality of communication between team members. Do people tell each other everything they need to know, including information about difficulties, mistakes, risks and problems? Do people say what they think?

- **Recognition** - Considers the long-term health of the team and whether the team members celebrate their successes, both corporately and by praising each other. The important thing is whether team members feel their good work is recognised

- **Morale** - Considers if team members are happy and want to be a part of the team - they are proud of it and of themselves in it. If morale is high, it is more likely that team members will achieve their potential and therefore, ultimately, so will the team

Team effectiveness is essential for organisational success. Through regular assessment and discussion teams can diagnose issues and develop solutions to achieve their combined potential.

The foregoing assessment methodology is a formal approach that a team supervisor can take. However, individual team members can also assess their contribution towards team performance - a self-assessment. This can be conducted by a team member within any team.

All that is required is an up-to-date, clear and simple job description and a set of objectives for the team or a specific time period. The documents used do not have to follow any particular form. The most useful job descriptions tend to indicate the approximate percentage of time devoted to each function. Similarly, the most valuable job objectives are expressed in measurable terms, such as 'deliver internal mail by 10.00' or 'update a marketing plan each quarter'. In carrying out a self-assessment using this format, the following essential elements should be followed:

- The assessment should be done regularly, which could include:
  - 15 minutes one day a week to review and record the week's successes and failures
  - One hour during the last week of the month to assess the month's successes and failures
  - One day each quarter to review results and develop a plan for personal development during the upcoming year

- The review should cover all aspects of the job. All jobs can be broken down into three broad categories:

  - Technical, e.g. sales, accounting

  - Administrative, e.g. budgeting, compliance with company procedures

  - Communication, e.g. keeping superiors informed, corresponding with customers and colleagues, listening to employees' suggestions

The individual team members appraising their own performance should develop a checklist that reflects all areas of the job to make sure that each task is competently performed. All results should be written down to permit team members to follow up, by working on those functions or activities that need improvement. This might mean more frequent reporting to the team superior, taking a brush-up course in some aspect of the job etc. During this process of self-assessment team members should involve their superior, asking them to review the self-assessment. This procedure for measuring individual team member's performance provides a way for judging and improving progress throughout the year, as well as a means for improving performance from one year to the next. Most people are good judges of themselves.

• ACTIVITY 11

What is self-assessment and how can it be used to improve team performance?

Leaders who offer vision inspire their team as much as if they were able to offer improved pay, position or authority. Vision inspires commitment and a feeling of common purpose. If you claim to have a vision you may be dismissed as an eccentric, but vision transforms a manager into a leader. It is vision that suggests that things can only get better and this inspires ordinary people. Leaders present their vision in such a way that others want to achieve it. Managers present ideas and proposals and may achieve their goals, but they are not demonstrating leadership.

Leaders take risks and invite their colleagues to join them in exploring those risks. This requires a great deal of commitment and willingness to accept the possibility that their vision will be rejected by those unable to share it. The leader's relationship with their team relies heavily on gaining the trust and support of all the members who may have to accept ideas that they would not previously have considered. If a team has been treated well in the past they will have faith that they are being led in the right direction.

Testing your knowledge

1. How should communication skills be used to lead a team?

2. Why is it important that team objectives are achievable?

3. How can team members be involved in agreeing team goals and objectives?

4. How do individual objectives relate to the achievement of team objectives?

5. What are the benefits of encouraging creativity and innovation in team members?

6. How is a team lead when the team supervisor has not been given the authority to do so?

7. What is the purpose of a team?

8. What methods can be used to deal with conflict within the team and what are the advantages and disadvantages of each method?

9. What are leadership styles and how do they differ from one another?

10. How can you recognise the different motivational methods applicable to individuals within your team?

11. What are the types of problems that can be encountered with leading a team?

Skills

contact with them and to communicate all aspects of the tasks and activities that the team has been set. This is a delicate balance of skills to perform as you need to appear to be in control of how the team is operating but not controlling to the point that you stifle creativity and innovation from members of the team. Team members must be given the freedom to contribute, in their own way, to advance the objectives of the task / activity to reach the achievement. It the objectives have not been agreed by most members of the team it will be difficult for them to have a sense of ownership of the team activities they are being asked to perform. A team that has contributed to agreeing objectives is one that is committed and can work as a single body rather than as an entity with many different ideas of what has to be achieved. The process of setting objectives comes down to setting in motion the tools for leading your team to complete tasks and activities positively and successfully.

• ACTIVITY 12

Think about members of your own team. Which leadership style would be most effective with each of them? Write an explanation of your reasons in each case.

Working with a group of employees in a team is an opportunity for the supervisor to exploit the strengths of team members, but also the opportunity to develop team members' weaker skills. Development of your team is an important task which should be encapsulated by the feedback and appraisal system you set up to evaluate the performance of team members from project to project. The team members need to be supported at all times, particularly those who are being developed in areas where their skills and knowledge are weakest. A good leader will usually have an 'open-door' policy, whereby team members can approach their supervisor to resolve problems or seek enlightenment on what they have to do. Team members, having agreed their objectives, will need to know the standard of work they will be required to deliver to achieve the outcomes of their objectives, e.g. when a job needs to be completed by or the format the job needs to be completed in.

• ACTIVITY 13

Choose someone who has inspired you. This could be someone you know personally, a celebrity or a historical figure. Write about the leadership qualities that person displayed and why these were effective in their leadership style.

Working with employees in a team offers changing dynamics. Employees may come to work one day feeling energised while on other days they may be a little depressed. Each of these behaviours will not only affect the individual performance of team members but it will affect the team as a whole. Too much energy can lead to overconfidence, which is just as likely to lead to the creation of mistakes as a depressed environment, where team members do not care as much as they should. The supervisor's job is to make sure the team is motivated to the level of tasks and activities the team has to undertake. They will also need your direction so they can achieve their objectives successfully.

• ACTIVITY 14

Review your leadership of team activities over the period of one month with your line manager. Evaluate the outcome of the review, identifying targets that have been met and areas for improvement or development.

Leadership, direction and motivation are the tools the supervisor uses to inspire their team and get the most out of team members' contributions to achieving the team's objectives. However, working in a team under your supervision is also an opportunity for each member of the team to appraise their own development as a means of confirming their development. Does every team member want to develop? Some may be very happy working within the sphere of development. It is up to the supervisor to inspire their team members to develop their skills and knowledge so they are able to offer the team, the organisation and themselves a higher level of skills and knowledge.

Testing your skills

1. How did you use your communication skills to supervise your team?

2. What were the objectives that your team set to achieve?

3. How did the objectives change, if they did, and how did you manage this transition?

4. How did you relate individual objectives to the achievement of team objectives?

5. How did you encourage creativity and innovation from your team members?

6. How did you exercise authority over your team?

7. What did you expect your team to achieve?

8. How did you monitor the achievement of team goals?

9. How did you resolve conflict from within your team?

10. What were the legal, regulatory and ethical requirements your team had to work within?

11. How did you provide relevant advice and support to your team members?

12. How would you describe your style of leadership?

13. How could you improve your style of leadership?

14. How did you motivate individual team members to achieve the team's goals?

Ready for assessment?
To achieve this Level 3 unit of a Business & Administration qualification, learners will need to demonstrate that they are able to perform the following activities:

1. Communicated with people in a team during work activities

2. Supervised work goals and planned work objectives, priorities and responsibilities for a team and individuals

3. Identified, agreed and supervised opportunities for others to work to achieve agreed outcomes

4. Scheduled activities and resources

5. Allocated work tasks and supervised best use of abilities within a team

6. Agreed quality measures and timescales for a team

7. Provided support to members of a team, as required

8. Showed respect for individuals in a team

9. Supervised production of work to agreed quality standards and timescales

10. Identified and solved problems and disagreements, or referred them, if necessary

11. Assessed and evaluated the work of a team and individuals to identify strengths and areas for improvement

12. Made sure team members had opportunities to assess their own work for strengths and areas for improvement

13. Shared feedback and outcomes of assessing work with individuals and a team

14. Made and agreed suggestions for improving the work of individuals and a team

15. Made sure individuals and a team were encouraged to improve work as an outcome of assessing work

You will need to produce evidence from a variety of sources to support the performance requirements of this unit.

If you carry out the 'ACTIVITIES' and respond to the 'NEED TO KNOW' questions, these will provide some of the evidence required.

Links to other units

While gathering evidence for this unit, evidence **may** also be used from evidence generated from other units within the Business & Administration suite of units. Below is a **sample** of applicable units; however, most units within the Business & Administration suite of units will also be applicable.

QCF NVQ

Communications

Communicate in a business environment (Level 3)

Develop a presentation

Deliver a presentation

Core business & administration

Evaluate and improve own performance in a business environment (Level 3)

Solve business problems (Level 3)

Work in a business environment (Level 3)

Work with other people in a business environment (Level 3)

Contribute to decision-making in a business environment

Negotiate in a business environment (Level 3)

Customer service

Deliver, monitor and evaluate customer service to internal customers

Deliver, monitor and evaluate customer service to external customer

SVQ

Communications

Plan how to communicate in a business environment

Develop a presentation

Deliver a presentation

Core business & administration

Solve business problems

Review and maintain work in a business environment

Support other people to work in a business environment

Contribute to decision-making in a business environment

Contribute to negotiations in a business environment

Customer service

Deliver, monitor and evaluate customer service to internal customers

Deliver, monitor and evaluate customer service to external customers

15

Deliver, monitor and evaluate customer service to internal customers

DELIVER, MONITOR AND EVALUATE CUSTOMER SERVICE TO INTERNAL CUSTOMERS

'Deliver, monitor and evaluate customer service to internal customers' is an <u>optional unit</u> which may be chosen as one of a combination of units to achieve a Qualifications and Credit Framework (QCF), National Vocational Qualification (NVQ) or Scottish Vocational Qualification (SVQ).

The aims of this unit are to:

- Understand the meaning of 'internal customer'

- Know the types of products and services relevant to internal customers

- Understand how to deliver customer service that meets or exceeds internal customer expectations

- Understand the purpose of quality standards and timescales for delivering customer service

- Understand how to deal with internal customer service problems

- Understand how to monitor and evaluate internal customer service and the benefits of this

- Be able to build positive working relationships with internal customers

- Be able to deliver customer services to agreed quality standards and timescales

- Be able to deal with internal customer service problems and complaints

- Be able to monitor and evaluate customer services to internal customers

To achieve the above aims of this unit, learners will be expected to provide evidence through the performance of work-based activities.

Knowledge

What is meant by internal customers?

To excel at or exceed in the delivery of customer service is a mantra that is often heard in management speak; however, excellent customer service lies at the heart of any successful business. **Internal customers** are people and processes that are being supplied with services, information or products / parts of products, completed in other parts of the organisation - it is every employee who has a stake in achieving success for the organisation. It is working with other employees or other departments within the organisation. It is providing other departments with a service, information or product that helps them do their jobs. It is also about treating other employees as customers and giving them the same respect and service as external customers. It is listening to and understanding the concerns of others within the organisation. It is solving problems for other employees to help the organisation succeed. In the manufacturing industry other departments might include offices, workshops for developing machines or parts of machines and a warehouse for storage and transport. The employees working in these departments are all part of a chain of service made up of internal customers, this is known as the **service chain** and is a key factor in running a profitable and happy business that promotes achievement and growth to make sure customer service is at the heart of the organisation. Internal customer service brings employees together as a team.

The delivery of good internal customer service is about meeting the of fellow employees within the organisation. Delivering good internal customer service will enable the organisation to succeed in meeting its objectives. The delivery of excellent internal customer service helps to improve employees' morale, productivity and the delivery of excellent external customer service. Ultimately, it drives the organisation to establish greater financial security and viability. And employees who receive excellent internal customer service recognise that they are valued by other employees and the organisation as a whole. When employees value one another, the result is increased performance, which contributes to the success of the entire organisation and creates a positive and productive working environment.

• ACTIVITY 1

To work within an organisation employees not only want to meet the requirements of their job role but want to be satisfied in the overall contribution they not only offer but receive from other employees.

Internal customer service is a two-way process in a linear progression of service from one employee to another employee, which may involve many employees as part of a **service chain**, see figure 15.1. For example, an employee may need assistance completing a report so they approach another employee for information, which that employee may only be able to provide a part of, so, in turn, they approach another employee etc., so the report can be completed.

Service Chain ➡ Internal Customers ➡ External Customers

Figure 15.1 Service Chain

The customer service aspect is how employees behave towards one another, e.g. act with courtesy, offer a smile. Such behaviour induces respect between employees and contributes to feeling valued within a culture of inclusion. In many respects, good internal customer service is symbiotic, as each employee becomes dependent on one another, building a happy and respectful work environment and improving overall customer service to all stakeholders doing business with the organisation. Any work environment can help to improve the delivery of internal customer service by empowering employees to communicate freely and act against the need to build protective walls around themselves. Training should be provided by the organisation to instil a culture to employees of working co-operatively with one another. Employees who interact positively with one another are less stressed, especially if they feel they can interact with other employees without fear of rejection. Employees who are able to help one another feel satisfied and this makes them feel better about themselves.

• ACTIVITY 2

What should an organisation do to deliver excellent internal customer service?

An integral skill required to facilitate excellent internal customer service is establishing an environment of open communication between employees. For example, using internal forums or the organisation's intranet keeps employees communicating while working. Also, meetings and emails keep all employees informed of important events / situations that arise within the organisation. It is how an employee behaves when another employee asks for information they need to complete tasks of the day; it is what an employee says when an employee from another department asks for information, e.g. how an employee will respond to their manager when they ask for something to be done very quickly. Each of these interactions could be interpreted as an interruption to their work, to their 'real' job. However, all aspects of work are vital to the success of the organisation. If there is a gap between the 'real' job and servicing the needs of other employees within the organisation, then ultimately there is a mismatch between the aspirations of the employee and the aspirations of the organisation. By helping other employees in the organisation, each employee is helping the organisation to succeed.

Customer service is a major focus of many successful organisations, where there is a focus on making employees happy, as it leads to excellent customer service.

> Employee satisfaction equals customer satisfaction at UPS.
> - *Kent Nelson, CEO*

Achieving employee satisfaction

Just as customer service leads to external customer satisfaction, internal customer service leads to **employee satisfaction**. Customer satisfaction is one of the most important outcomes in customer service. This leads to internal customer loyalty whereby employees feel empowered by the trust and commitment that the organisation and its employees offer one another. It is more expensive for an organisation to recruit and select new employees than to retain old ones. As mentioned above, perhaps the most restricting force within organisations for achieving excellent internal customer service is created when employees build walls around themselves in the mistaken belief that they are protecting their 'real' work. This is a powerful argument used by employees in organisations to protect their job role and agreed outputs. There are three approaches that can be used to disabuse employees of this practice, namely:

Create forums to share information

This can be done by any employee within an organisation if they have the level of authority to do so or seek permission to do so. The more employees know about the objectives of the organisation, and how each department contributes to accomplishing those objectives, the less likely they are to feel a need to 'protect' themselves and their jobs by building walls around themselves. One way a football player enables their team to execute successful goals is by making sure every player understands what their teammates are doing in the game. Members of a football team do not advance the ball by keeping their plans secret from one another. Employees in the organisation do not advance their plans by withholding information or assistance from one another. Departments in an organisation are interdependent from one another. Forums for sharing information can include: organisation-wide meetings, al fresco meetings, passing one another in a corridor, a shared lunch between two departments, emails outlining what a particular department is doing and why.

Practice proactive information-sharing

Employees should be able to supply information to other employees so that it is freely available without them having to come looking for it. Do not wait for employees to ask for information they need to do their jobs. Offer it to them. Offer it before they need it. Offer it before they know they need it. Think of ways that the information and data collected and stored by an employee can be disseminated to other employees within the organisation. Invest this function as part of a job description, delivering a service or product to an external customer. Employees doing this will be acknowledged for their interest and openness, which could help to knock down other employees' walls.

> Create, or contribute to, an environment in which status is accorded to employees who share freely and do not build walls

Most employees who build walls do it to protect their turf from encroachment by others in the organisation. They fear that if other employees have what they have those other employees may make them obsolete. Make that fear groundless by rewarding employees and colleagues who do not protect their turf, but instead work to fulfil the objectives of the company. Reward behaviours, e.g. employee of the month, compliments, pats on the back, commendations at meetings that lead to open information-sharing. Make it clear that territorial behaviour sabotages the efforts of the organisation, while treating colleagues like valued customers contributes to the organisation's success.

• ACTIVITY 3

What strategies can be employed to break down employees building walls to protect their job?

Many organisations focus vast budgets on promoting the value of their external customer service in the hopes of wooing new customers and retaining current customers; however, they pay scant attention to the effect poor internal customer service is having on overall customer satisfaction and loyalty. Customer service starts internally within an organisation and spreads outwards to external customers. For an organisation to achieve superlative customer service, their commitment to external customer service care has to be matched by their commitment to internal customer service care. It refers to the level of responsiveness, quality, communication, teamwork and morale employees within an organisation are able to offer with equanimity.

The strength of the organisation's internal customer service is built on how well employees not only work within their own department but also with other departments. When an employee has to work within their own department, if working in a larger organisation, do they approach it with trepidation or with relish as an opportunity to either work with employees they have not worked with before or renew contacts? When an employee has to work with another department do they approach it with trepidation or with relish as an opportunity to either work with employees they have not worked with before or renew contacts? Sometimes there can be internal wars between departments within the organisation, which may have arisen because departments have missed deadlines or have provided less than standard work filled with errors and oversights. Poor teamwork, poor communication and outmoded thinking can lead to the hardening of positions over time. Ironically, in such environments, departments equally care about the service or finished product they have contributed to but departments have put pressure on each other without realising it.

When working with other departments it is important to reaffirm not only the objectives of the project that departments are working to achieve but also alignment with the organisation's objectives. Employees should understand what they are being asked to contribute by the service they are being asked to provide. They need to ask the following questions:

- What is required?
- When is it required?
- In what form is it required?
- To whom should the object of the service be given to?
- Is any follow up required?

Confirming this information will make sure that there are no misunderstandings in what is expected of one another. The service being provided is always a partnership. For a partnership to work effectively one partner must be aware of what it is they are to provide or else the service provided will achieve the wrong objectives, which is a waste of the organisation's resources and both partners' resources. Time is becoming an increasing valuable commodity which cannot be inadvertently siphoned away on needless activities.

• ACTIVITY 4

Why is it important to understand the needs of the internal customer to whom a service is being provided? How would an employee confirm that they can provide the required service?

Departments and their employees should seek to confirm that their objectives are one and the same; that communication channels should remain open and not regard contact as a nuisance, a distraction or a drain of valuable time away from the 'real' job; and see the greater good that comes from employees helping each other to work together and agree how this can best be done to achieve a win / win for the greater good of all customers being served by the organisation. Employees should learn to take pride in the opportunities they are given to help other employees or departments to look good. This should not be done at the expense of themselves failing to achieve their agreed outcomes. Helping others is not about one employee winning and the other losing. Helping other employees and other departments to succeed can have a payback for those who have helped in the future.

Good internal customer service starts with good morale within a team or department. Managers or project managers have a duty of care to make sure that all members of their department or team are looked after and are happy. Employees should be encouraged to feel good about themselves and the contributions they make to achieve the objectives of their department and / or team. Managers should make sure employees have been given the correct training for them to feel confident in their performance. Contented and happy employees are: productive, and, more importantly, customers will notice their positive behaviour when they are being served by them; they are also better team players. Employees should be as happy and positive when finishing their day as they are when they start their day. This shows great morale and that employees like their jobs. It also shows an organisation that values its employees and treats them with good customer care. The more an organisation cares about its internal customers the more it can expect its internal customers to care about serving their external customers.

All in all, all employees are customers of their managers, and in many respects they are partners: sometimes junior, sometimes senior, but always partnered together to achieve the same outcome. Internal customer service is a process of collaboration with all employees working in the same direction to achieve the objectives which have been set by their organisation. The interaction between employees of whatever status within the organisation should be one of real engagement, real conversation, a genuine exchange of content and affection. The partnership is providing a service to each other, not servility. The organisation can help to strengthen the service being offered by its internal service providers, its employees, by making sure employees:

- Never complain within earshot of customers, as this gives the customer the impression that the organisation is not run well, undermining their confidence in the service and products offered by the organisation

- Refrain from complaining to internal customers about other departments' employees, as this will undermine morale and the respect that employees offer one another

- Strive to build bridges between departments, which can be achieved by cross-training, development days, parties as well as day-to-day niceties

- Utilise post-mortems after joint projects so all employees involved can learn from the experience. Fences can be mended and new understandings can be gained when all employees or team members review what went right ... or wrong. By doing so after the project the immediate pressure is off, yet stronger bonds can be forged while the experience is fresh in everybody's minds. Not doing so can result in lingering animosities that will exacerbate future collaborations

- Experience being a customer by becoming 'customer for a day', a practice which is often offered to employees in the hospitality sector so they can see first-hand the service they will be expected to provide to their customers

• ACTIVITY 5

What can organisations do to strengthen the internal customer services it can offer?

The drive within the organisation is to excel and provide superior customer service compared with other organisations. To do this the organisation needs to create an environment of sharing and helping, which can be achieved by implementing the following strategies:

- **Employees should listen -** Carefully, if not actively, to the customer they are aiming to serve so they can articulate what is required. By listening to the customer and understanding their issues, the employee is halfway to providing the service that the customer is looking to receive

- **Employees should develop a rapport with their internal customers -** Employees should try to get to know the customer with whom they are going to provide the service. Chat with them to open them up and get to know them. As a result, they may give more information than expected

- **Employees should begin any transaction or interaction using their own perspective -** Employees should regard other employees and other departments as their customers. They should understand that helping their colleagues to do their jobs more successfully helps both the organisation and themselves. Other employees are always a customer and should be treated as VIPs

- **Employees should not consider interruptions as nuisances, but as opportunities to serve their internal customers -** Identifying what are necessary and unnecessary interruptions. A necessary interruption is when an employee is seeking help of some kind to enable them to complete their objectives which will add to the value to the project, the organisation and themselves, e.g. if an employee interrupts an employee to ask for sales figures needed to analyse sales team performance. An unnecessary interruption is one that adds little value to achieving the objectives of the organisation; however, it may have some other personal benefits, e.g. exchanging gossip which, although not entirely beneficial to the organisation, may act as a release of energy and smooth the road ahead. An employee should take pride in helping other employees and enjoy their role in sharing information and providing services that help other employees to get their jobs done. In most cases, an employee's willingness to help other colleagues get their jobs done will lead them to assist that employee when needed in the future

- **Employees should exceed their internal customers' expectations** - When expectations are exceeded most employees feel delighted, excited and very positive about that employee and their organisation. Employees need to think of what they can accomplish for their organisation by exceeding their fellow employees' expectations e.g. if HR asks for overtime by 17.00, provide the information by 15.00 so HR can relax, knowing they have everything in hand

- **Say 'thank you'** - Express appreciation of the service that has been provided. Explain how it has made achieving a job much easier. Show delight when expectations have been exceeded

• ACTIVITY 7

What can organisations do to provide excellence in the internal customer service they provide?

Manage internal customer service problems
Sometimes the delivery of internal service does not go according to plan. If service is not provided correctly to internal customers problems may arise. As the delivery of internal customer service is a synthesis between 1. process, the relationship established between the two partners collaborating to achieve the service; and 2. the product, the specifics of the service being asked for, problems may occur within either of these two areas as a result of:

- Deadlines not being met

- Poor-quality work

- Poor communication

- Lack of trust between employees

- Negative inter-departmental past histories of working with each other, e.g. they do things not preferable to the internal customer, things they do not do but wish they did , or do things a differ way from how they normally carry them out

- Personal frictions between employees

- Misunderstanding of the service required

Employees should be observant and mindful of the service they have been asked to provide to other employees of departments within their organisation to anticipate or prevent problems from occurring. Early identification of internal customer service problems is the key to a successful solution. In the event of a problem arising with service to internal customers, employees should act swiftly and proactively to solve the problem and gain the internal customer's trust. Employees should strive to build a complaint-friendly environment where issues can be discussed objectively and positively by diagnosing the root problem. Strategies should be applied to resolving the problem which is specific to the internal customer and the situation. The employee should negotiate with the internal customer the most effective strategy for resolving the problem using their communication skills and other interpersonal skills. To militate against problems from occurring with internal customers, employees should strive to:

- Recognise the benefits of improving the service offered to internal customers

- Define who key and non-key internal customers are

- Create an effective customer experience statement

- Communicate positively with internal customers by recognising the benefits of communicating effectively with internal customers

- Use internal customers' physical experiences to meet and exceed internal customers' likely expectations

- Use assertive behaviour to manage conflict in a given scenario

- Recognise the benefits of taking a structured approach towards the implementation of internal customer service

- Create an internal customer service plan

- Set appropriate standards for internal customer service in a given scenario

- Use the appropriate types of questions to obtain internal customer feedback

If there is a catastrophic breakdown between the employee and the internal customers, the latter may decide to make a formal complaint against the level of service that they have received. To facilitate the successful resolution of complaints, the organisation should have in place a complaints procedure so that all complaints lodged by internal customers are responded to effectively and preventative action is taken to prevent similar complaints from arising again in the future.

If you look after your internal customers you do not have to worry about the external customers.
- *Richard Branson*

Monitoring internal customer satisfaction

An internal customer satisfaction survey is a process undertaken by the organisation to monitor the satisfaction quotient of their employees. An internal satisfaction survey tracks the return on organisational investments in keeping their employees happy, investing in a quality culture and providing a healthy environment in which their employees can work to achieve their objectives. Most importantly, the internal customer satisfaction survey helps to find the critical areas which need improvement. The need for internal customer satisfaction surveys to be conducted usually arises because of:

- A rapidly growing organisation

- A high or growing turnover rate

- Excessive rumour's

- A highly competitive industry

- Planned and recent organisational changes

The objectives of conducting an internal customer satisfaction survey is to find out the level of satisfaction among the internal customers:

- To know the present status of the internal service providers in terms of the products and services they provide

- To collect and evaluate ideas / views and expectations of the internal customers for the improvement of the internal service provider's performance

- To make the organisation's internal service providers aware of the dissatisfaction experienced by their internal customers

- To find out the most prominent areas of dissatisfaction

- To enhance communication and cooperation between the internal service providers and their internal customers

The benefits that can be derived from an internal customer satisfaction survey for the organisation include:

- Creating better teamwork and a much improved work process

- Higher output and superior-quality products and services

- Decreasing turnover through greater internal customer loyalty

- Reducing overheads and increasing customer satisfaction levels across the department of the organisation

- Enhancing communication and therefore improving team building, which reinforces a concerted and shared purpose

- Improving employee attitude and boosting morale, particularly if it is a well-planned survey

• ACTIVITY 7

What are some of the objectives and benefits from conducting an internal customer satisfaction survey?

It is desirable for the organisation to develop a process to better meet the needs and expectations of its internal customers. This could be accomplished by introducing a process to survey the needs and expectations of internal customers and to measure their current level of satisfaction. This information, in conjunction with an evaluation of the resources available and the way internal customers' needs and expectations are addressed, are important inputs to devising a plan for future improvement. Survey evaluations can function to focus on three performance characteristics:

- **Technical expertise**

- **Organisational role** - By focusing on the evaluation of department's operations and the part this plays in supporting external customer satisfaction and being an active player in the overall corporate environment

- **Intangible know-how** - Of meeting or exceeding the expectations of internal customers without employing excessive resources

While an internal customer survey can include many of the measures of performance identified above, the most effective survey tool is one that does not burden potential participants with hundreds of items. The ideal survey is a one-page survey form. The survey could include the performance measures of different tasks and then refine them over time. To collect the most useful information, put in place a built-in mechanism to solicit input from internal customers, e.g. provide opportunities for internal customers to raise issues that are perceived to be important by them, but may be overlooked by the initial survey. The survey form should ask internal customers questions such as, 'What can the department do improve the service that it provides?' and ask for comments on low-scoring items. A better approach would be to arrange a follow-up meeting to discuss the items. The survey is a tool that can be updated as the department and employees respond to and overcome deficiencies in the service provided to internal customers.

The survey should specify the level of service performed by a department or an employee that has actually been received by internal customers and requests internal customers to specify the required performance level of the activities, given the resources available. This approach is consistent with the spirit of excellent customer service, where excessive activities that do not add value to the organisation should be eliminated. Any differences between the actual and required level of services reported should be the internal service provider and internal customers. After obtaining a better understanding of the needs and expectations of internal customers through survey results, internal service providers should be equipped to focus on the performance areas that need to be improved to better satisfy the internal customer and achieve superior customer service. The survey is only a tool to assist the internal service provider to identify internal customers' requirements.

The process to be put in place to monitor internal customer service should involve the following functions:

- Identify internal customers
- Evaluate the role of the internal service provider within the organisation - a self evaluation
- Determine actual performance levels through a survey of internal customers

- Determine the level of satisfaction required within the organisation through a survey of internal customers

- Measure the satisfaction level of internal customers with respect to their needs and expectations

- Identify improvement opportunities required in work processes

- Determine what needs to be changed and develop action plans for better service

- Monitor, control and update the process

The achievement of quality customer service can only be obtained if corrective actions are taken.

• ACTIVITY 8

What functions should be addressed in the process to monitor internal customer service?

The internal service providers within the organisation should seek to improve the customer chain. They should look at their internal customers and consider the quality of service that they have provided to them and how this can be improved. This is not a mammoth task; in fact, it should be an ongoing evaluation to improve performance. It is by paying close attention to small details that contributes to providing a quality service:

- Responding to people without being chased by them - calendar a date, make a telephone call

- Keeping colleagues informed about what is happening on a project - copy them in on an email

- Arriving on time for meetings so others do not waste time waiting

Internal service providers should ask their internal customers if their service has added value to their work and offer any improvements that the internal service provider could implement. This will have a benefit for the organisation and the employee - seeking ways of improving the service they provide - but will also demonstrate how getting it right first time mean less work for everybody in the long run. Sometimes there are good reasons why work cannot be delivered to meet an internal customer's ideal specification; however, by clarifying the specification it will stop the internal customer from blaming the service provider for their inefficiency and improve their working relationship. **In summary, internal service providers can better serve their internal customers by:**

- Arriving at work on time

- Being polite

- Answering telephone calls quickly or within the agreed number of rings

- Responding to each other promptly with replies to queries

- Providing clear guidelines of what is expected of each other

- Defining roles and responsibilities

- Being professional at all times

- Going the 'extra mile' and exceeding internal customers' expectations

- Holding customer focus surgeries to discuss each other's needs

- Saying 'thank you'

The importance of internal customer service can never be underestimated. Without serving internal customers well, employees will never be able to provide and exceed the service expectations of external customers and maintain the competitive position of their organisation.

Testing your knowledge

1. What does an internal customer service provider do?

2. How are internal customers and external customers connected?

3. How can internal customer service providers be supported by the organisation?

4. What is the service chain?

5. How can employee satisfaction be achieved for

   5.1 the internal customer service provider

   5.2 the internal customer?

6. How can internal customer service problems be identified?

7. How can internal customer service problems be resolved?

8. How is internal customer service monitored in an organisation?

9. How can internal service providers better serve their internal customers?

Skills

Every employee in an organisation is an internal customer and also an internal customer service provider who, in their own way, provides information, products and / or services for delivery to external customers of the organisation. Ultimately, providing an excellent customer service to our colleagues, our fellow service providers, is strengthening all employees as well as the organisation, as it works to achieve its objectives. It is in all our best interests to be positive to one another, as this brushes off on each one of us. By behaving towards one another we enrich the customer service that we are able to provide throughout the organisation. This almost becomes a passive strategy which enriches the relationships that we can form in an organisation, department or team.

When providing customer service for an internal customer always find out from the internal customer what it is they want you to do or provide. This may not always be something that you can do independently of others. If this is the case, enquire of others as to how they can assist you. This harks back to the service chain, where internal customer service providers are linked to one another to resolve the service being provided.

• ACTIVITY 9

Answer the questions listed below, relating your answers to the delivery of your internal customer services. If possible, find someone else to complete this activity with so you can compare lists. Ideally, this should be someone who does not work in your team, because you want to get a fresh perspective on your issues:

Do you suffer from similar problems?

How much are the problems a matter of where you happen to be standing at the time?

Do the problems come from a difference of opinion over the right way to do things?

Are the problems being magnified because you do not know the individuals you are dealing with, especially over the telephone, so you tend to assume the worst of them?

Are there misunderstandings because you do not really know what other departments do or are allowed to do?

Which items on your lists can, at least in theory, be improved?

What would be the benefits to the organisation and yourself if these improvements are made?

What would it take to achieve each of those improvements?

Having agreed the parameters of the service that you are going to provide you should set about accomplishing this in the agreed time and to the agreed standards. If there are unforeseen circumstances that may not permit the service being delivered as agreed, communicate this with the internal customer. Your communication skills will be paramount in the delivery of the customer service you provide to your internal customers. With each service you provide to internal customers, which meets the objectives of the service, you are adding to the strength and morale of the organisation. In many respects, you are improving the brand of the company by the services that you provide.

It is important that you evaluate the service that you provide to internal customers. Your managers should also undertake this activity. Set up a system so that internal customers who have benefited from the service you have provided are surveyed to find out if they are satisfied with the level of service that you provided. These evaluations are opportunities for you to improve the level of service that you can provide in the future to make sure that the objectives and the purpose of the organisation are achieved by providing excellent customer service to their internal customers.

Testing your skills

1. How does your organisation recognise the value of internal customers?

2. How do you build positive relationships with the internal customers you service?

3. When you interact with internal customers what do you do to make sure you are able to provide the service they expect to receive?

4. How do you manage the process of providing customer service to internal customers?

5. If things go wrong when you are providing service to your internal customers, what do you do to resolve issues?

6. What is your organisation's procedure for handling complaints about internal customer service?

7. How many complaints have you received about the service you have provided to internal customers, if relevant? How were these resolved?

8. What system does your organisation have to evaluate the satisfaction of its internal customers?

9. What feedback have you had about the service you have provided to your internal customers?

10. How has the delivery of the service you provide to your internal customers improved over the past 12 months?

11. Where can you strengthen the skills of the service you provide to your internal customers?

Ready for assessment?
To achieve this Level 3 unit of a Business & Administration qualification, learners will need to demonstrate that they are able to perform the following activities:

1. Identified internal customers

2. Confirmed internal customers' needs in terms of products and services

3. Confirmed internal customers' needs in terms of quality standards and timescales

4. Agreed procedures to be followed if internal customers' needs were not met

5. Provided customer service to agreed quality standards

6. Provided customer service to agreed timescales

7. Checked internal customers' needs and expectations were met

8. Followed procedures, within an agreed timescale, to:

    8.1. Process problems and complaints

    8.2. Resolve problems and complaints

    8.3. Refer problems and complaints, where necessary

9. Obtained and recorded internal customers' feedback

10. Analysed and evaluated internal customers' feedback

11. Took action that lead to improvement in customer service to internal customers

You will need to produce evidence from a variety of sources to support the performance requirements of this unit.

If you carry out the 'ACTIVITIES' and respond to the 'NEED TO KNOW' questions, these will provide some of the evidence required.

Links to other units

While gathering evidence for this unit, evidence **may** also be used from evidence generated from other units within the Business & Administration suite of units. Below is a **sample** of applicable units; however, most units within the Business & Administration suite of units will also be applicable.

QCF NVQ
Communications
Communicate in a business environment (Level 3)
Develop a presentation
Deliver a presentation
Core business & administration
Manage own performance in a business environment (Level 3)
Evaluate and improve own performance in a business environment
Solve business problems (Level 3)
Work with other people in a business environment (Level 3)
Contribute to decision-making in a business environment
Contribute to negotiations in a business environment

SVQ
Communications
Communicate in a business environment
Develop a presentation
Deliver a presentation
Core business & administration
Plan how to manage and improve own performance in a business environment
Review and maintain work in a business environment
Solve business problems
Support other people to work in a business environment
Contribute to decision-making in a business environment
Contribute to negotiations in a business environment

16

Deliver, monitor and evaluate customer service to external customers

DELIVER, MONITOR AND EVALUATE CUSTOMER SERVICE TO EXTERNAL CUSTOMERS

'Deliver, monitor and evaluate customer service to external customers' is an <u>optional unit</u> which may be chosen as one of a combination of units to achieve a Qualifications and Credit Framework (QCF), National Vocational Qualification (NVQ) or Scottish Vocational Qualification (SVQ).

The aims of this unit are to:

• Understand the meaning of 'external customer'

• Know the types of products and services relevant to external customers

• Understand how to deliver customer service that meets or exceeds external customer expectations

• Understand the purpose of quality standards and timescales for delivering customer service

• Understand how to deal with external customer service problems

• Understand how to monitor and evaluate external customer service and the benefits of this

• Be able to build positive working relationships with external customers

• Be able to deliver customer services to agreed quality standards and timescales

• Be able to deal with external customer service problems and complaints

• Be able to monitor and evaluate customer services to external customers

To achieve the above aims of this unit, learners will be expected to provide evidence through the performance of work-based activities.

Knowledge

What is meant by external customers?

An external customer is any person who is not part of or affiliated with a particular organisation and who requires products and / or services or is given information about that organisation. There are two types of external customers that need to be considered: first, those external customers who are existing external customers who have requested products and / or services supplied by the organisation in the past and continue to be retained as repeat customers, and second, potential external customers who the organisation hopes to attract in order to supply the products and / or services provided by the quality of the external customer service their employees offer.

Organisations are characterised by their commitment to meeting the expectations of their external customers, if not exceeding these expectations to create an excellent, quality and superior **external customer service**.

External customer service can be provided:

* In **person**, interacting physically with the external customer

* **Online**, interacting virtually with the external customer

* **Telephonically**, interacting vocally with the external customer

Every time a person requests products and / or services from the organisation they are engaging with the organisation's external customer service, e.g. the maître d' greeting their customers as they enter a restaurant, a receptionist in a business, cashiers at department stores. External customer service is the ability of the organisation to constantly and consistently meet and, if possible, exceed customers' needs and expectations accurately and concisely. An organisation should focus on providing a service to their external customers that will make them happy and encourage them to return to use further products and / or services supplied by the organisation - repeat business is the lifeblood of organisations and is the strength of its profit margin. The organisation will also hope that this happy external customer will be dazzled by the quality of the service they have received and remain loyal to the organisation. Customer loyalty is seen as the key to success in an organisation as the customer will return again and again. Also, the customer is highly likely to advertise their service experience to others, encouraging new external customers to join and interact with the organisation.

Not all organisations want repeat business, but the importance of satisfying the customer is still the same, e.g. working for the NHS in the Accident and Emergency section - the service provided might include taking down patient details and explaining what will happen next, it might also include explaining to relatives and directing them to a ward where a patient has been taken. The service provider in this situation will try to raise the external customers' expectations by giving reassurance and the satisfaction of knowing that the service provider has done their job properly, with respect and care.

There are three different types of experiences external customer service can be given, which are:

- **Excellent** - Which produces external customers who positively advertise the quality products and services provided by the organisation. External customers who receive this type of customer service feel that not only was their custom valued but all their expectations were exceeded. An external customer who received this type of service will tell at least eight other people about the organisation

- **Good** - Which produces external customers who feel that their expectations of service were met by the service provider of the organisation. Ironically, despite the fact that this type of external customer is content with this positive service, it is the least memorable service offered by the organisation

- **Bad** - Which produces external customers who feel that their needs and expectations have not been met. This is not good for the organisation as it can ruin its reputation and incur loss of business to the organisation as external customers move their purchasing power to other organisations

Of these experiences, the organisation and its employees should strive to provide excellent external customer service.

• ACTIVITY 1

What is an external customer?

It is not easy to define what a **satisfied external customer** is as external customers come in all shapes and sizes, with different personalities, behaviours, attitudes and moods which will affect the way they engage with an organisation's service providers. However, to meet the demands of external customers requires service providers to behave in a **positive, open** and **professional manner** so external customers' needs can be addressed individually. Professionalism extends not only to what a service provider says but how they say it, making sure they engage in courteous conversation and behaviour, e.g. a good professional manner makes sure that an external customer is able to engage with the service provider as they answer and anticipate their needs. There are four components of **positive imaging** which can be used to make a good **first impression** with external customers - using the **personal assets** of a service provider to meet the needs and expectations of customers, namely:

- **Appearance** - Taking care of body language, clothing and the physical body

- **Personality** - Behaviours, communication skills and style and attitude towards external customers

- **Competencies** - Making sure that skills and knowledge are commensurate with the tasks and activities to be performed, providing service to external customers

- **Uniqueness** - What separates one service provider from another and what is their unique selling point (USP)

External customers can be immediately impressed by the way service providers present themselves. Unfamiliar external customers will evaluate service providers based on their appearance and personality. This first impression is critical for packaging the way service providers are able to brand the service they provide: what they have to contribute and how they interact with others. By strengthening these elements, the service provider also strengthens their confidence by providing a service that is familiar and true to themselves. Service providers should be well prepared, e.g. prepare a script they can use to answer frequently asked questions; rehearse the way they present themselves physically and vocally; and provide supplementary advice, guidance and information prior to it being requested - they need to learn how to anticipate the customer's needs. This applies equally to service providers who are interacting with external customers online or telephonically.

When the above personal assets are integrated with each other they become the USP of the service provider, which differentiates them from other service providers and makes a unique impression on the external customer. The service provider will be working from a position of strength and increasing their confidence in the service they provide. As service providers cultivate their assets, their impressions and the professional manner they want to display, they take charge of how they present themselves and act. However, it is important to remember that customers vary and may require handling in different ways, which the service provider will need to constantly assess and adapt to.

• ACTIVITY 2

How can service providers capitalise on their personal assets to offer excellent service?

As discussed in the previous unit on **internal customers**, quality external customer service stems from quality internal customer service, where employees feel just as appreciated and valuable as all the different types of customers that they are asked to serve. Like internal customer service, employees providing external customer service need to be fully aware of the organisation's objectives. To keep external customers happy, external service providers should:

- Present a positive image of themselves and the organisation

- Treat external customers with courtesy and respect regardless of their disposition, e.g. personality, external customers with special needs, foreign visitors, the elderly

- Make the customer feels important and help them

- Make sure they are fully stocked with products, e.g. enough change in the till

- Provide correct and up-to-date information

- Make sure equipment to provide the service is functioning, e.g. cash register, computer

- Refrain from making negative comments about a product, service or the organisation in front of external customers

- Seek ways of improving the way they interact with external customers

• ACTIVITY 3

What can a service provider do to make sure their external customers are happy?

Whereas an internal customer will have a good idea of what it is they are expecting from the service being provided by the internal service provider, many external customers are **speculative customers**, who may not necessarily know if they want anything at all, e.g. window shoppers who enter a department store with little intention of purchasing a product. Despite their lack of focus as the service provider engages with the external customer, they need to recognise at all times that the 'customer is always right!' What does this mean? Is the external customer always right? Well, not always; however, the service provider's role is to satisfy their needs and meet their expectations. A service provider is not a critic and should keep their thoughts to themselves - these should only be shared in private. Alternatively, external customers may:

- Have a precise idea of what they want but need the service provider to **facilitate** and **expedite** the service, e.g. purchase the product, deliver the service or communication information and data

- Have some idea of what they want but need some **advice** by confirming their choice (s)

- Have no idea of what they want and seek **guidance** by providing alternative choice (s)

To administer to the needs of external customers, external service providers may use the following strategies to understand and accommodate what the external customer wants, by asking the following questions:

- What is required by the external customer - a product, a service or information?

- Is the product / service / information available?

- Can the product / service / information be readily made available?

- Are the appropriate service providers available to deliver the service?

- Do they know where to find products or information?

- Do they know who to ask for further information to assist the external customer?

- Is it important or urgent?

It is incumbent on the service providers to make sure that the service they provide to their external customers remains of a high quality and is able to meet the needs and expectations of their external customers, if not anticipate them. Service can be maintained and improved by:

Upgrading skills and knowledge
Which are most appropriate for the delivery of quality service:

- **Communication skills** - Including active listening skills, e.g. knowing when and when not to be deflected by idle chatter

- **Interpersonal skills** - Building trust

- **Social skills** - Establishing rapport with external customers

- **Organisational and planning skills**

- **Time management skills** - Arriving at the service desk on time

- **Problem-solving skills** - Knowing when a problem is a problem

- **Coping with pressure and stress** - Knowing when to ask for assistance or support from others

- **The organisation's systems and procedures** - Keeping up to date with changes to product specifications

- **Standards of customer service delivery** - Knowing the level of service the organisation expects its employees to deliver constantly and consistently. The organisation may have standards centred on the way **telephone calls** are answered, usually stating what they will do and what they will do next if they cannot do the opening statement:

  - Aim to answer all telephone calls within a certain time of the first ring, e.g. after five seconds

  - Make sure telephone calls are answered. If they are not, what can be done to enable the caller to leave a message so someone can call them back

  - Make sure an enquiry is answered when the external customer telephones. If this is not possible, the organisation will tell them when they can expect to receive a response

- Make sure telephone calls are only transferred a specific number of times, e.g. once. If a telephone call cannot be transferred to the correct person straight away, the external customer's message will be recorded and answered

- When answering the telephone, employees will clearly state their name and department or team

- When returning telephone calls, employees will clearly state their name, their department or team and their reason for calling

• ACTIVITY 4

Why are communication skills so important to the delivery of external customer service?

Working more co-operatively with other service providers

A positive frame of mind is equally as important when working with other employees as it is working with external customers. Employees should strive to achieve constructive working relationships with other service providers they work with by recognising what it is both employees need from each other, working productively together and helping and supporting each other when things get tense or difficult. Learn to proactively help other service providers before being asked to assist them when they are stretched or under pressure. Provide a quality service to other employees so all employees can provide a better-quality service to their external customers.

Taking an interest in the products, services and information that is being offered to external customers.

The service provider should consider themselves to be experts in the field of the service they are providing. If it is a product they are selling they should know how it works, the market of the product, the advantages and disadvantages between different models of the product and any warranty attached to the sale of the product. If it is a service, understand the service that is being provided, how long it will take, the different types of service that could be offered and why they are different. If it is information, keep up to date with how information and data is changing. Skills and knowledge can be updated by:

- Reading leaflets about products and services

- Asking questions about products and services

- Discussing with other employees the advantages and disadvantages of products and services

- Observing and listening to employees with more experience and greater expertise

- Searching the Internet to see how information is changing and the new products and services being promoted by competitors

- Copying the way other service providers deliver their 'patter'

Empathise with the external customer
Service providers should put themselves in their external customers' shoes so they can acknowledge the quality of service they are providing.

Deal with external customers under extreme conditions
If an external customer is telephoning for an emergency service, it is no good telling them that there are no service providers available to service their fault. The service provider should know what to do in emergencies within their field, who to contact and the procedures to be followed to satisfy the external customer.

• ACTIVITY 5

What can a service provider do to maintain and improve the delivery of their external customer service?

Deal with external customer service problems
It is inevitable that external customers will provide their fair share of problems and be somewhat disgruntled with the service they have been given. They may identify problems with the level of service they have received or with the product - if it is not delivering what it promised it would. The product may be broken and missing some parts; the product may not be the right size, colour, shape; the service may not have delivered the whole specification of work; the service providers may have arrived late; the service providers may have left a mess causing damage to their property; or the information supplied was incorrect which has had a devastating effect. However large or small the problem it is very real and means something to the external customer or they would not have brought it up with the organisation to resolve.

Regardless of how good the organisation's products and services are or how committed external service providers are to provide the best customer service, problems will occur. At all times when faced with a problem situation it is best to diffuse the situation to create a loyal customer, the lifeblood of any organisation. There are rules that all service providers should implement when faced with problems:

- Remain calm and do not get caught up in the emotions of the moment - it is not personal. Use assertive skills, listen carefully, be firm but polite and allow the external customer to vent their spleen. Show your understanding of the situation and the problem and that something positive can be done to fix it. By focusing on the external customer they will realise that the employee is interested in their problem and calm down and move forward

- Apologise and empathise with the external customer even if the employee does not agree with the complaint. The customer will feel validated and will work more positively to help resolve the situation. This also helps to dilute the emotions from the situation. Empathise with the external customer and when the employee fully understands the problem relate this back to the external customer for their confirmation so both parties know they are working on the same problem

- Always work within the level of your authority, and if help is needed from managers, request it. The organisation will usually have policies and systems in place to help resolve a wide range of different types of problems; however, they may not cover everything. If the problem is accelerated to a higher level let the external customer know so they are aware of how committed the organisation is to resolving their issues

- Catalogue everything by writing it down, i.e. dates, times, names, operator ID numbers, telephone numbers, so there is a permanent and detailed outline of the circumstances of the problem so this can be used in the future to substantiate arguments both for and against the organisation

- Never promise what cannot be delivered! Whatever promises are made to the external customer to resolve their issues, make sure they are followed up. An employee should stick to their work and do what they said they were going to do. Even if a resolution has not been reached the external customer should be updated so the external customer knows the external service provider is keeping their word. This reinforces to the external customer that their business is important to the organisation and that the organisation is actively working towards resolving the problem

- Thank the external customer for bringing this problem to the attention of the organisation. The employee should thank the external customer at the beginning, middle and end of the negotiations as they work to resolve the problem

• ACTIVITY 6

How should service providers deal with external customer problems?

Most organisations will have a customer service charter establishing the procedures that they will implement in the event of complaints being raised. A customer service charter will usually have a vision or mission statement and the commitment they offer their external customers backed up with the values they believe are important to delivering quality customer service by their organisation:

- We will put you at the heart of everything we do
- We will be friendly, approachable and professional
- We will respond quickly and efficiently to requests for service and enquiries
- We will provide straightforward information about our services
- We will correct things promptly if they go wrong and learn from complaints
- We will promote equality and fair treatment
- We will strive to offer value for money
- We will aim to continuously improve our services through customer consultation

Service providers should do all that they can to resolve a problem before it escalates into a complaint. Complaints may be either major or minor and, depending on which kind of complaint it is, will require different approaches so they are resolved to the customer's satisfaction. However, whatever the kind of customer complaint, they should both be treated with equal importance so they can be resolved as quickly and satisfactorily as possible. Organisations should have a systematic and precise approach to resolving complaints which is consistently applied and adhered to by all employees within the organisation. The benefits of this to the organisation and the external customer are:

- Providing a customer-sensitive approach which contains the complaint in emotive-free communication or the taking of a defensive position, e.g. 'It is not my fault!' The aim of this approach is to minimise escalation of the complaint into the formal process the organisation will need to implement

- Reassuring external customers that their complaint is being taken seriously, with the expectation that it will be resolved by the employees of the organisation

Customer complaints come in many different forms; however, customer complaints have common characteristics, which are:

- **Emotive** - External customers are aggrieved and determined to get satisfaction

- **Multi-causal** - There may be a number of reasons for a product or service failing to meet the quality the organisation aims to deliver, e.g. traffic jams, so delivery companies are unable to deliver a package at the requested time. Causes may be within or outside the control of the organisation

- **Not always justified** - The external customer may be mistaken

- **Source of information** - To inform organisation practice in the future, which can be captured in a formal document, which acts as a checklist, a record and the basis for a reminder

When responding to an external customer's complaint, employees should adhere to the following systematic procedure:

- Listen

- Sympathise

- Clarify

- Re-clarify

- Provide a solution

- Follow-up actions

- Resolve the customer complaint

The charter will usually set out the standards of service they expect to deliver in a number of contexts, e.g. telephone calls, emails, letter and personal callers.

• ACTIVITY 7

What is a customer charter used for?

The customer charter may also have an attachment which sets out the procedures of the customer service complaints process which will inform external customers of:

- What they need to do if they want to make a complaint
- What they can expect to happen once they have made a complaint
- How their statutory rights may be affected by making a complaint
- The mediation process to follow, if necessary

Most customer complaints procedures will have a nominated person who will manage the process of customer complaints. This will set out:

- The responsibilities of employees of the organisation to resolve customer complaints
- The aspiration of the organisation to deal with customer complaints swiftly, courteously and to completion
- How customer complaints will be recorded
- The time within which a customer can expect to receive a response from the organisation about their complaint
- The follow-up action to pursue if a customer complaint has not been resolved satisfactorily within a specified amount of time agreed by the organisation, or at all
- The process for dealing with unjustified customer complaints
- The arbitration or legal process to be followed if no resolution to the customer complaint can be agreed
- The process of cooperating with any intermediary consulted by the external customer attempting to resolve the customer complaint
- The process of mediation to be followed by the organisation and the external customer making a complaint

> I know that you understand what you think I said, but I am not sure you realise that what you heard is not what I meant.
> - US President Nixon

Monitor and evaluate external customer service

For an organisation to continue to offer its business, its survival depends on retaining old customers and enticing new customers to purchase their range of products, services or information. To make sure that the organisation continues to offer excellent external customer service they need to monitor and evaluate the service being provided by their employees who are directly involved with the frontline of delivering external customer service.

Although some organisations, e.g. the NHS and other public sector services, would not be particularly interested in enticing new customers away from other organisations, they would want to monitor and evaluate the delivery of their services to make sure that they are delivering customer satisfaction to their external customers. These organisations will monitor and evaluate the delivery of their external customer service to get feedback about the quality of service their employees are providing to their external customers so they can improve the service for future external customers. If the organisation did not get the delivery of their external customer service right this time they want to make sure they do the next time round. When the organisation gets feedback from external customers about the service they are given it is not necessarily all bad or focused on problems and complaints. Some feedback is positive and reassuring. Feedback from external customers may be solicited or unsolicited and may be internal or external to the organisation. Feedback can take any of the following methods:

- **Unsolicited letters of complaint or compliment** - Recording and analysing problems external customers have written or telephoned about, which may also offer ways of improving the service the organisation delivers

- **Internal or external suggestion box** - Where all customers are given the opportunity to comment on the quality of the service they have received from the organisation

- **Comment cards** - Which will be located within the areas where the organisation delivers its service

- **Customer surveys** - Which may involve engaging directly with current and peripatetic external customers using **telephone interviews**, **talking to** and questioning them outside the building where they offer their service, using **web surveys**, which is a quick and easy way of collating and assessing results immediately, or postal **mail shots**, targeting specific demographics. A telephone call to external customers for feedback will give them a sense of contributing to how the business is run, which encourages them to continue to do business with the organisation. External customers may also be asked to fill out surveys at the end of their experiences to determine if they were pleased with the level of external customer service provided by employees. Surveys should not only target external customers to reflect on the overall service they received but also offer solutions

- **Mystery shoppers** - A trained and independent person who visits the organisation as a typical external customer to evaluate the service they are providing, e.g. they may walk into a restaurant and order a meal or challenge a specific area of service to test the flexibility of customer service. They will record detailed notes of their experiences which are forwarded to managers for analysis and discussion with employees. A mystery shopper is trained to be objective and present both negative and positive opinions based on industry standards. Mystery shoppers may present challenging behaviour, acting hard to please or attempting to return merchandise without proper receipts. The response of service providers to this type of behaviour can help managers to assess the quality of service being provided by their employees

- **Monitor and record telephone calls** - Listen to external customer service telephone calls to identify indicators to measure the quality of external customer service. The different kinds of indicators include: time to solve a problem, the number of issues handled over a certain time frame, a comparison between the level of external service provided by employees over a certain time frame, how cordially external customers are treated

- **Internal employee feedback and performance** - Ask employees to assess not only their level of external service provision but also of other employees they work with. Carry out one-to-one performance reviews with employees acting as an external customer engaging employees in a typical external customer service call. This allows managers to determine firsthand the employee's ability to handle the situation and how they use language

- **Review emails sent to external customers** - Lke recorded telephone calls, reviewing emails is an excellent way to see what language is being used with external customers

• ACTIVITY 8

What are the methods that can be used to monitor and evaluate the quality of external customer service?

The feedback information provided by any of the above methods is then evaluated to make sure that future external customer service is improved. The evaluation may focus on:

- **Level of sales** - Are sales levels increasing or decreasing?

- **Repeat customers** - How many customers return, and why?

- **New customers** - How many new customers are they getting, and why?

- **Level of complaints / compliments** - How many complaints or compliments does the organisation receive in and across specific time periods or seasons?

- **Employee turnover** - Do staff constantly leave, and why? High levels of turnover may indicate that the organisation is not a good organisation to work for, depressing morale and weakening collaborative and partnership working between employees

The organisation will want to monitor and evaluate the level of external service for:

- **External customers** - To make sure they provide a quality of service that aspires to excellence by being consistent and reliable

- **Internal customers** - To make sure employees are satisfied with their jobs and improve the working environment

- **The organisation** - To make sure it improves and provides the highest level of care to external customers, maintains and attracts new employees, maintains old external customers and attracts new ones, increases profits and continues to comply with legal obligations and regulatory standards

The whole process of monitoring and evaluating the quality of service the organisation provides to its external customers is a learning experience for the whole organisation. It is an opportunity for change and innovation. Anything that can be done to correct imbalances in the quality of service provided to external customers will allow the organisation to exercise control over the direction of its business which should ultimately increase profits or raise its level of external customer care to be recognised as an organisation that provides excellent external customer service.

Testing your knowledge

1. What is the difference between an internal customer and an external customer?

2. What do internal and external customer providers have in common?

3. What difference will there be in the service provided to external customers in person, online and telephonically?

4. How can customer service be offered in a positive, open and professional manner to external customers?

5. What are the three different types of external customer service that can be delivered?

6. How can a service be provided that satisfies the needs of external customers?

7. How can external customer service problems be identified?

8. How can external customer service problems be resolved?

9. How can external customer services be monitored in an organisation?

10. What is the difference between an external customer problem and a complaint?

11. How can external service providers improve the service they provide to their external customers?

12. What is the purpose of an organisation monitoring and evaluating the quality of service it provides to its external customers?

Skills

An employee of the organisation that provides customer service to external customers will always be expected to provide a service which meets the needs and, if possible, exceeds these by anticipating the external customers' desires, by always behaving in a professional manner, foremost of which is maintaining and projecting a positive image of themselves and their organisation, and remaining calm under pressure. You represent the organisation and everything that you say or do to the external customer will reflect back on the organisation. It is important to achieve satisfaction for the external customer as the organisation aims to retain this customer. Through your customer service your organisation wants to encourage them, either directly or indirectly, to spread the word about the organisation to encourage other customers to move their custom and allegiance to your organisation.

Providing your service is all about making sure you provide a quality product, be that making a sale, providing a service or disseminating information. The organisation you work in has to remain competitive and to do this they will always be thinking of ways of improving their products and the service they provide. If you need additional training to maintain and 'upskill' you should have this conversation with your manager. It is your responsibility to keep up with any changes that might affect the way you deliver the service you provide. This can be done by reading leaflets, searching the Internet for comparable products other organisations offer, from which you can compare your products favourably, talking up the advantages your product has over theirs. At all times your aim is to produce happy customers which you can do by strategically employing all your personal assets.

• ACTIVITY 9

Think of a situation when you were unable to resolve an external customer complaint. What would you do differently if a similar situation happened in the future?

Happy customers are produced by making sure that you understand what it is your external customers want. Always clarify with your external customers what their needs are afterwards if they are not clear to you. The external customer will not resent being prodded for additional information but, on the contrary, will feel more valued that you are taking your time to fulfil their needs. However, external customers may not always feel valued or feel that you have provided a valuable service. There are many reasons why problems may arise in the interaction between you and your external customer. Irrespective of the problems raised by external customers, always listen carefully to their complaint and do your best to resolve the issues without having to extend the situation by involving other employees. If you cannot do this, you will need to explain to the external customer what you are doing. The greatest asset you can offer an external customer when resolving problems and issues is to keep them informed of what you are doing. Never keep them in the dark, as they will find this frustrating and perhaps leave the organisation with a very negative view of the service that you offer, which they will broadcast to their friends, inhibiting potential new customers from using your organisation in the future. This applies to providing service to external customers in all forms of transactions, e.g. online, telephonically, where emphasis will be on using your skills in different ways, as you and the external customer will not be able to see each other.

• ACTIVITY 10

What motivates you to provide a quality service to your external customers? How dependent are you on others in your team to consistently provide quality external customer service?

If a customer service problem cannot be solved satisfactorily for external customers they may escalate this as a complaint. Complaints will arise from external customers which may be justified or not. Whatever the case, they need to be taken seriously and approached professionally using all the processes that the organisation has provided for this eventuality. As with problems, always listen carefully to what the external customer has to say, clarify what they have said, and write everything down so there is documented evidence of the conversation for future reference and as a means of providing evidence to improve the service if you or your organisation needs to do so in the future.

The future service you and your organisation can provide will be informed directly by your experiences and the experiences of your external customers. Your organisation will have formal and informal procedures in place to monitor and evaluate the levels of satisfaction your external customers experience, albeit real or imagined. Wherever external customers' feelings come from they need to be controlled and appeased so their experiences are not negatively advertised to other external customers your organisation hopes to retain or attract to the products they provide. Delivering service to external customers is a very important function of the organisation, it is what it is in business to deliver, because if it did not have any customers it would have no business, and it is your responsibility, as a service provider, to make sure that you continually improve the service you and other employees provide on behalf of the organisation.

The way to gain a good reputation is to endeavour to be what you desire to appear.
- Socrates

Testing your skills

1. How do you build positive relationships with external customers you service?

2. When you interact with external customers what do you do to make sure you are able to provide the service they expect to receive?

3. How do you manage the process of providing customer service to external customers?

4. If things go wrong when you are providing service to your external customers, what do you do to resolve issues?

5. What is your organisation's procedure for handling complaints about external customer service?

6. How many complaints have you received about the service you have provided to external customers, if relevant? How were these resolved?

7. What system does your organisation have to evaluate the satisfaction of its external customers?

8. What feedback have you had about the service you have provided to your external customers?

9. How has the delivery of the service you provide to your external customers improved over the past 12 months?

10. Where can you strengthen the skills of the service you provide to your external customers?

11. What standards does your organisation have for responding to telephone calls, written communication, email and face-to-face contact with external customers?

Ready for assessment?
To achieve this Level 3 unit of a Business & Administration qualification, learners will need to demonstrate that they are able to perform the following activities:

1. Identified external customers

2. Confirmed external customers' needs in terms of products and services

3. Confirmed external customers' needs in terms of quality standards and timescales

4. Agreed procedures to be followed if external customers' needs were not met

5. Provided customer service to agreed quality standards

6. Provided customer service to agreed timescales

7. Checked external customers' needs and expectations were met

8. Followed procedures, within an agreed timescale, to:

   8.1. Process problems and complaints

   8.2. Resolve problems and complaints

   8.3. Refer problems and complaints, where necessary

9. Obtained and recorded external customers' feedback

10. Analysed and evaluated external customers' feedback

11. Took action that lead to improvement in customer service to external customers

You will need to produce evidence from a variety of sources to support the performance requirements of this unit.

If you carry out the 'ACTIVITIES' and respond to the 'NEED TO KNOW' questions, these will provide some of the evidence required.

Links to other units
While gathering evidence for this unit, evidence **may** also be used from evidence generated from other units within the Business & Administration suite of units. Below is a **sample** of applicable units; however, most units within the Business & Administration suite of units will also be applicable.

QCF NVQ
Communications
Communicate in a business environment (Level 3)
Develop a presentation
Deliver a presentation
Core business & administration
Manage own performance in a business environment (Level 3)
Evaluate and improve own performance in a business environment
Solve business problems (Level 3)
Work with other people in a business environment (Level 3)
Contribute to decision-making in a business environment
Contribute to negotiations in a business environment

SVQ
Communications
Communicate in a business environment
Develop a presentation
Deliver a presentation
Core business & administration
Plan how to manage and improve own performance in a business environment
Review and maintain work in a business environment
Solve business problems
Support other people to work in a business environment
Contribute to decision-making in a business environment
Contribute to negotiations in a business environment

17

Contribute to innovation in a business environment

CONTRIBUTE TO INNOVATION IN A BUSINESS ENVIRONMENT

'Contribute to innovation in a business environment' is an <u>optional unit</u> which may be chosen as one of a combination of units to achieve either a Qualifications and Credit Framework (QCF), National Vocational Qualification (NvQ) or Scottish Vocational Qualification (SVQ).

The aims of this unit are to:

- Understand the purpose and benefits of innovation in a business environment

- Understand how to contribute to research, development and review ideas for new approaches and solutions

- Understand how to present suggestions for new approaches and solutions

- Be able to contribute to research and develop ideas

- Be able to present suggestions for new approaches and solutions

- Be able to evaluate, review and make suggestions for new approaches and solutions

To achieve the above aims of this unit, learners will be expected to provide evidence through the performance of work-based activities.

Knowledge

Innovation can be described as a 'flash of genius', a 'light-bulb moment' or 'a vision of pellucid clarity' where existing products and services can be converted from something which is already accepted to something that needs to be accepted and will meet the expectations of a society or an economy, the market place. Innovation, within a business environment, is focused on the process of improving, updating or creating a new system, which includes new ways of working or product development. Innovation is about changing the behaviour of people or customers and, as such, should be close to the market, focused on the market and driven by the market. It will exploit the knowledge of a particular field, e.g. information technology skills, processes, new systems, and evaluate the new idea to create or improve products or services offered by the organisation in a particular market.

Consideration also needs to be given to the effects of globalisation, as the world shrinks to a global village, and the impact this has not only on the tangible aspects but also the intangible aspects of a business. This also imposes the characteristic of 'time' forcing adjustments, adaptations and changes to a business as the organisation aims to maintain its competitive edge. The impact of globalisation on organisations is increasing the need for collaborative working. For example, many recent developments in technology are the result of combinations of different discoveries or insights that are unlikely to be found in a single company. Technological developments in information technology and communications make such collaboration easier all the time, e.g. social networks and the potential they have of reaching into the lives of organisations' loyal supporters. As the business world becomes less concrete and tangible due to the rise of the virtual business world, collaborative ways of working will become more widespread.

In the business world, innovation is extremely important as the key to growth. Innovation allows a business to surpass competitors and keep employees happy and productive. However, innovation can be neglected by allowing busy schedules and day-to-day activities to get in the way of developing and implementing new ideas. Organisations should have strategies in place to strengthen and encourage innovative practice:

- Pinpoint and evaluate problems or stagnation the business is currently experiencing through its adherence to maintaining the status quo

- Involve and encourage employees to contribute to the creation and evolution of innovation strategies, e.g. put forward new ideas in the best means possible

- Recruit help either internally or externally, employing the skills and knowledge to provide a more objective perspective and provide fresh ideas gained from working with other organisations

- Establish a common set of objectives, benchmarked and with a timeline, which are publicised to employees throughout the organisation to promote innovation as a priority

- Stay true to the organisation's core values to meet the expectations of core clients and customers

- Test new programmes of work and ideas on a small level first, by developing small pilot programmes to test the market or other limited ways of implementing and evaluating new ideas, products or services, to minimise risk as the innovation is realised

Innovation in business means that business practice is always changing, which can happen as a response to:

- **Changes and improvements in technology -** e.g. improvements in computer technology

- **External services used by the organisation -** e.g. telephone and communication services, courier services, cleaning services

- **Services and products provided by competitors**

- **Government, national and international influences** - e.g. health and safety legislation

• ACTIVITY 1

What is innovation?

One of the greater innovators of all time was Thomas Edison 1847-1931, who invented the light bulb, who always asked himself these questions:

- What needs do people have that I can fulfil?

- What trend or trends are present here?

- What opportunities do they present?

- What are the current gaps in the marketplace?

- What is the insight that can lead me to create greater value in this segment?

- How can I leverage what I know about this category or industry that makes sense for my laboratory and my brand name?

- How can I test the efficacy of my idea?

Whatever the project, Edison focused on how he could deliver the greatest possible value to the marketplace. He used a five-step process to launch his inventions:

- Identify trends in the marketplace, observing where and how needs are shifting

- Determine if there are any gaps created by these changing needs

- Identify the core insight - the 'aha!' factor - or need at the heart of each gap

- Link insights to capabilities of the organisation and strengths and weaknesses in relation to competitors

- Identify the hypothesis as an 'if-then' proposal for a practical experiment about the goal that is being sought to fulfil based on the linkages created

Edison's approach has close links to the concepts put forward by Drucker who followed him.

Innovation can be **proactive** or **reactive**. Proactive innovation is when the organisation is in control of its development and has a clear vision and strategy of remaining competitive and at the cutting edge of offering the products and services it produces. The size of a proactive operation will depend on the products and services that the organisation produces and in a highly technical area may have a dedicated research and development department who select people with the specific skills and knowledge to produce or redevelop high-end products and services. Organisations acting proactively will have developed business plans which clearly identify the scope of what has to be done over specific time frames. Reactive innovation is in many respects a more chaotic approach to the production or redevelopment of the organisation's products and services. The influence to change will be external to the organisation. The impetus for innovation may come from the politics, legislation - national or international - the environment, e.g. the effects of the BP oil spill in the Gulf of Mexico will influence how oil companies need to innovate products, systems, processes, health and safety, so that dangers, both social and economic, to the environment and people from oil spills and equipment are minimised, if not eliminated. It is difficult to predict how and when these changes might occur. However, it is important to keep pace with what is happening in the immediate business environment of the organisation so it reacts quickly so it remains competitive.

Many potential areas for change, or where change is more pronounced is driven by the impact of social and economic causes, e.g. the development of social networks has affected how organisations have the potential to penetrate new markets and target individual consumers, the recession of 2008 has created new financial regulation which will have an impact on the development of new financial products. Another main area of innovation is in the field of technology. This is a fast-paced environment where learning is a constant activity. It is important for an organisation to consider the evolution of all of these effects that can impact on the products and services offered by the organisation. Innovation will give the organisation the ability to envisage a vision of its future, employ the relevant skills and knowledge to translate this vision into concrete products and services and promote a business environment to foster new ideas. The process of innovation is about creating value for the organisation, i.e. an organisation that always provides valuable and beneficial products or services to its customers and potential customers.

• ACTIVITY 2

What can stimulate the drive to innovate?

Innovation is work. It requires commitment, diligence, persistence, knowledge, ingenuity, talent and a predisposition to working innovatively. Innovation is very meaningful for the development of a business as a means of keeping the organisation competitive and open for business. It involves finding a new and better way of doing something. Everyday life is influenced continually by the need to innovate. Linked with innovation is entrepreneurship, which involves looking for a new innovation and taking advantage of it. **Drucker**, a leading authority on innovation, has outlined **seven sources or places to look for innovative opportunities**. These should be monitored by those interested in starting an entrepreneurial venture. Drucker's seven sources of innovation opportunities are:

• **The unexpected** - Occurring from any source, e.g. success, failure or an unexpected external event to the organisation	
• **The incongruity** - Occurring as a discrepancy between reality and what everyone assumes it to be, or between what is and what ought to be	Internal influences that the organisation can **proactively** drive
• **Innovation based on process need** - Occurring when a weak link is evident in a particular process, but people work around it instead of doing something about it, an opportunity is available to the person or company willing to supply the 'missing link'	
• **Changes in industry or market structure** - Occurring when there is a fundamental change to the underlying foundation of the industry or if the market shifts	
• **Demographics** - Occurring when there are changes in the population's size, age structure, composition, employment, level of education and income	
• **Changes in perception, mood and meaning** - Occurring when a society's general assumptions, attitudes and beliefs change	External influences that the organisation **reacts** to as a result of changes to the social environment
• **New knowledge** - Occurring when advances in scientific and non-scientific knowledge can create new products and new markets	

Drucker also identified five principles of innovation, namely:

- Begin with an **analysis of the opportunity**. Conceptualise the opportunity, thinking through different sources of innovation opportunities. In different markets, different sources will have a different level of importance at different times. Systematically study and analyse innovation opportunities, which should be done regularly to maintain an organisation's competitive edge

- Analyse the opportunity to **see if people will be interested in using the innovation**. Go out to look, ask, listen and analyse what the innovation has to be to satisfy an opportunity. This should include analysing customers - the end-users - to see if the innovative approach will fit with customer values, needs, habits and expectations so they will want to use it

- Focus on a **specific need which is clear and simple**. It should be focused on a specific need that it satisfies and on a specific end result that it produces - it should aim to do only one thing

- **Start small**. By appealing to a small, limited market, a product or service requires little money and few people to produce and sell it. As the market grows, the organisation will have time to shape its processes to stay ahead of emerging competition. Innovation should concentrate on one specific thing, as there may be few resources, e.g. finance, people, or it may only have a small and limited market that can be diverted to realising the outcome of the innovation opportunity. Innovation takes time as adjustments and changes will need to be made to perfect the product or service. Adjustments and changes are easier to make if the scale of the innovation is small

- Aim for **market leadership**. If an innovation does not aim at market leadership from the beginning, the innovation is not likely to be innovative enough to successfully establish itself. Leadership can mean dominating a small market niche. Do not: try to be clever, as innovations have to be handled by ordinary customers; try to do too many things at once, as the people who realise the innovation have to understand each other; and, innovate for the present not the future, as the product or service needs to be applied immediately

• ACTIVITY 3

What are Drucker's five principles of innovation?

Drucker's sources of innovation and principles of innovation focus on the opportunity to innovate. The innovation opportunity is something that needs to be built into the purpose of the organisation through its mission and value statements which will inform the culture of the organisation and influence the way its employees go about their work to attract and maintain loyal customers through the products and services it offers. In this way the spur to innovate becomes organic and holistic to all employees working in an organisation. Innovation is nurtured and developed from within the organisation and thus is more able to respond to external influences over which the organisation has no control. Innovation is not an 'add on' but should be critical to the business strategy of an organisation so it can see what it needs to add, remove, increase or decrease to continue to maintain and build a loyal customer base. By taking such action the organisation engages in executing innovation within its business. Joyce Wycoff, 2004, argued for 10 practical steps to maintain the life of innovation within an organisation, which are:

- **Eliminate the fear** in the organisation. Innovation means doing something new, e.g. something new will probably fail if people are always overwhelmed with the fear of failure

- Make innovation a **part of the performance appraisal system** of each person. Ask employees about what potentially they could create or redevelop in the future, and then follow its progress. However, managers will need to be cautious in their assessments as some employees may not have the cognitive or emotional fit to innovate, so they will need to recognise what their employees are good at and focus them in that direction. It is building on strengths

- **Note and document** each innovation opportunity process and make sure everyone can understand their role in its creation

- Give **discretion to employees** to be able to explore new possibilities and collaborate with others, both within an organisation and outside the organisation

- Make sure all employees **understand the strategy of the organisation** to make sure that all innovation opportunities are in tune with the existing organisational strategy

- **Motivate everyone to be able to scan the environment**, e.g. new trends, technology or the changing mindset of a customer or society at large

- **Motivate everyone to appreciate diversity**, in style of thinking, perspectives, experience and expertise, as the innovation opportunity will present diverse activities which will be interconnected in the process of innovation

- **Determine the measurable criteria with a focus on the ideals of the organisation's future**. Strict criteria would only hinder the achievement of the ideals and preserve a variety of assumptions. Devote time to the development and success of the organisation to secure a bright future

- **Innovation teams** are different from regular project teams which requires different equipment and a different mindset. Adequate training should be provided so that everyone can work successfully to realise an innovation opportunity

- **Develop a management system idea** and develop and evaluate every idea with a variety of possibilities

• ACTIVITY 4

How can innovation in the organisation be maintained?

Innovation can be uncomfortable for employees within an organisation despite the best efforts of the organisation to promote the realisation of innovation opportunities. At a senior level within the organisation executives are focused on homogenising the culture of the organisation so that it can easily achieve its desired purpose. By reinforcing the need to innovate, an organisation can be constantly changing its culture to accommodate the process of finding, selecting and realising innovation opportunities. Innovation identifies within the organisation the idea that there may be an absence or shortage of the required skills for the business to realise its purpose, as innovation is about acknowledging breakthroughs in product or service development or recognising and anticipating how customer needs and wants in the future may change. As such, innovation requires a different set of skills from those that are promoted in the organisation, e.g. while there might be a scientific approach to innovation it is based on 'flashes of insight', which have risks attached to them and are by no means certain to pay off - there may be nothing to base the substance of the 'flash of insight' upon.

The concept of innovation is fairly unpredictable, as the organisation may not have been prepared to react to market forces. Senior executives within an organisation are focused on living in and promoting a stable business environment, whereas innovation is predisposed to nurturing an unpredictable business environment and an uncertain future. Innovation can be incredibly disruptive. Innovation can create a business environment of constant change which needs managing. Few senior executives are interested in managing the impact of this change as a result of perceived disruptive ideas, even if they do increase market share and meet the needs of their loyal customers. Many senior executives would happily swap regular, consistent growth in single digits for wild swings in growth based on occasional disruptive ideas.

Innovation is rarely in the hands of one person and is a process that will have shared responsibilities. This should be led by the vision of the senior executive; however, they will probably delegate functions within the innovative process which may feel to them as they do not have overall control of the innovation process - they will have to relinquish some of the decision-making process to other people. The more innovation is promoted within the organisation, the less control senior executives have about products, strategy and direction. This is why it is important for the organisation to align its innovative process with a clear strategy, goals and direction, so that innovation is completely governed by that vision.

Innovation can be perceived as being too risky for the organisation to continually implement in parallel with running the organisation to meet the day-to-day needs of the purpose for which the organisation has been established. However, contrary to such a perception, successful innovators tend not to be 'risk takers' as they clearly define the risks they have to take so they can be minimised; they confine risks to established areas; they systematically analyse the sources of innovative opportunity which they then focus in on and exploit to realise the vision of the organisation. Senior executives generally are more interested in using critical thinking to rescope the changing needs of an organisation, whereas   the innovative process relies on the synergy of critical thinking and creative thinking, the later being limitless in its results and not having to work along clear demarcations of output or outcomes.

Recent thinking towards realising a sensible approach for businesses of all sizes and across different sectors is to adopt the concept of **open innovation**. Open innovation is a model enabling businesses to create an innovation 'ecosystem' that uses networks of external partners and focuses on developing core internal competencies only in areas where they can add real value. This builds on past management thinking, e.g. business process re-engineering, outsourcing. Open innovation means not having total control over something that might be regarded as vital to the business, namely innovation and its results in realising new **intellectual property**. This model poses many challenges to the traditional concept of the organisation and how it manages its business.

Creative thinking
There are a number of theories that exist which focus on creative thinking, e.g. the work of Edward de Bono; however, this portion of the

chapter will focus on the work of Roger Von Oech, who has pioneered ways of becoming more creative since the 1980s.Von Oech argues that to think more creatively and allow a more innovative approach needs knowledge and the attitude of an enquiring mind that searches for new ideas or different ways of approaching old ideas and can manipulate existing knowledge and experience. Essentially, he is advocating working within yourself, through yourself and beyond yourself with limitless possibilities to approaching the ways an idea can be expressed. However, there are mental locks which prevent people from doing things differently more often then they could. Working within the organisation is working to the established routinisation of work, harnessing an employee's attitude to accomplish tasks and activities to the required standard, which is a repeated function an employee will continue to do from day to day. These routines are indispensible to an employee as they give structure and expected outcomes. But they also limit looking at how employees work and how processes and systems can be changed to improve the delivery of products and services.

• ACTIVITY 5

What is a mental lock?

Von Oech identifies 10 different kinds of mental locks, namely:

- **The right answer** - Only look for the one right answer rather than recognising that there may be a second right answer by asking **what if** - a question that can be used to release all of the mental locks that Von Oech outlines - playing the fool, reversing a problem, breaking the rules

- **That is not logical** - By relying excessively on a logical explanation, which is an important creative thinking tool in itself, especially when evaluating ideas and taking action with them, during the exploration of ideas it can short-circuit the creative process which should focus on the logic of the metaphorical - compare things - the fantastical, the elliptical and the ambiguous

- **Follow the rules** - Maintains pattern as they are. Creative thinking should allow the thinker to be constructive as well as destructive. Be flexible with rules. By breaking a rule other patterns may be discovered

- **Be practical** - The organisation and business world were built by practical people who used their imagination, so build on their ideas

- **Play it frivolous** - Play with a problem, as play is the father of invention

- **That is not my area** - May restrict thinking by depending too heavily on specialised areas of skills and knowledge which will limit the way an employee will look at a problem by only looking at ideas within spheres of understanding. As an antidote, develop an explorer's attitude, read fiction and read outside normal areas of interest

- **Avoid ambiguity** - Which is important for many roles, e.g. health and safety; however, too much specificity can stifle the imagination when searching for and playing with ideas

- **Do not be foolish** - By conforming and going along with groupthink. However, as much as these ways of thinking can be appropriate in some contexts, when working creatively, generating and investigating ideas, be a fool, destabilise habits, rules and conventions that keep people thinking in the same traditional fixed way

- **To err is wrong** - Be prepared to take a risk which may falter and be wrong, but use this mistake to galvanise an idea that may not have been explored. Differentiate between mistakes that can be one of 'omission' or 'commission', as the latter may be more costly than the former. Making mistakes is an important way of finding out how things work and aligns everybody to the purpose for which creative thinking is being used

- **I am not creative** - Try new things and build on these from what is found. The creative person believes their ideas will lead somewhere

• ACTIVITY 6

Outline one of Edward de Bono's approaches to thinking creatively and how this would encourage the creation of innovative ideas?

Von Oech argues that these are habits that have been learned, so the way to overcome them is quite simply to recognise what the habits are and either unlearn them or temporarily forget what we know so the familiar becomes unknowable, which should lead to enquiry or to a 'whack on the side of the head'. Examples of a 'whack on the side of the head' include:

- Being fired from a job

- A question that has not been thought of
- A joke
- Having an accident
- Being alerted to a talent in an area an employee never thought they had by being put on a project which uses this talent

As a guide to thinking creatively, Von Oech suggests:

- Be dissatisfied
- Map our your plans
- Take a whack at it
- Get rid of excuses
- Have something at stake
- Get support
- Sell, sell, sell
- Be courageous
- Get a deadline
- Fight for it
- Be persistent

There are no hard and fast strategies to be used when thinking creatively, as these will vary from person to person and be dictated by the situation that person finds themselves in. As with all things in life it should be tempered by the purpose for which thinking is being employed. Creative thinking could also be thought of as productive thinking or thinking outside the box. The process of creative thinking is further enriched by working with other employees who can challenge ideas shared within the discussion to question their rationale and how they meet the requirements of the project for which ideas are being exchanged. The idea of thinking of ideas being exchanged is helpful in recognising the worth of an idea, which may be too expensive for the organisation to implement, or it may take too much time given the parameters of a project or the organisation may not have all the resources required to realise an idea.

> Some people have ideas. A few carry them into the world of action and make them happen. These are the innovators.
> - *Andrew Mercer, innovator*

Work with others in the innovation process

An innovation opportunity can arise either individually or from within a group of colleagues. In the latter context, this may happen formally, e.g. a meeting is arranged to resolve a problem, or informally, e.g. a group of colleagues who meet when a new idea has been recognised as worthy of exploration. At both formal and informal meetings, people share points of view until a consensus is agreed. Each member of the group will contribute towards exploring ideas until an agreed innovation opportunity is agreed to be implemented. The aim of working in a group to explore innovation opportunities will:

- Define the innovation opportunities to be explored which are valid

- Share sources of information in the setting of innovation opportunities

- Help to explore a specific innovation opportunity through the diverse skills and knowledge a group can offer

- Identify the potential impact of innovation opportunities on various clients and internal and external customers

- Identify and share possible ideas to be explored

- Define the complexity of innovation opportunities

- Offer a consensus to the best ideas being put forward to realise innovation opportunities

Only the most suitable and relevant people should be involved in this process of sharing ideas.

• ACTIVITY 7

How can working with others in a group help the innovation process?

Advantages of working with others:

- **Increased output** - The more people there are the more skills, knowledge and experience can be pooled to find a solution

- **Exchange of ideas** - Ideas are explored that may not have been considered by one person

- **Reduced bias** - A group can explore unrealistic ideas that personal prejudice may not have considered

- **Risk taking** - As more people are involved in the discussion, individuals are more willing to take risks in sharing their ideas

- **Commitment** - In a group, commitment is improved as a result of sharing a common purpose

- **Communication** - In a group, communication is improved due to the involvement and expertise this brings to the exploration of innovative opportunities

- **Better solutions** - A stimulating environment is created which encourages the discussion of diverse ideas which lead to more solutions and better solutions to the innovative process

Disadvantages of working with others:

- **Competition** - In a group, competition may undermine the innovative process because the perception of behaviours encourages negative behaviour

- **Conformity** - People will reduce their thinking to the agreed ideas, they will not want to upset the group or be seen as different

- **Lack of direction** - Where a meeting to explore innovative opportunities has been arranged with no effective direction in place

- **Time** - Arranging a meeting to explore innovative opportunities can be a slow process. Having lots of different people adding lots of different ideas during the meeting can also take up valuable time

As part of the group a group member should aim to:

- **Contribute to creating an environment of mutual respect** - Group members may not participate in a discussion for different reasons: unfamiliarity, fear of criticism or reproach, ignorance, lack of interest, inability to think quickly or speak fluently, shyness, resentment of a group member etc. Treat fellow group members as individuals and frame contributions so that they draw on the resources of the group. Consider all ideas, using all points of view and evaluate possible answers to contribute to discussions

- **Promote open discussion within the group** - By **actively listening** and giving group members the opportunity to express their opinions without fear of criticism, which encourages group members to be less guarded in their responses and more open to sharing their ideas. There is no such thing as a bad idea and every idea is worthy of discussion

- **Know when to get involved** - Use the following skills to keep up to date with the discussions: **silence** - use it to allow independence of thinking within the discussion; **questions** - directed at group members, these should use the appropriate form and be non-threatening; and **summarise** - clarify the discussion points but do not put words in people's mouth. During the discussion use these skills to encourage other group members to remain involved in the discussion

- **Positively acknowledge responses from other group members** - As this will fertilise the discussion and maintain involvement from group members

• ACTIVITY 8

What are the advantages and disadvantages of working with others in the innovation process?

The innovative process can be improved by using the following procedures:

Identify and agree the purpose of innovative opportunities
Why has the need for innovation arisen? What is the context within which the innovation is being made? It is important to create a constructive environment within which all invited employees can attend to the innovation process. To make a constructive environment:

- **Define what needs to be achieved**

- **Agree how the final decision about the innovative opportunity will be made**

- **Involve the right people** - Consult appropriate stakeholders

- **Encourage people to contribute wholeheartedly to discussions** - The objective of the innovation process is to explore different ideas, which includes selecting the right people to be involved in the innovation process

- **Ask the correct questions** - Identify what the true issue is to be investigated before deciding on the idea to move forward with

- **Be creative** - Think from different perspectives, as this will generate new ideas and encourage new ways of exploring innovative opportunities

Gather all relevant information to generate ideas

What factors need to be considered from this information to make the right decision about ideas and the innovative opportunity?

Identify the criteria to judge the worth of exploring alternative ideas

What factors will form the basis for exploring ideas in greater depth.

Generate ideas

Use different methods to gather lots of different ideas. This is a critical stage in the innovation process. More alternatives will lead to more informed and innovative ideas which have considered all possibilities, even absurd ideas. This is an environment which should have no limits to creative thinking. Generating ideas is like mining, digging deeper and deeper to find that stream of gold! Some tools that can be used to generate ideas are:

- **Brainstorming** - Which facilitate the generation of lots of ideas. Group participants are encouraged to be as creative as possible without restriction. This results in more equal involvement from the group. The steps involved in brainstorming are:

  - Define questions, then ask group members to generate as many ideas about an innovation opportunity

  - Define Do not criticise any idea, regardless of how wild or crazy it appears

  - Define Do not discuss any proposed ideas until the brainstorming session is over

  - Define Encourage people to expand on proposed ideas

  - Define Collect all the ideas together so all group members can view them

- **Reverse brainstorming** - Ask people to brainstorm how to achieve the opposite outcome from the one wanted, and then reverse the action

- Define **Charette procedure:** gather and develop ideas from many stakeholders

- Gather different perspectives through:

  - Define **Reframing matrix:** using the **4Ps** - product, planning, potential and people - to gather different perspectives

  - Define **Concept fan:** if there are few options, or an unsatisfactory alternative to consider, this process approaches the exploration of innovative opportunities from a wider perspective

  - Define **Appreciative inquiry:** this approaches the factors from the point of view of what's 'going right', rather than what's 'going wrong'

  - Define **Organise ideas:** if there are a large number of ideas organise them into common themes

• ACTIVITY 9

How can ideas be generated in the innovation process?

Finding ideas can be a taxing occupation. If ideas are not flowing freely find external inputs to stimulate the mind. These external inputs can break down mental defences and stimulate creativity. For an external input to be useful it should have a quality of diversity - get diverse inputs to stimulate the mind, which will create connections between an input and the innovative opportunties being explored. External inputs that may be effective to create ideas include:

- Define **a clean and clear workstation -** This gives the opportunity to break away from the workspace, which gets blood pumping in the body. It removes clutter, which allows greater focus

- **An agreed deadline -** As it forces focus on a goal, which gives scope and perspective

- **Using different mediums of expression -** Change can have a big impact on creativity

- **Defining the situation clearly and focus on that**

- **Gathering together lots of materials -** e.g. sources of information that will be needed to make a decision. Sometimes, looking at something differently will generate a new idea

- **Relaxed breathing, cool the nerves** - It takes a clear, cool mind to generate great ideas. Breathing gives decision-makers a sense of control and boosts confidence

- **Creating a mind map** - Put down what is known and organise it. A mind map identifies what is known and what needs to be known

- **Asking a friend for advice**

- **Thinking with your eyes wide shut** - As this will push away visual distractions

- **Sleeping on it**

- **Using a search engine**

- **Asking questions**

- **Playing music**

- **Exercising**

- **Perspiration, not inspiration** - Thomas Edison said: "Genius is 1% inspiration and 99% perspiration." Eventually perspiration will lead to inspiration

• ACTIVITY 10

What is an external input and what strategies can be used to stimulate ideas?

Review and evaluate alternative innovations for cost impact
Make sure alternatives are realistic by evaluating each alternative for:

- **Risks** - As there is some degree of uncertainty in deciding which idea to develop, the risk needs to be manageable. Risks should be evaluated objectively through a risk analysis, which could be done using a **SWOT analysis**

- **Impact** - Evaluate the potential consequences of alternative ideas, which could be done using **De Bono's Six Thinking Hats method**

- **Validity** - Identify if resources are adequate, if the ideas match objectives and if the innovation is likely to work in the long term, which could be done using **Starbursting**, **Force Field Analysis** or **Cost-benefit Analysis**

Select the innovation to develop

Choose from among the above-mentioned options and agree alternative innovative approaches and decide the most appropriate one to action. If this is not clear cut, an analysis of alternatives can be done using the following methods:

- **Decision matrix** - Brings divergent factors into the decision-making process in a reliable and rigorous way

- **Paired comparison analysis** - Evaluates the relative importance of disparate factors. This compares unlike factors and decides which ones should carry the most weight in making a decision about ideas and innovative opportunities

- **Decision trees** - These help to choose between alternatives. They identify the likelihood of project success or a failure in the decision-making process

Check the innovation decision

Look at the innovation decisions about to be implemented objectively, for a final check, to make sure the innovation decision-making process has been thorough. The aim is to avoid any errors that may have crept into the innovation decision-making process. Test all the assumptions underlying the decision; make sure any decision-making errors, e.g. over-confidence, groupthink, have been identified and rectified; and check through the structure of the decision.

Communicate the innovation decision and action it

Explain to all stakeholders affected by the innovation why this innovation was selected. Provide as much information so all stakeholders are fully informed to minimise any risks and promote the outcome of the innovation to gain support for the innovation.

Review and evaluate the outcome of the innovation selected

What lessons can be learned from the decision taken to select an innovation and the innovation decision-making process of all those involved in making the decision? This will lead to the development of innovation and decision-making skills in the future.

Innovation is not something to be feared. It is an endeavour that should be embraced by the organisation and its employees. It will strengthen the organisation and the business as it aims to increase its market share. Innovation should be linked to the purpose of the organisation so it is encultured into the cognitive and emotional fabric of the organisation. The organisation should aim to encourage open thinking and support its internal customers so they can achieve the purpose of business with less stress and far greater business success.

> If you don't ask "why this?" often enough, somebody will ask, "why you?"
>
> *- Tom Hirshfield, Physicist*

Testing your knowledge

1. What are the different types of innovation? Show examples of each type.

2. Why is innovation important to the organisation?

3. What strategies can be employed to encourage innovation in the organisation?

4. What are the seven sources to look for innovative opportunities?

5. What can adversely affect the delivery of innovative practice in the organisation as a result of senior executive reservations?

6. What is open innovation?

7. Describe Von Oech's approach to creative thinking.

8. What processes can be used to improve the innovation process?

Skills

Working within any organisation will always provide the opportunity of reviewing the way that you work and the materials, processes and systems that you work with. You may find as you have got more familiar with them and, as your job role may have changed, you will have noticed that things could be improved so that you can work more efficiently and effectively, i.e. you are able to complete work ahead of schedule and more meaningfully. This could be as simple as noting the ergonomic management of your workstation to a computer program that you work with. As a member of the organisation, and feeding into the purpose of the organisation, it is important to remain vigilant of ways to improve working practices.

Aside from the individual contributions you can make to improving the ways things are done in your organisation, there will be the opportunity to work as a member of a team specifically to brainstorm ideas about improving existing processes, systems, products or services, working within a team to create these afresh. As such, you may be involved in different stages of the development of innovative opportunities. With this level of investigation, perhaps the most important way to approach this work is to remain totally open to any suggestions or ideas that may come into your head or from any other member of the innovation team. No matter how ridiculous it may sound, allow all ideas to filter into the discussion. You may find that a really bad idea may be the springboard for generating another idea. Use the ideas put forward by Van Oech to release manual locks to free your imagination. It is probably a good idea, when working with a group of people, to agree some ground rules up front, to allow ideas to be generated freely without fear of being censured if an idea sounds absurd. The environment for using your imagination and creativity should be open and free from criticism in the first stages of exploring ideas. Once options have been evaluated, then the team can expand on the pros and cons of an innovative idea. There should always be clear objectives for exploring innovative opportunities, which should conform to the purpose for which the opportunity to innovate is being addressed.

• ACTIVITY 10

Propose to your manager to spend one or two days next month doing something unusual. What would it be? What would make it worthwhile, from both your point of view and that of your manager, to undertake this activity - how would you propose it and sell it?

You will need to consider things such as making sure ideas fit with organisational vision and ethos, e.g. if working in an organisation that produces and promotes organic food, it would not be consistent with the vision and ethos of the organisation to suggest the use of insecticides as a means of increasing productivity of product; the time factor involved in generating ideas; the cost to the organisation to implement the improved or new innovation; the fit with client or customer expectations; any legislation that applies to your sector or industry; health and safety implications; and other specific requirements that your organisation insists on. It is important, when working on innovative opportunities, to be able to express and communicate your ideas succinctly and in a manner which sells the benefits of your ideas. The creative environment in which ideas will be generated and explored will allow you to contribute to other people's ideas and build on them. As you feedback and receive feedback, always take a constructive and positive attitude, as the innovative process can be a very sensitive process for all members of the innovation involved in generating ideas to reach the required innovation opportunity.

• ACTIVITY 12

What activity could you do to make yourself more creative?

It is important to remember that there may be excellent ideas but they may be discounted because of the parameters that the innovation process has set. File these ideas away, as they may be reshaped to meet the requirements of future innovation opportunities.

Testing your skills

1. How have you contributed to the innovation process?

2. How have you questioned ways of working within your area of work to come up with new ideas and innovations?

3. What sources of information have you used to identify potential innovation opportunities?

4. How did you contribute to moving from ideas to agreeing an innovation?

5. How were innovation opportunities managed so that they always met the purpose and vision of the organisation?

6. How did you know when an innovative opportunity was efficacious?

7. How did you sell your ideas for innovation opportunities?

8. How did the feedback from others affect the way you contributed to the development of innovation opportunities?

Ready for assessment?
To achieve this Level 3 unit of a Business & Administration qualification, learners will need to demonstrate that they are able to perform the following activities:

1. Questioned constructively existing ways of working in own area of responsibility

2. Contributed to researching and identifying possible improvements to working methods, products or services in own area of responsibility

3. Contributed to the collection of information that could be used to develop ideas for new approaches and solutions

4. Agreed criteria for evaluating ideas, including fit with organisational aims and objectives

5. Presented and sold suggestions for new approaches and / or solutions

6. Communicated risks to others in a suitable format

7. Contributed to the evaluation of ideas for new approaches and solutions using:

   7.1. Organisational aims and objectives

   7.2. Other agreed criteria

8. Evaluated ideas to challenge own assumptions and thinking about ways of working, products or services

9. Contributed to the selling of ideas to others

10. Sought feedback on ideas, analysed feedback and showed a willingness to compromise

11. Contributed to the assessment of an idea / ideas and decided whether a suggestion for a new approach / solution was possible

You will need to produce evidence from a variety of sources to support the performance requirements of this unit.

If you carry out the 'ACTIVITIES' and respond to the 'NEED TO KNOW' questions, these will provide some of the evidence required.

Links to other units

While gathering evidence for this unit, evidence may also be used from evidence generated from other units within the Business & Administration suite of units. Below is a sample of applicable units; however, most units within the Business & Administration suite of units will also be applicable.

QCF NVQ
Communications
Communicate in a business environment (Level 3)
Develop a presentation
Deliver a presentation
Core business & administration
Manage own performance in a business environment (Level 3)
Evaluate and improve own performance in a business environment
Solve business problems (Level 3)
Work with other people in a business environment (Level 3)
Contribute to decision-making in a business environment

SVQ
Communications
Communicate in a business environment
Develop a presentation
Deliver a presentation
Core business & administration
Plan how to manage and improve own performance in a business environment
Review and maintain work in a business environment
Solve business problems
Support other people to work in a business environment
Contribute to decision-making in a business environment

18 Design and produce documents in a business environment

DESIGN AND PRODUCE DOCUMENTS IN A BUSINESS ENVIRONMENT

'Design and produce documents in a business environment' is an optional unit which may be chosen as one of a combination of units to achieve either a Qualifications and Credit Framework (QCF), National Vocational Qualification (NVQ) or Scottish Vocational Qualification (SVQ).

The aims of this unit are to:

- Understand the purpose and value of designing and producing high-quality and attractive documents in a business environment

- Know what resources are available to design and produce documents and how to use them

- Understand the purpose and value of following procedures when designing and producing documents in a business environment

- Be able to design and produce documents to agreed specifications in a business environment

To achieve the above aims of this unit, learners will be expected to provide evidence through the performance of work-based activities.

Knowledge

The production of documents in a business environment should look professional and attractive. The document projects the image, branding and professionalism of an organisation, i.e. a professionally produced document shows the expertise and care an organisation will invest in its employees to deliver. This could have a vital effect on a customer's decision to do business with an organisation. When a document lands in front of a customer it needs to make an impact, it needs to grab the reader's attention. The effective production of documents is about helping important information to stand out. The document should be attractive enough to invite the audience for whom the document has been designed to want to read it, assimilate it and respond to it, if necessary. The document should be easy to read and look inviting. To achieve the effective production of the document requires a creative and innovative approach to the design of the document.

Documents need to be well designed so they are consistent in appearance across the organisation. This will require formatting into some form of **template**. When designing a document it must feature more than just **visual elements**, e.g. type, spacing, color, and tap into the reader's **learning styles, physiology** and **psychology** and **perception**. The reader should be seduced into the world of the document and not distracted by the designer's intent.

A well-designed document should bring together **prose, illustrations** and **typography** to instruct, inform or persuade the audience for whom they have been designed to perform the daily operations of their work. The reader's needs must drive the design of the document. As well as writing and designing a document, the document designer will also need to skillfully select, structure and emphasise the content that will maintain the reader's focus. While it is important for an organisation to promote its brand, as mentioned above, it should be done with subtlety and good taste, so the reader is not overwhelmed by the corporate identify.

• ACTIVITY 1

What is a template?

While many organisations require their employees to follow their '**house style**', certain documents will require an employee to use their imagination to design a response that is idiosyncratic to the communication they are responding to. In this respect they need to consider different elements of the design of the document, e.g. type and spacing.

Legibility is a document designer's main goal. And a legible document is a document that is **readable**, i.e. it is easy and inviting to read. A document's readability can be influenced by the choice of the design of individual typefaces and the subtleties of word and character spacing. Readability is also affected by the nature of the material and the reader's environment. The major factors affecting readability relate to the relative proportions of horizontal to vertical space:

- **Spaces between lines, words and letters -** There should be enough space between lines so that the eye can easily move in a horizontal direction, enough space between words so that they can be perceived as units and enough space between letters so that they can be distinguished. There must not be so much space that the eye fails to easily make the transition from the end of one line to the beginning of the next, so words do not flow easily into each other or letters do not compose visually into words

- **Type size** - Type that is too large for the column width limits the number of words that will fit on a line, creating uneven word spacing and excess use of hyphens. Type that is too small for the column forces the reader to move closer to the text

The key relationships for readability are, therefore, those that exist between visual type size, line length and line spacing.

• ACTIVITY 2

What are the benefits of designing documents that look professional and attractive?

The features that can be used to create and produce quality, professional and attractive documents are:

- **Preparation** - Before starting to produce any document make sure that there is a **rationale** for the development of the document, including any resources that will be needed to complete the document, e.g. the addition of images or diagrams. Every document must have a clearly defined purpose and objectives it is aiming to achieve for its audience. This should create a document that is meaningful and of value to the recipient, clear, concise and delivered by a set **deadline**. A deadline is when a document is due by a certain time, in a certain format and containing the required information. If a document is not delivered against these requirements it will appear unprofessional, particularly if lateness has not been discussed with the recipient, which could lead to loss of business. Having an agreed deadline will help to plan and prioritise tasks / activities

- **Information and content** - Organise information in the document so that it does not overwhelm the recipient. Make choices and give important content sufficient space within the document so it can be understood by the reader, e.g. placing content in a box or surrounding it with white space. Be selective about what information is included in a document. Create a theme using the appropriate software, that is, a coordinated set of fonts, colours and graphic effects that can be applied with one click. Use graphics to illustrate key points - which can be done using SmartArt

- **Style** - Many organisations have an agreed policy about the way their documents should look, so they are presented consistently and to the same quality, e.g. do not use abbreviations. This is often referred to as the '**house style**'

- **Accuracy** - A well-presented, correctly spelled, grammatical and accurately punctuated document will create a positive impression which will last. After producing a document it should be checked carefully, as errors in spelling or grammar could have a potentially disastrous effect. If in doubt about the intended meaning, refer back to the original author

- **Layout** - A document should have a layout with features that present the finished document in the agreed format, e.g. type of paper, margins, line spacing, type of font

The above features can be remembered using the pneumonic **PICSAL**. If documents are produced using **PICSAL** it will aid the process of communication between the senders and receivers of messages.

• ACTIVITY 3

It should be obvious to the reader how a document has been designed?

Circle the correct answer.

True   False

There is a wide range of software available that will help to produce the highest-quality documents possible. Each piece of software will have a number of different features that can be added to a document, e.g. images, graphs, tables, diagrams. During the production of the document, name it according to the organisation's policy on naming files. Regularly save the document throughout its creation so no work is lost in the event of software or electrical breakdown.

If the document being created is 'private and confidential', make sure it is identified as such and follows the organisation's policy on 'private and confidential' documents, e.g. the contents of the document should not be discussed publicly so unauthorised people can hear. Confidential information is information that has great value, is considered to be of a private nature and is only permitted to be seen by designated people within an organisation. 'Confidential information' can embrace commercial secrets as well as general information, e.g. medical records. An organisation can be damaged if its privacy of information is not upheld and respected, which could result in the organisation being devalued.

There is no single Act of Parliament defining 'confidential information' or governing how it is protected, or setting out rights and obligations in respect of it. However, the law on 'confidential information' is currently undergoing radical change as a result of developing European and UK legislation and decisions of the courts. Place 'confidentiality' warnings on standard communications, e.g. faxes or emails, to make sure if an individual receives the information by accident they are notified of its 'confidential' nature.

'Private and confidential' documents also includes commercially sensitive information, which needs to be protected from being read by an organisation's competitors. If the content of a document covers personal information it must conform to the requirements of the **Data Protection Act 1998**.

• ACTIVITY 4

Which of the following documents are likely to be confidential?

1. Brief notes of a meeting.
2. Report on absenteeism within the organisation.
3. Invitation to the staff Christmas party.
4. Fax copy of a confidentiality agreement.
5. Minutes of an executive directors' meeting.
6. Study on a potential merger.

All documents should be stored safely and securely according to the storage system being used within an organisation, e.g. a manual paper-based system, an electronic-based system or both. Documents should be stored in accordance with the organisation's policy on storing documents, so they are easily accessible when required. Organisations may have different means of codifying their documents. However, as a rule, the following will need to be in place to access documents:

* **Title or subject / category or reference number**

* **Dated** - Note should be taken of how a 'date' is written. In the UK,

the 7th September 2010 is written as 07.09.10. In America, it would be written as 09.07.10

- **Author**

Hard copies of documents can be stored manually using different methods:

- **Alphabetical** - Information is stored in order from A-Z. Files starting with the same letter are filed in order of the second letter: Aa, Ab, Ac etc. People's names are filed by their surnames, and if more than one has the same surname, by their first names. Names starting with 'The' are filed by ignoring the 'The'. Names beginning with 'Mac' or 'Mc' come before 'Ma', 'Mb' etc.

- **Numerical** - Information is coded using a numbering system, e.g. purchase orders, invoice

- **Alphanumerical** - Information is stored using a combination of letters and numbers, e.g. National Insurance numbers. Usually large databases hold this type of coded information, as they hold more information than numerical systems and are more flexible than alphabetical systems. The order of filing depends on the sequence of the file name. If file names start with letters followed by numbers, they are filed in alphabetical order first and numerical order within each letter

- **Chronological** - This method is often used within one of the other methods. For example, customers' records are filed alphabetically, but the information within the file is stored chronologically, usually with the latest at the front. This provides a history of all activities undertaken for a particular file of information. It can also be based on dates of birth or start dates

- **Geographical** - This is a method of sorting by areas, e.g. North West England, East Anglia or counties, towns, cities

- **By subject or category** - Some organisations need to sort their filing under topics rather than names. For example, a shoe manufacturer may keep files under product names such as Ladies, Gentlemen and Children

• ACTIVITY 5

What is the difference between filing documents numerically and alphanumerically?

Whichever method is adopted documents must be stored **accurately**, to allow people to find information easily and quickly. People should find what they are looking for in the place that they expect to find it. Documents should be stored as quickly as possible to allow access to users within an organisation. When amending information held electronically, saving the file will automatically update the previous version.

Types and styles of documents

There are several types of documents that may be produced in an organisation, which include:

Memos

These are used for internal communication within an organisation. They may vary in the level of formality in which they are written. They:

- May be addressed to more than one recipient

- Will usually not include addresses

- Will have a subject line, similar to 'emails'

- Will state the date, name of the recipient (s), the name of the sender and the content

- May have the recipient and sender's job titles and departments

- Will usually be produced on a template which reflects the organisation's 'house style'

Most organisations still use memos for important internal messages, if they have not been replaced by the use of 'emails'.

MEMORANDUM

To: All selling staff

From: Sales Manager

Date: 27th August 2010

Subject: Sales targets

Last week saw total sales of £127,436, an increase of 3.1% on last year. This week we have a challenging target of £148,000, or 3.7% on last year. This will require 100% effort from all of us, but I am confident we can do it.

REMEMBER: PROMOTE DISPOSABLE BARBECUES.

Faxes

A fax is any document that is sent using a telephone line, e.g. a memo, letter, invoice. Organisations may use a cover sheet to precede the document, which may include the name and fax numbers of the sender and recipient and the number of pages being sent.

FACSIMILE COVER SHEET

To: Peter Robinson
               Motor Vehicle Repairs

Fax No: 02274 55369

From: Ronald R. Barker
               Paving Co. Ltd.

Fax No: 02564 33465

No of Pages: 1 plus this cover sheet

Letters

Letters will usually be written on paper headed with the organisation's address. Letters may also need to follow the design and style set out in an organisation's 'house style'. Letters will normally:

- Be **addressed to one person**, e.g. 'Dear Sir' or 'Dear Madam'

- Be **dated**

- Contain a **salutation**, e.g. 'Dear ...'

- **Have a reference number / title / heading** - these are optional

- Contain the body of text for writing the letter

- End with a **closing statement** that summarises the main points for writing the letter

- Include a **compliment**, e.g. 'Yours sincerely'

- Include a **signature**

• ACTIVITY 6

A letter with the salutation, 'Dear Mrs Jones' should have which compliment?

Circle the correct answer.

1. Yours faithfully.

2. Yours sincerely.

3. Yours truly.

4. Best regards.

Business letters are usually produced:

- **Fully blocked -** All parts of the document start at the left-hand margin

- With **open punctuation -** Punctuation used only in the body of the letter, where it is essential for grammatical accuracy and understanding

Matthew and Son Builders
Allington Place
West Billington
WW1 1AD
Tel: 01632 566854

Our ref: GM / RA / 124
Your ref: VH / AK

13 August 2010

Mr V Harmison
Oval Walk
West Billington
WW2 1AX

Dear Mr Harmison

Thank you for your letter dated 6th August 2010 accepting our quotation to extend your office building.

The work will commence on 6th September 2010 and will be completed within 6 working weeks.

If you have any queries, please do not hesitate to contact me.

Yours sincerely

Graham Matthew
Director

• ACTIVITY 7

A document is fully blocked if:

Circle the correct answer.

1. All parts of the document start at the right-hand margin.
2. Punctuation is used only in the body of the letter.
3. All parts of the document start at the left-hand margin
4. Punctuation is used only at the beginning of the letter.

Reports

These are produced in response to a request for information. They may be formal or informal, depending on the audience they are being written for. For example, a report written to the Board of an organisation will generally be more formal than a report to the members of a club. A report is written to inform the reader of facts about a subject. The depth of information contained in a report will depend on the purpose of the report and its intended audience.

All reports will follow a similar structure, however detailed they may be:

- **Front page** - This contains the title of the report, the name of the author and the date

- **Contents** - This will list all the subjects covered in the report

- **Executive summary** - This gives a brief outline of the report

- **Background information** - This gives the reasons why the report was produced

- **Methodology** - This outlines the methods used to produce the data in the report, e.g. surveys, questionnaires

- **Findings** - These are the results of the methods used to explore the purpose of the report. Findings may be presented by:

  - Importance: where the central ideas are presented

  - Chronology: where ideas are presented in the order of events, starting either with the latest or the first

  - Sequence: where one idea follows from another

  - Comparison: where two ideas are compared in alternate paragraphs

- **Conclusion** - This outlines the conclusions that can be drawn from the findings of the research

- **Recommendations** - This outlines the actions that are recommended to be taken as a result of the conclusion

- **Acknowledgements** - This records the contribution others have made to the report

- **Bibliography** - This outlines the source material used in the research. There are a number of different ways that a bibliography can be drawn up

- **Appendices** - This sets out all the information referred to in the report which is too detailed to be given in full without distracting from the purpose of the report

The content of a written report will vary in how it is organised, using the above headings depending on the purpose of the written report. For example, a short report may only include the 'main content' and 'recommendations'.

There are a number of ways of ordering the contents of a report. These include, by:

- Importance: beginning with the central idea

- Chronology: in order of events, starting either with the latest or the first

- Sequence: where one idea follows from another

- Comparison: where two ideas are compared in alternate paragraphs

You may be able to set up templates for standard documents on your personal computer (PC), this will save time when you are asked to produce the same type of document at a later date.

• ACTIVITY 8

What are the different ways the content of a report can be ordered?

Resources

The resources required to finish a document will depend on the purpose for which the document has been designed. Everyone in an organisation will have a workstation equipped with a PC. To produce a finished document in hard copy the following will be required:

- **Paper** - Headed, letter quality or copy quality. If there is more than one page, consideration needs to be given to how these will be held together, if at all

- **Printer** - Gives choice of paper; quality settings: best, normal or draft and colour or black and white

- **Envelopes** - Letters to external addresses will need good-quality envelopes, while internal memos may be sent using internal envelopes which can be used a number of times. Consideration should be given to the size of envelope needed and if using a transparent window. In the latter case, the document should be typed using the organisation's template. Documents with several pages should be placed unfolded in an envelope

- **Attachments** - Consideration needs to be given to how these will be held together: paper clip or staple

Researching content of the document

There should be a thorough search of available data and information that will respond to the communication that the document has to address. The level of detail that will need to be researched will vary according to the experience and expertise of the person writing the document. Preparing a document also provides different levels of learning opportunities.

The data and information that is researched should be relevant and reliable. An initial investigation of source data and information should be conducted to gather as much appropriate content before making a decision about what should be included in the document. Sources of information data may be collected from to inform the topic are:

Previous research carried out by the researcher or the organisation

This will require previous research to have been stored accurately, e.g. in the organisation's library or archived conveniently to allow easy access. For simple research proposals there is a good chance that most of the information will be freely available and held in a database or spreadsheet. A simple research proposal may be one that is done fairly regularly throughout a year, so it just requires updating the information. A more complex research proposal will involve more time and a greater depth and breadth of research. In a complex research proposal research may have taken place in the past which may be a good point to start the current information research. If the research proposal is only looking at internal information it will be found within the organisation. However, a complex research proposal will normally require information to be researched both inside and outside of the organisation.

Paper-based reference material

For example, books, industry / sector magazine articles, newspapers, brochures, leaflets, government papers. Each of these types of publication will have varying levels of relevance to the research proposal. These are shortcuts, saving time, to looking up information in reference books:

- **The preface** - An initial review to see if the source will be relevant

- **The publication date** - Tells the researcher how current the information is

- **The index** - Uses keywords

- **The contents** - Uses chapter headings

- **The bibliography** - Uses other books related to the same subject area

Electronic-based reference material

For example, using the Internet. The Internet holds information on almost everything; however, as there is so much information, it can be difficult to find exactly what is required. Use a good 'search engine', e.g. 'Google', 'Yahoo'. To narrow the research:

- Think of keywords that would appear in an article

- Avoid using lengthy combinations of keywords

- Start with seven words

- Spell the keywords correctly

- Use a 'thesaurus' to choose keywords

- Use lower-case letters

In all searches for information consider copyright and confidentiality. Any published work is likely to be subject to copyright, whereby the work belongs to the person / people who wrote it. If a quote from reference material is going to be used it must be acknowledged, to avoid accusations of **plagiarism**.

People

This may be an informal approach where key members of staff are asked for their opinions or a formal approach where a questionnaire is specifically designed to ask questions to explore the research proposal. Talk to everybody who may have useful knowledge. Work colleagues bring lots of information from their previous experience and expertise gained in other jobs, which may be applicable to the research proposal. It may be necessary to liaise with other departments to obtain information which they may hold in databases. All personal data will be subject to the **Data Protection Act 1998**.

• ACTIVITY 9

What are the possible sources of information that can be researched to design and produce a finished document?

In undertaking any research for the completion of a document, consideration needs to be given to the following areas:

- The **volume** of data and information required - Consider all types of data and information that will help to satisfy the document being prepared Do not get sidetracked by irrelevant information

- The **depth and breadth** of the data and information to be researched

- **When** the data and information is required

- How the data and information should be **formatted**

- How the data and information should be **reported**

- If the data and information is relevant to its **intended audience**

Always remain focused on the purpose of the content being researched and the purpose it is aiming to achieve.

All data and information researched should be:

- **Relevant** - Information that is applicable to the research

- **Valid** - Information is what it claims it is. It is the 'truth'

- **Reliable** - Information that is consistent

In undertaking the research, always be guided by the purpose of the research - the aims and objectives that the document is aiming to achieve.

There is no need to be scrupulous in searching for data and information, i.e. it does not have to be a belt and braces search, as new ideas may come from unexpected places and this degree of creativity and innovation is to be welcomed in the formation of the content of a document. Gather together the relevant facts and figures that will form the basis of the document for the audience it is being designed to be delivered to.

The document should cover all points of information being requested.

This could include anticipating possible questions that may arise as a result of the response document.

Formatting the document

Gather together all the information that needs to be included in a document. This may come from any number of sources, including the letter being replied to, previous reports, databases, the Internet etc. Having decided the content, it will need to be organised so that it can be found when required. It may be useful to produce a first draft to see where the content fits into the whole. For long or complex documents, plan a draft of the document using topics or headings to organise the content before writing the detail. Consideration will then need to be given to:

- **The size of paper to use** - Most documents are printed on A4 paper, 210mm x 297mm. However, A5, half of A4, could be used for memos, leaflets and brochures. A3, twice the size of A4, can be used for providing large spreadsheets of information or posters

- Whether to present a document in **portrait** or **landscape** form. Most standard documents are presented in portrait form. Landscape is generally used for tables and spreadsheets, where it is helpful to be able to see the full row of information at a glance

- Any **diagrams** or **tables** to be inserted into the document. Diagrams

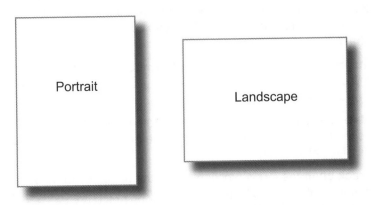

will usually be imported from elsewhere. Tables may be produced in a document or imported from elsewhere. Tables are produced from the 'Table' menu

• ACTIVITY 10

When could a document be presented in either portrait or landscape, and why?

A PC provides a lot of functions that allow a document to be easily edited:

- **Delete** - Ctrl+delete - This allows a single letter, group of letters or whole parts of a document to be deleted

- **Paste** - Ctrl+v - This is used in combination with either the 'cut' or 'copy', see below, instruction. Paste will add the last data selected to the document 'copied' or stored on the 'clipboard', which will provide other recently 'copied' information

- **Cut** - Ctrl+x - This is used to highlight a piece of text and remove it from the document. It can then be 'pasted', see above, to another part of the document or a new document

- **Copy** - Ctrl+c - This is used to highlight a piece of text and copied. It can then be 'pasted', see above, to another part of the document or a new document

- **Find and replace** - Ctrl+f - This function is used to change all the examples of a particular word to another word. For example, replace the word 'company' with the word 'organisation', there is no need to retype every example, use 'find' and / or 'replace' to make all the changes

- **Inserting special characters and symbols** - This function enables the use of other alphabets, e.g. Arabic ﺵﺀﺓﻙﻕ and other signs / symbols, e.g. o, û, ©, %

- **Mail merge** - This function is useful if the same letter is going to several recipients, as it can just change the name and address of each recipient

- **Track changes** - This function allows the originator of a document to share it with other colleagues, inviting them to make changes which can be tracked by name and highlighted

- **'Widows** and **orphans'** - These are words or short lines at the beginning or end of a paragraph which are left dangling at the top or bottom of a column, separated from the rest of the paragraph. A 'widow' can be either a paragraph-opening line that appears by itself at the bottom of a page / column or a word, part of a word or very short line that appears by itself at the end of a paragraph. An 'orphan' is a paragraph-ending line that falls at the beginning of the following page / column, thus separated from the remainder of the text. Orphaned lines generally happen first in a text at the start of paragraphs and widowed lines happen at the end of paragraphs. Documents should avoid 'widows and orphans'. Some techniques to eliminate 'widows' include:

- Forcing a page break early, producing a shorter page

- Adjusting the space between lines of text

- Adjusting the spacing between words to produce 'tighter' or 'looser' paragraphs

- Adjusting the hyphenation of words within the paragraph

- Adjusting the page's margins

- Subtle scaling of the page

- Rewriting a portion of the paragraph

- Adding a figure to the text, or resizing an existing figure

An 'orphan' is cured more easily, by inserting a blank line or forcing a page break to push the orphan line onto the next page to be with the rest of its paragraph. Most full-featured word processors and page layout applications include a paragraph setting to automatically prevent 'widows and orphans'.

At any stage during the production of a document the format of the text can be changed. There are various options available in the format menu, e.g. font, which allows the font to be changed to different styles, sizes or colour. It is possible to format characters, pages or whole sections of a document. A part of a document can be formatted and used again later in the document by selecting 'styles and formatting', and the software will show what formatting has been used previously in the document.

If text is being produced which will have more than one page, it is advisable to use a '**header and footer**', with required information and / or '**page numbers**'. Using both functions will allow the title to be put onto each page with a page number. It is also possible to '**number paragraphs**' and include an '**index**' or '**table of contents**' to help the reader find their way around the text.

• ACTIVITY 11

What are the following abbreviations of?

- incl

- adv.

- plc

- ft.

- yd.

- corp.

Any '**picture**', '**diagram**' or '**table**' already held on your hard drive or on a disk can be imported. 'Tables' are an excellent way to organise information. They look great and they are simple to manage. They can hold text, graphics or other tables. They can simplify even the most complex layouts. 'Tables' are a powerful and flexible function.

'**Footnotes**' or '**endnotes**' can be used to support information. **Objects** can also be imported from other software on a PC, through a connected scanner or digital camera or from the Internet. Care will need to be taken when importing non-text objects. In a letter, 'less is more' where 'pictures' and 'diagrams' are concerned. In a report, 'pictures' and 'diagrams' can certainly add to the impact. 'Pictures' and 'diagrams' should be used wisely, and only when they are relevant and make the content more meaningful. Their positioning and size must also be carefully considered.

Some tips when using a software program:

- Use 'styles' - avoid direct formatting

- Use 'templates'

- Do not use line feeds to make space between paragraphs

- Do not use the 'spacebar' to make spaces or align text

- Use only one 'space' after a full stop

- Do not manually number pages

- Minimise the use of 'sections'

- Avoid manual 'page breaks'

Checking the document

Once a document has been completed it is essential that it is checked for accuracy. On completing the check make any changes as necessary. Most software programs contain spell checking and grammar checking facilities. Use these first to correct the more obvious errors; however, they must not be relied on entirely as some will be programmed with the default to use American spelling and grammar. For example, the PC will accept 'color' and reject 'colour'. When the automatic checking is complete, read the document carefully to look for missed errors, and also for correct use of paragraphs, headings and subheadings, style and formatting. Remember the 'Five Cs' when checking documents:

- **Conciseness** - Have the amount of words been minimised to clearly express points of information?

- **Completeness** - Is everything the recipient needs there?

- **Courtesy** - Is the tone of the document polite?

- **Clarity** - Will the recipient understand the points being made?

- **Correctness** - Are all statements accurate and true?

Be particularly careful to proofread numbers, dates, times and amounts. Check for errors between similar words, such as 'affect' and 'effect' or 'less' and 'fewer'.

• ACTIVITY 12

Type up the following handwritten notice to place it on the noticeboard. Correct the errors in spelling, punctuation and grammar. Produce a notice that will be attractive and inviting to the audience that it is intended for. List the spelling mistakes which would not be picked up by a PC using the spell check function.

Mrs. Wilson will knot be avalaible to give the lectern on Friday 15th she is sic he wil be replased by Mr, Jefferson who will know be giving the lecture on Adminastration in the motor industry. The thyme of the lectur has also changed it will not be at 11.00 am butt at 14.00 pm. Note the ours have chainged.The plaice of the meating has not changed as it will still be held on the 5th flaw in the charity room.

If the document has been completed for another person, make sure that they check for the accuracy of statements and details. For example, if the author has dictated 'we will sell petrol only to people in a metal container', you should suggest rewording this to clarify that it is not necessary for the purchasers of petrol to be inside a metal container at the time of purchase.

• ACTIVITY 13

Which of the following are correct? Correct the incorrect statements.

1. Would we have fewer problems if we had less departments?
2. Either Edinburgh or Sunderland is in England.
3. The customers are always right.
4. The customer's always right.
5. The ships crew was up to it's full complement.
6. The customer's is always right.

The completed document will need to be presented either for despatch or for the original author by the agreed deadline and in the style agreed. If unforeseen circumstances mean that the style or content has been changed, or if unable to meet the agreed deadline, it is important that this is reported as soon as the situation arises. It is too late to be told that a deadline will not be met when the deadline arrives. It is not acceptable to lower the agreed quality standards in order to meet the deadline.

Whatever type of document is produced, always confirm the purpose, content, style and quality of the document has been designed to meet the agreed standards and deadline.

Testing your knowledge

1. What is meant by readability of a document?

2. What influences the readability of a document?

3. What is meant by legibility?

4. What is the difference between readability and legibility?

5. What is meant by layout?

6. What is the intention of designing documents that conform to a specific 'house style'?

7. Which function is used to replace words on a PC?

8. When would it be appropriate to use graphs?

9. How are images integrated into a report?

10. What is the difference between the layout of memos and emails?

11. What are the five Cs?

12. What is the value in researching content for a document?

13. What is the best way of organising content of a document?

14. What is the best way of organising electronic files, and why?

Skills

The main purpose for designing and producing a document is for the document to be readable and legible. These two aspects of design and production should be your mantra for everything that you do in the design and production of any document.

Before starting work on the design and production of any document in a business environment, make sure you are clear and agreed about:

- The purpose of the document

- The content of the document

- The style of the content

- The deadlines within which the document needs to be completed

Each of these aspects of preparing to design and produce a document will help to inform the planning of the work you will need to do for either yourself or, if you are designing and producing the document on behalf of someone else, its original author. Organise your work around all the tasks that you have to complete so you finish the document at the agreed time. Once you are clear about what has to be done, gather together all the resources you will require to complete the task. Make sure there is sufficient stationery to complete your tasks and, if it has run out, report it to the appropriate colleague so it can be replenished.

Think about the content of the document, as it is the most important aspect of the work you are doing designing and producing the document. Is it in response to another piece of correspondence? If so, be guided by the form and content of that communication in your response. If it is an original piece of communication be very clear about what you are aiming to achieve with the design and production of this document in whatever style it will be presented. Remember to implement the five Cs.

You may also be asked to design and produce documents which are not in response to correspondence that you have received or are doing on behalf of your manager. For example, you may have to prepare an advertising brief, a company flier or a report for the AGM. Each of these tasks will require a different focus and approach, as the purpose of the design and production of this type of document is different. Always be guided by the requirement of the brief for designing and producing the document.

• ACTIVITY 14

Write a report to your supervisor suggesting ways in which your current filing systems can be improved. Consider the best way to order the contents of the report.

When designing and producing the document on your PC, make sure you are fully up to date with the functions of your software so you can add images, tables etc., effectively and efficiently. Chat to someone who is very confident in this area, or your supervisor / manager, to check that you are fully conversant with the functionality of the technology you are using. This will not only save you time but make your document look more professional and readable. Be judicious about the images etc., that you include in your document.

Make sure you have sufficiently researched the data and information that you need to inform the design and development of your document. Search the most appropriate sources of data and information. You do not want to overwhelm the recipient of the document with too much inappropriate data and information. Remember to produce a document which will give sufficient data and information to the recipient. That alone will impress them. Adding too much data and information will not impress them and they may not finish reading your document.

Make sure that you are agreed about the style, layout and format that you wish, or the original author wishes, the document to take. Clarify all these components of your document. Integrate the non-text objects so that they make the information that you are presenting very clear, legible and, above all, readable. Make sure, when importing or integrating non-text objects, you use the technology effectively so that the objects are in line with the appropriate text in the document and do not jump about to different places when you are working on the document.

If you are working on a large document, check through what you will include in the content of the document. If necessary, produce a draft document and check through this with the original author to make sure it meets all the requirements that they are aiming to achieve. Check through the document to make sure that it accurately presents data and information, i.e. there are no spelling mistakes. Make sure your PC is set to the correct defaults, the grammar has been correctly used and edit the text for conciseness. Check against the five Cs.

Once you have checked the document, check the aims of the document with the original author, to make sure that they have been achieved. When working on the production of the document, if you are not sure, at any stage of its development, that it is progressing along the right track, pause and reflect on what the document is aiming to achieve. Check with the original author - if it is not you. If anything changes with the development of the document check with the original author that they are happy with the change of direction that the document may have to take. This should include the deadline within which it was agreed the document would be completed.

• ACTIVITY 15

Select a number of documents that you have produced which you feel demonstrate your competence in using correct layout, spelling, punctuation and grammar. Consider the question of confidentiality in making your selection. Check through these with your supervisor / manager.

Testing your skills

1. Where would you look to find the relevant content of a document?

2. Do you know how to select options on your printer?

3. What types of documents do you produce?

4. How do you access databases?

5. How do you layout a formal letter?

6. What is the 'house style' of your organisation? How effective do you think it is?

7. How do you use your word processing package?

8. Could you find appropriate images for a report on the Brazil Olympics 2016?

9. How do you manipulate images to fit the purpose of the document?

10. How and when do you use spell check and grammar check?

11. How do you check that your spelling, punctuation and grammar have been used correctly?

12. What sources of information have you used in the design and production of your documents?

13. If you were filing vehicle records by registration number, which filing method would you use?

14. What is your organisation's convention for naming electronic files?

15. What are the filing methods used in your organisation? How effective are they?

Ready for assessment?
To achieve this Level 3 unit of a Business & Administration qualification, learners will need to demonstrate that they are able to perform the following activities:

1. Confirmed the purpose, content, styles and deadlines for documents

2. Identified and prepared the required resources needed to design and produce documents

3. Researched and organised the required content for documents

4. Used available technology appropriate to the design and production of documents

5. Designed, formatted and produced documents to an agreed style

6. Integrated non-text objects in the agreed layout, where required

7. Checked texts and objects for accuracy

8. Edited and corrected texts and objects, as required

9. Clarified documents' requirements, if necessary

10. Stored documents safely and securely following organisational procedures

11. Presented documents to the required format and within the agreed deadlines

You will need to produce evidence from a variety of sources to support the performance requirements of this unit.

If you carry out the 'ACTIVITIES' and respond to the 'NEED TO KNOW' questions, these will provide some of the evidence required.

Links to other units

While gathering evidence for this unit, evidence **may** also be used from evidence generated from other units within the Business & Administration suite of units. Below is a **sample** of applicable units; however, most units within the Business & Administration suite of units will also be applicable.

QCF NVQ
Communications
Communicate in a business environment (Level 3)
Make and receive telephone calls
Use electronic message systems
Core business & administration
Manage own performance in a business environment (Level 3)
Improve own performance in a business environment (Level 3)
Work in a business environment (Level 3)
Work with other people in a business environment (Level 3)
Document production
Prepare text from notes
Prepare text from notes using touch typing (60 wpm)
Prepare text from shorthand (80 wpm)
Prepare text from recorded audio instruction (60 wpm)

SVQ
Communications
Communicate in a business environment
Make and receive telephone calls
Use electronic message systems
Core business & administration
Plan how to manage and improve own performance in a business environment
Review and maintain work in a business environment
Support other people to work in a business environment
Document production
Prepare text from notes
Prepare text from notes using touch typing (60 wpm)
Prepare text from shorthand (80 wpm)
Prepare text from recorded audio instruction (60 wpm)

19

Prepare text from notes using touch typing (60 wpm)

PREPARE TEXT FROM NOTES USING TOUCH TYPING (60 WPM)

'**Prepare text from notes using touch typing (60 wpm)**' is an <u>optional unit</u> which may be chosen as one of a combination of units to achieve either a Qualifications and Credit Framework (QCF), National Vocational Qualification (NVQ) or Scottish Vocational Qualification (SVQ).

The aims of this unit are to:

- Understand the preparing of text from notes using touch typing

- Understand the purpose and benefits of following procedures when preparing text using touch typing

- Be able to prepare for tasks

- Be able to prepare text using touch typing at 60 wpm

To achieve the above aims of this unit, learners will be expected to provide evidence through the performance of work-based activities.

Knowledge

Touch typing

Before starting to use the keyboard always make sure that the workstation is ergonomically prepared to meet the individual requirements of the keyboard user - sit up straight, feet flat on the floor, elbows close to the body, wrists straight and forearms parallel to the work surface. And remember to take regular breaks from touch typing.

The attraction of touch typing is to increase typing speed, which will ultimately increase productivity. While speed may be a major aim of touch typing, the main aim is accurate touch typing. The benefits derived from touch typing come from no requirement of conscious thought or visual confirmation. For example, when typing a letter there is no need to interrupt the thought pattern by having to look at the keyboard. Or the touch typist can copy text directly from the source text without having to divide their attention between the source material, the computer screen and the keyboard.

When learning to touch type the learner should always rest their fingers lightly on the 'home row' of the keyboard. The **F** and **J** keys usually have small raised bumps on the two keys so the fingers can feel that they are resting on the correct keys of the home row.

THE HOME ROW									
LEFT HAND					RIGHT HAND				
LLF	LRF	LMF	LIF	LIF	RIF	RIF	RMF	RRF	RLF
A	S	D	F	G	H	J	K	L	;

- The **left index finger (LIF)** will control the **F** and **G** keys, and the **right index finger (RIF)** will control the **J** and **H** keys

- The **left middle finger (LMF)** will control the **D** key, and the **right middle finger (RMF)** will control the **K** key

- The **left ring finger (LRF)** will control the **S** key, and the **right ring finger (RRF)** will control the **L** key

- The **left little finger (LLF)** will control the **A** key, and the **right little finger (RLF)** will control the **;** key

- The **spacebar** is controlled by the **right thumb**

The locations of all the other keys on the keyboard are learned in relation to the **home keys**. Touch typing relies finding the home keys and working from them to type in the other keys on the keyboard. When learning to touch type get used to finding the home keys without looking at the keyboard. Try not to look at the keyboard when learning each of the keys on the keyboard. Focus should be on the text that is being typed, which can be seen on the computer screen. Take time to relax and just feel where the fingers are resting on the **F** and **J** keys in relation to the rest of the keyboard.

THE QWERTY ROW									
LEFT HAND					RIGHT HAND				
LLF	LRF	LMF	LIF	LIF	RIF	RIF	RMF	RRF	RLF
Q	W	E	R	T	Y	U	I	O	P
A	S	D	F	G	H	J	K	L	;

- The **LIF** will control the **R** and **T** keys, and the **RIF** will control the **U** and **Y** keys

- The **LMF** will control the **E** key, and the **RMF** will control the **I** key

- The **LRF** will control the **W** key, and the **RRF** will control the **O** key

- The **LLF** will control the **Q** key, and the **RLF** will control the **P** key

The **QWERTY row** is perhaps the hardest-working row on the keyboard, because it has four vowels: **E, I, O** and **U**.

THE FIRST ROW									
LEFT HAND					RIGHT HAND				
LLF	LRF	LMF	LIF	LIF	RIF	RIF	RMF	RRF	RLF
Q	W	E	R	T	Y	U	I	O	P
A	S	D	F	G	H	J	K	L	;
Z	X	C	V	B	N	M	,	.	/

- The **LIF** will control the **V** and **B** keys, and the **RIF** will control the **M** and **N** keys

- The **LMF** will control the **C** key, and the **RMF** will control the **,** key

- The **LRF** will control the **X** key, and the **RRF** will control the **.** key

- The **LLF** will control the **Z** key, and the **RLF** will control the **/** key

Once the first row on the keyboard is learned, all the alpha keys on the keyboard will have been learned.

THE NUMBER ROW									
LEFT HAND					RIGHT HAND				
LLF	LRF	LMF	LIF	LIF	RIF	RIF	RMF	RRF	RLF
1	2	3	4	5	6	7	8	9	0
Q	W	E	R	T	Y	U	I	O	P
A	S	D	F	G	H	J	K	L	;
Z	X	C	V	B	N	M	,	.	/

- The **LIF** will control the **4** and **5** keys, and the **RIF** will control the **7** and **6** keys

- The **LMF** will control the **3** key, and the **RMF** will control the **8** key
- The **LRF** will control the **2** key, and the **RRF** will control the **9** key
- The **LLF** will control the **1** key, and the **RLF** will control the **0** key

The **number row** is the furthest row from the typist's fingers' resting position, the **home row**.

THE NUMBER ROW - UPPERCASE									
LEFT HAND					RIGHT HAND				
LLF	LRF	LMF	LIF	LIF	RIF	RIF	RMF	RRF	RLF
!	"	£	$	%	^	&	*	(	)
Q	W	E	R	T	Y	U	I	O	P
A	S	D	F	G	H	J	K	L	;
Z	X	C	V	B	N	M	,	.	/

The number row has two sets of symbols on it: numbers and symbols. To access the symbols use the appropriate shift key.

Capitals - the keyboard should have two shift keys, one to the left and one to the right. Use the little finger of the inactive hand to work one of the shift keys when capitals are needed. For example, if typing a capital A, strike the A key with the index finger of the left hand while depressing the shift key with the little finger of the right hand. This can feel a little awkward in the beginning, but it will feel natural after sufficient repetition of use.

Some tips when first starting out to learn how to touch type:

- **Never look at the keyboard!** Check the computer for accuracy
- Always check for the starting position of the fingers on the **F** and **J** keys in the **home row**, and feel the bumps on the keys
- Do not worry about typing non-words at first, as this is to gain familiarity with the keys of the keyboard
- Measure your **typing speed periodically**, to see when you have achieved 40 wpm. The speed being typed should avoid any mistakes, and this is what you are aiming to achieve - **accuracy**. Aim

always to reduce the number of mistakes while increasing your touch typing speed

- Speed is measured in **words per minute (wpm)**, where a word is represented by five key strokes, including using the space bar and the shift bar

- Both your accuracy and speed will improve with practice

- A good phrase to use when practicing is, '**The quick brown fox jumped over the lazy dog**', as this uses all the letters of the alphabet

- **Practice! Practice! Practice!**

• ACTIVITY 1

Type the following passages aiming to reach a speed of 60 wpm. Aim to eliminate any mistakes. Type the whole passage in each exercise, including the brackets containing the number of words and character spaces:

Exercise 1.
Of 1,000 children chosen at random, on average 10 have a particular special educational need. Of these 10 children with the need, around nine will obtain a positive result in a diagnostic test. Of the 990 without the special need, around 99 will also obtain a positive test result. If all 1,000 children are tested, and a child you know is one of the 108 obtaining a positive result, what is the probability that they have the special need? The quality and quantity of numbers collected will depend on the cohort of children studied. This will depend on the size of each cohort of children selected for the experiment. (101 words, 618 character spaces)

Exercise 2.
We expect 501 tonnes of vegetables in different sizes and containers over the next 12 months. This will represent 75% of the stock that we will need over the next 12 months, which is being exported from West Venezuela and North Belize. In the first quarter, 35% of the order will be delivered at a cost to the department of £456,398.00 or US$730,236.80, which meets the requirements of the original quote we were quoted. The remaining quarters of the year will have the following budgets: the second quarter £492,381.00 or US$787,809.60; the third quarter £187,295.00 or US$299,672.00; and the final quarter £89,174.00 or US$142,678.40. The total cost will be £1,225,248.00 or US$1,960,396.80. This represents an increase of 15.25%*.

*This is based on figures from 2009 / 2010. (127 words, 778 character spaces)

Exercise 3.
The psychological implication of this erudite study tells us that we cannot always trust what we see or what we think we have seen. The visual system will attend to stimuli in our environment that we focus on. In this experiment, in the control group a large number of participants did not see the zebra (a man in a zebra costume) mix with the group of people. The attention of the control group was focused discriminately, and the participants' visual system narrowed its search to the stimuli that the experimenter had asked them to focus on. However, in the experimental group, where the experimenter had asked participants to look for a zebra, all participants identified the zebra. Their visual system had been attenuated to the suggested stimuli and that is what the participants focused on. This experiment has been replicated in many different contexts and the results have remained consistent, whether data has been interpreted parsimoniously or generously. (157 words, 961 character spaces)

Different types of documents that can be produced from notes

Different types of organisations working in many different sectors will have the need to produce text from notes. These will include emails, memos, letters, reports and minutes of meetings. Notes will have been produced from a variety of sources, e.g. shorthand, audio recordings.

Many text documents will be prepared from handwritten notes which can be made by an author who will:

- **Prepare the text** - This should be relatively easy to transcribe as the person preparing the text is translating handwritten notes which they have made, so legibility and shortcuts should not be a problem

- **Not prepare the text** - This may be a little more difficult to transcribe as the person preparing the text is not translating their own handwritten notes. They may not understand the handwriting or the shortcuts that the author has made. If this occurs, the person transcribing the text should clarify from the author any script that is not legible

Before preparing the transcription of any notes into text make sure that the purpose, format and deadline of the text has been agreed. A deadline is when a document is due by a certain time, in a certain format and containing the required information. It is important that all parties involved in the production of text are all agreed on what the finished product will look like and when it can be expected. Before starting to produce any text from notes, include resources that will be needed to complete the text, e.g. the addition of images or diagrams.

The text should be clear. If a document is not delivered against these requirements it will appear unprofessional, particularly if lateness has not been discussed with the recipient, and this could lead to loss of business. Having an agreed deadline will help to plan and prioritise tasks / activities. Whatever source material is going to be used, documents will be produced from the following formats:

Memos

These are used for internal communication within an organisation. They may vary in the level of formality in which they are written. They:

*   May be addressed to more than one recipient

*   Will usually not include addresses

*   Will have a subject line, similar to 'emails'

*   Will state the date, name of the recipient (s), the name of the sender and the content

*   May have the recipient and sender's job titles and departments

*   Will usually be produced on a template which reflects the organisation's '**house style**'

Most organisations still use memos for important internal messages, if they have not been replaced by the use of 'emails'.

MEMORANDUM

To: All selling staff

From: Sales Manager

Date: 27th August 2010

Subject: Sales targets

Last week saw total sales of £127,436, an increase of 3.1% on last year. This week we have a challenging target of £148,000, or 3.7% on last year. This will require 100% effort from all of us, but I am confident we can do it.

REMEMBER: PROMOTE DISPOSABLE BARBECUES.

Business letter

These are usually printed on paper headed with the organisation's address and business details. There is a recognised format to letter writing; however, an organisation may choose to adopt its own 'house style'. Letters will normally:

- Be **addressed to one person**, e.g. 'Dear Sir' or 'Dear Madam'
- Be **dated**
- Contain a **salutation**, e.g. 'Dear ...'
- **Have a reference number / title / heading** - these are optional
- Contain the body of text for writing the letter
- End with a **closing statement** that summarises the main points for writing the letter
- Include a **compliment**, e.g. 'Yours sincerely'
- Include a signature

Matthew and Son Builders
Allington Place
West Billington
WW1 1AD
Tel: 01632 566854

Our ref: GM / RA / 124
Your ref: VH / AK

13 August 2010

Mr V Harmison
Oval Walk
West Billington
WW2 1AX

Dear Mr Harmison

Thank you for your letter dated 6th August 2010 accepting our quotation to extend your office building.

The work will commence on 6th September 2010 and will be completed within 6 working weeks.

If you have any queries, please do not hesitate to contact me.

Yours sincerely

Graham Matthew
Director

Business letters are usually produced:

- **Fully blocked** - All parts of the document start at the left-hand margin

- With **open punctuation** - Punctuation used only in the body of the letter, where it is essential for grammatical accuracy and understanding

A letter addressed to Mrs Jayne Wilcox, 12 Manver's Street, London SW19 7ER can be sent using the following salutations and complimentary phrases:

SALUTATION	Dear Jayne	Dear Mrs Wilcox	Dear Madam
COMPLIMENT	Kind regards	Yours sincerely	Yours faithfully

If someone knows Jayne Wilcox well they will probably use Jayne. If a sender does not know Jayne well they may feel more comfortable addressing her as Mrs Wilcox. If they do not know Mrs Wilcox at all, they will probably usually the formal term 'Madam'. As the salutation becomes more formal so does the complimentary close.

With the advent of electronic means of communication the number of letters written and received by organisations has declined. Letters will probably be written if there is no access to an email address on an organisation's website, for legal reasons or the sender may want a formal record of the communication.

• ACTIVITY 2

Why are business letters 'fully blocked'?

Reports
These are produced in response to a request for information. They may be formal or informal, depending on the audience they are being written for. For example, a report written to a Board of an organisation will generally be more formal than a report to the members of a club. A report is written to inform the reader of facts about a subject. The depth of information contained in a report will depend on the purpose of the report and its intended audience.

All reports will follow a similar structure, however detailed they may be:

- **Front page** - This contains the title of the report, the name of the author and the date

- **Contents** - This will list all the subjects covered in the report

- **Executive summary** - This gives a brief outline of the report

- **Background information** - This gives the reasons why the report was produced

- **Methodology** - This outlines the methods used to produce the data in the report, e.g. surveys, questionnaires

- **Findings** - These are the results of the methods used to explore the purpose of the report. Findings may be presented by:

  - Importance: where the central ideas are presented

  - Chronology: where ideas are presented in the order of events, starting either with the latest or the first

  - Sequence: where one idea follows from another

  - Comparison: where two ideas are compared in alternate paragraphs

- **Conclusion** - This outlines the conclusions that can be drawn from the findings of the research

- **Recommendations** - This outlines the actions that are recommended to be taken as a result of the conclusion

- **Acknowledgements** - This records the contribution others have made to the report

- **Bibliography** - This outlines the source material used in the research. There are a number of different ways that a bibliography can be drawn up

- **Appendices** - This sets out all the information referred to in the report which is too detailed to be given in full without distracting from the purpose of the report

Minutes

These are a record of the discussions and agreed actions that will need to be followed up as a result of a meeting. Minutes can be recorded in a number of different forms:

- **Verbatim** - Where everything is recorded word for word

- **Narrative** - Where a summary of the meeting is recorded. Formal resolutions will be recorded verbatim

- **Resolution** - Where a motion which has been voted on and passed gives details of the proposer and seconder of the motion, with a verbatim recording of the resolution

- **Action** - Where only the action and the name of the person or persons responsible for carrying out the action are recorded

ACTIVITY 3

Someone working in the HR department has left a note for you to type up the following information:

Data has been identified regarding the following members of staff in the organisation. I will need a table of the following figures:

In 1994 there were 36 retirements, 3 types of other employment, 6 employees on maternity leave, 10 employees on long-term sickness, which meant 55% of the workforce were fully employed in the organisation.

In 1995 there were 3 retirements, 5 types of other employment, 5 employees on maternity leave, 10 employees on long-term sickness, which meant 57% of the workforce were fully employed in the organisation.

In 1996 there were 35 retirements, 3 types of other employment, 6 employees on maternity leave, 12 employees on long-term sickness, which meant 56% of the workforce were fully employed in the organisation.

In 1997 there were 36 retirements, 4 types of other employment, 5 employees on maternity leave, 13 employees on long-term sickness, which meant 58% of the workforce were fully employed in the organisation.

In 1998 there were 18 retirements, 6 types of other employment, 6 employees on maternity leave, 19 employees on long-term sickness, which meant 48% of the workforce were fully employed in the organisation.

In 1999 there were 17 retirements, 6 types of other employment, 6 employees on maternity leave, 19 employees on long-term sickness, which meant 48% of the workforce were fully employed in the organisation.

In 2000 there were 15 retirements, 5 types of other employment, 5 employees on maternity leave, 17 employees on long-term sickness, which meant 43% of the workforce were fully employed in the organisation.

In 2001 there were 13 retirements, 4 types of other employment, 4 employees on maternity leave, 19 employees on long-term sickness, which meant 41% of the workforce were fully employed in the organisation.

Organise this information into a short report using two different methods to present the information.

Accuracy of text prepared from notes

Any piece of text produced from notes should be a quality piece of work. It should be executed with the correct spelling, the use of grammatical rules and the correct application of punctuation to produce a product that both gives a good impression of the organisation and, more importantly, conveys the intended message of the text.

Spelling

A computer will automatically check the spelling of words and highlight them in the document being worked on. However, spell check cannot:

- Differentiate between American and English spelling of words, so make sure that the spell check default is aligned to the correct country

- Differentiate between words that are spelled correctly but used incorrectly, e.g. using 'through' when it should be 'threw'. Some of the most commonly confused words are:

  - We are pleased to accept your donation
    Everyone made a donation except Mr Jones

  - Never listen to advice from your parents
    I would advise you always to listen to your parents

  - The increase in interest rates will affect everyone
    The effect of the increase was felt by everyone

  - She thought she was eligible for a grant
    The letter she received was illegible

  - You must ensure that your car is insured

  - Lowestoft is farther east than Birmingham
    I need further information on the location of Hull

- There are <u>fewer</u> days in February than in June
  It is <u>less</u> likely to rain today than it was yesterday
- My <u>personal</u> opinion is that it will rain today
  The HR Department deals with <u>personnel</u>
- I visited the local doctors' <u>practice</u> this morning
  I need to <u>practise</u> my spelling more often
- The <u>principal</u> cause of heart disease is overeating
  The minister resigned over a matter of <u>principle</u>
- The traffic on the M6 was <u>stationary</u> for two hours
  We need to order some more <u>stationery</u> this week
- This week's sales were better <u>than</u> last week's
  We will look at this week's plan, <u>then</u> next week's
- The girls picked up <u>their</u> handbags
  The boys will be over <u>there</u> tomorrow
  <u>They're</u> planning to visit next week

• ACTIVITY 4

Circle the correct spelling in the following list of words:

1. Participative	participertive	particsipative
2. Calasthenets	calisthenics	calisthenicks
3. Originate	oridginate	originatte
4. Pergured	perfoured	perjured
5. Perigrinate	peregrinate	peragrinate
6. Sadled	sadaled	saddled
7. Zephyr	zefr	zephir
8. Asignation	assignation	assegnation
9. Vertigenous	vertiganous	vertiginous
10. Bucolic	bucolick	buccolic

Grammar

Grammar can loosely be defined at the 'rules of language'. However, in English, the 'rules' are not consistent, which makes it complicated to learn and apply. Grammar is important to make sure that the intended meaning of a sentence is communicated to the recipients of the communication. For example, 'Use both lanes when turning right' actually requires drivers to straddle the two lanes, which is a highly dangerous manoeuvre to carry out. The correct sentence construction should be: 'Use either lane when turning right'.

There are five parts of speech which are commonly used:

- **Nouns** - These are the names of a person, place or thing, e.g. 'book', 'television', 'Sunday', 'Norfolk'

- **Pronouns** - These are used instead of a noun, e.g. instead of saying 'John' in a paragraph that refers only to him, use 'he' or 'him'

- **Verbs** - These are words that express doing things, e.g. 'ran', 'run' or 'running'

- **Adverbs** - These words give information about how a verb was executed, e.g. 'he ran <u>quickly</u>' or 'he ran <u>fast</u>'. Note that while most adverbs will be formed by the addition of '-ly' to the end of a verb, it is not always the case, as can be seen by the second example in this paragraph

- **Adjectives** - These describe nouns, e.g. 'an <u>interesting</u> book', '<u>reality</u> television'

• ACTIVITY 5

What is a gerund?

Sentences are formed by linking parts of speech together. Simple sentences contain a subject and a verb, e.g. 'I am', where 'I' is the subject and 'am' is the verb. More complicated sentences will have a subject, verb and object, e.g. 'I am going to London', where the object of the sentence is London. Sentences must start with a capital letter and end with some form of punctuation, e.g. a full stop, question mark. Capital letters are also used to indicate **proper names**, e.g. America, Anthony; **titles**, e.g. Mr, Mrs, Lord; **days of the week or months of the year** and **acronyms** (RAF, CIA, FBI, MI5, RAC).

A paragraph is formed by linking two or more sentences together. If the subject of a paragraph changes, it is advisable to start a new paragraph.

• ACTIVITY 6

Proofread and correct the following and produce a corrected version. Switch off the spell check function on the computer.

Our ref: DT/GY/1256

Mr S Williamson
Apart 21
The shore
Manchster

M6 7yu

Dear serena williamon

Account number 45678956 -Flat 24 te maltings, Mancester

Thankyoy for you're resent enqiry regarding you mortgage, and theintrst rates available to you. I am encloseing a quotetion showing what yur new paymemts would be at a new rat of interst. Yhjis has been calculated on and Interest only Basis.

At the moment you're monthly payments is ^189.23 vased ib a rate if 6.75%. Should you decide to exce0pt our offer (details) attached, your new repayments would be approx $206.933. The admin fee of £120.00 gas veeb added ti your balasnce for quotation's pirposes o9nly.

This iffer is valid for 14 days from the date of the enclosed quotation. you should of receved further details yesterday.

Transferring yourmortgage onto the new rate couldnt be easer, Simply return the Deed of Variation encl9osed, signed by all partied to the mortgage.

We will charge you the aministration fe of £120.00, This sim can be added to the lan or may be paid by check if you wish.

If you have any quest6ions, plesse contact me on 02356 56998 Monday to Friday between 9.00pm and 5.00pm.

Yours faithfyully

W Gaines
Consutant Mortgage Provider

Punctuation

As with grammar, the correct use of punctuation will make it easier for people to understand the content of a piece of communication. For example, if someone said 'Fred, the dog is ill', they would be telling someone called Fred that the dog is unwell. If they said 'Fred the dog is ill', they would be telling someone that the dog called Fred is unwell. Three of the most common punctuation marks in use are:

- **Full stops** - These are used to mark the end of a sentence or after abbreviations

- **Commas** - These are used to separate words in a list or phrases in a sentence, or to make sentences easier to read

- **Apostrophes** - There are two uses of the apostrophe: to replace a missing letter, e.g. 'I'm, he's, don't' or to indicate something belongs to someone, the possessive case, e.g. 'Jim's book, Pauline's shoes, women's clothing, babies' bottles'

Whatever text is produced, it is important that it is checked for accuracy before being distributed.

Formatting the text

At any stage during the production of text, formatting will be necessary. This can be as simple as changing the type of font used in the text to using text effects, e.g. 'strikethrough'.

It is possible to format:

- **Characters** - By selecting 'font' it allows the following functions to be carried out: style, colour and size of letters, **embolden**, *italicise*, <u>underline</u>, change the s p a c i n g

- **Paragraphs** - Align text using the 'centre' or 'justify' options, or by selecting 'bullets and numbering' add bullet points or numbers. Other amendments can be made by selecting 'borders and shading', or by altering the line spacing, tabs and indent

- **Pages** - Changes can be made to the 'size', 'orientation' and 'margins' of pages. 'Page numbers' can be inserted as well as 'headers and footers' or the 'date and time'. 'Insert page breaks' can be made to indicate where a new page should begin, or 'columns' can divide the page vertically

- **Sections** - It is not necessary for the whole text to be in the same format. Different sections of text can use different formats

If part of the text is formatted in a certain way and this style is to be used later in the text, select 'styles and formatting' and the software will show what has been used previously in the document. This will help to give consistency to the design of the text.

Checking and editing text

As identified previously, text from notes can be accomplished in two ways. If the transcription of notes is being undertaken on behalf of someone else who has made the notes, check with them to clarify any meanings or phrases which are not clear. Make sure the correct interpretation of words and phrases is agreed as early on in the process as possible, so to minimise the amount of changes that have to be made to a document. To help with the process of transcribing the notes, produce a 'draft' copy, so that the originator can check what has been produced matches with what was intended. Make sure that the draft is free from errors.

Most word processing packages contain spell checking and grammar checking facilities. Use these first to correct the obvious errors, but do not rely on them entirely. Check to make sure that the spell check default is not using American spelling and grammar, as the document will accept 'color' and reject 'colour' etc. When the automatic checking is complete, read the document carefully to look for missed errors, and also for correct use of paragraphs, headings and subheadings, style and formatting. Be particularly careful to proofread numbers, dates, times and amounts. Check for errors between similar words, such as 'affect' and 'effect' or 'less' and 'fewer'.

Look for errors of context and content. The draft text will be returned by the originator indicating where any changes need to be made to the document. Changes may come about as a result of:

- **Input errors**

- **Errors in the source material**

- **Amendments to the content**

Changes may have been agreed not necessarily because of poor transcription skills but because the originator of the notes wants to make changes to the document to improve the tone and meaning.

A computer provides a lot of functions that allow text to be easily edited:

- **Delete** - Ctrl+delete - This allows a single letter, group of letters or whole parts of a document to be deleted

- **Paste** - Ctrl+v - This is used in combination with either the 'cut' or 'copy', see below, instruction. Paste will add the last data selected to the document 'copied' or stored on the 'clipboard', which will provide other recently 'copied' information

- **Cut** - Ctrl+x - This is used to highlight a piece of text and remove it from the document. It can then be 'pasted', see above, to another part of the document or a new document

- **Copy** - Ctrl+c - This is used to highlight a piece of text and copied. It can then be 'pasted', see above, to another part of the document or a new document

- **Find and replace** - Ctrl+f - This function is used to change all the examples of a particular word to another word. For example, replace the word 'company' with the word 'organisation', there is no need to retype every example, use 'find' and / or 'replace' to make all the changes

- **Inserting special characters and symbols** - This function enables the use of other alphabets, e.g. Arabic شءكةق and other signs / symbols, e.g. o, û, ©, %

- **Mail merge** - This function is useful if the same letter is going to several recipients, as it can change the name and address of each recipient

- **Track changes** - This function allows the originator of a document to share it with other colleagues inviting them to make changes which can be tracked by name and highlighted

At any stage during the transcription of text from notes the format of the text can be changed. There are various options available in the format menu, e.g. font, which allows the font to be changed to different styles, sizes, colour. It is possible to format characters, pages or whole sections of a document. A part of the text can be formatted and used again later in the document by selecting '**styles and formatting**', and the software will show what formatting has been used previously in the text.

If text is being produced which will have more than one page, it is advisable to use a '**header and footer**', with required information and / or '**page numbers**'. Using both functions will allow the title to be put onto each page with a page number. It is also possible to 'number paragraphs' and include an '**index**' or '**table of contents**' to help the reader find their way around the text..

• ACTIVITY 7

Correct the following piece of text:

Minutes of learning and development team meeting held on 10 September, 2010, Hyatt Regis Hotel, Mayfair, W1, 10.00-16.00.

Present
Jason Henderson (Chair)
Beverly Thompson
Iris Angelli
Anita Sebastian
Dorothy Kennedy
Hope Zeigler
Harry Morrison

Apologies were received from:
Anthony Mitchell
David Kerr
Sophia Wright

minutes of the last meeting were questioned and amended in line with agreed decisions

Matters arising: the implications of the 'spending review' were considered in line with department objectives for the year ahead. It was agreed that a further meeting should take place in two weeks time to specifically address the impact of the 'spending review' on projects for the next twelve months. Everyone was in agreement with this suggestion. This is an extraordinary meeting and weekly meetings will continue as planned.

The new year is fast approaching with the introduction of new systems for the HR department. Everyone was reminded of the implications of this for their various work objectives.

New induction packs were agreed and will be printed.

Next meeting on Wednesday, 1 December, 2010.

Having made all the requested alterations, produce a final draft and pass that to the originator. Hopefully there will be no further amendments at this stage. Once this has been signed off it can be printed to the quality standard requested, not forgetting that a copy of the text should be stored in the appropriate storage system.

Storing text

Every piece of text will probably need to be stored in some way. This can be done using a manual paper-based system, an electronic-based system or both. A computer will have its own in-built sorting and storing mechanisms. Text should be stored accurately in the approved locations so anyone can find it quickly and easily. Folders should be used that can be held within the main directory of the computer system. Folders should be used to group files together to speed up their retrieval. Paper copies will be stored manually using one of the following methods:

- **Alphabetical** - Information is stored in order, from A-Z. Files starting with the same letter are filed in order of the second letter: Aa, Ab, Ac etc. People's names are filed by their surnames, and if more than one has the same surname, by their first names. Names starting with 'The' are filed by ignoring the 'The'. Names beginning with 'Mac' or 'Mc' come before 'Ma', 'Mb' etc.

- **Numerical** - Information is coded using a numbering system, e.g. purchase orders, invoices

- **Alphanumerical** - Information is stored using a combination of letters and numbers, e.g. National Insurance numbers. Usually large databases hold this type of coded information, as they hold more information than numerical systems and are more flexible than alphabetical systems. The order of filing depends on the sequence of the file name. If file names start with letters followed by numbers, they are filed in alphabetical order first and numerical order within each letter

- **Chronological** - This method is often used within one of the other methods. For example, customers' records are filed alphabetically, but the information within the file is stored chronologically, usually with the latest at the front. This provides a history of all activities undertaken for a particular file of information. It can also be based on dates of birth or start dates

- **Geographical** - This is a method of sorting by areas, e.g. North West England, East Anglia or counties, towns, cities

- **By subject or category** - Some organisations need to sort their filing under topics rather than names. For example, a shoe manufacturer may keep files under product names such as Ladies, Gentlemen and Children

What methods could be used to store texts where records need to be identified through dates and postcodes?

The original source material from which the text has been typed will also need to be filed and stored if it needs to be referred to at a later date. An organisation may have its own system of referencing documents which should be followed. If using a system to reference documents, make sure that the original source material is referenced with the same reference number as the completed text. The source material should be stored in a logical manner:

- Handwritten notes can be attached to the file copy of the typed document

- Shorthand notebooks should be stored chronologically, with the start and end date written on the front

- Audio tapes should be stored chronologically and labelled with the date

If the document being created is 'private and confidential', make sure it is identified as such and follows the organisation's policy on 'private and confidential' documents, e.g. the contents of the document should not be discussed publicly so unauthorised people can hear. Confidential information is information that has great value, is considered to be of a private nature and is only permitted to be seen by designated people within an organisation. 'Confidential information' can embrace commercial secrets as well as general information, e.g. medical records. An organisation can be damaged if its privacy of information is not upheld and respected, which could result in the organisation being devalued.

There is no single Act of Parliament defining 'confidential information' or governing how it is protected, or setting out rights and obligations in respect of it. However, the law on 'confidential information' is currently undergoing radical change as a result of developing European and UK legislation and decisions of the courts. Place 'confidentiality' warnings on standard communications, e.g. faxes or emails, to make sure if an individual receives the information by accident they are notified of its 'confidential' nature.

'Private and confidential' documents also includes commercially sensitive information, which needs to be protected from being read by an organisation's competitors. If the content of a document covers personal information it must conform to the requirements of the **Data Protection Act 1998**.

Testing your knowledge

1. What are the different uses of memos, reports, minutes and letters?

2. What is meant by 'fully blocked'?

3. Why is it necessary to meet deadlines?

4. What type of document will always have a signature?

5. What forms can minutes take?

6. What is the sequence of content that can be presented in a report?

7. What do you understand by an 'appendix'?

8. What punctuation is used in a letter using 'open' punctuation?

9. What is meant by proofreading?

10. What types of amendments might be made to a draft?

11. Why is the source material filed as well as the completed document?

12. Why it is important to be able to locate the source material if requested?

13. What does 'confidential' mean in terms of text storage?

Skills

Make sure that you have organised your workstation so that your posture is fully supported when you are touch typing. Follow your organisation's policy for good ergonomic practice in the work environment. Place your keyboard so that your arms are parallel to your work surface and your elbows are close to your body.

Before starting work of the typing of any piece of text, make sure you are clear about:

* The purpose of the text

* The format of the text

* The deadlines within which the text needs to be completed

• ACTIVITY 9

Attend an event where you are expected to report back to your team about the content of the event and how the team need to think about it in the work that they are doing. Take notes that you will need to type into text. Produce a short typed report from the notes. The report will be shared with work colleagues to give them an understanding of the importance of the event you attended, so consider the best way of presenting this information.

Time yourself inputting the text and count the number of words. Proofread the document and calculate the net wpm.

Each of these aspects will inform the planning of the work you will need to do for either yourself or if you are typing the text from original source material. Organise your work around all the tasks that you have to complete so you finish the touch typing transcription of the text at the agreed time. Once you are clear about what has to be done, gather together all the resources you will require to complete the task.

• ACTIVITY 10

Write a report to your supervisor / manager suggesting ways in which team meetings can be organised, run and minuted. Consider the best way to order the contents of the report.

When touch typing text from notes make sure you are fully up to date with the functions of your software so you can edit the text effectively and efficiently. Chat to someone who is very confident in this area, or your supervisor / manager, to check that you are fully conversant with functionality of the technology you are using. This will not only save you time but make your text look more professional.

Make sure that you are clear about the style, layout and format that you wish, or the original author wishes, the text to take. Clarify all these components of your text.

• ACTIVITY 11

Select a number of texts that you have produced which you feel demonstrate your competence in using correct layout, spelling, punctuation and grammar. Share these with your supervisor / manager to get their feedback on the quality of your work.

Type up a draft document and check through this with the original author to make sure it meets all the requirements that they are aiming to achieve. Check through the document to make sure that it accurately presents information, that is, there are no spelling mistakes. Make sure your computer is set to the correct defaults and that grammar and punctuation have been used correctly.

Once you have checked the typed text, check with the original author to make sure that the aims of the typed text have been achieved. When working on the typing of text, if you are not sure, at any stage of its development, that the text is progressing along the right track, pause and reflect on what the text is aiming to achieve. Check with the original author - if it is not you. If anything changes with the development of the text check with the original author that they are happy with the change of direction that the text may have to take. Complete the final draft of the typed text and present this to the author of the original source material if it is not yourself.

Make sure the text has been referenced in line with your organisation's procedures. Then file it using whatever storage system your organisation uses.

Testing your skills

1. How do you check that your typing has used correct spelling, punctuation and grammar?

2. How is the content of a report laid out?

3. How would you insert symbols into your text?

4. If you were asked to emphasise a paragraph in a report, how would you do it?

5. How do you proofread your own work?

6. When would you use printers' correction symbols?

7. What functions would you use to edit text, and why?

8. When would you use mail merge?

9. Why should you produce a final draft of your text?

10. Why is it important to raise any queries with the originator of the original source material before producing the final draft?

11. How does your organisation reference text documents?

12. Why does your organisation use the system (s) of storing text documents that it uses?

Ready for assessment?

To achieve this Level 3 unit of a Business & Administration qualification, learners will need to demonstrate that they are able to perform the following activities:

1. Agreed the purpose, format and deadlines for typing of texts

2. Inputted texts using touch typing at a minimum speed of 60 wpm

3. Formatted texts to an agreed style and layout, making efficient use of available technology

4. Clarified text requirements, when necessary

5. Read and checked texts, as required

6. Edited and corrected texts, as required

7. Stored texts and the original notes safely and securely following organisational procedures

8. Presented texts in the required format within agreed deadlines

You will need to produce evidence from a variety of sources to support the performance requirements of this unit.

If you carry out the 'ACTIVITIES' and respond to the 'NEED TO KNOW' questions, these will provide some of the evidence required.

Links to other units

While gathering evidence for this unit, evidence **may** also be used from evidence generated from other units within the Business & Administration suite of units. Below is a **sample** of applicable units; however, most units within the Business & Administration suite of units will also be applicable.

QCF NVQ
Communications
Communicate in a business environment (Level 2)
Make and receive telephone calls
Use electronic message systems
Core business & administration
Manage own performance in a business environment (Level 2)
Improve own performance in a business environment (Level 2)
Work in a business environment (Level 2)
Work with other people in a business environment (Level 2)
Document production
Design and produce documents in a business environment
Prepare text from shorthand (80 wpm)
Prepare text from recorded audio instruction (60 wpm)
Manage information and data
Store and retrieve information

SVQ

Communications

Prepare to communicate in a business environment

Make and receive telephone calls

Use electronic message systems

Core business & administration

Agree how to manage and improve own performance in a business environment

Undertake work in a business environment

Work with other people in a business environment

Document production

Design and produce documents in a business environment

Prepare text from shorthand (80 wpm)

Prepare text from recorded audio instruction (60 wpm)

Manage information and data

Store and retrieve information

20

Prepare text from shorthand (80 wpm)

PREPARE TEXT FROM SHORTHAND (80 WPM)

'**Prepare text from shorthand (80 wpm)**' is an optional unit which may be chosen as one of a combination of units to achieve either a Qualifications and Credit Framework (QCF), National Vocational Qualification (NVQ) or Scottish Vocational Qualification (SVQ).

The aims of this unit are to:

- Understand the task of preparing text from shorthand

- Understand the purpose and value of following procedures when preparing text from shorthand

- Be able to prepare for tasks and use shorthand to take dictation

- Be able to produce texts from shorthand in 80 wpm

To achieve the above aims of this unit, learners will be expected to provide evidence through the performance of work-based activities.

Knowledge

Prepare text from shorthand

Shorthand is a system of taking notes of the spoken word quickly and efficiently using handwriting, using different symbols for the sound of words. There are different systems of shorthand which use a variety of techniques, including simplifying existing letters or characters and using special symbols to represent phonemes, the sound units of a word, words and phrases of words.

Two of the most popular shorthand systems include:

Pitman Shorthand

Devised by Sir Isaac Pitman, 1813-1897, it was first published in 1837. Since then it has been improved upon and adapted for 15 different languages. The notable features of the Pitman system are:

- It is **phonetic** - It records the sounds of speech rather than the spelling. For example, the sound **F** in 'form', 'ele**ph**ant' and 'rou**gh**' is written the same for each word

- **Vowel sounds are optional** - They are written with small dots, dashes or other shapes next to the main strokes, which helps to increase writing speed because most words can be identified from their consonants only

- The **thickness**, **length** and **position** of strokes are all significant

- There are many **special abbreviations** and other **tricks** to increase writing speed

The record speed for Pitman shorthand is 350 wpm, tested in 1922.

Gregg Shorthand
Invented by John Robert Gregg, 1867-1948, it was first published in 1888. Since then many different versions have appeared. Gregg's shorthand is still used in the USA. Some of the notable features of the Gregg system are:

- **It is phonetic, as with Pitman**

- **Vowels are written as 'hooks'**

- **Consonants are written as 'circles'**

• ACTIVITY 1

Ask a colleague to read a document containing at least 600 words to you at dictation speed, where the speed of dictation should create at least 80 words per minute, this should take no more than 10 minutes. Take notes in shorthand. Type the document from the notes. Proofread the typed version against the original shorthand notes.

When taking shorthand notes make sure that the workstation being worked from has been modified to the ergonomic requirements of the user. The shorthand notebook should be held in a convenient position, e.g. on a lap or on a desk. Have a sharp pencil to use to take shorthand notes, and spares. Listen very carefully to what is being said. If a word is missed or not fully understood, ask for clarification immediately. If someone is dictating too quickly, particularly if they are a person new to dictation, ask them to slow down a little until you are used to their delivery. It is better to clarify this as the dictation goes along rather than to wait until the end of the dictation session. Building a rapport with the person giving dictation makes it easier to understand what they mean and enables you to record it efficiently.

Different types of documents that can be produced from notes
Different types of organisations working in many different sectors will have the need to produce text from notes. These will include emails, memos, letters, reports and minutes of

meetings. Notes will have been produced from a variety of sources, e.g. shorthand, audio recordings.

Many text documents will be prepared from handwritten notes which can be made by an author who will:

- **Prepare the text** - This should be relatively easy to transcribe as the person preparing the text is translating handwritten notes which they have made, so legibility and shortcuts should not be a problem

- **Not prepare the text** - This may be a little more difficult to transcribe as the person preparing the text is not translating their own handwritten notes. They may not understand the handwriting or the shortcuts that the author has made. If this occurs, the person transcribing the text should clarify from the author any script that is not legible

Before preparing the transcription of any notes into text make sure that the purpose, format and deadline of the text has been agreed. A deadline is when a document is due by a certain time, in a certain format and containing the required information. It is important that all parties involved in the production of text are all agreed on what the finished product will look like and when it can be expected. Before starting to produce any text from notes, include resources that will be needed to complete the text, e.g. the addition of images or diagrams. The text should be clear. If a document is not delivered against these requirements it will appear unprofessional, particularly if lateness has not been discussed with the recipient, and this could lead to loss of business. Having an agreed deadline will help to plan and prioritise tasks / activities.

Whatever source material is going to be used, documents will be produced from the following formats:

Stenography alphabet

	A B C D E F G H I J K L M N O P Q R S T U V W X Y Z
Antiquity	
M.Ages	
1.Wills	
Mavon	
Macaulay	
Byrom	
Nash	
Cossard	
Roe	
Fayet	
Taylor	
Pitman	
Gabelsberger	

Memos

These are used for internal communication within an organisation. They may vary in the level of formality in which they are written. They:

- May be addressed to more than one recipient

- Will usually not include addresses

- Will have a subject line, similar to emails

- Will state the date, name of the recipient (s), the name of the sender and the content

- May have the recipient and sender's job titles and departments

- Will usually be produced on a template which reflects the organisation's 'house style'

MEMORANDUM

To: All selling staff

From: Sales Manager

Date: 27th August 2010

Subject: Sales targets

Last week saw total sales of £127,436, an increase of 3.1% on last year. This week we have a challenging target of £148,000, or 3.7% on last year. This will require 100% effort from all of us, but I am confident we can do it.

REMEMBER: PROMOTE DISPOSABLE BARBECUES.

Most organisations still use memos for important internal messages, if they have not been replaced by the use of emails

Business letters
These are usually printed on paper headed with the organisation's address and business details. There is a recognised format to letter writing; however, an organisation may choose to adopt its own 'house style'. Letters will normally:

- Be **addressed to one person**, e.g. 'Dear Sir' or 'Dear Madam'

- Be **dated**

- Contain a **salutation**, e.g. 'Dear ...'

- **Have a reference number / title / heading** - these are optional

- Contain the body of text for writing the letter

- End with a **closing statement** that summarises the main points for writing the letter

- Include a **compliment**, e.g. 'Yours sincerely'

- Include a **signature**

Matthew and Son Builders
Allington Place
West Billington
WW1 1AD
Tel: 01632 566854

Our ref: GM / RA / 124
Your ref: VH / AK

13 August 2010

Mr V Harmison
Oval Walk
West Billington
WW2 1AX

Dear Mr Harmison

Thank you for your letter dated 6th August 2010 accepting our quotation to extend your office building.

The work will commence on 6th September 2010 and will be completed within 6 working weeks.

If you have any queries, please do not hesitate to contact me.

Yours sincerely

Graham Matthew
Director

Business letters are usually produced:

- **Fully blocked** - All parts of the document start at the left-hand margin

- With **open punctuation** - Punctuation used only in the body of the letter, where it is essential for grammatical accuracy and understanding

A letter addressed to Mrs Jayne Wilcox, 12 Manver's Street, London SW19 7ER can be sent using the following salutations and complimentary phrases:

SALUTATION	Dear Jayne	Dear Mrs Wilcox	Dear Madam
COMPLIMENT	Kind regards	Yours sincerely	Yours faithfully

If someone knows Jayne Wilcox well they will probably use Jayne. If a sender does not know Jayne well they may feel more comfortable addressing her as Mrs Wilcox. If they do not know Mrs Wilcox at all, they will probably usually the formal term 'Madam'. As the salutation becomes more formal so does the complimentary close.

With the advent of electronic means of communication the number of letters written and received by organisations has declined. Letters will probably be written if there is no access to an email address on an organisation's website, for legal reasons or the sender may want a formal record of the communication.

• ACTIVITY 2

What does 'open punctuation' mean?

Reports

These are produced in response to a request for information. They may be formal or informal, depending on the audience they are being written for. For example, a report written to a Board of an organisation will generally be more formal than a report to the members of a club. A report is written to inform the reader of facts about a subject. The depth of information contained in a report will depend on the purpose of the report and its intended audience.

All reports will follow a similar structure, however detailed they may be:

- **Front page** - This contains the title of the report, the name of the author and the date

- **Contents** - This will list all the subjects covered in the report

- **Executive summary** - This gives a brief outline of the report

- **Background information** - This gives the reasons why the report was produced

- **Methodology** - This outlines the methods used to produce the data in the report, e.g. surveys, questionnaires

- **Findings** - These are the results of the methods used to explore the purpose of the report. Findings may be presented by:

  - Importance, where the central ideas are presented

  - Chronology, where ideas are presented in the order of events, starting either with the latest or the first

- Sequence, where one idea follows from another

- Comparison, where two ideas are compared in alternate paragraphs

- **Conclusion** - This outlines the conclusions that can be drawn from the findings of the research

Recommendations - This outlines the actions that are • recommended to be taken as a result of the conclusion

- **Acknowledgements** - This records the contribution others have made to the report

- **Bibliography** - This outlines the source material used in the research. There are a number of different ways that a bibliography can be drawn up

- **Appendices** - This sets out all the information referred to in the report which is too detailed to be given in full without distracting from the purpose of the report

Minutes

These are a record of the discussions and agreed actions that will need to be followed up as a result of a meeting. Minutes can be recorded in a number of different forms:

- **Verbatim** - Where everything is recorded word for word

- **Narrative** - Where a summary of the meeting is recorded. Formal resolutions will be recorded verbatim

- **Resolution** - Where a motion which has been voted on and passed gives details of the proposer and seconder of the motion, with a verbatim recording of the resolution

- **Action** - Where only the action and the name of the person or persons responsible for carrying out the action are recorded

Accuracy of text prepared from notes

Any piece of text produced from notes should be a quality piece of work. It should be executed with the correct spelling, the use of grammatical rules and the correct application of punctuation to produce a product that both gives a good impression of the organisation and, more importantly, conveys the intended message of the text.

Spelling

A computer will automatically check the spelling of words and highlight them in the document being worked on. However, spell check cannot:

- Differentiate between American and English spelling of words, so make sure that the spell check default is aligned to the correct country

- Differentiate between words that are spelled correctly but used incorrectly, e.g. using 'through' when it should be 'threw'. Some of the most commonly confused words are:

  - We are pleased to <u>accept</u> your donation
    Everyone made a donation <u>except</u> Mr Jones

  - Never listen to <u>advice</u> from your parents
    I would <u>advise</u> you always to listen to your parents

  - The increase in interest rates will <u>affect</u> everyone
    The <u>effect</u> of the increase was felt by everyone

  - She thought she was <u>eligible</u> for a grant
    The letter she received was <u>illegible</u>

  - You must <u>ensure</u> that your car is <u>insured</u>

  - Lowestoft is <u>farther</u> east than Birmingham
    I need <u>further</u> information on the location of Hull

  - There are <u>fewer</u> days in February than in June
    It is <u>less</u> likely to rain today than it was yesterday

  - My <u>personal</u> opinion is that it will rain today
    The HR Department deals with <u>personnel</u>

  - I visited the local doctors' <u>practice</u> this morning
    I need to <u>practise</u> my spelling more often

  - The <u>principal</u> cause of heart disease is overeating
    The minister resigned over a matter of <u>principle</u>

  - The traffic on the M6 was <u>stationary</u> for two hours
    We need to order some more <u>stationery</u> this week

  - This week's sales were better <u>than</u> last week's
    We will look at this week's plan, <u>then</u> next week's

- The girls picked up <u>their</u> handbags
  The boys will be over <u>there</u> tomorrow
  They're planning to visit next week

• ACTIVITY 3

Circle the correct spelling in the following list of words:

1. Participative	participertive	particsipative
2. Calasthenets	calisthenics	calisthenicks
3. Originate	oridginate	originatte
4. Pergured	perfoured	perjured
5. Perigrinate	peregrinate	peragrinate
6. Sadled	sadaled	saddled
7. Zephyr	zefr	zephir
8. Asignation	assignation	assegnation
9. Vertigenous	vertiganous	vertiginous
10. Bucolic	bucolick	buccolic

Grammar

Grammar can loosely be defined at the 'rules of language'. However, in English, the 'rules' are not consistent, which makes it complicated to learn and apply. Grammar is important to make sure that the intended meaning of a sentence is communicated to the recipients of the communication. For example, 'Use both lanes when turning right' actually requires drivers to straddle the two lanes, which is a highly dangerous manoeuvre to carry out. The correct sentence construction should be: 'Use either lane when turning right'.

There are five parts of speech which are commonly used:

- **Nouns** - These are the names of a person, place or thing, e.g. 'book', 'television', 'Sunday', 'Norfolk'

- **Pronouns** - These are used instead of a noun, e.g. instead of saying 'John' in a paragraph that refers only to him, use 'he' or 'him'

- **Verbs** - These are words that express doing things, e.g. 'ran', 'run' or 'running'

- **Adverbs** - These words give information about how a verb was executed, e.g. 'he ran <u>quickly</u>' or 'he ran <u>fast</u>'. Note that while most adverbs will be formed by the addition of '-ly' to the end of a verb, it is not always the case, as can be seen by the second example in this paragraph

- **Adjectives** - These describe nouns, e.g. 'an <u>interesting</u> book', '<u>reality</u> television'

What are the different types of verbs?

Sentences are formed by linking parts of speech together. Simple sentences contain a subject and a verb, e.g. 'I am', where 'I' is the subject and 'am' is the verb. More complicated sentences will have a subject, verb and object, e.g. 'I am going to London', where the object of the sentence is London. Sentences must start with a capital letter and end with some form of punctuation, e.g. a full stop, question mark. Capital letters are also used to indicate **proper names**, e.g. America, Anthony; **titles**, e.g. Mr, Mrs, Lord; **days of the week or months of the year** and **acronyms** (RAF, CIA, FBI, MI5, RAC).

A paragraph is formed by linking two or more sentences together. If the subject of a paragraph changes, it is advisable to start a new paragraph.

• ACTIVITY 5

Proofread and correct the following and produce a corrected version.
Switch off the spell check function on the computer.

Our ref: DT/GY/1256

Mr S Williamson
Apart 21
The shore
Manchster
M6 7yu

Dear serena williamon

Account number 45678956 -Flat 24 te maltings, Mancester

Thankyoy for you're resent enqiry regarding you mortgage, and theintrst
rates available to you. I am encloseing a quotetion showing what yur new
paymemts would be at a new rat of interst. Yhjis has been calculated on
and Interest only Basis.

At the moment you're monthly payments is ^189.23 vased ib a rate if
6.75%. Should you decide to exce0pt our offer (details) attached, your
new repayments would be approx $206.933. The admin fee of £120.00
gas veeb added ti your balasnce for quotation's pirposes o9nly.

This iffer is valid for 14 days from the date of the enclosed quotation. you
should of receved further details yesterday.

Transferring yourmortgage onto the new rate couldnt be easer, Simply
return the Deed of Variation encl9osed, signed by all partied to the
mortgage.

We will charge you the aministration fe of £120.00, This sim can be added
to the lan or may be paid by check if you wish.

If you have any quest6ions, plesse contact me on 02356 56998 Monday
to Friday between 9.00pm and 5.00pm.

Yours faithfyully

W Gaines
Consutant Mortgage Provider

Punctuation

As with grammar, the correct use of punctuation will make it easier for
people to understand the content of a piece of communication. For
example, if someone said 'Fred, the dog is ill', they would be telling

someone called Fred that the dog is unwell. If they said 'Fred the dog is ill', they would be telling someone that the dog called Fred is unwell. Three of the most common punctuation marks in use are:

- **Full stops** - These are used to mark the end of a sentence or after abbreviations

- **Commas** - These are used to separate words in a list or phrases in a sentence, or to make sentences easier to read

- **Apostrophes** - There are two uses of the apostrophe: to replace a missing letter, e.g. 'I'm, he's, don't' or to indicate something belongs to someone, the possessive case, e.g. 'Jim's book, Pauline's shoes, women's clothing, babies' bottles'

Whatever text is produced, it is important that it is checked for accuracy before being distributed.

Formatting the text

At any stage during the production of text, formatting will be necessary. This can be as simple as changing the type of font used in the text to using text effects, e.g. 'strikethrough'.

It is possible to format:

- **Characters** - By selecting 'font' it allows the following functions to be carried out: style, colour and size of letters, **embolden**, *italicise*, underline, change the s p a c i n g

- **Paragraphs** - You can align text using the 'centre' or 'justify' options, or by selecting 'bullets and numbering' add bullet points or numbers. Other amendments can be made by selecting 'borders and shading', or by altering the line spacing, tabs and indent

- **Pages** - Changes can be made to the 'size', 'orientation' and 'margins' of pages. 'Page numbers' can be inserted as well as 'headers and footers' or the 'date and time'. 'Insert page breaks' can be made to indicate where a new page should begin, or 'columns' can divide the page vertically

- **Sections** - It is not necessary for the whole text to be in the same format. Different sections of text can use different formats

If part of the text is formatted in a certain way and this style is to be used later in the text, select 'styles and formatting' and the software will show what has been used previously in the document. This will help to give consistency to the design of the text.

Checking and editing text

As identified previously, text from notes can be accomplished in two ways. If the transcription of notes is being undertaken on behalf of someone else who has made the notes, check with them to clarify any meanings or phrases which are not clear. Make sure the correct interpretation of words and phrases is agreed as early on in the process as possible, so to minimise the amount of changes that have to be made to a document. To help with the process of transcribing the notes, produce a 'draft' copy, so that the originator can check what has been produced matches with what was intended. Make sure that the draft is free from errors.

Most word processing packages contain spell checking and grammar checking facilities. Use these first to correct the obvious errors, but do not rely on them entirely. Check to make sure that the spell check default is not using American spelling and grammar, as the document will accept 'color' and reject 'colour' etc. When the automatic checking is complete, read the document carefully to look for missed errors, and also for correct use of paragraphs, headings and subheadings, style and formatting. Be particularly careful to proofread numbers, dates, times and amounts. Check for errors between similar words, such as 'affect' and 'effect' or 'less' and 'fewer'.

Look for errors of context and content. The draft text will be returned by the originator indicating where any changes need to be made to the document. Changes may come about as a result of:

- **Input errors**

- **Errors in the source material**

- **Amendments to the content**

Changes may have been agreed not necessarily because of poor transcription skills but because the originator of the notes wants to make changes to the document to improve the tone and meaning.

A computer provides a lot of functions that allow text to be easily edited:

- **Delete** - Ctrl+delete - This allows a single letter, group of letters or whole parts of a document to be deleted

- **Paste** - Ctrl+v - This is used in combination with either the 'cut' or 'copy', see below, instruction. Paste will add the last data selected to the document 'copied' or stored on the 'clipboard', which will provide other recently 'copied' information

- **Cut -** Ctrl+x - This is used to highlight a piece of text and remove it from the document. It can then be 'pasted', see above, to another part of the document or a new document

- **Copy -** Ctrl+c - This is used to highlight a piece of text and copied. It can then be 'pasted', see above, to another part of the document or a new document

- **Find and replace -** Ctrl+f - This function is used to change all the examples of a particular word to another word. For example, replace the word 'company' with the word 'organisation', there is no need to retype every example, use 'find' and / or 'replace' to make all the changes

- **Inserting special characters and symbols -** This function enables the use of other alphabets, e.g. Arabic شةةكق and other signs / symbols, e.g. o, û, ©, %

- **Mail merge -** This function is useful if the same letter is going to several recipients, as it can change the name and address of each recipient

- **Track changes -** This function allows the originator of a document to share it with other colleagues inviting them to make changes which can be tracked by name and highlighted

At any stage during the transcription of text from notes the format of the text can be changed. There are various options available in the format menu, e.g. font, which allows the font to be changed to different styles, sizes, colour. It is possible to format characters, pages or whole sections of a document. A part of the text can be formatted and used again later in the document by selecting 'styles and formatting', and the software will show what formatting has been used previously in the text.

If text is being produced which will have more than one page, it is advisable to use a 'header and footer', with required information and / or 'page numbers'. Using both functions will allow the title to be put onto each page with a page number. It is also possible to 'number paragraphs' and include an 'index' or 'table of contents' to help the reader find their way around the text.

• ACTIVITY 6

Correct the following piece of text:

minutes of senor executive meting helod on 2 Novembr 2010, Rusel Sqare Hotel, Russell sq, London WC1, 9.30-4.0

Presnt
Jill St Jon (Chair)
Basil Pilot
Felicty Adamsr
Loretta Hedderson
Andrw Jones
Michael Higgns
Trry Jackson

Apologes were recieved from:
Adelaide Stephens
Martin James

minuts of the last mee4ting were apprved

None matt4ers arisng.

It was sugested thast a farther meeting be he4ld in jan to agre the final steppes of th sales plane for the new year. All 7 present agred.

Christmas is fest aproaching and it well be very busy. As Peter will be leave it will effect the way the te4am will work.

New stationary to be ordered for the team.

Next meeting on Tues, 78 des 2010.

Having made all the requested alterations, produce a final draft and pass that to the originator. Hopefully there will be no further amendments at this stage. Once this has been signed off it can be printed to the quality standard requested, not forgetting that a copy of the text should be stored in the appropriate storage system.

Storing text

Every piece of text will probably need to be stored in some way. This can be done using a manual paper-based system, an electronic-based system or both. A computer will have its own in-built sorting and storing mechanisms. Text should be stored accurately in the approved locations so anyone can find it quickly and easily. Folders should be used that can be held within the main directory of the computer system. Folders should be used to group files together to speed up their retrieval. Paper copies will be stored manually using one of the following methods:

- **Alphabetical** - Information is stored in order, from A-Z. Files starting with the same letter are filed in order of the second letter: Aa, Ab, Ac etc. People's names are filed by their surnames, and if more than one has the same surname, by their first names. Names starting with 'The' are filed by ignoring the 'The'. Names beginning with 'Mac' or 'Mc' come before 'Ma', 'Mb' etc.

- **Numerical** - Information is coded using a numbering system, e.g. purchase orders, invoices

- **Alphanumerical** - Information is stored using a combination of letters and numbers, e.g. National Insurance numbers. Usually large databases hold this type of coded information, as they hold more information than numerical systems and are more flexible than alphabetical systems. The order of filing depends on the sequence of the file name. If file names start with letters followed by numbers, they are filed in alphabetical order first and numerical order within each letter

- **Chronological** - This method is often used within one of the other methods. For example, customers' records are filed alphabetically, but the information within the file is stored chronologically, usually with the latest at the front. This provides a history of all activities undertaken for a particular file of information. It can also be based on dates of birth or start dates

- **Geographical** - This is a method of sorting by areas, e.g. North West England, East Anglia or counties, towns, cities

- **By subject or category** - Some organisations need to sort their filing under topics rather than names. For example, a shoe manufacturer may keep files under product names such as Ladies, Gentlemen and Children

• ACTIVITY 7

What is the difference between storing texts alphabetically and chronologically?

The original source material from which the text has been produced will also need to be filed and stored if it needs to be referred to at a later date. An organisation may have its own system of referencing documents which should be followed. If using a system to reference documents, make sure that the original source material is referenced with the same reference number as the completed text. The source material should be stored in a logical manner:

- Handwritten notes can be attached to the file copy of the completed document

- Shorthand notebooks should be stored chronologically, with the start and end date written on the front

- Audio tapes should be stored chronologically and labelled with the date

If the document being created is 'private and confidential', make sure it is identified as such and follows the organisation's policy on 'private and confidential' documents, e.g. the contents of the document should not be discussed publicly so unauthorised people can hear. Confidential information is information that has great value, is considered to be of a private nature and is only permitted to be seen by designated people within an organisation. 'Confidential information' can embrace commercial secrets as well as general information, e.g. medical records. An organisation can be damaged if its privacy of information is not upheld and respected, which could result in the organisation being devalued.

There is no single Act of Parliament defining 'confidential information' or governing how it is protected, or setting out rights and obligations in respect of it. However, the law on 'confidential information' is currently undergoing radical change as a result of developing European and UK legislation and decisions of the courts. Place 'confidentiality' warnings on standard communications, e.g. faxes or emails, to make sure if an individual receives the information by accident they are notified of its 'confidential' nature.

'Private and confidential' documents also includes commercially sensitive information, which needs to be protected from being read by an organisation's competitors. If the content of a document covers personal information it must conform to the requirements of the **Data Protection Act 1998**.

Testing your knowledge

1. Why does the content of reports differ from report to report?

2. What is meant by 'fully blocked'?

3. Why is it necessary to meet deadlines for the production of text documents?

4. What type of document will always have a signature?

5. What forms can minutes take?

6. What is the sequence of content that can be presented in a report?

7. What do you understand by a 'bibliography'?

8. What punctuation is used in a letter using 'open' punctuation?

9. What is meant by proofreading?

10. What is the purpose of creating a draft document?

11. Why is the source material filed as well as the completed final document?

Skills
Before starting work on the transcription of any piece of text from shorthand notes, make sure you are clear about:

- The purpose of the text

- The format of the text

- The deadlines within which the text needs to be completed

• ACTIVITY 8

Attend a meeting - this could be a team meeting at work, a social club meeting, a meeting at college - and take shorthand notes of what is said OR obtain notes that need to be transcribed into text. Produce a short typed report from the shorthand notes. Time yourself inputting the text and count the number of words. Proofread the document and calculate the net words per minute.

Each of these aspects of preparation before starting work on transcriptions will help to inform the planning of the work you will need to do for either yourself or someone else - if you are producing the text from shorthand notes made by someone else. Organise your work around all the tasks that you have to complete so you finish the transcription of the shorthand notes at the agreed time. Once you are clear about what has to be done, gather together all the resources you will require to complete the task.

• ACTIVITY 9

Write a report to your supervisor suggesting ways in which your organisation's work areas can be kept more safe and secure. Consider the best way to order the contents of the report.

When transcribing text from shorthand notes make sure you are fully up to date with the functions of your software so you can edit the text effectively and efficiently. Chat to someone who is very confident in this area, or your supervisor / manager, to check that you are fully conversant with functionality of the technology you are using. This will not only save you time but make your text look more professional.

Make sure that you are clear about the style, layout and format that you wish, or the original author wishes, the text to take. Clarify all these components of your text.

• ACTIVITY 10

Select a number of texts that you have produced from shorthand notes which you feel demonstrate your competence in using correct layout, spelling, punctuation and grammar. Share these with your supervisor / manager to get their feedback on the quality of your work.

Produce a draft document and check through this with the original author to make sure it meets all the requirements that they are aiming to achieve. Check through the document to make sure that it accurately presents information. that is, there are no spelling mistakes. Make sure your computer is set to the correct defaults and that grammar and punctuation have been used correctly.

Once you have checked the text, check the aims of the text with the original author, to make sure that they have been achieved. When working on the production of the text, if you are not sure, at any stage of its development, that the text is progressing along the right track, pause and reflect on what the text is aiming to achieve. Check with the original author - if it is not you. If anything changes with the development of the text check with the original author that they are happy with the change of direction that the text may have to take. Complete the final draft of the text and present this to the author of the original source material if it is not yourself.

Make sure the text has been referenced in line with your organisation's procedures. Then file it using whatever storage system your organisation uses.

Testing your skills

1. How do you make sure that spelling, punctuation and grammar has been used correctly?

2. How is the content of a memo laid out?

3. How and when would you use the home menu?

4. If you were asked to emphasise a sentence in a report how would you do it?

5. How do you proofread your own work?

6. When would macros be used?

7. Why would you use 'page layout' when formatting your text document?

8. What do you do with a draft copy of your text?

9. Why is it important to raise any queries with the originator of the original source material before producing the final draft?

10. How does your organisation reference text documents?

11. What system (s) of storing text document does your organisation use, and why?

Ready for assessment?
To achieve this Level 3 unit of a Business & Administration qualification, learners will need to demonstrate that they are able to perform the following activities:

1. Agreed the purpose, format and deadlines for preparing text from shorthand

2. Took dictation using shorthand at a minimum speed of 80 wpm

3. Clarified text requirements, when necessary

4. Inputted and formatted texts to an agreed format from shorthand notes

5. Made efficient use of technology, as required

6. Read and checked texts for accuracy

7. Edited and corrected the text, as required

8. Stored texts and original shorthand notes safely and securely following organisational procedures

9. Presented texts to the required format and within the agreed deadlines

You will need to produce evidence from a variety of sources to support the performance requirements of this unit.

If you carry out the 'ACTIVITIES' and respond to the 'NEED TO KNOW' questions, these will provide some of the evidence required.

Links to other units

While gathering evidence for this unit, evidence **may** also be used from evidence generated from other units within the Business & Administration suite of units. Below is a **sample** of applicable units; however, most units within the Business & Administration suite of units will also be applicable.

QCF NVQ
Communications
Communicate in a business environment (Level 2)
Make and receive telephone calls
Use electronic message systems
Core business & administration
Manage own performance in a business environment (Level 2)
Improve own performance in a business environment (Level 2)
Work in a business environment (Level 2)
Work with other people in a business environment (Level 2)
Customer service
Handle mail
Document production
Produce documents in a business environment
Prepare text from notes using touch typing (40 wpm)
Prepare text from shorthand (60 wpm)
Prepare text from recorded audio instruction (40 wpm)

SVQ

Communications

Prepare to communicate in a business environment

Make and receive telephone calls

Use electronic message systems

Core business & administration

Agree how to manage and improve own performance in a business environment

Undertake work in a business environment

Work with other people in a business environment

Customer service

Handle mail

Document production

Produce documents in a business environment

Prepare text from notes using touch typing (40 wpm)

Prepare text from shorthand (60 wpm)

Prepare text from recorded audio instruction (40 wpm)

21

Prepare text from recorded audio instruction (60wpm)

PREPARE TEXT FROM RECORDED AUDIO INSTRUCTION (60 WPM)

'Prepare text from recorded audio instruction (60 wpm)' is an optional unit which may be chosen as one of a combination of units to achieve either a Qualifications and Credit Framework (QCF), National Vocational Qualification (NVQ) or Scottish Vocational Qualification (SVQ).

The aims of this unit are to:

- Understand the task of preparing text from recorded audio instruction

- Understand the purpose and value of following procedures when preparing text from recorded audio instruction

- Be able to produce texts from audio recordings at 60 wpm

To achieve the above aims of this unit, learners will be expected to provide evidence through the performance of work-based activities.

Knowledge

Before starting to use the keyboard always make sure that the workstation is ergonomically prepared to meet the individual requirements of the keyboard user - sit up straight, feet flat on the floor, elbows close to the body, wrists straight and forearms parallel to the work surface. And remember to take regular breaks from typing.

The equipment and skills required to type up notes from a recorded audio machine includes:

- A computer and all its associated equipment

- A headset

- A foot pedal - preferably the USB kind

- Depending on the format used, e.g. DVD, mp3, cassette, microcassette, additional equipment may be required for audio playback

- A good typing speed and good listening skills

Audio recordings are used greatly in the legal and medical profession, which may impose some compliance issues to content with, e.g. if creating a medical transcription, will HIPPA compliance issues be involved?

Some issues that need to be considered when typing from an audio recording:

- Sound quality

- Multiple speakers

- Accents

- People talking over each other and audience interaction, as this can slow down the transcription process causing frustration and reducing productivity

- Use of 'templates' within organisations

- Focus to exclude other functions, e.g. no telephone calls or tweets

- If 'real-time' transcription is required, the client will need to be available at the same time of transcription, which does not allow much time for editing or breaks

- Verbatim transcription or an edited version, deleting 'umms' and other unfinished thoughts

• ACTIVITY 1

Using any pre-recorded text, e.g. a talking book, type for 10 minutes. Ask a colleague to proofread your version against the recording. Count the number of words you have typed and calculate the net words per minute.

Different types of documents that can be produced from recorded audio instructions

Different types of organisations working in many different sectors will have the need to produce text from audio recordings. Many text documents will be prepared from audio recordings which can be made by a speaker (s) who will:

- **Prepare the text -** This should be relatively easy to transcribe as the person preparing the text is translating audio recordings which they have made, so the quality of the voice and vocal shortcuts should not be a problem to transcribe

- **Not prepare the text -** This may be a little more difficult to transcribe as the person preparing the text is not translating their own audio recording. They may not understand the vocal landscape or the vocal shortcuts of the audio recording. Clarify any vocal idiosyncrasies

Before preparing the transcription of any audio recording into text make sure that the purpose, format and deadline of the text has been agreed. A deadline is when a document is due by a certain time, in a certain format and containing the required information. It is important that all parties involved in the production of text are all agreed on what the finished product will look like and when it can be expected. Before starting to produce any text from the audio recording, include resources that will be needed to complete the text, e.g. the addition of images or diagrams. The text should be clear. If a document is not delivered against these requirements it will appear unprofessional, particularly if lateness has not been discussed with the recipient, which could lead to loss of business. Having an agreed deadline will help to plan and prioritise tasks / activities.

Whatever source material is going to be used, documents will be produced in the following formats:

Memos

These are used for internal communication within an organisation. They may vary in the level of formality in which they are written. They:

- May be addressed to more than one recipient

- Will usually not include addresses

- Will have a subject line, similar to 'emails'

- Will state the date, name of the recipient (s), the name of the sender and the content

- May have the recipient and sender's job titles and departments

- Will usually be produced on a template which reflects the organisation's 'house style'

MEMORANDUM

To: All selling staff

From: Sales Manager

Date: 27th August 2010

Subject: Sales targets

Last week saw total sales of £127,436, an increase of 3.1% on last year. This week we have a challenging target of £148,000, or 3.7% on last year. This will require 100% effort from all of us, but I am confident we can do it.

REMEMBER: PROMOTE DISPOSABLE BARBECUES.

Most organisations still use memos for important internal messages, if they have not been replaced by the use of 'emails'.

Business letters

These are usually printed on paper headed with the organisation's address and business details. There is a recognised format to letter writing; however, an organisation may choose to adopt its own 'house style'. Letters will normally:

- Be **addressed to one person**, e.g. 'Dear Sir' or 'Dear Madam'

- Be **dated**

- Contain a **salutation**, e.g. 'Dear ...'

- **Have a reference number / title / heading** - these are optional

- Contain the body of text for writing the letter

- End with a **closing statement** that summarises the main points for writing the letter

- Include a **compliment**, e.g. 'Yours sincerely'

- Include a **signature**

Matthew and Son Builders
Allington Place
West Billington
WW1 1AD
Tel: 01632 566854

Our ref: GM / RA / 124
Your ref: VH / AK

13 August 2010

Mr V Harmison
Oval Walk
West Billington
WW2 1AX

Dear Mr Harmison

Thank you for your letter dated 6th August 2010 accepting our quotation to extend your office building.

The work will commence on 6th September 2010 and will be completed within 6 working weeks.

If you have any queries, please do not hesitate to contact me.

Yours sincerely

Graham Matthew
Director

Business letters are usually produced:

- **Fully blocked** - All parts of the document start at the left-hand margin

- With **open punctuation** - Punctuation used only in the body of the letter, where it is essential for grammatical accuracy and understanding

A letter addressed to Mrs Jayne Wilcox, 12 Manver's Street, London SW19 7ER can be sent using the following salutations and complimentary phrases:

SALUTATION	Dear Jayne	Dear Mrs Wilcox	Dear Madam
COMPLIMENT	Kind regards	Yours sincerely	Yours faithfully

If someone knows Jayne Wilcox well they will probably use Jayne. If a sender does not know Jayne well they may feel more comfortable addressing her as Mrs Wilcox. If they do not know Mrs Wilcox at all, they will probably usually the formal term 'Madam'. As the salutation becomes more formal so does the complimentary close.

With the advent of electronic means of communication the number of letters written and received by organisations has declined. Letters will probably be written if there is no access to an email address on an organisation's website, for legal reasons or the sender may want a formal record of the communication.

• ACTIVITY 2

What does 'open punctuation' mean?

Reports
These are produced in response to a request for information. They may be formal or informal, depending on the audience they are being written for. For example, a report written to a Board of an organisation will generally be more formal than a report to the members of a club. A report is written to inform the reader of facts about a subject. The depth of information contained in a report will depend on the purpose of the report and its intended audience.

All reports will follow a similar structure, however detailed they may be:

- **Front page** - This contains the title of the report, the name of the author and the date

- **Contents** - This will list all the subjects covered in the report

- **Executive summary** - This gives a brief outline of the report

- **Background information** - This gives the reasons why the report was produced

- **Methodology** - This outlines the methods used to produce the data in the report, e.g. surveys, questionnaires

- **Findings** - These are the results of the methods used to explore the purpose of the report. Findings may be presented by:

  - Importance: where the central ideas are presented

  - Chronology: where ideas are presented in the order of events, starting either with the latest or the first

- Sequence: where one idea follows from another

- Comparison: where two ideas are compared in alternate paragraphs

- **Conclusion** - This outlines the conclusions that can be drawn from the findings of the research

- **Recommendations** - This outlines the actions that are - recommended to be taken as a result of the conclusion

- **Acknowledgements** - This records the contribution others have made to the report

- **Bibliography** - This outlines the source material used in the research. There are a number of different ways that a bibliography can be drawn up

- **Appendices** - This sets out all the information referred to in the report which is too detailed to be given in full without distracting from the purpose of the report

Minutes

These are a record of the discussions and agreed actions that will need to be followed up as a result of a meeting. Minutes can be recorded in a number of different forms:

- **Verbatim** - Where everything is recorded word for word

- **Narrative** - Where a summary of the meeting is recorded. Formal resolutions will be recorded verbatim

- **Resolution** - Where a motion which has been voted on and passed, which gives details of the proposer and seconder of the motion, with a verbatim recording of the resolution

- **Action** - Where only the action and the name of the person or persons responsible for carrying out the action are recorded

Accuracy of text prepared from recorded audio instructions

Any piece of text produced from audio recordings should be a quality piece of work. It should be executed with the correct spelling, the use of grammatical rules and the correct application of punctuation to produce a product that both gives a good impression of the organisation and, more importantly, conveys the intended message of the text.

Spelling

A computer will automatically check the spelling of words and highlight them in the document being worked on. However, spell check cannot:

- Differentiate between American and English spelling of words, so make sure that the spell check default is aligned to the correct country

- Differentiate between words that are spelled correctly but used incorrectly, e.g. using 'through' when it should be 'threw'. Some of the most commonly confused words are:

  - We are pleased to <u>accept</u> your donation
    Everyone made a donation <u>except</u> Mr Jones

  - Never listen to <u>advice</u> from your parents
    I would <u>advise</u> you always to listen to your parents

  - The increase in interest rates will <u>affect</u> everyone
    The <u>effect</u> of the increase was felt by everyone

  - She thought she was <u>eligible</u> for a grant
    The letter she received was <u>illegible</u>

  - You must <u>ensure</u> that your car is <u>insured</u>

  - Lowestoft is <u>farther</u> east than Birmingham
    I need <u>further</u> information on the location of Hull

  - There are <u>fewer</u> days in February than in June
    It is <u>less</u> likely to rain today than it was yesterday

  - My <u>personal</u> opinion is that it will rain today
    The HR Department deals with <u>personnel</u>

  - I visited the local doctors' <u>practice</u> this morning
    I need to <u>practise</u> my spelling more often

  - The <u>principal</u> cause of heart disease is overeating
    The minister resigned over a matter of <u>principle</u>

  - The traffic on the M6 was <u>stationary</u> for two hours
    We need to order some more <u>stationery</u> this week

  - This week's sales were better <u>than</u> last week's
    We will look at this week's plan, <u>then</u> next week's

  - The girls picked up <u>their</u> handbags
    The boys will be over <u>there</u> tomorrow
    They're planning to visit next week

• ACTIVITY 3

Circle the correct spelling in the following list of words:

1. Participative	participertive	particsipative
2. Calasthenets	calisthenics	calisthenicks
3. Originate	oridginate	originatte
4. Pergured	perfoured	perjured
5. Perigrinate	peregrinate	peragrinate
6. Sadled	sadaled	saddled
7. Zephyr	zefr	zephir
8. Asignation	assignation	assegnation
9. Vertigenous	vertiganous	vertiginous
10. Bucolic	bucolick	buccolic

Grammar

Grammar can loosely be defined at the 'rules of language'. However, in English, the 'rules' are not consistent, which makes it complicated to learn and apply. Grammar is important to make sure that the intended meaning of a sentence is communicated to the recipients of the communication. For example, 'Use both lanes when turning right' actually requires drivers to straddle the two lanes, which is a highly dangerous manoeuvre to carry out. The correct sentence construction should be: 'Use either lane when turning right'.

There are five parts of speech which are commonly used:

- **Nouns -** These are the names of a person, place or thing, e.g. 'book', 'television', 'Sunday', 'Norfolk'

- **Pronouns -** These are used instead of a noun, e.g. instead of saying 'John' in a paragraph that refers only to him, use 'he' or 'him'

- **Verbs -** These are words that express doing things, e.g. 'ran', 'run' or 'running'

- **Adverbs -** These words give information about how a verb was executed, e.g. 'he ran <u>quickly</u>' or 'he ran <u>fast</u>'. Note that while most adverbs will be formed by the addition of '-ly' to the end of a verb, it is not always the case, as can be seen by the second example in this paragraph

- **Adjectives -** These describe nouns, e.g. 'an <u>interesting</u> book', '<u>reality</u> television'

• ACTIVITY 4

What is a preposition?

Sentences are formed by linking parts of speech together. Simple sentences contain a subject and a verb, e.g. 'I am', where 'I' is the subject and 'am' is the verb. More complicated sentences will have a subject, verb and object, e.g. 'I am going to London', where the object of the sentence is London. Sentences must start with a capital letter and end with some form of punctuation, e.g. a full stop, question mark. Capital letters are also used to indicate **proper names**, e.g. America, Anthony; **titles**, e.g. Mr, Mrs, Lord; **days of the week or months of the year** and **acronyms** (RAF, CIA, FBI, MI5, RAC).

A paragraph is formed by linking two or more sentences together. If the subject of a paragraph changes, it is advisable to start a new paragraph.

• ACTIVITY 5

Proofread and correct the following and produce a corrected version. Switch off the spell check function on the computer.

Our ref: DT/GY/1256

Mr S Williamson
Apart 21
The shore
Manchster
M6 7yu

Dear serena williamon

Account number 45678956 -Flat 24 te maltings, Mancester

Thankyoy for you're resent enqiry regarding you mortgage, and theintrst rates available to you. I am encloseing a quotetion showing what yur new paymemts would be at a new rat of interst. Yhjis has been calculated on and Interest only Basis.

At the moment you're monthly payments is ^189.23 vased ib a rate if 6.75%. Should you decide to exce0pt our offer (details) attached, your new repayments would be approx $206.933. The admin fee of £120.00 gas veeb added ti your balasnce for quotation's pirposes o9nly.

This iffer is valid for 14 days from the date of the enclosed quotation. you should of receved further details yesterday.

Transferring yourmortgage onto the new rate couldnt be easer, Simply return the Deed of Variation encl9osed, signed by all partied to the mortgage.

We will charge you the aministration fe of £120.00, This sim can be added to the lan or may be paid by check if you wish.

If you have any quest6ions, plesse contact me on 02356 56998 Monday to Friday between 9.00pm and 5.00pm.

Yours faithfyully

W Gaines
Consultant Mortgage Provider

Punctuation

As with grammar, the correct use of punctuation will make it easier for people to understand the content of a piece of communication. For example, if someone said 'Fred, the dog is ill', they would be telling someone called Fred that the dog is unwell. If they said 'Fred the dog is ill', they would be telling someone that the dog called Fred is unwell. Three of the most common punctuation marks in use are:

- **Full stops** - These are used to mark the end of a sentence or after abbreviations

- **Commas** - These are used to separate words in a list or phrases in a sentence, or to make sentences easier to read

- **Apostrophes** - There are two uses of the apostrophe: to replace a missing letter, e.g. 'I'm, he's, don't' or to indicate something belongs to someone, the possessive case, e.g. 'Jim's book, Pauline's shoes, women's clothing, babies' bottles'

Whatever text is produced, it is important that it is checked for accuracy before being distributed.

Formatting the text

At any stage during the production of text, formatting will be necessary. This can be as simple as changing the type of font used in the text to using text effects, e.g. 'strikethrough'.

It is possible to format:

- **Characters** - By selecting 'font' it allows the following functions to be carried out: 'style', 'colour' and 'size' of letters, **embolden**, *italicise*, underline, change the s p a c i n g

- **Paragraphs** - Align text using the 'centre' or 'justify' options, or by selecting 'bullets and numbering' add bullet points or numbers. Other amendments can be made by selecting 'borders and shading', or by altering the line spacing, tabs and indent

- **Pages** - Changes can be made to the 'size', 'orientation' and 'margins' of pages. 'Page numbers' can be inserted as well as 'headers and footers' or the 'date and time'. 'Insert page breaks' can be made to indicate where a new page should begin, or 'columns' can divide the page vertically

- **Sections** - It is not necessary for the whole text to be in the same format. Different sections of text can use different formats

If part of the text is formatted in a certain way and this style is to be used later in the text, select 'styles and formatting' and the software will show what has been used previously in the document. This will help to give consistency to the design of the text.

Checking and editing text

As identified previously, text from notes can be accomplished in two ways. If the transcription of notes is being undertaken on behalf of someone else who has made the notes, check with them to clarify any meanings or phrases which are not clear. Make sure the correct interpretation of words and phrases is agreed as early on in the process as possible, so to minimise the amount of changes that have to be made to a document. To help with the process of transcribing the notes, produce a 'draft' copy, so that the originator can check what has been produced matches with what was intended. Make sure that the draft is free from errors.

Most word processing packages contain spell checking and grammar checking facilities. Use these first to correct the obvious errors, but do not rely on them entirely. Check to make sure that the spell check default is not using American spelling and grammar, as the document will accept 'color' and reject 'colour' etc. When the automatic checking is complete, read the document carefully to look for missed errors, and also for correct use of paragraphs, headings and subheadings, style and formatting. Be particularly careful to proofread numbers, dates, times and amounts. Check for errors between similar words, such as 'affect' and 'effect' or 'less' and 'fewer'.

Look for errors of context and content. The draft text will be returned by the originator indicating where any changes need to be made to the document. Changes may come about as a result of:

- **Input errors**

- **Errors in the source material**

- **Amendments to the content**

Changes may have been agreed not necessarily because of poor transcription skills but because the originator of the notes wants to make changes to the document to improve the tone and meaning.

A computer provides a lot of functions that allow text to be easily edited:

- **Delete** - Ctrl+delete - This allows a single letter, group of letters or whole parts of a document to be deleted

- **Paste** - Ctrl+v - This is used in combination with either the 'cut' or 'copy', see below, instruction. Paste will add the last data selected to the document 'copied' or stored on the 'clipboard', which will provide other recently 'copied' information

- **Cut** - Ctrl+x - This is used to highlight a piece of text and remove it from the document. It can then be 'pasted', see above, to another part of the document or a new document

- **Copy** - Ctrl+c - This is used to highlight a piece of text and copied. It can then be 'pasted', see above, to another part of the document or a new document

- **Find and replace** - Ctrl+f
  This function is used to change all the examples of a particular word to another word. For example, replace the word 'company' with the word 'organisation', there is no need to retype every example, use 'find' and / or 'replace' to make all the changes

- **Inserting special characters and symbols** - This function enables the use of other alphabets, e.g. Arabic شةككق and other signs / symbols, e.g. o, û, ©, %

- **Mail merge** - This function is useful if the same letter is going to several recipients, as it can change the name and address of each recipient

- **Track changes** - This function allows the originator of a document to share it with other colleagues, inviting them to make changes which can be tracked by name and highlighted

At any stage during the transcription of text from notes the format of the text can be changed. There are various options available in the format menu, e.g. font, which allows the font to be changed to different styles, sizes, colour etc. It is possible to format characters, pages or whole sections of a document. A part of the text can be formatted and used again later in the document by selecting 'styles and formatting', and the software will show what formatting has been used previously in the text.

If text is being produced which will have more than one page, it is advisable to use a 'header and footer', with required information and / or 'page numbers'. Using both functions will allow the title to be put onto each page with a page number. It is also possible to 'number paragraphs' and include an 'index' or 'table of contents' to help the reader find their way around the text.

• ACTIVITY 6

Correct the following piece of text:

minuts of sals and marketing team held on 92th August 2010, Imperil Hotl, Russel sq, london Wc1, 99.30

Present
Jeremy smith (chair
Benita Aporia
john jones
Charlie Charls
Keth Campbell
Jennifer Hislop
Larry Lamb

Apologes were recieved from:
Lewis Michaelson
Josef Josefs

minuts of the last meting were aproved

None maters arising.

It was suggested that a father meeting be held in sept to agree the final steppes of th sales plain for the new year. All 7 presnt agred.

Chrismas is fast aproaching and it will be very bisy. As peter will be leave it will effect way the team will work.

New stationary to be ordered for the department

Next meeting on Tues, 24 Sept 2010.

Having made all the requested alterations, produce a final draft and pass that to the originator. Hopefully there will be no further amendments at this stage. Once this has been signed off it can be printed to the quality standard requested, not forgetting that a copy of the text should be stored in the appropriate storage system.

Storing text

Every piece of text will probably need to be stored in some way. This can be done using a manual paper-based system, an electronic-based system or both. A computer will have its own in-built sorting and storing mechanisms. Text should be stored accurately in the approved locations so anyone can find it quickly and easily. Folders should be used that can be held within the main directory of the computer system. Folders should be used to group files together to speed up their retrieval. Paper copies will be stored manually using one of the following methods:

- **Alphabetical -** Information is stored in order from A-Z. Files starting with the same letter are filed in order of the second letter: Aa, Ab, Ac etc. People's names are filed by their surnames, and if more than one has the same surname, by their first names. Names starting with 'The' are filed by ignoring the 'The'. Names beginning with 'Mac' or 'Mc' come before 'Ma', 'Mb' etc.

- **Numerical -** Information is coded using a numbering system, e.g. purchase orders, invoices

- **Alphanumerical -** Information is stored using a combination of letters and numbers, e.g. National Insurance numbers. Usually large databases hold this type of coded information, as they hold more information than numerical systems and are more flexible than alphabetical systems. The order of filing depends on the sequence of the file name. If file names start with letters followed by numbers, they are filed in alphabetical order first and numerical order within each letter

- **Chronological -** This method is often used within one of the other methods. For example, customers' records are filed alphabetically, but the information within the file is stored chronologically, usually with the latest at the front. This provides a history of all activities undertaken for a particular file of information. It can also be based on dates of birth or start dates

- **Geographical -** This is a method of sorting by areas, e.g. North West England, East Anglia or counties, towns, cities

- **By subject or category -** Some organisations need to sort their filing under topics rather than names. For example, a shoe manufacturer may keep files under product names such as Ladies, Gentlemen and Children

• ACTIVITY 7

What is the difference between storing text documents by subject or category and numerically?

The original source material from which the text has been produced will also need to be filed and stored if it needs to be referred to at a later date. An organisation may have its own system of referencing documents which should be followed. If using a system to reference documents, make sure that the original source material is referenced with the same reference number as the completed text. The source material should be stored in a logical manner:

- Handwritten notes can be attached to the file copy of the completed document

- Shorthand notebooks should be stored chronologically, with the start and end date written on the front

- Audio tapes should be stored chronologically and labelled with the date

If the document being created is 'private and confidential', make sure it is identified as such and follows the organisation's policy on 'private and confidential' documents, e.g. the contents of the document should not be discussed publicly so unauthorised people can hear. Confidential information is information that has great value, is considered to be of a private nature and is only permitted to be seen by designated people within an organisation. 'Confidential information' can embrace commercial secrets as well as general information, e.g. medical records. An organisation can be damaged if its privacy of information is not upheld and respected, which could result in the organisation being devalued.

There is no single Act of Parliament defining 'confidential information' or governing how it is protected, or setting out rights and obligations in respect of it. However, the law on 'confidential information' is currently undergoing radical change as a result of developing European and UK legislation and decisions of the courts. Place 'confidentiality' warnings on standard communications, e.g. faxes or emails, to make sure if an individual receives the information by accident they are notified of its 'confidential' nature.

'Private and confidential' documents also includes commercially sensitive information, which needs to be protected from being read by an organisation's competitors. If the content of a document covers personal information it must conform to the requirements of the **Data Protection Act 1998.**

Testing your knowledge

1. Why are there different types of text documents that can be produced?

2. What is meant by 'fully blocked'?

3. Why is it necessary to meet deadlines for the production of text documents?

4. What type of document will always have a signature?

5. What forms can minutes take?

6. What is the sequence of content that can be presented in a report?

7. What do you understand by an 'acknowledgement'?

8. What is meant by proofreading?

9. What types of amendments might be made to a draft?

10. Why is the source material filed as well as the completed document?

11. What is the difference between a draft document and a final document?

12. What does 'confidential' mean in terms of text storage?

Skills

Before starting work on the transcription of any piece of text, make sure you are clear about:

- The purpose of the text

- The format of the text

- The deadlines within which the text needs to be completed

• ACTIVITY 8

Attend a meeting - this could be a team meeting at work, a social club meeting, a meeting at college - and record the conversation / discussion. Transcribe the recordings into text. Produce a short typed report from the recordings. Time yourself inputting the text and count the number of words. Proofread the document and calculate the net words per minute.

Each of these aspects of preparing to transcribe text will inform the planning of the work you will need to do for either yourself or if you are producing the text from original source material. Organise your work around all the tasks that you have to complete so you finish the transcription of the text at the agreed time. Once you are clear about what has to be done, gather together all the resources you will require to complete the task.

• ACTIVITY 9

Write a report to your supervisor suggesting ways in which your current filing systems can be improved. Consider the best way to order the contents of the report.

When transcribing text from audio recordings make sure you are fully up to date with the functions of your software so you can edit the text effectively and efficiently. Chat to someone who is very confident in this area, or your supervisor / manager, to check that you are fully conversant with functionality of the technology you are using. This will not only save you time but make your text look more professional. Make sure that you are clear about the style, layout and format that you wish, or the original author wishes, the text to take. Seek clarification of how to use a 'template' if your organisation uses them. Clarify all these components of your text.

• ACTIVITY 10

Select a number of texts that you have produced which you feel demonstrate your competence in using correct layout, spelling, punctuation and grammar. Share these with your supervisor / manager to get their feedback on the quality of your work.

Produce a draft document and check through this with the original author to make sure it meets all the requirements that they are aiming to achieve. Check through the document to make sure that it accurately presents information, that is, there are no spelling mistakes. Make sure your computer is set to the correct defaults and that grammar and punctuation have been used correctly.

Once you have checked the text, check the aims of the text with the original speaker, to make sure that they have been achieved. When working on the production of the text, if you are not sure, at any stage of its development, pause and reflect on what the text is aiming to achieve. Check with the original speakers. If anything changes with the development of the text check with the original speaker that they are happy with the change of direction that the text may have to take. Complete the final draft of the text and present this to the speaker of the original source material.

Make sure the text has been referenced in line with your organisation's procedures. Then file it using whatever storage system your organisation uses.

Testing your skills

1. How do you make sure that spelling, punctuation and grammar has been used correctly?

2. How is the content of a business letter laid out?

3. How and when would you use the format menu?

4. If you were asked to emphasise a sentence in a report how would you do it?

5. How do you proofread your own work?

6. When would you use printers' correction symbols?

7. What functions would you use to edit text, and why?

8. Why is it important to raise any queries with the originator of the original source material before producing the final draft text document?

9. How does your organisation reference text documents?

10. What system (s) of storing text documents does your organisation use?

Ready for assessment?
To achieve this Level 3 unit of a Business & Administration qualification, learners will need to demonstrate that they are able to perform the following activities:

1. Agreed the purpose, format and deadlines for texts

2. Inputted text from audio recordings at a minimum speed of 60 wpm

3. Formatted texts to the agreed format, making efficient use of available technology

4. Clarified text requirements, when necessary

5. Read and checked texts for accuracy

6. Edited and corrected texts, as required

7. Stored texts and original recordings safely and securely following organisational procedures

8. Presented texts in the required format and within the agreed deadlines

You will need to produce evidence from a variety of sources to support the performance requirements of this unit.

If you carry out the 'ACTIVITIES' and respond to the 'NEED TO KNOW' questions, these will provide some of the evidence required.

Links to other units

While gathering evidence for this unit, evidence **may** also be used from evidence generated from other units within the Business & Administration suite of units. Below is a **sample** of applicable units; however, most units within the Business & Administration suite of units will also be applicable.

QCF NVQ
Communications
Communicate in a business environment (Level 2)
Make and receive telephone calls
Use electronic message systems
Core business & administration
Manage own performance in a business environment (Level 2)
Improve own performance in a business environment (Level 2)
Work in a business environment (Level 2)
Work with other people in a business environment (Level 2)
Document production
Produce documents in a business environment
Prepare text from notes using touch typing (40 wpm)
Prepare text from shorthand (60 wpm)
Prepare text from recorded audio instruction (40 wpm)
Manage information and data
Store and retrieve information

SVQ

Communications

Prepare to communicate in a business environment

Make and receive telephone calls

Use electronic message systems

Core business & administration

Agree how to manage and improve own performance in a business environment

Undertake work in a business environment

Work with other people in a business environment

Document production

Produce documents in a business environment

Prepare text from notes using touch typing (40 wpm)

Prepare text from shorthand (60 wpm)

Prepare text from recorded audio instruction (40 wpm)

Manage information and data

Store and retrieve information

22

Plan and organise an event

PLAN AND ORGANISE AN EVENT

'**Plan and organise an event**' is an <u>optional unit</u> which may be chosen as one of a combination of units to achieve either a Qualifications and Credit Framework (QCF), National Vocational Qualification (NVQ) or Scottish Vocational Qualification (SVQ).

The aims of this unit are to:

*   Understand the role of an event organiser in planning an event

*   Understand the arrangements to be made when planning and organising an event

*   Understand the different types of venues and resources needed for different types of events

*   Be able to plan and organise an event

To achieve the above aims of this unit, learners will be expected to provide evidence through the performance of work-based activities.

Knowledge

What is an event?

An event can be defined as a **very large meeting** which can be organised for business, a social occasion or a combination of both. An event will be organised to bring together a group of people for a common purpose, usually to present new or re-formed information, at a specific time and location. Planning an event is time consuming and can be a stressful affair; it can also be costly to undertake. Events can be planned to take place for small or large groups of people, numbering in their thousands. Events can be planned and organised by teams within an organisation or by 'event management' organisations who have specialised skills and knowledge to undertake this function. The event will be planned and organised to engage with its audience, its stakeholders, so they walk away buying in to what has been presented to them. As with meetings, events will focus on some form of **change**.

More specifically, events can be organised to:

- Raise awareness about particular issues or focus on someone else's issues, e.g. at a big international conference, encouraging people to think differently about issues

- Build alliances to provide opportunities for people to participate

- Create strong visual images of products / ideas

- Widen an organisation's / product's appeal by communicating directly to people's emotions and intellect

- Empower people, e.g. build a feeling that great things can be achieved by acting together with particular focus

- Have fun!

The benefits to an organisation that can be achieved by holding an event are:

- Communicating directly with targeted stakeholders

- Building on an organisation's reputation and profile

- Reinforcing an organisation's values

- Delivering against the aims of promoting an organisation's / product's aims

• ACTIVITY 1

Events may be either:

- **Major -** A more complex combination of elements that will require detailed organisation. This will take many months to plan. This may also involve a number of different organisations

- **Minor -** Less complex than a major event and will have less elements to organise. This will take less time to plan. This will probably be limited to being offered by one organisation

Events will vary in:

- **Size -** This may refer to the **physical size** of the venue being used or to the number of **delegates** that will be invited to the event

- **Duration -** This may last one day or for more than a week, e.g. the Ideal Home Exhibition, which runs for nearly two weeks

- **Purpose** - This may vary from marketing a product or the organisation, building business relationships to raising money or a celebration

  - **Planning** - Will vary depending on the size of the event to be organised, which could take from as much as 18 months to plan and organise to as little as one month

  - **Cost** - Budgets may vary in size from less than £1,000 to £50,000

The organisation of an event will vary from event to event, depending on the **purpose** of holding the event:

- **Conferences** - Events arranged to last at least one day which will be based around a specific theme, e.g. an annual conference based on new policies that an organisation is about to launch

- **Exhibitions** - Events arranged to display an organisation's products or services

- **Product launches** - Events arranged to launch a new product or service

- **Prize / award presentations** - Events arranged to award employees or customers with honours for their efforts on behalf of the organisation

- **Seminars** - Similar to conferences but smaller and of a shorter duration

- **Briefing sessions** - Events arranged to provide information to delegates on a topic

- **Party** - Events arranged to celebrate specific themes, e.g. a staff Christmas party

- **Development day** - Events arranged as part of a 'learning and development' plan to gather employees together to share and discuss changes within the organisation

Whatever the size or purpose of the event it will require some degree of **planning**.

• ACTIVITY 2

How does the purpose of an event effect the planning of an event?

Planning an event

Most events will have an **event planner** or event organiser. They will be dedicated to organising a successful event. They will aim to organise all relevant resources to be in place and available for the delegates who will be invited to the event. The event planner may have a team to support the implementation of the event plan. However, the level of support that the event planner will need will vary depending on the complexity of the event being planned. The event support team will contribute to the implementation of the plan. They may be asked to take responsibility for specific elements of the event plan, e.g. search for the venue. They may be given specific tasks to complete which cover different elements of the event plan. Their level of responsibility will vary from task to task, where they may take a lead role or a subordinate role. Whatever their role, the support team will be dedicated to implementing an event plan that will lead to a successful event. The event planner will organise meetings to feedback on the completion of tasks to make sure the plan is being delivered to the agreed timetable. The event plan will be a document with some or all of the following features:

- **Management arrangement for the event** - Details of everything, e.g. security arrangements, access arrangements, parking

- **Site plan** - Details of the venue, e.g. entrance and exits, toilets, information booths

- **Risk assessment plan** - The **objective** of a risk assessment plan is to remove risks entirely or to reduce risk to an acceptable level.

The **purpose** of risk assessment is to identify **hazards** - anything which has the potential to cause harm to people. As part of risk assessment, identify **risks** - the likelihood of the harm from a hazard being realised and the extent of it - that may arise from identified hazards. A decision will then need to find suitable strategies / measures to eliminate or control the risks. All decisions that relate to the findings of the risk assessment must be recorded if five or more people are employed. It will also be necessary to visit the event venues to identify any hazards. A risk assessment is completed for an event because:

- There is a responsibility to the public to make sure events are run safely and in an appropriate manner

- It makes sure safety implications of events have considered all risks and identified all possible steps to reduce them

- It will act on its findings to reduce the chance of problems occurring

- For legal reasons, it will show that every precaution has been taken to predict and remove identified risks if a claim or prosecution relating to health and safety was brought against the event organisers

When completing a risk assessment make sure:

- Only one person is responsible for health and safety

- All event employees are briefed on the health and safety plan and risk assessment

- A logical process is followed. Ask 'What if ...?', thinking through the whole event to cover all elements of its organisation. Do not complicate it

• ACTIVITY 3

What is a risk assessment plan?

A **simple** risk assessment has five steps:

- 1 - Identify hazards associated with activities contributing to the event, where the activities are carried out and how the activities are to be undertaken. Consider what could go wrong and write them down without worrying how it sounds. Consider how severe the hazard would be if it happened - low, medium or high. Consider the likelihood of the hazard happening, i.e. how likely will the hazard happen if no action is taken to reduce the risk beyond the controls which are already in place

- 2 - Identify who may be harmed, and how

- 3 - Identify existing precautions, e.g. venue design, operational procedures

- **4** - Evaluate risks
- **5** - Decide what further actions may also be required, e.g. improvement in venue design

Control measures will be required, i.e. the actions that need to be taken to remove the risk or reduce it to an acceptable level. Look for a simple or common-sense solution to the problem. It needs to be identified and must be carried out every time that risk is present, i.e. identify the realistic actions that can be taken to reduce the risk. As there may be many solutions to contain a risk, select the most appropriate solution, bearing in mind the risk rating and the event specifics, including manpower and financial considerations.

When completing a risk assessment plan, the event planner will need to consider:
- The authority / budget / capabilities required to reduce the risk

- If taking an action, will it eliminate or reduce the risk to an acceptable level? If 'no', remove the risk area from the event or change it to provide a solution that eliminates or reduces it

• ACTIVITY 4

What five steps should be taken to complete a simple risk assessment?

Contingency arrangements
Contingency planning should follow from the risk assessment plan that is completed for events. It should identify types of emergencies that may occur at a particular event and a plan of how to deal with them, e.g. evacuation plan, communication arrangements, medical responses. The following should be considered when completing a contingency plan:

- **Event location** in relation to services and infrastructure needed in an emergency, e.g. electricity, telephones, water, shelter, proximity to hospitals and availability of emergency services. It is best to have them available or nearby

- **Access routes** for emergency vehicles ideally separate from access routes for the public

- **A designated emergency control point** where members of the event management team and emergency services can meet in the event of an incident

- **A designated single point of contact to liaise with any emergency services**

- **Brief stewarding, security, contractors / stallholders** and medical staff on procedures to be taken in the event of a significant incident

- **An evacuation plan**, identifying where public and employees should assemble and evacuate to and agree evacuation routes, signage and public address systems

- **Security precautions** to cover VIPs, subversive action from individuals or groups

- **Specific individual and organisational roles and responsibilities in an incident**

- **Manage and utilise resources** if there is an incident

- **Plan for dealing with the media**

- **Any other relevant documents -** Any other relevant documentation, e.g. copies of qualification certificates of people working at the venue

• ACTIVITY 5

What is the difference between a risk assessment plan and a contingency plan?

An event planner will:
- **Agree the event brief -** Agree with the client what they are aiming to achieve at their event, how they are aiming to achieve it, when it will occur etc. The event planner will work with their client, who may be internal or external to the organisation, and will advise the kind of event they require; when  and where it is to take place; any partners that can be allied with; the target population of people to attend and influence; approximately how many people will attend; and how to get the target audience. This information will form the basis of an event brief. The event planner will need to get this brief agreed in writing with as much detail as possible, identifying who is going to carry out the tasks / activities

- **Agree an agenda for the event** - This should set out each agenda item that will be presented throughout the event, how it will be presented, how much time it will take to present the item, type of layout required etc

- **Negotiate a budget** - There may be a fixed sum or specific criteria that needs to be met. The event planner will agree the budget with the client and identify any potential overspends. The budget may be agreed when the client has identified either:

- A maximum sum of money available to pay for the whole event. The event planner will provide the best event within that budget

- Specific requirements for the location, standard of accommodation, levels of equipment, duration and season for the event etc. The event planner will agree the best price to meet the client's requirements

- **Identify the type of event required** - An event can be outdoor, indoor, site based, a meeting or a demonstration. The event may be time critical or bound by weather conditions

- **Locate suitable venues** - Consider size, location, resources and facilities for delegates with special requirements, price etc. The decision on the venue will depend on factors such as:

  - The purpose of the event

  - The budget of the event

  - The number of delegates to be invited

  - The size of the event space, as this will have an effect on sightlines, which will influence audience engagement

  - Perspective of the event space - is there room for a photographer / cameraman to shoot effectively, e.g. a photograph that includes presenters, products, name of the target

  - The ability to provide interactive versus static imaging

  - The standard of venue required to suit the delegates

  - The geographic location of the delegates

  - Using the organisation's in-house facilities or contracting externally from the organisation

  - The potential disruption to the business

  - Safety issues, e.g. traffic, public access, police permission to use public thoroughfares, if applicable

- Content and tone of the event, e.g. interacting with the audience using costumes

Selecting a venue space in-house or near to the host organisation has the advantage of saving travelling time and costs for people based on the premises. If the venue is external to the organisation obtain quotes from suitable suppliers. Other factors that need to be considered when selecting a venue include:

- Availability of break-out rooms

- Size of main meeting space

- Number and type of meeting rooms and facilities - OHP, data projector, flip chart, whiteboard

- Accommodation - on site or off site

- Secure office

- Registration area

- Crèche / child care

- Communications - telephone, fax, photocopy, computers, Internet access

- Access to phones for delegates

- Disabled access

- Booking arrangements and contract commitments

- Audio-visual equipment, PA system, power point access, screens

- Social facilities - bars, quiet areas, separate party area

- Licensing

- ISDN line / access to computers

- Parking

• ACTIVITY 6

What does the event planner need to consider when planning and organising an event?

There are many organisations that conduct venue searches free of charge. This service could be used to select suitable venues that match the requirements of an event. Venues that have been used in the past could also be used or search for a new venue by carrying out a search on the Internet.

When searching for the right venue for an event make sure the standard of hospitality and catering is appropriate. Make sure the menu chosen meets the expectations of the delegates. Make sure it is clear exactly what is being provided. Have alternative menus agreed for vegetarians, halal, gluten free etc. Catering arrangements may be tied to the venue or independent from the venue. Consideration needs to be given to meal times, areas for refreshment breaks and the size of the dining areas to allow networking.

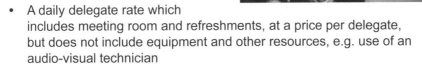

Many venues will offer a choice of different delegate tariffs:

- A daily delegate rate which includes meeting room and refreshments, at a price per delegate, but does not include equipment and other resources, e.g. use of an audio-visual technician

- A daily delegate rate which includes meeting room, equipment, lunch and refreshments, at a price per delegate

- A 24-hour delegate rate which includes meeting room, equipment, lunch and refreshments, dinner, accommodation and breakfast, at a price per delegate

- An executive rate which includes all of the above plus superior accommodation and meals, at a price per delegate

• ACTIVITY 7

What factors need to be considered when selecting a venue for events?

Once all the information about costs, size etc., have been collected from potential venues, the event planner will make a shortlist. The event planner should visit as many shortlisted venues as possible to make sure descriptions are accurate. If the event planner knows of someone who has used the venue in the past, they could ask for their feedback on venue standards.

There will also be a choice of room layout to be decided. This will be determined by the various purposes of the agreed agenda items. The event may require different types of set up throughout its duration.

• ACTIVITY 8

Why would the following room layouts be used?

1. Boardroom
2. Classroom
3. Cabaret
4. Banquet

Arrange the hire of the venue
Discuss with the venue the plans for the event, e.g. provisional numbers of delegates, which will be confirmed as agreed. The venue coordinator will require a purchase order from the event planner confirming an agreement to their booking terms and conditions. This will form the basis of a contract between the organisation or the event planner, and the venue, which will be subject to contract law. This will cover charges for cancellations or changes to arrangements subsequent to confirmation. There will usually be a sliding scale of charges depending on changes to the event plan. The event planner will need to check through the contract to make sure it is correct and as agreed.

Organise the necessary resources
Discuss with the venue the resources they can provide and those which will have to be outsourced. Design a brand motif if appropriate, organise and confirm speakers / demonstrators / layout of the venue etc. Speakers will need to be agreed with the client. Some speakers may be booked up in advance, so it is best to agree these speakers as soon as possible, e.g. motivational speakers or Master of Ceremonies for the event. The event planner will organise with each speaker when the final copy of their presentation needs to be agreed and signed off. This will need to be done before material for the delegate pack is printed. The presentations will need to make sure they have the right tone and do not present anything controversial or oppose anything being presented in other parts of the event.

Organise with the client what resources they will need on the day of the event. This may include:

- Laptop and multi-media projector

- Overhead projector and screen

- Video and monitor

- Microphones for the head tables and for delegates asking questions (make sure the speaker system has been organised so it does not deafen delegates)

- Flip chart and easel

- Free-standing lectern

- Public address system

- Post-it notes

- Pencils / pens / paper for delegates

- Bowl of sweets for delegate tables to help keep the throat lubricated

Different types of events will require different resources, depending on the purpose of the event. These may also include accommodation, car-parking facilities etc.

Arrange the attendance of delegates
Agree on the delegates to be invited, design the invitation, send it out and collate the responses from the delegates. Delegates should be invited to the event as soon as possible. This will give enough time for the delegates to record the event in their diary and advise whether or not they are able to attend. They can also advise if they have a replacement. At this stage they will be asked if they have any special requests - these are additional arrangements that will need to be made, e.g. access to the venue or dietary needs. Delegates may also be asked to nominate attendance at seminars that will be held throughout the event.

Prepare a delegate list and delegate sign-in list
Once all the responses have been received from delegates invited to attend the event. Make a note of any special requirements, e.g. dietary, mobility, hearing or vision impairment, travel and accommodation. These will need to be discussed with the venue management team to make sure they can all be catered for. Confirm each delegate's attendance via a letter and, at the same time, also send out relevant information

about the event to each delegate, e.g. a map showing directions and the location of the event, car parks and the nearest railway station.

Organise delegate materials

Once the agenda has been agreed for the event, decisions will need to be made about the materials that will be given out to delegates. These will vary depending on the type of event, however, a normal template of documents would be:

- **Pre-event:**
  - Delegate invitation
  - Draft agenda
  - Directions to the event venue
  - Dietary requirements
  - Any accessibility issues, e.g. if a person is blind
- **Event:** the delegate pack, which will normally include:
  - Event agenda
  - Agenda item documents
  - Seminar materials, if appropriate
  - Expenses claim form, if necessary
  - Feedback form

Help to coordinate the event

Attend the event and offer any services as required.

Help to vacate the venue at the end of the event

Remove all equipment and other resources that do not belong to the venue.

Evaluate the event

Design a feedback form which is given to delegates with their delegate pack. At some stage throughout the day, ask delegates to complete the feedback form. This may need to be repeated a few times throughout the event to get delegates to cooperate. Collate and analyse the feedback from delegates.

Prepare accounts comparing actual cost with the budget

Keep track of how the budget was spent.

Provide delegates with any follow-up material

Either provide electronic or hard-copy versions of handouts, sales brochures, order acknowledgements or appointments etc., to delegates.

Agree promotional material and public relations (PR)

Sign off the advertising campaign for the event and agree which exhibitors want to set up a booth at the event.

The event planner will also need to cover health, safety and security during the event, legislation surrounding any contracts with the venue or suppliers of hired equipment, insurance, if appropriate and coping with problems that arise prior to, during and after the event.

The event planner will delegate the above tasks to members of their support team. The event planner will delegate tasks / activities according to a person's strengths and weaknesses. This may be an opportunity for someone to develop new skills and knowledge. The support team will take responsibility for the tasks they have been asked to complete. This is an integral part of event planning. The event planner will come to rely on their support team and build relationships between all the members of the support team to execute all aspects of the event plan. The support team will keep the event planner informed of progress and any problems through the organisation and planning of the event. As with most things in a business, the strength of an event's success will depend on the quality of its communication.

When planning an event the event planner, once they have agreed and confirmed the venue and suppliers they wish to engage with, will need to agree a **contract of services**. Most contracts of service will have the following points of information that will need to be agreed:

- Names of all parties involved
- Description of the event
- Premises to be used
- Term and use - dates and times
- Fees - charges for facility rent and other associated costs
- Payment schedule

- Description of services

- Property not removed

- Maintenance and facilities

- Destruction of the premises or materials provided by the venue

- Force majeure, providing for cancellation for reasons beyond the parties' control

- Indemnity and liability insurance

- Licensor's access to premises

- Licensor's remedies

- Conditions to licensor's obligations

- Miscellaneous provisions

Contracts, once they have been drawn up and agreed, should be reviewed and approved by the appropriate authority within the organisations, which will usually include the event planner, budget holder and the legal department within the organisation, if there is one. The contract will then need to be signed off by the appropriate authority. This may not always be the event planner but the budget holder, who may be different from the event planner. Insurance requirements will vary depending on the type of event being planned and organised and individual organisational procedures. In some cases, special licences or permits may be required for an event. If music is to be played at an event, this may be copyrighted, which may require a fee. However, there is also non-copyrighted music available.

The following is an example of what an event planner will need to plan for a large event starting 12 months in advance of the event:

6 to 12 months ahead

- Decide event purpose
- Choose a theme
- Visit potential sites
- Research / appoint an event coordinator
- Research / select presenters / chairperson (s)
- Get cost estimates - site rental, food, drinks, sound / lights etc.
- Get recommendations for entertainment - hold auditions
- Get bids for entertainment
- Get bids for decorations
- Get bids for design / printing
- Get bids for other major items
- Finance committee drafts initial budget
- Decide on admission cost
- Create sponsorship amounts / levels
- List items to be underwritten and possible sources
- Research / approach sponsors
- Compile a mailing list
- Check proposed date for potential conflicts, finalise date in writing
- Get written contracts for site, entertainment etc.
- Develop alternative site - if event is outdoors
- Consider pre-party event for publicity or underwriting
- Invite / confirm VIPs
- Select graphic artist - begin invitation design
- Create logo for event with graphic artist
- Set marketing / public relations schedule
- Develop press release and calendar listings
- Select photographer and arrange for photos of VIPs etc.
- Get biographical information on VIPs etc.
- Investigate need for special permits, licences, insurance etc.

3 to 6 months ahead

- Begin monthly committee meetings
- Write / send requests for funding or underwriting to major donors, corporations, sponsors
- Request logos from corporate sponsors for printing
- Review with graphic artist invitations, programmes, posters etc.
- Prepare final copy for invitations etc.
- Prepare final copy for tickets
- Complete mailing lists for invitations
- Order invitations, posters, tickets etc.
- Sign contract with event company
- Make list of locations for posters
- Finalise mailing lists
- Begin soliciting corporations and major donors
- Obtain lists from VIPs
- Obtain radio / TV sponsors, public service announcements, promos
- Set menu with caterer for food and beverages
- Secure permits and insurance
- Get written confirmation of celebrity participation / special needs
- Finalise contract
- Select / order trophies / awards

2 months ahead

- Hold underwriting or preview party to coincide with mailing of invitations
- Invite media
- Assemble / address invitations
- Mail invitations
- Distribute posters
- Finalise transportation / hotel accommodation for staff, VIPs etc.
- Obtain contracts for decorations and rental items
- Confirm TV / radio participation
- Release press announcements about celebrities, VIPs etc.

- Follow up to confirm sponsorships and underwriting
- Obtain logos from corporate sponsors for programme printing
- Review needs for signs at registration, directions etc.
- All major chairpersons to finalise plans
- Hold walk-through of event with chairperson (s) and responsible site staff
- members at the event site
- Review / finalise budget, task sheets and tentative timeline
- Start phone follow-up for table sponsors

1 month ahead
- Phone follow-up of mailing list
- Place newspaper ads, follow up with news media, on-air announcements
- Confirm staff for registration, hosting, other
- Write to VIPs, celebrities, programme participants, confirm participation
- Complete list of contents for VIP welcome packs
- Get enlarged site plan / room diagram, assign seats / tables
- Give estimate of guests expected to caterer / food service
- Meet with all outside vendors and consultants to coordinate event
- Review script / timeline
- Continue phone follow-ups for ticket / table sales
- Continue assigning seats
- Confirm transportation schedules: airlines, trains, buses, cars, limos
- Confirm hotel accommodation
- Prepare transportation and accommodation - arrival time, flight number, airline, person assigned to meet flight etc.
- Confirm special security needed for VIPs, event presenters, delegates
- Prepare welcome packet for VIPs, chairmen and key staff
- Schedule deliveries of special equipment, rentals
- Confirm set-up and tear-down times with event site

- Finalise plans with party decorator
- Give caterer revised numbers
- Meet with chairpersons and key staff to finalise any of the above

1 week before
- Meet with all committees for last-minute details
- Finish phone follow-ups
- Confirm number attending
- Finish seating / table arrangements
- Hold training session with volunteers - finalise assignments
- Secure two or three volunteers to assist with emergencies
- Finalise registration staff
- Distribute seating chart, assignments to hosts / hostesses
- Schedule pickup or delivery of any rented or loaned equipment
- Double-check arrival time and delivery times with vendors
- Reconfirm event site, hotel, transportation
- Deliver final scripts / timelines to all programme participants
- Finalise catering guarantee, refreshments
- Confirm number of volunteers
- Make follow-up calls to news media for advance and event coverage
- Distribute additional fliers
- Final walk-through with all personnel
- Schedule rehearsals
- Schedule volunteer assignments for day of event
- Establish amount of petty cash needed for tips and emergencies
- Write cheques for payments to be made for the day of the event

Day before event
- Lay out all clothes that you will need the day of the event
- Recheck all equipment and supplies to be brought to the event
- Have petty cash and vendor checks prepared

Event day

- Arrive early
- Unpack equipment, supplies and make sure nothing is missing
- Be sure all VIPs are in place and have scripts
- Reconfirm refreshments/meal schedule for volunteers
- Go over all the final details with caterer and set-up staff
- Check with volunteers to make sure all tasks are covered
- Set up registration area
- Check sound / light equipment and staging before rehearsal
- Hold final rehearsal

Testing your knowledge

1. What is the role of an event planner?

2. What factors will impact on the planning of an event?

3. What is the difference between a hazard and a risk?

4. What is residual risk rating?

5. What is a control measure used for?

6. What will affect the choice of event venues?

7. What will affect the choice of a room layout for events?

8. What are all the functions carried out by an event planner?

9. What elements could be itemised in a contract for holding an event?

Skills

As the event planner you will plan and organise the event required by your particular clients within your organisation. The tasks that you will be asked to complete may vary in depth and breadth depending on the organisational procedures you are working within. Your immediate task will be to work with your stakeholder who wants you to organise the event. You should listen to what their demands are, go away and think about this to source resources and cost them and then return to the client to go over your plan to see if it is acceptable. Acceptability will cover quantitative issues, e.g. budget / cost, and qualitative issues, e.g. type and size of venue, location of venue, target audience. Depending on the size of your project you may be able to enlist a team to support your plans. This will need to be agreed with relevant people in your organisation if there is not a specific department that handles event planning.

The event planner will work with their client to make sure they realise the vision and purpose of the event the client wants to provide to their target audience. They will expect your advice and guidance as you will be the expert in this field. You will work with a budget and all your decisions will need to make sure that they do not push the costs over the budget. If costs are not realistic for the vision the client has for realising the event, you will need to discuss this with them to see if there are either ways of cutting expectations or increasing the size of the budget. The plans may need to be amended and the budget changed to accommodate an increase in the budget for particular tasks. The areas of work in the planning of an event that you will focus on will include:

* Locating suitable venues
* Arranging the hire of the venue
* Completing a risk assessment
* Completing contingency planning
* Organising the necessary resources
* Arranging the attendance of delegates
* Organising delegate materials
* Providing delegates with any follow-up material

- Agreeing promotional material and PR

- Reviewing, agreeing and signing off the contract for holding the event required by your organisational procedures

• ACTIVITY 9

You have been asked to source the venue for an event. You have been given the following information:

Budget: £50,000

Length of the event: 1-2 days

Space requirements: main hall for initial presentation and plenary; 10 additional seminar rooms; sufficient space for exhibitors to display their booths

Task to be completed by: one working day from when you have been assigned the task

1. What further pieces of information do you need to complete this task?
2. Explain if there is sufficient time to complete the task. If there is not sufficient time, what do you need to do?
3. How do you plan to complete this task?
4. What will you do?
5. Design a checklist to work with

Perhaps one of the most important issues that needs to be agreed with the client is the timing of the event and all aspects of realising the event. You will need to be very organised to make sure everything stays on track. This will include delegating tasks / activities to your support team, if you have one, and meeting on a timely basis with relevant stakeholders of the event to agree all resources. The event planner should devise a plan checklist which they can refer to at any time to update where they are at with the organisation of an event. The event planner will need to agree with their client:

- When you need to complete all tasks / activities

- The amount of budget you have

- The stakeholders you will be working with

- The support team you will be working with

- What to do in the event of any problems

- Attendance at planning meetings
- The amount of time you will spend on the assigned task (s) for the event project

• ACTIVITY 10

Design a template to conduct a risk assessment ?

It is important to keep communication channels open and to have a clear reporting system so that all stakeholders are appraised at any time of what is happening and what remains to be done. Delegate clearly and eliminate any ambiguity in your plans. Work with other members of your support team to resolve any issues. Always keep your clients up to date with progress of your plans. Seek the client's feedback to inspire confidence in the progress of the project at all times within the life of the project.

• ACTIVITY 11

You have been asked to prepare the materials for a delegate pack. You have been told the following about the event:

Budget: £1,500

Delegate pack layout: bound booklet

Task to be completed by: one week prior to the event

Contributions: there will be slide presentations from five speakers; materials for six seminars that are being offered

1. What further material (s) do you need to complete this task?
2. How do you plan to complete this task?
3. What will you do?
4. Are there any alternative approaches you could offer to complete the task?
5. You have been told by your event planner that the Director, who is giving the opening speech, has changed their presentation slides after the delegate pack has gone to print. What do you do?

Testing your skills

1. What did you do to implement the event plan?

2. How did you agree the budget for the event?

3. How did your tasks / activities meet the agreed objectives of the event plan?

4. How did you manage other people on the event team to complete the objectives of the event plan?

5. How did you achieve the budget objectives in the tasks / activities of the event plan?

6. How did you select the venue?

7. How did you conduct risk assessments of event venues?

8. What contingency plans did you draw up for events?

9. How did you organise the production and delivery of invitations and responses to and from delegates?

10. Which delegate materials did you organise for events, and how did you do this?

11. How did you use the event plan to complete your tasks / activities?

12. How did you complete your risk assessments?

13. What are the legal requirements your organisation expects you to complete when contracting with a vendor?

Ready for assessment?

To achieve this Level 3 unit of a Business & Administration qualification, learners will need to demonstrate that they are able to perform the following activities:

1. Agreed an event brief and budget

2. Agreed a plan for an event which met agreed objectives and addressed any identified risks and contingencies

3. Identified and agreed resources and support needed for organising an event

4. Agreed requirements for venues

5. Identified venue and agreed costings

6. Liaised with the venue to confirm event requirements and / or any special delegate requirements

7. Agreed requirements for resources

8. Coordinated resources and production of event materials

9. Made sure arrangements were in place for the event to meet relevant health, safety and security requirements

10. Made sure legal and organisational requirements for contracts were met

11. Made sure that all those involved were briefed and trained to fulfil their roles

12. Delegated functions to the event team, as required

13. Made arrangements for rehearsals to make sure the event ran smoothly, if required

14. Made sure invitations were sent out to delegates

You will need to produce evidence from a variety of sources to support the performance requirements of this unit.

If you carry out the 'ACTIVITIES' and respond to the 'NEED TO KNOW' questions, these will provide some of the evidence required.

Links to other units
While gathering evidence for this unit, evidence **may** also be used from evidence generated from other units within the Business & Administration suite of units. Below is a **sample** of applicable units; however, most units within the Business & Administration suite of units will also be applicable.

QCF NVQ
Communications
Communicate in a business environment (Level 3)
Core business & administration
Manage own performance in a business environment (Level 3)
Improve own performance in a business environment (Level 3)
Work in a business environment (Level 3)
Solve business problems (Level 3)
Work with other people in a business environment (Level 3)
Contribute to decision-making in a business environment
Contribute to negotiations in a business environment
Document production
Design and produce documents in a business environment
Events and meetings
Coordinate an event
Plan and organise meetings
Organise business travel or accommodation
Evaluate organisation of business travel or accommodation

QCF NVQ

Communications

Communicate in a business environment

Core business & administration

Plan how to manage and improve own performance in a business environment

Review and maintain work in a business environment

Support other people to work in a business environment

Solve business problems

Contribute to decision-making in a business environment

Contribute to negotiations in a business environment

Document production

Design and produce documents in a business environment

Events and meetings

Coordinate an event

Plan and organise meetings

Organise business travel or accommodation

Evaluate organisation of business travel or accommodation

23

Coordinate an event

COORDINATE AN EVENT

'Coordinate an event' is an optional unit which may be chosen as one of a combination of units to achieve a Qualifications and Credit Framework (QCF), National Vocational Qualification (NVQ) or Scottish Vocational Qualification (SVQ).

The aims of this unit are to:

- Understand the role of an event coordinator in managing an event to meet the objectives of the brief

- Understand the activities required when coordinating an event

- Be able to coordinate an event

To achieve the above aims of this unit, learners will be expected to provide evidence through the performance of work-based activities.

Knowledge

Prior to delegate arrivals

The event planner may or may not be the event coordinator. If they are not the same person, the event planner along with the event coordinator, if these two roles are separate, will be at the event to check the event plan is being implemented correctly to meet the agreed objectives of the event. These two people will normally be the first point of contact in the event of any problems happening during the event. Before arriving at the venue, all members of the team supporting the event coordinator will have been given tasks / activities to perform at the venue to make sure the event runs smoothly, according to the event plan, and is a success.

The event coordinator will normally arrive at the venue prior to the arrival of the delegates, along with all the members of the event support team, if there is one in place, to make sure all delegated tasks / activities have been completed according to the event plan and schedule. The event coordinator will make sure:

- All members of the **support team** have arrived and are well versed with the functions they will perform during the event

- Access to all areas in the event space is clear and all potential **hazards and risks** have been eliminated or reported to the venue management

- The **catering** is organised for the agreed times and location. If not, they will inform the Master of Ceremonies (MC) / host / chair etc., who will advise the delegates at the introduction of the event

- All of the **equipment** and **delegate materials** are in place and in working order. They will communicate with the audio-visual technician to see how they can contribute to the smooth flow of presentations throughout the event. They will communicate any changes to the speakers so they have a choice if they want to use any enhanced service

- All **resources** required for the event have been procured and are in place

- **Housekeeping** for the day is organised. This includes informing the MC / host / chair of the following:

  - **Access to toilets**

  - What to do if there is a **fire-alarm** test, including the location of exits and the assembly point

  - Any change to the **event agenda**

  - To remind delegates to check that BlackBerrys and mobile phones should be switched off

- There is **disabled access**

- There is someone responsible for **first aid**

- There is someone on the **venue management team** to answer any queries

- There are no **transport problems** that may delay the opening of the event

The event coordinator will have **pre-planned to meet the chair** and the speakers who will be making presentations at the event. They will need to be briefed about housekeeping and any last-minute changes, e.g. changes to their presentation which may need to be formatted and an announcement made to delegates that it will be different from the material in their delegate pack. They may have a memory stick that will need to be given to the audio-visual technician to update the slide show and to make sure it is compatible with the venue's equipment. If they are to use equipment with which they are not familiar they will need to be given the opportunity to make themselves comfortable with its use.

• ACTIVITY 1

What should the event coordinator check before delegates arrive at the venue?

Some events may require **delegates to stay overnight** prior to or after the event. If this is the case, check with the venue to make sure there will be enough staff to cope with the delegates' arrival and luggage. If check-in is not available until later in the day, storage for delegates' luggage will be necessary. It may be worth considering arranging pre-registration, where the venue is supplied with a list of delegates and completes registration forms for each prior to their arrival. Then the delegate only has to give their name at reception to be given their key. If delegates' accommodation will not be available at the time of arrival it is essential that a luggage storage room is provided for delegates arriving by public transport or taxi.

If there are sponsors of the event who have been promised space to **exhibit their stands** these will need to be placed in accordance with health and safety regulations. This should allow for access within the event space but also enough space for delegates to view the stands. This will form part of the floor plan that will be agreed between the event planner / coordinator and the venue management, as they will also make sure that health and safety is maintained. The exhibits should have been set up prior to the delegates' arrival.

The reception area should have been set up with **delegate badges**. The badges should be split alphabetically to ease any congestion as they are collected by delegates, especially if it is a very large event. Delegate sign-in lists should be arranged in the same order as the delegate badges. Support staff will have been given a certain range of delegate badges to hand to delegates as they arrive, if it is a large event. All members of the event support team will have been told of the running order and who to contact if there are any problems.

The event coordinator will run through their checklist with the venue management team to make sure everything is working according to the agreed plan.

Delegate arrivals

Most events will tell delegates when they can **register for the event**. As the delegates arrive for the event the event coordinator should:

- Be on hand to greet them
- Check whether they have any additional needs
- Show them where to sign in, if necessary
- Tell them where the cloakroom is
- Tell them where refreshments can be found
- Tell them the location of the event
- Tell them where they can store their luggage
- Tell them where the toilet facilities are
- Answer any questions they may have
- Distribute any identity badges
- Hand out delegate packs as the delegates arrive or advise them where they are to be collected, if these are being supplied
- Show the delegates where to find the seating plan, if relevant

• ACTIVITY 2

What should be done if the venue management team are not on hand to assist with the coordination of events?

Before informing the event organiser that the event can officially start, check to see how many delegates are yet to arrive. If there are a large number of delegates yet to arrive, a delay to the opening may be necessary. If not, arrange with the event support team managing the reception of delegates arriving at the event, to escort delegates into the event.

During the event

Once the event is under way, the event coordinator will facilitate the smooth running of the event. All members of the event support team will need to keep one step ahead of everything that is happening. Before the morning coffee break, check refreshments are available; check there are sufficient refreshments etc. Before lunch, check arrangements are in hand. Before each speaker begins their presentation, check everything is ready and working as required by the speaker.

Potential **problems** that may arise will include:

- **Speakers failing to arrive** - If booked speakers are experiencing travel difficulties they should telephone ahead and let the event planner know. Check with them for an estimated time of arrival so their presentation can be rescheduled and run other activities before they arrive

- **Refreshments not being on time or of an acceptable standard** - Liaise with the venue coordinator or caterer to deal with any of these problems. It may be that an individual delegate has not advised the venue of their special dietary requirement or the caterers may have forgotten to supply it. In this case, do the best to provide them with an acceptable alternative

- **Equipment failure** - Despite all checks that may have been made prior to the event starting, it is quite possible that something will fail to work when needed. If the equipment has been supplied by the venue, call the venue coordinator to deal with the problem. If the event planner has supplied the equipment, they may have an alternative piece of equipment which can be used

- **Heating, lighting or air-conditioning problems** - Every delegate will have a different comfort level regarding temperature. Some will always be too hot; some will always be too cold. Respond to individual issues but make sure the majority of delegates are happy. Make sure the equipment is functioning efficiently

Follow up with any delegates that do not arrive at all. If accommodation has been booked in their name, the venue will need to know they will not be using it. If they are able to reuse the accommodation, there may be a reduction in the cancellation charge.

• ACTIVITY 3

What problems can happen that may have an impact on the contract agreed with the venue management?

After the event - the clear up
Coordinate with the support team to search the venue area to see if there is any lost property and arrange for it to be returned to the original

owner, if possible. If not, take it back to the office and put it in lost property. A communication should be sent to all delegates informing them that an item has been found at the event and what they should do if the lost item belongs to them.

All the equipment used at the event will need to be sorted. Either pack up equipment that was provided by the organisation or check with the audio-visual technician or the venue management team to make sure everything is okay. If equipment has been supplied by the venue, hand it back in the same condition in which it was received. If equipment has been hired from elsewhere, check with the event planner to supervise its return or collection. If the organisation convening the event supplied the equipment, pack it up safely to take it back to the organisation.

If the delegates have stayed overnight, the support team will need to be on hand when they check out. Each delegate will be responsible for making sure their keys are returned and any extras paid for. The booking instructions will have clearly outlined which costs are included in the accommodation and which are the delegate's responsibility. If  delegates leave the venue without settling their bill, the venue will hold the organisation responsible. Make a note of these delegates so the organisation's finance department can invoice them for these services. However, it is much easier to deal with this situation before the delegate leaves.

• ACTIVITY 4

What should be done if a delegate informs you that their bag has been stolen?

The event coordinator will organise for any evaluation forms that delegates have left to be collected. These will need to be kept safe so they can be analysed and reported on later. There may be additional feedback forms that are sent after the event. Given that this will happen, it is wise to hold off completing the final analysis of the event for a week or so to capture all feedback. Feedback forms should be analysed objectively. Where individuals were less than satisfied with aspects of the event than other delegates consider whether this is simply a matter of being unable to please all of the people all of the time. Where common issues are raised, formulate an action plan to deal with them. Take on board the matters raised and resolve to improve these in future events. If they relate to the performance of invited speakers, pass on the feedback to the speaker, as they will be interested to learn what delegates thought of their performance. If they relate to aspects of the venue which can be improved, pass on the feedback to the venue management. If they relate to issues which cannot be changed, such as the location of the venue, make a note to take these into account when considering the venue for future events. The results of the feedback analysis can be shared with delegates; however, they will be shared with the event planner to inform how the planning and coordination of future events can be improved. Feedback will cover:

- Planning and coordination of the event

- Planning of the event agenda

- Quality and content of the speakers

- Quality and performance of all employees involved in the event, including the event management team

- Quality of the venue and resources provided by the event coordinator and the event management team

Thank the venue for their service and make sure everything has been cleared up, including any papers and spare delegate packs. If the event coordinator is not satisfied with any element of the service or quality of products being provided by the event management team these should be discussed at the time of the event so an agreement can be reached regarding how these issues can be resolved. This may have an impact on the cost of the event, which will need  to be amended for future invoicing. The event coordinator will work with the event planner to make sure that all aspects of the contract were completed as agreed. They should review all invoices against the contract specification to make sure that all charges are correct before the budget holder signs the invoice off.

If there are any documents which need to be circulated to delegates following the event, arrange for them to be copied and distributed, either electronically or via hard copy. Send copies to delegates who were unable to attend who indicated they would like details forwarded.

Throughout the event there will be endless calls on the time and initiative of the event coordinator and their support team. The event coordinator and their support team should use their full resources to keep on top of everything, adopting a professional and positive approach, to make sure delegate expectations can be met.

Testing your knowledge

1. What activities need to be organised by the event coordinator to manage the arrival of delegates to an event?

2. What would be the differences between coordinating the opening of a major and minor event?

3. What functions does the event coordinator need to do at the end of an event?

4. To whom should the event coordinator report details of 'housekeeping'?

5. What should an event coordinator do if over 50% of delegates are late arriving for the beginning of the event?

6. Why should an event coordinator access the venue for hazards and risks despite a risk assessment plan having been carried out?

7. Why is it important for an event coordinator to have excellent communication skills?

8. Why is feedback of an event carried out?

Skills

The event coordinator should work closely with the event planner to bring to life the vision of the event. The vision of an event will vary depending on the purpose of the event. The event coordinator should work through all the tasks that have been planned to take place and check with the venue management team. As with all plans, they are not static documents and the event coordinator can expect things to not run as smoothly as planned. A major function of the event coordinator is to be a troubleshooter, surveying or being kept in communication with their support team to anticipate any issues or problems they think may occur. Their mind has to be constantly questioning: Is that all right? What would happen if this was not so? Is there a potential hazard? What are the risks? These questions should recur despite the completion and agreement of the risk assessment plan and contingency plan.

As an event is being attended by people it is a highly volatile environment. It is an environment open to the physical and emotional movement of delegates. Who knows what will happen. Additional care needs to be taken at an event if delegates fall into conflicting groups opposing one another's opinions. These groups will need to be managed so that nothing unpleasant flares up. The event coordinator will have been appraised of delegates who should be kept separated from one another and they will continue to manage this situation. An event is like an organism. It is organic and can change and move in many different directions which will need to be managed. In many respects, the event coordinator is like a lighthouse illuminating the event with advice and guidance and being a point of reference for their support team, delegates and any other stakeholders involved in delivering the event. However, unlike a lighthouse the event coordinator should be invisible throughout all the activities they perform.

The event coordinator will be involved in the following functions, though not exclusively, as things will change on the day of the event:

- Arriving before the event starts to check that everything is in place. In the case of large events, they may be involved in the event set up for a day before the launch

- Setting up the main room and break-out rooms for seminars

- Distributing delegate packs and seminar materials
- Setting up the delegate reception area
- Organising the signing in of delegates
- Handing out delegates' badges
- Directing delegates to the main hall / refreshment area
- Making sure the MC / host and all presenters have arrived and are happy with facilities for their presentations
- Building positive relationships with the venue management staff
- Setting up all relevant equipment and resources
- Signing off any additional requirements that may occur throughout the day
- Making sure signage is in place and is correctly phrased
- Making sure the health and safety of all people attending the event has been managed
- Being on hand to assist delegates with any queries they might have
- Being on hand to assist the event support team and the event management team
- Managing the event management team to make sure the venue remains clean and tidy throughout the event
- Checking, checking and checking again to make sure the plan for the event is realised seamlessly

• ACTIVITY 5

You have to organise the delegate reception area. You know the following information:

Number of delegates: 500

1. What further pieces of information do you need to complete this task?
2. How much time do you think you will need to set up the reception area?
3. How do you plan to complete this task?
4. What do you need to complete this task?
5. Design a checklist to work with

As you go about your work in any of these areas, you will always be guided by the event plan. The event coordinator will have worked with the event planner, if they are two separate functions, to agree:

- An outline of the whole event so timings are clear

- When all activities need to be completed, or redone if they are recurring tasks

- The team you will work with

- What to do in the event of any problems

- Any supplementary activity to help other members of the team

By the time the event starts the event coordinator should be very familiar with the event plan. They will know what needs to be done on the day of the event and have worked out where things might go wrong. The most important function of the event coordinator is to be 'communicator extroadinaire'. They will be an accomplished communicator and know that they must never give preferential treatment to one delegate or a select group, but must attend to all delegates equally. You will need to make sure that the event agenda is followed precisely so that timings are adhered to. There is nothing worse than having an event close later than advertised, so make sure the event agenda is adhered to. Delegates who have to leave at the advertised time of closing will feel they are missing out on something, the venue may have plans for other events to follow yours, presenters will not want to be rushed as they have taken care and time to prepare their presentation etc.

You will need to make sure all presenters are ready to make their presentation and they have all the resources they need. Some presenters may be nervous and it will be your job to reassure them and build their confidence. You will need to remind people throughout the event of what they have to do or what is coming up that they need to be prepared for. You will need to remind presenters to remind delegates to complete the event feedback form at some time during the event, but preferably at the end so you can capture as much feedback about the event as possible. The event will stretch your energy resources so make sure you drink lots of water and remember to eat. You must remain positive throughout the event, even in the face of extreme adversity. Everyone will look to you to look after them, even the event management team. In essence, the event coordinator becomes the font of all knowledge for the event.

• ACTIVITY 6

You are in the main hall during the opening presentation when the sound system fails to work. What do you do?

As the event coordinator you will need to make sure that your support team is dressed correctly - this may include costumes for some events. If this is the case, particularly if they are wearing animal skins, you will need to make sure they have adequate rest periods and lots of water. The event coordinator is the public face of the organisation. You will need to make a good impression and strive to go beyond meeting all stakeholders' expectations.

• ACTIVITY 7

What aspects of your verbal communication skills will you need to focus on when you coordinate events?

At the end of the event make sure that the venue has been cleared, as agreed, to meet the requirements of the contract. Make sure all organisation papers have been collected and returned to the organisation. Organise to collect all the feedback forms and keep them secure so they are not lost. All those people who have been involved in making the event a success should be thanked, including the presenters and the MC / chair.

Once you have returned to the organisation you should undertake a review of your effectiveness coordinating the event. This will come through from the formal event feedback forms completed by the delegates, but you may also want to get feedback from your support team and manager. Agree any development points that you need to work on. Share any specific feedback diplomatically with people identified in the feedback forms. Decide with the event planner who is going to analyse the event feedback. Be on hand to advise the budget holder of any changes to invoices as a result of additional costs that might have occurred on the day, e.g. the venue doing additional photocopying.

Testing your skills

1. How did you prepare to coordinate events?

2. How did you prepare the event venue?

3. What resources did you make sure were in place?

4. What did you do before the event started (the first agenda item)?

5. What did you do throughout the event to make sure things ran smoothly?

6. How did you make delegates feel welcome?

7. How did you build confidence in all members who contributed to the event?

8. How did you respond to delegates' requests for assistance?

9. What problems did you deal with and how did you resolve them?

10. What were the most important communication skills that you used throughout the event?

11. How did you manage your support team, if you had one?

12. What follow-up activities did you do after the closing of the event?

13. What lessons have you learned from coordinating events?

Ready for assessment?
To achieve this Level 3 unit of a Business & Administration qualification, learners will need to demonstrate that they are able to perform the following activities:

1. Prepared the venue and made sure all necessary resources were in place

2. Coordinated activities during an event, in line with agree plans

3. Helped delegates to feel welcome

4. Responded to delegates' needs throughout an event

5. Resolved problems, as required

6. Oversaw the work of key staff during the event

7. Monitored compliance with relevant health, safety and security requirements

8. Liaised with the management of the venue to make sure facility resources were in place

9. Arranged any clearing up, and vacated the venue according to the terms of the contract

10. Prepared and circulated papers, or completed other follow-up actions following the event, if required

11. Reconciled accounts to budget, if required

12. Evaluated an event, identifying recommendations, and passed these on to relevant colleagues, where relevant

13. Agreed key learning points and used these to improve the running of future events

You will need to produce evidence from a variety of sources to support the performance requirements of this unit.

If you carry out the 'ACTIVITIES' and respond to the 'NEED TO KNOW' questions, these will provide some of the evidence required.

Links to other units

While gathering evidence for this unit, evidence **may** also be used from evidence generated from other units within the Business & Administration suite of units. Below is a **sample** of applicable units; however, most units within the Business & Administration suite of units will also be applicable.

QCF NVQ
Communications
Communicate in a business environment (Level 3)
Core business & administration
Manage own performance in a business environment (Level 3)
Improve own performance in a business environment (Level 3)
Work in a business environment (Level 3)
Solve business problems (Level 3)
Work with other people in a business environment (Level 3)
Document production
Design and produce documents in a business environment
Events and meetings
Plan and organise meetings
Organise business travel or accommodation

SVQ
Communications
Communicate in a business environment
Core business & administration
Plan how to manage and improve own performance in a business environment
Review and maintain work in a business environment
Support other people to work in a business environment
Document production
Design and produce documents in a business environment
Events and meetings
Plan and organise meetings
Organise business travel or accommodation

24

Plan and organise meetings

PLAN AND ORGANISE MEETINGS

'Plan and organise meetings' is an <u>optional unit</u> which may be chosen as one of a combination of units to achieve a Qualifications and Credit Framework (QCF), National Vocational Qualification (NVQ) or Scottish Vocational Qualification (SVQ).

The aims of this unit are to:

- Understand the arrangements and actions for planning and organising meetings

- Be able to prepare for a meeting

- Be able to support running a meeting

- Know how to follow up a meeting

To achieve the above aims of this unit, learners will be expected to provide evidence through the performance of work-based activities.

Knowledge

What is a meeting?

In a business or work environment a meeting is a gathering of people to present or exchange information, which may involve planning and making decisions. Almost every team activity or project requires meetings of some sort. A good meeting will help to generate enthusiasm for a project and build skills for future projects. It will also provide attendees with techniques that may benefit them in their future careers. Good meetings require good leaders who will encourage and direct attendees to achieve the purpose of the meeting.

Meetings will vary in size and frequency depending on the type of a business. Meetings can be:

- **Formal -** This type of meeting will be highly structured with clear aims and objectives to achieve. They may be convened at specific times of the year. They will follow an agenda and may have a large number of invited attendees. All outcomes will be recorded in some way. These types of meetings may include: board meetings; annual general meetings (AGMs); public forums, e.g. shareholder meetings; appraisal meetings; disciplinary hearings or team meetings. Generally, formal meetings are arranged for more than four people who need to inform others of decisions agreed at a meeting. The format for taking minutes will involve a lot of detail, not necessarily word for word, though this will depend on the reason for taking the minutes. This will vary, depending on the importance of attributing who said what and what actions were agreed to. In some instances, it is a legal requirement to record the outcomes of a meeting, e.g. public board meetings

- **Informal** - These types of meetings may include: one-to-one meetings or impromptu meetings. The format is less formal and may only record agreed actions to be taken

- **Physical** - All members of the meeting will be present in a room / venue. Everyone attending this type of meeting will clearly see and hear the contributions being made by other attendees at the meeting

- **Virtual** - Attendees will be located around different geographic locations linked up by videoconferencing or teleconferencing. This may be both cost- and time-effective for attendees. However, the technology needs to be organised and maintained throughout a meeting. Unlike physical meetings, body language can be difficult to interpret and this can compromise the quality of a meeting

• ACTIVITY 1

What is a meeting aiming to achieve?

Minutes of a meeting may be issued and made available to the public, if this is a legal requirement for the organisation or only available as a private record, e.g. within an organisation where commercial decisions are too sensitive to share publicly. Decisions that are made and the issues discussed during a meeting are crucial to the continued productivity of a business. It is important to keep a record of decisions and discussions in an **organised** and **methodical** fashion. While it may not be a legal obligation to maintain minutes, it is considered good practice to maintain them as verification of a formal approach to the decision-making process within an organisation.

A primary function of planning and organising a meeting is to nominate someone who is competent to take the minutes of a meeting. The degree of competence required by the minute taker will vary depending on the type of meeting that the minute taker is employed to minute. Nominating a minute taker is also an opportunity to identify and satisfy the development needs of employees who may have little experience of minuting.

The **Freedom of Information Act 2000** provides access by the public to records created by a Board and its employees, this includes minutes from a meeting. However, there are exemptions from the Act which allow non-disclosure of either full or partial information, depending on the commercial sensitivity of the information recorded in the minutes.

Types of meetings

There are many different types of meetings, including:

*   **Annual general meetings (AGMs)** - All companies with shareholders are obliged to hold a meeting at least once a year which all shareholders are invited to attend to give them the opportunity to question directors and vote on resolutions

*   **Extraordinary general meetings** - Additional meetings can be called if the holders of at least 10% of the shares want them to discuss issues that have arisen since the last AGM that cannot wait until the next, e.g. the change of the Board or to discuss the implications of a takeover / merger

*   **Board meetings** - Directors of a company meet regularly to discuss the strategic direction and general running of the organisation's business

*   **Management meetings** - Managers meet to discuss the day-to-day running of the organisation's business to decide how the strategy agreed by the Board is to be implemented

*   **Team meetings** - Meetings that discuss specific issues that affect a team and integrate information decided by senior management, e.g. the sales and marketing team, the customer service team, the communications team

*   **Staff meetings** - Meetings held to address issues that will affect everybody within the business. For example, a meeting called by a public sector organisation about the requirements relating to the distribution of information prior to an election

*   **Committee meetings** - There are many different types of committee meetings, ranging from the committee of a large organisation to committees of social clubs

*   **Project meetings** - These meetings will be organised to catch up with and report on project milestones to make sure the project is being managed successfully

• ACTIVITY 2

What are the differences in planning and organising an AGM and a team meeting?

Planning a meeting
Most meetings will be organised to achieve a specific purpose. This will be agreed before the meeting takes place. Agreeing the purpose of a meeting will help to facilitate how to plan for the resources and the environment that will be required to make the meeting a success. It is helpful to create a meeting brief to capture all the ideas for convening a meeting. A meeting brief will allow the meeting planner and organiser to coordinate all the meeting activities. It will also make decision-making quicker and easier and give the meeting planner confidence, making them feel in control and fully involved from the moment a meeting has been agreed to go forward.

• ACTIVITY 3

What are the benefits of having an agreed meeting brief?

Once the purpose of a meeting has been agreed, it will then need to be organised. To prepare to organise a meeting the meeting organiser will need to know the:

Purpose of the meeting
Meetings may be organised for the following purposes:

- Giving information

- Training

- Discussion

- Generating ideas

- Planning

- Workshops

- Consulting and getting feedback

- Finding solutions / solving problems

- Crisis management
- Performance reporting / assessment
- Setting targets and objectives
- Setting tasks and delegating
- Making decisions
- Conveying / clarifying policy issues
- Team building
- Motivating
- Special subjects - guest speakers
- Interdepartmental - process improvement

A list of interested attendees will be prepared who will confirm their interest in attending the meeting. Invitations will be sent to potential attendees with an RSVP. Once the RSVPs are returned they can be collated to identify how many attendees will be attending.

• ACTIVITY 4

What are some of the purposes for which a meeting may be organised?

Time of the meeting
If the meeting is relevant for a participant to attend, they will need to know if the time is convenient and does not clash with any other appointments they have in their diary.

Length of the meeting
Attendees will need to know how long the meeting is so they can plan their schedule of activities. The length of a meeting will depend on what the purpose of the meeting is aiming to achieve.

Size of the meeting
Once the purpose of the meeting has been agreed, the number of attendees will also need to be agreed to determine how big the room will need to be to accommodate the attendees.

Location of the meeting
This should include a map giving attendees directions to the meeting

venue, showing the location of the meeting, car parks, nearest railway station etc. Once the number of attendees at the meeting has been agreed a decision will need to be made about the location of the venue. This will be based on other factors, such as:

- The purpose of the meeting

- The seniority of the attendees

- The geographic location of the attendees

- Whether it should be in-house or external to the organisation. If the meeting can be arranged in-house it will be less costly to the business in time, finances, equipment, resources and people

- The potential disruption to the business

Once the type of meeting venue has been agreed it should be booked, identifying any specific location within a building, e.g. natural light or not; equipment, e.g. whiteboards; resources, e.g. documents and catering requirements. Different meeting venues need to be sourced to meet the agreed meeting brief and budget. Quotes for relevant meeting venues need to be obtained and a decision made on which venue will be the best to use. If possible, the meeting venue should be checked, or check with colleagues within the organisation who may have used the venue, to get their feedback. It is important to make sure the standard of hospitality and catering is appropriate. Identify exactly what the venue is providing. Check the status of equipment and catering: is it included or do separate arrangements need to be made? Decisions will also need to be made about how the meeting room is going to be organised. This will depend on the purpose of the meeting. There are three common layouts for meeting rooms:

Classroom

This is where the speaker stands in front of an audience seated round a number of tables. This is useful if attendees are to take part in a 'workshop'.

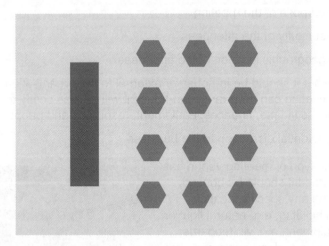

Boardroom, conference or council

This is where the whole group sit round a table. If attendees are to discuss ideas, reach a conclusion or coordinate activities this layout may be more appropriate.

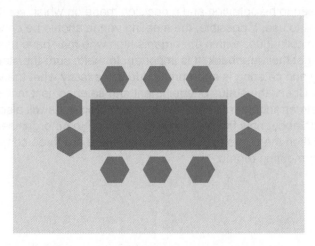

Theatre or auditorium

This is where a speaker stands in front of an audience seated in rows of seats. This layout is suitable for planning a meeting where attendees will be simply listening to a keynote speaker or watching a presentation on screen.

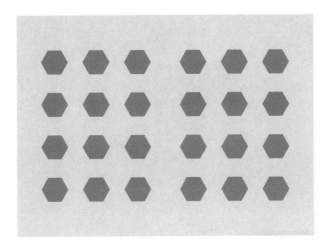

U shaped

This is a series of u-shaped tables, with seats all around, facilitating interaction between participants and the speaker.

Cabaret

This is a group of round tables seating 6 to 8, in a half-moon, for a lecture-type presentation and breakout groups.

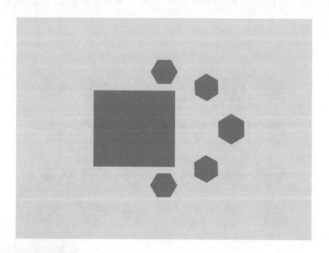

• ACTIVITY 5

What are the different types of room layouts and why would each layout be used?

When planning a meeting, design the meeting layout to create an environment that will be conducive to meeting the goals and objectives of the meeting. Create an environment that promotes interaction, engages attendees and provides a comfortable, safe space to meet. It is not always about accommodating the most people possible in the optimum space. Design and agree the meeting layout by considering the meeting's purpose, goals and objectives. The environment should create enjoyment, as this will encourage attendees to contribute more freely and creatively to the meeting. Consider the following when planning the room layout of a meeting:

- **Interaction** - Is the aim of the meeting to increase interaction among attendees? If so, create a layout that promotes interaction that allows attendees to see each other and share information. If people can see the faces of the other attendees, this increases the opportunity to interact and engage with others

- **Avoid creating a 'bowling alley' setting** - If there are more than 100 attendees, set the front of the room on the longest wall, to decrease the distance between the last row of the audience and the speaker. This will make it easier and more comfortable for attendees to see the stage and screen

- **Design seating that keeps people from clustering in the back and keeps emergency exits clear** - Often chairs are added to a room because people are standing at the back, when there are actually plenty of open seats in the middle of the room. Often those standing are clustered around doors, thereby creating an unsafe situation. Avoid this by using principles of audience-centred seating. Set the last row of seating on the back wall, leaving a wide aisle between it and the second-to-last row, which allows people to walk in front of the last row to get to the side aisles, but does not allow them to stand at the back, in front of those seated. Leave several feet at the end of each row to allow people to move up the sides and into empty seats - this is important, in case of emergency, and also helps those who might need to leave during the session. Create cut-in access aisles by removing a centre chair from each row, which allows people in the back to move up through several rows into those empty middle seats

- **Create a comfortable, safe environment** - Avoid locking seats together, as this limits the ability of the attendees to rearrange seating to be more comfortable and prevents them from forming small groups, if needed

At the completion of a meeting make sure that attendees are given the opportunity to feedback on the quality of the meeting, including the venue and catering. This feedback should then be given to the venue, even if it is very positive feedback. Appropriate records of this feedback should be stored to help inform choice of venues in the future. Feedback forms are usually created by the planner and handed out to attendees. This is a very formal tool to make sure that the meeting has reached its goals and satisfied attendees' expectations. The feedback form should provide the opportunity to identify qualitative and quantitative data. Feedback can be collected at the meeting or emailed / posted after the meeting.

As a result of feedback from a meeting, the meeting planner should be able to identify learning points to improve the organisation of future meetings. All the elements that the meeting planner needs to consider to run the meeting should form the template for attempting to 'future proof' the success of future meetings.

• ACTIVITY 6

A meeting has been planned and organised for 40 people who will be discussing the strategic direction of the team. The manager will set out the agenda for the day with a 30-minute presentation. It is expected that there will be various breakout sessions. What would be the best room layout to use to meet the requirements of the meeting?

Any special requirements
Attendees can advise the meeting organiser of any special requirements, e.g. dietary needs, if being catered for; disabled access to the meeting venue.

Equipment and other resources required at the meeting
Where a screen or flip chart is being used it is essential that everyone can see it. If arranging a meeting for a large number of attendees consider whether microphones are necessary. Make sure speakers are not placed where attendees may be deafened by the sound. Other equipment you may need to have available includes:

- A laptop, to allow a PowerPoint presentation to be shown

- A multi-media projector

- Whiteboards and dry-wipe markers, for brainstorming sessions

- An easel, to put the flip chart on

- Pencils, paper and maybe a dish of sweets for each table

- Duplicates of documents that attendees will need

Catering requirements
- Tea and coffee for morning or mid-afternoon breaks

- Lunch

- Dietary requirements of delegates attending the meeting

An agreed agenda for the meeting
An agenda can also be used as a planning tool for organising a meeting. It can also function to:

- Provide an outline of the meeting - how long to spend on agenda items

- Check that all information required for the meeting is covered
- Inform attendees of agenda items before the meeting, so they can arrive prepared for discussions or decisions
- Focus the objective of the meeting

An agenda will usually be made up of the following minimum headings:

- Attendees and apologies for absence
- The minutes of the past meeting
- Matters arising
- Any other business (AOB)
- Date and time of next meeting

A week before the meeting send an agenda and copies of any meeting papers to those who indicated they would be attending. The agenda of a meeting sets out, in a logical order, what is to be discussed at the meeting.

An agenda is the tool used for controlling a meeting.
Include all the relevant information and circulate it in advance. Formal agendas for board meetings and committees will normally have an established fixed format. Informal meetings focus on practicality and try to avoid formality.

Each agenda item should be explained priming attendees on how they can contribute to the discussion - decision-making, information. Agenda items that make up the meeting should be timed to facilitate the smooth running of the meeting and its completion on schedule. Even if an agenda does not have timings for agenda items, the planner and organiser of the meeting should plan timings so they can control the meeting. Agree a realistic time slot for each agenda item, as some agenda items might take longer to discuss / disseminate information than planned. The agenda should name guest speakers or presenters, plan coffee breaks and lunch breaks, if relevant. Avoid formal sit-down restaurant lunches as they add at least 30 minutes unnecessarily to the lunch break, and the whole thing makes people tired. Working lunches are a better idea as long as attendees have some time to get some fresh air. Make sure agendas have 'comfort' breaks every 45-60 minutes to keep attendees focused and the meeting productive. Allow attendees to contribute to the agenda items, if appropriate.

- **Satisfy any health and safety regulations and security requirements**
- **People who should be invited to attend the meeting**
- **Brief the chair of the meeting**

All meetings will require a 'pilot' to make sure that the agenda is followed and is completed on schedule, who is called the **chair** of the meeting. The chair may be someone from within the organisation or independent of the organisation. This will depend on the purpose of convening the meeting. The chair will need to be appraised of the agenda, if they have not been party to developing it. They will need to know the purpose of the meeting and how they need to steer the discussions to achieve the purpose of the meeting. They will need to be briefed on any specialised information / data / knowledge that is important to share with attendees of the meeting to help empower discussions. They will need to be brought up to date with any policy initiatives that will impact on the discussions surrounding the agenda items. The chair will need to work out with the meeting planner and organiser signals the chair can use if they are in difficulty and need assistance from the meeting planner. The chair will usually want to be made aware of any difficult personalities who may attend so they can think about strategies of how to manage these attendees.

• ACTIVITY 7

What are the most important elements that need to be managed when organising a meeting?

Prior to the time of the meeting, the meeting planner and organiser should have carried out the following mental checklist in preparation for the meeting to facilitate its success:

- Be clear about the purpose of the meeting
- Be sure meeting attendees are clear about the stated purpose of the meeting
- Establish a specific standard to measure success or failure of the meeting
- Establish only essential attendance to achieve the purpose of the meeting

- Build working relationships with attendees prior to the meeting
- Rationalise agenda items, as necessary, to achieve the purpose of the meeting
- Determine what must be done to make the desired vision of the meeting a reality
- Establish a meeting environment consistent with the purpose of the meeting
- Consult with any attendees, or others whose cooperation is necessary, to achieve the purpose of the meeting
- Establish a clear and appropriately detailed agenda, and circulate it with other materials in advance of the meeting
- Respect particular customs, rules and etiquette of the meeting

Once all the arrangements for the meeting are in place, on the day of the meeting, the planner of the meeting should aim to arrive early to carry out the following checks:

- Catering - Should be organised for the times as stated on the agenda
- Equipment and resources - Should be in place and it works. Make sure there are spare copies of the papers sent prior to the meeting available for those who have lost them, forgotten them or claim never to have received them. There may be other items for discussion at the meeting which were not included on the agenda. If this happens, make sure there are sufficient copies of relevant papers for the meeting, because these will not have been circulated in advance. These should be collated into the order in which they will be discussed and placed in position on the meeting tables. Sorting the papers into order will enable people to follow the agenda more easily and reduce the distraction that searching through piles of paper causes. Make sure everyone has a full set of papers. Arrange for the photocopying of papers during the meeting, if required, and deal with failures of power, equipment or catering

If the meeting is not in-house make sure the following is known:

- Where the toilets are
- Whether there is a fire alarm test arranged for that day
- Where the fire exits are
- Where the assembly point is

- Where lunch is going to be served

- If there are facilities for smokers

- Where the disabled access is

- Who is responsible for first aid

- What alarm system to use

When attendees start to arrive make sure someone is on hand to greet them, sign them in and give them a delegate's badge, if necessary. Guide attendees to where the cloakroom is, where refreshments can be found, the location of the meeting room and answer any questions they may have.

During the meeting, the key to success is keeping control. This is achieved by:

- Sticking to the agenda

- Managing relationships and personalities

- Concentrating on achieving the purpose of the meeting through its agenda items

At the beginning of the meeting remind the meeting attendees of the meeting's purpose. Throughout the meeting steer it towards making progress. Politely suppress the over-zealous and encourage the nervous. Make sure notes are taken, recording important points and the agreed actions, with names, measurable outcomes and deadlines. Focus on achieving the outcomes of the agreed agenda. Direct discussion to the purpose of the meeting as it moves through each agenda item, e.g. avoid hours of discussion if a simple decision is required from attendees or defer new issues to another time or meeting. Delegate to attendees, as necessary, to manage people, tasks and outcomes throughout the meeting. Observe how people are behaving in meetings - look for signs of tiredness, exasperation and confusion, and take necessary action. Always follow the meeting agenda, but be guided by the behaviour of attendees.

Throughout the meeting make sure the meeting has all the support it needs so it is not distracted or derailed by unintended events. Usher latecomers into the meeting, as appropriate, re-organise seating if required, make sure all attendees sign the sign-in sheet, make sure all attendees have all the required documents, obtain more documents / additional papers, resolve equipment that fails to work properly, think of alternatives to use if equipment breaks down, make sure there are sufficient refreshments for attendees etc. Be on hand to attend to any of these problems or any others that may arise.

Make a note of any lapses in service provided by the meeting venue, which can be followed up after the meeting is over. If the anticipated service has not been delivered negotiate this with the meeting venue management team. Make any notes to improve the way meetings might be organised and run in the future.

Once the meeting is over, thank attendees for attending the meeting. Make sure they know where the cloakroom is and fulfil any requests. Clear the room as required by organisational procedures. This will vary depending on whether the meeting has been held in-house or off site and the size of the organisation and the ancillary services that the organisation is able to provide if in-house.

Once the minutes have been agreed by the chairperson, distribute these, as requested, to attendees and those people who were unable to attend the meeting so they not only have a record of proceedings but can make any suggestions for the future.

• ACTIVITY 8

What are the differences between planning a meeting which takes place in-house as opposed to off site?

Testing your knowledge

1. What is a meeting brief?

2. What are the differences between informal meetings and virtual meetings?

3. What are benefits of agreeing the purpose of a meeting?

4. Why is an agenda created for a meeting?

5. Why are agendas divided into agenda items?

6. Why is the chair of a meeting briefed?

7. What is the reason for meetings having different room layouts?

8. What should be done if 75% of attendees of a meeting are unable to make the meeting due to travel disruption?

9. What types of equipment and resources may be needed at a meeting?

10. What type of problems could occur when planning and running a meeting?

11. What type of minutes should be taken for meetings?

Skills

As the person responsible for planning and organising the meeting, you will need to agree the meeting brief and the budget for the meeting. You will need to manage every aspect of the planning and organisation of the meeting. This may require you to delegate various tasks required to realise the plan, if you have a team to support the activities you have organised. You will need to make sure that the support team follow the meeting plan that has been set out. The tasks that you have organised for the planning of the meeting will also need to be balanced against other plans of work that you have been assigned.

When agreeing the meeting brief it is good practice to remember that it is a living document. It may need to change according to the changing purpose of the meeting. This may have an impact on the size of the budget that has been agreed for the meeting, if appropriate. The areas of work you will need to consider in planning a meeting will be, though not exclusively:

- Agreeing the budget and reviewing it against incoming costs to make sure the costs do not spiral out of control land exceed the budget

- Identifying and agreeing what the meeting plan is aiming to achieve - the purpose of the meeting

- Identifying and agreeing where the meeting is to take place - in-house or off site - and making sure that it comes within budget, if appropriate

- Agreeing the purpose of the meeting before sourcing a venue

- Sourcing an appropriate venue for the meeting

- Meeting with and briefing the chair about the meeting

- Checking to see if there are any travel requirements

- Identifying and agreeing what kind of room layout the meeting should have

- Organising all relevant equipment

- Organising any other resources

- Agreeing and organising the printing and dissemination of all relevant documents for the meeting

- Agreeing the meeting agenda, including giving attendees the opportunity to contribute towards its development

- Organising the printing of all documents required for the meeting

- Managing any special requirements for attendees

- Organising any catering requirements

- Making sure that all organisational procedures have been followed

- Making sure that all health and safety regulations have been built into the meeting plan

- Making sure that all security requirements have been built into the meeting plan

Make sure, on the day, that the venue has been laid out as agreed, that all equipment is in good working order and all documents have been compiled and placed for each attendee.

It would be appropriate and very helpful to aid the planning and organising of meetings to have a checklist you can follow to make sure that everything that you need to do has been agreed, organised and followed through. The checklist should cover everything to do with what has to be prepared before the meeting, e.g. the documents that need to be sent out to attendees in advance of the meeting; what needs to be considered during the running of a meeting, e.g. making sure that you are equipped to resolve problems that may arise during the meeting; and the follow-up activities that you will need to do as a result of the meeting, e.g. collect all feedback forms - if appropriate - and evaluate them to inform future planning and organisation of meetings.

• ACTIVITY 9

Design a checklist for planning and organising a meeting.

Use the checklist to make sure that you have planned and organised for all eventualities. This will help you in your work and build confidence with the team you are working with. Work with other members of your team to check that everything has been planned for and resolve any issues that you are not sure about.

• ACTIVITY 10

How would you plan and organise a meeting for training of HR development managers who are learning a new recruitment methodology? There will be 50 attendees coming from all four nations of the UK. The meeting will last two days. You will have a budget of £5,000 to organise the meeting.

Depending on the nature of the meeting, you will need to either develop a feedback form or use an existing template. The reason for using a feedback form is to check to see if the purpose of your meeting has been achieved, and if not, what you can learn from the experience so that planning and organising meetings in the future is more positive. The feedback form will also allow you to evaluate the external services that you have used - have they provided a good service and offered value for money. The feedback form will also give you the opportunity to reflect on good practice and your management skills. As with most experiences of working within an organisation, planning and organising meetings provides great learning opportunities. Use observations about your work practice to inform and develop better ways of working in the future. Write any learning opportunities into your learning and development plan, if your organisation does this. Even if it does not, make a note of what you need to think about in your future working and discuss this with your manager.

• ACTIVITY 11

How do you manage your support team, if you have one, to make sure the meeting is organised to meet its purpose? If you have no support team, how do you organise yourself to make sure the meeting purpose will be achieved?

Testing your skills

1. How did you create the meeting plan brief?

2. How did you organise the meeting agenda?

3. How did you confirm the meeting room was the correct size and configured to the agreed layout?

4. How did you organise invitations and responses from attendees?

5. What special needs did you need to make sure were organised? How did you do this?

6. How did you know what papers were needed to be organised for the meeting?

7. How did you prepare the meeting to maximise its success?

8. What did you do during the meeting?

9. What problems did you resolve prior to and during the meeting?

10. What health and safety regulations did you need to consider in supporting the organisation of the meeting?

11. What security arrangements did you need to consider for the organisation of the meeting?

12. How did you organise for any feedback in relation to meetings you planned and organised?

13. What did you learn from planning and organising meetings that will help to improve meetings in the future?

Ready for assessment?
To achieve this Level 3 unit of a Business & Administration qualification, learners will need to demonstrate that they are able to perform the following activities:

1. Agreed and prepared the meeting brief, checking with others, if required

2. Agreed a budget for the meeting, if required

3. Prepared and agreed an agenda and meeting papers

4. Organised and confirmed venue, equipment and catering requirements, when necessary

5. Invited attendees, confirmed attendance and identified any special requirements

6. Arranged catering, if required

7. Arranged the equipment and layout of the room, if required

8. Made sure the chair received appropriate briefing

9. Welcomed attendees and offered suitable refreshment, if required

10. Made sure attendees had a full set of papers

11. Made sure a person had been nominated to take minutes, if required

12. Provided information, advice and support when required

13. Produced records of meetings

14. Sought approval of meeting records and amended them, as required

15. Responded to requests for amendments and arranged recirculation of revised meting records

16. Followed action points, if required

17. Evaluated meeting arrangements and external service, where used

18. Evaluated attendee feedback from the meeting and shared results with relevant people, where used

19. Summarised learning points and used these to identify improvements that could be made to future meeting arrangements and support

You will need to produce evidence from a variety of sources to support the performance requirements of this unit.

If you carry out the 'ACTIVITIES' and respond to the 'NEED TO KNOW' questions, these will provide some of the evidence required.

Links to other units

While gathering evidence for this unit, evidence **may** also be used from evidence generated from other units within the Business & Administration suite of units. Below is a **sample** of applicable units; however, most units within the Business & Administration suite of units will also be applicable.

QCF NVQ
Communications
Communicate in a business environment (Level 3)
Core business & administration
Manage own performance in a business environment (Level 3)
Improve own performance in a business environment (Level 3)
Work in a business environment (Level 3)
Work with other people in a business environment (Level 3)
Document production
Design and produce documents in a business environment
Events and meetings
Plan an organise an event
Coordinate an event
Organise business travel or accommodation

SVQ
Communications
Communicate in a business environment
Core business & administration
Plan how to manage and improve own performance in a business environment
Review and maintain work in a business environment
Support other people to work in a business environment
Document production
Design and produce documents in a business environment
Events and meetings
Organise and coordinate events
Organise business travel or accommodation

25

Organise business travel or accommodation

ORGANISE BUSINESS TRAVEL OR ACCOMODATION

'Organise business travel or accommodation' is an optional unit
which may be chosen as one of a combination of units to achieve either
a Qualifications and Credit Framework (QCF), National Vocational
Qualification (NVQ) or Scottish Vocational Qualification (SVQ).

The aims of this unit are to:

- Understand the range of information, requirements and
  procedures that may be needed for all types of business travel or
  accommodation arrangements

- Understand the types of problems that may occur with business
  travel or accommodation arrangements and how to deal with them

- Be able to organise different types of business travel or
  accommodation arrangements

To achieve the above aims of this unit, learners will be expected to
provide evidence through the performance of work-based activities.

Knowledge
Businesses are increasingly expanding their operations
to offer their products and services in a globalised
community. To position a business within a globalised
community, an organisation may have to send their
employees to attend meetings, conferences etc., beyond
their local office. Employees may be expected to travel:

- **Domestically** - Within their national borders. This type of journey will
  not require visas or foreign currency, e.g. travelling to Scotland

- **Internationally** - Outside of their national borders. This type of
  journey may require visas or foreign currency, e.g. travelling to any
  nation within the EU will not require a visa, but foreign currency, the
  Euro, may need to be arranged

Business travel may be undertaken frequently or infrequently by
employees within an organisation. Depending on the length of the trip,
accommodation may also need to be arranged for an employee. In
some organisations, entrusted employees are empowered to undertake
organising their own business travel or accommodation arrangements.
However, it is important that they are supported in their endeavours,
which is the aim of the business travel or accommodation organiser.

An organisation may have a specific department that looks after all these arrangements, they may have employees within a team who are responsible for these arrangements as part of their job or they may outsource the work to a specialist business travel agent. It will depend on the size of the organisation and how the business is organised. However, whatever the size of the operation arranging business travel or accommodation, an organisation should have a business travel and accommodation policy which should describe:

- How this function is organised within the organisation

- The restrictions the organisation places on this function

- Health and safety requirements for employees when abroad

- The support given to employees to make the trip a success

- The information required to monitor and evaluate this function

The advantages of having a business travel and accommodation policy are:

- **Coherency** - Everyone follows the same process, which is seen to produce similar outcomes which fit the **personalised** requirements requested by employees

- **Employee support** - Employees feel **valued** and looked after in the knowledge that their business travel or accommodation arrangements will be organised in all eventualities

- **Consistent processes** - The processes involved in arranging business travel or accommodation can be seen to be **unbiased** and consistent as they apply to employees across the organisation

- **Cost-efficiencies** - Business travel or accommodation arrangements should be **negotiated** with employees and suppliers to provide value for money, which will minimise inconvenience to the business of the organisation

Planning business travel

When it has been agreed that an employee needs to travel they should approach the appropriate person with the following information:

- The **budget** for the trip

- **When** the trip is taking place. The departure date / time and the return date / time. Consideration will need to be given to the time it will take getting to and from the point of departure. This should factor in the potential for delays and the effect of different time zones, if travelling internationally

- The **destination** of the trip

- The best **form of travel**, which will depend on:

  - Budgets

  - Time constraints

  - Working practice expectations while travelling, e.g. working on the train

  - Access to the departure / arrival terminal

  - Frequency of the travel service

  - Convenience of the travel services - the ease of travel between travel terminals and the departure / destination points

  - Length of the journey

  - Potential problems that could occur when making a journey, e.g. delays

  - Amount of luggage or equipment that needs to be taken, although this could always be sent on ahead

  - Weather conditions for particular times of the year, e.g. travelling to the north of Scotland in the middle of winter with heavy snow forecast may mean driving is not the best travel option

Employees could travel by the following **systems of transport**:

- **Car -** Usually for travel within the home nation. This may be the best form of travel for destinations where there is either no access or difficult access to public transport. Decisions will need  to be made if the employee is to use their own car (mileage costs) or hire one (type of car); if they can accommodate others in the car; how long the journey will take (number of breaks to take so they are not too tired when they arrive) and the availability of parking on arrival

- **Rail -** Consideration will need to be given to the possible number of connections and if the traveller could work while travelling by train

- **Plane -** Consideration will need to be given to the closest terminal for the traveller (s), which is balanced with the costs and impact to the business

- **Ferry**

A mode of travel that may be used infrequently and will need to consider prevailing weather conditions

* The **number of people** who will be travelling

* Any **special requirements**, e.g. a seat on a train travelling in the direction of travel; extra leg room on a plane

* Clarify **suitable standards** of business travel or accommodation and compensation

Business travellers should be aware of the grade of travel they are entitled to use. This will often depend on the length of the journey and seniority of the employee concerned. There should be a similar statement for hotels. Consideration should be given to how the organisation policy manages partners accompanying employees on work-related business trips and whether benefits earned on frequent flyer programmes should be returned to the organisation or retained by the individual. Cost-of-living indexes for various cities should be monitored to control business expenses. Compensation for weekends and bank holidays spent abroad must be agreed with employees, and they must know how soon they are expected back at work after returning from their business trip.

• ACTIVITY 1

What is the most important information required from the traveller when arranging business travel or accommodation, and why?

There are many variables involved in planning and deciding on which form transport to use for business travel. There is no right or wrong way of doing it and it will depend on what the business travel and accommodation policy states for an organisation. However, consideration needs to be given to the **personal preferences of the traveller**:

* A car journey may be the cheapest option but the traveller may not have a driving licence

* If the traveller suffers from seasickness, travelling by ferry would not be a good option

* The traveller may have a phobia about a form of transport, e.g. a fear of flying

Sometimes a cheap option may appear to be the best option regarding cost but it may be more expensive in human terms, and this may have a knock-on effect to the success of the business to be conducted. The monetary cost may be low but the human cost may be very high. In planning the best form of travel or accommodation it is important to remember that the aim of the business travel is to successfully conduct business. This is being carried out by an employee of the organisation. The employee needs to arrive at their destination in the best mental and physical shape to conduct business successfully.

• ACTIVITY 2

The HR manager needs a trip organised to Australia and New Zealand. The itinerary for the trip has the following appointments:

- Sydney, 12th November, 10.00
- Canberra, 14th November, 14.30
- Ballarat, 15th November, 09.00
- Adelaide, 16th November, 09.00 and 14.30
- Fremantle, 18th November, 10.00
- Auckland, 21st November, 10.00
- Launceston, 21st November, 15.00
- London, 23rd November, 10.30

Research and cost all travel and accommodation arrangements offering the best value to the traveller and the organisation. What recommendations could be made to minimise costs and make the trip less strenuous for the traveller, and what would need to be considered to make these recommendations? Put together a revised itinerary based on these recommendations. Organise visas, if they are required, medical requirements and foreign currency - what is the budget for this?

International travel or accommodation
Frequently, employees will be asked to travel overseas to foreign destinations. This will require consideration of a number of factors when making business travel or accommodation arrangements, which include arranging the following:

Visas
A visa is a document which gives permission for a person to travel into a foreign country and stay there for an agreed period of time. Visas

are generally added to a traveller's passport or they may be held in separate documents. Visas should be safeguarded to make sure they are not separated from the traveller's passport, lost or stolen, as this will present problems to the traveller when leaving a foreign country. Some foreign countries waive the requirement for visas as they have a reciprocal arrangement with the traveller's home country. It is important to research visa requirements before travelling internationally, as organising this will take time and, in most cases, incur a cost to the traveller.

Visas are generally only valid for a set period of time. Visas may be extended or people may need to leave a country and re-enter it to receive a new visa. Visas may be for single or multiple entry into the country. There are restrictions on visas, e.g. some will only be given for business travel or tourism. Most foreign countries will restrict the amount of currency that can be brought into or leave a country. Visas may also be rejected for travellers who may suffer from infectious diseases. Some visas will require a photograph of the traveller or the photograph will be taken for the visa on entry to the foreign country.

Foreign currency
The traveller to a foreign country will need the local currency to maintain their stay in the foreign country. This should be costed and agreed within the budget for the traveller. Some countries have restrictions on the amount of foreign currency travellers are allowed to enter the country with or leave with. Depending on how the currency is bought it may incur a charge from the money changer. It is also advisable to be aware of the exchange rates before travelling, as these fluctuate on a daily basis, which may have an impact on the total cost of foreign currency.

Safety, medical requirements and insurance
The political climate of a country should be considered before planning foreign travel, to make sure there are no local insurrections going on that would compromise the safety of travellers. The Foreign Office provides information on foreign countries where it is not safe to travel to.

Other safety issues should also be considered, e.g. if a group of senior managers is intending to travel together, they should travel on separate modes of transport. Make sure employees travelling internationally for the first time receive a briefing on personal safety issues, e.g. on a plane, in the street, in a hotel, when taking taxis or driving themselves and about looking after money. Offer advice on measures that employees can take to protect their home and family while away.

There are many different health issues that need to be considered when travelling internationally. These include inoculations and other specific health risks in certain countries. Advice should be given to employees to deal with jet lag, tummy bugs and the sun. If appropriate, issue a first-aid kit to business travellers going to countries with unreliable medical services and an AIDS problem. Some countries may require foreign travellers to be inoculated against various diseases, e.g. malaria, cholera, TB. If a traveller does not have evidence that these inoculations have been carried out they may be barred from entering the country. Inoculations will need to be planned because some may have to be done a few weeks before travel or require a series of inoculations. Like visas, these documents should be kept safe to avoid either being barred from entry to the foreign country or having all the inoculations again at the destination.

Make sure that all types of insurance have been organised for the business traveller, particularly if they are to spend considerable time in the foreign country. The best insurance cover is all-year cover for all employees to cover all eventualities, e.g. when last-minute business trips have to be organised or when an employee has never travelled internationally before. Insurance policies should be checked to see what is covered and what the small print is. Minimise costs by shopping around and comparing costs for the best business travel insurance policies.

Description of the foreign environment

It is important, when travelling to a foreign country, to make sure that employees are aware of **local customs**, so they can facilitate business opportunities and create a positive environment to conduct business. Cultural mistakes can be costly in business as well as in personal terms. Keep up to date with useful publications and seminars. There are many gestures that you may be accustomed to but are frowned upon in other countries, where they may be seen as the opposite of their intention, e.g. the thumbs up 'OK' sign is interpreted negatively in other countries, such as parts of Italy and Greece. In the Far East the concept of saving face colours the way the locals will answer questions, which may undermine their position. **Dress like the locals** or so that you do not draw unwanted attention. This may be the case when travelling to locations that have religious requirements that must be observed. Avoid wearing expensive jewellery. Be **polite** and **non-demanding**. It may also be appropriate to organise for some language training for the business traveller, depending on time and budget and the nature of the business to be conducted.

• ACTIVITY 3

What factors need to be considered when organising international business travel or accommodation?

Planning accommodation

Some domestic and international reasons for travelling may require the traveller to stay for more than one night to conduct their business. In this situation, accommodation will also need to be organised.

An organisation's business travel and accommodation policy will advise on the type of accommodation that should be selected, which will require the following information:

- The **budget** for the accommodation

- **When** the accommodation is required

- **Where** the accommodation is required

- The **standard** and **type of accommodation** required

- The **number of people** requiring accommodation

- How **convenient the location** is to the travel service being used

- Any **special requirements**, e.g. a ground-floor room for someone who suffered from vertigo

As with making arrangements for travelling, employees need to be secure in the knowledge that they will arrive for their meeting capable of making good decisions and be able to move the business forward.

• ACTIVITY 4

What is the main reason for controlling the travel and accommodation budget for travellers?

Preparing an itinerary

The traveller or their manager will identify the business travel or accommodation requirements, specifying all the requirements to be met within budget. Once all the plans for business travel or accommodation have been agreed, a search should be completed fulfilling the requirements of the travel brief. This should present alternative routes of travel and the costs attached to each option. This will allow the traveller to make the most informed choice about which option to select. Once an option has been selected by the traveller, the organiser of the business travel or accommodation will draw up a full **itinerary** that clearly sets out the timelines for the full period of travel.

An itinerary sets out the entire travel or accommodation schedule prior to the trip. It helps to organise activities well in advance so time is not wasted due to unscheduled or unplanned actions. Having an itinerary helps the traveller to focus on the planned activities and purpose of the business trip rather than on the logistics of the travel arrangements. The itinerary makes sure that both the organiser and the traveller (s) is fully prepared, guaranteeing a productive use of time. The lack of an itinerary could result in last-minute activities that waste both time and money.

The itinerary should be checked with the traveller before the bookings are confirmed with the travel organiser. The traveller may have previous experience of the actual journey and be able to make suggestions about better options to explore. An itinerary could overlook certain requirements which the traveller will see when they review the itinerary. The itinerary should always be checked to avoid any possible cancellation charges.

• ACTIVITY 5

What is the purpose of agreeing an itinerary with travellers?

Searching for travel or accommodation options

There are many sites on the Internet which can be found to help with identifying different travel services and the costs attached to them, e.g. www.travelsupermarket.com. Each of these sites will provide a cost of the travel service or accommodation being considered. Alternatively, an organisation

may employ dedicated travel agents with whom they make all their travel arrangements. The most appropriate options, which fulfil the requirements of the travel brief and the agreed budget, can then be collated. This will allow a comparison to be made across the different options.

Confirming the booking

Once the itinerary and the appropriate options of travel and accommodation have been agreed, the booking can go ahead. How this is done will vary from organisation to organisation and depend on their travel and accommodation management policy. Possible arrangements that may be in place could be:

- **Special rates** with specific hotel chains. Contact the reservations department and give them the details of the number of rooms, number of nights, date of arrival and names of guests etc.

- **Online facilities** to book travel and accommodation. This will require the use of a company credit card, unless the organisation has an account or credit facility with the supplier

- A **travel agent** who will make all the travel arrangements

- Book **direct** with a hotel or travel company

- All **bookings**, once completed, will need to be confirmed with a booking reference

The traveller will need all their business travel or accommodation information as soon as possible. The traveller should be given the itinerary and all necessary documents in good time prior to travelling. The traveller will need to review all the documents to make sure they not only meet the requirements of the travel brief but also conform to the traveller's requirements. The traveller should then confirm that they are happy with all the itinerary and documents that have been provided. A business trip can be very stressful - for many different reasons, some of which the organiser may not be aware of - so it is important that the traveller is confident about all their travel arrangements. If any changes are needed there will still be time to make them. Last-minute changes are much more difficult to organise and often incur additional costs.

In order to keep track of business travel or accommodation arrangements and deal with any queries that may arise, all agreements and bookings should be maintained accurately in a recording system.

These may be held electronically, in hard copy or a combination of both. Copies of all bookings made should be kept in a 'live' file for ease of reference. When the trip has been completed all records should be archived. Records should also be maintained regarding feedback received about the accommodation, facilities and any other aspects of cultural interest for international business travel.

• ACTIVITY 6

Why should travel or accommodation bookings be confirmed?

Paying for the travel or accommodation arrangements
All forms of transport or accommodation will usually require payment in advance of travel. Every organisation has different approaches regarding how their travel or accommodation arrangements are paid for, which include:

- **Invoicing** - The travel company will invoice the organisation for all costs. The invoice will need to be paid within 28 days or other specific arrangement that has been agreed

- **Company credit card** - When the booking has been confirmed, the organiser will use an authorised company credit card. This offers greater flexibility when using travel websites

- **Travel account** - If using a travel agent, an account will normally be opened which will need to be paid at specific times agreed between both parties

When invoices and credit card statements are received these must be checked carefully against the bookings in the archived file. Any discrepancies should be reported to the supplier immediately. The organisation's procedures must then be followed to make sure of prompt payment. This will avoid any charges for late payment. It will also build a positive relationship with the supplier.

Some organisations will expect their employees to pay for accommodation using their personal credit card. This expense is then claimed back using an expense account. Expense accounts will normally be linked to a cost centre or specific budget code. Employees should be advised of the spending limits they are allowed to use when travelling for business on behalf of the organisation. They should also be advised of how their business travel or accommodation spending is claimed back from the organisation.

Dealing with travel problems

Many problems may arise in arranging travel or accommodation of which some are listed below:

- **Tickets may not arrive.** Chase up the company in time for replacements to be sent

- **Transport may be delayed.** The traveller should be told to check travel arrangements before they travel to make sure there are no problems

- **Transport may be cancelled.** The traveller should be told to check travel arrangements before they travel to make sure there are no problems. Alternative travel arrangements may need to be made

- People travelling by car may be **delayed** by roadworks or **breakdowns**, or may get lost in an unfamiliar area. In the case of a breakdown, arrangements should be in place for a recovery service to be used or obtaining an alternative hire car

- The hotel may have made a **mistake with the booking.** Speak to the hotel and resolve the matter. Arrange alternative accommodation if necessary

- The traveller's **luggage may be mislaid** at the airport. Deal with this as the traveller gets on with the purpose of their visit. If the visit is for several days, financial assistance may need to be organised

- A **travel company may go out of business.** Travel arrangements may need to be rebooked as the original travel arrangement may not be honoured

- A visa not being granted to the traveller

- The traveller losing all their travel documents in a foreign location

Whatever the problem, it will require some form of communication with the traveller to make sure they are able to reach their intended destination at the required time or have appropriate accommodation. If the travel organiser cannot contact the traveller, they may have to contact the appropriate company at the destination point to let them know what alternative arrangements have been made for the traveller. In the event of international business travel, this may require communicating with the British Consulate to let them know that travellers from the organisation will be in the foreign country for a certain period of time. It is up to the travel organiser to make sure the business trip runs as smoothly as possible so the traveller is in the best mental and physical form to conduct their business.

When making business travel or accommodation arrangements it is important to **safeguard the information** that has been acquired to make bookings. In some cases this could be extremely private information relating to an employee, which is covered by the Data Protection Act 1998. This information should be considered 'private and confidential' and safeguarded in line with organisational procedures for storing 'private and confidential' information.

Notes should be kept on the **quality of service** that has been provided by the suppliers of business travel or accommodation. These notes should be reviewed to evaluate and justify if suppliers should continue to be used for this service. Evaluation should be based on the quality of service and value for money that the supplier provides, e.g. service which is timely or will undertake to collect visas.

Testing your knowledge

1. What is the main reason for having a business travel and accommodation policy?

2. What factors need to be considered when organising business, travel or accommodation arrangements to international destinations?

3. What is the difference between organising business travel or accommodation arrangements for travellers to

    3.1. Domestic destinations?

    3.2. International destinations?

4. Why are records kept on business travel or accommodation arrangements?

5. What is a visa and why should it be organised when making business travel or accommodation arrangements to

    5.1. Domestic destinations?

    5.2. International destinations?

6. What are the components of a business itinerary?

7. What is the best way to organise foreign currency for a business traveller?

8. What needs to be checked before paying an invoice for business travel or accommodation arranged for business travellers?

9. What are the potential stresses that a business traveller may encounter?

Skills

You will organise and agree a plan and budget to arrange business travel or accommodation. This will be done with the travellers for whom you will be providing the service. The decisions that you will make will vary depending on the type of business travel or accommodation that is required, e.g. domestic travel will probably be cheaper and quicker to organise. The tasks that you will be asked to plan for will vary in depth and breadth of commitment depending on the types of business travel or accommodation required. These tasks will also need to be balanced against other plans of work that you have been assigned to complete. You should have a shared understanding of all the requirements of the plan and budget so you can make decisions that will benefit the traveller and show value for money. In some cases the traveller may not be the budget holder, so additional dialogue will need to be undertaken with their manager to agree the parameters of the business travel or accommodation arrangements.

• ACTIVITY 7

If you were arranging for someone to travel from London to Istanbul, Baghdad, Kabul, Islamabad and back to London, what factors would you need to consider when organising travel or accommodation arrangements?

Your expertise and judgement will be called for to make decisions with the traveller. Consider the parameters of the business travel or accommodation plans and make suggestions regarding how they can be improved. The areas of work that you will be involved in will cover the following:

- Agreeing the business travel or accommodation plan

- Agreeing the budget and making sure all costs are reasonable and remain within budget

- Managing your support team, if appropriate

- Making sure all bookings meet the requirements of the travellers brief

- Accommodating any changes to traveller requirements

- Searching for various business travel or accommodation options
- Working to find the best supplier of business travel or accommodation
- Aiming to achieve value for money in all your negotiations with suppliers
- Booking the business travel or accommodation options
- Paying for any travel or accommodation arrangements
- Developing an itinerary of travel arrangements or accommodation for the traveller
- Maintaining a record of all transactions
- Providing the traveller with the final itinerary which you will check through with them to make sure all the travel plans have been met as agreed
- Organising an appointment, e.g. visa application or medical inoculations, in the event of international travel
- Making sure all 'private and confidential' information is stored securely

• ACTIVITY 8

What is the quickest and most cost-effective way to travel from Paris to Padua in December? What factors would you need to consider to make sure the traveller was able to travel at this time?

As you go about your work in any of these areas, you will always be guided by the travel or accommodation suppliers and / or the travellers' needs. You will work with travellers to agree:

- An outline of the whole travel plan so timings are clear
- When you need to complete all tasks
- The manager you will report to
- The support team you will be working with, if appropriate
- What to do in the event of any problems
- Any supplementary activity that needs to be completed

It would be helpful for you to design a checklist to keep track of what you need to do, if necessary. Tick off each stage of your mini plan once the sub-tasks have been completed. This will help your work and build confidence with your support team, if appropriate. In the event of organising international travel or accommodation arrangements, organise a brief for the traveller of the cultural conditions in the foreign country they will be travelling to. Resolve any issues / problems as they arise, or if they occur closer to the time of travel, to help your travellers.

• ACTIVITY 9

Create a flow chart of the procedures and processes involved to successfully plan and organise events. Personalise the flow chart for the personnel involved in these procedures and processes in your current organisation.

Testing your skills

1. How did you agree the plan for organising business travel or accommodation?

2. How did you accommodate changes to your plans for business travel or accommodation?

3. What processes did you put in place to make sure that you were able to accommodate all the requirements of the business travel or accommodation plans?

4. What sources of information have you used to plan and organise your business travel or accommodation arrangements?

5. What is your organisation's policy on employees retaining points earned from frequent flyer programmes?

6. How does your organisation manage their business expenses?

7. Why have you used the suppliers of business travel or accommodation for your travel plans?

8. How did you negotiate terms and conditions with the suppliers of business travel or accommodation?

9. How did you organise travellers' visas?

10. Why do you use the hotel groups your organisation uses?

11. How have you resolved problems related to organising the whole process of business travel or accommodation?

12. How did you manage your support team, if appropriate?

Ready for assessment?

To achieve this Level 3 unit of a Business & Administration qualification, learners will need to demonstrate that they are able to perform the following activities:

1. Agreed the business travel or accommodation brief and budget with the traveller (s)

2. Checked the draft itineraries and schedules with the traveller (s)

3. Researched suitable business travel or accommodation options

4. Made business travel arrangements or booked accommodation, to the brief and budget, obtaining the best value for money

5. Made necessary payments or arranged payment facilities

6. Made additional arrangements for international travel and accommodation, if required

7. Obtained confirmation and recorded all details of arrangements

8. Collated all documents and other items

9. Kept business travel items, if required, safe and secure until handed over to the traveller (s)

10. Provided the traveller (s) with an itinerary and all required information and documentation in good time

11. Confirmed with the traveller (s) that all items provided met requirements

12. Resolved problems that may have arisen

You will need to produce evidence from a variety of sources to support the performance requirements of this unit.

If you carry out the 'ACTIVITIES' and respond to the 'NEED TO KNOW' questions, these will provide some of the evidence required.

Links to other units

While gathering evidence for this unit, evidence **may** also be used from evidence generated from other units within the Business & Administration suite of units. Below is a **sample** of applicable units; however, most units within the Business & Administration suite of units will also be applicable.

QCF NVQ

Communications

Communicate in a business environment (Level 3)

Core business & administration

Manage own performance in a business environment (Level 3)

Improve own performance in a business environment (Level 3)

Work in a business environment (Level 3)

Solve business problems (Level 3)

Work with other people in a business environment (Level 3)

Document production

Design and produce documents in a business environment

Events and meetings

Plan and organise an event

Coordinate an event

SVQ

Communications

Communicate in a business environment

Core business & administration

Plan how to manage and improve own performance in a business environment

Review and maintain work in a business environment

Support other people to work in a business environment

Document production

Design and produce documents in a business environment

Events and meetings

Organise and coordinate events

26

Evaluate the organisation of business travel or accommodation

EVALUATE THE ORGANISATION OF BUSINESS TRAVEL OR ACCOMMODATION

'Evaluate the organisation of business travel or accommodation' is an <u>optional unit</u> which may be chosen as one of a combination of units to achieve either a Qualifications and Credit Framework (QCF), National Vocational Qualification (NVQ) or Scottish Vocational Qualification (SVQ).

The aims of this unit are to:

- Understand the purpose and processes of evaluating business travel or accommodation arrangements

- Be able to evaluate business travel or accommodation arrangements

To achieve the above aims of this unit, learners will be expected to provide evidence through the performance of work-based activities.

Knowledge
Evaluation is the process of determining significance or worth which involves assigning values to the thing or person being evaluated. It involves making judgements, usually by careful appraisal and study. It is the analysis and comparison of actual progress versus prior plans and agreements, orientated towards improving plans for future implementation. There is sometimes a negative connotation that surrounds evaluation, as it is assumed that it is used primarily to improve performance by identifying under- or poor performance; however, evaluation is a double-edged sword which can equally improve performance by recording and reporting excellent performance, as well as issues that need to be resolved to improve performance.

Most business organisations work with external suppliers of products and services to provide the organisation with resources they need to carry out the aims and objectives of their various business units. For an organisation to remain efficient and effective - of worth and value - it needs to make sure that the quality of service and goods provided by external suppliers is supplied:

- At the **agreed time**

- At the **agreed price**

- In the **agreed quality**
- In the **agreed quantity**
- With the **agreed supplementary support services**
- **Problem-free** or the supplier responds to customer enquires quickly

Most organisations will endeavour to agree a **service level agreement (SLA)** with the external suppliers they contract with. This should be no less the case with services and goods provided to a business organisation when organising their business travel or accommodation arrangements. This will apply to service providers supplying the requirements of domestic or international business travel or accommodation.

• ACTIVITY 1

What are the parameters of quality service expected to be provided by a supplier of goods or services?

A SLA is an agreement or contract that defines the service suppliers must provide. Essentially, the SLA is aiming to safeguard the performance that the customer expects to be delivered by a supplier of goods or services. The SLA sets out the level of service to be delivered and its responsibilities and priorities. SLAs are **contractual obligations** and are often built into a contract. A SLA can be a complex document which should be well defined and drawn up and agreed with precision, highlighting the most critical components of the deal so the strictest penalties can apply to these clauses. A SLA should identify the number of **performance reviews** that will be taken and specify the conditions that will initiate such reviews. A SLA will typically set out:

- The **service** being provided
- The **standards of service**
- The respective **responsibilities of supplier** and **customer**
- Provisions for **legal** and **regulatory compliance**

- Mechanisms for **monitoring** and **reporting** on the service
- **Payment terms**
- How **disputes** will be resolved
- **Confidentiality** and **non-disclosure** provisions
- **Termination** conditions

If suppliers fail to meet agreed levels of service, the SLA will usually provide for compensation. A SLA should be updated constantly as the needs of a business change, as different performance criteria may be required. Improvements in technology should also be taken into account when reviewing a SLA.

• ACTIVITY 2

What is a SLA and what is it used for?

A SLA will usually operate in parallel with the organisation's business travel and accommodation policy, as the policy will describe:

- How this function is organised within the organisation
- The restrictions the organisation places on this function
- The health and safety requirements for employees when abroad
- The support given to employees to make the trip a success
- The information required to monitor and evaluate this function

The advantages of having a business travel and accommodation policy are:

- **Coherency** - Everyone follows the same process which is seen to produce similar outcomes which fit the personalised requirements requested by employees
- **Employee support** - Employees feel valued and looked after in the knowledge that their business travel or accommodation arrangements will be organised in all eventualities
- **Consistent processes** - The processes involved in arranging business travel or accommodation can be seen to be unbiased and consistent as they apply to employees across the organisation

- **Cost-efficiencies** - Business travel or accommodation arrangements should be negotiated with employees and suppliers to provide value for money, which will minimise inconvenience to the business of the organisation

• ACTIVITY 3

How can a SLA be used with an organisation's policy on organising travel or accommodation arrangements to effectively evaluate the service being provided when organising business travel or accommodation?

An organisation will have these two documents to work with to agree templates for monitoring and evaluating supplier performance. However, for an evaluation to reveal the level of performance or standards being offered, the organisation will need to rely on feedback from:

- Employees who interact directly with the service providers supplying business travel or accommodation arrangements. This can include members of a dedicated team who organise business travel or accommodation arrangements or members of the finance department who deal with financial issues

- Employees / travellers who are the beneficiaries of these services who are able to comment from their personal experience on the service provided to them

- Employees / travellers who are the beneficiaries of these services who are able to comment on the service they have received from their internal department responsible for organising travel or accommodation arrangements

From the perspective of the traveller, they will be able to comment on the service being provided by both the external supplier and the internal supplier of the travel or accommodation service being provided.

When deciding on which service providers to contract with, it is important that a review is undertaken of their success as a company and their solvency position. Consideration should also be given to the level of insurance cover their organisation is contracted for and if they are a member of a trade organisation, e.g. Association of British Travel Agents (ABTA) or Association of Independent Tour Operators (AITO). Most reputable tour operators and travel agents are members of a trade association. ABTA operates an arbitration scheme that attempts to resolve complaints between customers and tour operators. Being a member of ABTA also means a customer will be financially protected if the operator goes out of business.

When evaluating the services provided for business travel or accommodation, data and information can be collected:

- **Formally -** Using feedback forms which are completed by all stakeholders involved in providing the service or benefiting from the service. This is the most effective way of addressing supplier service, as facts and figures will support any under-performance of service. Lack of service can be addressed immediately with a manager who can telephone the travel company to discuss the situation or through agreed performance reviews set out in the SLA

- **Informally -** Using anecdotal evidence as and when it comes. This not the most effective way for a business to present its case for improving performance from its suppliers

• ACTIVITY 4

What are some advantages to be gained from formally evaluating the service of organising business travel or accommodation?

If performance reviews become an organic function of the department looking after the organisation of business travel or accommodation arrangements, an organisation will build a positive relationship with their service providers, which should prevent any legal interventions. Potential issues that could be a **problem** when organising business travel or accommodation include:

- Travel documents which are delivered late

- Travel documents which have an incorrect name

- Travel documents for an incorrect number of travellers

- Incorrect travel documents, e.g. a visa for tourism travel rather than business travel

- Incorrect information has been given about health requirements

- Personal preferences for travel or accommodation arrangements have been ignored

- Accommodation which has been organised for the wrong dates

- Standard of accommodation is less than expected or advertised
- Incorrect rates have been used
- Incorrect invoicing
- Slow payment of expenses to employees

• ACTIVITY 5

What other types of problems could be encountered with the service being provided to employees / travellers by internal and external suppliers?

Each one of these issues can either impact on the department responsible for organising business travel or accommodation or travellers, and should be avoided at all costs. The department responsible for organising business travel or accommodation needs to manage these issues by providing a seamless and good service both to its external suppliers and internal customers. There are problems that can occur which are out of control of both the internal and external supplier, called **force majeure**, which cannot be controlled, e.g. volcanic eruptions clouding the sky with debris restricting flight travel.

The **benefits from evaluating** the quality of service provided for organising business travel or accommodation can be felt across various aspects of a business, which include:

- Minimising disruption to the service being provided to employees / travellers
- Valuing employees / travellers by making sure travel or accommodation arrangements are correct all the time
- Maintaining good business relationships with external suppliers
- Maintaining good business relationships with internal customers / travellers
- Rationalising and minimising costs to the business
- Improving the quality of service provided by an organisation's internal suppliers

• ACTIVITY 6

What are some of the benefits of evaluating the service provided by all stakeholders when organising business travel or accommodation?

An evaluation of the service of organising business travel or accommodation should be carried out using data and information that is recorded and backed up with documentary evidence. An **incident report** needs to promptly outline the issues involved and should be date stamped. The department for organising travel or accommodation arrangement should design a form for cataloguing data and information. This could be done using an incident report, which should aim to capture issues promptly and be dated. Incident reports are helpful for identifying patterns of the service being provided by service providers. Having documentary evidence will also help to negotiate more advantageous services, goods or prices for the organisation. Issues or incidents should be investigated thoroughly to correctly identify the source of the service issues, e.g. airline, car rental company, traveller, as employees can blame others for their own travel booking mistakes.

An organisation could also appraise a supplier's performance by conducting an in-house company-wide survey. This gives all key stakeholders the opportunity to provide feedback about the service being provided. This could be done online or via hard copy. Information could be collected to cover travel patterns, number of journeys and the different suppliers that have been used. Opinions can also be requested from travellers about the effectiveness of the travel and accommodation policy and whether employees think that the procedures and rules are fair and delivered consistently.

All the data and information that has been collated to evaluate the service being provided by service providers should then be analysed. Once the analysis has been completed recommendations should be reached and agreed to share with the service providers.

Before discussing any service issues with service providers at a performance review, the evaluation report should be reviewed with senior managers to make sure it is accurate and reflects the concerns of the organisation. It should also help to develop the organisation's business travel and accommodation policy so its internal service can also be improved. This may have an impact on the systems and processes involved in organising business travel or accommodation. Records and evidence should be stored securely. Evaluation is an opportunity not only to improve the service being provided by suppliers but also to thank them for the excellence their service may provide.

Testing your knowledge

1. What criteria can be used to evaluate the service for organising business travel or accommodation?

2. What is a performance review?

3. What is an organisation business travel and accommodation policy?

4. Who are the stakeholders that would be involved in evaluating the organisation of business travel or accommodation?

5. Why should the service of organising business travel or accommodation be evaluated?

6. What is an incident report and what is it used for?

7. What is the difference between feedback and evaluation?

Skills

Evaluation is the opportunity to improve the working relationship you have with your suppliers. Working relationships can be improved by providing positive reinforcement of the service being supplied by the service provider as well as reporting areas where service can be improved.

When evaluating the service of organising business travel or accommodation, you should work from the records identifying performance from all suppliers. Reference should be made to SLAs, if they exist. If an issue can be resolved to improve performance by telephoning or visiting the supplier this should be done and a record of the meeting kept for future reference. Evaluation is not about blame but about mutually improving the quality of service that is provided to an organisation and its employees. You will make judgements about performance, but these judgements should be made objectively and free of bias. There needs to be a degree of flexibility that exists in the relationships you have evolved with your suppliers so they are given the opportunity to respond and improve the service they are providing to your organisation and to you.

All data and information should be collated where they evidence examples of under - or poor performance. These should be dated and stored away securely. Evidence could be codified in incident reports which help you to identify performance trends. You may also want to interview employees who have used your service for their feedback, as well as asking people who work in your department for their feedback.

• ACTIVITY 7

Create a template for an incident report.

All feedback about the organisation of travel or accommodation arrangements should then be evaluated objectively to determine the true worth of the service being supplied by the service provider. Once the service performance of the service provider has been evaluated and agreed, recommendations should be made to improve the service and any other policies, systems and processes.

• ACTIVITY 8

Create a survey for canvassing feedback from employees / travellers about the service you provide organising business travel or accommodation.

Testing your skills

1. What kinds of SLAs does your organisation have for organising business travel or accommodation arrangements with its external suppliers?

2. How often does your organisation carry out performance reviews with its suppliers who support the organisation of business travel or accommodation?

3. How often do you carry out an evaluation of the service being provided to support the organisation of business travel or accommodation?

4. What forms do you use to evaluate the service provided by suppliers who support the organisation of business travel or accommodation?

5. How effective are the services provided by the suppliers who support the organisation of business travel or accommodation?

6. How happy are your travellers with the service you have provided?

7. What do you take into consideration when making judgements on the quality of service provided by suppliers who support the organisation of business travel or accommodation?

8. What recommendations have you made to improve the performance provided by suppliers who support the organisation of business travel or accommodation?

9. How has your organisation's policy on travel and accommodation changed as a result of evaluations of the travel service you have provided?

Ready for assessment

To achieve this Level 3 unit of a Business & Administration qualification, learners will need to demonstrate that they are able to perform the following activities:

1. Used records of completed business travel or accommodation arrangements and services used and assessed their effectiveness

2. Used feedback from travellers to assess the effectiveness of business travel or accommodation arrangements made and services used

3. Recorded outcomes of evaluations to inform future service expectations

4. Made recommendations to the appropriate people to update business travel or accommodation policies and procedures

You will need to produce evidence from a variety of sources to support the performance requirements of this unit.

If you carry out the 'ACTIVITIES' and respond to the 'NEED TO KNOW' questions, these will provide some of the evidence required.

Links to other units
While gathering evidence for this unit, evidence **may** also be used from evidence generated from other units within the Business & Administration suite of units. Below is a **sample** of applicable units; however, most units within the Business & Administration suite of units will also be applicable.

QCF NVQ
Communications
Communicate in a business environment (Level 3)
Core business & administration
Manage own performance in a business environment (Level 3)
Improve own performance in a business environment (Level 3)
Work in a business environment (Level 3)
Solve business problems (Level 3)
Work with other people in a business environment (Level 3)
Events and meetings
Organise business travel or accommodation

QCF NVQ
Communications
Communicate in a business environment
Core business & administration
Plan how to manage and improve own performance in a business environment
Review and maintain work in a business environment
Support other people to work in a business environment
Events and meetings
Organise business travel or accommodation

27

Support the design and development of an information system

SUPPORT THE DESIGN AND DEVELOPMENT OF AN INFORMATION SYSTEM

'**Support the design and development of an information system**' is an optional unit which may be chosen as one of a combination of units to achieve either a Qualifications and Credit Framework (QCF), National Vocational Qualification (NVQ) or Scottish Vocational Qualification (SVQ).

The aims of this unit are to:

- Understand the purpose of supporting the design and development of an information system

- Understand how to contribute to the design and development of an information system

- Be able to contribute to the design and development of an information system

To achieve the above aims of this unit, learners will be expected to provide evidence through the performance of work-based activities.

Knowledge

Information systems are used within organisations to allow its employees to access and modify information and provide information to its external customers in whatever form is most appropriate for an organisation to organise and manage. Because of the speed of technological change and globalisation of markets, organisations increasingly need an information system to manage their operations, compete in the marketplace, supply services and augment personal lives, e.g. organisations use information systems to process financial accounts, manage human resources and market its products and services; government departments use information systems to provide services to their citizens, e.g. computerised access to calculate and submit yearly tax returns. Therefore, for an organisation or business to remain competitive it needs to make sure that its information system optimises all processes to provide the required data, information and knowledge to both its internal and external customers in a timely and required format. An organisation will store information on a variety of subjects, including:

- Sales
- Purchasing
- Accounts
- Personnel
- Payroll
- Stock
- Customers
- Suppliers
- Technical specifications
- Legislation
- Competitors
- Production
- Despatch
- Transport
- Company assets
- Insurance
- Archived records

An information system or management information system (MIS) refers to the wider systems of people, data and activities. An information system should be designed to **provide solutions to business problems**. An information system can be:

Computer based
Which has the following components:

- **Hardware -** Is the physical medium, e.g. circuit boards, keyboards, processors

- **Software -** Is a computer program, e.g. an operating system, an editor, which vary in size and complexity. Software allows the hardware to be used

- **Database -** An organised collection of related files or records that stores data

- **Network -** A system that connects different computers to enable the sharing of resources

An information system can be a combination of hardware and software used to process information automatically. However, an information system is more than just a computer system. An information system is an integrated set of components for collecting, storing, processing, analysing and communicating information. In most cases, the MIS operates behind the scenes.

An information system can be a website that processes transactions for an organisation or responds to requests for information from its customers. Most organisations will have a website which allows its customers or potential customers to communicate with it and gain access to information or services.

Manual based

Which use physical components and resources, e.g. cupboards, index systems, to manage the information that flows to and from an organisation. Where data and information is held in manual files which are the responsibility of different departments within  an organisation, there is a risk of inconsistency where one department is more efficient than another in updating the data and information. A manual-based information system does not have the flexibility of retrieval and reporting facilities as a computer-based information system. However, the focus of this chapter will be on computer-based information systems.

Common to both systems is the need to employ:

- **People** - Perhaps the most important aspect of any information system. At the heart of a computer-based information system are the people who maintain, monitor and use it

- **Procedures** - The strategies, policies, methods and rules for using the information system

• ACTIVITY 1

What is an information system?

An information system uses inputs and outputs. It processes the inputs and produces outputs that are sent to the user or the other systems that interface with the main systems of the information system. An information system works within an environment, e.g. an individual organisation, governmental departments, countries. When looking at information systems, it is important to note the differences between data, information and knowledge:

- **Data** - Is **raw facts** that are captured, recorded, stored and classified, but not organised to convey any specific meaning, e.g. flexitime, bank balances

- **Information** - Is a collection of facts / data, organised in a manner that is **meaningful** to a recipient. Information comes from data that has been processed, e.g. employee wages with hours worked, customer names with their bank balances

- **Knowledge** - Is information that has been organised and processed to convey **understanding**. It can include experiences, accumulated learning or expertise, as it applies to a current business problem to help inform the decision-making process. Information can be processed to extract critical implications and to reflect past experience and expertise for employees within an organisation. This knowledge may prevent managers from making the same mistakes other mangers have made

• ACTIVITY 2

What is the difference between data, information and knowledge?

Information systems store data and information in a form that enables it to be retrieved on demand and used to produce targeted information knowledgably for a variety of purposes. Organisations require an information system that can:

- **Classify data and information** - Name, address and National Insurance number

- **Sort data and information** - Into male employees and female employees

- **Summarise data and information** - Number of full-time and part-time employees

- **Manipulate data and information** - Calculate the total wage cost

- **Identify appropriate data and information** - Provide a list of employees earning over a selected figure

While these systems may be manual or electronic, electronic systems are easier and quicker to monitor and update and information is more quickly retrieved. To make data available it is important that it is retrievable from the application in which it is created. Most organisations will probably use a variety of database programs. Each database will have been selected to meet the needs of the individual user department; however, data produced by one database may not be compatible with data produced by other databases within the organisation. The solution to this situation is to create and design an information system which is able to download data from all the databases and manipulate it to produce the required management information. Small organisations may select an information system 'off the shelf' to meet its requirements or an information system that can be adapted to do so. Larger or more complex organisations will need to have a tailored bespoke information system designed specifically for their needs.

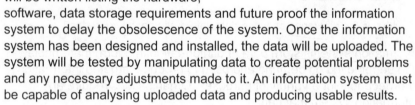

Any information system needs to be designed to meet the identified needs of the end-users. Specialist system analysts will be involved in designing the necessary program. A specification will be written listing the hardware, software, data storage requirements and future proof the information system to delay the obsolescence of the system. Once the information system has been designed and installed, the data will be uploaded. The system will be tested by manipulating data to create potential problems and any necessary adjustments made to it. An information system must be capable of analysing uploaded data and producing usable results.

All information systems will need to be continuously monitored to make sure they access data and information for the end-users accurately, in the format requested and on time. As data and information changes and evolves over time, it is important that the information system is designed to be capable of being continuously improved and updated to meet the changing demands of an organisation or business.

• ACTIVITY 3

What should an information system do for an organisation?

Computer-based information systems
There are a number of reasons for designing a computer-based information system, which include:

- The current system is **incapable of coping** with either the changing requirements of the business or the increased volume of data that needs to be processed

- **Cost savings -** A manual information system can be labour intensive, which a computer-based system will reduce. An electronic information system will also free up office space used by any additional clerical staff

- Senior management have identified a need for **better or faster management information** in order to enable more effective decisions to be made

- **Loss of competitive edge** to other organisations who have installed computer-based information systems, who are able to react more quickly to changes in the market and provide more efficient customer service

- **Investment** in more up-to-date technology to benefit the organisation

- **Branding** of an organisation to project itself as being at the cutting edge of technology

- **Changes in legislation** requiring organisations to produce greater amounts of information, e.g. Freedom of Information Act 2000

• ACTIVITY 4

Why are computer-based information systems designed for an organisation?

To decide on the design of a computer-based information system the following stakeholders should be involved in the decision-making process:

- **End-users of the existing information system -** Who will be able to explain exactly what the current system is able to provide and the input involved. They will also define what it is they would like the new information system to provide and where they see the opportunity for reduction in the input

- **Computer programmers** - Who take the information provided by the end-users and turn it into applications that will produce the outputs required

- **System analysts** - Who interpret the information provided by end-users and the computer programmers. They are able to understand the needs of the end-users and explain them in terms that the computer programmers can recognise. The **responsibilities** of the systems analyst are to:

  - Analyse the existing system to determine its information use and its requirements

  - Assess the feasibility of replacing the existing information system with a computer-based information system or upgrading the existing computer-based information system

  - Design a new computer-based information system specifying the programs, hardware, data, structures and controls required

  - Test the new computer-based information system to make sure it delivers the requirements

  - Oversee the installation of the new computer-based information system

  - Create the necessary user manuals and technical guides

  - Evaluate the computer-based information system

• ACTIVITY 5

Who should be involved in the design of a computer-based information system?

The implementation of a computer-based information system will pass through a number of different stages:

Stage 1
Agree the overall scope of the project. At this stage terms of reference are agreed:

- Which departments of the organisation need the computer-based information system?

- What are the problems that the computer-based system is required to address?

- When is the feasibility report to be delivered?

- What is the budget for producing the feasibility report?

Stage 2
Systems analyst to investigate the current information system.
System analysts will interview end-users of the information system and look at the documentation currently in use. End-users will have the opportunity to explain how the current information system works in practice, as opposed to how it is supposed to work in theory. A feasibility report will then be produced which indicates:

- A number of alternative solutions to the problems that the system is required to address

- The benefits and feasibility of each alternative and a broad estimate of the costs involved

Stage 3
Management review the feasibility report and make a decision whether to authorise more detailed analysis of the proposed solutions. If the go-ahead is given the systems analyst looks in detail at the process necessary to satisfy the objectives and functions of the system. This is called 'process analysis'. The systems analyst will then look at the data required to feed the process. This is called 'data analysis'. The result of stage 3 will be a logic model of the system, not in any way a physical representation.

Stage 4
End-users review the logic model and agree that it is capable of resolving the problems identified in stage 1. The systems analyst then designs the physical aspects of the system and suggests alternative designs based on different cost solutions with corresponding levels of benefit. Alternative solutions will be presented to management to commission one of them.

Stage 5

Detailed specification is written which provides a more accurate estimate of total costs. Management sign off this estimate and purchase orders can be raised for hardware and software and contracts written for programmers' time. Programs are commissioned, hardware is specified, the structure of the databases is specified and a schedule of implementation created.

The systems designer and analyst will be particularly concerned, at this stage, with:

- **Making the computer-based information system secure -** Security of the system involves making sure that it is protected from corruption, that it is complete in that it delivers all of the stated requirements, that the data it produces is accurate and that it can deliver continuous outputs

- **Making sure that the computer-based information system is user-friendly -** At each point at which the end-users come into contact with the information system it needs to be easy to use

Once all five stages have been completed, then:

- Hardware is purchased and installed

- Programs are written and tested

- Databases are created

- Historic data is loaded onto the databases

- Procedures are drafted

- Paperwork is designed

- Staff are trained in the requirements of the new procedures

- Security of the existing files is maintained

- The new system is tested

- The system is handed over to management

• ACTIVITY 6

What are the stages for implementing a computer-based information system?

There are many different ways of designing a computer-based information system, which can be found in the following table:

Information System	Description
Executive Support System (ESS)	Designed to help senior management make strategic decisions. This system gathers, analyses and summarises the key internal and external information used in the business
Management Information System (MIS)	Mainly concerned with internal sources of information. A MIS usually takes data from the TPS and summarises it into a series of management reports. Used mainly by middle management and operational supervisors
Decision-Support System (DSS)	Designed to help management make decisions in situations where there is uncertainty about the possible outcomes of those decisions. A DSS often involves the use of complex spreadsheets and databases to create models
Knowledge Management System (KMS)	Helps businesses to create and share information. A KMS is built around a system which allows efficient categorisation and distribution of knowledge, e.g. in word processing documents, spreadsheets and PowerPoint presentations. Information using a KMS would be shared using an organisation's intranet
Transaction Processing System (TPS)	Designed to process routine transactions efficiently and accurately, e.g. systems that deal with: • Sending invoices to customers • Calculating weekly and monthly payroll • Production and purchasing to calculate raw materials • Stock control
Office Automation System (OAS)	The aim of an OAS is to improve the productivity of employees who need to process data and information, e.g. systems that allow employees to work from home

Table 27.1 Different information systems

• ACTIVITY 7

What is the difference between a Transaction Processing System (TPS) and a Decision-Support System (DSS)?

What should the design of an information system provide?
To compete effectively and solve business problems, information
systems should be designed to provide the following capabilities:

- Processing fast and accurate transactions - Events that occur in
  a business are called transactions, e.g. the sale of products and
  services, issuing a pay cheque. Every transaction generates data
  which must be captured accurately and quickly. This data is usually
  processed through transaction processing and
  is processed in a TPS

- Large capacity fast access storage

- Fast communication, both technological and
  human - Networks enable employees and
  computers to communicate almost instantly
  around the world. High-transmission-capacity
  networks, those with high bandwidths, make fast communications
  possible. They also allow data, voice, images, documents and full-
  motion video to be transmitted simultaneously. Instantaneous access
  to information reduces lag time for decision-makers

- Reduce information overload - Information systems, particularly
  networks, have contributed to managers having too much
  information. The amount of information on the Internet increases at
  an exponential rate each year. Managers can feel overwhelmed with
  information and unable to make decisions efficiently and effectively.
  Information systems should be designed to reduce information
  overload, e.g. a system with software that prioritises managers'
  emails according to criteria

- **Span boundaries** - Information systems span boundaries inside
  organisations as well as between organisations. Inside the
  organisation, boundary spanning can facilitate decision-making
  across functional areas, communications etc. Boundary spanning
  facilitates can shorten cycle times for product delivery etc.

- **Support for decision-making**

- **A competitive weapon** - An information system can give an
  organisation an advantage over its competitors

• ACTIVITY 8

What should the design of a computer-based information system provide?

Testing a computer-based information system

The system will be tested by manipulating data to:

- Make sure that the needs of the organisation or business outlined in the agreed specification meet the required functionalities

- Create potential problems and resolve them with necessary adjustments to the information system

An information system must be capable of analysing uploaded data and producing usable results for the organisation to function competitively. The testing of any information technology project should be undertaken to meet the four following categories:

- **Business** requirements that define the goals and objectives that any I.T. solution has to support

- **Stakeholder** requirements that specify the needs of end-users

- **Solution** requirements that describe functions, information and specific qualities that the delivered technology has to provide

- **Transition** requirements that define behaviours to facilitate moving from the 'as-is' to the 'to-be' state of the project

• ACTIVITY 9

What are the four categories an information system should meet?

There are three stages involved in the testing of an information system, namely:

Plan testing activities

A test plan should be drawn up which answers the basic questions about the testing to be undertaken. Ideally, it should be drawn up in parallel with the agreement of the specification for the information system. Having a test plan will make sure that testing is structured and scheduled. A test is an integral part of the coherent requirements of an information system management process, which should:

- Enable a more reliable estimate of the testing to be undertaken
- Allow the project team time to consider ways to reduce the testing effort realistically
- Help to remove misunderstandings between developers and end-users before the solution is developed
- Create a verifiable system component that will become part of the specification
- Help to identify problem areas and focus the testing team's attention on the critical paths
- Reduce the probability of implementing non-tested components

Testing usually accounts for 45-75% of the time taken on the design and development of an information system. The responsibility for planning testing activities is different for unit, integration and acceptance testing. Testing will involve developers, managers, project leaders and end-users. Some organisations may have a quality assurance / testing group which will be involved in the testing process.

Test plans can exist on many different levels. There may be a test plan for the whole project or there may be individual test plans for different components of the information system, e.g. unit testing, acceptance testing, integration testing. Test plan activities may include:

- **Determine objectives of the test** - The what and why of tests
- **Determine testing techniques to be used** - The kind (s) of testing to be done, e.g. reviews, walk-throughs, walking data through code, computer execution
- **Select appropriate test cases** - The test cases to include in the test plan
- **Maximise scheduling of test runs** - this will vary according to the type of testing being done
- **Identify needed resources** - The kinds of resources needed, how many and for how long
- **Establish start and end dates** - Based on the specification
- **Secure the test environment** - Make sure everything: people, machines, time, needed is available when the test (s) is run
- **Write up a formal test plan** - Place all relevant information into a document

- **Review the test plan and obtain necessary approvals** - Review the test plan with relevant stakeholders

Each test plan should contain a set of activities which define **strategic** and **scheduling** components:

- **Strategic components** should include:

  - Agreement of test plan objectives

  - Description of potential risks to the organisation if test objectives cannot be achieved

  - Definition of the planned approach to achieve the test plan objectives

  - Scope of application components to be or not to be tested

  - Testing techniques, e.g. baseline testing, parallel testing

  - Resources required, e.g. hardware, software, people, training, testing tools, including when and why they are needed

  - Completion date, to avoid endangering the planned delivery date

  - List of those involved in the test plan, including a project manager

  - Instructions for reporting problems - how discrepancies will be recorded, reported and tracked

- **Scheduling components** should include:

  - Critical assumptions which, if not met, will influence the effort, duration or dates of testing

  - Planned date to begin testing

  - Planned date to complete testing

  - Estimated work required to execute tests

  - Expected duration of testing

  - Actual date to begin testing

  - Actual date to complete testing

• ACTIVITY 10

What is the difference between strategic and scheduling components?

Errors that may occur could include some of the following:

- **System works but the user dissatisfied** - The system may not be aesthetically pleasing; have no functional impact; may be misleading or redundant offering a small impact on performance; be dehumanising; have counter-intuitive sequences

- **System does not work correctly** - The system refuses legitimate transactions; loses track of transactions, losing accountability; or transactions are incorrectly processed

- **System is inherently unreliable** - The system has frequent and arbitrary occurrences of the above-mentioned errors; irrecoverable corruption of database occurs, serious thought to shutting system down; system fails, shuts down itself

- **System is out of control** - The system corrupts other systems without failing itself; influence exceeds system scope

Engineer test data
Focuses on selecting data values that have a higher probability of identifying an error than any similar set of data values. Whether the test data comes from production files, existing tests or is created by the tester, properly engineered data reduces the number of required test cases. The engineering of test data is undertaken to:

- Reliably predict the expected results in sufficient detail to avoid misinterpretation of the test results

- Create data that is more likely to find errors in the solution

- Establish a baseline for test coverage metrics

- Reduce the number of test cases needed to achieve testing goals

- Exercise the system components at their boundary points

- Make sure that the most likely causes of failure are avoided

- Establish a baseline for repeatable tests that deliver consistent results in regression

Data values that test system rules should be engineered once business rules have been established that define data constraints. Before starting unit, integration, system, performance, configuration, end-user acceptance or any other form of testing, the appropriate data should be engineered. Developers need to engineer the test data they use in unit and integration testing. Quality assurance, or any other test group, should engineer the data they need for system testing. End-users should engineer their data for effective acceptance testing.

Sometimes it is difficult to identify test cases or scenarios. If there is no system documentation, focus on **business expertise**, the **imagination** of members of the project team and **ask questions**. To help identify test cases or scenarios:

- **Brainstorm a list of business events** - Something that happens outside the control of the information system creating a reaction from the system - that the target application responds to, e.g. to test an accounting application identify the events required: customer pays invoice, customer does not pay in time, supplier delivers goods, marketing launches new product, end of fiscal year

- For each identified event, **select variations that need to be tested**. Identify what strange and unusual things might happen that are related to the business event. These variations will be the test scenarios, e.g. following the previous example, if the customer pays the invoice, scenarios to be tested could include, do they pay the correct amount, underpay or overpay?

- For each test scenario, **identify the expected system response** by creating **global responses** - responses triggered for all of the identified test scenarios - or **specific responses** - triggered for selected test scenarios, e.g. if a customer pays the correct amount, the global response could be to update the customer's account and post payment of the ledger accounts; however, there would be no specific response

- For each identified response, **identify the appropriate test data fields, inputs**, expected **outputs** and **stored data values** that will be affected. Equivalence class identification and boundary value analysis will identify the optimal values that need to be tested, e.g. when updating a customer's accounts, input data could include customer account number, payment amount, payment date; stored data could include previous amount due, current payment due date; and output data could include, new open balance, new due date

• ACTIVITY 11

How can test cases or scenarios be identified?

Execute tests

There are two ways to conduct tests: on a computer by executing selected programs or modules under controlled conditions and in the form of quality assurance walk-throughs. In either case, test execution is not complete until identified discrepancies have been documented in a problem report and distributed to the appropriate parties for resolution. Effective test execution:

• Is the only alternative to production disasters

• Reduces the cost of failure

• Decreases the probability of failure in production

• Increases the end-users' confidence that the solution works as designed

• Increases the developers' confidence in their solution

• Creates problem reports that pinpoint the work that developers have to do

• Captures statistical information that can be used to improve the overall development effort

Testing is needed throughout the system development life cycle. During the analysis and design phase, the most common form of testing is a quality assurance walk-through. A separate quality assurance group should be responsible for testing. The most commonly accepted practice is for developers to test their components while end-users test for business acceptance. The need for impartial testers increases as the complexity of the components or the need for quality increases. Techniques to execute tests include:

• **Problem reports** - A problem report is a document that records the discrepancy between an expected result and an actual result observed during test execution. The problem report needs to be documented to enable problem tracking and resolution; to establish a basis for quality metrics; and serves as a learning tool for developers and end-users. Potential components that can be used to evaluate problem reporting mechanisms include:

Problem report item	Definitions and examples
Problem report ID	Unique identifier for the problem report
Description of the problem	Short explanation of identified discrepancies
Test case ID	Unique identifier of the test case that was executed
Test plan name	Name of the test plan
Tester comments	Notes from the test executor regarding reproduction of the error
Test execution document reference	Identification and location of relevant documentation produced by the test
Requirement ID	Requirement statement regarding system behaviour that has been violated
Severity of error	Use software error categories
Who is assigned to resolve discrepancies	Project team member assigned to resolve reported discrepancies
Expected repair completion date	Estimated date defective components will be available for retesting
Status	Open: assigned; in progress; repaired Closed: deferred; fixed; non-reproducible
Problem resolution	Actions taken to resolve discrepancies
Actual repair completion date	Date defective components will be available for retesting

- **Walk-through** - An effective walk-through, a specific meeting, requires advanced preparation by the participants, a clear set of rules and the commitment by the organisation to utilise the results to improve the product and the process. The walk-through should involve the following roles:

  - **Moderator** who runs the meeting making sure everybody is heard and keeps the meeting focused on identifying errors

  - **Presenter** who presents the product being evaluated and responds to questions

  - **Reviewers** made up from all stakeholders who will use the information system

  - **Recorder** who captures identified issues, concerns and discrepancies

The critical success factors for a walk-through are:

- Prior to the meeting, expectations of the walk-through are established and managed throughout the session

- Prior to the meeting, all participants have access to the product or deliverable that is being evaluated for a sufficient period of time

- Prior to the meeting, all participants have been given the necessary tools and prerequisite knowledge to be able to evaluate the product

- There is a set time limit to any scheduled walk-through

- The emphasis of the meeting is on finding errors and *not* defining solutions

• ACTIVITY 12

What is the difference between a 'problem report' and a 'walk-through'?

As a result of testing, errors will be identified. The project team and end-users need to agree a range of **severity levels** that represent the relative severity, in terms of business / commercial impact, of a problem with the system found during testing. For example, the following description of problems ranges from most severe to least impact on the business:

- **Show stopper** - The error / bug is too severe to continue testing

- **Critical problem** - Testing continues but cannot go live with this problem

- **Major problem** - Testing continues but the problem will cause severe disruption to business processes in live operation

- **Medium problem** - Testing continues with the system going live with only minimal departure from agreed business processes

- **Minor problem** - Testing and live operations may progress. The problem should be corrected, but little or no changes to business processes are envisaged

- **Cosmetic problem** - e.g. colours; fonts; pitch size. If such features are key to the business requirements they will warrant a higher severity level

The users of the system must agree the responsibilities and required actions for each **category of problem**, e.g. problems that are most severe receive priority response and all testing will stop until this category problem is solved. Stakeholders and the project team must agree the maximum number of acceptable outstanding problems in any particular category.

The documentation of test cases makes them repeatable by people other than the person who designed them. The following table represents a list of potential components that can be used to evaluate a test case design:

Test Case Item	Definitions and Examples
Test case ID	A unique identifier for each test case
Test case description	A name or short sentence describing what this test case does
Purpose of the test	A short answer to the question, 'Why is this test needed?'
Resources required	List of all resources, e.g. hardware, software, people, training, testing tools, needed and why - role of the resource
Reaction to defects	Specific description of how the project team will react to reported discrepancies between expected and actual results
Risk category	Required to minimise the number of test cases
Interfacing systems	List of all systems that provide information to or receive information from the system in which the test is executed for this set of tests
Prerequisite test cases	List of test cases that must be successfully completed prior to executing this test case
Required data content	Data content that is required for test execution - set-up requirements
Estimated effort	Amount of work time required to execute the set of test cases
Expected duration	Amount of calendar time required to execute the set of test cases
Set-up steps	Audience-level detailed instructions for set up of the test
Execution steps	Audience-level detailed instructions for execution of the test
Evaluation steps	Audience-level detailed instructions for evaluation of the test results
Expected result	Verifiable result that should be achieved when this test is executed
Execution date / time	Date and time the test was executed
Executor ID	Name of the person executing the test
Actual result	Actual result achieved if it is different than the expected result
Actual effort	Amount of work time that was required to execute the test
Actual duration	Amount of calendar time that was required to execute the test
Test run status	Indicates whether the test was completed, interrupted, passed or failed

• ACTIVITY 13

What are the components of a test case design that can be used to repeat test cases?

Testing your knowledge

1. What is the purpose of an information system?

2. What subjects is an organisation likely to use an information system for?

3. What is the difference between a manual and a computer-based information system?

4. What are the components of a computer-based information system?

5. What is the difference between hardware and software?

6. What activities could be included in a test of an information system?

7. What are the two components a test plan should define?

8. What errors could occur when testing an information system?

9. Why is the engineering of test data undertaken?

10. What is the purpose of test execution?

11. Describe a way of identifying the severity of information system errors?

12. What are the three stages involved in the testing of an information system? Describe what each stage entails.

Skills

The first thing that needs to be done before an information system is tested is to agree what the information system is being designed to deliver. This will probably be a project-based activity which will be run by a project manager. You will have been selected because of your skills and knowledge to contribute to this project. You may be involved in either the design or development of the system or the testing of the system. It is generally good practice to separate the members of the team to deliver these two functions before an information system can be signed off as meeting the agreed specification. However, no information system is every really complete as technology is constantly changing, as are the needs of organising, storing and providing data and information to the various stakeholders of any organisation.

To design an information system you must find out what data and information the organisation wants to have available to its various stakeholders. You may be involved in identifying the documentation required for the system and how this needs to function. This will require you to focus on your business expertise and knowledge of the organisation and how it functions and the purpose that it has been designed to deliver to its customers. You will need to use your imagination and think about functionality and the possible requirements that the functionality must provide for end-users. Finally, you must interrogate as many stakeholders as you know to find out what their expectations are for how the system should work for them. It is helpful when asking such questions to preface them with, 'what if …?' This will allow your imagination to establish different types of scenarios that a system may need to respond to.

• ACTIVITY 14

How have you contributed to the design of an information system? Outline what you did, why you did it and the impact of what you did?

Throughout all of your work, as you contribute to the design and development of information systems, is the importance of involving the end-user for whom the information system is being designed. If the system does not work, i.e. does not provide all the functionalities required of the system, because it has not been thoroughly investigated, the system is out of date already and will not be able to provide the organisation with the data and information its stakeholders require. While it might appear that the end-user knows all that is required, sometimes they do not. This is why it is important to continually interrogate the requirements of information systems by asking end-users: why?, why?, why? This will not only give you an understanding of the requirements of information systems but challenge end-users to make sure that the functionalities that they require of systems is being developed.

Once it has been agreed how the design of information systems is developed, you will be asked to contribute to the testing of the system to make sure that it works. At this stage you will want to establish if the end-users are happy with what has been developed; that the system is working as it has been designed to provide; that the system is working reliably; and that the system is not out of control. You will be asked to test scenarios to establish system errors and resolve these. Once an error has been discovered it should be assessed to identify the level of risk it presents to the system. Errors should then be prioritised to enable their resolution depending on how severe they are. At all stages of testing you should be supported by your project manager. You should make sure that you have devised relevant documentation to guide the testing of the system, so these can be signed off by the project manager.

• ACTIVITY 15

How did you contribute to the development and subsequent testing of an information system?

Testing your skills

1. How did you involve stakeholders in the design of an information system?

2. What did you contribute to the agreement of the specification of the design of the information system?

3. What did the specifications for the design and development of information systems that you were involved with cover?

4. How did you support the development of information systems?

5. How did you support the testing of information systems? Which tests did you carry out?

6. What kinds of errors did you find when testing information systems?

7. How did you contribute to resolving information system errors?

8. How successful were information systems that you have worked on in achieving the agreed design specification?

9. What kind of legal constraints did you have to work under, if any?

Ready for assessment?

To achieve this Level 3 unit of a Business & Administration qualification, learners will need to demonstrate that they are able to perform the following activities:

1. Identified and agreed the information to be managed

2. Contributed to the design and development of an information system that met agreed specification requirements

3. Supported testing of the information system

4. Identified and reported faults of the information system

5. Remedied faults of the information system, within limits of own authority

You will need to produce evidence from a variety of sources to support the performance requirements of this unit.

If you carry out the 'ACTIVITIES' and respond to the 'NEED TO KNOW' questions, these will provide some of the evidence required.

Links to other units

While gathering evidence for this unit, evidence **may** also be used from evidence generated from other units within the Business & Administration suite of units. Below is a sample of applicable units; however, most units within the Business & Administration suite of units will also be applicable.

QCF NVQ
Communications
Communicate in a business environment (Level 2)
Core business & administration
Manage own performance in a business environment (Level 2)
Improve own performance in a business environment (Level 2)
Work in a business environment (Level 2)
Work with other people in a business environment (Level 2)

SVQ
Communications
Prepare to communicate in a business environment
Core business & administration
Agree how to manage and improve own performance in a business environment
Undertake work in a business environment
Contribute to working with others in a business environment

28

Monitor information systems

MONITOR INFORMATION SYSTEMS

'**Monitor information systems**' is an <u>optional unit</u> which may be chosen as one of a combination of units to achieve either a Qualifications and Credit Framework (QCF), National Vocational Qualification (NVQ) or Scottish Vocational Qualification (SVQ).

The aims of this unit are to:

- Understand how to monitor an information system

- Understand how to review and further develop an information system

- Be able to monitor an information system

To achieve the above aims of this unit, learners will be expected to provide evidence through the performance of work-based activities.

Knowledge

Information systems are used within organisations to allow its employees to access and modify information and provide information to its external customers in whatever form is most appropriate for an organisation to organise and manage.

Because of the speed of technological change and globalisation of markets, organisations increasingly need an information system to manage their operations, compete in the marketplace, supply services and augment personal lives, e.g. organisations use information systems to process financial accounts, manage human resources and market its products and services; government departments use information systems to provide services to their citizens, e.g. computerised access to calculate and submit yearly tax returns. Therefore, for an organisation or business to remain competitive it needs to make sure that its information system optimises all processes to provide the required data, information and knowledge to both its internal and external customers in a timely and required format. An organisation will store information on a variety of subjects, including:

- Sales

- Purchasing

- Accounts

- Personnel

- Payroll

- Stock

- Customers

- Suppliers

- Technical specifications

- Legislation

- Competitors

- Production

- Despatch

- Transport

- Company assets

- Insurance

- Archived records

An information system or management information system (MIS) refers to the wider systems of people, data and activities. An information system should be designed to provide solutions to business problems. An information system can be:

Computer based
Which has the following components:

- **Hardware** - Is the physical medium, e.g. circuit boards, keyboards, processors

- **Software** - Is a computer program, e.g. an operating system, an editor, which vary in size and complexity. Software allows the hardware to be used

- **Database -** An organised collection of related files or records that stores data

- **Network -** A system that connects different computers to enable the sharing of resources

An information system can be a combination of hardware and software used to process information automatically. However, an information system is more than just a computer system. An information system is an integrated set of components for collecting, storing, processing, analysing and communicating information. In most cases, the MIS operates behind the scenes.

An information system can be a website that processes transactions for an organisation or responds to requests for information from its customers. Most organisations will have a website which allows its customers or potential customers to communicate with it and gain access to information or services.

Manual based

Which use physical components and resources, e.g. cupboards, index systems, to manage the information that flows to and from an organisation. Where data and information is held in manual files which are the responsibility of different departments within an organisation, there is a risk of inconsistency where one department is more efficient than another in updating the data and information. A manual-based information system does not have the flexibility of retrieval and reporting facilities as a computer-based information system. However, the focus of this chapter will be on computer-based information systems.

Common to both systems is the need to employ:

- **People** - Perhaps the most important aspect of any information system. At the heart of a computer-based information system are the people who maintain, monitor and use it

- **Procedures** - The strategies, policies, methods and rules for using the information system

•ACTIVITY 1

Why do organisations have different types of information systems?

An information system uses inputs and outputs. It processes the inputs and produces outputs that are sent to the user or the other systems that interface with the main systems of the information system. An information system works within an environment, e.g. an individual organisation, governmental departments, countries. When looking at information systems, it is important to note the differences between data, information and knowledge:

- **Data** - Is **raw facts** that are captured, recorded, stored and classified, but not organised to convey any specific meaning, e.g. flexitime, bank balances

- **Information** - Is a collection of facts / data, organised in a manner that is **meaningful** to a recipient. Information comes from data that has been processed, e.g. employee wages with hours worked, customer names with their bank balances

- **Knowledge** - Is information that has been organised and processed to convey **understanding**. It can include experiences, accumulated learning or expertise, as it applies to a current business problem to help inform the decision-making process. Information can be processed to extract critical implications and to reflect past experience and expertise for employees within an organisation. This knowledge may prevent managers from making the same mistakes other mangers have made

• ACTIVITY 2

What is the difference between data and knowledge?

Information systems store data and information in a form that enables it to be retrieved on demand and used to produce targeted information knowledgably for a variety of purposes. Organisations require an information system that can:

- **Classify data and information** - e.g. name, address and National Insurance number

- **Sort data and information** - e.g. into male employees and female employees

- **Summarise data and information** - e.g. number of full-time and part-time employees

- **Manipulate data and information** - e.g. calculate the total wage cost

- **Identify appropriate data and information** - e.g. provide a list of employees earning over a selected figure

While these systems may be manual or electronic, electronic systems are easier and quicker to monitor and update and information is more quickly retrieved. To make data available it is important that it is

retrievable from the application in which it
is created. Most organisations will probably
use a variety of database programs. Each
database will have been selected to meet
the needs of the individual user department;
however, data produced by one database
may not be compatible with data produced
by other databases within the organisation.
The solution to this situation is to create an
information system which is able to download

data from all the databases and manipulate it to produce the required
management information. Small organisations may select an information
system 'off the shelf' to meet its requirements or an information system
that can be adapted to do so. Larger or more complex organisations will
need to have a tailored bespoke information system designed for them.

Any information system needs to be designed to meet the identified
needs of the end-users. Specialist system analysts will be involved in
designing the necessary program. A specification will be written listing
the hardware, software, data storage requirements and future proof
the information system to delay the obsolescence of the system. Once
the information system has been designed and installed, the data will
be uploaded. The system will be tested by manipulating data to create
potential problems and any necessary adjustments made to it. An
information system must be capable of analysing uploaded data and
producing usable results.

All information systems will need to be continuously monitored to make
sure they access data and information for the end-users accurately, in
the format requested and on time. As data and information changes and
evolves over time, it is important that the information system is designed
to be capable of being continuously improved and updated to meet the
changing demands of an organisation or business.

Computer-based information systems
There are a number of reasons for designing a computer-based
information system, which include:

* The current system is **incapable of coping** with either the changing
  requirements of the business or the increased volume of data that
  needs to be processed

* **Cost savings** - A manual information system can be labour
  intensive, which a computer-based system will reduce. An electronic

information system will also free up office space used by any additional clerical staff

- Senior management have identified a need for **better or faster management information** in order to enable more effective decisions to be made

- **Loss of competitive edge** to other organisations who have installed computer-based information systems, who are able to react more quickly to changes in the market and provide more efficient customer service

- **Investment** in more up-to-date technology to benefit the organisation

- **Branding** of an organisation to project itself as being at the cutting edge of technology

- **Changes in legislation** requiring organisations to produce greater amounts of information, e.g. Freedom of Information Act 2000

To decide on the design of a computer-based information system the following stakeholders should be involved in the decision-making process:

- **End-users of the existing information system** - Who will be able to explain exactly what the current system is able to provide and the input involved. They will also define what it is they would like the new information system to provide and where they see the opportunity for reduction in the input

- **Computer programmers** - Who take the information provided by the end-users and turn it into applications that will produce the outputs required

- **System analysts** - Who interpret the information provided by end-users and the computer programmers. They are able to understand the needs of the end-users and explain them in terms that the computer programmers can recognise. The **responsibilities** of the systems analyst are to:

  - Analyse the existing system to determine its information use and its requirements

  - Assess the feasibility of replacing the existing information system with a computer-based information system or upgrading the existing computer-based information system

- Design a new computer-based information system specifying the programs, hardware, data, structures and controls required

- Test the new computer-based information system to make sure it delivers the requirements

- Oversee the installation of the new computer-based information system

- Create the necessary user manuals and technical guides

- Evaluate the computer-based information system

The implementation of a computer-based information system will pass through a number of different stages:

Stage 1 - Agree the overall scope of the project

At this stage terms of reference are agreed:

- Which departments of the organisation need the computer-based information system?

- What are the problems that the computer-based system is required to address?

- When is the feasibility report to be delivered?

- What is the budget for producing the feasibility report?

Stage 2 - Systems analyst to investigate the current information system

System analysts will interview end-users of the information system and look at the documentation currently in use. End-users will have the opportunity to explain how the current information system works in practice, as opposed to how it is supposed to work in theory. A feasibility report will then be produced which indicates:

- A number of alternative solutions to the problems that the system is required to address

- The benefits and feasibility of each alternative and a broad estimate of the costs involved

Stage 3 - Management review the feasibility report and make a decision whether to authorise more detailed analysis of the proposed solutions

If the go-ahead is given the systems analyst looks in detail at the process necessary to satisfy the objectives and functions of the system. This is called 'process analysis'. The systems analyst will then look at the data required to feed the process. This is called 'data analysis'. The result of stage 3 will be a logic model of the system, not in any way a physical representation.

Stage 4 - End-users review the logic model and agree that it is capable of resolving the problems identified in stage 1

The systems analyst then designs the physical aspects of the system and suggests alternative designs based on different cost solutions with corresponding levels of benefit. Alternative solutions will be presented to management to commission one of them.

Stage 5 - Detailed specification is written which provides a more accurate estimate of total costs

Management sign off this estimate and purchase orders can be raised for hardware and software and contracts written for programmers' time. Programs are commissioned, hardware is specified, the structure of the databases is specified and a schedule of implementation created. The systems analyst will be particularly concerned at this stage with:

* **Making the computer-based information system secure** - Security of the system involves making sure that it is protected from corruption, that it is complete in that it delivers all of the stated requirements, that the data it produces is accurate and that it can deliver continuous outputs

* **Making sure that the computer-based information system is user-friendly** - At each point at which the end-users come into contact with the information system it needs to be easy to use

Once all five stages have been completed, then:

* Hardware is purchased and installed

* Programs are written and tested

* Databases are created

* Historic data is loaded onto the databases

* Procedures are drafted

* Paperwork is designed

* Staff are trained in the requirements of the new procedures

- Security of the existing files is maintained
- The new system is tested
- The system is handed over to management

There are many different ways of designing a computer-based information system, which can be found in the following table:

Information System	Description
Executive Support System (ESS)	Designed to help senior management make strategic decisions. This system gathers, analyses and summarises the key internal and external information used in the business
Management Information System (MIS)	Mainly concerned with internal sources of information. A MIS usually takes data from the TPS and summarises it into a series of management reports. Used mainly by middle management and operational supervisors
Decision-Support System (DSS)	Designed to help management make decisions in situations where there is uncertainty about the possible outcomes of those decisions. A DSS often involves the use of complex spreadsheets and databases to create models
Knowledge Management System (KMS)	Helps businesses to create and share information. A KMS is built around a system which allows efficient categorisation and distribution of knowledge, e.g. in word processing documents, spreadsheets and PowerPoint presentations. Information using a KMS would be shared using an organisation's intranet
Transaction Processing System (TPS)	Designed to process routine transactions efficiently and accurately, e.g. systems that deal with: • Sending invoices to customers • Calculating weekly and monthly payroll • Production and purchasing to calculate raw materials • Stock control
Office Automation System (OAS)	The aim of an OAS is to improve the productivity of employees who need to process data and information, e.g. systems that allow employees to work from home

Table 28.1. Different information systems

What should an information system provide?

To compete effectively and solve business problems, information systems should be designed to provide the following capabilities:

- **Processing fast and accurate transactions** - Events that occur in a business are called **transactions**, e.g. the sale of products and services, issuing a pay cheque. Every transaction generates data which must be captured accurately and quickly. This data is usually processed through **transaction processing** and is processed in a **TPS**

- Large capacity fast access storage

- **Fast communication, both technological and human** - Networks enable employees and computers to communicate almost instantly around the world. High-transmission-capacity networks, those with high bandwidths, make fast communications possible. They also allow data, voice, images, documents and full-motion video to be transmitted simultaneously. Instantaneous access to information reduces lag time for decision-makers

- **Reduce information overload** - Information systems, particularly networks, have contributed to managers having too much information. The amount of information on the Internet increases at an exponential rate each year. Managers can feel overwhelmed with information and unable to make decisions efficiently and effectively. Information systems should be designed to reduce information overload, e.g. a system with software that prioritises managers' emails according to criteria

- **Span boundaries** - Information systems span boundaries inside organisations as well as between organisations. Inside the organisation, boundary spanning can facilitate decision-making across functional areas, communications etc. Boundary spanning facilitates can shorten cycle times for product delivery etc.

- **Support for decision-making**

- **A competitive weapon** - An information system can give an organisation an advantage over its competitors

• ACTIVITY 3

What should an information system be monitored to deliver?

Training for users

For an organisation's employees to deliver 'on-time' or 'real-time' information they must be able to access the information system within their organisation with the required level of expertise. Not only must an employee develop the expertise but they must also factor in the time required to keep up to date with how their organisation's intranet and Internet develops. The intranet will hold all information that relates to how an employee, the internal customer, can work and function within their organisation. The Internet provides the vision of selected and appropriate components of an organisation's internal world to their external customers.

For an employee to use an information system effectively to provide data, information and knowledge to help provide solutions to business problems and aid the decision-making process, they will need to have the required training to add further value to an organisation. However, it is  worth remembering that, allied with training, an employee will need to have adequate supervision, procedures in place, job aids, briefings and an awareness of management expectations to make sure they fully embrace their understanding and applications of an information system.

Training should come in the form of:

- **Induction to new recruits -** It is imperative that when an employee starts their new role that their supervisor / manager checks that they have had the relevant induction training for the systems that they have access to and will use. Make it **simple**

- **Ongoing training needs analysis -** This may be isolated training given to an employee who moves to a new department where they will have added responsibility to use functions in an information system that they have not had before, e.g. being promoted from one department to a new department. Make it **routine**

- **System updates or replacements -** This may be conducted as an information system is overhauled in an organisation and every employee needs the training to work the system correctly. Make it **timely**

It is important for all employees to have the required training for them to be able to carry out the responsibilities of their role with confidence and expertise. This is allied to the positive impression an employee will want to communicate to both their internal and external customers. Employees should be supported by the needs of the business of an organisation to make sure that their skills and knowledge are at a level where they can contribute effectively to the successful dissemination of information and application of functionality within their job roles. This should be administered by managers from across the organisation who are responsible for the development and monitoring of systems and the policy that supports their implementation. Support to employees should be delivered on demand, on time and in the best form to engage learning. It is important that an employee is able to use an information system effectively and not abuse it either accidentally or by design. Employees should use the information system within the guidance set out by their organisation and any legal constraints, e.g. when it comes to the security of use to:

- Protect their user id and system from unauthorised use

- Access information with the correct authorisation or clearance level, or that is publicly available

- Use only legal versions of copyrighted software in compliance with vendor licence requirements

- Be responsible for all activities on their user id or that originate from their system

- Not monopolise systems, overload networks with excessive data, degrade services or waste computer time

Failure to comply with these requirements could lead to unnecessary waste, increased financial costs to the organisation, reputational costs to the organisation, undermining an organisation's competitive edge etc. It could also affect the motivation of employees. All training should contribute to fulfilling company aims and objectives. The training mission must be clear and individual roles and responsibilities need to be clearly defined to produce competent and professional employees. Training facilities, equipment and materials should be supplied to effectively support training activities. Training records should be maintained to support management information needs and provide required historical data. The training staff should possess the technical and instructional knowledge, skills and attitudes to fulfil their assigned training duties. Trainers should maintain and improve the technical and instructional knowledge and skills.

Training should maintain and improve the knowledge and skills of employees. It should be based on evaluation feedback, changes in regulatory requirements, changes in job scope, results of external evaluations and inspections, changes in operational procedures and changes in operational systems and equipment etc. A systematic process should be used to determine job performance requirements to specify training content, prepare training materials and maintain required training. Training should be conducted in a setting suitable for the training content. Training delivery and employees who have undertaken training should be evaluated to make sure that they have met the aims of the training and improved the bottom line of the organisation.

• ACTIVITY 4

Why is it important to support the training of staff to use information systems effectively?

Whatever the purpose of the information system, any data or information that is stored within the system will need to meet the requirements of the **Data Protection Act 1998** and be accessible and in the format prescribed by stakeholders under the **Freedom of Information Act 2000**.

Monitor an information system

Once a computer-based information system is in place it will need to be monitored to make sure that it is still able to respond to the needs for which it has been designed. Any system will need to make sure that it maintains agreed:

Levels of **security** or **protection** by:

*   Making sure all critical systems must have the most recently released, appropriate software patches to protect against exploitation and compromise of cardholder data by malicious individuals and malicious software. Many of these vulnerabilities are fixed by vendor provided security patches, which must be installed by the entities that manage the systems. Appropriate software patches are those

that have been evaluated and tested sufficiently to determine that they do not conflict with existing security configurations. For in-house developed applications, numerous vulnerabilities can be avoided by using standard system development processes and secure coding techniques

- Making sure all system components and software have the latest vendor supplied security patches installed

- Establishing a process to identify newly discovered security vulnerabilities

- Developing software applications in accordance with PCI DSS, e.g. secure authentication and logging, and based on industry best practices and incorporate information security throughout the software development life cycle. These processes should include the following:

  - Testing all security patches and system and software configuration changes before deployment, including the following:

    - Validation of all input to prevent cross-site scripting, injection flaws, malicious file execution etc.

    - Validation of proper error handling

    - Validation of secure cryptographic storage

    - Validation of secure communications

    - Validation of proper role-based access control (RBAC)

  - Separating development / test and production environments

  - Separating duties between development / test and production environments

  - Removing of test data and accounts before production systems become active

  - Removing of custom application accounts, usernames and passwords before applications become active or are released to customers

- Reviewing of custom codes prior to release to production or customers in order to identify any potential coding vulnerability

  - Following change control procedures for all changes to system components. The procedures should include the following:

    - Documentation of impact

- Management sign-off by appropriate parties
- Testing of operational functionality
- Back-out procedures

- Developing all web applications based on secure coding guidelines. Prevent common coding vulnerabilities in software development processes including:

  - Cross-site scripting (XSS)
  - Injection flaws, particularly SQL injection, LDAP and Xpath injection flaws
  - Malicious file execution
  - Insecure direct object references
  - Cross-site request forgery (CSRF)
  - Information leakage and improper error handling
  - Broken authentication and session management
  - Insecure cryptographic storage
  - Insecure communications
  - Failure to restrict URL access

- Addressing new threats and vulnerabilities for public-facing web applications on an ongoing basis and making sure these applications are protected against known attacks by either of the following methods:

  - Reviewing public-facing web applications via manual or automated application vulnerability security assessment tools or methods, at least annually and after any changes
  - Installing a web-application firewall in front of public-facing web applications

• ACTIVITY 5

Why is it important to continually monitor the security of an information system?

Quality of the stored data by:

- **Making sure the system always conforms to its definition -** A system should make sure that the stored data always conforms to its definition, i.e. the definition as understood by the end-users. Database quality can be threatened by erroneous input or improper update actions. If errors are not detected the quality of the stored data and information will be degraded. End-users also use this information to properly interpret the data and establish what to expect from the system. It will undermine end-user confidence in the system if the definition of certain data characteristics, e.g. alpha or numeric type data fields, does not conform to the declared type. Systems can store a:

  - **Skeleton database definition:** this makes it easy for the system to check for conformance. End-users are responsible for testing additional conditions which should be satisfied for the data to be valid

  - **Comprehensive definition:** a comprehensive definition means more work for the system but also means higher-quality data. This can generate greater end-user confidence in the database and its management system

- **Validating the stored data and the input data -** Data validation means comparing data to an expression of what the data should look like. For stored data, the definition represents validity conditions. A more comprehensive definition of the stored data provides bases for better quality control. In addition to testing data for conformance to its definition, validation of input data before it is used to update the database can increase the quality of the database. It is generally easier and more efficient to validate input transactions than to continuously monitor the database against a comprehensive database definition. The database must still conform to its definition

- **Controlling the execution of update processes, making sure proper authorisation, controlling concurrent update and synchronising update of multiple copies -** Processes which change the database can disrupt the information system by destroying the quality of the database. Threats may result from multiple processes attempting to update the same data concurrently, a runaway update process, an incompletely debugged program or an update initiated by an unauthorised user. These threats identify the need to control the development, cataloguing, initiation and execution of update processes. Various levels of update may demand different levels of control. Merely adding data to a database is not generally as disruptive as changing the existing data. Tighter controls may be needed on processes which delete data, particularly whole records or files. Not every employee in an organisation should freely update the database. The independent and uncontrolled execution of the concurrent update processes can threaten the quality of the database. The solution of allowing a process to lockout concurrent update processes can lead to deadlock. Update synchronisation is required when data is stored redundantly, in multiple copies. Besides the obvious cost of additional storage space, the major cost of data redundancy is in synchronising updates. These costs must be weighed against the benefits of increased availability of data, faster response to requests for data and better recovery with the redundant data back-up

• ACTIVITY 6

How could the quality of an information system be monitored?

It can be seen from the above that there are two main aims of monitoring an information system:

Maintenance

Of which there are four types:

- **Corrective** - Probably the main focus of most maintenance work, i.e. up to about 75%, that will be carried out on a system, which adds no value to the system

- **Adaptive** - Which probably takes up about 8% of maintenance work, which adds value to the system

- **Perfective** - Which probably takes up about 12% of maintenance work, which adds value to the system

- **Preventative** - Which probably takes up about 5% of maintenance work, which adds value to the system

This can be an active or passive process. The **active process** occurs when there are requests from employees to take corrective action and make changes to a system, identifying what parts of the system need to be changed. Different resources will be required to implement changes. Changes may need to be designed, coded and tested before implementation. Any changes to an information system should be documented, user guides updated and make sure employees within an organisation are made aware of the changes made to the system. The **passive process** occurs when there are procedures in place to monitor information systems periodically and systematically throughout a year.

Update or **enhance** the system's functionality as a result of technological improvements that impact on components of the system:

- **Hardware** - Maintained through a maintenance contract either with the supplier or with a specialist hardware maintenance company

- **Software** - Maintained by resolving faults which have become apparent with use, making alterations to the program to improve efficiency or meeting amended system requirements

• ACTIVITY 7

Explain why information systems are monitored?

Any type of system will need to make sure that it is able to continually **classify, sort, summarise, manipulate** and **identify** data and information that meets the needs of individual departments within an organisation as well as their internal and external customers. However, it may not always be possible to monitor every task carried out by the system, so some form of sampling should be designed to cope with this task. There are a number of methods of sampling:

- **Random sample** - Where a process is randomly checked. The advantage of this method is that no one within an organisation can prepare to carry out particular processes correctly

- **Structured sample** - Where a grid of processes and time is drawn up and a pattern of sampling established. The advantage of this method is that everything is checked over a period of time; however, it suffers from the disadvantage of employees predicting when checks will be carried out

- **Informed structured sample** - Where a grid is drawn up, as in the structured sample, but the level of sampling is adjusted over time to reflect the results of the sampling. Processes which regularly indicate problems are sampled more often than those which are always up to date. The advantage of this method is that the sampling is directed towards areas that require attention; however, it suffers from the disadvantage that processes that have historically been no problem may develop problems unnoticed

Foolproof systems don't take into account the ingenuity of fools.
- Gene Brown

The benefits that can be achieved from monitoring an information system include:

- **Rationalisation and minimisation of costs** to provide a complete solution for the creation, delivery and continuous updating of data and information

- **Increased management control** using document tagging etc., which could integrate quality, health and safety and environmental management systems leading to decreased bureaucracy, conflict, confusion, duplication and inefficiency

- **Making end-user interface** easy to access, so information can be obtained when needed

- **Increased security** by customising a level of security that can model organisation structures and adapt to changing requirements

- **Increased flexibility** by redefining the structure of an information system quickly

- **Managing resources** to provide a complete infrastructure for managing customer information systems

• ACTIVITY 8

What are some of the benefits that can be achieved from monitoring an information system?

Testing your knowledge

1. Why it is important that information is managed effectively and efficiently?

2. What are the criteria for selecting an information system?

3. Why should end-users be involved in the monitoring of an information system?

4. What problems may occur with information systems?

5. Why is it important to continuously improve information systems?

6. What methods can be used to identify training needs?

7. What are the alternative processes that can be used to monitor an information system?

8. How can problems with information systems be dealt with?

9. What is the role of a systems analyst?

10. Why would a feasibility study be commissioned?

Skills

Before monitoring an information system it is vital that you become familiar with its architecture and that you are fully aware of what the system has been designed to deliver. An organisation may have more than one type of information system, so it is important that you know which information system you will be monitoring. Your main function in monitoring a system is to either maintain the system or to upgrade the system. In both instances, your focus will be on making sure the system performs to meet the expectations of its end-users. So you will need to make sure you know what the end-users are expecting from a system to minimise or eliminate any frustrations they may feel, which could be totally misplaced, e.g. the end-users may not have either been trained correctly or at all in using a computer-based application. However, an HR department in any organisation should have a record of the training interventions that all of its employees have undergone. It may be possible, as the person responsible for monitoring information systems, to keep a record of training yourself; however, this could also duplicate work, which would be a waste of time and energy.

• ACTIVITY 9

Monitor an existing information system in your organisation for an agreed period. If possible, select a manual system or a computerised system that has limited functions. Evaluate the effectiveness of the processes to achieve the purpose of the system.

The continuing support that you will need to give to end-users as a result of the changes that may have been made to an information system should be planned and fall in line with the passive monitoring that you will undertake periodically throughout the year. You should also review if the organisation has contracted any external suppliers of the information system that you will have to work with when monitoring the system. You may be part of a large team within the organisation and only work within limited areas of an information system. Check with your manager what your responsibilities are and what you are expected to achieve autonomously.

• ACTIVITY 10

Investigate an information system by interviewing the end-users and examining any relevant documentation used within an organisation to use a system. Consider the benefits that could be gained by replacing or updating the current system.

Organisations are not static and they will respond to the market forces which surround their business. They will need to make sure that the way they manage the organisation and dissemination of data and knowledge meets the expectations of their internal and external customers. To that end, the original specification for the design of the information system will change over time. Your responsibility will be to make sure that the design specification for the information system remains viable and can be successfully implemented within the organisation. As well as an organisation responding to market forces, it will also need to make sure that it conforms to legal requirements that arise, e.g. the Freedom of Information Act 2000, as this will have an impact on how data and information is stored, retrieved and disseminated to both its internal and external customers. As a result of your monitoring function of information systems, it is imperative that end-users are continually kept up to date with changing procedures and written guidance. If there are major changes to an information system you may be required to either write or contribute towards the development of a new specification to redesign an information system.

With the monitoring of any information system it is imperative that all end-users using the system know what the system has been designed for them to do or access. Above all, you will want to maintain confidence in the information system.

Testing your skills

1. How is information managed in your organisation? Could it be improved?

2. What criteria did your organisation use for selecting its information system?

3. What types of information does your organisation manage?

4. How have you involved end-users in the monitoring of your organisation's information system?

5. What problems have you had to resolve with information systems? How did you resolve them?

6. How have you made sure end-users are trained to use information systems which have changed as a result of monitoring information systems?

7. What processes have you used to monitor information systems?

8. What are the features of the information system used within your organisation? Can any of these features be improved?

9. How has the legislation of the Data Protection Act 1998 and Freedom of Information Act 2000 impacted on your organisation's information systems?

Ready for assessment?
To achieve this Level 3 unit of a Business & Administration qualification, learners will need to demonstrate that they are able to perform the following activities:

1. Identified the information to be monitored and the resources available to do so

2. Contributed to designing a system specification

3. Provided training on the use of an information system

4. Provided ongoing support to users

5. Monitored the use of an information system

6. Made sure legal and organisational requirements for handling information were followed

7. Made sure a system was maintained and updated, if required

8. Identified, analysed and resolved problems when they occurred

9. Collected feedback on the performance of an information system

10. Provided information to enable further system development to met agreed specifications

You will need to produce evidence from a variety of sources to support the performance requirements of this unit.

If you carry out the 'ACTIVITIES' and respond to the 'NEED TO KNOW' questions, these will provide some of the evidence required.

Links to other units

While gathering evidence for this unit, evidence **may** also be used from evidence generated from other units within the Business & Administration suite of units. Below is a **sample** of applicable units; however, most units within the Business & Administration suite of units will also be applicable.

QCF NVQ
Communications
Communicate in a business environment (Level 3)
Develop a presentation
Deliver a presentation
Core business & administration
Manage own performance in a business environment (Level 3)
Evaluate and improve own performance in a business environment
Solve business problems (Level 3)
Work with other people in a business environment (Level 3)
Contribute to decision-making in a business environment
Contribute to negotiations in a business environment

SVQ
Communications
Communicate in a business environment
Develop a presentation
Deliver a presentation
Core business & administration
Plan how to manage and improve own performance in a business environment
Review and maintain work in a business environment
Solve business problems
Support other people to work in a business environment
Contribute to decision-making in a business environment
Contribute to negotiations in a business environment

29

Analyse and report data

ANALYSE AND REPORT DATA

'Analyse and report data' is an <u>optional unit</u> which may be chosen as one of a combination of units to achieve either a Qualifications and Credit Framework (QCF), National Vocational Qualification (NVQ) or Scottish Vocational Qualification (SVQ).

The aims of this unit are to:

- Understand how to organise and evaluate data that has been researched

- Understand how to report data that has been researched

- Be able to analyse and evaluate data

- Be able to report data

To achieve the above aims of this unit, learners will be expected to provide evidence through the performance of work-based activities.

Knowledge

Organisations gather together and research information about themselves and other organisations to maintain and build on their market share and find out what is happening in their particular sector. The amount of data that can be researched by an organisation is limitless. For example, job satisfaction, management, change, the effectiveness of a training intervention, labour market information. Once all the data has been collected it must be analysed to make sense of the research materials collected. From this analysis, conclusions and recommendations will be made as appropriate. All this information will be catalogued in a report which will be formatted for the audience the research is aiming to reach.

An employee will be asked to undertake a research project. They will be asked to complete this piece of research to:

- Meet an agreed **purpose** - the aims and objectives of the research

- Be **formatted** in a specific way

- Be **reported** to conform to the organisation's '**house style**'

- Be completed within agreed **time frames**

- Meet the needs of its **intended audience**

The research project can be broken down into:

The research brief

Every research brief will identify a question that needs to be answered. This will be the purpose of the research. For example, how has the trend for women reaching senior management level in the organisation changed over the past three years?

Research design

The methodology that will be undertaken to extract data, which could include the following practices:

- **Searching existing literature sources** - Search the literature using databases, the Internet, text and expert sources. This should be broad and in-depth, showing a comprehensive search of the problem area

- **Critical appraisal of the literature** - Review the literature in a systematic way

- **Developing questions and / or hypotheses** - A more specific research question and / or hypothesis may be developed from the literature review that aims to provide answers to the question / hypothesis posed

- **Theoretical base** - Research may employ a theoretical base to examine problems, e.g. social sciences, psychology

Data collection

Depending on which form of research method is used for the research project, data will be collected and organised. Data will either be:

- **Numeric -** This is data that is in the form of numbers, which results from quantitative research

- **Non-numeric or narrative -** This is data that is in the form of narrative statements, which results from qualitative research

Data analysis

Data that is collected and then analysed to find causal relationships from which conclusions and recommendations about the data can be written. There are many different ways of analysing data, which depends on whether the data is numerical or non-numerical.

Project report

Once all the data has been collected a report will be written which will analyse the findings and make conclusions and recommendations. This may have to follow an organisation's 'house style'.

• ACTIVITY 1

What is the purpose of analysing data?

Data analysis

All data that is collected as a result of the research methodology employed to explore the research questions should be:

- **Relevant** - Data that is applicable to the research, e.g. if the research is being based in the hospitality sector, data should only be collected from that sector, though comparisons could be made across other sectors

- **Valid** - Data that is what it claims it is. It is the 'truth', e.g. data to forecast a sales plan will be based on data about sales over the past 12 months

- **Reliable** - Data that consistently provides the same value, e.g. temperature of an office

It is this data that will be analysed to answer the research question. There are two types of data that can be collected, **numerical data** and **narrative data**, which are:

Numerical

Is basically 'numbers'. Numerical data is gathered from employing a **quantitative** design. Quantitative designs methods, more commonly known as the **scientific approach**, arose as a result of new thinking that grew out of the **age of enlightenment**. The numerical data that can be collected from employing a quantitative design can be either:

- **Descriptive statistics** - Which is the basic way of analysing collected data. This chapter will focus on **measures of central tendency**, which gives the researcher an indication of the **typical score** of samples of data. There are three types of measures of central tendency which are important for analysing numerical data:

  - **The mean:** Generally known as the average. The mean is calculated by adding together all the scores collected in a sample of data and then dividing the total by the number of scores collected, e.g. 2, 2, 3, 4, 7, 10 will be:

$$\frac{2 + 2 + 3 + 4 + 5 + 7 + 8 + 9}{8} = 5$$

- The mean is a popular choice for describing data as it is a figure that is based on actual scores. However, it has the disadvantage of being skewed if the sample of scores has extreme scores, e.g. changing the above example to include one extreme score:

$$\frac{2 + 2 + 3 + 4 + 5 + 7 + 8 + 27}{8} = 7.25$$

The effect of having an extreme score can be seen to increase the mean from **5** to **7.25**, which does not reflect the composition of the data. In this instance, the extreme score could be deleted from the scores to calculate the mean so the mean is more reflective of the typical score in the sample - by doing this in the above example, the mean would change to **4.4**. However, the choice to delete the extreme score should be recorded and reported in the final report

- **The median:** which is the score which lies in the middle of a sample of scores, The median is calculated by ranking all the scores of the sample of scores in ascending order and selecting the middle score, e.g.

Scores	2	2	3	4	5	7	8	9
Ranking position	1.5	1.5	3	4	5	6	7	8
Rank	1	2	3	4	5	6	7	8

If there are more than two scores of the same value, their rank is calculated by adding the rank of the scores together to get the ranking position, e.g. score **2** in the above example is ranked 1 and 2 but has a ranking position for each value of 1.5, which is calculated by adding the two ranks together and dividing by two. As the above example has no central score an average has to be taken of the two scores in the middle to find the median, which in this example is **4.5**.

The median is not sensitive to extreme scores, and therefore could be used in the example under the heading of 'The Mean' with the extreme score, e.g. the median would be **4.5**, which reflects the typical score in the sample that the mean figure of **7.25** does not. However, the median is not based on actual scores but the ranking of scores.

- **The mode:** which is the most frequently occurring score in a sample of scores, e.g. in the above example, the mode would be **2**, as it is the score that occurs most frequently. Does the mode of 2 give a good indication of the typical scores in this sample of example scores? No. Of all the measures of central tendency used in the example above, the best one to use would be the **median**, as it reflects the typical score in the sample of scores.

- It is important to remember that for some sample of scores there is no typical score and therefore none of the measures of central tendency described above should be used. In this event, it may be more practical to use **percentages** to describe or compare the data collected from which meaningful information can be **deduced**. The great advantage of percentages is that they allow comparisons across different cases or people relative to each other. This cannot be done with raw numbers.

For example, the following table represents data that has been collected from a questionnaire which has been organised into percentages. Working with percentages also provides an opportunity to report raw data as well.

		Total responses	Category responses	Percentage
UK Nations	England	250	200	80%
	Scotland		26	10.4%
	Wales		22	8.8%
	N. Ireland		2	0.8%
Size of organisations	1-5	218	20	9.17%
	6-20		9	4.13%
	21-50		19	8.72%
	50-250		65	29.82%
	250-1000		61	27.98%
	1000+		44	20.18%
Type of organisation	Private sector	222	175	78.829%
	Public sector		40	18.018%
	Voluntary / Charity		0	0%
	Other		7	3.153%

Percentages can be used in the following ways:

- Rounded up or down. Is the percentage rounded off to zero, one, two, three etc., decimal points? Whatever decision is made it may have an impact on the data that is being reported. It may inflate or deflate percentages, which will not represent the data as accurately as it should be

- Converted to a decimal equivalent, e.g. 15% becomes 0.15. These conversions are important to compute discounts, interest due or interest paid

- Created from converting ratios, e.g. .789 becomes 78.9% by moving the decimal points two places forward

- Multiplied together by converting the product into decimals and then converted back into a percentage, e.g. .14 x .25 = .035 or 3.5%

- Collapsing data to present different percentages. Sometimes it may be appropriate to collapse information for the purpose of analysis, e.g. in the above example, in size of organisations, the first four scores could be collapsed into one percentage to reflect the percentage of organisations represented by 'small and medium enterprises (SME)' - usually defined as businesses with up to 250 employees - which would be 51.84%. This decision would be determined by the purpose of the analysis that was being undertaken

The type of measure of central tendency that can be used will be determined by the data that has been collected. And this will in turn be determined by the need to identify scores that are typical of the range of scores within the sample of scores collected.

- Inferential statistics - Which aims to generalise findings from samples to populations. Because of the level of complexity associated with inferential statistics it will not be discussed in this chapter

• ACTIVITY 2

Which measure of central tendency would be used when a sample of scores has a few large / extreme scores?

Narrative

Is basically information given by from participants that explain their behaviours or attitudes or feelings about concepts, ideas etc. While this can be done asking questions using the **Likert scale**, forced response choices which provide quantitative data, most methodologies will also stretch participants to follow up with an explanation of why they have answered the way they have, to provide **qualitative** opinions. There are many different types of qualitative methods which can be used, e.g. grounded theory, discourse analysis, case studies. However, this chapter will not focus on any particular theory but consider the essence of what most of these theories aim to do, namely, to **code** data thematically to help explain phenomena. Unlike the quantitative approach, qualitative methodology is more **inductive** in its approach - it is about explaining the absence or present of phenomena.

Data is coded by identifying various categories that the data can be categorised to. When designing a questionnaire most researchers will have already decided the themes they wish to investigate. However, within these themes participants will respond with explanations which will identify sub-themes. Themes should be identified using the words or phrases that participants have provided in their responses.

The following is data collected from the review of the Council for Administration National Occupational Standard, '***Deal with internal and external customers***', where participants were asked to identify any gaps they thought were in the standard.

1. *Communication skills*

2. *Include, 'providing an appropriate response to a customer following a complaint'*

3. *Title: could you use 'stakeholders' rather than 'customers'? The standard's knowledge and understanding relates to the ability to do a job. However, it would be beneficial for learners if a bit more focus was placed on analytical skills especially in relation to quality assurance*

4. *No gaps, excellent standard*

5. *Health and Safety. Both external and internal customers need to be aware of an organisation's H&S policy. Also disabled requirements, are the external customers informed prior to visiting the organisation?*

6. *I believe the points required to cover are thorough and reflect a true Customer Service function*

7. *Specific skill of reporting - to effect change?*

8. *Topics required are all covered but too much repetition in the Knowledge questions*

9. *Knowledge of how to draw up Customer Agreements and Contracts*

10. *No real gaps*

11. *Agreeing of timescales and quality standards should be expanded. This should include defining / specifying and monitoring quality standards and timescales for delivery of services*

12. *Good standard*

The analysis of this data would be undertaken with reference to the standard in question. However, an analysis of the responses could be framed in the following way:

"It can be concluded that participants questioned about gaps in this standard, on the whole, recorded that they felt there were no major gaps. However, attention was drawn to the following areas:

- Title: use stakeholder rather than customer

- More about communication skills

- Add something about responding to customer complaints

- Add something about health and safety

- Add something about customer agreements and contracts

- Add something about monitoring quality standards

It is recommended that consideration should be given to 'responding to customer complaints'."

It is important to remember when analysing data that it should be approached objectively. The analyst should avoid biasing conclusions and recommendations to suit their purpose rather than report the findings of responses honestly so as to subsidise any hidden agendas.

The analysis of data should always be led by the data that has been extracted from the research. Conclusions and recommendations should only be deducted / induced from the data that has been collected. If not, any conclusions or recommendations will be considered to be spurious and not worthy of consideration by the audience reading the final report. Whatever methodology is used in the collection of data will influence the quality of the analysis of the data. Primary research methodologies should be designed so that they extract the correct kinds of data that the researcher will be looking to analyse. The levels of analysis will be dictated by these choices.

• ACTIVITY 3

What is the difference between quantitative and qualitative methods of research?

Report data

However research data is gathered, it needs to be condensed, summarised and organised in a meaningful way ready for analysis and interpretation by its intended audience in a final report. Data will be collected as the results of the research question. Data at this stage will be 'raw' - it has not been collated, summarised or processed in any way. Data that is collected quantitatively should be presented graphically according to two principles:

- **Exclusiveness** - No observation should be classified into more than one category

- **Inclusiveness** - Every observation is classified into a category

This means that when organising observations there should be enough categories coded to fit all observations. This also means that each category is coded precisely so every observation can only be placed in one category, e.g. see the table below, which categorises the total revenue for each functional area within an organisation.

• ACTIVITY 4

What are the two principles for representing data graphically?

Numerical data can be presented in different graphical formats:

Tables

A list of figures or scores which give precise data, but this can be very difficult to make sense of, see below:

	2009	2010	Difference
Sales	£15,552	£20,353	-£4,801
Maintenance	£205	£584	-£379
Telephone	£315	£263	£52
Stationery	£504	£72	£432
Total expenses	£1,024	£919	£105
Sales - Expenses	£14,528	£19,434	-£4,906

Pie charts

A pie chart is the best graphical display for displaying data arranged in categories. Each category is represented by a wedge of the pie and the size of each wedge is in proportion to the percentage of each category. Pie charts should:

- Organise data into a few categories. Too many categories will make the chart difficult to interpret

- Display the pieces of the pie in either ascending or descending order of magnitude

- Be used to display percentages

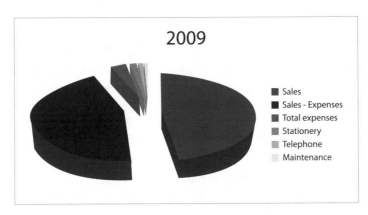

2009

- Sales
- Sales - Expenses
- Total expenses
- Stationery
- Telephone
- Maintenance

In the above example, the categories have been reordered so the data is presented in decreasing order of magnitude.

Bar charts

A bar chart or histogram shows frequencies or percentages in a chart. Frequencies should be shown along the vertical axis of the chart and the categories on the horizontal axis of the chart. Bar charts should:

- Start the vertical scale at '0', to avoid distorting the graph

- Have rectangles constructed over each category, with the height of the rectangle equal to the number of observations in the category

- Leave a space between each category for clarity of reading

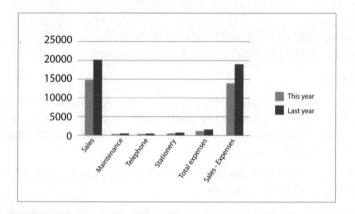

• ACTIVITY 5

Which format is best to use to display data arranged in categories?

Non-numerical data, qualitative data, will also need to be organised. This is done in a similar way as with numerical data, except that with qualitative data categories are given numerical intervals. These numerical intervals are called **class intervals**. The class intervals should be designed in such a way that every measurement falls in one and only one interval, conforming to the principles of inclusiveness and exclusiveness. For example, here is a list of ages of employees that were involved in a change programme:

> Stewart, 55; David, 42; Michael, 34; Veronica, 37; Susanna, 52; Thomas, 65; Kylie, 31; John, 53; Harvey, 56; Martin, 33; Robert, 43; and Charles, 48.

To make sense of this data, a table needs to be created to arrange the data by intervals. This will clearly show how many employees of each age group were involved in the change programme. In this instance, the data will be arranged in five-year intervals:

Age Group	Number of Employees
31-35	3
36-40	1
41-45	2
46-50	1
51-55	3
56-60	1
61-65	1
Total	12

When identifying which class interval to use:

- Decide on the number of intervals necessary to describe the data

- Choose class intervals with no gaps between them - as in the above example

- Choose class intervals with a common width - using five in the above example

- Locate the first interval so that it includes the smallest score

Using the above example, a class interval of 3, 10, 15 etc., could have been used, which would have changed how the table could be organised. Quantitative data can also be written in the narrative form, e.g. it may be appropriate to represent the data in more than one of the above formats. This will depend on the complexity of the data being presented. It may be helpful to have both a table and a graph in a report, because the effect of the data may not be apparent from a table and it may be more effectively illustrated in a chart or graph.

• ACTIVITY 6

What is a class interval and what should be considered in determining which class interval to use?

At this stage of the research project no decision has been made about what data will be presented in the final report. Some of the data could be inserted into the main part of a document or in an appendix. It will depend on how much detail the final report is going to present, which will depend on the audience for whom the report is being designed. The presentation of the data

needs to be organised in a final report. The type of report required to organise all the data that has been collected will vary depending on the purpose of the research and the 'house style' of an organisation. A report is required to present information in a logical order. Some reports could be as simple as a memo or an email response. If the project is a complex one, a report will need to be written. If a report is to be written, an outline structure for the report needs to be agreed. Most reports will have the following headings:

- **Title of the report** - This should succinctly contextualise the central themes of information that will be presented in the report

- **Executive summary** - This is optional, depending on an organisation's requirements

- **Introduction** - This section outlines the background to the report and gives an overview of what the report contains

- **Methodology** - This section records the research methods used to collect the research data, e.g. questionnaires conducted online and over the telephone

- **Findings / results** - This section outlines all the findings from the research. This should be written in a logical way that leads the reader clearly to the conclusion (s) and recommendation (s)

- **Conclusions** - This section will present the results of the analysis, stating what the research has led to and why. Conclusions should only be drawn from the data and information presented in the report, not from any previously held personal opinions

- **Recommendations** - This section should state any action (s) that should be taken as a result of the conclusion (s)

- **Acknowledgements** - This section should thank those who have assisted with the research project

- **Bibliography** - This will include references used during 'desk' research. Source material should be referred to. This should be listed alphabetically by author and the date of publication given

- **Appendix** - This should include raw data. It may also include information referred to in the report which is too detailed to be given in full without distracting from the purpose of the report

In the first instance, a **draft report** should be written. This should identify initial findings etc. The draft report should be shown to the person for whom the report is being compiled. Agree with them that the final report will probably contain more detailed information. Agree with them what this content should be.

• ACTIVITY 7

How are original statements made by another author, which are cited in a report, formatted?

On completing a final report make sure it is proofread before having it printed and distributed. Most word-processing packages contain spell-check and grammar-check facilities. Use these first to correct any obvious mistakes; however, do not rely on them completely as they are not foolproof systems of correction. The dictionary may default to use American spelling and grammar, so will accept, for instance, 'color' and reject 'colour'. Set the default to use the English, UK, dictionary in the options a computer gives for the spell-check function. When the automatic checking is complete, reread the document carefully to look for missed errors. Correct the document so that it is consistently formatted in the same style throughout, e.g. use of paragraphs, headings, subheadings. Take extra care when reviewing numbers, dates, times and amounts. Check for errors between similar words, such as 'affect' and 'effect' or 'less' and 'fewer'.

The researcher may have to present this report in more meaningful chunks of information to an invited audience who may not have had access to the report before attending the presentation. Create an appropriate presentation which outlines the main points of the report, e.g. the title, conclusion and recommendations, and provide handouts, if appropriate.

When the final report has been completed, decide if and how it is going to be archived. Review the information and decide whether it is worth keeping for future reference. If it is archived, review it from time to time and throw away anything that is out of date.

There are many ways of analysing and reporting data. Always analyse relevant, valid and reliable pieces of data obtained from the research. Once data has been analysed, organise the extracted data in a way that meets the requirements of the person for whom the research has been completed. Create the final report in the in the most user-friendly way which conforms to an organisation's 'house style' and meets the expectations of its intended audience.

Testing your knowledge

1. What is a measure of central tendency?

2. Which measure of central tendency is sensitive to extreme scores?
   - Mode
   - Median
   - Mean
   - None of the above

3. What is the mean?

4. What is the mean of the following scores: 13, 21, 34, 51, 64, 74, 83, 92, 101?
   - 58.9
   - 59.2
   - 64
   - 533

5. What is the median?

6. What is the mode?

7. Given the following set of data: 2, 5, 3, 7, 10, 2, 3, 4, 2, 16, what are the mean, median and mode?
   - 5.4, 3.5, 2
   - 5.4, 3.6, 3
   - 5.3, 3.5, 2
   - 5.4, 3.5, 3

8. Given the following set of data: 2, 2, 3, 3, 4, 5, 6, 7, 10, 75, what is the most sensible indicator of central tendency?
   - Mean
   - Median
   - Mode
   - None of the above

9. When could percentages be used when analysing data?

10. What is inferential statistics?

11. What is the purpose of a final report?

12. How should a bibliography be organised in a report?

Skills

The quality of your analysis of data will always be influenced by the quality of data that has been collected. It is important to make sure when designing the primary research methodologies that you will be carrying out that they ask the right kinds of questions to give you the information that will inform the purpose of your research. You will need to agree the logistical aspects of the research, how much research is required, what sources of information should be checked, what should be extracted from these sources of information etc. Data that you will be asked to analyse can range from small chunks of data to large chunks of data which has been collected as a result of a questionnaire. Always check the level of analysis that is required for a report, bearing in mind that a report could be as small as an email to as large as a full report beginning with an executive summary. If appropriate, always present your data and offer images that will to appeal to a range of different learning styles of your intended audience. The aim of your analysis is to gain support for your conclusions and recommendations. Include tables and different types of diagrams, e.g. flow diagrams are very helpful for your audience to understand how the process you are describing will work.

• ACTIVITY 8

Negotiate a research project at work with your line manager. Agree the aims and objectives of the research, the time you can take to carry out the research and the way you are going to report the findings and recommendations to your line manager.

Once you have decided on the sources of information that you will analyse, read through them and extract the appropriate data that will produce an argument which can be elaborated on in the report. Some data may already be in an appropriate format, so it can just be imported. However, other data may not be in the most appropriate format, to make it clear what the data it telling you, so this could be changed into another format. The choice of how data is analysed will depend on the type of data that you will be analysing. Some data will be sourced through primary research, where data has been identified by participants who may have completed a questionnaire, been interviewed over the telephone or been in a focus group. This data will need to be made meaningful by being formatted appropriately. You may want to use more than one format to allow you to analyse the data from different perspectives, which will offer your audience a wider view of the data that has been collected.

Data that has been collected can be either numerical or non-numerical - which can be formatted in a narrative style, where participants who were involved in answering a questionnaire etc., have given opinions about what they think. When reporting non-numerical data it is important to look at the answers given by participants to make sure they have answered the given question correctly.

Participants may not necessarily answer the question, but their answers may be appropriate to other questions that have been asked. A note of this should be made and cross-referenced. If this is a recurring theme, it needs to be reported to the lead researcher, because something may be wrong with the way the question has been written. Looking at all the narrative answers, you will need to start assembling them into different themes or subject areas. This will allow the data to be analysed and reported in logical and meaningful ways.

Check the data that has been extracted or collected from primary research is adequate, accurate - valid and reliable - and relevant to the research topic before beginning your analysis. Remember, with research there is always a question seeking an answer. Your organisation of the data will lead to the correct approach to take to analyse the data to answer the research question. Having satisfied all parties that the collected data has been analysed and formatted accurately, decide on what kind of report needs to be completed to present the information. Use any templates your organisation has designed for writing reports. If a full report is not required there may be elements of the report template that can be used, e.g. findings and conclusions. It will depend on the depth and breadth of the research being undertaken. If you need feedback on your analysis, check with someone who has the expertise to help you.

Once you have completed your report check that it has answered the research question. Go over your analysis to make sure all statements can be supported by the data that has been collected. This may require going over the analysis of your data to make sure it is correct or going over the narrative of your report to make sure your report has accurately defined what the information you are reporting is saying / doing.

Make a final report and prepare a presentation, if one is requested.

• ACTIVITY 9

You have just got a new job as an administrator in a small company producing components. These components range from small, relatively light-weight parts to bulky, heavy items. The components are distributed worldwide and you are concerned that the organisation is not using the most cost-effective methods of distribution. Research the alternatives and produce a report.

Testing your skills

1. How have you organised your data for analysis?
2. How do you know if the data you are analysing is valid and reliable?
3. What tools have you used to analyse data?
4. How do you make sure your report is not biased in any way?
5. How do you check that the analysis you have conducted is accurate and fair?
6. What feedback have you got from the reports you have completed?

Ready for assessment?
To achieve this Level 3 unit of a Business & Administration qualification, learners will need to demonstrate that they are able to perform the following activities:

1. Organised data so that it was analysed and reported
2. Selected relevant, valid and reliable data to analyse
3. Applied analysis and evaluation techniques, as required
4. Reviewed data to produce accurate, unbiased results and conclusions
5. Checked the accuracy of the analysis and made adjustments if required
6. Obtained feedback on data analysis, if required
7. Presented data in an agreed format
8. Presented data to an agreed timescale

You will need to produce evidence from a variety of sources to support the performance requirements of this unit.

If you carry out the 'ACTIVITIES' and respond to the 'NEED TO KNOW' questions, these will provide some of the evidence required.

Links to other units

While gathering evidence for this unit, evidence **may** also be used from evidence generated from other units within the Business & Administration suite of units. Below is a **sample** of applicable units; however, most units within the Business & Administration suite of units will also be applicable.

QCF NVQ
Communications
Communicate in a business environment (Level 3)
Core business & administration
Evaluate and improve own performance in a business environment (Level 3)
Solve business problems (Level 3)
Work in a business environment (Level 3)
Work with other people in a business environment (Level 3)
Contribute to decision-making in a business environment
Contribute to negotiations in a business environment (Level 3)
Document production
Design and produce documents in a business environment
Manage information and data
Organise and report data
Research information
Store and retrieve information

SVQ

Communications

Communicate in a business environment

Core business & administration

Solve business problems

Review and maintain work in a business environment

Support other people to work in a business environment

Contribute to decision-making in a business environment

Contribute to negotiations in a business environment

Document production

Design and produce documents in a business environment

Manage information and data

Organise and report data

Research information

Store and retrieve information

30

Contribute to running a project

CONTRIBUTE TO RUNNING A PROJECT

'**Contribute to running a project**' is an <u>optional unit</u> which must be chosen as one of a combination of units to achieve either a Qualifications and Credit Framework (QCF), National Vocational Qualification (NVQ) or Scottish Vocational Qualification (SVQ).

The aims of this unit are to:

* Understand how to contribute to agreeing a project brief

* Understand how to contribute to a project

* Understand the purpose of contributing to the evaluation of a project

* Be able to contribute to preparing and planning a project

* Be able to contribute to running a project

To achieve the above aims of this unit, learners will be expected to provide evidence through the performance of work-based activities.

Knowledge

What is project management?

A **project** is a series of activities designed to achieve a specific outcome within a set budget, time frame and resources. A project will have a definite beginning and end, unlike the day-to-day work that an employee will be expected to perform. Most organisations will plan and organise their activities around projects. Projects will vary in size and length depending on the outcomes that the project is expected to achieve. As a project is a means of planning and organising specified outcomes, there is no guarantee that the outcome of a project will be achieved as it was originally envisaged. An employee may be involved in more than one project at any time within their responsibilities. They will also be allocated specific responsibilities, e.g. administration of the budget. Project management in the last decade of the 20th century has become very sophisticated, having developed computer programs, e.g. PRINCE, which is widely utilised in the public sector, as a means of controlling the inputs and outputs of a project, e.g. budget, staffing.

Projects will generally fall into one of four groups:

- **Manufacturing projects** - The final result is a piece of equipment, e.g. a ship, an aircraft

- **Construction projects** - The final result is building a conveyance or structure, e.g. a road, a building

- **Management projects** - The final result may not have any tangible outcomes, e.g. the relocation of the organisation, the introduction of a new system

- **Research projects** - The final result will be based on tenuous objectives that may have unpredictable results, e.g. Christopher Columbus's project set out to discover the Indies not America

Every project will be planned and organised to achieve a specific purpose. The purpose of the project will identify aims and objectives that the project will need to achieve.

• ACTIVITY 1

What is the difference between a project and project management?

The project manager
Generally, a project will have a nominated project manager who will have overall responsibility for the management of the project. The project manager rarely works in isolation and will be supported by a project team which they will select, although this may vary depending on the nature of the project and the requirements of the organisation.

The project manager guides the project team in the right direction. The purpose of the project must be agreed by all project members so that everyone has the same aims and level of commitment, which will be gained through continuous communication. The project manager should communicate any changes as soon as they are known so as not to waste time, resources, money and maintain commitment from all project team members. The project manager will assist project team members with the implementation of their goals and delegated activities throughout the term of the project. Successful project teams consist of team members with a common goal. The project manager should develop team members by recognising individual good performance of team members in front of the whole team - but delivering any necessary criticism or feedback in private - and praising the whole team so that all project team members feel a part of the success.

Most project teams will develop through the following stages:

- **Forming** - Project team members asking themselves, **'why am I here?'**

- **Storming** - Project team members asking themselves, **'what is my status in the team?'**

- **Norming** - Project team members asking themselves, **'how will we work together?'**

- **Performing** - Project team members asking themselves, **'what can I do now?'**

If it is a long-term project, the project team will go through two more stages, **boring** and **mourning**. Project team members may stop looking for new challenges or ways of doing things. At this point, the project manager will need to encourage innovation, possibly adopting a change for their own sake, to prevent stagnation. If a project team member leaves a project, the rest of the project team may miss their presence. The project manager should give the project team members an opportunity to get involved in the selection and induction of the replacement. This will have the added benefit of helping the newcomer to integrate into the project team. Some project managers may be externally selected as a consultant for the sole purpose of managing a project and will inherit a project team when they join the project. There will usually be a time frame within which a project has to be completed.

• ACTIVITY 2

What are the stages of project team formation?

The project manager needs the following skills to be successful:

- Strategic focus with excellent delegation skills

- Perception, so they can spot potential problems before they become too damaging

- Be prepared to question all information they are given without supporting evidence

- Be familiar with project management techniques, including appropriate software applications

- Be 'hands on', as projects cannot be managed solely from behind a desk
- Excellent motivators of project team members and other project stakeholders
- Good organisers
- Ability to chair and control meetings
- Excellent communicators
- Excellent negotiators
- Gain cooperation with the management, client and all stakeholders involved in the project

The project manager will aim to make sure that objectives of the project are met in the following three categories:

- **Performance** - The client's needs must be met
- **Budget** - The client's needs must be met within the agreed costs
- **Time** - The client's needs must be met within the agreed time

The client, whether external or internal to the organisation, will know what they want. They will not know exactly what is possible - if they did, they would not need a project manager. To successfully manage a project, the project manager will need to define the project goals and be sure they are achievable. The project manager must be able to answer, with confidence, how much the project will cost; how many people it will need; how long it will take; and if it will be cost-effective.

If the project manager is to meet the objectives in all three categories, those objectives must be clearly defined. The client and the project manager will discuss the client's requirements and a preferred solution will be agreed. This solution forms the basis of the **project specification**. This project specification must cover all the requirements of the project.

• ACTIVITY 3

What are the functions of a project manager?

The four stages of project management

Every project will usually involve the following stages:

1. The project specification

This is the beginning of the project management process, when the need to initiate a project is agreed. At this stage, various stakeholders - both internal and external - will ratify the need for the project and confirm the purpose and outcomes that the project will aim to achieve. The project specification will set out in minutiae all the planning requirements of the project, which will include, though not exclusively, the allocation of the following:

Identify the project purpose

This will identify the results that the project is aiming to achieve. Built into this should be a mission statement which can be referred to throughout the project by all members of the project team to make sure they are still on target. This should align the purpose of the project to the core values of the organisation.

Analyse the environment within which the project will be implemented

This is a kind of stocktaking to establish the parameters or limitations - both internal and external to the organisation - of the project. This will require some form of analysis, e.g. a SWOT analysis - SWOT is an acronym for considering the organisation's strengths, weaknesses, opportunities and threats.

Establish the objectives, goals and tasks of the project

This will be based on the analysis and be aligned to the overall mission of the project. The aims, objectives and goals should build on the strengths of the project to take advantage of opportunities, while overcoming weaknesses and warding off threats. It is important to understand the difference between aims, objectives and goals, which can be defined as:

- **Objectives** - Are specific accomplishments that must be achieved in full, or in some combination to achieve the purpose of the project plan. Objectives are usually '**milestones**' that need to be achieved during the implementation of the project plan. Objectives are selected to be timely and indicative of progress towards goals. Each objective should be assigned to whoever has overall responsibility for its achievement, with deadlines set for meeting each responsibility

- **Goals** - Are specific accomplishments that must be achieved in full, or in some combination, in order to achieve some larger, overall result preferred by the organisation, e.g. the mission of an organisation. Goals are outputs from the project and will have strategies in place to achieve them

- **Tasks** - Team members are delegated various activities that will need to be achieved during the implementation of the project plan

Objectives and goals should be written using the principles of the **SMARTER** acronym, which means:

SPECIFIC - Clearly identify **what needs to be done**

MEASURABLE - Clearly identify the **scope** of what needs to be done

ACCEPTABLE - Involve project members in the decision-making process so they **accept that they are achievable**

REALISTIC - Identify the **usefulness** of what has to be achieved

TIME FRAME - Identify **how long** it will take to achieve

EXTENDING - Build in some **stretch** to develop the skills and knowledge of project team members

REWARDING - Identify the **tangible** and **intangible rewards** that can be achieved from completing objectives / goals

One of the most important things to plan is who does what. Project team members will be given specific tasks. The skills of each project team member need to be taken into account. Once roles and responsibilities are established, each individual project team member must be given terms of reference, stating what they have to do, who they report to, who reports to them and what they are expected to deliver. Project teams must be briefed so that everyone knows what everyone else is responsible for and how that affects their role within the project team.

• ACTIVITY 4

What does the acronym SMARTER mean?

Establish strategies to achieve aims, objectives and goals
This will identify what has to be done in terms of affordability, practicality and efficiency.

Write up the project plan

The above information should be documented into the project plan.

Sign off the project plan

All relevant stakeholders should be given the opportunity to feedback and agree the final project plan and sign it off. This endorsement recognises that the project plan is relevant and achievable within the stated time frame and identified resources. This is the opportunity of confirming with the client if the specification meets their requirements. The client must then agree that what has been proposed is acceptable.

If it is an internal client, the agreement will need to cover what resources will be required from within the organisation and how they will be made available. It may be necessary to obtain the agreement of others within the organisation affected by this use of resources for the project.

Communicate the project plan

The project plan should be communicated to all relevant stakeholders who will either be involved in the project or impacted by the project.

The project specification is a statement of what the end result of the project will be, the timescales and the budget. It is based on the requirements of the client and must contain the following:

- **Start date** - The agreed date the project is to take place. From this point the client is responsible for the costs involved

- **End date** - The agreed completion date of the project. There may be penalty clauses inserted into the contract if the project fails to achieve its objectives by the end date

- **Budget** - The agreed total amount that the client is prepared to invest in the project. Agreement should be reached in advance of implementing the project in the event of overruns on the original budget and how this will be managed

- **Completion criteria** - The criteria - quality measures - that identify when the project has been completed. If the project is for an external client, this states exactly what must be achieved if the client is to accept responsibility for paying for the project. For an internal client, this is the point at which the project can be handed over to the user

- **Terms and conditions** - Defines who is responsible for what and when. It may include a staged handover of parts of the project, staged payments and the parameters for later amendments

- **Legal and safety requirements** - Specifies who is responsible for making sure that all legislation that may be appropriate to the project is met

- **Quality measurements** - Defines the standard to which the work involved must be achieved

A detailed project specification will make implementation and monitoring and controlling the project much easier to manage.

• ACTIVITY 5

What are the standard contents of a project specification?

It is important to remember that a project plan is just that, a plan: it is not set in stone. Things will change in the normal dynamics of organisational activity. A project plan should be an iterative and reflexive document that has the flexibility to withstand the pressure of change and adaptation. This will be built into the **monitor and control** stage of a project. During the lifetime of the project client's needs may change, so the project plan will need to adapt to these changing circumstances. However, it is expected that a project will be achieved within the agreed timescales and to budget. If not, the client should have been regularly updated through written communication to apprise them of the changing situation. The project manager should always make sure that any changes are allowed for in arrangements with the client.

2. Implementation

Many projects are implemented and managed using **milestones**. Milestones are not activities in themselves. They are identifiable points in the life of the project, e.g. start date and end date of a milestone. They are useful when monitoring progress in terms of time and cost. The project manager can compare progress towards a milestone with the plan using the percentage of the work completed and cost incurred to date as a basis. This can be illustrated on a milestone chart - see figure 30.1.

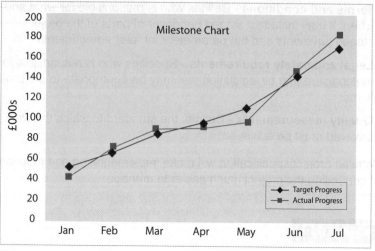

Figure 30.1. Milestone Chart

Using the horizontal axis to illustrate time and the vertical axis to illustrate cost, milestones can be plotted graphically. A line can be drawn joining the milestones to illustrate the planned progress in terms of time and cost. As each milestone is achieved it can be plotted on the chart and a line drawn to illustrate actual progress. The horizontal difference between the two lines indicates time slippage; the vertical difference cost slippage.

• ACTIVITY 6

What is a milestone and what is the purpose of a milestone chart?

Project team members responsible for activities or milestones must report to the project manager regularly. Reports should include:

- The current position
- Achievements since the last report
- Identified and resolved problems
- Potential problems
- Opportunities or threats to milestones

Problems are usually caused by events outside the control of the project or project manager. If the project manager has correctly identified the risks to the project, they should be able to identify warning signs and reduce the damage these problems may have on the project by acting quickly. A common area of risk is where the project depends on the actions of someone who is not part of the project team. They do not report to the project manager or anyone else in the project team. They will have their own goals and objectives and their own ways of working. If communication has not been effective, they may not have all of the information they need. The project manager will need to keep on top of everything all the time to successfully manage risk.

It will be easier for a project manager to deal with the unexpected if it is expected to happen. It may not be possible to plan for every contingency, but the more a project manager has considered the less threat it will pose to the project. If the project manager or project team members are inexperienced at project management, they should seek advice from colleagues who may have more experience of this activity. They may be able to give advice on dealing with potential problems. This may have an impact on the planning of the project, which will need to be factored into a change of plan.

Information should be collated into a project management report to summarise the current position of a milestone or project. The milestone chart will enable the project manager or project team members to draw some conclusions:

- A project on time but over budget suggests extra effort is being put in to overcome problems

- A project on budget but behind time suggests a lack of priority being given to the project

- A project which is behind and over budget suggests there are problems which are not being overcome

Throughout the implementation stage of a project all members of the project team should devise a checklist so they are able to prioritise and follow all activities in their milestone or the project, particularly if there are dependencies contingent on achieving tasks and activities.

3. Monitor and control

It is hoped that from the implementation of a project it will run smoothly, with no deviations from the original project specification; however, this is rarely the case. There are many types of unplanned events that can happen at any time during the project. The project manager will need to:

Control any changes that happen

To maintain stability of the project, all agreements must be recorded in **control documents**, which aims to control changes that may seriously harm a project and distinguish an error - in the implementation of the project or in the documentation in the project, from a change - a modification to the way an agreement, workflow or agreed system is implemented in the project, which may affect the whole project or parts of it. Control documents may include:

- Organisational objectives, priorities of objectives, strategies and goals

- Project objectives, priorities of objectives, strategies, goals and constraints

- Business requirements

- Workflow requirements

- System requirements

Any changes to agreements must be evaluated to see how they impact on the project. Control documents should be monitored by a **project management board**, which will include the project manager along with other relevant stakeholders. This board can then agree and install systems to monitor the implementation of the project. Changes must be introduced in a disciplined fashion. Any changes should be documented and then reviewed and approved by the project management board. The changes will be implemented and relevant quality assurance put in place. If, as a result of the agreed changes, there are functional changes, these will need to be incorporated into the implementation of the project. User manuals describing the function should be updated and changes to business policies should be recorded.

Systems should be put in place to control the tasks and activities to be completed in a project. A simple principle to adhere to is the **Kiss Principle** - keep it simple! If reports are being generated they should be meaningful and contribute towards the progress of a project.

• ACTIVITY 7

What is the purpose of control documents?

Manage any risks

During the running of the project to:

- Identify risks, potential project problems, as early as possible

- Identify when goals may not be met

- Identify when constraints may be violated

- Make sure that contingency plans occur before unrecoverable problems occur

- Provide and receive project status for the phases and the total project

Any identified risks should be reported to the relevant manager. Risks should be risk rated to manage the impact they will have on the project. Risks may be either identified or not identified. Allied with risk rating, there should be **contingency plans** put in place for when risks become actual problems. Risks may be identified as:

- **Important** - These should never be a problem, as the project manager should have factored them into the risk assessment

- **Unimportant** - Which may change into a high risk - they should be recorded and revisited to check they are not turning into a problem

- **Latent** - Which have the potential to become a problem - they should be monitored constantly by the project manager

Risks to the organisation may include:

- Interruption of normal business to facilitate the project

- Diversion of resources, including people, to the project

- Bypassing organisational procedures as the project does not fit into the normal structure

- A change in the prevailing financial situation. This may arise from the project itself or from external influences, such as interest rates, government policy or stock market fluctuation

- The effect on the organisation's reputation if the project is unsuccessful

Three major risk areas that the project manager will need to keep a careful eye on are:

1. Budget

For a project to be successful all types of resources must be in place and available when required. The project manager should check that the agreed budget of the project specification is realistic.

2. Resources

Identified in the project specification and includes everything in the initial estimate required to deliver the project. The project manger should be realistic in the estimates they make of all resources required to achieve the project, including employee time. A costing method should be agreed at the beginning of the project and applied consistently, e.g. if a person has to work on the project everyday for 10 days, but only for two hours a day, the cost is 20 hours at their hourly rate, not 10 days. The project manager should always weigh up alternatives to minimise the cost of resources. Accurate records should be maintained of all project-related expenditure to check that the budget is on track.

3. Time

However well planned a project might be, people are not machines and will invariably run into problems. It is unlikely that all of the activities involved in the project will start at the same time. Breaking the project down into its milestones, and then grouping the activities, will show the project manager how they fit together into a logical sequence. This will help to estimate how many people will be needed and the skills they will be required to have. If everyone understands their role there will be fewer misunderstandings. The project manager will estimate how long activities are likely to take within milestones, making a note of the maximum and minimum times estimated, as these may be useful if flexibility is needed later. A poor estimate at the beginning can cause serious problems as the project develops. The project manager will track progress against the original plan, as slippage will need to be communicated to the project team members, this will impact on if they are involved in achieving a milestone.

External factors

Being a part of a project may only be a part of the daily functions of a project manager or their project team. The project manager will need to consult with many different stakeholders in the project who will have competing demands placed on them as they work within their organisations. The project manager will need to make sure that the achievement of their project is the number-one priority for them and their stakeholders.

It is important for anyone intimately connected with the delivery of a project or milestones within it that they continue to identify and assess anything that may be a risk to the project and take remedial action to rectify any inconsistencies with the original plans in the project specification. The purpose of **project management** is to minimise, contain or counter the risks and organise resources. To evaluate risks, one method is to multiply the probability of the risk occurring by the cost of correcting the resulting problem. Once a risk has been identified and managed it is no longer a threat to the achievement of the project or milestones within it. It is not cost-effective to spend more eliminating a risk than the cost of dealing with the problem.

• ACTIVITY 8

What is a risk and how will contingency plans mitigate against it becoming a problem?

4. Completion

This is the opportunity to acknowledge completion, celebrate success and evaluate the project to see what lessons can be learned. The latter is important to inform the planning of future projects. If everything has gone well, or everything that has gone wrong has been managed, the project will end on time and on budget. Probably the most effective way of judging the success of this is from the client's point of view. If the client is happy, the project has achieved its main goal. However, the success of a project should be reviewed through other perspectives. Even if the project was completed on time and to budget it is likely that there will be areas where improvements could have been made.

Throughout the life of the project, the project manager will have been gathering different types of information. When the project is complete this information will be useful in analysing every part of the project. As well as using this statistical evidence, a series of debriefing meetings should be held with the project team to monitor and control the project. At these meetings, the project manager should discuss:

- What is known about the individuals, the team and the organisation as a result of the project?

- What could be done differently if a similar project was carried out?

- Was the planning right, or, if not, where did it go wrong?

- What has been learned about processes or management from the project?

The project manager should record everybody's thoughts and input so that the evaluation of the project can be as thorough as possible. A comprehensive project report should be completed detailing the strengths and weaknesses identified by the evaluation of the project. If the project was internal, this should be made available to all the relevant stakeholders so that it can inform decisions on future projects. The final report should be honest and objective, minimising the attachment of blame or deflection of criticism as a result of the less successful components of the project. The aim of the final project report is to improve future project management practice.

Estimates

An important element of any project for a project manager is the **estimates** they must make for the costs of resources and the time activities will take to achieve. For an estimate to be accurate, the project manager needs to be realistic. There are three different types of estimates:

- **Ballpark** - Estimates are made when there is only a rough outline of information available or made when an emergency exists. Ballpark estimates might achieve an accuracy of plus or minus 25%

- **Comparative** - Estimates are made comparing the current project costs to previous similar projects and are commonly used as a basis for tenders. Comparative estimates might achieve an accuracy of plus or minus 15%

- **Feasibility** - Estimates are made once the specification has clearly identified the parameters of the project. Feasibility estimates might achieve an accuracy of plus or minus 10%

An estimate must avoid either being **underestimated** or **overestimated**, although the latter option is preferable to the former. In making estimates for a project, the project manager must consider the complexity of the project. They will need to factor into their estimates unexpected events or high-priority unscheduled work. To properly estimate how long each activity will take, the project manager must consider all the components that will make it up, allowing for any:

- Liaison with outside bodies

- Meetings

- Quality assurance

- Accidents and emergencies

- Staff holidays

- Staff sickness

- Equipment breakdowns

- Late deliveries

- Interruptions

• ACTIVITY 9

What is an estimate and what should be considered to make an accurate estimate?

Tools to monitor and control a project - Gantt charts and critical path analysis

In any project there will be activities that cannot start until another

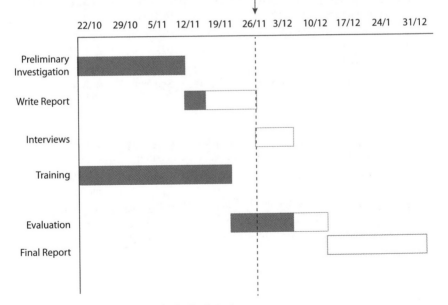

Figure 30.2. Example of a Gantt chart

is completed. These are known as **dependencies**. They exist both within the project and between the project and external influences. Dependencies dictate the timescale of the whole project. The overall length of the project can be determined by the use of **Gantt charts**, which help the project manager to plan tasks to be achieved, give them a basis for scheduling those tasks, help them to allocate resources and work out the critical path to complete a project. To draw a Gantt chart, first list all the activities in the project. For each activity show the earliest start date, an estimate of how long it will take and whether it is **parallel** - can be carried out at the same time as another activity - or **sequential** - is dependent on another activity being completed. If the activity is sequential, the Gantt chart should indicate which other activities it depends on.

• ACTIVITY 10

Plot a Gantt chart using the list of activities for creating an information system in the table below. Schedule actions in the Gantt chart so that sequential actions are carried out in the required sequence. Dependent activities cannot start until the activities they depend on are complete.

	Activity	Resources available	Length	Type	Dependent on
1	Write programs	Week 1	3 weeks	Parallel	
2	Test programs	Week 1	1 week	Sequential	Activity 1
3	Create databases	Week 1	2 weeks	Sequential	Activities 1 and 2
4	Load data	Week 1	2 weeks	Sequential	Activities 1, 2, 3 and 7
5	Draft procedures	Week 1	2 weeks	Sequential	Activity 1
6	Design paperwork	Week 1	1 week	Sequential	Activities 1 and 5
7	Train staff	Week 1	3 weeks	Sequential	Activities 1 and 2
8	Test system	Week 1	1 week	Sequential	Activities 1, 2, 3, 4 and 7
9	Hand over			Sequential	Activities 1–8

Critical path analysis (CPA) is a method used to assess:

- The tasks to be carried out

- Areas where tasks can be performed in parallel

- The resources needed for the project

- Priorities within the project

- The correct sequence of activities

- How to schedule and time activities

- The shortest time in which a project can be completed

- Ways of shortening urgent projects

To draw a CPA chart, first list all the activities in the project. For each activity show the earliest start date, an estimate of how long it will take and whether it is **parallel** - can be carried out at the same time as another activity - or **sequential** - is dependant on another activity being completed. If the activity is sequential, indicate which other activities it depends on.

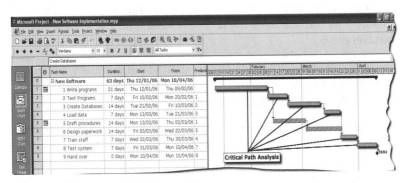

Figure 30.3. Example of a critical path analysis

Once the activities have been listed, create a circle and arrow diagram in which circles show events, i.e. the start and finish of an activity, and an arrow running between two circles shows the activity. A description of the activity should be written below the arrow and the length of the task above it. All arrows run left to right. See figure 30.3.

Where one activity cannot start until another has been completed, the arrow for the dependent activity starts at the completion event circle of the previous activity. The diagram above shows that the earliest the system can be handed over is at the end of week 9. This depends on all of the estimates of the length of activities being met. It may be that having created the CPA the total time from start to finish is not acceptable. The critical path - the longest route from start to finish - shows anyone where allocating additional resources will be effective. Having extra staff drafting procedures and designing paperwork will not reduce the overall project length. Allocating additional resources to reduce the time needed to create databases and load data can reduce the critical path.

• ACTIVITY 11

What is Critical Path Analysis?

The benefits of CPA over Gantt charts is that they help to identify the minimum length of time needed to complete a project and where projects can be accelerated to reduce this minimum time. There is an alternative to CPA, called **Program Evaluation and Review Technique (PERT)**, which takes a more sceptical view of the time activities will take. To use PERT, take the shortest time an activity can take, the most likely time and the longest time. Use the following formula to calculate the actual time each activity will take. Shortest time + 4 x likely time + longest time ÷ 6.

While all of the above methods can be carried out manually, software programs can also be used, e.g. Microsoft Project, which will greatly reduce the time needed to calculate the critical path.

Most projects will be temporary, drawing on specific project teams that will have been selected for their skills and knowledge. A project will have a finite time for its completion which everyone involved with it will expect to see achieved. It is this that the project manager will manage, making sure the project keeps on track. This is important not only for the client, either internal or external to the organisation, but also for the competing demands that members of the project team will need to juggle. To make sure the project remains on track boils down to planning and managing the implementation of the plan so each member of the project team knows how and what they will contribute.

Testing your knowledge

1. What is the purpose of project management and how may this vary from organisation to organisation?

2. What is the difference between projects and everyday work?

3. What is the difference between a project objective and a project goal?

4. What objectives must all projects meet?

5. Why is it helpful to plot milestones in the progress of a project?

6. How is a milestone chart created?

7. What is a dependency in a project?

8. What skills should a successful project manager aim to posses?

9. What risks are involved in managing projects?

10. How can risks be reduced in a project?

11. What is the difference between using a Gantt chart and Critical Path Analysis?

12. How are projects evaluated?

Skills

As a member of a project team, you will have been selected for your special skills and knowledge to add value to the achievement of the project's purpose, objectives and goals. At the beginning of the project you will contribute to delivering some aspects of the project. This will vary in depth and breadth depending on your project manager. The project manager will have agreed an outline specification with the client. After a broad outline has been agreed with the client, the project manager should involve you in planning the specification of the project, as it is divided into various milestones and activities. Your skills and knowledge will add insight into the estimation of resources, costs and time that various milestones and milestone activities will take to complete that you may be given responsibility to deliver within the project.

• ACTIVITY 12

You have been asked to organise the makeover of your office, which includes new office furniture, carpeting and painting of the walls. Write a project specification for these activities.

Before any project moves forward, all stakeholders who will contribute or be impacted by the project should be notified and included in the planning of the project. This will help to minimise problems from occurring as everyone will be apprised of what is expected to happen. It cannot be overstressed how important maintaining good communications is to any project. Everyone needs to know if any changes have taken place, as these may have a knock-on effect to other dependencies of the project. There is no time that can be wasted, as most projects will have been planned down to the knuckle to make sure that there is no wastage. You will want to review with your project manager the scope of the work that you will need to undertake and how this relates to the overall achievement of the project. You will need to make sure that for whatever aspect of the project falls within your responsibility you know when it needs to be completed by so you can manage your resources to achieve its aims and objectives.

•ACTIVITY 13

Choose either CPA or PERT to carry out an analysis of the project specification you have written for ACTIVITY 14 below. You can create the path manually or use a software application.

Regardless of the responsibilities you are given within a project, you should work with the control documents and any systems that the project manager has agreed should be used throughout the implementation of the project. It would be helpful to have a checklist to help you manage the achievement of your tasks and activities. These tools will help you to monitor and control your areas of responsibility. You must be resolute in your observation of what is going on to minimise or eliminate problems that may arise throughout the project. If you do not have the skills and knowledge to overcome a problem, seek advice from your manager. You should use these tools as a record of all agreements throughout the implementation of the project. Throughout the implementation of the project you should provide interim reports. A fundamental part of your job will be to minimise and eliminate any risks to a project.

•ACTIVITY 14

You have been asked to work with the project manger to help reorganise your office space to accommodate a further 10 desks. Your office currently has 112 desks. Assist with the writing of a project specification, estimating time and budget requirements. Include all aspects of the office reorganisation, including furniture and equipment, connection of new hardware, implications for electricity and the I.T. team, and advise customers that the office will be closed for two days.

Depending on your project manager, you may be involved in the evaluation of the project. Did the project achieve what it planned to achieve within time and to budget? The interim reports that you have provided throughout the project will help in this analysis.

•ACTIVITY 15

Carry out a risk assessment to identify the possible problems or risks of ACTIVITY 14 above.

Testing your skills

1. What kind of stakeholders were you involved with in your projects?

2. What projects have you contributed towards achieving?

3. How have you contributed to projects that you have been involved in?

4. How did you contribute to establishing objectives and goals of projects?

5. What risks did you identify in the projects you worked on?

6. How effectively did your project manager manage you and the project? What recommendations could you make to improve their performance?

7. What tools were used to monitor and control the projects you were involved in?

8. What factors did your project managers use to evaluate the success of projects?

9. How were final project reports structured in the projects you have been involved with?

10. Describe the dynamics of the four stages of project team formation you have experienced?

Ready for assessment?

To achieve this Level 3 unit of a Business & Administration qualification, learners will need to demonstrate that they are able to perform the following activities:

1. Confirmed the purpose of the project with all stakeholders

2. Confirmed project scope, timescales, aims and objectives

3. Contributed to the preparation of a project specification

4. Confirmed all types of resources for all stakeholders

5. Confirmed with all stakeholders the project plan and timed use of all types of resources for an area of work

6. Contributed to identifying risks and developed contingency plans for an area of work

7. Implemented a project

8. Communicated with all stakeholders involved with or affected by a project

9. Adapted project plans for stakeholders to respond to unexpected events and risks

10. Provided interim reports on project progress to relevant stakeholders

11. Achieved required outcomes for relevant stakeholders on time and to budget

12. Sought advice in response to unexpected events, if required

13. Kept records of project activity

14. Evaluated the project for all stakeholders

15. Reported on the degree to which a project had met its aims and objectives for all stakeholders

16. Reported on the project strengths and areas for improvement for all stakeholders

You will need to produce evidence from a variety of sources to support the performance requirements of this unit.

If you carry out the 'ACTIVITIES' and respond to the 'NEED TO KNOW' questions, these will provide some of the evidence required.

Links to other units

While gathering evidence for this unit, evidence **may** also be used from evidence generated from other units within the Business & Administration suite of units. Below is a **sample** of applicable units; however, most units within the Business & Administration suite of units will also be applicable.

QCF NVQ
Communications
Communicate in a business environment (Level 3)
Develop a presentation
Deliver a presentation
Core business & administration
Manage own performance in a business environment (Level 3)
Evaluate and improve own performance in a business environment
Solve business problems (Level 3)
Work with other people in a business environment (Level 3)
Contribute to decision-making in a business environment
Contribute to negotiations in a business environment

SVQ
Communications
Communicate in a business environment
Develop a presentation
Deliver a presentation
Core business & administration
Plan how to manage and improve own performance in a business environment
Review and maintain work in a business environment
Solve business problems
Support other people to work in a business environment
Contribute to decision-making in a business environment
Contribute to negotiations in a business environment

INDEX